# The Politics
# of Women's Spirituality

# The Politics
# of Women's Spirituality

## ESSAYS ON THE RISE
## OF SPIRITUAL POWER
## WITHIN THE FEMINIST
## MOVEMENT

Edited by Charlene Spretnak

ANCHOR BOOKS
ANCHOR PRESS/DOUBLEDAY
GARDEN CITY, NEW YORK

This is the first publication of *The Politics of Women's Spirituality*, published simultaneously in hardcover and paperback editions. Anchor Press edition: 1982

Library of Congress Catalog Card Number 80-2876
ISBN (hardcover): 0-385-17770-4
ISBN (paperback): 0-385-17241-9


Library of Congress Cataloging in Publication Data
Main entry under title:

The Politics of women's spirituality.

Bibliography.
1. Feminism — Moral and religious aspects — Addresses, essays, lectures. 2. Spirituality — Addresses, essays, lectures. 3. Women (in religion, folklore, etc.) — Addresses, essays, lectures. I. Spretnak, Charlene, 1946–   .
HQ1154.P6     305.4'2     AACR2

# Acknowledgments

The idea for this book grew out of several months of work I did for *Chrysalis: A Magazine of Women's Culture* in 1977 and 1978. Kirsten Grimstad, executive editor, invited me to write an article on the politics of women's spirituality. I began with a review of the literature which grew so extensive that the editorial board decided to divide the piece into "The Politics of Women's Spirituality" and a "Catalog of Women's Spirituality" (*Chrysalis*, no. 6, Nov. 1978). In designing and writing the capsule reviews for what became a 24-page catalog, I was assisted by the following staff members at *Chrysalis*: Linda Palumbo, Joanne Parrent, Maurine Renville, and Terry Wolverton.

In the early stages of this book, I received helpful information from Carol P. Christ, Daniel Goleman, Kathy Barry, and later from Ann Forfreedom and Joseph Meeker.

I especially wish to thank all of the many contributors who did more than they were asked to do, the women who accompanied their material with notes or phone calls of support. Sisterhood in action.

I am very grateful to the following feminist colleagues for their encouragement and thoughtful responses to various portions of the manuscript: Judy Grahn, Wendy Cadden, Fritjof Capra, Judith Todd, and Rita Moss. David Tiers contributed both typing assistance and responses.

For daily, in-the-trenches support while I worked on this book, I deeply thank my rather amazing daughter, Lissa Merkel, and my neighbor Barbara Riggs, whose friendship has spanned three continents and a dozen years. Also, Ann Flanagan often supplied a much appreciated boost to morale, and Carolyn and Jim Scott provided support services.

Darlene Pagano, the Question Authority, and Natalie Lando, both of A Woman's Place bookstore in Oakland, supplied reference assistance on many occasions.

I was fortunate in researching my article on the Christian Right to have received assistance from activists in many parts of the country: Deirdre English, Georgia Fuller, Evelyn Hailey, Nadine Hansen, Charlotte Hendee, Sonia Johnson, Judy Koretsky, Lawrence Lader, Ruth McGill, Andy Merton, Chris Miller, and David Tiers.

I also wish to acknowledge the work of my agent, Frances Goldin, who is warm, tough, and very savvy — in short, a quintessential New Yorker.

Both of my editors at Anchor/Doubleday have been veritable Goddess-sends for this project. Marie D. Brown, Senior Editor, originally acquired the book and handled the formidable job of securing permissions; she was assisted by Tim McGinnis and Cy Keith Jones. After Ms. Brown left to become the editor-in-chief of a new magazine, the book came under the auspices of Loretta A. Barrett, Executive Editor of Anchor Press, assisted by Paul Aron and Dave Gernert. The editorial assistant for *The Politics of Women's Spirituality* was Laura Van Wormer. The copy editor was Rosalyn Badalamenti; the designer was Paul Randall Mize. I thank all of these people for their advice, assistance, and enthusiasm.

# Contents

Acknowledgments   v

Introduction / *Charlene Spretnak*   xi

PART ONE: DISCOVERING A HISTORY OF POWER

WHAT THE GODDESS MEANS TO WOMEN

Poem / *Ntozake Shange*   3
Preface   5
The Great Goddess: Who Was She? / *Merlin Stone*   7
Women and Culture in Goddess-Oriented Old Europe / *Marija Gimbutas*   22
Prepatriarchal Female/Goddess Images / *Adrienne Rich*   32
The Origins of Music: Women's Goddess Worship / *Sophie Drinker*   39
Witchcraft as Goddess Religion / *Starhawk*   49
From the House of Yemanja: The Goddess Heritage of Black Women / *Sabrina Sojourner*   57
The Three Faces of Goddess Spirituality / *Merlin Stone*   64
Why Women Need the Goddess: Phenomenological, Psychological, and Political Reflections / *Carol P. Christ*   71

MYTHIC HERAS AS MODELS OF STRENGTH AND WISDOM

Prose Poem / *Robin Morgan*   87
Preface   89
Ancient Mirrors of Womanhood / *Merlin Stone*   91
The Amazon Legacy / *Phyllis Chesler*   97
Tales of a Reincarnated Amazon Princess: The Invincible Wonder Woman! / *Gloria Steinem*   114

Growing Up with Legends of the Chinese Swordswomen / *Siew Hwa Beh*  121

Meanings of Matriarchy / *Margot Adler*  127

Drawing from Mythology in Women's Quest for Selfhood / *Bella Debrida*  138

Our Heritage Is Our Power / *Judy Chicago*  152

PART TWO: MANIFESTING PERSONAL POWER

CONSCIOUSNESS/ENERGY/ACTION

Poem / *Judy Grahn*  159

Preface  161

A Consciousness Manifesto / *Nancy F. W. Passmore*  163

Consciousness, Politics, and Magic / *Starhawk*  172

The Metaphors of Power / *Barbara Starrett*  185

Womanpower: Energy Re-Sourcement / *Sally Gearhart*  194

Gyn/Ecology: Spinning New Time/Space / *Mary Daly*  207

Feminist Witchcraft: Controlling Our Own Inner Space / *Naomi Goldenberg*  213

Contemporary Feminist Rituals / *Kay Turner*  219

Honor and Ceremony in Women's Rituals / *E. M. Broner*  234

SELF-IMAGES OF STRENGTH AND WHOLENESS

Poem / *Marge Piercy*  245

Preface  247

Images and Models—in Process / *Juanita Weaver*  249

Martial Art Meditations / *Emily E. Culpepper*  258

From Sacred Blood to the Curse and Beyond / *Judy Grahn*  265

The Healing Powers of Women / *Chellis Glendinning*  280

Expanding Personal Power Through Meditation / *Hallie Iglehart*  294

Feeding the Feminist Psyche Through Ritual Theater / *Batya Podos*  305

See for Yourself: Women's Spirituality in Holistic Art / *Mary Beth Edelson*  312

Images of Spiritual Power in Women's Fiction / *Carol P. Christ and Charlene Spretnak*  327

# PART THREE: TRANSFORMING THE POLITICAL

THE UNITY OF POLITICS AND SPIRITUALITY

Prose Poem / *Adrienne Rich*   347
Preface   349
Sisterhood as Cosmic Covenant / *Mary Daly*   351
The Personal Is Political / *Sheila D. Collins*   362
Dimensions of Spirituality / *Judy Davis and Juanita Weaver*   368
Politics, Spirituality, and Models of Change / *Dorothy I. Riddle*   373
The Politics of Feminist Spirituality / *Anne Kent Rush*   382
Metaphysical Feminism / *Robin Morgan*   386
The Politics of Women's Spirituality / *Charlene Spretnak*   393
Feminist Spirituality: The Politics of the Psyche / *Judith Antonelli*   399
The Unnatural Divorce of Spirituality and Politics / *Hallie Iglehart*   404
Ethics and Justice in Goddess Religion / *Starhawk*   415


APPLICATIONS OF SPIRITUALITY AS A POLITICAL FORCE

Poem / *June Jordan*   423
Preface   425
WITCH: Spooking the Patriarchy during the Late Sixties   427
On Common Ground: Native American and Feminist Spirituality Approaches in the Struggle to Save Mother Earth / *Judith Todd*   430
Spiritual Dimensions of Feminist Anti-Nuclear Activism / *Gina Foglia and Dorit Wolffberg*   446
Spiritual Techniques for Re-Powering Survivors of Sexual Assault / *Carolyn R. Shaffer*   462
The Christian Right's "Holy War" Against Feminism / *Charlene Spretnak*   470
The Voice of Women's Spirituality in Futurism / *Baba Copper*   497
Women's Collective Spirit: Exemplified and Envisioned / *Grace Shinell*   510

Appendix: Two Debates

I. Does Hierarchy Have a Place in Women's Spirituality?  531

    Spiritual Hierarchies: The Empress' New Clothes? / *Gloria* Z.
      *Greenfield*  531
    *Response by* Z. *Budapest*: The Vows, Wows, and Joys of the High
      Priestess or What Do You People Do Anyway?  535

II. Are Goddesses and Matriarchies Merely Figments of Feminist Imag-
    ination?  541

    Myths and Matriarchies / *Sally R. Binford*  541
    *Responses by Merlin Stone and Charlene Spretnak*  550
    *Counter-Response by Sally R. Binford*  558
    *Post-Counter-Response by Charlene Spretnak*  560

Afterword: Feminist Politics and the Nature of Mind / *Charlene Spretnak*  563

Notes on the Contributors  575

A Bibliography of Feminist Spirituality  581

# Introduction

Whose purposes are served by patriarchal religion? Analysts in both the first and second waves of feminism have exposed the sexism behind Judeo-Christian symbolism, ideology, structure, and ministry, but such revelations have often been dismissed by the feminist movement at large as wastes of energy that would better be spent on *real* political work. The message, however, that was voiced initially by Matilda Joslyn Gage in *Woman, Church and State* (1893) and by Elizabeth Cady Stanton and the Revising Committee in *The Woman's Bible* (1895) is not that patriarchal religion is merely "unfair" in itself: The lies about the nature and function of woman that are intrinsic to patriarchal religion have informed the legal, educational, political, economic, and medical/psychiatric systems of our society and are accepted as "natural truths" by even the most modern and/or atheistic citizens. Anyone who has been resisting this feminist insight during the past eighty-five years will surely have to reconsider now that the Christian Right is acting out a predictable, yet disconcerting, scenario on the stage of national politics: Masses of fundamentalist Christians *and other concerned citizens* have been mobilized to defeat the Equal Rights Amendment to the United States Constitution, and other pro-feminist legislation at all levels, because it would upset "God's natural law" and disturb the "natural" roles of the sexes.

There is nothing natural about patriarchal religion. It is a relatively recent invention. Abraham, the first patriarch of the Judeo-Christian tradition, is dated at *c.* 1800 B.C. and Mohammed at *c.* 600 A.D.; male gods (as the omnipotent ruler, rather than as the son/consort of the Goddess or as minor vegetation deities) were introduced in India, the Middle and Near East, Eastern Europe, and later in Greece, by barbarian invaders who spread out in waves from the Eurasian steppes, beginning around 4500 B.C.[1] In contrast, artifacts related to the religion of the Goddess are dated as early as *c.* 25,000 B.C. and have been discovered in all of the regions mentioned above, plus numerous others.

Humankind's earliest artifacts, the numerous female statues from the Upper Paleolithic period, document the awe our ancestors felt for women and their mysteries, e.g., bleeding painlessly in rhythm with the moon, drawing *people* from their bodies, producing food from their bodies for the young. Since paternity was not recognized for a long, long while (well into the twentieth century, the native Australians still believed that women are impregnated by spirits in the wind), the matrilineal clan was the bonding unit of matrifocal culture. Such a culture developed sacred myths and spiritual practices based on a macrocosmic application of the mysteries they observed at hand: Earth is the bountiful female, the ever-giving Mother, Who sends forth food on Her surface in cyclical rhythms and receives our dead back into Her womb. Rituals in Her honor took place in womb-like caves, often with vulva-like entrances and long, slippery corridors. The elemental power of the female was the cultural focus as far back as we can trace.

At the moment this awe turned to envy, resentment, and fear, patriarchy was born. Why or how we do not know.[2] What we do know, all too well, is the nature of patriarchy and its destructive effects on both sexes. Men had once felt a secure sense of connection with the essential life processes, through the womb of the Great Mother, but under the patriarchal system they become mere outsiders observing the powerful flow of nature in its procreative cycles. Their response to this separation and alienation may constitute the very core of misogyny. The objective of patriarchy was and is to prevent women from achieving, or even supposing, our potential: that we are powerful in both mind *and* body and that the totality of those powers is a potent force. All of the myriad varieties of patriarchal oppression — co-opting and replacing the Goddess, imposing patrilineal descent and ownership of woman's womb, restricting and mutilating woman's body, denying woman education and legal rights, forbidding her control of her body, and portraying that body as a pornographic toy — *all* of these acts are motivated by one desperate drive: to prevent woman from experiencing her power.

They almost succeeded. Women raised under patriarchy are trained early on to regard themselves as "the other," as Simone de Beauvoir observed in 1949. We were never exposed to models of female power, except for strong female figures who dutifully supported the patriarchal order, such as the revisionist Olympian version of Athena. A woman under patriarchy receives daily variations of the message that her only hope in life is to attach herself to a man who possesses, actually or potentially, economic, legal, intellectual, and spiritual power — seemingly as a natural birthright. After all, he is the same sex as lawmakers, presidents, kings, priests, and even God Himself.

Since men could never possess the elemental power that women have, they sought to hoard all the cultural, i.e., invented, power. Toward this end, they created ludicrous myths that belie the truths of nature, e.g., Zeus giving birth to His daughter Athena by having Her spring from His forehead (fully armed and ready to defend Daddy's property!), and Yahweh/God the Father birthing the Earth and all its creatures by performing some tricky sleights of hand. Patriarchal culture also denigrated the formerly sacred menstrual blood and childbirth, declaring that both render women categorically "unclean." Still, power is power — and the reason the feminist movement makes many men extremely uneasy on a visceral level is that women are regaining cultural power *along with our elemental power*. ("Men do look to destroy every quality in a woman which will give her the powers of a male, for she is in their eyes already armed with the power that she brought them forth, and that is a power beyond measure." — Norman Mailer) Fortunately for the patriarchs, the female mind uses power in more positive, life-affirming ways than the patriarchal "an eye for an eye, a tooth for a tooth." In short, justice and cultural sanity interest us, not vengeful degradation and reverse oppression.

Insights into the intrinsic nature of patriarchal religion and culture can be deduced from recent neuropsychological research. When experimental psychologists study the sexes' functioning in the areas of senses and attention, as well as in the traditional area of study, cognitive skills, they conclude that man is a "manipulative animal" who tends to express himself in actions, while woman is a "communicative animal," who prefers to remember, share, and transmit signs and symbols to others. From infancy, males are fascinated with objects, females with human faces, voices, and music; later, females are more empathetic and socially responsive.[3] If a person is born with a mind that does not readily perceive "connectedness" with other people and is raised in a culture that does not encourage such perceptions, he will probably go through life seeing only separations, struggling with the frustrations of this worldview ("Hell is other people." — Jean-Paul Sartre) and accepting its corollaries as truth ("War is the nature of man." — G. Gordon Liddy, lecturing to college students after serving his Watergate prison term).

Often when women are asked to describe their ideal state, they speak of harmonious relations with family, friends, and colleagues and of satisfying work. In contrast, men often say something like, "Being in control, no boss over me. Being able to do whatever I want at any given time." With such psychological bents, it is not difficult to understand why the "manipulative animal" perceives the concept of supreme deity, i.e., ultimate power, as The Great Manipulator, the jealous, fierce, judgmental Father who keeps records of everyone's behavior and must be obeyed completely if one is to escape damnation.

Correspondingly, patriarchal religion and society are built on the notion of hierarchical control: God the Father → Jesus → man → woman (and, where applicable, other "not-full-beings" such as people of color) → children → animals → nature. (Diane McGuinness' article on aggression and dominance, cited in Footnote 3, includes evidence that males, even at pre-school age, organize themselves into a linear dominance system, in which all males submit to Male A, Male B submits to Male A but no others, etc.) If the impulse to manipulate and control is more highly developed in the average male than is the impulse toward empathy, communion, and harmony, perhaps it follows that most men physiologically *feel good* when they dominate a neighbor's army, a football team, a business associate, a woman's body. Patriarchal culture is rather brilliantly suited to male proclivities, but its values do not resonate with the female mind — nor with a number of men's, for the neurophysiologists stress emphatically that they are expressing averages, not absolutes.

Living under patriarchy, then, women have had to cope with prevailing attitudes that are alien to us. As Andrea Dworkin has wryly observed, "Women have had two choices: lie or die. Feminists are trying to open up the options a bit." Women who refused to lie about the "wisdom" of patriarchal religion and culture were, indeed, often sentenced to torture and/or death, e.g., the brutal slaughter of the Goddess-worshipping Pagans in the Biblical accounts, the massive Witch-burnings in Europe during the Renaissance, the psychiatric incarceration and electroshock therapy of post-World-War-II housewives who refused to adapt to a submissive role. Moreover, all the millions of women who did opt to live the patriarchal lies also died — a death of the spirit, of their inner wisdom and mature sense of being, of their potential for growth. We were told by church, law, and society to maintain our "natural" station as the childlike, obedient helpmate to our husbands — to be the "lesser vessel" in a patriarchal marriage. Inner development and communion with "the powers that be" were reserved for men, who declared we were incapable of such activities.

Contemporary feminists have continued the work of the first wave by exposing the woman-hating in patriarchal religion and its shallow historical legitimacy. Many women are fighting valiantly to become Judeo-Christian clergy and are attempting to reform the sexist language and concepts of that tradition.[4] Others of us, however, have concluded that Judeo-Christian spirituality is too relentlessly patriarchal — in origin, content, form, and implication — to be redeemed. Although it has certainly been successful as an arm of patriarchal politics, we feel that patriarchal religion has failed, and failed with disastrous effects on humans and on the Earth, at perceiving and communing with "the higher powers" in a constructive and life-affirming way. We are committed to the evolution of postpatriarchal spirituality. "Opening up the options" is the subject of this book.

That patriarchal religion is unhealthy for the female psyche is rather obvious. Beyond that, however, many people wonder, "Why *any* spirituality? It's all hype. Western religion has been used to control the masses, and Eastern mysticism is too esoteric to be relevant."

In truth, there is nothing "mystical" or "other worldly" about spirituality. The life of the spirit, or soul, refers merely to functions of the mind. Hence spirituality is an intrinsic dimension of human consciousness and is not separate from the body; e.g., the Greek concept of *pneuma* meant breath or spirit or soul, and *spirit* comes from the Latin root for "to breathe". From one perspective, we realize that we need food, shelter, and clothing; from another that some sort of relationship among people, animals, and the Earth is necessary; from another that we must determine our identity as creatures not only of our immediate habitat but of the world and the universe; from another that the subtle, suprarational reaches of mind can reveal the true nature of being: All is One, all forms of existence are comprised of one continuous dance of matter/energy arising and falling away, arising and falling away. Only the illusions of separation divide us. The experience of union with the One has been called cosmic consciousness, God consciousness, knowing the One Mind, etc.

One cluster of spiritual approaches, e.g., Judaism, Christianity, Islam, much of Hinduism, maintains that people will be united with God in the afterlife (or afterlives, in the case of Hinduism) and that, meanwhile, the separations among beings are of tantamount importance. Man is a sinful creature (and woman even more so) who is far below Yahweh, God the Father, Allah, or Brahma/Vishnu/Krishna and can only hope to win His favor by appealing to the priestly caste with its power-over rituals. Infidels, "unclean" or even "untouchable" neighbors, *goyim,* and non-believers are not considered to be full persons; neither are the women within these traditions.[5] Placating the judgmental Father God and obeying "His will" is the essence of this spiritual practice; fear, guilt, and alienation are some of the results.

Another cluster of spiritual approaches stresses the intrinsic unity of all forms of being, the "life force" or "life energy." Experiences of union with the One are accessible to everyone here and now; the truth of oneness is expressed in the consciousness of everyday existence. In this cluster are women's spirituality, Goddess spirituality, Wicca, Native American spirituality, Taoism, Buddhism, Sufism, and yoga. (The last two pre-date Islam and Hinduism, which absorbed them; the entire cluster includes prepatriarchal imagery and concepts that survived even through the patriarchal era.[6]) Also included are "natural philosophy," which has persisted in Western culture, although definitely as a minority voice,[7] and the spiritual implications of the discoveries of modern physics.[8]

The second cluster may be thought of as the integrative, or holistic, path. All experience is "grist for the mill," is the stuff of wisdom and growth *as an ongoing process.* Inner development is encouraged as a profound adventure, but only within the sphere of oneness and the realization that all of our fates are inextricably linked. This orientation is the opposite of the egocentric I-me-my mentality. The holistic approaches may be serious and/or reverential toward their concepts (called in Buddhism "the Dharma," which merely means the way things really are, the "naked truth," as opposed to illusions of separation, stasis, etc.), but they are also joyful and playful. Their refusal to be grim has irritated many Western/patriarchal critics for, as Theodore Roszak has observed, those men simply cannot bring themselves to endorse a system of spirituality or psychology that has no sense of sin at its center: "Fallenness, fear and trembling — so they have learned from St. Paul and St. Augustine, Calvin and Kierkegaard, Freud and Sartre, *et al.* — are the credentials of serious knowledge. Without the whiplash of guilt, there is no way to enforce self-denial; and without self-denial, there is no basis for moral conduct."[9] As we know, however, there is indeed another basis: Moral conduct can follow from one's moral identity. If we believe, and experientially *know* through various practices such as meditation and holistic ritual, that neither our sisters and brothers nor the rest of nature is "the other," we will not violate their being, nor our own. Ethics of mutual respect would not allow coercion or domination, such as forcing someone to give birth or to kill.

The only holistic approach that involves an anthropomorphized concept of deity is Goddess spirituality.[10] However, just as the matrifocal cultures were communal, harmonious, and peaceful (Minoan Crete, for example, enjoyed a thousand years without war, and the settlements of Old Europe were unfortified for millennia before the invasions), thereby differing very substantially from patriarchal cultures, so the meaning of the Goddess differs substantially from that of God. No one is interested in revering a "Yahweh with a skirt," a distant, judgmental, manipulative figure of power who holds us all in a state of terror. The revival of the Goddess has resonated with so many people because She symbolizes *the way things really are:* All forms of being are One, continually renewed in cyclic rhythms of birth, maturation, death. That is the meaning of Her triple aspect — the waxing, full, and waning moon; the maiden, mother, and wise crone. The Goddess honors *union and process,* the cosmic dance, the eternally vibrating flux of matter/ energy: She expresses the dynamic, rather than static, model of the universe. She is *immanent* in our lives and our world (see "Consciousness, Politics, and Magic" by Starhawk). She contains both female and male, in Her womb, as a male deity cannot; all beings are *part of Her,* not distant creations. She also symbolizes the power of the female body/mind. There is no "party line" of Goddess worship; rather, each person's process of perceiving and living Her truth is a movement in the larger dance — hence the phrase "The Goddess Is All."

Women's spirituality is not synonymous with Goddess spirituality; some practitioners of the former are uncomfortable with any anthropomorphizing of the One.[11] In many cases, their spirituality is comprised of the truths of naturalism and the holistic proclivities of women. The theme of women's elemental power runs throughout this book, and by that I do not mean "merely" our power to form people from our very flesh and blood and then to nourish them from our breasts, or the fact that we run on cosmic time, i.e., share the cycles of the moon. I mean that there are many moments in a woman's life wherein she gains experiential knowledge, in a powerful body/mind union, of the holistic truths of spirituality.[12] First of all, neuropsychologists have demonstrated that females are predisposed from a very early age to perceive *connectedness* in life, e.g., females are more empathetic, and they remain more aware of subtle, contextual "data" in interpersonal contacts throughout adulthood. Second, the purpose of many spiritual practices such as meditation, ritual, music, and dance is to move one's consciousness beyond the mundane perception of illusion, i.e., that all beings are separate, mechanistic entities, to the consciousness of oneness. This "altered" mindstate occurs to varying degrees when women experience "reclaimed" menstruation (see "From Sacred Blood to the Curse and Beyond" by Judy Grahn); orgasm (the sense of having no boundaries in the postorgasmic state is often described by women as a peaceful, expansive mindstate, by men as fearsome, vulnerable, or even terrifying); and pregnancy, natural childbirth, and motherhood (as Nancy Passmore observes in "A Consciousness Manifesto," "Certainly the distinction between me and not me becomes a little blurry, to say the least, when one has been inhabited as a mother.") The experiences inherent in women's sexuality are expressions of the essential, holistic nature of life on Earth; they are "body parables" of the profound oneness and interconnectedness of all matter/energy, which physicists have discovered in recent decades at the subatomic level. Every woman who has practiced meditation and is aware of the holistic composition of the universe — whether through Goddess spirituality, Eastern religion, or modern physics — recognizes that her postorgasmic mindstate is something quite different from what males have described as *le petit mort* (the little death); rather, the boundary-less, free-floating, nondiscriminating sense of oneness that females experience could more accurately be called *le petit satori* (the little glimpse of enlightenment). In a culture that honored, rather than denigrated such "body truth," the holistic realities would be guiding principles of ethics and structure.[13]

Men, too, experience moments of heightened awareness when everything seems different, more vividly alive. They have often written that such instances occur during the hunting of a large animal, the landing/killing of a large fish, the moments just before and during combat. Not feeling intrinsically involved in the processes of birthing and nurture, nor strongly predisposed toward empathetic communion, men may have turned their attention, for many eras, toward the other aspect of the cycle, death. Certainly much of men's art and literature has shown an obsession with this theme, and the male-orchestrated global arms race is suicide on a grand scale. But many men, too, have life-affirming "awakenings," often related to naturalism, and, like women, report spiritual experiences in near-death situations wherein one feels sublimely peaceful and is drawn toward union with a compelling light or union with one's family members who died previously.

That there are similarities and very real differences between the sexes is not news. What is new is our refusal to accept patriarchal perceptions and interpretations of those differences. To achieve a sane society that reflects, spiritually and culturally, holistic truths, we must encourage awareness, or "mindfulness," of such truths. Admittedly, women seem to have an elemental advantage, but men may consider that old feminist saw: Biology is not destiny. All minds contain all possibilities. The sexes are not opposites or dualistic polarities; the differences are matters of degree, whether negligible or immense. Inner growth, not war, is our natural state, and much could be done to foster it. For example, during the past decade men have been encouraged to be with their wives/lovers during labor and delivery, and they report feeling a much stronger bond with those children in whose birthing they had participated than with the older siblings from whose births the fathers had been banned by patriarchal custom. A holistic orientation would also include teaching children the connectedness among all beings through raising them with non-sexist principles.[14]

Every person contains the entire range of options for thinking and behaving; s/he may be predisposed to some more than others, and cultural values will encourage or discourage the development of various options. A popular, patriarchal approach to spiritual integration, Jungian psychology, has, in my opinion, obfuscated the issue of cultivating one's possibilities. C. G. Jung theorized that one grouping of human traits and tendencies is *intrinsically feminine,* comprising the "anima," while another group is *intrinsically masculine,* the "animus." The first is called "passive," the second "active." Jungian analysts commonly identify a woman's career activities, for instance, as an expression of "the active, masculine part of her self." ("Man is defined as a human being and woman as a female — whenever she behaves as a human being, she is said to imitate the male." — Simone de Beauvoir) This identification has pervaded nearly all areas of contemporary life, to the extent that school counselors often advise girls not to go into the "masculine" fields because it would be too much of a strain on their predominantly "passive" nature. Jung himself said, ". . . in taking up a masculine calling, studying, and working in a man's way, woman is doing something not wholly in agreement with, if not directly injurious to, her feminine nature."

First of all, what is intrinsically "masculine" about mentally rotating a three-dimensional object (a visual-spatial task at which men excel), and what is intrinsically "feminine" about processing information quickly (a task at which females surpass males)? And what about the extremely active behavior of women fiercely defending their young from time immemorial? Do not such attacks or counterattacks stem directly from their motherhood? Who would ever deduce that women are acting "masculine" at such times except someone peering through a filter of patriarchal values that requires all courageous, laudatory acts to somehow be associated with the male nature?

Not only is there no commonsense reasoning for Jung's labeling of specific traits and actions as "feminine" or "masculine," but his scheme is not supported by experiential truth. At the moments when I have acted assertively, or downright aggressively when faced with physical violence, I did not feel "masculine" in any fiber of my being; I simply felt like a strong woman. Likewise, I imagine that when men give nurturing and affection, they do not feel "feminine"; they are simply being loving men. Moreover, the New Age rallying cry of "Balance the masculine and feminine parts of your mind in order to be whole" has actually accomplished relatively little.[15] After hearing such advice extolled for ten years now, most men still consider the "masculine" traits to be essential, positive, and admirable, while the "feminine" traits are seen, if the truth be told, as peripheral, weak, and often contemptible.[16] As for women, we have made considerable progress in shedding patriarchal conditioning and letting our own strong selves emerge, but I do not know of any of us who wish to develop a more "masculine" frame of reference.

In spite of all false advice from patriarchal experts, psychological balance is a desirable goal, and the recent research by neuropsychologists suggests a way to break the spell of Jung's biased notions of the "eternal feminine" and "eternal masculine": One could simply say that most women naturally possess *integrative* skills and most men naturally possess *analytical* skills. Each person contains both areas in varying proportions, and both should be developed.[17] In achieving balance, as in perceiving holistic spiritual truths, women again have an advantage: We possess contextual perception and integrative skills from birth and then spend twelve or twenty or more years developing our analytical skills in patriarchal school systems.[18] Those schools merely increase the imbal-

ance with which men are born *and* do considerable harm to all students
by teaching separation, friction, fear, and competition.

I am not suggesting that all the mysteries of the human psyche will
ever be revealed in a laboratory, merely that what can be known should
be. The path of women's spirituality does not involve an artificial
search for "masculine" traits. We look, instead, to our elemental power.

My own patterns of awakening in the evolution of women's spirituality parallel those of many other feminists. I began life firmly en-
trenched in the Judeo-Christian tradition, experienced a disappointing
emptiness in that orientation, and finally began making personal discoveries of the spiritual dimensions of life. Those discoveries acquired a
frame of reference when I learned of the ancient prepatriarchal myths
and religions that had honored female access to spiritual realities and
personal power. As I began to meet other women who were making
similar discoveries and who were quick to see the political implications,
I knew we would never be lost again.

Women's spirituality evolved as an independent spiritual option only
by first passing through a necessary stage of reacting to the sexism of
patriarchal religion.[19] After *The Church and the Second Sex* by Mary
Daly appeared in 1968, a spate of well-argued books continued the
feminist critique. In 1973, Daly's *Beyond God the Father* both reacted
irrefutably against the Church's philosophy *and* pioneered postpatriarchal spirituality: "The conflict is on the level of being and non-being." Much of "New Age spirituality" was also found to be sexist; see,
for instance, "The Politics of Wholeness: Feminism and the New Spirituality" by Susan Leigh Star in *Sinister Wisdom,* Spring 1977.

In recent years nearly every major feminist magazine has featured an
issue on women's spirituality, e.g., *Heresies: A Feminist Publication on
Art and Politics,* no. 5; *Chrysalis: A Magazine of Women's Culture,* no.
6; and *Quest: A Feminist Quarterly,* vol. 1, no. 4 and vol. 4, no. 3. In
addition, two feminist journals specifically concerned with spirituality,
and its implications for our politics, have flourished: *WomanSpirit* and
*Lady-Unique-Inclination-of-the-Night.* Although not exclusively feminist, *Anima: An Experiential Journal,* edited by Harry M. Buck and
Rebecca Nisley, has published articles by many of the theorists included in this anthology.

*WomanSpirit* was founded in the autumn of 1974 by two inscru-
tably wise crones, Jean and Ruth Mountaingrove. Every season since
then, a quarterly issue of *WomanSpirit* has emanated from their office

in Wolf Creek, Oregon, where they are assisted by several other women. They have published many of "the great debates" (see Footnote 4 and Appendix) and myriad accounts of women all over the country discovering and applying their elemental power. On the opposite side of the continent, *Lady Unique* began publication in the autumn of 1976 and has appeared annually. It is edited by Kay Turner and beautifully produced by the Lady Unique Collective in New Brunswick, New Jersey. Also in 1976, Nancy F. W. Passmore founded *The Lunar Calendar,* a thirteen-month calendar and compendium of art and essays on spirituality which is published each summer by The Luna Press in Boston.

The misperception of women's spirituality as an apolitical "cop-out" from feminist struggles has sometimes taken comic twists.[20] A member of the Matriarchal Study Group in London told me that while planning a special issue of *Shrew* on spirituality, their meetings were infiltrated by a Marxist feminist who subtly but persistently tried to get them to see "the error of their ways"! Conversely, feminist spirituality buffs have done some infiltrating of their own. Mary Beth Edelson (see "See for Yourself: Women's Spirituality in Holistic Art") laughingly confessed that she had joined the *Heresies* magazine collective to make sure a spirituality issue would be produced. The collective, all hard-core Manhattanites, was nervous about such a topic and nearly canceled it, but when the issue, titled "The Great Goddess," was published in September 1978, it sold out immediately in bookstores around the country and was one of the most successful issues of *Heresies.*

All of the pieces in this anthology are active rather than reactive, are revolutionary rather than reformist, and express broad political awareness. Many of them have come to be considered feminist classics; nearly half of the essays and articles were commissioned specifically for this volume and are appearing for the first time. No one book could include all the current aspects of women's spirituality, and much excellent work that does not fit the particular framework of this anthology is recommended in the bibliography. Just as there are thousands of books on patriarchal spirituality, we can look forward to thousands on holistic, postpatriarchal spirituality! I doubt that any one of the contributors, myself included, would agree completely with *all* of the diverse ideas expressed within the range of this anthology. This is not a source of dissension, for we are not seeking any sort of *ex cathedra* doctrine. Rather, we value the insights that occur when women share the spiritual *process* that they experience, when women think about postpatriarchal spirituality and speak their truths. From these most deeply held truths grow our political convictions: "What would happen if one woman told the truth about her life? The world would split open." — Muriel Rukeyser.

The title *The Politics of Women's Spirituality* refers to our attitude toward life on Earth (i.e., spirituality) and the perception, manifestation, and use of power (i.e., politics) that stem from that attitude. The worldview inherent in feminist spirituality is, like the female mind, holistic and integrative. We see *connectedness* where the patriarchal mentality insists on seeing only separations. An excellent example of the integrative approach to issues was the unity statement of the Women's Pentagon Action in November 1980, which addressed the network of horrors that flow from patriarchal values, the domination and exploitation of "the other": foreign countries, women, minorities, and the Earth (see "Spiritual Dimensions of Feminist Anti-Nuclear Activism").

The global feminist movement is bringing about the end of patriarchy, the eclipse of the politics of separation, and the beginning of a new era modeled on the dynamic, holistic paradigm. In working toward those goals, we have many allies among men. Radical feminists envision that era, and the long process leading toward it, as a *comprehensive* transformation. The gains that we make in legal, economic, medical, and educational areas will be shortlived unless they are grounded in collective action that is continually fueled by a strong sense of our personal power and its elemental source. In fact, without that sense of inner power, without the sense that *we* are the source of change, our vision will not prevail.

As we enter the second decade of the second wave of feminism, we are faced with a growing backlash from the reactionary forces in our society. Politically, they are determined to block all programs and legislation that would establish equal rights for women. Culturally, the backlash takes the form of patriarchal censorship. In recent weeks, I have read three reviews in respected journals that began or ended with a variation of this judgment: "There is no need, really, for the reader to pay any attention to this book [or sculptural exhibition, or play, or record album] since it was obviously created by a feminist . . . and everyone *knows* what we can expect from a source like that." Yes: truth, the way things really are. Although no one system of analysis explains everything in life, feminism explains a great deal of what we see each day, and women's truth, whether artfully expressed or baldly declared, is a message that has always and everywhere terrified the guardians of patriarchy. They will continue to try to crush us. To survive and evolve as free women, we must maintain unity and draw on our inner resources.

In my own life, for instance, I know intellectually that the perception of time as a linear continuum with three neat divisions of past, present, and future is merely an artifice, a mental device; I have read the words of the physicists and the Eastern metaphysicians explaining that all time (and space) is of one essence, is now. But I never *felt* that knowledge as an experiential truth until I encountered women's spirituality and discovered that temporal boundaries can be rather simply dissolved by the female mind's propensity for empathetic comprehension and bonding. Through ritual moments and countless meditations, through absorbing the sacred myths of our prepatriarchal foremothers and passing them on to my daughter, through experiencing in my own daughter/mother mind and body the mysteries celebrated in the ancient rites, I have come to know, to *feel,* oneness with all the millions of women who have lived, who live, and who will live. I contain those millions. Each of us does. Every moment. Such a power cannot be stopped.

CHARLENE SPRETNAK
Berkeley
November 9980*

---

* In "9978: Repairing the Time Warp and Other Related Realities" (*Heresies,* no. 5, Sept. 1978), Merlin Stone pointed out that Christian dating skews time in a manner that makes the A.D. era the "real" time and the B.C. era, which is enormously larger, "a vast emptiness of the unknown or unreal." The truly momentous event for the human race was the development of agriculture [by women, who had been the gatherers of plants, seeds, and roots] during the Proto-Neolithic period, 9000–7000 B.C. Since that radical shift in our ancestor's way of living, there has been a continuous, though not always wise or truly progressive, development of technology and culture. [Most of the sophisticated art, science, and architecture of the Neolithic period was Goddess-oriented; see Marija Gimbutas' article.] Stone proposes that we acknowledge the midpoint of the Proto-Neolithic period, 8000 B.C., as the actual beginning of our cultural history, after the long hunter-gatherer stage. Counting the years by the A.D.A. system (After the Development of Agriculture) brings us now to 9980 and, asserts Stone, makes us aware of that important part of our heritage. I have used patriarchal dating for the bibliographical references throughout this book, but I apply Stone's suggestion here so that readers might think about the fact that even our sense of time has been molded by patriarchal religion.

NOTES

1. See "Proceedings of the International Conference on the Transformation of European Culture at 4500–2500 B.C.," Dubrovnik,
   12–17 Sept. 1979, edited by Marija Gimbutas, *Journal of Indo-
   European Studies*, vol. 8, 1980. Also see Merlin Stone, *When God
   Was a Woman* (1976).
2. One can pinpoint the patriarchal revolution in Europe, Asia, and
   North Africa to the invasions of the barbarian horsemen — but what
   was the cause in other areas, where there is evidence that the same
   shift occurred? Were peaceful, advanced, agrarian, matrifocal cultures universally overrun by nomadic, patriarchal hordes during the
   Neolithic period? This is a major puzzle of human history. Theories
   abound, but most patriarchal, and some feminist, scholars cannot
   come to grips with the archaeological and anthropological evidence
   cited, for instance, by Marija Gimbutas in "Women and Culture in
   Goddess-Oriented Old Europe." In *The Mermaid and the Minotaur:
   Sexual Arrangements and the Human Malaise* (1976), Dorothy Dinnerstein proposed that women's functioning as the primary, omnipotent parent during everyone's first years necessarily results in hatred
   of women, male dominance, and hatred of nature. Applying this
   theory, Dinnerstein doubts that matriarchal societies (or even societies "free of male dominion") could ever have existed unless men
   were the primary givers of infant care, which of course seems very
   unlikely, or unless "the relatively limited and rational power that fathers necessarily represent for mother-raised offspring seemed at that
   time a power too finitely human to be relied upon in any central
   way." But we know that matriarchal or matrifocal cultures did exist;
   the beings who gave life, milk/food, protection, comforting body
   contact, and comprised the societal clan structure, i.e., women, were
   the nexus of power. However, the art, artifacts and sacred myths
   from the prepatriarchal cultures do not express matrifocal power as
   an oppressive, terror-inspiring phenomenon (see *Ancient Mirrors of
   Womanhood: Our Goddess and Heroine Heritage* by Merlin Stone,
   *Lost Goddesses of Early Greece* by Charlene Spretnak, and the forthcoming *The Great Goddess, Giver of All* by Marija Gimbutas and
   Barbara Bradshaw). The matrifocal art and culture *celebrated* the female body. Dinnerstein's book is a good account of the ramifications
   of body-hating in our patriarchal culture, but one cannot assume that
   such attitudes prevailed in the matrifocal societies since the evidence
   indicates the opposite. In addition, recent psychological studies (see
   the articles cited in Footnote 3) suggest that female and male infants

may experience the primary parent's presence and actions quite differently. Boys in groups organize themselves into hierarchical dominance systems as young as age three, so their tendency to perceive dominance in relationships may be present from birth. Infant girls are much more receptive and responsive than boys to voice and facial expressions, i.e., the mother's expressions of love, and do not organize themselves according to any patterns of linear dominance within the play clusters they later form in pre-school. Therefore, it is possible that female infants' primary perception of mothering is that of being loved, while male infants' may be that of being dominated. (If further studies support this extrapolation from the recent research, much of Freudian theory on the humiliations of infancy should be viewed as valuable contributions to the psychology of the male, but not fully relevant to that of the female.) Dinnerstein's solution of shared parenting in itself would not solve "the human malaise" because boys would simply grow up resenting *both* giants who had dominated them in infancy. What is also needed are cultural affirmations of the powers of love — *and the acceptance of being loved*, which would be quite a different orientation than the self-hatred, fragmentation, and violence encouraged by patriarchal culture. However, even with the current conditioning that men receive, many of them, although seemingly a minority, exhibit considerable empathy and gentleness, do love women, and report that they do not resent and/or hate their mothers; in fact, the mother-son bond expressed by such men appears to be genuinely deep and loving. Studies of the kind of parenting that those men received would be valuable information for society.

3. See Daniel Goleman, "Special Abilities of the Sexes: Do They Begin in the Brain?," *Psychology Today*, Nov. 1978; see Diane McGuinness and Karl Pribram, "The Origins of Sensory Bias in the Development of Gender Differences in Perception and Cognition," *Cognitive Growth and Development: Essays in Memory of Herbert G. Birch* (New York: Brunner/Mazel, 1979); see Jo Durden-Smith, "Male and Female: Cracking the Code to Sexuality," *Quest*, Oct. 1980. Also see Diane McGuinness, "The Nature of Aggression and Dominance Systems," *Absolute Values and the Search for the Peace of Mankind: Proc. of the Ninth Internatl. Conference on the Unity of the Sciences*, Miami Beach, Florida, 27–30 Nov. 1980 (New York: Internatl. Cultural Foundation, 1982) for evidence that female primates, like female humans, are more "socially responsive." Earlier primate researchers (e.g., DeVore, 1965) mistakenly perceived dominant males organizing and herding females because the observers did not stay in the field long enough to determine kinship

relationships. Subsequent work by Japanese and American primatologists has revealed that the situation is exactly the reverse: Females constitute the socially cohesive group and are often related; males are occasionally permitted to remain or to join the group from the outside after a consensus has been taken. Females select males with low aggressivity, and highly aggressive males are not tolerated in a social sphere. Perhaps this mode of social organization prevailed throughout our evolutionary journey from primates to hominids to *homo sapiens*.

These research data, and numerous similar reports of recent years, indicate that the female and male personality structures are *not* solely the result of conditioning, as some feminists currently insist. In attempting to deduce the reasons for women's nearly exclusive responsibility for childrearing, Nancy Chodorow has asserted that women assume primary parenting because of intrafamily dynamics and public socialization rather than any "instinctive nurturance" (see *The Reproduction of Mothering*, 1978). This is probably true since many women have no interest in mothering. However, there *are* psychobiological differences between the sexes; the above neurophysiological research has established that most females are more empathetic than most males, even when only a few days old and their responses to human voices are observed. This certainly does not limit women to childcare; the capacity for empathy enhances the wisdom of a judge, a physician, a professor, an executive, or a Cabinet member in charge of any area involving human beings. Although patriarchal conditioning obviously distorts and manipulates the natural bents of the female and male psyches, our goal should not be to stamp out empathy and "connectedness" in women in order to make us more isolated and competitive, better players in the patriarchal game. Rather, the social structure itself would be less cruel and destructive if the female propensities were recognized as the more sensible, humane course for everyone. That is why we protest *en masse* at the Pentagon and elsewhere that we refuse to send our children to fight our sisters' children in other countries: We *feel* that connectedness. We insist upon it.

4. For a reformist feminist critique of feminist spirituality, see Rosemary Radford Ruether, "A Religion for Women: Sources and Strategies," *Christianity and Crisis*, 10 Dec. 1979. Although that journal declined to publish a thorough response by Carol P. Christ, readers can find it in the Summer and Fall 1980 issues of *WomanSpirit*; the Summer issue also features responses by Naomi Goldenberg, Kay Gardner, Z. Budapest, and others. Meanwhile, Ruether had written a more vitriolic version of her critique, "Goddesses and Witches: Liberation and Countercultural Feminism," which was published in *The*

*Christian Century,* 10–17 Sept. 1980. In it she asserts that feminists
involved with postpatriarchal spirituality, whom she tries to relegate
to being peripheral and "countercultural" as opposed to the true
feminism within the Church, are dangerous, immature — and immod-
est! Ruether explained to readers that Goddess-oriented feminists believe all men are by nature evil (absolutely false), that we are a
separatist movement (absolutely false), and that we are fascistic! *The
Christian Century* published several brief responses in their 26 Nov.
issue, all favorable except for Z. Budapest's; among them was a disconcerting letter from a male Methodist minister who opined that all
such silly talk of a women's spirituality is unnecessary since Dorothy
Dinnerstein has already solved the problem of sexism by proposing
her "joyous" solution of shared parenting! Although extremely important, shared parenting most certainly is not a panacea for the myriad
manifestations of patriarchal corruption in our society. Finally, the
issue of 7–14 Jan. 1981 featured a response by Shirley Ann Ranck, a
Unitarian Universalist minister, who corrected several of Ruether's
distortions of feminist spirituality and the history of religion. "Be like
me — or else!" sentiments on either side are sad and clearly divisive.
A feminist's decision to live within or without patriarchal religion
must be honored as a deeply felt expression of her self-determination.
We honor multiplicity within unity — which many of us feel is most
accurately symbolized by the procreative Goddess from Whose womb
comes the multiplicity who are of the One.

5. Some sects may affirm a direct relation with the Divine in this lifetime, e.g., "Jesus is in my heart and is always with me," but their
   lack of bonding with all the "non-believers" does not encourage harmonious relations; the "other" is fair game for hatred, exploitation,
   and aggression.

6. See, for instance, Ellen Marie Chen, "Tao as the Great Mother and
   the Influence of Motherly Love in the Shaping of Chinese Philosophy," *History of Religions,* vol. 14, no. 1, 1974–75.

7. See *The New Natural Philosophy Reader,* edited by Joseph Meeker
   (forthcoming).

8. See Fritjof Capra, *The Tao of Physics* (1975).

9. Theodore Roszak, "If This Be Narcissism," *The Berkeley Monthly,*
   June 1980.

10. Those holistic traditions (e.g., Sufism and yoga, which means
    "union") that were absorbed by the newer, patriarchal religions
    thereafter had to call the One by the name of "God," but that is a
    thin veneer.

11. "Goddess" is capitalized throughout this book, unlike in patriarchal
    usage, not to imply that all the contributors are Goddess-worshippers,

although many are, but, rather, that we honor the values She embodies. After all, since we have a custom in our language of capitalizing the name of the supreme deity, it only makes sense to pay respect to the Original One as well as the Recently Invented One. Similarly, Goddess-worshipper, Pagan, and Witch are capitalized since those spiritual orientations are just as authentic and honorable (and much older) as those whose followers are called Jew, Catholic, Protestant, etc.

12. Beware the patriarchal "wisdom" that has invaded some of the holistic approaches; for instance, a well-known Japanese teacher in the U.S. reasons that women are obviously the more spiritually evolved sex so they can stay in the kitchen preparing meals while the men meditate! In fact, however, *everyone* raised with the alienation inherent in patriarchal culture can benefit from meditation.

13. In the preface to *Womanspirit Rising,* Carol P. Christ and Judith Plaskow tell of the intense opposition that they and other female graduate students at the Yale Divinity School encountered from male professors in the early Seventies when they proposed incorporating women's *experience* into their theological explorations. Never! The Judeo-Christian tradition is comprised of divine truths from which one may extrapolate, they were told, and that is all. The women eventually concluded, rightly, that Judeo-Christian theology is indeed based on experience — men's experience.

14. See Letty Cottin Pogrebin, *Growing Up Free* (1980), for an insightful discussion of the far-reaching damage wrought by sexist child-rearing; the tension encouraged between each sex and the unfathomable "other" strains all social, political, business, and love relationships. Reactionaries are quite wrong in accusing feminists of furthering a unisex society. Such a goal would be psychologically impossible even if it were desirable, which it is not. What we are striving for is wholeness, no more crippling of the psyche by sexism.

15. Unfortunately, most New Age thinkers have extended the erroneous Jungian association to their understanding of the Taoist concept of *yin* and *yang.* The Western notions of "passive" and "active" are not accurate translations of Chinese thought. *Wu wei,* literally "non-action," means refraining from actions against nature, thus acting in harmony with the Tao. The Chinese associated this consciousness of oneness with the female, *yin.*

16. Recently I observed an exchange between two people, both long-time adherents of New Age, holistic principles, that demonstrated the firmly rooted connotations of patriarchal labels. The man exhibited a lovely viola he had made of polished dark wood with graceful curves. The woman said, "It's beautiful! So earthy!" He said, "Yeah, it's re-

ally masculine and gutsy." She said again, with genuine admiration, "So beautiful and earthy!" He said again, with unmistakable satisfaction, "Yeah, really masculine and gutsy." An observer unacquainted with patriarchal values would have been hardpressed to explain how the viola could be considered "masculine" since its curves resembled the woman's body much more than the man's. As for me, I found myself smiling at the thought of just how "gutsy" that particular man would be while birthing a nine-pound baby, assuming, of course, that he had chosen to do it without anesthesia, as so many of us have.

17. Developing as many areas of the mind as possible and encouraging holistic values may be sufficient for postpatriarchal generations, but those of us who are living through, and causing, this transition period must also devote considerable attention to healing the psychological wounds inflicted by patriarchy, principally the lack of self-love that plagues most women and many men.

18. See Rosalie A. Cohen, "Conceptual Styles, Culture Conflict, and Nonverbal Tests of Intelligence," *American Anthropologist*, vol. 71, 1969. Studies show that girls are more likely than boys to combine the "parts-specific" (analytical) and the "global/gestalt/relational" modes of cognition. In addition, McGuinness and Pribram have discovered that females are better able to coordinate the activities of the left (verbal) and right (visual) hemispheres of the brain than are males.

19. I realize that "postpatriarchal" is itself a reactive name for the "new" women's spirituality. However, to call it simply "holistic," which it is, would render invisible the fact that this orientation is a clear and sensible alternative to patriarchal religion, which many women and men mistake as the only option for spirituality. That is an extremely important message right now.

20. Sometimes the misunderstandings about women's spirituality are not so light-hearted. A loosely knit faction of feminists who sometimes refer to themselves as "materialist feminists" (Marxists and other anti-spirituality folks) insists that a feminist is either spiritual *or* political. We, of course, do not see such a separation. Many of the contributors to this book, for example, are unequivocally activist on a broad range of issues. We simply consider inadequate any political vision that fails to incorporate the spiritual dimensions of life. For more on this topic, see the last exchange in the Appendix. For a convergence point of creeping socialism and creeping paganism, see the essays in this volume by Sally Gearhart and Grace Shinell.

# PART ONE

# Discovering a History of Power

# What the Goddess Means to Women

i found god in myself
& i loved her / i loved her fiercely

— Ntozake Shange

# What the Goddess Means to Women

When I was traveling in the Middle East and Central Asia in 1969, the people I met, mostly peasants, would often ask about my home, my family, and my religion. Being a retired Catholic with an interest in Buddhist meditation, I attempted to express my feelings about spirituality and nearly always they would ask, "Do you have a book?" They felt that a holy book of any sort — the Koran, the Upanishads, the Sutras, the Bible — would signify legitimacy. Sometimes I sense that same reaction among contemporary theologians and people in general toward Goddess spirituality — to which I respond: We are older, much older, than books.

Many of the sacred myths of the Goddess that were told by our prepatriarchal ancestors have survived and are now being gathered into books, although much of the Old Religion has been destroyed during the suppression of the patriarchal era. Ancient Mirrors of Womanhood: Our Goddess and Heroine Heritage and Lost Goddesses of Early Greece are examples of such collections. To sift through the surviving fragments of the ancient Goddess spirituality is a sobering experience. How close we came to losing that wisdom forever, to believing the pa-

*triarchal assertions that their politics of separation are the natural — the only — way to live.*

*Patriarchal governments and religions regard the current Goddess revival with deep-seated fear. Nothing threatens their power structure so resoundingly as the ancient consciousness that they believed had been crushed. In panicked tones, they declare that we are the demonic anti-Christ or that we are "unnatural" or "indecent." In England, for instance, the artist Monica Sjoo was nearly brought to trial in 1970 and again in 1973 for exhibiting a painting titled* God Giving Birth *(1968), which features a large female figure in the process of giving birth while the planets revolve nearby. This the British authorities found deserving of a blasphemy and obscenity charge!*

*Feminists do not claim to own the Goddess. She has meaning for all people as a symbol of the holistic nature of life on Earth, in which all forms of being are intrinsically linked and are one (see Introduction). She also has special meaning for women as an expression of the power of the female body/mind. As such, it is not difficult to deduce why almost none of the history presented in the following selections appears in patriarchal textbooks. I am not suggesting a "conspiracy" among scholars but, rather, a pervasive cultural attitude that all prepatriarchal religions were less worthy than the Judeo-Christian system. For example, one never reads of "the religion of Artemis" and "the cult of Jesus"; it is always the other way around. Similarly, the ancient Near Eastern words for "sanctified women" or "holy women" were translated by patriarchal scholars as "temple prostitutes."*

*Yet, thanks to the work of J. J. Bachofen, Jane Ellen Harrison, Robert Briffault, Helen Diner, G. Rachel Levy, Erich Neumann, E. O. James, Elizabeth Gould Davis, and scores of others after them — especially Marija Gimbutas and Merlin Stone — the history of the Goddess has been saved. Contemporary Goddess spirituality, with its roots in prepatriarchal culture, embodies a multiplicity of meaning for women. She is ever, She is all, She is us.*

C.S.

# The Great Goddess: Who Was She?

# Merlin Stone

Her religion had existed and flourished in the Near and Middle East for thousands of years before the arrival of the patriarchal Abraham, first prophet of the male deity Yahweh. Archaeologists had traced the worship of the Goddess back to the Neolithic communities of about 7000 B.C., some to the Upper Paleolithic cultures of about 25,000 B.C. From the time of its Neolithic origins, its existence was repeatedly attested to until well into Roman times. Yet Bible scholars agreed that it was as late as somewhere between 1800 and 1550 B.C. that Abraham had lived in Canaan (Palestine).

Who was this Goddess? Why had a female, rather than a male, been designated as the supreme deity? How influential and significant was Her worship, and when had it actually begun? As I asked myself these questions, I began to probe even deeper into Neolithic and Paleolithic times. Though goddesses have been worshiped in all areas of the world, I focused on the religion as it evolved in the Near and Middle East, since these were the lands where Judaism, Christianity, and Islam were born. I found that the development of the religion of the female deity in this area was intertwined with the earliest beginnings of religion so far discovered anywhere on earth.

## DAWN IN THE GRAVETTIAN GARDEN OF EDEN

The Upper Paleolithic period, though most of its sites have been found in Europe, is the conjectural foundation of the religion of the Goddess as it emerged in the later Neolithic Age of the Near East. Since it precedes the time of written records and does not directly lead into an historical period that might have helped to explain it, the information on the Paleolithic existence of Goddess worship must at this time remain speculative. Theories on the origins of the Goddess in this period are founded on the juxtaposition of mother-kinship customs to ancestor worship. They are based upon three separate lines of evidence.

The first relies on anthropological analogy to explain the initial development of matrilineal (mother-kinship) societies. Studies of "primitive" tribes over the last few centuries have led to the realization that some isolated "primitive" peoples, even in our own century, did not yet possess the conscious understanding of the relationship of sex to conception. The analogy is then drawn that Paleolithic people may have been at a similar level of biological awareness.

Jacquetta Hawkes wrote in 1963 that ". . . Australian and a few other primitive peoples did not understand biological paternity or accept a necessary connection between sexual intercourse and conception." In that same year, S. G. F. Brandon, Professor of Comparative Religion at the University of Manchester in England, observed, "How the infant came to be in the womb was undoubtedly a mystery to primitive man . . . in view of the period that separates impregnation from birth, it seems probable that the significance of gestation and birth was appreciated long before it was realized that these phenomena were the result of conception following coition."

"James Frazer, Margaret Mead, and other anthropologists," writes Leonard Cottrell, "have established that in the very early stages of man's development, before the secret of human fecundity was understood, before coitus was associated with childbirth, the female was revered as the giver of life. Only women could produce their own kind, and man's part in this process was not as yet recognized."

According to these authors, as well as many authorities who have written on this subject, in the most ancient human societies people probably did not yet possess the conscious understanding of the relationship of sex to reproduction. Thus the concepts of paternity and fatherhood would not yet have been understood. Though probably accompanied by various mythical explanations, babies were simply born from women.

If this was the case, then the mother would have been seen as the singular parent of her family, the lone producer of the next generation. For this reason it would be natural for children to take the name of their mother's tribe or clan. Accounts of descent in the family would be kept through the female line, going from mother to daughter, rather than from father to son, as is the custom practiced in Western societies today. Such a social structure is generally referred to as matrilineal, that is, based upon mother-kinship. In such cultures (known among many "primitive" peoples even today, as well as in historically attested societies at the time of classical Greece), not only the names, but titles, possessions, and territorial rights are passed along through the female line, so that they may be retained within the family clan.

Hawkes points out that in Australia, in areas where the concept of paternity had not yet been understood, ". . . there is much to show that matrilineal descent and matrilocal marriage (the husband moving to the wife's family home or village) were general and the status of women much higher." She writes that these customs still prevail in parts of Africa and among the Dravidians of India, and relics of them in Melanesia, Micronesia, and Indonesia.

The second line of evidence concerns the beginnings of religious beliefs and rituals and their connection with matrilineal descent. There have been numerous studies of Paleolithic cultures, explorations of sites occupied by these people, and the apparent rites connected with the disposal of their dead. These suggest that, as the earliest concepts of religion developed, they probably took the form of ancestor worship. Again an analogy is drawn between the Paleolithic people and the religious concepts and rituals observed among many of the "primitive" tribes studied by anthropologists over the last two centuries. Ancestor worship occurs among tribal people the world over. Johannes Maringer states that even at the time of his writing, 1956, certain tribes in Asia were still making small statues known as *dzuli*. Explaining these he says, "The idols are female and represent the human origins of the whole tribe."

Thus, as the religious concepts of the earliest *homo sapiens*\* were developing, the quest for the ultimate source of life (perhaps the core of all theological thought) may have begun. In these Upper Paleolithic societies — in which the mother may have been regarded as the sole parent of the family, ancestor worship was apparently the basis of sacred ritual, and accounts of ancestry were probably reckoned only through the matriline — the concept of the creator of all human life may have been formulated by the clan's image of the woman who had been their most ancient, their primal ancestor and that image thereby deified and revered as Divine Ancestress.

The third line of evidence, and the most tangible, derives from the numerous sculptures of women found in the Gravettian-Aurignacian cultures of the Upper Paleolithic Age. Some of these date back as far as 25,000 B.C. These small female figurines, made of stone and bone and clay and often referred to as *Venus figures,* have been found in areas where small settled communities once lived. They were often discovered lying close to the remains of the sunken walls of what were probably the earliest human-made dwellings on earth. Maringer claims that niches or depressions had been made in the walls to hold the figures. These statues of women, some seemingly pregnant, have been found throughout the widespread Gravettian-Aurignacian sites in areas as far apart as Spain, France, Germany, Austria, Czechoslovakia, and Russia. These sites and figures appear to span a period of at least ten thousand years.

"It appears highly probable then," says Maringer, "that the female figurines were idols of a 'great mother' cult, practiced by the non-nomadic Aurignacian mammoth hunters who inhabited the immense Eurasian territories that extended from Southern France to Lake Baikal in Siberia." (Incidentally, it is from this Lake Baikal area in Siberia that the tribes which migrated to North America, supposedly about this same period [there developing into the American Indians], are believed to have originated.)

Russian paleontologist Z. A. Abramova, quoted in Alexander Marshak's *Roots of Civilization,* offers a slightly different interpretation,

---

\* The term *homo sapiens* (literally "knowing or knowledgeable *man*") illustrates once again the scholarly assumption of the prime importance of the male, in this case to the point of the total negation of the female population of the species so defined. If all *"homo sapiens"* had literally been just that, no sooner than the species had developed would it have died out for lack of the capability to reproduce its own kind.

writing that in the Paleolithic religion, "The image of the Woman-Mother . . . was a complex one, and it included diverse ideas related to the special significance of the woman in early clan society. She was neither a god, an idol, nor the mother of a god; she was the Clan Mother . . . The ideology of the hunting tribes in this period of the matriarchal clan was reflected in the female figurines."

## THE NEOLITHIC MORNING

The connections between the Paleolithic female figurines and the later emergence of the Goddess-worshiping societies in the Neolithic periods of the Near and Middle East are not definitive, but are suggested by many authorities. At the Gravettian site of Vestonice, Czechoslovakia, where Venus figures were not only formed but hardened in an oven, the carefully arranged grave of a woman was found. She was about forty years old. She had been supplied with tools, covered with mammoth shoulder blade bones, and strewn with red ocher. In a proto-Neolithic site at Shanidar, on the northern stretches of the Tigris River, another grave was found, this one dating from about 9000 B.C. It was the burial place of a slightly younger woman, once again strewn with red ocher.

One of the most significant links between the two periods are the female figurines, understood in Neolithic societies, through their emergence into the historic period of written records, to represent the Goddess. The sculptures of the Paleolithic cultures and those of the Neolithic periods are remarkably similar in materials, size, and, most astonishing, in style. Hawkes commented on the relationship between the two periods, noting that the Paleolithic female figures ". . . are extraordinarily like the Mother or Earth Goddesses of the agricultural peoples of Eurasia in the Neolithic Age and must be directly ancestral to them." E. O. James also remarks on the similarity, saying of the Neolithic statues, "Many of them are quite clearly allied to the Gravettian-Paleolithic prototypes." (But perhaps most significant is the fact that Aurignacian sites have now been discovered near Antalya, about sixty miles from the Neolithic Goddess-worshiping community of Hacilar in the Cilician plains of Anatolia, near present day Konya; James Mellaart discovered no less than forty shrines, dating from 6500 B.C. onward.) The culture of Çatal Hüyük existed for nearly one thousand years. Mellaart reveals, "The statues allow us to recognize the main deities worshiped by Neolithic people at Çatal Hüyük. The principal deity was a goddess, who is shown in her three aspects: as a young woman, a mother giving birth, or as an old woman." Mellaart suggests that there may have been a majority of women at Çatal Hüyük, as evidenced by the number of female burials. At Çatal Hüyük, too, red ocher was strewn on the bodies; nearly all of the red ocher burials were of women. He also suggests that the religion was primarily associated with the role of women in the initial development of agriculture, and adds, "It seems extremely likely that the cult of the goddess was administered mainly by women . . ."

By about 5500 B.C. houses had been built with groups of rooms around a central courtyard, a style used by many architects even today. These were found in sites along the northern reaches of the Tigris River, in communities that represent what is known as the Hassuna period. There, as in other Neolithic communities, archaeologists found agricultural tools, such as the hoe and sickle, storage jars for corn, and clay ovens. And once again, H. F. W. Saggs reports, "The religious ideas of the Hassuna period are reflected in clay figurines of the mother goddess."

One of the most sophisticated prehistoric cultures of the ancient Near and Middle East was situated along the banks of the northern Tigris and westward as far as the Habur River. It is known as the Halaf culture and appeared in various places by 5000 B.C. At these Halaf sites, small towns with cobbled streets have been discovered. Metal was in use, which would place the Halaf cultures into a period labeled by archaeologists as Chalcolithic.

Saggs writes that, judging from a picture on a ceramic vase, "It is probably from the Halaf period that the invention of wheeled vehicles date." Goddess figurines have been found at all Halaf sites, but at the Halafian town of Arpachiyah these figures were associated with serpents, double axes, and doves, all symbols connected with Goddess worship as it was known in historical periods. Along with the intricately designed polychromed ceramic ware, at Arpachiyah buildings known as *tholoi* appeared. These were circular shaped rooms up to thirty-three feet in diameter with well-engineered, vaulted ceilings. The round structures were connected to long rectangular corridors up to sixty-three feet in length. Since it was close to these *tholoi* that most of the Goddess figurines were discovered, it is likely that they were used as shrines.

By 4000 B.C., Goddess figures appeared at Ur and Uruk, both situated on the southern end of the Euphrates River, not far from the Persian Gulf. At about this same period the Neolithic Badarian and Amratian cultures of Egypt first appeared. It is at these sites that agriculture first emerged in Egypt. And once again in these Neolithic communities of Egypt, Goddess figurines were discovered.

From this point on, with the invention of writing, history emerged in both Sumer (southern Iraq) and Egypt — about 3000 B.C. In every area of the Near and Middle East the Goddess was known in historic times. Though many centuries of transformation had undoubtedly changed the religion in various ways, the worship of the female deity survived into the classical periods of Greece and Rome. It was not totally suppressed until the time of the Christian emperors of Rome and Byzantium, who closed down the last Goddess temples in about 500 A.D.

## GODDESS — AS PEOPLE TODAY THINK OF GOD

The archaeological artifacts suggest that in all the Neolithic and early Chalcolithic societies the Divine Ancestress, generally referred to by most writers as the Mother-Goddess, was revered as the supreme deity. Now She provided not only human life but a controllable food supply as well. C. Dawson, writing in 1928, surmised that "The earliest agriculture must have grown up around the shrines of the Mother-Goddess, which, thus, became social and economic centers, as well as holy places and were the germs of future cities."

W. Schmidt, quoted by Joseph Campbell in *Primitive Mythology*, says of these early cultures, "Here it was the women who showed themselves supreme; they were not only the bearers of children but also the chief producers of food. By realizing that it was possible to cultivate, as well as to gather, they had made the earth valuable and they became, consequently, its possessors. Thus, they won both economic and social power and prestige." In 1963, Hawkes added that "There is every reason to suppose that under the conditions of the primary Neolithic way of life mother-right and the clan system were still dominant, and the land would generally have descended through the female line."

Though at first the Goddess appears to have reigned alone, at some yet unknown point in time, She acquired a son or brother (depending upon the geographic location), who was also Her lover and consort. He is known through the symbolism of the earliest historic periods and is generally assumed to have been a part of the female religion in much earlier times. Professor E. O. James writes, "Whether or not this reflects a primeval system of matriarchal social organization, as is by no means improbable, the fact remains that the Goddess at first had precedence over the young god with whom she was associated as her son or husband or lover."

It was this youth who was symbolized by the male role in the sacred annual sexual union with the Goddess. (This ritual is known from historic times but is generally believed to have also been known in the Neolithic period of the religion.) Known in various languages as Damuzi, Tammuz, Attis, Adonis, Osiris, or Baal, this consort died in his youth, causing an annual period of grief and lamentation among those who paid homage to the Goddess. Wherever this dying young consort appears as the male deity, we may recognize the presence of the religion of the Goddess, the legends and lamentation rituals of which are extraordinarily similar in so many cultures. This relationship of the Goddess to Her son, or in certain places to a handsome youth who symbolized the son, was known in Egypt by 3000 B.C.; it occurred in the earliest literature of Sumer, emerged in later Babylon, Anatolia, and Canaan, survived in the classical Greek legend of Aphrodite and Adonis and was even known in pre-Christian Rome as the rituals of Cybele and Attis, possibly there influencing the symbolism and rituals of early Christianity. It is one of the major aspects of the religion which bridges the vast expanses covered both geographically and chronologically.

But just as the people of the early Neolithic cultures may have come down from Europe, as the possible descendants of the Gravettian-Aurignacian cultures, so later waves of even more northern peoples descended into the Near East. There has been some conjecture that these were the descendants of the Mesolithic (about 15,000–8000 B.C.), Maglemosian, and Kunda cultures of northern Europe. Their arrival was not a gradual assimilation into the area, as the Goddess peoples' seems to have been, but rather a series of aggressive invasions, resulting in the conquest, area by area, of the Goddess people.

These northern invaders, generally known as Indo-Europeans, brought their own religion with them, the worship of a young warrior god and/or a supreme father god. Their arrival is archaeologically and historically attested by 2400 B.C., but several invasions may have occurred even earlier. The pattern that emerged after the invasions was an amalgamation of the two theologies, the strength of one or the other often noticeably different from city to city. As the invaders gained more territories and continued to grow more powerful over the next two thousand years, this synthesized religion often juxtaposed the female and male deities not as equals but with the male as the dominant husband or even as Her murderer. Yet myths, statues, and documentary evidence reveal the continual presence of the Goddess and the survival of the customs and rituals connected to the religion, despite the efforts of the conquerors to destroy or belittle the ancient worship.

Although the earliest examples of written language yet discovered anywhere on earth appeared at the temple of the Queen of Heaven in Erech in Sumer, just before 3000 B.C., writing at that time seems to have been used primarily for the business accounts of the temple. The arriving northern groups adopted this manner of writing, known as *cuneiform* (small wedge signs pressed into damp clay), and used it for their own records and literature. Edward Chiera comments, "It is strange to notice that practically all the existing literature was put down in written form a century or two after 2000 B.C." Whether this suggests that written language was never considered as a medium for myths and legends before that time or that existing tablets were destroyed and rewritten at that time remains an open question. But unfortunately it means that we must rely on literature that was written after the start of the northern invasions and conquests. Yet the survival and revival of the Goddess as supreme in certain areas, the customs, the rituals, the prayers, the symbolism of the myths, as well as the evidence of temple sites and statues, provide us with a great deal of information on the worship of the Goddess even at that time. And to a certain extent, they allow us, by observing the progression of transitions that took place over the next two thousand years, to extrapolate backward to better understand the nature of the religion as it may have existed in earlier historic and Neolithic times.

As I mentioned previously, the worship of the female deity has for the most part been included as a minor addition to the study of the patterns of religious beliefs in ancient cultures, most writers apparently preferring to discuss periods when male deities had already gained prominence. In many books a cursory mention of the Goddess often precedes lengthy dissertations about the male deities who replaced Her. Most misleading are the vague inferences that the veneration of a female deity was a separate, minor, unusual, or curious occurrence. Since most books are concerned with one specific geographic area, this is partially the result of the fact that the Goddess was identified by a specific name or names which were native to that location and the overall connections are simply never mentioned.

Upon closer scrutiny, however, it becomes clear that so many of the names used in diverse areas were simply various titles of the Great Goddess, epithets such as Queen of Heaven, Lady of the High Place, Celestial Ruler, Lady of the Universe, Sovereign of the Heavens, Lioness of the Sacred Assembly, or simply Her Holiness. Often the name of the town or city was added, which made the name even more specific. We are not, however, confronting a confusing myriad of deities, but a variety of titles resulting from diverse languages and dialects, yet each referring to a most similar female divinity. Once gaining this broader and more overall view, it becomes evident that the female deity in the Near and Middle East was revered as Goddess — much as people today think of God.

In Strong and Garstang's *Syrian Goddess* of 1913, some of the connections are explained. "Among the Babylonians and northern Semites She was Ishtar; She is Ashtoreth of the Bible, and the Astarte of Phoenicia. In Syria, Her name was Athar and in Cilicia it had the form Ate (Atheh)."

In Robert Graves's translation of *The Golden Ass* by the Roman writer Apuleius of the second century A.D., the Goddess Herself appears and explains:

I am Nature, the universal Mother, mistress of all elements, primordial child of time, sovereign of all things spiritual, queen of the dead, queen also of the immortals, the single manifestation of all gods and goddesses that are. My nod governs the shining heights of Heaven, the wholesome sea breezes, the lamentable silences of the world below. Though I am worshipped in many aspects, known by countless names, and propitiated with all manner of different rites, yet the whole round earth venerates me.

The primeval Phrygians call me Pessinuntica, Mother of the gods; the Athenians sprung from their own soil, call me Cecropian Artemis; for the islanders of Cyprus I am Paphian Aphrodite, for the archers of Crete I am Dictynna; for the tri-lingual Silicians, Stygian Proserpine; and for the Eleusinians their ancient Mother of Corn. Some know me as Juno, some as Bellona of the Battles; others as Hecate, others again as Rhamnubia, but both races of Aethiopians, whose lands the morning sun first shines upon, and the Egyptians who excel in ancient learning and worship me with ceremonies proper to my godhead, call me by my true name, namely Queen Isis.

Ironically, Isis was the Greek translation for the Egyptian Goddess Au Set.

The similarities among the statues, titles, and symbols — such as the serpent, the cow, the dove, and the double axe — the relationship of the son/lover who dies and is mourned annually, the eunuch priests, the sacred annual sexual union, and the sexual customs of the temple all reveal the overlapping and underlying connections between the worship of the female deity in areas as far apart in space and time as the earliest records of Sumer to classical Greece and Rome.

The deification and worship of the female divinity in so many parts of the ancient world were variations on a theme, slightly differing versions of the same basic theological beliefs, those that originated in the earliest periods of human civilization. It is difficult to grasp the immensity and significance of the extreme reverence paid to the Goddess over a period of either twenty-five thousand (as the Upper Paleolithic evidence suggests) or even seven thousand years and over miles of land, cutting across national boundaries and vast expanses of sea. Yet it is vital to do just that to fully comprehend the longevity as well as the widespread power and influence this religion once held.

According to Robert Graves, "The whole of Neolithic Europe, to judge from surviving artifacts and myths, had a remarkably homogenous system of religious ideas based on the many-titled Mother Goddess, who was also known in Syria and Libya . . . The Great Goddess was regarded as immortal, changeless, omnipotent; and the concept of fatherhood had not yet been introduced into religious thought."

Much the same religion that Graves discusses existed even earlier in the areas known today as Iraq, Iran, India, Saudi Arabia, Lebanon, Jordan, Israel (Palestine), Egypt, Sinai, Libya, Syria, Turkey, Greece, and Italy as well as on the large island cultures of Crete, Cyprus, Malta, Sicily, and Sardinia. There were instances of much the same worship in the Neolithic periods of Europe, which began at about 3000 B.C. The Tuatha de Danaan traced their origins back to a Goddess they brought with them to Ireland, long before the arrival of Roman culture. The Celts, who now comprise a major part of the populations of Ireland, Scotland, Wales, and Brittany, were known to the Romans as the Gauls. They are known to have sent priests to a sacred festival for the Goddess Cybele in Pessinus, Anatolia, in the second century B.C. And evidence of carvings at Carnac and the Gallic shrines of Chartres and Mont St. Michel in France suggests that these places were once sites of the Great Goddess.

## "FROM INDIA TO THE MEDITERRANEAN . . . SHE REIGNED SUPREME"

The status and origins of the Great Goddess have been discussed in several studies of ancient worship. The primary interest of most of these scholars was in the son/lover and the transition from the female to the male religions, but each of their statements reveals that the original status of the Goddess was as supreme deity.

In 1962, James Mellaart described the cultures of 9000 to 7000 B.C. in *Earliest Civilizations of the Near East*. As I mentioned previously, he pointed out that at that time, "Art makes its appearance in the form of animal carvings and statuettes of the supreme deity, the Mother Goddess." He writes that at Çatal Hüyük of the seventh millennium, "The principal deity was a goddess . . ." In describing the site of ancient Hacilar, a Neolithic community by 5800 B.C., he directs our attention to the fact that "The statuettes portray the goddess and the male occurs only in a subsidiary role as child or paramour."

One figure of the Goddess from Hacilar is now in the museum in Ankara, which houses most of the pieces found at Hacilar and Çatal Hüyük by Mellaart's excavations, their antiquity contrasting strangely with its contemporary architecture and decor. This particular sculpture of the Goddess appears to depict Her in the act of making love, though the male figure is broken and represented only by a small fragment of his waist, thighs, and one leg. There is the possibility that this is an older child being held close, but it appears more likely to be an adolescent youth, perhaps intended to portray the son/lover of the female deity some eight thousand years ago.

In *The Lost World of Elam*, published in 1973, Walther Hinz, Director of the Institute of Iranian Studies at the University of Goettingen in Germany, also discusses the worship of the Goddess in the Near and Middle East. The nation of Elam was just east of Sumer and in early historic periods the two cultures were in close contact. Hinz writes that "Pride of place in this world was taken by a goddess — and this is typical of Elam . . . She was clearly the 'great mother of the gods' to the Elamites. The very fact that precedence was given to a goddess, who stood above and apart from the other Elamite gods, indicates a matriarchal approach in the devotees of this religion."

Hinz describes the Goddess as She was known in various centers of the Elamite territories and then tells us, "In the third millennium these 'great mothers of the gods' still held undisputed sway at the head of the Elamite pantheon, but a change came during the course of the second. Just as the age-old matriarchy of Elam had once yielded in the face of a gradual rise in the position of men, so corresponding arrangement took place among the gods . . . During the third millennium, he [Humban, the consort of the Goddess] still occupied the third place, but from the middle of the second millennium he stood at the head of the pantheon."

Explaining the precedence of the female deity among the Semites, which include both the Arab and Hebrew peoples, Robertson Smith, in his prophetic work of 1894, *Religion of the Semites,* asserted that the female divinity in Semitic religion was deified as a direct result of the juxtaposition of ancestor worship and a female kinship system. At that time he wrote:

Recent researches into the history of the family render it in the highest degree improbable that the physical kinship between the god and his worshippers, of which traces are found all over the Semitic area, was originally conceived as fatherhood. It was the mother's, not the father's blood which formed the original bond of kinship among the Semites as among other early people and in this stage of society, if the tribal deity was thought of as the parent of the stock, a goddess, not a god, would necessarily have been the object of worship.

"In Mesopotamia, the goddess is supreme," wrote Henri Frankfort in his 1948 publication of *Kingship and the Gods,* "because the source of all life is seen as female. Hence, the god, too, descends from her and is called her son, though he is also her husband. In the ritual of the sacred marriage, the goddess holds the initiative throughout. Even in the condition of chaos, the female Tiamat is the leader and Apsu merely her male complement."

Within his twelve extensive volumes of research on ancient and "primitive" religion, published in 1907, Sir James Frazer wrote of the Egyptian Goddess Isis (Au Set) and Her brother/husband Osiris (Au Sar). In addition to the volumes of *The Golden Bough,* he published a separate book, *Attis, Adonis and Osiris,* a title also used for several of the sections of *The Golden Bough.* In both works he asserted that, according to Egyptian mythology, Isis was the stronger divinity of the pair. He related this to the system of property and descent practiced in Egypt, which he described as "mother-kinship." He referred to the young lover of the Goddess as "the mythical personification of nature," and explained that it was required that this figure should be sexually coupled with the supreme female divinity. Of the lad's status and position within the religion, he commented, "In each case [Attis, Adonis and Osiris] it appears that originally the goddess was a more powerful and important personage than the god."

In his 1928 *Handbook of Greek Mythology,* H. J. Rose discussed the role of the young male in the sacred sexual union and described him as "her inferior male partner," observing, "So far we have been dealing

with legends which represent the goddess, not as married but as forming more or less temporary unions with someone much inferior to herself, a proceeding quite characteristic of Oriental goddesses who are essentially mothers but not wives and beside whom their lovers sink into
comparative insignificance."

A description of the relationship between the Goddess and Her
son/lover was included by E. O. James in his 1960 publication, *The
Ancient Gods*. He explained Her supremacy in this way:

It was She who was responsible for his recovery and his resuscitation on
which the renewal of nature depended. So that in the last analysis In-
anna/Ishtar, not Damuzi/Tammuz was the ultimate source of life and regeneration, though the young god as her agent was instrumental in the
process . . . With the establishment of husbandry and domestication, however, the function of the male in the process of generation became more apparent and vital and the Mother Goddess was then assigned to a spouse to
play his role as the begetter, even though as in Mesopotamia for example he
was her youthful son/lover or her servant. From India to the Mediterranean, in fact, she reigned supreme, often appearing as the unmarried
goddess.

Arthur Evans, eminent Oxford scholar and noted archaeologist, who
located, unearthed, and even partially reconstructed the royal complex
at Knossos on the island of Crete, commented in 1936, "It is certain
that, however much the male element had asserted itself in the domain
of government, by the great days of the Minoan civilization, the religion still continued to reflect the older matriarchal stage of social development. Clearly the goddess was supreme . . ."

Discussing Anatolia, which was closely related to Minoan Crete
through colonization and trade, Evans wrote, "Throughout a large part
of Anatolia, again we recognize the cult of the same great mother with
her male-satellite husband, lover or child, as the case may be." Another
Oxford scholar of the late-nineteenth century, L. R. Farnell, wrote
about Crete as early as 1896. In his series of volumes *The Cults of the
Greek States*, he commented, "We may then safely conclude from the
evidence so far available that the earliest religion of civilized Crete was
mainly devoted to a great goddess, while the male deity, always inevitable in goddess cult, was subordinate and kept in the background."

Robertson Smith wrote of the position of the Goddess in Arabia, who
he had previously suggested was originally deified as the parent of the
stock. He described the transition of power that then took place: "In
Arabian religion a goddess and a god were paired, the goddess being

supreme, the god, her son, a lesser deity. Gradually there was a change whereby the attributes of the goddess were presented to the god, thus lowering the position of the female below the male."

Smith pointed out that the Goddess was still known in later patriarchal religion and claimed that Her worship was attached to "cults" which found their origins in the "ages of mother-kinship." He then discussed the time when:

. . . the change in the law of kinship deprived the mother of her old preeminence in the family and transferred to the father the greater part of her authority and dignity . . . women lost the right to choose their own partners at will, the wife became subject to her husband's lordship . . . at the same time her children became, for all purposes of inheritance and all duties of blood, members of his and not her kin. So far as the religion kept pace with the new laws of social morality due to this development, the independent divine mother necessarily became the subordinate partner of a male deity . . . or if the supremacy of the goddess was too well established to be thus undermined, she might change her sex as in Southern Arabia where Ishtar was transformed into the masculine Athtar.

Summing up, he observed that, upon the acceptance of male kinship, the woman was placed in a subordinate status and the principal position in the religion was no longer held by the Goddess, but by a god. Though Smith presented the change as taking place rather naturally, the transition was actually accomplished by violent aggression, brutal massacres, and territorial conquests throughout the Near and Middle East.

# Women and Culture in Goddess-Oriented Old Europe

## Marija Gimbutas

With the growing realization of the necessity to distinguish the Neolithic and Copper Age pre-Indo-European civilization from the Indo-Europeanized Europe of the Bronze Age, I coined, ten years ago, the new term "Old Europe." This term covers, in a broad sense, all Europe west of the Pontic steppe before the series of incursions of the steppe (or "Kurgan") pastoralists in the second half of the fifth, the fourth, and the beginning of the third millennium B.C., for in my view Europe is not the homeland of the Indo-European speakers. In a narrower sense, the term Old Europe applies to Europe's first civilization, i.e., the highest Neolithic and Copper Age culture, which was focused in the southeast and the Danubian basin and was gradually destroyed by repeated Kurgan infiltrations.

© Marija Gimbutas, 1980. Excerpted from "Old Europe in the Fifth Millennium B.C.: The European Situation on the Arrival of Indo-Europeans," a lecture Dr. Gimbutas delivered at the conference on "The Indo-Europeans in the Fourth and Third Millennia B.C.," University of Texas at Austin, 4–5 Feb. 1980; the complete text appears in the proceedings of the conference, Vol. 14 of the Studia Series published by Karoma Pub., Ann Arbor, MI, 1981. This excerpt is published by permission of the author.

The two cultural systems were very different: The first was matrifocal, sedentary, peaceful, art-loving, earth- and sea-bound; the second was patrifocal, mobile, warlike, ideologically sky oriented, and indifferent to art. The two systems can best be understood if studied before the period of their clash and melange, i.e., before c. 4500–4000 B.C.

## SOCIAL ORGANIZATION

Old European societies were unstratified: There were no contrasting classes of rulers and laborers, but there was a rich middle class which arose as a consequence of metallurgy and expansion of trade. Neither royal tombs, distinct in burial rites from those of the rest of the population, nor royal quarters, distinguished by extravagance, have been discovered. I see no evidence of the existence of a patriarchal chieftain system with pronounced ranking of the Indo-European type. Instead, there were in Old Europe a multitude of temples with accumulations of wealth — gold, copper, marble, shells, and exquisite ceramics. The goods of highest quality, produced by the best craftspeople, belonged not to the chief, as is customary in chiefdoms, but to the Goddess and to Her representative, the queen-priestess. The social organization represented by the rise of temples was a primary centrifugal social force.

The question of governmental organization is, as yet, difficult to answer. Central areas and secondary provinces can be observed in each culture group. Some of the foci were clearly more influential than others, but whether centralized government existed we do not know. I favor the theory of small theocratic kingdoms, or city-states, analogous to Etruscan *lucomonies* and Minoan palaces, with a queen-priestess as ruler, and her brother or husband as supervisor of agriculture and trade. The basis of such structure was more social and religious in character than civil, political, or military.

There is absolutely no indication that Old European society was patrilinear or patriarchal. Evidence from the cemeteries does not indicate a subordinate position of women. There was no ranking along a patriarchal masculine-feminine value scale as there was in Europe after the infiltration of steppe pastoralists, who introduced the patriarchal and the patrilinear system. The study of grave equipment in each culture group suggests an egalitarian society. A division of labor between the sexes is demonstrated by grave goods, but not a superiority of either. The richest graves belong to both men and women. Age was a determining factor; children had the lowest number of objects.

A strong support for the existence of matrilinearity in Old Europe is the historic continuity of matrilinear succession in the non-Indo-European societies of Europe and Asia Minor, such as the Etruscan, Pelasgian, Lydian, Carian, and Basque. Even in Rome during the monarchy, royal office passed regularly through the female line — clearly a non-Indo-European tradition, most probably inherited from Old Europe. Polybius, in the second century B.C., speaking of the Greek colony Lokroi on the toe of Italy, observed, "All their ancestral honors are traced through women." Furthermore, we hear from Greek historians that the Etruscans and prehistoric Athenians had "wives in common" and "their children did not know their own fathers." The woman in such a system was free to marry the man of her choice, and as many as she pleased (there was no question of adultery; that was a male invention). Children's lineage was traced through the mother only. This evidence led George Thomson to the assumption that group marriage was combined with common ownership in prehistoric Aegean societies.[1] Matrilinear succession on some Aegean islands, e.g., Lesbos, Skyros, is reported by written records in the eighteenth century A.D. and continues in partial form to this very day. Matrilinear succession to real property and prenuptial promiscuity were practiced in isolated mountainous regions of southwestern Yugoslavia up to the twentieth century.[2] Such customs are certainly unthinkable in present patriarchal society; only a very deeply rooted tradition could have survived for millennia the counterinfluence of the patrilinearity of surrounding tribes.

A matrifocal society is reflected by the Old European manifestations of the Goddess and Her worship. It is obvious that the Goddess, not gods, dominated the Old European pantheon; the Goddess ruled absolutely over human, animal, and plant life. The Goddess, not gods, spontaneously generated the life-force and created the universe. As demonstrated by the thousands of figurines and temples from the Neolithic through the Copper Ages, the male god was an adjunct of the female Goddess, as consort or son.[3] In the models of temples and household shrines, and in actual temple remains, females are shown supervising the preparation and performance of rituals dedicated to the various aspects and functions of the Goddess.[4] Enormous energy was expended in the production of religious equipment and votive gifts. Some temple models show the grinding of grain and the baking of sacred bread. The routine acts of daily existence were religious rituals by virtue of replicating the sacred models. In the temple workshops, which usually constituted half the building or occupied the floor below the temple proper, females made and decorated quantities of the various pots appropriate to different rites. Next to the altar of the temple stood a vertical loom on which were probably woven the sacred garments and temple appurtenances. The most sophisticated creations of Old Europe — the most exquisite vases, sculptures, etc., now extant — were women's work (the equipment for decoration of vases so far is known only from female graves). Since the requirements of the temple were of primary importance, production for the temple must have doubled or tripled the general level of productivity, both stimulating and maintaining the level of female craftsmanship.

## RELIGION

### Temples

The tradition of temple building began in the seventh millennium B.C. A remarkable series of temple models and actual rectangular temples from the sixth and fifth millennia B.C. bear witness to a great architectural tradition.

At present about fifty models from various culture groups and phases are known. They are more informative than the actual temple remains, since they present details of architecture, decoration, and furnishings otherwise unavailable to prehistoric archaeology. Actual remains of sanctuaries suggest that miniature models in clay were replicas of the real temples. They almost always were found at the altars, probably as gifts to the Goddess. The seventh- and sixth-millennia temple models seemed to have conceived of the temple literally as the body or the house of the deity.

The figurines portrayed (in clay models) and found in actual shrines are shown to perform various religious activities — ritual grinding, baking of sacred bread, attending offerings — or are seated on the altar, apparently used for the reenactment of a particular religious ceremony. In the mid-fifth-millennium Cucuteni (Early Tripolyte) shrine at Sabatinivka in the valley of Southern Bug in the Ukraine, sixteen female figurines were sitting on chairs on the altar, all with snake-shaped heads and massive thighs. One held a baby snake. Another group of sixteen were in action — baking, grinding, or standing at the dish containing remains of a bull sacrifice. In the corner next to the altar stood a life-size clay throne with a horned back support, perhaps for a priestess to supervise the ceremony.[5] At Ovčarovo near Trgovište in northeastern Bulgaria, twenty-six miniature religious objects were found within the remains of a burnt shrine. They included four female figurines with upraised arms, three altar screens (or temple facades) decorated with symbols, nine chairs, three tables, three lidded vessels, three drums, and several dishes larger than figurines. Such objects vividly suggest ceremonies with music and dances, lustrations, and offerings.[6]

The production of an enormous variety of religious paraphernalia — exquisite anthropomorphic, zoomorphic, and ornithomorphic vases, sacrificial containers, lamps, ladles, etc. — is one of the very characteristic features of this culture and may be viewed as a response to the demands of a theocentric culture where most production centered around the temple. The consideration of these creations is unfortunately beyond the scope of this article. Regarding the technological and aesthetic skills, nothing similar was created in the millennia that immediately followed the demise of Old Europe.

## Ceremonial Costumes and Masks

A wealth of costume details is preserved on the clay figurines. Deep incisions encrusted with white paste or red ocher affirm the presence of hip-belts, fringe, aprons, narrow skirts, blouses, stoles; a variety of hair styles, and the use of caps, necklaces, bracelets, and medallions. Whether these fashions were worn commonly or were traditional garb for priestesses or other participants in ritual celebrations can only be conjectured. The latter was probably the case; most of the figurines seem to have been characters in tableaux of ritual. But ritual or not, the costumes reflect stylistic conventions of dress and taste characteristic of the period.

In the female costume several dress combinations recur persistently: Partly dressed figures wear only a hip-belt, or a hip-belt from which hangs an apron or panels of an entire skirt of fringe; others wear a tight skirt with shoulder straps or a blouse. A number of figurines show incised or painted stoles over the shoulders and in front and back. The skirt, which generally begins below the waist and hugs the hips, has a decorative texture of white encrusted incisions, showing net-pattern, zigzags, checkerboard, or dots. The skirt narrows below the knees, and on some figurines wrappings around the legs are indicated. It may be that the skirt was slit in front below the knees and fastened between the legs with woven bands. This type of skirt gives the impression of constraining movement and very likely had a ritualistic purpose.

The figurines tell little about male attire: Males are usually portrayed nude, except for a large V-shaped collar and a belt. In the last phase of the Cucuteni culture, male figures wear a hip-belt and a strap passing diagonally across the chest and back over one of the shoulders.

Special attention to coiffure and headgear is evidenced. The Bird and Snake Goddesses in particular, or devotees associated with Their images, had beautiful coiffures, a crown, or decorative headbands. Vinča and Butmir female figurines have hair neatly combed and divided symmetrically in the center, the two panels perhaps separated by a central ribbon. Late Cucutenian female figurines, primarily nude, but some wearing hip-belt and necklace, have a long, thick coil of hair hanging down the back and ending in a large, circular bun or with an attached disc, reminiscent of the style favored by Egyptian ritual dancers of the third millennium B.C. A typical item of dress is a conical cap on which radial or horizontal parallel incisions perhaps represent its construction of narrow ribbon-like bands.

Figurines were portrayed wearing masks representing certain aspects of the Goddess, gods, or their sacred animals, or else they were simply shown as bird-headed (with beaked faces on a cylindrical neck), snake-headed (with a long mouth, round eyes, and no nose), ram- or other animal-headed. Frequently occurring perforations of the mask were obviously intended to carry some sort of organic attachment. Plumes, flowers, fruits, and other materials could have been employed in this way.

## Deities

In the literature on prehistoric religion the female figures of clay, bone, and stone are usually considered to be the "Mother-Goddess." Is She indeed nothing more than an image of motherhood? The term is not entirely a misnomer if we understand Her as a creator or as a cosmogenic woman. It must be emphasized that from the Upper Paleolithic onward the persona of the Goddess splintered in response to the developing economy, and the images of deities portray far more than the single maternal metaphor. Study of the several stereotypical shapes and postures of the figurines and of the associated symbolism of the signs incised upon them clearly shows that the figurines were intended to project a multiplicity of divine aspects and a variety of divine functions.

There were, in my opinion, two primary aspects of the Goddess (not necessarily two Goddesses) presented by the effigies. The first is "She Who Is the Giver of All" — giver of life, of moisture, of food, of happiness — and "Taker of All," i.e., death. The second aspect of the Goddess is Her association with the periodic awakening of nature: She is springtime, the new moon, rebirth, regeneration, and metamorphosis. Both go back to the Upper Paleolithic. The significance of each aspect is visually supported on the figurines by appropriate symbols and signs. The first aspect of the Goddess as Giver and Taker of All, that is, as both beginning and end of life, is accompanied by aquatic symbols — water birds, snakes, fish, frogs, and animals associated with water — and by representations of water itself in the form of zigzag bands, groups of parallel lines, meanders, nets, checkerboards, and running spirals. The second aspect of the Goddess as rebirth, renewal, and transcendence is accompanied by the symbols of "becoming": eggs, uteri, phalluses, whirls, crescents, and horns which resemble cornucopias. The Goddess often appears in the form of a bee, butterfly, or caterpillar. This second group involves male animals, such as bulls and dogs.

Hybrids of the human female with a bird or snake dominated mythical imagery throughout the Upper Paleolithic, Neolithic, Chalcolithic, and Copper Age from c. 26,000 to the end of Old Europe at c. 3000 B.C., but lingered in the Aegean and Mediterranean region through the Bronze Age and later; at least forty percent of the total number of figurines belong to this type. The Fish, Bird, and Snake Goddesses were interrelated in meaning and function. Each is Creator and Giver. They are, therefore, inseparable from cosmogonic and cosmogenic myths, such as water birds carrying cosmic eggs. She, as the Mother or *Source*, is the giver of rain, water, milk, and meat (plus hides and wool). Her portrayals usually show exaggerated breasts marked with parallel lines, or a wide-open beak or round hole for a mouth. Her large eyes are a magical source and are surrounded by aquatic symbolism (usually groups of parallel lines). Beginning in the Neolithic, the ram (the earliest domesticated animal, a vital source of food and clothing) became Her sacred animal. The symbols of this aspect of the Goddess on spindle whorls and loom weights suggest She was the originator or guardian of the crafts of spinning and weaving. Metaphorically, as "the spinner and weaver of human life," She became the Goddess of Fate.

Along with the life-giving aspect of the Goddess, Her life-taking or death-giving aspect must have developed in pre-agricultural times. The images of vultures and owls are known from the Upper Paleolithic and from the earliest Neolithic (in the frescoes of Çatal Hüyük, in central Anatolia, vultures appear above headless human beings). The figurines of the nude Goddess with large pubic triangle, folded arms, and face of an owl, well known from Old European graves, may be representations of the Goddess in the aspect of night and death.

In early agricultural times, the Giver of All developed another function, a function vital to tillers of the soil: Giver of Bread. Her images were deposited in grain silos or in egg-shaped vases, where they were indispensable insurance for the resurgence of plant life. She also appears as a pregnant woman, Her ripe body a metaphor of the fertile field. She was worshipped with Her sacred animal, the pig. The fattening of the pig was associated with the growth and ripening of crops and fertility in general.

Richly represented throughout the Neolithic, Chalcolithic, and Copper Age is still another aspect of the Goddess: Birth-giving Goddess. She is portrayed with outstretched legs and upraised arms in a naturalistic birth-giving posture. This stereotypic image appears in relief on large vases and on temple walls; carved in black and green stone or alabaster, it was worn as an amulet.

The "periodic regeneration" aspect of the Goddess may be as ancient as the Giver of All aspect, since symbols of "becoming" are present in the Upper Paleolithic: Crescents and horns appear in association with Paleolithic nudes. Because regenerating the life-force was Her main function, the Goddess was flanked by male animals noted for physical strength — bulls, he-goats, dogs. In Her incarnation as a crescent, caterpillar, bee, or butterfly, She was a symbol of new life; She emerged from the body or horns of the bull as a bee or butterfly.

The female principle was conceived as creative and eternal, the male as spontaneous and ephemeral. The male principle was represented symbolically by male animals and by phalluses and ithyphallic animalmasked men — goat-man or bull-man. They appear as adjuncts of the Goddess. The figurines of ecstatic dancers, goat- or bull-masked, may represent worshippers of the Goddess in rituals enacting the dance of life.

## THE PATRIARCHAL INVASIONS

Old Europe was rapidly developing into an urban culture, but its growth was interrupted and eventually stopped by destructive forces from the East: the steadily increasing infiltration of the semi-nomadic, horse-riding ("Kurgan") pastoralists from the Pontic steppe. Periodic waves of infiltration into civilized Europe effected the disintegration of the first European civilization. Only on the islands, such as Crete,

Thera, and Malta, did the traditions, symbols, and syllabic script of Old
Europe survive for almost two millennia. The Bronze Age culture that
followed north of the Aegean, however, was an amalgam of the Old
European substrate plus totally different elements of an Eastern culture.

Thanks to a growing number of radiocarbon dates, archaeologists can
ascertain the periods of Kurgan penetration into Europe. There was no
single massive invasion, but a series of repeated incursions concentrated
into three major thrusts: *c.* 4400–4300 B.C.; *c.* 3400–3200 B.C.; and *c.*
3000–2900 B.C.[7]

The steppe people were, above all, pastoralists. As such, their social
system was composed of small patrilinear units that were socially
stratified according to the strategic services performed by its male
members. The grazing of large herds over vast expanses of land necessi-
tated a living pattern of seasonal settlements or small villages affording
sufficient pasturage for animals. The chief tasks of a pastoral economy
were executed by men, not by women, as was characteristic of the indigenous agricultural system.

It was inevitable that an economy based on farming and another
which relied on stock-breeding would produce unrelated ideologies.
The upheaval of the Old European civilization is registered in the
abrupt cessation of painted pottery and figurines, the disappearance of
shrines, the termination of symbols and signs, the abolition of matrifocal culture, and the annihilation or co-optation of the Goddess
religion.

Old European ceramics are readily identified with the rich symbolic
signs and decorative motifs that reflect an ideology concerned with cos-
mogony, generation, birth, and regeneration. Symbols were compartmentalized or interwoven in myriad combinations — meanders and spirals, chevrons and zigzags, circles, eggs, horns, etc. There were a
multitude of pictorial and sculptural representations of the Goddess and
subordinate gods, of worshippers, and sacred animals. In contrast, Kurgan pottery is devoid of symbolic language and of aesthetic treatment in
general because it obviously did not serve the same ceremonial purposes
as that of Old Europe. The Kurgan stabbing and impressing technique
is quite primitive and seems to focus on only one symbol, the sun. Occasionally, a schematized fir tree occurs, which may symbolize a "tree of
life."

Mythical images that were in existence on the Eurasian steppe dis-
persed now over a large part of Europe and continued to the beginning

of Christianity and beyond. The new ideology was an apotheosis of the horseman and warrior. The principal gods carried weapons and rode horses or chariots; they were figures of inexhaustible energy, physical power, and fecundity. In contrast to the sacred myths of pre-Indo-European peoples which centered around the moon, water, and the female, the religion of pastoral, semi-sedentary Indo-European peoples was oriented toward the rotating sky, the sun, stars, planets, and other sky phenomena, such as thunder and lightning. Their sky and sun gods shone "bright as the sky"; they wore starry cloaks adorned with glittering gold, copper, or amber pendants, torques, chest plates, and belts. They carried shining daggers, swords, and shields. The Indo-Europeans glorified the magical swiftness of arrow and javelin and the sharpness of the blade. Throughout the millennia, the Indo-Europeans exulted in the making of weapons, not pottery or sculpture. They believed that the touch of the axe blade awakened the powers of nature and transmitted the fecundity of the Thunder God; by the touch of His spear tip, the God of War and the Underworld marked the hero for glorious death.

Notes

1. George Thomson, *The Prehistoric Aegean: Studies in Ancient Greek Society* (London: Lawrence and Wishart, 1978 edition), pp. 97 ff.
2. Conversation with Djuro Basler, Sarajevo, 1968.
3. Marija Gimbutas, *The Gods and Goddesses of Old Europe, 7000–3500 B.C.: Myths, Legends and Cult Images* (London: Thames and Hudson, 1974; Berkeley: University of California Press, 1974).
4. Marija Gimbutas, "Temples of Old Europe," *Archaeology*, Nov./Dec. 1980, pp. 41–50.
5. M. L. Makarevich, "Ob Ideologicheskikh Predstavleniyakh u Tripol'skikh Plemen'," *Zapiski Odesskogo Arkheol. Obshchestva*, Odessa, 1960.
6. Henrieta Todorova, *Ovčharovo*, Izdatelstvo "Septemvri," Sofia, 1976.
7. Marija Gimbutas, "The Three Waves of the Steppe People into East Central Europe," *Arch. suisses d'anthrop. gén.*, Geneva, 43, 2 (in press 1980). Also consult "Proceedings of the International Conference on the Transformation of European Culture at 4500–2500 B.C.," Dubrovnik, 12–17 Sept. 1979, ed. by Marija Gimbutas, *Journal of Indo-European Studies*, vol. 8, 1980.

# Prepatriarchal
# Female/Goddess Images

# Adrienne Rich

The question "Was there ever true universal matriarchy?" seems to me to blot out, in its inconclusiveness, other and perhaps more catalytic questions about the past. I, therefore, use the term *gynocentric* in speaking of periods of human culture which have shared certain kinds of woman-centered beliefs and woman-centered social organization. Throughout most of the world, there is archaeological evidence of a period when Woman was venerated in several aspects, the primal one being maternal, when Goddess worship prevailed, and when myths depicted strong and revered female figures. In the earliest artifacts we know, we encounter the female as primal power.

Leave aside for the moment whether those images were made by women's or men's hands: They express an attitude toward the female charged with awareness of her intrinsic importance, her depth of meaning, her existence at the very center of what is necessary and sacred.*

Selection is reprinted from *Of Woman Born, Motherhood as Experience and Institution*, by Adrienne Rich, with the permission of W. W. Norton & Company, Inc. Copyright © 1976 by W. W. Norton & Company, Inc.

* Some illustrative photographs of such images may be found in the early sections of the *Larousse World Mythology*, edited by Paul Grimal; in Paul Radin's

She is beautiful in ways we have almost forgotten, or which have become defined as ugliness. Her body possesses mass, interior depth, inner rest, and balance. She is not smiling; her expression is inward-looking or ecstatic, and sometimes her eyeballs seem to burn through the air. If, as very often, there is a child at her breast, or on her lap, she is not absorbed in contemplation of him (the "Adoration of the Virgin" with the Son as center of the world, will come later). She is not particularly young, or rather, she is absolutely without age. She is *for-herself* even when suckling an infant, even when, like the image of the Ephesian Diana, she appears as a cone of many breasts. Sometimes she is fanged, wielding a club, sometimes she is girdled by serpents; but even in her most benign aspect the ancient Goddess is not beckoning to her worshipers. She exists, not to cajole or reassure man, but to assert herself.

Let us try to imagine for a moment what sense of herself it gave a woman to be in the presence of such images. If they did nothing else for her, they must have validated her spiritually (as our contemporary images do not), giving her back aspects of herself neither insipid nor trivial, investing her with a sense of participation in essential mysteries. No *Pietà* could do this, nor even the elegant queen of the Amarnan divine family of Egypt, in which the Sun-King stands with his hand patriarchally on his son's head, while his consort — regal as she is — remains clearly a consort. The images of the prepatriarchal goddess-cults did one thing: They told women that power, awesomeness, and centrality were theirs by nature, not by privilege or miracle; the female was primary. The male appears in earliest art, if at all, in the aspect of a child, often tiny and helpless, carried horizontally in the arms, or seated in the lap of the Goddess, or suckling at her breast.*

---

*African Folktales and Sculpture;* in Reynold Higgins, *Minoan and Mycenean Art.* See also (for descriptive text) E. O. James, *The Cult of the Mother-Goddess* (New York: Praeger, 1959).

* In her suggestive and closely documented book *The Gate of Horn: Religious Conceptions of the Stone Age,* G. Rachel Levy discusses the types of tracings found in Neolithic caves from Siberia to southern France. She sees the female symbolism and images in many of these paintings — some linear, some fully painted and gloriously immanent with power — along with the female statuettes found in the caves, as suggesting not just a "cult of the Mother Goddess" but a later identification of the caverns with the body of a Mother of Rebirth. She points out that the cave was not simply a shelter in the secular sense, but a religious sanctuary; that its most exquisite and mysterious images are found, not in the general domestic dwelling area, but in labyrinthine corridors, difficult to reach, and clearly sacred zones. The cave itself as a whole was perceived as the body of the Mother, but within it there

Now it can be argued that these figures — Neolithic, pre-Columbian, Cypriot, Cycladic, Minoan, predynastic Egyptian — can tell us nothing of woman's early perception of *herself,* that they are the work of men, the casting into symbolic form of man's sense of *his* relation to Earth and nature. Erich Neumann, a Jungian analyst (1905–60), inclines to this view. First of all, he sets up a triad of relationships characterized by (1) "the child's relationship to its mother, who provides nourishment . . ."; (2) "an historical period in which man's dependence on the earth and nature is at its greatest"; and (3) "the dependence of the ego and consciousness on the unconscious."[1]* Then, according to Neumann, "the Feminine, the giver of nourishment, becomes everywhere a revered principle of nature, on which man is dependent in pleasure and pain. *It is from this eternal experience of man,* who is as helpless in his dependence on nature as the infant in his dependence on his mother, *that the mother-child figure is inspired forever anew.*" (Emphasis mine.)[2] In other words, we again have woman reduced to bearer and nourisher, while man depicts his vision of her, and himself in relation to her, in a different kind of creation — the images of art.†

---

is also an abundance of vaginal imagery, a triangular symbol in particular, which is found at the entrance to enclosed spaces, and which seems to demarcate profane from sacred areas. Although figures of male hunters occasionally appear, they are not cult-objects; "the underlying principle [of the Aurignacian culture] was feminine."

* Unfortunately, this triad depends on a too-familiar dualism, between man/culture/consciousness and woman/nature/unconsciousness. As a woman thinking, I experience no such division in my own being between nature and culture, between my female body and my conscious thought. In bringing the light of critical thinking to bear on her subject, in the very act of *becoming more conscious* of her situation in the world, a woman may feel herself coming deeper than ever into touch with her unconscious and with her body. Woman-reading-Neumann, woman-reading-Freud, woman-reading-Engels or Lévi-Strauss, has to draw on her own deep experience for strength and clarity in discrimination, analysis, criticism. She has to ask herself, not merely, "What does my own prior intellectual training tell me?" but "What do my own brain, my own body, tell me — my memories, my sexuality, my dreams, my powers and energies?"

† Neumann, though a Jungian, has gone much further than Jung in trying to understand and bring into focus the role of the feminine in culture and to acknowledge the force of misogyny. However, like Jung, he is primarily concerned with integrating the feminine into the masculine psyche (again, as in Marcuse's coinage, "the femalization of the male") and his bias is clearly masculine. Nevertheless, I find Neumann's interleaving of several aspects of experience useful as a way of keeping in mind that we are talking at one and the same time about the physical realm of human biological reproduction and nurture, the cultural/historical realm

Neumann was, however, writing before an event which changed accepted ideas about the age of the earliest cultures. Recent archaeological excavations in the Near East, at such sites as Jericho in Israel and Anatolia in Turkey, revealed cultures existing in Asia Minor two thousand or more years before the presumed Neolithic cultures of Iraq, Iran, Syria, and Palestine, and producing evidence of a "proto-Neolithic" cult of worship, including figurines and "symbolically ornamented chapels — revealing, in superb display, practically all the basic motifs of the great Mother Goddess mythologies of later ages."[3] James Mellaart, an archaeologist active in the unearthing of the town of Çatal Hüyük in Anatolia, believes that the Goddess figurines, as well as the other art discovered there, were the work of women:

What is particularly noteworthy . . . is the complete absence of sex [he means sexuality] in any of the figurines, statuettes, plaster reliefs, or wall-paintings. The reproductive organs are never shown, representations of phallus and vulva are unknown, and this is the more remarkable as they were frequently portrayed both in the Upper Paleolithic and in the Neolithic and post-Neolithic cultures outside Anatolia. It seems that there is a very simple answer to this seemingly puzzling question, for emphasis on sex in art is invariably connected with male impulse and desire. If Neolithic woman was the creator of Neolithic religion, its absence is easily explained and a different symbolism was created in which breast, navel, and pregnancy stand for the female principle, horns and horned animal heads for the male.[4]*

We can find some support for this hypothesis indirectly in both Robert Briffault and Neumann, who cite numerous examples to show that the deeply reverenced art of pottery-making was invented by women, was taboo to men, was regarded as a sacred process and that "the making of the pot is just as much a part of the creative activity of the feminine as is the making of the child. . . . In pottery-making the woman

---

of what human beings have invented, prescribed, designed in their efforts to live together, and the realm that exists within the individual psyche. Like Briffault, Neumann has brought together an enormous mass of material relating to woman, specifically as mother, and many of their materials reinforce each other in suggesting certain aspects of prepatriarchal life.

* It is tempting to ask why sexuality in art — Neolithic or otherwise — should "invariably (be) connected with male impulse and desire." But this is not the place in which to follow up that query. I quote from Mellaart to suggest that there is some documentation for the idea that the early images of women were created by women.

experiences . . . primordial creative force . . . we know how great a role the sacred vessel played in the primordial era, particularly as a vehicle of magical action. In this magical implication the essential features of the feminine transformation character are bound up with the vessel as a symbol of transformation."[5] Briffault describes the actual molding of pots by Zuñi women in the shape of a breast; he further states that "the manufacture of pots, like most operations in primitive society . . . partakes of a ritual or religious character" and that "the pot's identity with the Great Mother is deeply rooted in ancient belief through the greater part of the world."[6]

It does not seem unlikely that the woman potter molded, not simply vessels, but images of herself, the vessel of life, the transformer of blood into life and milk — that in so doing she was expressing, celebrating, and giving concrete form to her experience as a creative being possessed of indispensable powers. Without her biological endowment, the child — the future and sustainer of the tribe — could not be born; without her invention and skill, the pot or vessel — the most sacred of handmade objects — would not exist.

And the pot, vessel, urn, pitcher was not an ornament or a casual container; it made possible the long-term storage of oils and grains, the transforming of raw food into cooked; it was also sometimes used to store the bones or ashes of the dead. The potential improvement and stabilization of life inherent in the development and elaboration of pottery-making could be likened to the most complex innovations of a technological age — the refining of crude petroleum, the adaptation of nuclear energy — which invest their controllers with immense power. And yet, even this analogy fails us, because the relationship of the potter to the pot, invested with both an intimate and a communal spirit, is unknown in present-day technology.

Because of speculations like Erik Erikson's (wittily dissected by Kate Millett) as to the meaning and value of woman's "inner space," it is difficult to talk about women in connection with "containers" without evoking a negative if not derisive response.[7] The old associations start pouring in: Woman is "receptive," a "receptacle"; little girls "instinctively" want to play with dollhouses while boys do not; woman's place is the "inner space" of the home; woman's anatomy lays on her an ethical imperative to be maternal in the sense of masochistic, patient, pacific; women without children are "unfulfilled," "barren," and "empty" women. My own negative associations with male derivations from female anatomy were so strong that for a long time I felt distaste, or profound ambivalence, when I looked at some of the early Mother Goddess figures emphasizing breasts and belly. It took me a long time to get beyond patriarchally acquired responses and to connect with the power and integrity, the absolute nonfemininity, of posture and expression in those images. Bearing in mind, then, that we are talking not about "inner space" as some determinant of woman's proper social function, but about primordial clusters of association, we can see the extension of the woman/vessel association. (It must be also borne in mind that in primordial terms the vessel is anything but a "passive" receptacle: It is *transformative* — active, powerful.)

A diagram may be useful here:

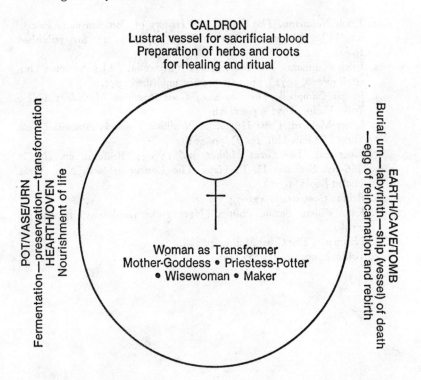

**CALDRON**
Lustral vessel for sacrificial blood
Preparation of herbs and roots
for healing and ritual

POT/VASE/URN
HEARTH/OVEN
Fermentation—preservation—transformation
Nourishment of life

EARTH/CAVE/TOMB
Burial urn—labyrinth—ship (vessel) of death
—egg of reincarnation and rebirth

Woman as Transformer
Mother-Goddess • Priestess-Potter
• Wisewoman • Maker

The transformations necessary for the continuation of life are thus, in terms of this early imagery, exercises of female power. According to Neumann, "the magical caldron or pot is always in the hands of the female mana figures, the priestess, or later, the witch."[8] The earliest religious activity had as its impulse not the contemplation of eternity but the struggle for survival; it was "practical, not speculative," as Briffault says, having to do with daily needs. And women were the people who filled those needs. He suggests further that sex inequality in our terms was unknown in prepatriarchal society; the kinds of administrative and bureaucratic power relationships which developed in patriarchy simply did not exist.[9] Thus, not power *over others*, but *transforming* power was the truly significant and essential power, and this, in prepatriarchal society, women knew for their own.

## Notes

1. Erich Neumann, *The Origins and History of Consciousness* (Princeton, N.J.: Princeton University Press, 1971), p. 43; first published 1949.

2. Erich Neumann, *The Great Mother* (Princeton, N.J.: Princeton University Press, 1972), pp. 129–31; first published 1955.

3. Joseph Campbell, *The Masks of God: Primitive Mythology* (New York: Viking, 1972), pp. vi–vii.

4. James Mellaart, *Çatal Hüyük: A Neolithic Town in Anatolia* (New York: McGraw-Hill, 1967), pp. 201–2.

5. Neumann, *The Great Mother*, pp. 135–37; Briffault, *op. cit.*, I: 466–67. See also H. R. Hays, *The Dangerous Sex* (New York: Pocket Books, 1972).

6. Briffault, *op. cit.*, I: 473–74.

7. Kate Millett, *Sexual Politics* (New York: Doubleday, 1970), pp. 210–20.

8. Neumann, *The Great Mother*, p. 288.

9. Briffault, *op. cit.*, II: 513, 490.

# The Origins of Music: Women's Goddess Worship

## Sophie Drinker

After the rock paintings, the next historical evidence of human activity is found in pottery vessels used for domestic purposes, mortuary urns, and little idols of men, women, and children. These have been excavated in the Indus Valley, in Sumer, in Egypt, and in Europe. They are frequently decorated with male and female symbols. The umbilical cord as the life line is a favorite design. Others are the triangle and spiral, which are also feminine symbols. Often vases were made in the form of a lyre — one of the oldest of the moon-woman symbols — or in the shape of a woman actually giving birth to a child. There are many figurines of women holding musical instruments — clappers, drum, cymbals, or flute. Other figurines represent women weeping or wailing. Most significantly, the images of musicians are generally female. Scholars suggest that the people of those times believed the images, when placed in a grave, to be capable of bringing about the rebirth by means of magic music.

But what happened in those years when the primitive mothers were uniting and linking their families to make cities and states? Did they keep on singing to the moon and weaving songs of lamentation and of triumph? Did the primitive mother evolve with evolving society into the queen and priestess? And when there began to be great religious ceremonies, with thousands of people participating in vast temples with massive pillars of carved stone and hundreds of lights at the altar, was there still a singing to the moon? And were women as priestesses leading it? We have every evidence that this was so, even in some cases down to Christian times, for in the first picture writings, statues, and paintings there is the Moon-Mother-Musician Goddess in the full flower of Her glory.

This Goddess, as She appears at the time when written and pictorial records become numerous, is the climax of a long development. She sums up and crystallizes what women did, what they wished to do, and what men believed they could do in the preliterate period when ancient mythology was being elaborated and handed down by word of mouth.

When, about five thousand years ago, unknown scribes began to write the first histories (in the form of stories designed to be sung), they told about superhuman beings who created the world, founded civilizations, and performed heroic deeds. In these epics, women played a lively part, frequently a greater part than that attributed to men. To many people these deities of ancient times seem to be creations of poetic imagination, with no relation to actual conditions. Gods and goddesses were ideal images, it is true, but the ideals expressed in them indicated existing values. A goddess standing on a crescent moon, for instance, represented the close association of women with new life. But at the same time the deities were generally reflections of the people — real men and women being prototypes of gods and goddesses.

The great driving energy that is the fount of all life was to many Hindus a female force. They gave it a name — *sakti*. In later times, in this section of Hinduism, every god had to be accompanied by his *sakti* and was often so depicted. Her energy manifested itself with particular power in the persons of the Great Mothers. They were sevenfold — the Seven Mothers, whose cult exists among many of the more primitive groups today. The large number of female figurines that come from the Indus Valley civilization suggests that a Goddess-Mother was worshiped three thousand years ago. In Egyptian history no time is known when four of the mighty mothers were not already there. Néït, the Weaver, thought to be of Libyan origin, had for a title "The Old One Who Was When Nothing Was" or "The One Born Before There Was

Birth." Cat-headed Bastet had a name that meant Love. Nekhbiyet — Eileithyia to the Greeks — was the goddess of birth. She was the moon, the bringer of life. The Egyptians honored Her by calling one of their towns after Her. Hat-hor was "The Great One; eye of the sun-lady of heaven; mistress of all the gods." With the same authority, the Sumerian Inanna carried civilization and the arts to new centers. And under another name, the Great Mother in Sumer created the world and everything in it. The idea that woman gives the final touch which endows human beings with capability is also found in primitive tribes. It is an exciting one for a girl to realize and might well be incorporated into the teaching of history.

These Goddess-Mothers were generally represented as giving speech, music, and the art of gesture to humanity, and as being themselves dancers and musicians. The reason the mother was thought of as the giver of speech and music may be easily understood if we again work backward from what we know of simple societies today. For where life is very simple, the baby is almost inseparable from the mother until after the age when it can speak and can begin to sing and imitate patterns of gesture. Mothers often carry their babies on their backs while working or while dancing and singing in religious ceremonies. The child drinks in speech and music with its mother's milk. So Bhāratī and Sarasvati, divine representatives of the dark-eyed women of early India, were thought of as giving all their people speech, music, and ritual. Sarasvati gave poetry and music and arranged musical tones into scales. Bhāratī taught the union of dancing with singing and is often called the Mother of the Bards.

In certain ancient invocations to deities, these two goddess-musicians were summoned with Ilā, goddess of the rite itself, and were spoken of as a group of three. Since they were deities of speech, gesture, music, and ritual, it seems clear that poetry, dance, and the occasion were enhanced by music and that they were integrated then, as they are now in India when the temple dancing girls add songs to their rhythmic gestures. The fact that these ancient deities were goddesses, not gods, implies that before their time women had been active in the making of rites, dances, and songs.

In Egypt, cat-headed Bastet held the sistrum and delighted in dancing and in music. Hat-hor, the Great One, was "mistress of the dancing, lady of music and wreathing of garlands, mistress of songs." They were matched by Inanna in Sumer, who was described as organizing rites, wailing to bring new life, lamenting over the dying year, and rejoicing over the rebirth. "She of the Beautiful Voice" made the lamentations and the incantations for the magic rituals. "O singer" are the words with which people began their appeals for mercy and compassion. The link between the real woman and the ideal in these representations was such a goddess as the Chinese Nukua. With her fine, gold-tinted skin and tilted eyes, she has been identified as an empress, wife of the emperor Fohi. About 2500 B.C. these two interested themselves in making musical reforms, and to the Empress is attributed the creation of a tonal system for the use of musicians. In legend, the real woman became a goddess who mythically performed what the good Empress had already achieved.

These oldest goddesses, spirits, symbols, and even names represent the type of woman normal for the period *before* written history begins. The women of the ancient world of seven and eight thousand years ago — in China, India, and on the Mediterranean shores — were themselves the prototypes of the deities. The hierarchy of divine and semidivine spirits represented the institutionalized role of women in that type of society. If a goddess was supreme in her circle, a queen and high priestess had previously had authority in her tribe or clan, settling a new territory, perhaps, selecting a sacred grove, finding times and places for the cult dances and songs. As the Goddess Isis did, so might a queen have led the people to abandon cannibalism and to eat the bread she taught them to bake. If a goddess was able to help a woman in childbirth or to make grain grow by means of her incantations, then women had previously been skilled in medicine and in agricultural magic. If many goddesses danced and sang, lamented and rejoiced over the waxing and waning moon, or over decaying and sprouting vegetation, then many more priestesses had contributed to the development of those elaborate rituals and had been singing and dancing in choirs. There can be no doubt that women were creative musicians in that age which preceded the epoch of written history. Superhuman or human, women had economic and spiritual authority and could do what people expected to be done with music.

Women's religion, women's customs in primitive tribes, traditions handed down by men's secret societies, and the symbols of divine women in early mythology all point directly to the conclusion that men had not yet seriously put their minds upon the development of rituals, domestic work, and music until after women had established their own conception of a life of the spirit, including expression in music.

For creative expression in music there must be a free flow between the plane of daily experience and the plane of thought and fantasy. One must be able to transfer into universal and ideal terms one's vital personal experience. To the extent to which the ideal plane is restricted or distorted, the creative energies of the individual are devitalized or even poisoned.

Women in pre-Christian times all over the world had simply and naturally evolved a grand religious idea out of their greatest experience — the experience of birth. And just as simply and naturally, they assumed that the life of the universe could be expressed in terms of a woman's experience. Surely, they thought, the universal life must be a mother. It might unite with a father. But the motherhood of the deity was to them more obvious and more really important than the fatherhood. They were not restricted, as Western women later were for nineteen hundred years, to a single male god. On the contrary, they had a representation of what they, as women, knew of life. They had a means of idealizing and universalizing their own highest impulses.

Women were preeminent in the creation of music in these early times. They are not preeminent now. For in those days, they were also preeminent in the formulation of religious ideas. They did not take their religion from men, or leave it to men to make their music.

To understand what happened to women later, one must understand the kind of religious images that women had as an inspiration for the outpouring of their songs. In all the myths, rituals, sculpture, painting, and literature of antiquity, there is an all-pervading woman presence. Whether she is called Cybele or Ishtar or Isis or Hera, or some name foreign to our ears, she represents woman power as an active beneficent principle in all life, sometimes as life itself, the ultimate being, mother of all living things. A realized truth generates creative power. From these noble images of women, energy flowed back to the individual woman, releasing and strengthening her imagination and her artistic impulse at this deep level where music is conceived.

Behind the rites of primitive people everywhere today, and in all very early religions, there is the womanspirit. In the great early civilizations of Egypt, Babylonia, and Crete, the Great Mother acquired a grand, all-embracing personality, and was loved and worshiped with a passionate faith. In Rome the cult of the Great Mother persisted and resisted the powerful onslaught of the growing Christian Church until the fifth century. In Greece, where the tendency was to bring all gods down to earth and turn them into human beings, the personality of the

Great Mother was split up into a number of divine feminine figures and lovingly individualized, by the Greek talent for character delineation, into ideal women, clearly distinguished from each other in temperament, appearance, and the kind of interest they took in human affairs — but all of them noble, benignant, all-powerful.

The Great Goddesses, by whatever name they were called, had their own rites, in which music and dancing were always conspicuous, their own liturgies, their own myths, and their own insignia. One had the spiral; others carried the plume, jewels, an ear of corn, the three-stalked flower, a musical instrument. One was crowned with the sun's halo, one held the sky cape above her, another a sea shell. One stood surrounded by the swiftly flowing rivers of the world. Many were accompanied by lions — symbols of the strength inherent in womanhood. All the Great Goddesses represented the rhythm of life and the moon.

These Goddesses, in their many beautiful impersonations, with their various symbols, represent three mighty facts of nature, akin to each other in their character and manifestations, which seemed to these early human beings, and especially to women, to hold the key to life. One was the waxing and waning of the moon, its three nights of darkness, its effulgent period of resplendent light making night for the brief period of the full moon a kind of heavenly day full of mystery and magic. The second was the fact that, in nature, death is the prelude to new birth. When the flower petals fall, there remains the seed from which new flowers will spring. And the third was the kinship of the woman — in all those biological details that distinguish her from the male — to the moon cycle and to the something that gives birth throughout all nature. Hence, the divine life was naturally and inevitably feminine and woman was its natural priestess. She knew how to speak to it in her incantations; she knew the rhythms, the gestures, and the symbols, the spirit behind all things that would understand and heed.

As mate, mother, provider for the household through industry, and guardian of home and community hearths, the woman sang at the altar to invoke the universal life for the protection of lives under her care. So she was, by necessity of her motherhood, a musician. In every country of the ancient world, divine symbols represented women in their role as dancers, instrumental players, and, especially, as singers.

The dance had many feminine and few masculine impersonations. All nymphs, fairies, and forest mothers danced. In India, the Apsaras were in perpetual motion. In Greece, the Horae danced to mark the

march of time. The Charites, the Horae, and the Graces — symbols of
the bloom of youth — moved with measured steps under their own
leader, Thalia. The Greeks portrayed religious dance as a matron. In
Crete, the great Mother Rhea "invented" the steps that made the Cretan youth famous for centuries. In Egypt, Hat-hor was Goddess of the
Moon and Goddess of the Dance.

Musical instruments were often the property of spirits and
Goddesses. A certain type of drum was sacred only to Sarasvati, giver of
speech and music to humanity, but various types of drums, tambourines, and cymbals belonged to the company of deified musicians.
The Bacchae always carried them, and Cybele, the All-Begetting
Mother, beat a drum to mark the rhythm of life. Flutes were also
played by the Bacchae and by many others. A legend tells that Athene
invented the instrument that blew the breath of life. To Isis was attributed the invention of the sistrum, a glorified type of rattle. Lyres
and harps of different types were associated with supernatural musicians, especially Artemis. In Persia, the spirit of the harp was personified by Azada, whose music echoed the harmony of the spheres.

Singing was the genius of goddesses. Each separate step in the making of magic song became deified. The wail, the cry of joy, the imitation of natural sounds all had feminine impersonation. Every type of
song — incantation, epic, lament — had a special feminine spirit.

As a result of its constant use upon occasions of birth and rebirth, the
wail received impersonation. Little figures of clay or marble, representing women as wailers and weepers, have been found in the graves and
on the sarcophagi of many peoples. When her son Ruadan was born,
the Celtic Goddess Anu gave the first wail ever heard in Ireland. Ishtar
wailed "like a woman in travail" in her effort to bring about the return
of creative energy to the sleeping earth. Isis invented the wail and
taught it to the women of her country as a magical device to bring
about birth. The Great Wailer herself, accompanied by Nephthys, her
sister, the Less Wailer; Neget, a goddess known as the crier; Nëit and
Nūt, two of the Great Mothers; Selket, protectress of the dead; and two
lesser deities, Ibwet and Tayet, stood in the temple of Hat-hor at Den-
derah in the room consecrated to lamentations, ready to wail the image
of Osiris back to life.

Wail songs, or laments, were composed by many supernatural
women. All nymphs, forest mothers, and other semidivine creatures
sang laments. The sirens, as playmates of Persephone, Goddess of
Death, personified death lamentations — incantations to bring about re-

birth. But whenever sirens appeared upon tombstones, they were depicted as both lamenting and rejoicing. In the earliest times they assumed the form of bird-women, and as such may be relatives of Sírin and Alkonóst, the two Russian bird-women from whom came all laments and songs of joy.

A link between fantastical bird-women and real women singers is the common myth of women turning into birds. In Greece there were two such legends. In one, Aedon killed her son by mistake and prayed to be turned into a bird. "Daughter of Pandareus, the brown bright nightingale," wrote the poet, "pours forth her full-voiced music, bewailing her child." In the other myth, two sisters are turned into birds and bemoan their sorrows. Philomela became a swallow and Procne a nightingale. (Ovid twisted the names — probably on purpose, as Philomela is the prettier sound.) Both bird-sisters lament. Pausanias, always interested in the origin of myths, explained: "The tradition of the change into the nightingale and swallow is, I think, because these birds have a melancholy song like a lament." The significance of Pausanias' interpretation is that neither he nor anyone else, apparently, thought it odd for a woman to be identified with a songbird when in reality only male birds sing.

The same association is found in Lithuania, where the verb "to cuckoo" signifies "to lament" and where the cuckoo is nearly always compared to a woman. The reason this identification did not seem incongruous is undoubtedly because the association of women with the singing of laments was so strong that the sex of the bird dwindled into unimportance. All Mother-Goddesses, too, sang the laments and the songs of rejoicing. In Egypt, Isis and her sister Nephthys composed the laments that became the models for both informal and formal dirges. In other countries the name of the mother is mentioned in the lament as the one who is mourning and rejoicing.

Other types of incantations — those for achieving any purpose — often assumed human guise. The singing Sirens, for example, could influence the behavior of people, animals, and even natural phenomena. They could inspire some men to great and noble deeds; they could lure others from their chosen pursuits and chain them fast. Only the Great Mothers surpassed them in the art of making incantations. Nearly every one had a subtitle such as "Lady of Incantations."

In the mythology of ancient Rome, the Carmentes were personifications of the fortune or luck of the mother in childbirth, but they were also projections of the incantations made by midwives, whose chief means of assistance at childbirth was music. The Carmentes got their name from the word *carmen*, meaning a charm, and incantation or song. *Carmen* is derived from the name of a real person, Carmenta or Nicostrata, an ancient poetess of Latium, who is said to have introduced religion, poetry, and agriculture. She seems to have been a prophetess, bard, and cult heroine. To us the translation of *carmen* is more familiar as "song" than as "magic formula for aid in childbirth." The shift from the original specific meaning to the more generic one must have resulted from the innumerable incantations or songs made through the ages by women for aid in childbirth.

Not only each separate department of music had a special goddess, but the art itself was generally given a feminine impersonation. As we have already seen, some of the very ancient goddesses combined music with their other life-giving functions. Hat-hor, Bastet, Sarasvati, Bhāratī, Inanna, Artemis, and the Muses were all identified with singing and dancing and the playing of certain instruments.

The Muses, at first only three in number, had names that indicated their business. One was called Invention, or She Who Invents the Words and Musical Phrases. Another was known simply as Song, or The One Who Sings. The third Muse answered to Memory, or She Who Remembers, an important quality in an age when song and story were passed orally from singer to singer. This one inherited her name, her faculty, and her function from her mother, Mnemosyne. One very old set of their names was Nete, Mese, and Hypate. These also signify the low, middle, and high tones in the Greek system of scales. Such designations would not have been associated with feminine spirits if an identity with music had not been intended. In the oldest depictions of the Muses, they stand with a woman leader, sometimes Mnemosyne, sometimes Athene, sometimes an unknown figure — possibly Artemis. Throughout their long history the Muses, from whose very name the word music is derived, kept their musical authority. Around Zeus's altar they alone chanted the epic of the world's origin. Thamyris, the bard, was struck blind for daring to challenge them in song. Even after Apollo had acquired the title "God of Music," he rarely dared appear without their encircling support.

Mate, mother, worker, communal guardian, musician, and free soul — such was woman's picture of herself in the thousands of years in which she worked out her own idealizations of her own functions and sang freely at altars of her own building to the Great Goddesses and their hosts of spirit attendants. Mirrors of woman in her different natures, avatars of the strength that can alter — as the moon alters — and yet preserve the feminine core, they also symbolized life in its many manifestations. What the natural woman was, what she did, became the highest object of religious devotion, and so idealized and universalized, became an ever revered inspiration to effort and invention.

Before these spirits, the holy hymn of an ancient faith was chanted. Worshiping nature's rhythmic laws and striving to keep in touch with the life-force, which is beyond human comprehension, men and women set a spiritual value on woman's natural way. Men and women both lived according to the principle that woman is creative in body and spirit. In the independence and originality of the spirit of collective womanhood, which was and remains the glory of primitive religion, a woman may have faith and courage — and the heart — to sing. When Artemis strikes Her lyre, She sings no man's composition, and lifts Her eyes to no man's heaven. She sings for Herself, out of the deepest truths She knows as a woman, in the reassuring and lovely splendor of the moon at its full.

# Witchcraft as Goddess Religion

## Starhawk

Witchcraft has always been a religion of poetry, not theology. The myths, legends, and teachings are recognized as metaphors for "That-Which-Cannot-Be-Told," the absolute reality our limited minds can never completely know. The mysteries of the absolute can never be explained — only felt or intuited. Symbols and ritual acts are used to trigger altered states of awareness, in which insights that go beyond words are revealed. When we speak of "the secrets that cannot be told," we do not mean merely that rules prevent us from speaking freely. We mean that the inner knowledge literally *cannot* be expressed in words. It can only be conveyed by experience, and no one can legislate what insight another person may draw from any given experience. For example, after participating in a certain ritual, a woman said, "As we were chanting, I felt that we blended together and became one voice; I sensed the oneness of everybody." Another woman said, "I became aware of how different the chant sounded for each of us, of how unique each person is." A man said simply, "I felt loved." To a Witch, all of these statements are equally true and valid. They are no more contradictory than the statements, "Your eyes are as bright as stars" and "Your eyes are as blue as the sea."

The primary symbol for "That-Which-Cannot-Be-Told" is the Goddess. The Goddess has infinite aspects and thousands of names — She is the reality behind many metaphors. She *is* reality, the manifest deity, omnipresent in all of life, in each of us. The Goddess is not separate from the world — She *is* the world, and all things in it: moon, sun, earth, star, stone, seed, flowing river, wind, wave, leaf and branch, bud and blossom, fang and claw, woman and man. In Witchcraft, flesh and spirit are one.

As we have seen, Goddess religion is unimaginably old, but contemporary Witchcraft could just as accurately be called the New Religion. The Craft, today, is undergoing more than a revival, it is experiencing a renaissance, a re-creation. Women are spurring this renewal, and actively reawakening the Goddess, the image of "the legitimacy and beneficence of female power."[1]

Since the decline of the Goddess religions, women have lacked religious models and spiritual systems that speak to female needs and experience. Male images of divinity characterize both Western and Eastern religions. Regardless of how abstract the underlying concept of God may be, the symbols, avatars, preachers, prophets, gurus, and Buddhas are overwhelmingly male. Women are not encouraged to explore their own strengths and realizations; they are taught to submit to male authority, to identify masculine perceptions as their spiritual ideals, to deny their bodies and sexuality, to fit their insights into a male mold.

Mary Daly, author of *Beyond God the Father*, points out that the model of the universe in which a male god rules the cosmos from outside serves to legitimize male control of social institutions. "The symbol of the Father God, spawned in the human imagination and sustained as plausible by patriarchy, has, in turn, rendered service to this type of society by making its mechanisms for the oppression of women appear right and fitting."[2] The unconscious model continues to shape the perceptions even of those who have consciously rejected religious teachings. The details of one dogma are rejected, but the underlying structure of belief is imbibed at so deep a level it is rarely questioned. Instead, a new dogma, a parallel structure, replaces the old. For example, many people have rejected the "revealed truth" of Christianity without ever questioning the underlying concept that truth is a set of beliefs revealed through the agency of a "Great Man," possessed of powers or intelligence beyond the ordinary human scope. Christ, as the "Great Man," may be replaced by Buddha, Freud, Marx, Jung, Werner Erhard, or the Maharaj Ji in their theology, but truth is always seen as coming from someone else, as only knowable secondhand. As feminist scholar Carol P. Christ points out, "Symbol systems cannot simply be rejected, they must be replaced. Where there is no replacement, the mind will revert to familiar structures at times of crisis, bafflement, or defeat."[3]

The symbolism of the Goddess is not a parallel structure to the symbolism of God the Father. The Goddess does not rule the world; She *is* the world. Manifest in each of us, She can be known internally by every individual, in all Her magnificent diversity. She does not legitimize the rule of either sex by the other and lends no authority to rulers of temporal hierarchies. In Witchcraft, each of us must reveal our own truth. Deity is seen in our own forms, whether female or male, because the Goddess has Her male aspect. Sexuality is a sacrament. Religion is a matter of relinking, with the divine within and with Her outer manifestations in all of the human and natural world.

The symbol of the Goddess is *poemagogic,* a term coined by Anton Ehrenzweig to "describe its special function of inducing and symbolizing the ego's creativity."[4] It has a dreamlike, "slippery" quality. One aspect slips into another: She is constantly changing form and changing face. Her images do not define or pin down a set of attributes; they spark inspiration, creation, fertility of mind and spirit: "One thing becomes another,/In the Mother . . . In the Mother . . ." (ritual chant for the winter solstice).

The importance of the Goddess symbol for women cannot be overstressed. The image of the Goddess inspires women to see ourselves as divine, our bodies as sacred, the changing phases of our lives as holy, our aggression as healthy, our anger as purifying, and our power to nurture and create, but also to limit and destroy when necessary, as the very force that sustains all life. Through the Goddess, we can discover our strength, enlighten our minds, own our bodies, and celebrate our emotions. We can move beyond narrow, constricting roles and become whole.

The Goddess is also important for men. The oppression of men in Father God-ruled patriarchy is perhaps less obvious but no less tragic than that of women. Men are encouraged to identify with a model no human being can successfully emulate: to be minirulers of narrow universes. They are internally split, into a "spiritual" self that is supposed to conquer their baser animal and emotional natures. They are at war with themselves: in the West, to "conquer" sin; in the East, to "conquer" desire or ego. Few escape from these wars undamaged. Men lose touch with their feelings and their bodies, becoming the "successful male zombies" described by Herb Goldberg in *The Hazards of Being Male*: "Oppressed by the cultural pressures that have denied him his feelings, by the mythology of the woman and the distorted and self-destructive way he sees and relates to her, by the urgency for him to 'act like a man,' which blocks his ability to respond to his inner promptings both emotionally and physiologically, and by a generalized self-hate that causes him to feel comfortable only when he is functioning well in harness, not when he lives for joy and personal growth."[5]

Because women give birth to males, nurture them at the breast, and in our culture are primarily responsible for their care as children, "every male brought up in a traditional home develops an intense early identification with his mother and, therefore, carries within him a strong feminine imprint."[6] The symbol of the Goddess allows men to experience and integrate the feminine side of their nature, which is often felt to be the deepest and most sensitive aspect of self. The Goddess does not exclude the male; She contains him, as a pregnant woman contains a male child. Her own male aspect embodies both the solar light of the intellect and wild, untamed animal energy.

Our relationship to the earth and the other species that share it has also been conditioned by our religious models. The image of God as outside of nature has given us a rationale for our own destruction of the natural order, and justified our plunder of the earth's resources. We have attempted to "conquer" nature as we have tried to conquer sin. Only as the results of pollution and ecological destruction become severe enough to threaten even urban humanity's adaptability have we come to recognize the importance of ecological balance and the interdependence of all life. The model of the Goddess, who is immanent in nature, fosters respect for the sacredness of all living things. Witchcraft can be seen as a religion of ecology. Its goal is harmony with nature, so that life may not just survive, but thrive.

The rise of Goddess religion makes some politically oriented feminists uneasy. They fear it will sidetrack energy away from direct action to bring about social change. But in areas as deeply rooted as the relations between the sexes, true social change can only come about when the myths and symbols of our culture are themselves changed.

The symbol of the Goddess conveys the spiritual power both to challenge systems of oppression and to create new, life-oriented cultures.

Modern Witchcraft is a rich kaleidoscope of traditions and orientations. Covens, the small, closely knit groups that form the congregations of Witchcraft, are autonomous; there is no central authority that determines liturgy or rites. Some covens follow practices that have been handed down in an unbroken line since before the Burning Times. Others derive their rituals from leaders of modern revivals of the Craft — the two whose followers are most widespread are Gerald Gardner and Alex Sanders, both British. Feminist covens are probably the fastest-growing arm of the Craft. Many are Dianic, a sect of Witchcraft that gives far more prominence to the female principle than the male. Other covens are openly eclectic, creating their own traditions from many sources. My own covens are based on the Faery Tradition, which goes back to the Little People of Stone Age Britain, but we believe in creating our own rituals, which reflect our needs and insights of today. In Witchcraft, a chant is not necessarily better because it is older. The Goddess is continually revealing Herself, and each of us is potentially capable of writing our own liturgy.

In spite of diversity, there are ethics and values that are common to all traditions of Witchcraft. They are based on the concept of the Goddess as immanent in the world and in all forms of life, including human beings.

Theologians familiar with Judeo-Christian concepts sometimes have trouble understanding how a religion such as Witchcraft can develop a system of ethics and a concept of justice. If there is no split between spirit and nature, no concept of sin, no covenant or commandments against which one can sin, how can people be ethical? By what standards can they judge their actions, when the external judge is removed from his place as ruler of the cosmos? And if the Goddess is immanent in the world, why work for change or strive toward an ideal? Why not bask in the perfection of divinity?

Love for life in all its forms is the basic ethic of Witchcraft. Witches are bound to honor and respect all living things, and to serve the life-force. While the Craft recognizes that life feeds on life and that we must kill in order to survive, life is never taken needlessly, never squandered or wasted. Serving the life-force means working to preserve the diversity of natural life, to prevent the poisoning of the environment and the destruction of species.

The world is the manifestation of the Goddess, but nothing in that concept need foster passivity. Many Eastern religions encourage quietism not because they believe the divine is truly immanent, but because they believe She/He is not. For them, the world is Maya, Illusion, masking the perfection of the Divine Reality. What happens in such a world is not really important; it is only a shadow play obscuring the Infinite Light. In Witchcraft, however, what happens in the world is vitally important. The Goddess is immanent, but She needs human help to realize Her fullest beauty. The harmonious balance of plant/animal/human/divine awareness is not automatic; it must constantly be renewed, and this is the true function of Craft rituals. Inner work, spiritual work, is most effective when it proceeds hand in hand with outer work. Meditation on the balance of nature might be considered a spiritual act in Witchcraft, but not as much as would cleaning up garbage left at a campsite or marching to protest an unsafe nuclear plant.

Witches do not see justice as administered by some external authority, based on a written code or set of rules imposed from without. Instead, justice is an inner sense that each act brings about consequences that must be faced responsibly. The Craft does not foster guilt, the stern, admonishing, self-hating inner voice that cripples action. Instead, it demands responsibility. "What you send, returns three times over" is the saying — an amplified version of "Do unto others as you would have them do unto you." For example, a Witch does not steal, not because of an admonition in a sacred book, but because the threefold harm far outweighs any small material gain. Stealing diminishes the thief's self-respect and sense of honor; it is an admission that one is incapable of providing honestly for one's own needs and desires. Stealing creates a climate of suspicion and fear, in which even thieves have to live. And, because we are all linked in the same social fabric, those who steal also pay higher prices for groceries, insurance, taxes. Witchcraft strongly imparts the view that all things are interdependent and interrelated and, therefore, mutually responsible. An act that harms anyone harms us all.

Honor is a guiding principle in the Craft. This is not a "macho" need to take offense at imagined slights against one's virility — it is an inner sense of pride and self-respect. The Goddess is honored in oneself, and in others. Women, who embody the Goddess, are respected, not placed on pedestals or etherealized, but valued for all their human qualities. The self, one's individuality and unique way of being in the world, is highly valued. The Goddess, like nature, loves diversity. Oneness is attained not through losing the self, but through realizing it fully. "Honor the Goddess in yourself, celebrate your self, and you will see that Self is everywhere."

In Witchcraft, "All acts of love and pleasure are My rituals." Sexuality, as a direct expression of the life-force, is seen as numinous and sacred. It can be expressed freely, so long as the guiding principle is love. Marriage is a deep commitment, a magical, spiritual, and psychic bond. But it is only one possibility out of many for loving, sexual expression.

Misuse of sexuality, however, is heinous. Rape, for example, is an intolerable crime because it dishonors the life-force by turning sexuality to the expression of violence and hostility instead of love. A woman has the sacred right to control her own body, as does a man. No one has the right to force or coerce another.

Life is valued in Witchcraft, and it is approached with an attitude of joy and wonder, as well as a sense of humor. Life is seen as the gift of the Goddess. If suffering exists, it is not our task to reconcile ourselves to it, but to work for change.

Magic, the art of sensing and shaping the subtle, unseen forces that flow through the world, of awakening deeper levels of consciousness beyond the rational, is an element common to all traditions of Witchcraft. Craft rituals are magical rites: They stimulate an awareness of the hidden side of reality, and awaken long-forgotten powers of the human mind.

The magical element in Witchcraft is disconcerting to many people. I would like to speak to the fear I have heard expressed that Witchcraft and occultism are in some way a revival of Nazism. There does seem to be evidence that Hitler and other Nazis were occultists — that is, they may have practiced some of the same techniques as others who seek to expand the horizons of the minds. Magic, like chemistry, is a set of techniques that can be put to the service of any philosophy. The rise of the Third Reich played on the civilized Germans' disillusionment with rationalism and tapped a deep longing to recover modes of experience Western culture had too long ignored. It is as if we had been trained, since infancy, never to use our left arms: The muscles have partly atrophied, but they cry out to be used. But Hitler perverted this longing and twisted it into cruelty and horror. The Nazis were not Goddess worshippers; they denigrated women, relegating them to the position of breeding animals whose role was to produce more Aryan warriors. They were the perfect patriarchy, the ultimate warrior cult — not servants of the life-force. Witchcraft has no ideal of a "superman" to be created at the expense of inferior races. In the Craft, all people are already seen as manifest gods, and differences in color, race, and customs are welcomed as signs of the myriad beauty of the Goddess. To equate Witches with Nazis because neither are Judeo-Christians and both share magical elements is like saying that swans are really scorpions because neither are horses and both have tails.

Mother-Goddess is reawakening, and we can begin to recover our primal birthright, the sheer, intoxicating joy of being alive. We can open new eyes and see that there is nothing to be saved *from*, no struggle of life *against* the universe, no God outside the the world to be feared and obeyed; only the Goddess, the Mother, the turning spiral that whirls us in and out of existence, whose winking eye is the pulse of being — birth, death, rebirth — whose laughter bubbles and courses through all things and who is found only through love: love of trees, of stones, of sky and clouds, of scented blossoms and thundering waves; of all that runs and flies and swims and crawls on her face; through love of ourselves; life-dissolving world-creating orgasmic love of each other; each of us unique and natural as a snowflake, each of us our own star, her Child, her lover, her beloved, her Self.

NOTES

1. Carol P. Christ, "Why Women Need the Goddess," *Womanspirit Rising: A Feminist Reader in Religion,* Carol P. Christ and Judith Plaskow, eds. (San Francisco: Harper & Row, 1979), p. 278.
2. Mary Daly, *Beyond God the Father* (Boston: Beacon Press, 1973), p. 13.
3. Christ, *op. cit.,* p. 275.
4. Anton Ehrenzweig, *The Hidden Order of Art* (London: Paladin, 1967), p. 190.
5. Herb Goldberg, *The Hazards of Being Male* (New York: Signet, 1977), p. 4.
6. *Ibid.,* p. 39.

# From the House of Yemanja: The Goddess Heritage of Black Women

## Sabrina Sojourner

It is difficult, if not impossible, to be raised in the United States without having Christian value judgments invade one's life. Until recent times, it was doubly hard for Black Americans to escape this intrusion because of the intrinsic political and social, as well as religious, role the Black church has played in our community. It was only as late as my parents' generation that countless Black women and men began leaving the church, no longer believing in the salvation offered by a white god and savior. Now many women of my own generation are discovering that God is not only not white, She has never even been considered male until relatively recently!

### RECLAIMING OUR SPIRITUAL MOTHER

Seboulisa mother goddess with one breast
eaten away by worms of sorrow and loss
see me now

> your severed daughter
> laughing our name into echo
> all the world shall remember.

— Audre Lorde[1]

The lack of information about Black Goddesses in most works on Goddess worship might lead one to believe that such information does not exist. This simply is not so! We of African descent have a rich Goddess and matrifocal heritage. While it is true that many tribes maintained a kingship for centuries before the notion of written history, more often than not, the king received his legitimacy from a magic-sacerdotal female clan. In other instances, the power of the king was channeled through the figure of a "dowager queen" or wifely queen. With some tribes, the kingship was not a position desired by most men because the king was ritually murdered every six months to a year.[2]

The information I have gathered about African Goddesses, heroines, and Amazons is a synthesis of bits and pieces of information from a variety of sources. The following profiles are taken primarily from the works of three women: Merlin Stone,[3] Audre Lorde,[4] and Helen Diner.[5]

*Yemanja* is the mother Goddess of the Orisha and, as such, is related to Mawu. Yemanja is the Goddess of the oceans; rivers are said to flow from Her breasts. River-smoothed stones are Her symbol. The sea is sacred to Her followers. In Brazil She is worshipped as Iamanja and is honored on the eve of Summer Solstice.

*Mawu* is known as the creator of the universe. As mother of the Vodu, She is related to Yemanja. Another form of Mawu is that of Mawulisa (Mawu-Lisa), the inseparable twins of the universe. For the Dahomean people, Mawulisa is the female-male, sky goddess-god principle, also represented as west-east, night-day, moon-sun. Where She is known as Mawu, Lisa is called either Her first son/consort or Her twin brother. Other manifestations of Mawu are Seboulisa and Sogbo.

*Ala* is a goddess of the Ibo people of Nigeria. She is called the provider of life and the mother who receives again in death. It is Ala who proclaims the law that is the basis for all moral human behavior. It is a Nigerian custom to have life-size images of Ala sitting on the porch of a small wooden house in the village visible to all who pass by.

*Jezanna* is the Goddess of the Moshona people of Zimbabwe. Her symbol is the moon and Her high priestess is Her primary representative.

*Songi* is the Great Mother of the Bantu people of central and southern Africa. A sacred legend holds that Nsomeka, a young woman, met Mother Songi in the forest one day. Songi notched Nsomeka's teeth. That evening, from the notches sprang forth livestock, fruit trees, houses, and shade trees. When the men of the village beat their wives for not producing these things for them, Nsomeka gathered all the women in her field and notched their teeth. None of the men could join them until they had promised to treat the women with respect.

*Mboze* is the First Mother of the Woyo people of Zaire. Her sacred story expresses women's attempts to keep tradition in the face of betrayal. Mboze has a daughter, Bunzi, by Her son/lover, Makanga. When Her husband, Kuitilkuiti (who had changed his black skin for white), learns that Makanga is the father, he beats Mboze to death. Bunzi grows older to do the work Her mother had once done, rewarding the faithful with bountiful rains and harvests.

*Mbaba Mwana Waresa* is the Goddess of the Zulu people of Natal. Among Her gifts, this holy Rain Goddess of the Heavens also gave Her people beer so that they might better celebrate their joyous times.

*Tji-Wara* (or *Chi-Wara*) is said to have introduced agriculture to the Bambara people. A good harvest is assured through pleasing Her.

## AFRICAN AMAZONS OF THE GODDESS LANDS

As with Amazon cultures of Goddess-oriented Anatolia, much of what we know about the Amazons of Libya (a term that once referred to all of Africa) centers around their fierceness as warriors. Through legend, mythology, and historical facts, we know of Merina,[6] for instance, and her peaceful march east through Egypt. Once in Syria, she conquered the Arabs, settlement after settlement. She led her Amazon troops through Phrygia and up the coast of the Mediterranean. In their path of triumph, they founded towns and colonies. Lesbos and other eastern Mediterranean islands are said to have fallen to Merina. Cast ashore at Samothrace after a terrific storm, Merina named the island and erected a temple to the Mother-Goddess (probably Neith), celebrated mysteries in Her honor, built altars, and made sacrifices. These were all in accordance with a vow she had taken during her hour of peril.[7]

The trek to Samothrace had been long and arduous. Their exhaustion benefited Greek forces led by Mompsus, a Thracian, and Sypylus, a Scythian. At their hands Merina was defeated and killed, ending the ferocious nation of Libyan Amazons. Most of her followers returned to North Africa. There they continued to honor Neith. The Libyan Amazons also worshipped Pallas Athena and Pallas Promochos, the Vanguard Goddess, as their goddess. As before the death of Merina, women were expected to remain virgins (unmarried) while in active service.[8]

## REVIVAL OF YORUBAN THEOLOGY AMONG BLACK AMERICAN WOMEN

The African belief in a pantheon of goddesses and gods did not die when the Africans were brought to the "New World"; it merely changed. Traces of Yoruban culture survive in the West Indies, the United States, and South America. In the late Sixties, transmitters of this tradition began to be sought out by Black intellectuals wanting to reclaim a lost part of their spiritual heritage. Now a third group has emerged: women who are challenging the present patriarchal structure of the religion. It is their belief that half-truths and false taboos have been imposed on them and the Yoruban manifestations of the Goddess, that undue power has been placed in the hands of men, and that it is their duty as the daughters of Yemanja, Oshun, and Oya to restore their mothers as the heads of the House and regain respect for women.

Two such women are Luisah Teish and Robin Pearson. Teish has lived in the San Francisco Bay Area since 1971. She was not born into the Yoruban culture, but does not approach it completely as an outsider; during her childhood in the Delta region of Louisiana, remnants of it were all around her. Her formal interest began in the mid-Sixties when she began dancing with Katherine Dunham. Upon her arrival in the Bay Area, Teish started teaching Afro-Haitian dance. Since much of the dance is rooted in religion, Teish also provided her classes with information about the religious culture. In 1977 she started teaching classes on the Yoruban goddesses, mostly to women.

Teish believes that Oshun, the Yoruban goddess of love, beauty, and female power, has been wronged by contemporary patriarchs of the Yoruban culture. "Oshun is usually depicted as the very delicate, very conceited and jealous female," observes Teish; but many aspects of this goddess are kept hidden. For instance, Teish explains, "We are told that Oshun's bird is the peacock whose only value is its outward appearance. However, if you listen carefully, you may also hear Her associated with the vulture." Teish adds with a sly smile, "And we all know how powerful the jaws and the claws of a vulture are."

Robin Pearson lives in Jamaica Plains, Massachusetts. Like Teish, Pearson was not born into the Yoruban culture. She joined a communal house in the mid-Seventies that is oriented toward female spirituality. Pearson has since left the strictly ordered house and is working on her own. Both she and Teish hope to become priestesses; the complex ceremony of initiation can span five years. Because the initiators have tremendous influence over the outcome, both women hope to go to Africa, make contact with women who keep the old ways, and return to this country to open feminist Yoruba houses, centers that again will honor the Mother and Her daughters.

## REDEFINING OUR SPIRITUAL HERITAGE

> I come like a woman
> who I am
> spreading out through nights
> laughter and promise
> and dark heat
> warming whatever I touch
> that is living
> consuming
> only
> what is already dead.

> — AUDRE LORDE[9]

The Africans who adopted Christianity maintained their African spiritual sensibilities. Thus, with their conversion began the tapestry of Black theology and folk religion, comprised of threads of African religions and culture, Western civilization, and Christianity. It is colored with the practices, rituals, and philosophies of white, Christian theology and the African tradition that religion permeates all aspects of life with no final distinctions between what is secular and what is sacred.[10]

It is the latter aspect that accounts for the spiritual aspect of Black art, theater, music, and literature. This is why, even though raised outside the Church, there is rarely a Black individual who does not understand the Church's significance to the Black culture and community. Black theology and folk religion, like traditional African religions, seeks the power or the spirit of God (Divine Energy) in all times and places and things; without that power, one is helpless.[11] Because the Church has succeeded in providing for its community a "heaven on earth" — a sense of joy in the face of adversity — it has maintained its central position. By attuning yourself to the Spirit, or its manifestations, you become one with that power. Thus, when Black Christians talk about putting themselves in the hands of God, they are generally referring to their need, desire, or ability to tap into a divine source of energy and utilize that energy to push/pull themselves through a situation. This is not much different from the Pagan process of channeling energy, which many women are reviving today.

Perhaps the Amazons who rode into Europe from the Russian steppes were fierce, blonde, blue-eyed women. My Amazons have always been dark. It is not easy growing up in a society whose language and laws fear, despise, and dehumanize the rainbow of people who are of darker hues. It is not easy trusting alliances with women who continue a *status quo* negation of one's racial/cultural/ethnic/class background. The dark-skinned women who rode, thousands strong, across the African continent and through the Arab world are my reminder that I am the ancestral daughter/sister of a powerful nation of women. Whether their battles were merely for the sport and spoils of war or for the preservation of Mother Right is immaterial. It is their fight and strength that I cling to. For me, this image has been an amazing source of courage, conviction, and freedom.

The works of Diner and Stone are a very helpful and encouraging beginning, but there is much more that needs to be uncovered. Black women must tend to this cultural history; because it is our own, we are more likely to intuit the threads of truth that join the surviving facts. Several Black women writers have already begun to explore the mythical/spiritual realm of our existence: Zora Neal Hurston in *Their Eyes Were Watching God* and *Of Mules and Men*, as well as in most of her anthropological writings; Marita Bonner in her play *The Purple Flower*; Audre Lorde in "Uses of the Erotic: The Erotic as Power," *The Black Unicorn, Coal*, and more than can be named here; Toni Cade Bambara in *The Salt Eaters*; Ntozake Shange in *for colored girls who have considered suicide/when the rainbow is enuf*, the short story "Sassafrass," and numerous poems; Pat Parker in *Movement in Black*; and Joyce Carol Thomas in her play *Ambrosia*, a powerful tale of spiritual reincarnation.

The chasm that exists between the matrifocal cultures of yesterday and the brutal subjugation of our African sisters today, which includes widespread genital mutilation, is treacherously deep. Numerous institutions and individuals have been complicit in leading us to believe that the latter is the "natural" way things have always been. What they try to ignore and we often fail to remember is that patriarchal religion and cultural mores are only a few thousand years old — hardly worthy of the term "forever"! Improving the quality of women's lives around the world requires more than economic and/or political theory. It is my hope that as more and more Third World women read Diner, Stone, Lorde, and others, they will begin to fill in the names, rituals, and deeds — the realities — of the Goddess-worshipping and woman-honoring cultures of our ancestors. I long for a discussion of spiritual, as well as economic and political, structures among Third World women, among all women.

NOTES

1. Audre Lorde, "125th Street and Abomey," *The Black Unicorn* (New York: W. W. Norton & Co., 1978), p. 12.

2. Helen Diner, *Mother and Amazons: The First Feminine History of Culture* (Garden City, N.Y.: Anchor Press/Doubleday, 1973), pp. 177–181.

3. Merlin Stone, *When God Was a Woman* (New York: The Dial Press, 1976) and *Ancient Mirrors of Womanhood: Our Goddess and Heroine Heritage* (New York: New Sibylline Books, 1979/80).

4. Audre Lorde, *The Black Unicorn.*

5. Helen Diner, *op. cit.*

6. Merina is most widely known as Myrine, her Greek name, but the former is her Libyan name.

7. Guy Cadogan Rothery, *The Amazons in Antiquity and Modern Times* (London: Francis Griffiths, 1910), p. 113.

8. See Rothery, p. 113, and Diner, pp. 108–109.

9. Audre Lorde, "The Women of Dan Dance With Swords In Their Hands To Mark The Time When They Were Warriors," *The Black Unicorn*, p. 14.

10. Joseph R. Washington, Jr., *Black Sects and Cults* (Garden City, N.Y.: Anchor Press/Doubleday, 1973), p. 20.

11. *Ibid.*

# The Three Faces of Goddess Spirituality

# Merlin Stone

In considering the already widespread and increasing interest in the diverse manifestations of Goddess spirituality within the feminist movement, it may be helpful to clarify at least three emerging aspects of this relatively new phenomenon. These three aspects, of what may be the most unexpected occurrence within feminism, have developed, separately and together, in a rather incredibly organic "grass roots" manner. Perhaps only within the flexibility of a feminism that is continually evolving out of the process of consciousness raising in its truest sense has this outgrowth of feminist consciousness been able to develop and grow.

Since all three of these aspects of Goddess spirituality appear to be simultaneously growing from one central trunk, I drew lots (a method used at the prophecy-providing shrines of the Goddess in ancient times) to decide their linear placement. This placement in no way implies that one aspect is of greater importance than another or precedes the others in actual development and, as you will see, many connections link the three.

© Merlin Stone, 1978. Reprinted by permission of the author from *Heresies: A Feminist Publication on Art and Politics*, no. 5, 1978.

The first aspect of Goddess spirituality is the emerging interest in the history and prehistory of ancient cultures that worshipped a female deity and in the laws and customs of those societies. Through research in archaeology, history, anthropology — and using this information to analyze ancient literature and mythology — we have begun to discover that far from the generally accepted idea that the Judeo-Christian religions rescued women from supposedly more barbarian and anti-woman societies, women have actually lost a great deal of status and physical and material autonomy since the inception of these and other male-worshipping religions. As a result of this research, which covers the period from the Neolithic Goddess shrines of about 8000 B.C. to the closing of the last Goddess temples in the early Christian periods of Byzantium, we have learned that many Goddess-worshipping societies were matrilineal, matrilocal, and matrifocal. In many of these societies, women owned property, engaged in business, and held the highest positions of the clergy. In such societies children automatically belonged to their mother's clan and took their mother's family name.

Through this research we are discovering the roots of today's attitudes toward women's bodies and minds. These attitudes become clear as we study them within the context of the original institution of patrilineal, patrilocal, and patrifocal systems under the aegis of the worship of a supreme deity as male. Though it required many millennia to suppress the Goddess religion and its social customs, this ancient religion was eventually designated as "pagan," and its remaining vestiges were obliterated by early Christian emperors, medieval inquisitions, and Witch burnings.

In our growing interest and efforts to explore the truth about the past, we are building, and hopefully we will continue to build, a body of evidence that bears witness to the many millennia in which the Creator was regarded as female and in which women held a much higher status than we have known since that time. This aspect of Goddess spirituality within the feminist movement is motivated by much the same feeling that has encouraged us to rediscover and reclaim female artists, writers, scientists, political leaders, and other important women who were ignored by the writers of the history books with which we were educated. This information affords an entirely new perspective on current stereotypes of women. It provides a broader view, as the perspective which allows us to look into the past also allows us to see further ahead.

The second aspect is that of a growing concern with a feminist per-

ception of spirituality and theology. It has emerged from feminist consciousness, an inkling or more of the first aspect and the perhaps ever-
present search for answers to such theological questions as the possible
purposes (or nonpurpose) of existence, the true nature of morality (or
immorality), birth, death, and the nature of mind as it is revealed in intelligence, intuition, and reason. For many centuries women have been
taught that if they cared to consider these questions at all (the implication being that such questions were actually too abstract for female
minds), answers were to be found in the words and writings of male
priests, male ministers, male rabbis, and male gurus — all of whom supposedly had greater spiritually contemplative abilities as well as more
direct access to knowledge of The Divine Plan or Cosmic Process.

A feminist contemplation of spiritual and theological questions soon
makes us painfully aware that the answers with which we have so far
been provided have existed in close relationship to, or more often
within, a personified life-force that is nearly always linguistically, and
more often actually, considered to be of the male gender. Not too surprisingly, "answers" about divine intentions are often as male-oriented
as the men who provide them. The exceptional rate of growth of
feminist concerns with Goddess spirituality in itself reveals a level of
consciousness that refuses and refutes this male-designed hierarchy and
its appropriation of theological and spiritual considerations — and the
subsequent "divine" decrees.

So far, and let us hope in the future as well, feminists concerned
with Goddess spirituality have seldom offered absolute or pat answers to
theological questions. What has been happening is the experiencing,
and at times the reporting, of these personal or group experiences: how
it feels to regard the ultimate life-force in our own image — as females;
how it feels to openly embrace and to share our own contemplations
and intuitive knowledge about the role of women on this planet; how it
feels to gain a sense of direction, a motivating energy, a strength, a
courage — somehow intuited as coming from a cosmic female energy
force that fuels and refuels us in our struggle against all human oppression and planetary destruction.

Some say they find this force within themselves; others regard it as
external. Some feel it in the ocean, the moon, a tree, the flight of a
bird, or in the constant stream of coincidences (or noncoincidences)
that occur in our lives. Some find access to it in the lighting of a can-
dle, chanting, meditating — alone or with other women. From what I
have so far read, heard, or experienced myself, I think it safe to say that

all women who feel they have experienced Goddess spirituality in one way or another also feel that they have gained an inner strength and direction that temporarily or permanently has helped them to deal with life. Most women interested or involved in feminist concepts of spirituality do not regard this spirituality as an end in itself but as a means of gaining and giving strength and understanding that will help us to confront the many tangible and material issues of the blatant inequities of society as we know it today.

The third aspect of Goddess spirituality is concerned with the more circumspect observation of the organized male-worshipping, male-clergied religions of today — an examination of the specific ways in which these religions have instituted and maintained a secondary status for women. Involvement in Goddess spirituality has encouraged us to take a more careful look at the scriptures, rituals, and the gender of the decision-making level of the clergy of the religions in which we were raised and/or those that affect the society in which we live.

Some of the most urgent issues confronting contemporary women all over the planet are those concerning economic survival, abortion, contraception, rape, clitorectomy, infibulation, divorce, attitudes toward "illegitimacy," lesbian rights, social pressure to marry and to have children, physical and psychological violence, attitudes toward women's bodies, and the stereotypes of woman as follower rather than leader and as sexual and reproductive being rather than as total human being.

A careful reading of the Bible still used by Judeo-Christian congregations reveals the ancient origins of many of these important feminist issues. The proclamation in Gen. 3:16 informs both women and men that women are expected, as the result of a "divine" decree, to be sexually faithful and subservient to their husbands and that the pains of childbirth are to be regarded as "divine" retribution — the "will of God" as it is asserted over the will of woman.

Deut. 22:28, 29 requires that a raped virgin be *married* to the man who raped her. Deut. 22:22–24 stipulates that a raped betrothed woman should be *put to death* (unless the rape occurred in the deserted countryside). Deut. 22:20–22 states that a bride discovered not to be a virgin should be dragged from the house and *stoned to death*. Deut. 22:22 declares that a married woman should be *put to death* if found lying with a man (no excuse for rape is mentioned). Deut. 24:1 decrees that a man has the right to divorce his wife on his decision alone, while *no* provision is made for a woman who desires to divorce her husband. Each of these biblical laws reveals the intense efforts made to control reproductive capacities, and, thus, the sexual activities of women, by the men who wrote these laws and by those who followed them.

Our understanding and analysis of these biblical laws and their subsequent effects on contemporary women become clear only in the context of historical information which reveals that these laws were devised at much the same time that matrilineal customs were being destroyed and patrilineal systems initiated. In a patrilineal system, knowledge of paternity is vital. This knowledge takes on even greater import when the system is declared to be an integral aspect of The Divine Plan and, thus, any challenge to the patrilineal system and certain knowledge of paternity may be considered blasphemy — at times punishable by death. Even today, socio-religious attitudes toward "unwed mothers" and "illegitimacy" have not yet been thoroughly examined and challenged as a vital feminist issue.

The institution and maintenance of a patrilineal system were further abetted by biblical laws such as Num. 30 requiring that a daughter's or a wife's vow must be regarded as null and void unless confirmed by father or husband — making it impossible for most women to engage in business activities and thus limiting their access to economic autonomy. Num. 27 explains that the rights to family inheritance are accessible only to sons, unless there are no male heirs, and Num. 36 decrees that if a woman does inherit in such a situation, she must then marry only within her father's tribe. Written about 3,000 years ago, these laws still exist in the Old Testament of the Judeo-Christian Bible. Though the last few generations may have forgotten or rejected these laws, can we afford to ignore them in our efforts to understand the origins of attitudes toward women as wage earners today?

Judeo-Christian laws and decrees have deeply affected the secular laws and attitudes of our contemporary patrilineal society. All too often we discover them to be the probable origins of many of the problems we face today, such as the right of each woman to be able to control her own physical body and its functions; access to abortion; in some countries, access to contraception and divorce; the concept of "illegitimacy" and the social and legal pressures surrounding it; social and legal attitudes on lesbian love; physical violence against women, stereotypes of whore and madonna; double standards for premarital virginity and marital fidelity; attitudes toward women's access to earning power (including choice of vocation, education, advancement in chosen field, and levels of economic recompense) and the so-called "natural" assumption of male leadership in political, intellectual, and spiritual spheres.

Each of these issues is an anger-provoking reminder of the long-standing power of male-oriented, male-dominated religions. It is for this reason that it is vital to fully understand the connections between these attitudes, biblical laws, and the initial institution of the patrilineal system in which we live. The supremacy of "Father in Heaven" is a mere reflection of the supremacy of "father on earth." The status of father is magnified beyond biological reality by the patrilineal system, and it is this system that is the underlying foundation of all *patri*archal ideas and actions. Refusing to acknowledge paternal identity may be one of the most revolutionary acts possible.

Even today, the absence or extreme minority of women in decision-making levels of the clergy of nearly all Jewish, Catholic, and Protestant congregations ensures that these biblical decrees and subsequent attitudes will retain their original power. Perhaps more important, we must remember that biblical laws and attitudes have extended far beyond the walls of any specific church or temple and are now deeply embedded within so-called secular law and social custom. Despite the supposed separation of church and state, women's demands in early feminist struggles for women's suffrage were continually challenged and obstructed by clergymen who claimed sole access to knowledge of The Divine Plan — and women voting was not part of it.

It is also of interest that along with sexist attitudes, racism and slavery were justified by the "religious" idea that heathens had no souls — thus allowing "good" Christians to invade the land of the Native Americans, decimating them as a people and appropriating their property, and to kidnap Africans and to use them as slaves. Male-oriented religion's passive acceptance of racism is still to be seen in the racial segregation of churches.

Goddess spirituality offers us the immediate and inherent refutation of the institutionalized "religious" values that have for too long been used as weapons of oppression. From this third aspect of Goddess spirituality grows the consciousness of, and the direct challenge to, these "religious" laws and attitudes that have played such a large part in formulating the roles of women in contemporary society.

In all of its aspects, Goddess spirituality has grown from our continually feeling, speaking, comparing, analyzing, feminist-consciousness-raising process — the very core of our new perceptions and, thus, our motivating energies. Our consciousness has now been raised — to the point where we can no longer ignore the suppression or perversion of evidence on the roles of women in the ancient Goddess-worshipping cultures; the trivializing of women's thoughts and ideas on spiritual and theological considerations of existence, from personal to planetary; and the oppression of women as it has been instituted and maintained within the patrilineal, male-worshipping religions and the effect this has had on society.

Though some may want to question the political viability of Goddess spirituality within the feminist struggle, few would deny its existence within the feminist community. Goddess spirituality has grown from our consciousness-raising process; it has grown from US. It may be the ultimate heresy — and it may ultimately be what allows us to succeed where so many others have failed.

# Why Women Need the Goddess: Phenomenological, Psychological, and Political Reflections

## Carol P. Christ

At the close of Ntozake Shange's stupendously successful Broadway play *for colored girls who have considered suicide / when the rainbow is enuf,* a tall beautiful Black woman rises from despair to cry out, "I found God in myself and I loved her fiercely."[1] Her discovery is echoed by women around the country who meet spontaneously in small groups on full moons, solstices, and equinoxes to celebrate the Goddess as symbol of life and death powers and waxing and waning energies in the universe and in themselves.[2]

From *Womanspirit Rising* by Judith Plaskow and Carol P. Christ. Copyright © 1979 by Judith Plaskow and Carol P. Christ. Reprinted by permission of Harper & Row, Publishers, Inc. Dr. Christ presented this essay as the keynote address at the conference titled "The Great Goddess Re-Emerging," University of California at Santa Cruz, 31 March–2 April 1978.

It is the night of the full moon. Nine women stand in a circle, on a rocky hill above the city. The western sky is rosy with the setting sun; in the east the moon's face begins to peer above the horizon. . . . The woman pours out a cup of wine onto the earth, refills it and raises it high. "Hail, Tana, Mother of mothers!" she cries. "Awaken from your long sleep, and return to your children again!"[3]

What are the political and psychological effects of this fierce new love of the divine in themselves for women whose spiritual experience has been focused by the male God of Judaism and Christianity? Is the spiritual dimension of feminism a passing diversion, an escape from difficult but necessary political work? Or does the emergence of the symbol of Goddess among women have significant political and psychological ramifications for the feminist movement?

To answer this question, we must first understand the importance of religious symbols and rituals in human life and consider the effect of male symbolism of God on women. According to anthropologist Clifford Geertz, religious symbols shape a cultural ethos, defining the deepest values of a society and the persons in it. "Religion," Geertz writes, "is a system of symbols which act to produce powerful, pervasive, and long-lasting moods and motivations"[4] in the people of a given culture. A "mood" for Geertz is a psychological attitude, such as awe, trust, and respect, while a "motivation" is the *social* and *political* trajectory created by a mood that transforms mythos into ethos, symbol system into social and political reality. Symbols have both psychological and political effects, because they create the inner conditions (deep-seated attitudes and feelings) that lead people to feel comfortable with or to accept social and political arrangements that correspond to the symbol system.

Because religion has such a compelling hold on the deep psyches of so many people, feminists cannot afford to leave it in the hands of the fathers. Even people who no longer "believe in God" or participate in the institutional structure of patriarchal religion still may not be free of the power of the symbolism of God the Father. A symbol's effect does not depend on rational assent, for a symbol also functions on levels of the psyche other than the rational. Religion fulfills deep psychic needs by providing symbols and rituals that enable people to cope with limit situations[5] in human life (death, evil, suffering) and to pass through life's important transitions (birth, sexuality, death). Even people who consider themselves completely secularized will often find themselves sitting in a church or synagogue when a friend or relative gets married, or when a parent or friend has died. The symbols associated with these important rituals cannot fail to affect the deep or unconscious structures of the mind of even a person who has rejected these symbolisms on a conscious level — especially if the person is under stress. The reason for the continuing effect of religious symbols is that the mind abhors a vacuum. Symbol systems cannot simply be rejected, they must be replaced. Where there is not any replacement, the mind will revert to familiar structures at times of crisis, bafflement, or defeat.

Religions centered on the worship of a male God create "moods" and "motivations" that keep women in a state of psychological dependence on men and male authority, while at the same time legitimating the *political* and *social* authority of fathers and sons in the institutions of society.

Religious symbol systems focused around exclusively male images of divinity create the impression that female power can never be fully legitimate or wholly beneficent. This message need never be explicitly stated (as, for example, it is in the story of Eve) for its effect to be felt. A woman completely ignorant of the myths of female evil in biblical religion nonetheless acknowledges the anomaly of female power when she prays exclusively to a male God. She may see herself as like God (created in the image of God) only by denying her own sexual identity and affirming God's transcendence of sexual identity. But she can never have the experience that is freely available to every man and boy in her culture, of having her full sexual identity affirmed as being in the image and likeness of God. In Geertz' terms, her "mood" is one of trust in male power as salvific and distrust of female power in herself and other women as inferior or dangerous. Such a powerful, pervasive, and longlasting "mood" cannot fail to become a "motivation" that translates into social and political reality.

In *Beyond God the Father,* feminist theologian Mary Daly detailed the psychological and political ramifications of father religion for women. "If God in 'his' heaven is a father ruling his people," she wrote, "then it is the 'nature' of things and according to divine plan and the order of the universe that society be male-dominated. Within this context, a *mystification of roles* takes place: The husband dominating his wife represents God 'himself.' The images and values of a given society have been projected into the realm of dogmas and 'Articles of Faith,' and these, in turn, justify the social structures which have given rise to them and which sustain their plausibility."[6]

Philosopher Simone de Beauvoir was well aware of the function of patriarchal religion as legitimater of male power; she wrote, "Man enjoys the great advantage of having a god endorse the code he writes; and since man exercises a sovereign authority over women it is especially fortunate that this authority has been vested in him by the Supreme Being. For the Jew, Mohammedans, and Christians, among others, man is Master by divine right; the fear of God will, therefore, repress any impulse to revolt in the downtrodden female."[7]

This brief discussion of the psychological and political effects of God religion puts us in an excellent position to begin to understand the significance of the symbol of Goddess for women. In discussing the meaning of the Goddess, my method will first be phenomenological. I will isolate a meaning of the symbol of the Goddess as it has emerged in the lives of contemporary women. I will then discuss its psychological and political significance by contrasting the "moods" and "motivations" engendered by Goddess symbols with those engendered by Christian symbolism. I will also correlate Goddess symbolism with themes that have emerged in the women's movement, in order to show how Goddess symbolism undergirds and legitimates the concerns of the women's movement, much as God symbolism in Christianity undergirded the interests of men in patriarchy. I will discuss four aspects of Goddess symbolism here: the Goddess as affirmation of female power, the female body, the female will, and women's bonds and heritage. There are, of course, many other meanings of the Goddess that I will not discuss here.

The sources for the symbol of the Goddess in contemporary spirituality are traditions of Goddess worship and modern women's experience. The ancient Mediterranean, pre-Christian European, Native American, Mesoamerican, Hindu, African, and other traditions are rich sources for Goddess symbolism. But these traditions are filtered through modern women's experiences. Traditions of goddesses, subordination to gods, for example, are ignored. Ancient traditions are tapped selectively and eclecticly, but they are not considered authoritative for modern consciousness. The Goddess symbol has emerged spontaneously in the dreams, fantasies, and thoughts of many women around the country in the past several years. Kirsten Grimstad and Susan Rennie reported that they were surprised to discover widespread interest in spirituality, including the Goddess, among feminists around the country in the summer of 1974.[8] *WomanSpirit* magazine, which published its first issue in 1974 and has contributors from across the United States, has expressed the grass roots nature of the women's spirituality movement.

In 1976, a journal, *Lady Unique*, devoted to the Goddess emerged. In 1975, the first women's spirituality conference was held in Boston and attended by 1,800 women. In 1978, a course on the Goddess at the University of California at Santa Cruz, drew over 500 people. Sources for this essay are these manifestations of the Goddess in modern women's experiences as reported in *WomanSpirit, Lady Unique,* and elsewhere, and as expressed in conversations I have had with women who have been thinking about the Goddess and women's spirituality.

The simplest and most basic meaning of the symbol of Goddess is the acknowledgment of the legitimacy of female power as a beneficent and independent power. A woman who echoes Ntozake Shange's dramatic statement, "I found God in myself and I loved her fiercely," is saying "Female power is strong and creative." She is saying that the divine principle, the saving and sustaining power, is in herself, that she will no longer look to men or male figures as saviors. The strength and independence of female power can be intuited by contemplating ancient and modern images of the Goddess. This meaning of the symbol of Goddess is simple and obvious, and yet it is difficult for many to comprehend. It stands in sharp contrast to the paradigms of female dependence on males that have been predominant in Western religion and culture. The internationally acclaimed novelist Monique Wittig captured the novelty and flavor of the affirmation of female power in her mythic work *Les Guérillères:*

> There was a time when you were not a slave, remember that. You walked alone, full of laughter, you bathed bare-bellied. You say you have lost all recollection of it, remember . . . you say there are no words to describe it, you say it does not exist. But remember. Make an effort to remember. Or, failing that, invent.[9]

While Wittig does not speak directly of the Goddess here, she captures the "mood" of joyous celebration of female freedom and independence that is created in women who define their identities through the symbol of Goddess. Artist Mary Beth Edelson expressed the political "motivations" inspired by the Goddess when she wrote,

> The ascending archetypal symbols of the feminine unfold today in the psyche of modern Everywoman. They encompass the multiple forms of the Great Goddess. Reaching across the centuries we take the hands of our Ancient Sisters. The Great Goddess, alive and well, is rising to announce to the patriarchs that their 5,000 years are up — Hallelujah! Here we come.[10]

The affirmation of female power contained in the Goddess symbol has both psychological and political consequences. Psychologically, it means the defeat of the view engendered by patriarchy that women's power is inferior and dangerous. This new "mood" of affirmation of female power also leads to new "motivations"; it supports and undergirds women's trust in their own power and the power of other women in family and society.

If the simplest meaning of the Goddess symbol is an affirmation of the legitimacy and beneficence of female power, then a question immediately arises, "Is the Goddess simply female power writ large, and, if so, why bother with the symbol of Goddess at all? Or does the symbol refer to a Goddess 'out there' who is not reducible to a human potential?" The many women who have rediscovered the power of Goddess would give three answers to this question: (1) The Goddess is divine female, a personification who can be invoked in prayer and ritual; (2) the Goddess is symbol of the life, death, and rebirth energy in nature and culture, in personal and communal life; and (3) the Goddess is symbol of the affirmation of the legitimacy and beauty of female power (made possible by the new becoming of women in the women's liberation movement). If one were to ask these women which answer is the "correct" one, different responses would be given. Some would assert that the Goddess definitely is *not* "out there," that the symbol of a divinity "out there" is part of the legacy of patriarchal oppression, which brings with it the authoritarianism, hierarchicalism, and dogmatic rigidity associated with biblical monotheistic religions. They might assert that the Goddess symbol reflects the sacred power within women and nature, suggesting the connectedness between women's cycles of menstruation, birth, and menopause, and the life and death cycles of the universe. Others seem quite comfortable with the notion of Goddess as a divine female protector and creator and would find their experience of Goddess limited by the assertion that she is not *also* out there as well as within themselves and in all natural processes. When asked what the symbol of Goddess means, Starhawk, a feminist priestess, replied, "It all depends on how I feel. When I feel weak, She is someone who can help and protect me. When I feel strong, She is the symbol of my own power. At other times I feel Her as the natural energy in my body and the world."[11] How are we to evaluate such a statement? Theologians might call these the words of a sloppy thinker. But my deepest intuition tells me they contain a wisdom that Western theological thought has lost.

To theologians, these differing views of the "meaning" of the symbol

of Goddess might seem to threaten a replay of the trinitarian contro-
versies. Is there, perhaps, a way of doing theology which would not
lead immediately into dogmatic controversy, which would not require
theologians to say definitively that one understanding is true and the
others are false? Could people's relation to a common symbol be made
primary and varying interpretations be acknowledged? The diversity of
explications of the meaning of the Goddess symbol suggests that symbols have a richer significance than any explications of their meaning
can express, a point literary critics have long insisted on. This phenomenological fact suggests that theologians may need to give more than
lip service to a theory of symbol in which the symbol is viewed as the
primary fact and the meanings are viewed as secondary. It also suggests
that a *thealogy*[12] of the Goddess would be very different from the
*theology* we have known in the West. But to spell out this notion of the
primacy of *symbol* in thealogy in contrast to the primacy of the *explanation* in theology would be the topic of another paper. Let me simply
state that women, who have been deprived of a female religious symbol
system for centuries, are, therefore, in an excellent position to recognize
the power and primacy of symbols. I believe women must develop a
theory of symbol and thealogy congruent with their experience at the
same time as they "remember and invent" new symbol systems.

A second important implication of the Goddess symbol for women is
the affirmation of the female body and the life cycle expressed in it.*
Because of women's unique position as menstruants, birthgivers, and
those who have traditionally cared for the young and the dying,
women's connection to the body, nature, and this world has been obvious. Women were denigrated because they seemed more carnal, fleshy,
and earthy than the culture-creating males.[13] The misogynist anti*body*
tradition in Western thought is symbolized in the myth of Eve who is

---

* Editor's Note: On a psychophysiological level, William Irwin Thompson has
expressed a view of sexuality that would seem to lead men, too, to Goddess spirituality: "The gigantic egg sits, and the frantic and tiny sperm flagellates its tail
to cross vast distances on its quest for dissolution in the huge egg. This is another
version of 'Woman is, Man does,' another version of the death-defying quest of
the male for ultimate dissolution in the Great Mother." Woman is *and* does, though
perhaps with more elemental security than that experienced by man. Nonetheless,
Thompson's perception of sexuality suggests an impulse that surely could reach
resolution only in a Goddess-oriented culture, wherein all life springs from the
Earth-Womb of the Mother to which we all return and dissolve when we die. Of
course, there are also many other reasons why the holistic symbol of the Goddess
resonates with postpatriarchal men. — C.S.

traditionally viewed as a sexual temptress, the epitome of women's carnal nature. This tradition reaches its nadir in the *Malleus Maleficarum* (*The Hammer of Evil-Doing Women*), which states, "All witchcraft stems from carnal lust, which in women is insatiable."[14] The Virgin Mary, the positive female image in Christianity does not contradict Christian denigration of the female body and its powers. The Virgin Mary is revered because she, in her perpetual virginity, transcends the carnal sexuality attributed to most women.

The denigration of the female body is expressed in cultural and religious taboos surrounding menstruation, childbirth, and menopause in women. While menstruation taboos may have originated in a perception of the awesome powers of the female body,[15] they degenerated into a simple perception that there is something "wrong" with female bodily functions. Menstruating women were forbidden to enter the sanctuary in ancient Hebrew and premodern Christian communities. Although only Orthodox Jews still enforce religious taboos against menstruant women, few women in our culture grow up affirming their menstruation as a connection to sacred power. Most women learn that menstruation is a curse and grow up believing that the bloody facts of menstruation are best hidden away. Feminists challenge this attitude to the female body. Judy Chicago's art piece "Menstruation Bathroom" broke these menstrual taboos. In a sterile white bathroom, she exhibited boxes of Tampax and Kotex on an open shelf, and the wastepaper basket was overflowing with bloody tampons and sanitary napkins.[16] Many women who viewed the piece felt relieved to have their "dirty secret" out in the open.

The denigration of the female body and its powers is further expressed in Western culture's attitudes toward childbirth.[17] Religious iconography does not celebrate the birthgiver, and there is no theology or ritual that enables a woman to celebrate the process of birth as a spiritual experience. Indeed, Jewish and Christian traditions also had blood taboos concerning the woman who had recently given birth. While these religious taboos are rarely enforced today (again, only by Orthodox Jews), they have secular equivalents. Giving birth is treated as a disease requiring hospitalization, and the woman is viewed as a passive object, anesthetized to ensure her acquiescence to the will of the doctor. The women's liberation movement has challenged these cultural attitudes, and many feminists have joined with advocates of natural childbirth and home birth in emphasizing the need for women to control and take pride in their bodies, including the birth process.

Western culture also gives little dignity to the postmenopausal or aging woman. It is no secret that our culture is based on a denial of aging and death, and that women suffer more severely from this denial than men. Women are placed on a pedestal and considered powerful when they are young and beautiful, but they are said to lose this power as they age. As feminists have pointed out, the "power" of the young woman is illusory, since beauty standards are defined by men, and since few women are considered (or consider themselves) beautiful for more than a few years of their lives. Some men are viewed as wise and authoritative in age, but old women are pitied and shunned. Religious iconography supports this cultural attitude toward aging women. The purity and virginity of Mary and the female saints is often expressed in the iconographic convention of perpetual youth. Moreover, religious mythology associates aging women with evil in the symbol of the wicked old Witch. Feminists have challenged cultural myths of aging women and have urged women to reject patriarchal beauty standards and to celebrate the distinctive beauty of women of all ages.

The symbol of Goddess aids the process of naming and reclaiming the female body and its cycles and processes. In the ancient world and among modern women, the Goddess symbol represents the birth, death, and rebirth processes of the natural and human worlds. The female body is viewed as the direct incarnation of the waxing and waning, life and death cycles in the universe. This is sometimes expressed through the symbolic connection between the twenty-eight-day cycles of menstruation and the twenty-eight-day cycles of the moon. Moreover, the Goddess is celebrated in the triple aspect of youth, maturity, and age, or maiden, mother, and crone. The potentiality of the young girl is celebrated in the nymph or maiden aspect of the Goddess. The Goddess as mother is sometimes depicted giving birth, and giving birth is viewed as a symbol for all the creative, life-giving powers of the universe.[18] The life-giving powers of the Goddess in Her creative aspect are not limited to physical birth, for the Goddess is also seen as the creator of all the arts of civilization, including healing, writing, and the giving of just law. Women in the middle of life who are not physical mothers may give birth to poems, songs, and books, or nurture other women, men, and children. They, too, are incarnations of the Goddess in Her creative, life-giving aspect. At the end of life, women incarnate the crone aspect of the Goddess. The wise old woman, the woman who knows from experience what life is about, the woman whose closeness to her own death gives her a distance and perspective on the problems of life, is celebrated as the third aspect of the Goddess. Thus, women learn to value youth, creativity, and wisdom in themselves and other women.

The possibilities of reclaiming the female body and its cycles have been expressed in a number of Goddess-centered rituals. Hallie Iglehart and Barbry My Own created a summer solstice ritual to celebrate menstruation and birth. The women simulated a birth canal and birthed each other into their circle. They raised power by placing their hands on each other's bellies and chanting together. Finally they marked each other's faces with rich, dark menstrual blood saying, "This is the blood that promises renewal. This is the blood that promises sustenance. This is the blood that promises life."[19] From hidden dirty secret to symbol of the life power of the Goddess, women's blood has come full circle. Other women have created rituals that celebrate the crone aspect of the Goddess. Z. Budapest believes that the crone aspect of the Goddess is predominant in the fall, especially at Halloween, an ancient holiday. On this day, the wisdom of the old woman is celebrated, and it is also recognized that the old must die so that the new can be born.

The "mood" created by the symbol of the Goddess in triple aspect is one of positive, joyful affirmation of the female body and its cycles and acceptance of aging and death as well as life. The "motivations" are to overcome menstrual taboos, to return the birth process to the hands of women, and to change cultural attitudes about age and death. Changing cultural attitudes toward the female body could go a long way toward overcoming the spirit-flesh, mind-body dualisms of Western culture, since, as Rosemary Ruether has pointed out, the denigration of the female body is at the heart of these dualisms. The Goddess as symbol of the revaluation of the body and nature, thus, also undergirds the human potential and ecology movements. The "mood" is one of affirmation, awe, and respect for the body and nature, and the "motivation" is to respect the teachings of the body and the rights of all living beings.

A third important implication of the Goddess symbol for women is the positive valuation of will in a Goddess-centered ritual, especially in Goddess-centered ritual magic and spellcasting in womanspirit and feminist Witchcraft circles. The basic notion behind ritual magic and spellcasting is energy as power. Here the Goddess is a center or focus of power and energy; She is the personification of the energy that flows between beings in the natural and human worlds. In Goddess circles, energy is raised by chanting or dancing. According to Starhawk, "Witches conceive of psychic energy as having form and substance that can be perceived and directed by those with a trained awareness. The power generated within the circle is built into a cone form and, at its peak, is released — to the Goddess, to reenergize the members of the coven, or to do a specific work such as healing."[20] In ritual magic, the energy raised is directed by willpower. Women who celebrate in Goddess circles believe they can achieve their wills in the world.

The emphasis on the will is important for women, because women traditionally have been taught to devalue their wills, to believe that they cannot achieve their will through their own power, and even to suspect that the assertion of will is evil. Faith Wilding's poem "Waiting," from which I will quote only a short segment, sums up women's sense that their lives are defined not by their own will, but by waiting for others to take the initiative:

> Waiting for my breasts to develop
> Waiting to wear a bra
> Waiting to menstruate
> . . .
> Waiting for life to begin, Waiting—
> Waiting to be somebody
> . . .
> Waiting to get married
> Waiting for my wedding day
> Waiting for my wedding night
> . . .
> Waiting for the end of the day
> Waiting for sleep. Waiting . . .[21]

Patriarchal religion has enforced the view that female initiative and will are evil through the juxtaposition of Eve and Mary. Eve caused the fall by asserting her will against the command of God, while Mary began the new age with her response to God's initiative, "Let it be done to me according to Thy word" (Luke 1:38). Even for men, patriarchal religion values the passive will subordinate to divine initiative. The classical doctrines of sin and grace view sin as the prideful assertion of will and grace as the obedient subordination of the human will to the divine initiative or order. While this view of will might be questioned from a human perspective, Valerie Saiving has argued that it has particularly deleterious consequences for women in Western culture. According to Saiving, Western culture encourages males in the assertion of will, and, thus, it may make some sense to view the male form of sin as an excess of will. But since our culture discourages females in the assertion of will, the traditional doctrines of sin and grace encourage women to remain in their form of sin, which is self-negation or insufficient assertion of will.[22] One possible reason the will is denigrated in a patriarchal religious framework is that both human and divine will are often pictured as arbitrary, self-initiated, and exercised without regard for other wills.

In a Goddess-centered context, in contrast, the will is valued. *A woman is encouraged to know her will, to believe that her will is valid, and to believe that her will can be achieved in the world,* three powers traditionally denied to her in patriarchy. In a Goddess-centered framework, a woman's will is not subordinated to the Lord God as king and ruler, nor to men as his representatives. Thus, a woman is not reduced to waiting and acquiescing in the wills of others as she is in patriarchy. But neither does she adopt the egocentric form of will that pursues self-interest without regard for the interests of others.

The Goddess-centered context provides a different understanding of the will than that available in the traditional patriarchal religious framework. In the Goddess framework, will can be achieved only when it is exercised in harmony with the energies and wills of other beings. Wise women, for example, raise a cone of healing energy at the full moon or solstice when the lunar or solar energies are at their high points with respect to the earth. This discipline encourages them to recognize that not all times are propitious for the achieving of every will. Similarly, they know that spring is a time for new beginnings in work and love, summer a time for producing external manifestations of inner potentialities, and fall or winter a time for stripping down to the inner core and extending roots. Such awareness of waxing and waning processes in the universe discourages arbitrary ego-centered assertion of will, while at the same time encouraging the assertion of individual will in cooperation with natural energies and the energies created by the wills of others. Wise women also have a tradition that whatever is sent out will be returned, and this reminds them to assert their wills in cooperative and healing rather than egocentric and destructive ways. This view of will allows women to begin to recognize, claim, and assert their wills without adopting the worst characteristics of the patriarchal understanding and use of will. In the Goddess-centered framework, the "mood" is one of positive affirmation of personal will in the context of the energies of other wills or beings. The "motivation" is for women to know and assert their wills in cooperation with other wills and energies. This of course does not mean that women always assert their wills in positive and life-affirming ways. Women's capacity for evil is, of course, as great as men's. My purpose is simply to contrast the differing attitudes toward the exercise of will *per se,* and the female will in particular, in Goddess-centered religion and in the Christian God-centered religion.

The fourth and final aspect of Goddess symbolism that I will discuss here is the significance of the Goddess for a revaluation of woman's bonds and heritage. As Virginia Woolf has said, "Chloe liked Olivia," a statement about a woman's relation to another woman, is a sentence that rarely occurs in fiction. Men have written the stories, and they have written about women almost exclusively in their relations to men.[23] The celebrations of women's bonds to each other, as mothers and daughters, as colleagues and co-workers, as sisters, friends, and lovers, is beginning to occur in the new literature and culture created by women in the women's movement. While I believe that the revaluing of each of these bonds is important, I will focus on the mother-daughter bond, in part because I believe it may be the key to the others.

Adrienne Rich has pointed out that the mother-daughter bond, perhaps the most important of woman's bonds, "resonant with charges . . . the flow of energy between two biologically alike bodies, one of which has lain in amniotic bliss inside the other, one of which has labored to give birth to the other,"[24] is rarely celebrated in patriarchal religion and culture. Christianity celebrates the father's relation to the son and the mother's relation to the son, but the story of mother and daughter is missing. So, too, in patriarchal literature and psychology the mothers and the daughters rarely exist. Volumes have been written about the Oedipus complex, but little has been written about the girl's relation to her mother. Moreover, as de Beauvoir has noted, the mother-daughter relation is distorted in patriarchy because the mother must give her daughter over to men in a male-defined culture in which women are viewed as inferior. The mother must socialize her daughter to become subordinate to men, and if her daughter challenges patriarchal norms, the mother is likely to defend the patriarchal structures against her own daughter.[25]

These patterns are changing in the new culture created by women in which the bonds of women to women are beginning to be celebrated. Holly Near has written several songs that celebrate women's bonds and women's heritage. In one of her finest songs she writes of an "old-time

woman" who is "waiting to die." A young woman feels for the life that
has passed the old woman by and begins to cry, but the old woman
looks her in the eye and says, "If I had not suffered, you wouldn't be
wearing those jeans/Being an old-time woman ain't as bad as it
seems."[26] This song, which Near has said was inspired by her grandmother, expresses and celebrates a bond and a heritage passed down
from one woman to another. In another of Near's songs, she sings of
"a hiking-boot mother who's seeing the world/For the first time with
her own little girl." In this song, the mother tells the drifter who has
been traveling with her to pack up and travel alone if he thinks "traveling three is a drag" because "I've got a little one who loves me as much
as you need me/And darling, that's loving enough."[27] This song is
significant because the mother places her relationship to her daughter
above her relationship to a man, something women rarely do in patriarchy.[28]

Almost the only story of mothers and daughters that has been transmitted in Western culture is the myth of Demeter and Persephone that
was the basis of religious rites celebrated by women only, the Thesmophoria, and later formed the basis of the Eleusinian mysteries, which
were open to all who spoke Greek. In this story, the daughter, Persephone, is abducted away from her mother, Demeter, and raped by the
God of the Underworld. Unwilling to accept this state of affairs, Demeter rages and withholds fertility from the Earth until Her daughter
is returned to Her. What is important for women in this story is that a
mother fights for her daughter and for her relation to her daughter.
This is completely different from the mother's relation to her daughter
in patriarchy. The "mood" created by the story of Demeter and Persephone is one of celebration of the mother-daughter bond, and the
"motivation" is for mothers and daughters to affirm the heritage passed
on from mother to daughter and to reject the patriarchal pattern where
the primary loyalties of mother and daughter must be to men.

The symbol of Goddess has much to offer women who are struggling
to be rid of the "powerful, pervasive, and long-lasting moods and motivations" of devaluation of female power, denigration of the female
body, distrust of female will, and denial of the women's bonds and heritage that have been engendered by patriarchal religion. As women
struggle to create a new culture in which women's power, bodies, will,
and bonds are celebrated, it seems natural that the Goddess would re-
emerge as symbol of the newfound beauty, strength, and power of
women.

NOTES

1. From the original cast album, Buddah Records, 1976.
2. See Susan Rennie and Kirsten Grimstad, "Spiritual Explorations Cross-Country," *Quest*, 1975, vol. 1, no. 4, 1975, pp. 49–51; and *WomanSpirit* magazine.
3. See Starhawk, "Witchcraft and Women's Culture," in *Womanspirit Rising*.
4. "Religion as a Cultural System," in William L. Lessa and Evon V. Vogt, eds., *Reader in Comparative Religion*, 2nd ed. (New York: Harper & Row, 1972), p. 206.
5. Geertz, p. 210.
6. Boston: Beacon Press, 1973, p. 13, italics added.
7. Simone de Beauvoir, *The Second Sex*, trans. H. M. Parshleys (New York: Alfred A. Knopf, 1953).
8. Grimstad and Rennie, *loc. cit.*
9. *Les Guérillères*, trans. David LeVay (New York: Avon Books, 1971), p. 89. Also quoted in Morgan MacFarland, "Witchcraft: The Art of Remembering," *Quest*, 1975, vol. 1, no. 4, p. 41.
10. "Speaking for Myself," *Lady Unique*, 1976, Cycle 1, p. 56.
11. Personal communication.
12. A term coined by Naomi Goldenberg to refer to reflection on the meaning of the symbol of Goddess.
13. This theory of the origins of the Western dualism is stated by Rosemary Ruether in *New Woman: New Earth* (New York: Seabury Press, 1975), and elsewhere.
14. Heinrich Kramer and Jacob Sprenger (New York: Dover, 1971), p. 47.
15. See Rita M. Gross, "Menstruation and Childbirth as Ritual and Religious Experience in the Religion of the Australian Aborigines," in *The Journal of the American Academy of Religion*, 1977, vol. 45, no. 41, Supplement, pp. 1147–1181.
16. *Through the Flower* (New York: Doubleday & Company, 1975), plate 4, pp. 106–107.
17. See Adrienne Rich, *Of Woman Born* (New York: Bantam Books, 1977), chaps. 6 and 7.
18. See James Mellaart, *Earliest Civilizations of the Near East* (New York: McGraw-Hill, 1965), p. 92.
19. Barbry My Own, "Ursa Maior: Menstrual Moon Celebration," *Moon, Moon*, Anne Kent Rush, ed. (Berkeley, Calif., and New York: Moon Books and Random House, 1976), pp. 374–387.

20. Starhawk, in *Womanspirit Rising.*
21. Judy Chicago, *op. cit.,* pp. 213–217.
22. "The Human Situation: A Feminine View," *Journal of Religion,* 1960, vol. 40, pp. 100–112.
23. *A Room of One's Own* (New York: Harcourt Brace Jovanovich, 1928), p. 86.
24. Rich, *op. cit.,* p. 226.
25. De Beauvoir, *op. cit.,* pp. 448–449.
26. "Old Time Woman," lyrics by Jeffrey Langley and Holly Near, from *Holly Near: A Live Album,* Redwood Records, 1974.
27. "Started Out Fine," by Holly Near from *Holly Near: A Live Album.*
28. Rich, *op. cit.,* p. 223.

# Mythic Heras* as Models of Strength and Wisdom

We *are* the myths. We are the Amazons, the Furies, the Witches. We have never not been here, this exact sliver of time, this precise place.

There is something utterly familiar about us.

We have been ourselves before.

— ROBIN MORGAN

* While I was compiling the research for *Lost Goddesses of Early Greece*, I discovered that the word *hera* (a pre-Hellenic name for the Goddess) predates the masculine form, *hero*, a term for the brave male Heracles (later Hercules) who carried out the bidding of his Goddess, Hera. The derivative form *heroine* is, therefore, completely unnecessary! Bella Debrida, a classics scholar, informs me that this connection between Hera, Heracles and hero is acknowledged in the standard French and German etymological dictionaries, edited by Chantraine and Frisk, respectively. Of course, a good feminist case can be made for eliminating all unnecessary gender distinctions, i.e., using only one form of this word for everyone who acts courageously. — C.S.

From *Going Too Far: The Personal Chronicle of a Feminist,* by Robin Morgan. Copyright 1968, 1970, 1973, 1975, 1977 by Robin Morgan. Reprinted by permission of Random House, Inc.

# Mythic Heras as Models of Strength and Wisdom

*Perhaps the most dynamic aspect of the feminist movement has been the discovery — and the creation — of possibilities, both personal and collective. Jerome Bruner, a developmental psychologist, has observed that possibilities themselves comprise the content of myth, which is "a corpus of images and identities and models that provide the pattern to which growth may aspire — a range of metaphoric identities"; myth is "the tutor, the shaper of identities." Patriarchal culture holds that a strong, courageous, independent woman is an aberration, an unfortunate freak of nature. We know this to be a lie because we have discovered widespread traditions of mythic and historic women of power, our potential shapers of identity.*

*Their very power is the reason that heras were twisted into villainous or treacherous characters in patriarchal, revisionist legends. The Sirens enticed men to their death; Medusa turned them to stone. And, of course, the Witches in fairy tales were always portrayed as "wicked" since they constituted the resistance movement against the patriarchy. In those tales, the powerful, hence monstrous, females are outnumbered by far by the docile, helpless ones who have relinquished all* power, the "good girls," who spend the first part of their lives waiting to be rescued and the rest being grateful. After the patriarchy invented such tales (and repressed and co-opted the prepatriarchal ones), they proudly pointed to them — and still do — as "authentic revelations of the feminine psyche."*

Having peeled back the lies, however, we are no longer entertained by such stories. A few years ago, a renowned male mythologist was about to retire from a women's college where he had taught for decades. At the end of a lecture on the Arthurian quest legends about the Holy Grail, one of his students asked why there were no roles in the legends with which women could identify. The professor was puzzled and pointed out that women are present as the hero's mother, the hero's queen, and the damsel-in-distress. "What more do you want?" he asked. "I want to be the hero, of course!" the student replied. The professor was quite taken aback and muttered that he was "glad to be retiring." But there is nowhere to hide.

Recognizing myth as "the pattern to which growth may aspire," we value its power as a spiritual force. It offers multi-faceted answers to "What is our true nature?" "What is possible?" Those answers are not static; their richness increases as our own wisdom grows. Our history of power is a grounding for our present and future evolution.

C.S.

* See "Problems with Jungian Uses of Greek Goddess Mythology," *Anima*, Fall 1979.

# Ancient Mirrors of Womanhood

## Merlin Stone

Nothing would be more interesting in connection with *The Woman's Bible* than a comparative study of the accounts of creation held by people of different races and faiths.

— CLARA COLBY, commenting on Genesis,
*The Woman's Bible,* 1895

There has been an ever growing consciousness of the advantages of being able to personally identify with positive images and role models, in developing the self-esteem that encourages the fulfillment of individual potential. This consciousness has made us increasingly aware of the general lack of strong and positive images of women, in the literature and traditions, both sacred and secular, of our own society. In reaction to these realizations, some of us have been searching in the obscure records of the last few centuries, reclaiming the histories of important women who have been all but ignored. Others have been developing fantasies of the future, inventing new images of woman, in the hope that they will be there for the women of today and tomorrow. These efforts and contributions are of immense value to the building of a body of positive female role models, but is this truly all that is available to us, as we search for role models and inspiring images of womanhood?

The hopeful request quoted above, made by Clara Colby, editor of the nineteenth-century *Woman's Tribune,* was written as women were initially confronting and challenging the gender biases and roles of women in the Hebrew Scripture (the Old Testament) and the New Testament — and the negative effects that various aspects of these religious scriptures have had upon women. With just a slight knowledge of Mexican, Scandinavian, and Algonquin beliefs, Clara Colby observed that images of womanhood seemed to be somewhat different in the religious lore of non-Judeo-Christian cultures, and, thus, suggested that a further exploration of this lore might produce some valuable insight and information.

Yet many women of today suspect, or even firmly believe, that a study of the religious accounts "of different races and faiths" would probably result only in finding that womanhood has always been perceived and portrayed as secondary to manhood. Statements, some even by well-educated feminists, often convey the idea that if actual accounts from societies that regarded woman as powerful, as supreme creator, or as important culture heroine, ever did exist, such information is now buried in the dust of prehistory — a Goddess name here or there all that is left to ponder.

The gradual formation of these attitudes has been accomplished in various ways. One has been to confine grade school and high school studies primarily to what has existed in relatively recent, generally Caucasian, male-oriented societies. Another has been through reassurances by university teachers, and texts, that if some cultures had viewed woman as supreme deity, or had had a female clergy that had deeply influenced moral and social structure, indication of this occurs only in the scantiest (and, therefore, inconclusive) of references. A more subtle factor at work has been the rejection of all things "religious" or "spiritual," by many who might agree with the need for finding positive images of woman but would prefer not to discover them in other than secular sources — thus ignoring the power and influence that contemporary male-oriented religions have upon even the most atheistic or agnostic of women today. Though stemming from an almost antithetical set of values, the above attitude manifests itself in a manner that is almost identical to that of the orthodox or devout Catholic, Jew, Protestant, or Muslim, who chooses to ignore any information that might bring long-held religious beliefs into question. An even further buttressing of these attitudes has been provided by the few scholars who were aware of a wider body of knowledge on the subject of Goddess reverence, and/or female clergy, in a particular period or area, but continually referred to this material as "mythology" — thereby relegating it to a topic closer to fairy tale or fantasy than the religious beliefs of a particular society. These factors, along with several others, have combined to quite efficiently smother the fires of motivation to search. After all, it is pointless to look for something that one has been taught to believe does not exist, is sinful, or is not especially pertinent or meaningful to "real" life.

After about eight years of research on deified and heroic images of women, I began to write about what I had found and was soon working on an introduction to point out the similarities, differences, influences, and transitions within the context of historical data, and the effects of migrations and invasions, upon Goddess reverence. It was this "introduction" that eventually became a volume in itself, originally published in London as *The Paradise Papers: The Story of the Suppression of Women's Rites,* later published in the United States as *When God Was a Woman.* I had already collected a vast amount of material, evidence of Goddess worship and heroic accounts of legendary mortal women from nearly every area of the world. This was the material that *When God Was a Woman* had initially been based upon, but only a very small portion of it was included in the actual text (which rather organically developed into an historical analysis of the suppression of Goddess reverence in the Near and Middle East — the areas in which Judaism, Christianity, and Islam first emerged).

After *When God Was a Woman* was published, I returned to the problem of how to present all else that I had found — most of it discovered in fragmented and piecemeal bits of information. This problem of a mode of presentation was more challenging to me than all the years of research had been. How to best present each piece of evidence, each fact that pertained to a specific Goddess or heroine name — in a way that would share the overwhelming sense of a long hidden heritage — as well as the enormous number of specific details? In writing the introduction that eventually became a book, I had drawn upon methods learned during many years of writing college ·term papers and theses, replete with quotations and references. But how to structure such a mass of fragmented, diverse, and, generally, unfamiliar bits of documentation, gleaned from such an enormous number of disparate sources? There were prayers and parts of prayers, rituals and parts of rituals, legends and parts of legends, titles, epithets, symbols, and inscriptions that had each been gleaned from translations of *cuneiform* tablets, translations of papyri and carved inscriptions, ethnological and anthropological studies that included accounts of spiritual beliefs, and translations of the early literature of Mexico, Scandinavia, China, Ireland, Iran, Wales, Japan, India, Greece, and Rome. In addition to this written information, there were my personal observations of sacred artifacts that I had studied at the museums of the United States, Europe, and the Near and Middle East, as well as my personal observations of ancient temple sites. Each provided evidence of images of womanhood that ranged all the way from the creation of the entire universe and all life — to the winning of a horse race and giving birth to twins at the finish line.

Once familiar with all the accounts of Goddess reverence and legends of heroines from so many cultures, the reader soon becomes aware that no simple archetype, or duality of archetypal aspects (e.g., Good Mother vs. Terrible Mother, as in Erich Neumann's work), or simple stereotype, or duality of stereotypes (e.g., madonna vs. whore) could possibly encompass all the images and perceptions of woman as they have actually been known. It is in the rich diversity, the almost astonishing multitude of various traits and aspects — many often attributed to the same deity — that the consciousness of what images of woman have been, and what images of woman can be, emerges most clearly. I believe that it is this diversity, and the acknowledgment and celebration of it, that offers the firmest foundation for our growing strength as we move ahead in our consciousness of ourselves as women and of our potential as human beings on this planet. As the dishonest canvas rips and the dishonest carved marble cracks apart, we are each better able to declare ourselves as the unique, multi-faceted beings we are, leaving behind all false or simplistic portraits that were said to symbolize *all* womanhood.

Symbols such as the moon, the sun, the various stars and planets, volcanoes, caves, springs, rivers, lakes, ocean, lioness, serpent, heifer, mare, whale, heron, raven, vulture, dove, fig tree, laurel, corn, marigolds, meteorites, obsidian, Earth Mother, Sea Goddess, Queen of Heaven, the force of existence, the flow of existence, traits that appear to mesh, traits that appear to conflict — each is a part of the full and wondrous treasure. Images of the creator of the universe, the creator of life, the one who takes in death, the one in whom our twin spirits unite until we are reborn, provider of law and cosmic pattern, provider of herbs and healing, the one who is compassionate, the one who is wrathful, the essence of wisdom, the guiding holy spirit, Liberty, Victory, Justice, Destiny, Lady Luck, and Mother Nature — all have been known in the form of woman. As anthropomorphic huntress, judge, warrior, tribal ancestress, inventor of writing, protector of animals, prophetess, inventor of fire, guardian of the celestial chamber of grain, teacher of carpentry and masonry, scribe of the tree of life — and as the more transcendental, metaphysical female principle that brought existence into being and continues to cause all to occur — each concept attests to images of womanhood that refute generalized archetypes, stereotypes, and simplistic dualities.

There are accounts of mothers mating with their sons, such as in Bachue, Fire Woman, and Inanna; of daughters both helping and defying their fathers, such as in Mella and Golden Lotus; of rituals for the Goddess including lesbian relationships, such as in the Mysteries for the Greek Goddess Gynacea and the Roman Bona Dea; of the Goddess choosing a mortal male for a mate and living happily ever after, such as in Mbaba Mwana Waresa; of the women of an entire tribe leaving the males to set up a community of their own, such as in Lia; of the worship of both Mother and Daughter as the sacred pair, such as in Lato and Artemis, Demeter and Persephone, Mahuea and Hina; of reverence for the Mother, two daughters and a granddaughter, such as in the Sun Goddess of Arinna. However one attempts to construct a mold, it will not fit them all.

Along with the pride of regained heritage, in becoming familiar with these many accounts of images of womanhood, we may also gain some insight into the various efforts made to suppress and alter these images, even to erase the very memory of them, by various male-worshipping groups. In the earliest periods there are the Sumerian transitions, from the most ancient Creator Goddess Nammu to the less powerful Inanna, and the loss of power by the Goddess Ereshkigal through the trickery and violence of the male deity Nergal. Kuan Yin, whose image may be derived from the preBuddhist Creator Goddess Nu Kwa, is described as having once been a male boddhisatva, who decided to return to Earth as Kuan Yin. The Arabian Goddess Attar, associated with the Semitic Ishtar and the Egyptian Hathor, is described in later South Arabian inscriptions as a male deity. The effects of early Judaism are noticeable in the accounts of the Goddess of the Semites as Asherah and Ashtart; Ashtart (Ashtoreth) was used as a name of a demon in the Middle Ages, though the gender was also changed to male. Early Christians made the Goddess Bridget into a Catholic saint, but doused Her eternal flame at Kildare; later Christians burned the holy books of the Mayans, but appropriated the Tepeyac shrine of the Goddess Coatlicue and dedicated it to the Virgin Mary as the Lady of Guadalupe. Long after St. Patrick destroyed the sacred cairn of the Cailleach Bheur in County Covan, missionaries in Hawaii encouraged converts to defy the Goddess Pele by throwing stones into the crater that was sacred to Her.

Thus as we become familiar with images of womanhood that were once held as sacred, we also come to realize how various male worshipping groups degraded and/or erased their existence. For those who question just what effects these images might have had upon the status and perceptions of womanhood in the societies that had revered these images, we might in turn ask why the male-oriented religions were so anxious to hide or deny them by these various means — and why the once almost universal existence of female clergy, which accompanied Goddess reverence, is a precept that today draws ridicule and dissent from so many.

The knowledge of these images of womanhood, and old/new ways of perceiving ourselves as women of this world, is our inheritance, our legacy of pride and self-esteem. Whether atheist or minister, scholar or carpenter, avowed feminist or fence-sitter, nine or ninety, we can all grow stronger on the treasures of our worldwide heritage that have been kept from us for far too long.

# The Amazon Legacy

## Phyllis Chesler

### AMAZONS: THE UNIVERSAL MALE NIGHTMARE

Men have written about and believed in Amazons just as they have believed in the existence of an earthly Paradise: as something marvelous and incredible, as an unbelievable and yet remembered phenomenon. From century to century and on all continents, men have described Amazons and Amazon customs with enough fear, guilt, and confusion to render them "legendary." Amazons are a universal male nightmare, exorcised by ridicule or disbelief. Or by subtle transformation: Behind each of these fiercely heroic and man-like warriors, behind each of these original "Belle Dames Sans Merci," is the most wondrous Mother of them all, the most powerful of Goddess-saviors, more beautiful and more compassionate than any male divinity. Precisely in their moments of greatest fear or murderousness, men crave grace, demanding to be rescued from evil by women, by the biological "other."

Many ancient Greek and Roman (male) historians, geographers, statesmen, philosophers, and poets described Amazons in Africa, in the European Caucasus, and in Greece itself. French, Portuguese, and

Spanish explorers in the sixteenth and seventeenth centuries returned from North and South America, from Eastern Europe, Russia, and Africa with "astonishing" tales of female warriors, queens, and priestesses and with the insistent reports, given by natives, of a legendary Amazon state — often just beyond the next river or mountain or, more often, in a region that the guide-informant was afraid to explore.

We have no tangible written record of the deeds and thoughts of legendary Amazon societies. Either such records never existed or they were completely destroyed. Perhaps they have yet to be unearthed. What we know about Amazons comes to us only through men — and men who wrote, traveled, fought, and painted in fiercely patriarchal cultures. As such, it is remarkable that any "proof" of Amazons exists at all. What proof does exist must be viewed as a combination of phobic male denials and hasty, guilty admissions, as a somewhat distorted and suppressed record of both fact and feeling, and as an inevitably romantic confusion of matriarchal and Amazon themes — a justifiable confusion, perhaps. Thus, for example, the mythical or magical prowess attributed to Amazon archers (especially by the Greeks) may have been a way of minimizing military defeats that resulted from the initially superior Asiatic weaponry that Amazons and other "eastern" groups, such as the Hittites and Scythians, introduced into Greece. In attributing magical powers (of horse-handling, courage, height, and strength) to Amazons, the Greeks may have been rationalizing their defeat by *women* and, conversely, maximizing the importance of victories over "mere" women. Then, too, the ambivalence and guilt probably felt by early patriarchs in violating the Great Mother-Goddess and Her cultures could be resolved and exorcised by repeatedly slaying Her in Her most terrible aspect, all the while justifying such destruction by distinguishing between the Terrible Woman (Amazons) and the Good Woman (the real mothers and sisters) — a deceptive distinction since it was against the latter that sons and brothers were historically and psychologically waging a war in earnest.

Reports about Amazons from (male) Christian Europeans present still other problems. The ancients were closer — historically, geographically, and psychologically — to such matriarchal phenomena as female ownership and inheritance of land and crops, female "ownership" of children, and female control of reproduction and religion. Ancients would not so quickly take such phenomena as proof of a supernatural or Amazon culture. Such phenomena, however, would indeed be "astonishing" to Christian Europeans. For example: Celtic and Gothic ("barbarian") women leading and joining their men in battle and in all political decisions; Indian women of North and South America fighting and trading with Columbus and Pizarro; Eastern European, Mediterranean, Central Asian, and African women alone, without men, in their nomadic camps, or in mountain and island "villages," who could and did defend their homes against attack — such women would have appeared to constitute an all-female state, to be in effect, Amazons. In such a scheme of things, men must have seemed to the Europeans as oppressed and debased as women in fact were in Judeo-Christian Europe. In much the same way, from the fifteenth to the nineteenth centuries, European male explorers "saw" Amazons in many a peaceful Indian village in the Americas.

And yet many South American and African informants, who were presumably out of touch with Greek mythology and history, insisted on the existence of "legendary" or classical Amazons in their own countries. Central European explorers in the seventeenth century heard reports of Amazons in the Black Sea and Caucasus regions and offered all sorts of "proof" that they really existed: armor, weapons, clothing, grave-sites, temple celebrations, the observed prowess of women warriors, queens, priestesses, politicians, and a multitude of Amazon-like customs. Such proofs are highly controversial and can be explained in many ways, but the geographical universality and historical longevity of the belief in legendary Amazonism is almost more important proof of their ancient existence than are various artifacts. Strong beliefs — legends that won't die — are always some sort of race-memory. The lasting belief in Amazons embodies a universal history of male-female conflict, and the Amazon myths presuppose the existence of the Great Mother cultures as well as the revolt of both daughters (Amazons) and sons (patriarchs).

## AMAZONS: A PSYCHO-HISTORICAL PERSPECTIVE

Isocrates and Aristeides praise the Greek victory over the Amazons as more important than that over the Persians or any other deed in history; the wars between the Greeks and Persians were wars between two male-dominated societies. In the Amazon war, the issue was which of the two forms of life was to shape European civilization in its image. . . . Persians and other enemies had merely been driven from the country, but the Amazons had been driven from human nature.

— HELEN DINER

Amazonism is a universal phenomenon. It is not based on the special physical or historical circumstances of any particular people but on conditions that are characteristic of all human existence. Amazonian phenomena are interwoven with the origins of all peoples. They may be found from Central Asia to the Occident, from the Scythian north to West Africa.

—J. J. Bachofen

At one time, legendary Amazons existed on every continent. They eventually died out — mysteriously, accidentally, inevitably — their customs either absorbed or banished by later societies. Perhaps Amazons (daughters) were defeated by patriarchs (sons) in wars of sibling rivalry. Perhaps just when daughters could afford to question a certain lack of passion, boldness, and freedom in matriarchal culture, sons found it possible to rebel against female rule — despite its "civilizing" features and in a way that would have been unthinkable to the most rebellious of daughters.

Some theorists view Amazonism as an extreme form of matriarchy (and, within their perspective, it is either "degraded" or advanced); to such thinkers, it is an excess of female power, which ultimately precipitates a male, or patriarchal, revolt. Other theorists see Amazonism as the female attempt to restore matriarchy or gynocracy just as men, seeking either to "progress" to another form of society or to "regress" to an earlier cultural stage, were in the process of abolishing female rule.* Still other theorists feel that Amazonism was necessary in order to force men — and women — to progress away from the early chaos of hetaerism to the later order of matriarchy. Certain theorists suggest that "outbursts" of legendary Amazonism occur in male-dominated cultures each time that *some* women perceive the cults of "femininity" — the worship

---

* The various myths and epic poems about the Amazon presence at the Battle of Troy are most important for what they reveal about the historic confrontation of matriarchy, Amazonism, and patriarchy. Presumably, Troy was a more matriarchal civilization than Athens, and, psycho-historically, the Amazons were defending matriarchy against patriarchal encroachments. In the *Oresteia*, Aeschylus gives a clear depiction of the forces at play in this contest. Agamemnon, leader of the Greek forces, sacrifices his daughter Iphigenia, as an offering to the gods for his troops. His wife, Clytemnestra — a matriarchal figure who is thus naturally closer to her daughter than to her husband — kills him. Her son, Orestes — a patriarchal hero — murders her to avenge the death of his father. To a matriarchal society, there is no more extreme crime than matricide; to a patriarchal society, patricide or husband-killing are the extreme crimes. Orestes' crime is pardoned, mainly through the intercession of Athena — a version of the Goddess unthinkable in a matriarchal society, a goddess who has no mother and protects only male heroes.

of the patriarchal version of Aphrodite or Dionysius — for what they really represent: a bogus "sexual revolution" that sacrifices women to allow men civilization — and access to "natural" infantile, disorderly, or bestial behaviors. The female revolt against such a sexual revolution and the male definitions of "civilization" that accompany it have often been derided as Amazonism or Puritanism. The patriarchal victories over such female revolts have just as often been called "male backlash" or patriarchal excesses.

According to some theorists, our earliest form of social organization was matriarchal in response to women's power to produce people and nourishment for them. Others propose that the first stage of human culture was "hetaeric": chaotic, disorganized, pre-agricultural, and sexually abusive to women — who probably were more exhausted (as a result of being continually pregnant) than "offended" by male or female sexual "promiscuity" or by male sexual violence. Matriarchal culture represented the female desire for a more securely ordered, fruitful, lawful, ethical, and spiritual way of life. "Great Mothers" invented a culture based on biological motherhood, agriculture, religion, and on *female* control of production and reproduction. And such female rule may have been kinder to both men and women than male rule has been to either of the sexes. Such female rule may indeed have accepted, developed, and valued both male and female biology as well as the special alliance with the inner and spiritual world that women seem to have — an alliance long shunned by our excessively male culture.

The mother-daughter relationship was at the heart of matriarchal culture. Men, as mates, were essentially peripheral to their wives' and daughters' family-grouping; as sons and brothers they were, in a spiritual sense, their mothers' and sisters' "servants."* If men were to gain more power, or to redefine civilization, they would have somehow to gain control of the family. To gain political and spiritual power, men would have to pit the *concept* of Fatherhood against the *fact* of Motherhood. And they would have to overthrow the Great Mother-Goddess — that bountiful giver of life, that terrible thief of life. The Great Mother-Goddesses (their mothers and sisters) were too powerful, too all-encompassing, too set in their ways. Men had to find a way to keep the Good Mother (nature) "good," while somehow destroying or minimizing the "bad" aspects: death, disease, and female control of the

---

* It must be kept in mind that "matriarchs" did not hate men — or even, in their culture's terms, "suppress" men.

means of production (agriculture) and reproduction. Through a violent and unnatural act of will, Fathers, not Mothers, would be the starting point of culture and knowledge. Had Amazonism triumphed, perhaps a similar "unnatural will" not solely based on reproductive maternity would have been at the basis of modern culture — but, of course, it did not.

The Amazon or daughter rebellion was more complicated and difficult. Amazons had both less and more cause to deny certain matriarchal principles: less cause if their own power base was being threatened by males; more cause if such a power base bequeathed them the luxury of wanting more, or of "seeing" new things.* For women to revolt against a female-dominated past would take enormous energy, supreme self-denial, and great visionary ardor. Amazons were interested in founding a culture that incorporated many matriarchal values and customs — but it was a culture that would not be based simply on biological and spiritual "givens." Unlike patriarchs, heroic Amazons had to deal with not one but two "enemies": their own ties to female biology, spirituality, and matriarchal culture, and the male revolt against any kind of female rule.

Amazonism, like patriarchy, must essentially have been a valiant, heroic, and dangerous rebellion against nature and tradition. Nature and biology were no longer experienced as inherently just, reasonable, inevitable, or sacred. Nature could be controlled and used for new ends. Perhaps even Amazons could not conceive of how self-destructively harsh, how dangerously narrow and unrelenting men would be toward both nature and spirituality after patriarchal "victory." Matriarchs, and even their passionately individualistic Amazon daughters, might not have foreseen their sons' and brothers' need to debase so totally all that was previously sacred (nature and women), in order to experience themselves as divine, in order to found a civilization based on their own sacredness.

## ETYMOLOGY

To ancient Greek mythographers and historians, as well as in later South American, Indian, and Eastern European accounts, "Amazon" usually meant belligerent or physically powerful women united in self-

---

* Regardless of the circumstances, for women to fight, or to *need* to fight, with men is already a major departure from the spirit of matriarchy.

governing politics and showing an aversion to any kind of permanent matrimonial tie, although this aversion varied in gradation from group to group. The word "Amazon," possibly Scythian in origin, could have many meanings and derivations. The Cherkassian *Emetchi* simply means "those who count by the mother," indicating matriarchal kinship and inheritance practices. In the Kalmuck language, a healthy, strong, heroic woman is called *Aemetzaine*. Europeans in the Caucasus region told an eighteenth-century traveler that their people had once been at war with the *Emmetsh* — a female tribe full of warlike spirit that welcomed any woman who cared to share its wanderings and join its heroic guild. Another eighteenth-century traveler was told about the *Emazuhn* in the mountains of Great Tartary; these women were accomplished hunters and warriors and kept their husbands in a subservient position. And, in the sixteenth and seventeenth centuries, South American informants referred to manlike women or women without husbands as "Amazons."

If the term "Amazon" was derived from *Amazosas,* it means "opposed to man." Homer called the Amazons *antianeirai* — "mannish" or "man-hating." (The difference is, of course, crucial.) If "Amazon" is derived from *Amastos* or *A-Mazo,* it means "those without a breast." Many writers describe the Amazon practice of burning off the right lacteal gland in childhood, presumably in order to become better archers or more strongly muscled in the right arm. Perhaps this rite can also be interpreted as a way of cutting off the "right" (or "male") side* and absorbing it androgynously. Amazon could also be related to *Azona,* which means "chastity belt"; in Amazon life, this was the symbol of an autonomous, unmarried state rather than of a virginal or sexually innocent condition. When Greek patriarchal adventurers (such as Hercules and Theseus) came to rob the Amazon Queen of her "belt," they were attempting to usurp her power, to plunder her geographical territory and independence, as well as her biological (child-bearing) "territory."

Whatever the derivation of the word, the point is that it was used in widely scattered geographical regions to signify a particular kind of culture or type of woman. Its usage may signify the existence of one original culture (or type of woman) or of many independently originated cultures. Or it may indicate the geographical migration either of such cultures or of the myths about them. Whatever the case, the wide use

---

* "Left" is traditionally the female side and, in our culture, usually has negative meanings. "Left" is mysterious, sinister, radical, wrong; right is "right."

and recognition the term has had suggests some kind of historical justification for the myth-makers.

## THE LEGENDARY AMAZONS

Classical or legendary Amazon societies were either all-female or female-dominated. In matriarchal fashion, the women controlled the means of production and reproduction and were also physically bold and politically autonomous. Commonly, such societies are depicted as having two queens — one for military affairs, the other for domestic.

Amazons were related to men and maternity in a variety of ways. Perhaps not every Amazon had to reproduce herself; perhaps only once was enough. Amazon societies engaged in annual rituals of "indiscriminate" sexual intercourse with certain male neighbors. They usually kept the female offspring and returned the male infants to their fathers. More radical Amazon societies killed all male infants, or crippled them in various ways and kept them as servants. Among the African Amazons, only the Gorgons maintained a pure, man-hating, Amazon state.* Other African Amazons maintained some men in their military camps. According to Helen Diner:

The Libyan Amazons, who removed their right breasts, had compulsory military service for all girls for a number of years, during which time they had to refrain from marriage. After that, they became a part of the reserves and were allowed to take a mate and reproduce their kind. The women monopolized government and other influential positions. In contrast to the later Thermondontines, however, they lived in a permanent relationship with their sex partners, even though the men led a retiring life, could not hold public office, and had no right to interfere in the government of the state or society.

According to the ancient Greeks and Romans, legendary Amazons arose in two main geographical regions and at two different times. The earliest group originated in northwestern Africa at the foot of the Atlas Mountains — areas then known as "Libya" and "Numidia," which now correspond to Morocco, Tunisia, and Algeria. The second major Amazon culture occurred somewhat later and arose in the Black Sea region

---

* Medusa was one of their queens: It is little wonder that she has come down to us through male eyes as a horrible monster, one who could turn men to stone and who was, of course, defeated by a patriarchal hero, Perseus.

— either on its European or Asiatic side. They were "Thermodon" Amazons.*

It was the Thermodon Amazons, led by Queen Penthesilea, whom certain Greek poets and artists often placed at the Battle of Troy, which may have occurred any time from 1270 B.C. to 1134 B.C.† Thus, these later Amazons may have flourished at the time of the female-dominated Minoan culture (c. 1600 B.C.), the Bronze Age in Greece, and the seventeenth and eighteenth dynasties in Egypt, which would place them after or partly co-existent with the Babylonian Dynasty in Mesopotamia.

The North African-based Amazons presumably arose independently during a much earlier period. They wore red leather armor and snakeskin shoes and carried python-skin shields. Legend has it they founded a city near Lake Triton, where they practiced animal husbandry but had no agriculture, living almost exclusively on meat and milk. A great part of Libya and Numidia was under their domination. Herodotus, writing as late as the fifth century B.C., described many Amazon-like customs in the Lake Triton area, such as girls, still wearing red leather clothes, engaging in military combat practice with each other. Much later, Strabo commented on the tradition in Africa of many generations of "belligerent women" who wore helmets and dressed in clothing made from animal skins. Strabo also described a supposed battle between the African Gorgon Amazons and another Amazon group, led by Queen Myrine. Myrine was victorious and, after the Gorgon war, conquered large areas in Egypt and Arabia: Syria, Phrygia, and all the lands along the Caicus River seacoast. She began building cities — often the same cities that the later Thermodon Amazons re-conquered or occupied. Islands such as Samos, Lesbos, Parthenos, and Samothrace may also have been conquered by Myrine.

The Thermodon (Caucasus-based) Amazons were the women Greeks meant when they wrote about, drew, and sculpted Amazons.

---

* Homer and Strabo place the Thermodon Amazons in countries that now correspond to Turkey, Yugoslavia, and Hungary — then called Scythia, Hercanium, Caspia, Thrace, etc. Hesiod places them on the Asiatic side of the Euxine (Black Sea). Diodorus Siculus places the African Amazons on the island of Hisperia, or "Tritonia," somewhere near the modern Canary Islands. One legend has it that Tritonia — like Atlantis — was submerged in the sea, and the Amazons with it.

† According to Philostrates, Hiera fought at Troy as a leader of the Mycian women's troops but Homer did not mention her in *The Iliad* because she would have "outshone his heroine, Helen."

Amazons depicted in classical Greek art are often shown in Asiatic (Oriental or Scythian) costumes: long, narrow, checkered trousers, or leggings; soft, high, and often fur-topped boots; Phrygian caps or mantles; and long belted tunics, often with stars on them. Amazon weapons included axes, usually the famous double-edged variety, an androgynous symbol of many female-dominated nations, sabres, bows and arrows, spears, and moon-shaped shields (sometimes decorated with animals such as panthers, lions, and dogs). These Amazons are also shown wearing greaves and Attic or Thracian helmets. Sometimes they are shown barefoot, or wearing supporting ankle-straps; sometimes they are wearing short chitons and are depicted as wounded.

Amazons were often depicted on horseback or driving chariots, and the horse was long considered as one of their "magical symbols."* And, in fact, Amazons were said to have invented cavalry and cavalry battle techniques. Hippocrates described the Scythian women of his time as excellent horsewomen who used bow and arrow even when riding at full speed.†

The Ionian tradition refers to the Thermodon Amazons as the founders of cities and sanctuaries: Smyrna, Sinope, Cyme, Gryne, Ephesus, Pitania, Magnesia, Clete, Pygela, Latoreia, and Amastris all boasted Amazons as godmothers and founders.

## THE GREEK AMAZON MYTHS

At the psychological heart of every major Greek Amazon myth are two important themes. First, there is the theme of women sacrificing and killing men: in battle, because they are "enemies"; in religious ceremonies, to appease or honor female divinities; in infancy, because they, like infant girls in patriarchal cultures, are less important or too burdensome to raise; or in the slower and less "violent" death of lifelong domesticity and political subservience. The other theme is that of

---

* Many Greek transliterations of Amazon (Scythian) names contained the Greek word *hippos,* meaning horse: Alcippa, Melanippa, Hippolyte, Dioxippa, Lysippe, Hippomache, and Hippothoe.

† Herodotus, Hippocrates, and Pliny the Elder similarly described Amazon or Amazon-like women in the Black Sea area variously called Scythia and Sauromatia. Herodotus, in his day, commented that "the women of this region still ride horseback with their husbands, still take the field in war, and dress like men." Similar Amazon customs are described in the same region in the sixteenth, seventeenth, and eighteenth centuries A.D.

the ultimate male triumph over such female acts: by slaughtering and defeating the Amazons in battle, or by converting them to male-worship of Dionysius or the patriarchal version of Aphrodite. Sometimes the Amazons "fall in love" with their male opponents, put down their arms, and desert their comrades to become wives and mothers. It is important to note, however, that Greek *men* do not "fall in love" with Amazons until *after* the women are wounded and dying. Achilles, for example, who fought with Queen Penthesilea at the Battle of Troy, was suddenly and romantically overcome by her valor and beauty — as she lay dying before him.

Like all myths, these themes shape, re-create, and explain both societal and individual history. Thus, for example, female children must still give up or minimize supposedly "male" activities, must "naturally" desert preadolescent or adolescent female comrades if they are to please boys, get married, and become mothers. And male children certainly never fall in love with or marry "Amazons" — at least, not until such women are safely disarmed.

The most famous Greek Amazon myths concern the territorial exploits of Bellerophon, Hercules, and Theseus against the Amazons, and the subsequent Amazon invasion of Athens, their retreat, and their later presence at the Battle of Troy. Another type of Greek Amazon myth concerns female revolt against fathers and husbands — as typified by the Danaïds and the women of Lemnos.

In the first instance, the ninth labor of Hercules was to steal the Amazon Queen Hippolyte's girdle — a "magic" belt given to her by her father Mars (Ares), the God of War. Hercules (or Hercules and Theseus, in some accounts) tricks or forces the relatively peaceful Amazons into battle. Hippolyte is vanquished, and Theseus abducts her sister Antiope, taking her with him to Athens. Some versions of the myth have Antiope falling in love with Theseus and later fighting by his side in Athens against the Amazons, who kill her. Oreithyia, the third sister and the Amazon military queen, has been away. Too late, she rushes back with her army, but the marauding Greeks have already left. She decides to march on Athens. The Amazons invade the city, besiege the Acropolis, and occupy the Areopagus. The fighting is intense, and both sides suffer heavy losses. Finally, a compromise is reached. The Amazons depart — some say broken-heartedly — without achieving the avenging destruction of Athens (or of patriarchy). During their march back to the Thermodon region, Oreithyia and/or Hippolyte die of grief and shame. The presence of Amazon troops at the Battle of Troy is attributed to the resulting long-lasting Amazon hatred of everything Greek.

The second instance of Greek Amazon myth—the revolt of the women of Lemnos—concerns the female desertion of classical Aphrodite-worship.* Aphrodite punishes the women by making them sexually unattractive to their men. The men promptly enslave some Thracian girls for sexual and domestic purposes—and are as promptly slain by the Lemnian women. The Lemnian revolt represents the militant reaction of outraged matriarchs whose men had begun to "adventure" abroad. Pillaging and raping, these men were violating the marriage bond and, in their treatment of wife and slave-girl alike, debasing the female sex.

Various Greek (male) poets have presented the Lemnian women as "regretful" and "lonely" afterward, as eager for new marriages—even with such patriarchs as Jason. It is Jason who has a love affair with the Lemnian Queen Hypsiplye. Of course, Jason leaves her, just as he leaves Medea, just as Odysseus leaves Penelope and Aeneus leaves Dido, Queen of Carthage, because in order to continue his heroic pilgrimage—in this case, the search for the Golden Fleece—he *must.* In patriarchy, men must always leave their mothers, their sisters, and, of course, their wives and mistresses, for adventures and "advancement" outside the family.

The myth of the Danaïds—the fifty daughters of Danaus—belong to a whole cycle of blood weddings in which the bridegrooms are killed. The Danaïds are forced, against their will, into marriage. Their revolt is a murderous and remorseless one. Of course, there is one non-murderer: Hypermnestra. Originally, this non-murdering Danaïd was the contemptible exception; in later versions, she became the only heroine. These later versions also condemn the other forty-nine Danaïds to Hades, where they must forever pour water into a jar with holes in it.

## THE HISTORICITY OF THE GREEK AMAZON MYTHS

Specific "proof" of Amazon exploits has understandably become a very controversial matter. Plutarch, in his *Life of Theseus*, apologizes for indulging in mythical history, but, in John Forsdyke's words, "when he [Plutarch] comes to the Amazonian attack on Athens, he

---

* Lemnos was, historically, a matriarchal culture from pre-Hellenic times.

writes as a serious historian." Plutarch notes that the enterprise was no "slight or womanish" endeavor:

The Athenians were routed and gave way before the women, as far as to the temple of the Furies, but, fresh supplies coming in from the Palladium, Ardettus, and the Lyceum, [the Athenians] charged their right wing and beat them back to their tents, in which action a great number of the Amazons were slain. At length, after four months, a peace was concluded between them by mediation. . . . That this war, however, was ended by a treaty is evident . . . from the ancient sacrifice which used to be celebrated to the Amazons the day before the Feast of Theseus. The Megarians also show a spot in their city where some Amazons were buried. . . . It appears further that the passage of the Amazons through Thessaly was not without opposition, for there are yet shown many tombs of them near Scotussa and Cynoscephalae.

Herodotus did not doubt the reality of Amazons, but thought they were extinct, having crossed the Black Sea from the Thermodon to the Tanaïs (Don) and become the progenitors of the Sarmatians. The Sarmatians of his day were a Scythian people living east of the Crimea. Their women were still Amazon-like, "frequently hunting on horseback with their husbands, sometimes even unaccompanied; in war taking the field and wearing the same dress as the men."* Some stories of Ionian cities sacked or founded by the Amazons may have come from such experiences. The dress and weapons that the Greeks assigned to Amazons were the same as those of the Scythians in Xerxes' army, whom Herodotus described as "wearing trousers and having on their heads tall stiff caps rising to a point."

Pausanias believed in the existence of the legendary Amazons. He stated that the Megarians of his day (the second century A.D.) still believed that the tomb of Queen Oreithyia and/or Hippolyte was located in Megara; and he had no reason to doubt their belief. Pausanias also tells us that, according to Pindar, the temple of Artemis at Ephesus was founded by those Amazons involved in the siege at Athens. The Roman historian Tacitus also connected the origins of the Temple of Ephesus with Amazons. But, in Pausanias' own opinion, the temple was much older, and its Amazon associations were derived from Amazons who simply took refuge there.

---

* Herodotus also claimed that some Amazons plundered the temple of Aphrodite (Astarte) at Ascalon and were consequently afflicted by that goddess with a "sexual aberration," from which their descendants in Scythia still "suffered" (lesbianism and homosexuality).

Strabo also accepted the reality of Amazons, relating that in the Ilian plain there was a hill dedicated to the Amazon Queen Myrine, supposedly for her feats of horsewomanship. Earlier, Homer had placed the grave of an Amazon Queen named Myrine in Troad.

Greek writers probably suppressed certain proofs of Amazon existence. Some denied it entirely. Still others "explained" these proofs as some other kind of phenomena: for example, as nothing more than the Persian and Eastern invasions of the Greek world, which, although undertaken primarily by men, sometimes included women.

Certainly, the sight of women who were physically fit and militarily capable was not startling to ancient Greek and Roman writers. The playwright Euripides, for example, describes the daughters of Sparta as "shameful"; "they are never home, they mingle with the young men in wrestling matches, their clothes cast off, their hips all naked." And Herodotus describes an African-based culture that honors its goddess by staging battles between women. "The girls are divided in two groups and fight with one another. . . . Maidens who die of their wounds are considered impure. The girls who conduct themselves with the greatest bravery are decorated with a Corinthian helmet, put on a chariot, and led all the way around the lake." Virgil, in *The Aeneid*, describes Thracian, Tyrian, and Spartan girls as swift runners and excellent horsewomen who dress as huntresses, wearing animal skins or simple tunics and carrying bows and arrows.

Such women would not be mistaken by the ancients as Amazons. But sixteenth- and seventeenth-century missionaries and explorers would be less well equipped to make the distinction. Still, Father Cristobal D'Acuña, a sixteenth-century missionary, described a group of Brazilian Indians as Amazons:

Women of great valor who had always preserved themselves without the ordinary intercourse with men; and even when men, by agreement, come every year to their land, they receive them with arms in their hands such as bows and arrows, which they brandish about for a time, until they are satisfied that the Indians come with peaceful intentions . . . the Indians return to their own country, repeating their visits every year at the same season.

Few, however, could offer eye-witness accounts. Sir Walter Raleigh, for example, was *told* "about an all-female state in the province of Topago"; in legendary fashion, the women supposedly engaged in "promiscuous" ritual intercourse for procreative purposes, returning the sons to their fathers and keeping only the daughters. Between the sixteenth and eighteenth centuries, some Spanish and English explorers actually set out to find legendary Amazons in South America, but again, their evidence was hearsay. Hernando de Ribera, in Peru, Anthony Knivet and Charles Marie de La Condamine, in Brazil, and Father Gili, in Guiana, were all *told* about warrior women who lived alone, were excellent arrow-makers and archers, mated only ritually, and had knowledge of "magical" herbs. Some cut off their right breasts, and some possessed great mineral wealth.

Two sixteenth-century missionaries working independently of each other in Abyssinia — Fathers Alvarez and Bermudez — heard about a group of women in the province of Damute who were "much addicted to war and hunting and much more daring than the men of their country." The women were described as searing off their right breasts, rarely marrying, and sending male children back to their fathers. Their queen, worshipped as Goddess, remained a virgin.

Withal, not all reports were second-hand. A temporary Amazon state may once have existed in Africa in the region of the Congo. A priest, one Father Cavazzi, told of a period in African Jaga history during which young girls were trained militarily and were prohibited from making permanent marriages, while their queen killed each of her lovers after a brief dalliance, eventually ordering the sacrifice of infant males. And according to various sixteenth-century Portuguese observers, a group of female warriors existed in the Congo region and they were very adept militarily; their king assigned certain districts to them in which they reared female children exclusively.

Although matriarchal and female-dominated states existed throughout India, the only unmistakable account of Indian Amazons is contained in the poem *The Mahabharata*, probably rewritten many times by Brahmin patriarchs. The poem depicts the encounter of its male hero, Arjuna, with a militarily and economically powerful all-female state. The young girls are described as dazzlingly lovely "warrior-maidens"; the older women received and entertained men but killed them if they remained for longer than a month. They did not rear male infants.

A number of writers have described a temporary but legendary-style Amazon state in European Bohemia (a Thermodon Amazon region) during the reigns of Queens Libussa and Dlasta (or Valesca). Libussa, born in approximately 680 A.D., instituted a political-religious "council of virgins," raising many women to high public office. Upon Libussa's death in 738 A.D. Dlasta, her chief confidante, headed a temporarily successful "woman's revolt." Dlasta ordered that only women be militarily trained, and she attempted to render male infants and adolescents unfit for warfare by blinding them in one eye. Dlasta is said to have reigned for seven years, after which time the Bohemian nation resumed "its normal course." For years, ruins of Mount Vidovole, known as *Divin-Hrad* (the Virgin's City), were pointed out as Dlasta's headquarters.

## MATRIARCHAL AND GYNOCRATIC SOCIETIES

To understand the meaning of Amazonism, it is essential to view its relationship to other kinds of female-dominated societies. There is no question that matriarchies and gynocracies existed — in early history as well as in more complicated and powerful forms in later history — or that matriarchal "themes" and customs have been present in both male- and female-dominated societies and on all continents.* Various matriarchal and gynocratic societies were to be found at one time in Lycia, Athens, Crete, Lemnos, Locris, Elis, Mantinea, Lesbos, Catabria, Egypt, Tibet, Central Asia, and India. Despite enormous variations, an essential spirit of matriarchy was everywhere widely retained: a superior female alliance with both the material-natural universe and the supersensory or spiritual universe. Within this context, both women and men could be sexually chaste or sexually "insatiable" at certain times of their lives, at certain times in the year, or during their entire lives. Within this context, women and men could be warriors, agriculturalists, and hunters — or not; child-rearers — or not; military and political decision-makers — or not. Divinities and their worldly representatives in the religious and political realm, however, were essentially female. Male priests served priestesses and female deities; royal kings received their power only through their mothers and sisters, whom they sometimes married, as in Egypt. Some matriarchies — in India, Africa, and South America — had only queens, never kings.

In matriarchal or somewhat matriarchal societies, it was not uncommon for women and men to live separately for long periods of time, or

---

* Even in patriarchal Greece and Rome, women retained many matriarchal practices. For example, they worshipped female divinities and served as oracles, seers, and priestesses. Matriarchy in Egypt may have applied mainly to its royal caste rather than to the general population. And Egyptian dynastic (royal) history presents a long record of the decline of matriarchy and the rise of patriarchy.

for men to visit their wives' homes as "guests," usually for specific sexual or family purposes. What, in our terms, would be seen as role reversals were, in matriarchal societies, not exceptional.* Women were priestesses and goddesses, warriors and military leaders, hunters and politicians in various matriarchal cultures. Men were sometimes — but perhaps more rarely than we would like to suppose — the cooks, child-rearers, and "sex-objects." In matriarchal societies, sons and brothers respected and worshipped their mothers and sisters — who, in turn, did not "hate" men. Brothers had sacred responsibilities to sisters; sons were "protected" by their mothers in many ways. Only the husband-wife relationship was relatively less important. Eventually, men were valued by women for their procreative, hunting, and warrior functions, none of which they were forced to do without female participation. In matriarchies, women did not despise the conception and rearing of children, making of pottery, chores of agriculture, food-gathering, and cooking. These activities sustained the family and the group. More than hunting and warfare, these activities were what the group was about.

Such matriarchal themes were retained in many later and more patriarchal cultures. Certain customs common to some matriarchal and all Amazon cultures were also continued — specifically, the custom of having a queen and the custom of women warriors.

---

* Herodotus, for example, writing in the fifth century B.C., reports that in Egypt of his day, "the women attend to the mercantile business, conducting trade and providing for the family, while the men sit at home at the loom." He also adds, "In Egypt, sons need not support their parents but daughters must." And Strabo noted: "In North Africa, the women were not in the army any more but they ruled the country politically, while the men were still without significance in the state, occupying themselves largely with body care and hair-do [and] greedy for golden jewelry."

# Tales of a Reincarnated Amazon Princess: The Invincible Wonder Woman!

## Gloria Steinem

Comic books were not quite respectable, which was a large part of the reason I read them: under the covers with a flashlight, in the car while my parents told me I was ruining my eyes, in a tree or some other inaccessible spot; any place that provided sweet privacy and independence. Along with cereal boxes and ketchup labels, they were the primers that taught me how to read. They were even cheap enough to be the first items I could buy on my own; a customer whose head didn't quite reach the counter but whose dignity was greatly enhanced by making a selection (usually after much agonizing) and offering up money of her own.

If, as I have always suspected, children are simply short people — ancient spirits who happen to be locked up in bodies that aren't big enough or skillful enough to cope with the world — then the superhuman feats in comic books and fairy tales become logical and necessary. It's satisfying for anyone to have heroes who can see through walls or leap over skyscrapers in a single bound, but it's especially satisfying if our worldview consists mostly of knees and tying our shoes is still an exercise in frustration.

The trouble is that the comic book performers of such superhuman feats — and even of only dimly competent ones — are almost always heroes. Literally. The female child is left to believe that, even when her body is as grown-up as her spirit, she will still be in the childlike role of helping with minor tasks, appreciating men's accomplishments, and being so incompetent and passive that she can only hope some man will come to her rescue. Of course, rescue and protection are comforting, even exhilarating experiences that should be and often are shared by men and boys. Even in comic books, the hero is frequently called on to protect his own kind in addition to helpless women. But dependency and zero accomplishments get very dull as a steady diet. The only option for a girl reader is to identify with the male characters — pretty difficult, even in the androgynous years of childhood. If she can't do that, she faces limited prospects: an "ideal" life of sitting around like a technicolor clothes horse, getting into jams with villains, and saying things like "Oh, Superman! I'll always be grateful to you," even as her hero goes off to bigger and better adventures. It hardly seems worth learning to tie our shoes.

I'm happy to say that I was rescued from this plight at about the age of seven or eight, rescued (great Hera!) by a woman. Not only was she as wise as Athena and as lovely as Aphrodite, she had the speed of Mercury and the strength of Hercules. Of course, being an Amazon, she had a head start on such accomplishments, but she had earned them in a human way by training in Greek-style contests of dexterity and speed with her Amazon sisters. (Somehow it always seemed boring to me that Superman was a creature from another planet, and, therefore, had bullet-proof skin, x-ray vision, and the power to fly. Where was the contest?) This beautiful Amazon did have some fantastic gadgets to help her: an invisible plane that carried her through dimensions of time and space, a golden magic lasso, and bullet-proof bracelets. But she still had to get to the plane, throw the lasso with accuracy, and be agile enough to catch bullets on the steel-enclosed wrists.

Her creator had also seen straight into my heart and understood the secret fears of violence hidden there. No longer did I have to pretend to like the "pow!" and "crunch!" style of Captain Marvel or the Green

Hornet. No longer did I have nightmares after reading ghoulish comics filled with torture and mayhem, comics made all the more horrifying by their real-life setting in World War II. (It was a time when leather-clad Nazis were marching in the newsreels *and* in the comics, and the blood on the pages seemed frighteningly real.) Here was a heroic person who might conquer with force, but only a force that was tempered by love and justice. She converted her enemies more often than not. And if they were destroyed, they did it to themselves, usually in some un-bloody accident.

She was beautiful, brave, and explicitly out to change "a world torn by the hatreds and wars of men."

She was Wonder Woman.

Looking back now at these Wonder Woman stories from the Forties, I am amazed by the strength of their feminist message. One typical story centers on Prudence, a young pioneer in the days of the American frontier. (Wonder Woman is transported there by her invisible plane, of course, which also served as a time machine.) Rescued by Wonder Woman, Prudence realizes her own worth and the worth of all women: "I've learned my lesson," she says proudly in the final scene. "From now on, I'll rely on myself, not on a man." In yet another epi-sode, Wonder Woman herself says, "I can never love a dominant man who is stronger than I am." And throughout the strips, it is only the de-structive, criminal woman — the woman who has bought the whole idea that male means aggression and female means submitting — who says, "Girls want superior men to boss them around."

Many of the plots revolve around evil men who treat women as infe-rior beings. In the end, all are brought to their knees and made to rec-ognize women's strength and value. Some of the stories focus on weak women who are destructive and confused. These misled females are converted to self-reliance and self-respect through the example of Won-der Woman. The message of the strips is sometimes inconsistent and al-ways oversimplified (these are, after all, comics), but it is still a passable version of the truisms that women are rediscovering today: that women are full human beings; that we cannot love others until we love our-selves; that love and respect can only exist between equals.

Wonder Woman's family of Amazons on Paradise Island, her band of college girls in America, and her efforts to save individual women are all welcome examples of women working together and caring about each other's welfare. The idea of such cooperation may not seem partic-

ularly revolutionary to the male reader: Men are routinely depicted as
working well together. But women know how rare and, therefore, exhilarating the idea of sisterhood really is.

Wonder Woman's mother, Queen Hippolyte, offers yet another welcome example to young girls in search of a strong identity. Queen
Hippolyte founds nations, wages war to protect Paradise Island, and
sends her daughter off to fight the forces of evil in the world. Perhaps
most impressive in an age fraught with Freudian shibboleths, she also
marshals her queenly strength to protect her daughter in bad times.
How many girl children grew to adulthood with no experience of a
courageous and worldly mother, except in these slender stories? How
many adult women disdain the birth of a female child, believe it is
"better" to bear male children, and fear the competition and jealousy
they have been conditioned to believe is "natural" to a mother and
daughter? Feminism is just beginning to uncover the sense of anger
and loss in girls whose mothers had no power to protect them in the
world, and so trained them to be victims, or left them to identify with
their fathers if they had any ambitions outside the traditional female
role.

Wonder Woman symbolizes many of the values of the women's culture that feminists are now trying to introduce into the mainstream:
strength and self-reliance for women, sisterhood and mutual support
among women, peacefulness and esteem for human life, a diminish-
ment both of "masculine" aggression and of the belief that violence is
the only way of solving conflicts.

Of course, the Wonder Woman stories are not admirable in all ways.
Many feminist principles are distorted or ignored. Thus, women are
converted and saved. Mad scientists, foreign spies, criminals, and other
male villains are regularly brought to the point of renouncing violence
and, more often, of saying, "You're right, Wonder Woman. I'll never
make the mistake of thinking women are inferior again." Is the reader
supposed to conclude women are superior? The Wonder Woman stories not only depict women as culturally different (in ways that are
sometimes constructive and sometimes not), they also hint that women
are biologically, and, therefore, immutably, superior to men.

Few modern feminists would agree. There are as yet no perfectly cul-
ture-free tests to prove to us which traits come from conditioning and
which do not, but the consensus seems to be that society, not biology,
assigns some human traits to males and others to females. Women have

suffered from being taught to develop what society considers the less-valued traits of humanity, but this doesn't mean we want to switch to a sole claim on the "more valuable" ones either. That might accomplish nothing more than changing places with men in the hierarchy. Most feminist philosophy supposes that the hierarchy itself must be eliminated, that individuals who are free of roles assigned because of sex or race will also be free to develop the full range of human qualities. It's the multitudinous differences in individuals that count, not the localized differences of sex or race.

For psychologist William Moulton Marston — who, under the pen name of "Charles Moulton," created Wonder Woman — females were sometimes romanticized as biologically and unchangeably superior. "Women," he wrote, "represent love; men represent force. Man's use of force without love brings evil and unhappiness. Wonder Woman proves that women are superior to men because they have love in addition to force." If that's the case, then we're stuck with yet another social order based on birth.

For the purposes of most Wonder Woman stories, however, the classic argument of nature versus nurture is a mere intellectual quibble. Just helping women to respect themselves, to use their strength and refuse domination by men is time-consuming enough: Wonder Woman rarely has the leisure to hint at what the future social order ought to be. As for men, we do get the idea that they have some hope — even if vague — of collective redemption. "This man's world of yours," explains Wonder Woman, "will never be without pain and suffering until it learns respect for human rights." Put in more positive terms, this does seem to indicate that humanized men will have full membership in the new society.

Some of the Wonder Woman stories preach patriotism in a false way, but much of the blame rests with history. Wonder Woman was born in 1941, just about the time that World War II became a reality for most Americans, and she, therefore, had to spend much of her time protecting this country from foreign threats. Usually, that task boiled down to proving that women could be just as brave and loyal as men in the service of their country. Even when her adventures took place in other countries or at other times, they still invariably ended with simplistic commercials about democracy. Although Wonder Woman was shocked by America's unjust patriarchal system — a shock she recorded on her arrival here from Paradise Island — she never had much opportunity to follow up on it; a nation mobilized for war is not a nation prepared to accept criticism. In fact, her costume was patterned after the American flag, and her wartime adventures sometimes had highly jingoistic and even racist overtones, especially when she was dealing with Japanese and Germans.

Compared to the other comic book characters of the period, however, Wonder Woman is still a relief. Marston invented her as a counter to the violence and "bloodcurdling masculinity" that pervaded most comic books, and he remained true to his purpose. Wonder Woman and her sisters were allowed to use violence, but only in self-defense and only if it stopped short of actually killing someone. Most group conflicts between men and women were set not in America, but in a mythological past. Thus Mars, the God of War, periodically endangered the Amazon community and sometimes tried to disarm Queen Hippolyte through the ruses of love. Mars, of course, was the "heavy." He preached that women "are the natural spoils of war" and must remain at home, the helpless slaves of the male victors. Marston used Mars as the symbol of everything Wonder Woman must fight against, but he also gave the God of War a rationale for his beliefs that was really the female superiority argument all over again: If women were allowed to become warriors like the Amazons, they would grow stronger than men and put an end to war. What future for an unemployed god?

The inconsistencies in Wonder Woman's philosophy are especially apparent in her love life. It is confused, to say the least. Sometimes her adventures with Steve, the pilot she is supposedly "in love" with, bear a feminist message. And sometimes they simper and go conventional in a way that contradicts everything that has gone before. In her American disguise as mild-mannered Diana Prince (a clear steal from Superman), she plays the classic feminine role: secretary, nurse, and worshipful, unrequited sidekick to Steve. The implicit moral is that, at least as Wonder Woman, she can love only an equal. But an equal never turns up, and sometimes she loses her grip on herself and falls for the masculine notion that there must be a permanent winner and a permanent loser, a conqueror and a conquered. "Some girls love to have a man stronger than they are to make them do things," she muses aloud. "Do I like it? I don't know, it's sort of thrilling. But isn't it more fun to make a man obey?"

I remember being worried by these contradictions. How could Wonder Woman be interested in Steve, who seemed so weak and so boring? Did women really have to live in a community by themselves — a separate country like Paradise Island — in order to be both happy and courageous? The very fact that the ideal was an island — insular, isolated, self-contained, cut-off — both pleased and bothered me. And why, when she chose an earthly disguise, did Wonder Woman have to pick such a loser? How could she bear to be like Diana Prince? Did that mean that all women really had to disguise their true selves in weak feminine stereotypes in order to survive?

But all these doubts paled beside the relief, the sweet vengeance, the toe-wriggling pleasure of reading about a woman who was strong, beautiful, courageous, and a fighter for social justice. A woman who strode forth, stopping wars and killing with one hand, distributing largesse and compassionate aid with the other. A Wonder Woman.

Wonder Woman may be just one small, isolated outcropping of a larger human memory. And perhaps the girl children who love her are responding to one small echo of dreams and capabilities in their own forgotten past.

# Growing Up with Legends of the Chinese Swordswomen

## Siew Hwa Beh

The universe is made of stories, not of atoms.
— MURIEL RUKEYSER

I grew up colonized, living out projected images invented by others for their self-serving mythologies. I have found that the process of knowing myself and creating a personal mythology is also a process of rediscovering a forgotten one.

A decade of outward seeking closed one sunny day in 1976 in San Francisco when I retraced my steps into an airline office. I felt a sudden urge to head home to Malaysia. Later, I realized that my mother had been twenty-nine when I was born, my exact age on that day I turned homeward. A circle was complete. With her, came flashes of many beginnings. The movies of the mind came to rest on mother's "talking stories" throughout our childhood. After the day's work, she rested on her square porcelain headrest flipping through Chinese comic books while we kids bustled behind her for the best visual position. She thumbed through the 4″ x 5″ series explaining and embellishing the exploits of the monkey god and the adventures of the swordswomen, a Chinese literary tradition since the ninth century. I was the customary look-out for the comic book peddler, who passed by every few days clinging his bell on a tricycle heaped full of comic books grouped in serials by rubber bands. I usually chose the evening's entertainment, selecting books with dynamic illustrations about the swordswomen — who were *girls* having exciting adventures! I felt my mother told these stories particularly well, emphasizing the bravery and prowess of these women warriors.

These heras were usually virtuous, brave, beautiful, and skilled in the martial arts. Their life-long mission was that of avengers whose face-saving journeys righted wrongs done to their families, villages, and communities. They were trained early and arduously in acrobatics and fighting tactics. Their destiny was to be ready for the day of reckoning when they would be called to champion the poor and oppressed against bandits, warlords, and evil swordfighters. Their moral fiber was constantly tested by temptations and incredible obstacles on their way to rescuing a maiden from rape or a misjudged man from death. Unlike the bionic woman, who is only a casing for the real hero, six million dollars' worth of technological devices, the swordswomen were painstakingly trained in physical, intellectual, and spiritual skills. When the swordswomen exhibited supernatural feats, their magical powers revealed a high level of spiritual evolution.

The swordswomen were often shrouded in mystical and mysterious aspects. Their mentors were usually older swordswomen or wise old men. Their training was secret. Their names were Red Peony, The Blade That Spares None, The Black Butterfly, The Invisible Sabre, The Lady with a Sword. Their multiple transformations further disguised their identities. During the day they were housewives, daughters, sisters, nuns, fiancées, waitresses, or workers in the fields. Humble facades were essential protection for their single-minded missions by night, when they transformed themselves into strong, beautiful warriors clad usually in red, black, purple, or sky-blue hues.

Although sophisticated in battle tactics and worldly ways, these swordswomen retained a chaste and innocent stance toward sexuality. Their disposition was one of dignity, reticence, and reservation toward potential mates. But as women of mystery and champions of the martial arts, the swordswomen were perceived as sexual challenges. As powerful, unattainable opposites, they were a constant source of frustration, fascination, and hypnotism. Such reactions from the men were used, in turn, by these women warriors at crucial moments when annihilation seemed imminent. The men's downfalls were usually caused by a boomerang of their own uncontrolled aggression when faced with sexual rejection.

A favorite tale my mother often told with relish was the story of Fa Mu Lan, the great army general who fought victorious battles dressed as a man. She painted her face half white and half black, symbolizing the balance of yin and yang, and led her army brilliantly. She was discovered to be a woman by a fellow general who fell in love with her. During a certain campaign, she gave birth in the battlefield and resumed fighting while nurturing her child. This was the legend that Maxine Hong Kingston skillfully retold as part of her personal fantasy in *The Woman Warrior*.[1] In the chapter titled "White Tigers," Hong Kingston created a personal mythology through a collage of variations on the theme of the swordswomen, ending with the story of Fa Mu Lan. Through her imaginative mediation, the reader shares the woman warrior's psyche, her predicaments, and her solutions. By culling aspects of the different stories, Hong reshaped the myth as ritualistic grounding for inner strength.

Another popular tale was about Madam White Snake. She was a brilliant swordswoman who had the magical power of turning into a snake. She had caused the death of her husband by shocking him during one of her snake transformations. In order to bring him back to life, she had to take on the whole heavenly army in her quest for the magic mushroom. Her solo battles were legendary and were often performed by a top star in the Beijing Opera.

Other swordswomen stories have been recalled by Lily Tom in "Swashbuckling Swordswomen of the Silver Screen."[2] She told of Black Butterfly, whose calling card was a black butterfly pin. She was a waitress in her father's inn by day, but was also the nocturnal masked bandit who robbed the rich to feed the poor. Then there was The Lady Hermit, a reclusive fighter who lived in parts unknown, spurning male attempts to aid her. In the tale of The Lady with the Sword, the woman warrior took her own fiancé to court for murdering her sister. Tom also told of the fourteen female warriors of the Yang family, who led the Sung army to victory over foreign invaders. This story was related in the Chinese revolutionary periodical *Women of China*.

Enamoured of these myths I grew up with, I pursued my heras in live operas, puppet shows, and movies. When the operas came to town,

I remember going early in order to catch glimpses of the star swords-woman backstage. On one occasion, the beautiful actress invited me into her dressing room. I stared with awe at the glittering costumes elaborately sequined with intricate designs. I touched the flashy swords and fighting staffs and the complicated warrior headgear with the springing long antennae swishing about like banners. I watched her apply highly stylized makeup as she told me about herself and her work. She had been in the opera since childhood. Coming from a theatrical family, she had been trained specifically to play the swordswoman. However, by the time we met, the late Fifties, audiences were dwindling and the future of the cast was uncertain. The actress motioned to me to remain silent just before she donned her elaborate headpiece. She entered a meditative state, and I realized I was witnessing a deeply spiritual moment as she contemplated the spirit of the particular swordswoman. As I watched her brilliant performance later, I also saw the struggling woman behind the mask.

The closest I ever came to being a groupie was a journey I made to Hong Kong to visit Chen Pei Pei, the star of a popular Shaw Brothers' film *Come Drink with Me*. She was a predecessor of Bruce Lee, and the film was an early innovation of "the Bruce Lee genre" of fast cutting on action, rapid pacing, numerous close-ups, and dynamic choreography. In the film, she played an innkeeper's adopted daughter whose secret mission was vengeance on those who had killed her real family. She fell in love with a scholar, whom she constantly had to rescue from trouble created by his naiveté. Chen Pei Pei was known especially for her versatility in the martial arts. Like Bruce Lee, she was extremely attractive, dark, and intense. Unlike Bruce Lee, she did not receive the pot of gold the patriarchy awards to its warrior heroes. She might have fared better economically if she had played a sexual image. The Shaw studios were housed in a series of factory-like buildings much like the early studios of Warner Brothers or Paramount. Actors lived in one- or two-bedroom apartments on the lot, were paid a fairly low salary, and were under stringent contracts. I had thought a star like Chen Pei Pei would be treated differently. Used to the magnificence of her celluloid image, I was surprised to encounter a soft-spoken woman and was jolted by the reality of our equal size on a physical plane. She was vaguely dissatisfied but tactful about her life as a contracted worker under the Shaw monopoly. She was paid $300 a month, plus room and board. Her lavish lifestyle was an invention of the publicity department.

In my search for heras, I was confronted with ambiguities. These women in real life found meaning in their daily struggles against obstacles, not unlike their mythical counterparts. Still, I wonder about the mixed messages the myths themselves present. During all the centuries in which these legends have been told, how many real changes occurred in the lives of most women? These mythic figures were often based on historical facts, e.g., the fourteen women warriors of the Yang family who fought successfully against foreign invasions, but such feats were exceptions of emancipated womanhood. Moreover, the value of personal emancipation can be questioned if they fought to uphold the *status quo*. The double messages and contradictions woven into these legends are attested to by the necessity for the swordswomen's transformations. These powerful figures had to lead dual lives as imposters, and sometimes as transvestites, with a public and private face. They had to hide their strengths behind feminine weakness and passivity. Their housebound submission was a controlled disposition concealing martial skills verging on the magical. I came to realize that the very society that oppressed women also compensated them with fantasies of infinite possibilities.

I remembered gazing at my mother's feet as she told me stories of these brave women. Her feet were small and partially deformed; finding suitable shoes was a continual problem. How could my mother ever be a swordswoman, I wondered? She told us that her parents had attempted foot-binding when she was a child, but, being spirited, she had unraveled the bandages while they were out working. Her struggle had continued until it was too late to crush the bones. She made certain that her illiteracy and aborted foot-binding were never to be her daughters' fate. Yet I look at my own feet, not too different from my mother's, deformed by "toe shoes" at the age of seven when a French-English ballet teacher had discovered an early talent and insisted I dance in them. Women were creatures of air and had to appear immune to the laws of gravity. The similarity of women's fates continues to surface in ironic ways. At each level of awareness we are met by a more intricate and complex trap, but our progression is always upward.

Mythology comprises a significant fiber of our lives. Stories, like dreams, can serve to relieve unconscious pressures. Seeking the legacy of the warrior, women contribute to the creation and re-creation of a positive female mythology. The building of a vocabulary of images is an essential element in our political evolution. Imaging is a radical tool that can help us build inner confidence and dissipate crippling fears.

Maxine Hong Kingston, for example, sought integration by interweaving aspects of the swordswoman myth in order to allow the hera/herself to be a successful warrior/writer. To realize our goals, we must first imagine them fully.

## NOTES

1. Maxine Hong Kingston, *The Woman Warrior* (New York: Alfred A. Knopf, 1976).
2. Lily Tom, *"Swashbuckling Swordswomen of the Silver Screen,"* Ms., April 1973.

# Meanings of Matriarchy

## Margot Adler

It is not surprising that spiritual feminists, in their explorations of the hidden and distorted history of women, have been attracted by the idea of a universal age of Goddess worship or a universal stage of matriarchy. These women have been reexamining those philosophers, historians, anthropologists, and psychologists who have argued that women in the ancient world held a position of relative power. Sometimes that power is political, as in the Marxist theories of a prehistorical classless society (as stated, for example, by Friedrich Engels and, more recently, Evelyn Reed); sometimes it is mythic or religious or psychological, as in the theories of J. J. Bachofen, Helen Diner, C. G. Jung, Erich Neumann, Robert Graves, and Esther Harding.[1]

The idea of matriarchy has ramifications that go beyond the question of whether or not the matriarchy ever existed in reality. When a feminist reads Strabo's description of an island of women at the mouth of the Loire, or when she reads an account of an ancient college of priestesses or Sappho's academy on Lesbos, or the legends of the Amazons, a rich and possibly transforming event takes place.

It is easy to get sidetracked by details, and that is the game many scholars play. We will play it also for a while. Prehistory is a wide open field. There is little agreement on what the word *matriarchy* means, and even less on whether ancient matriarchies existed, or if they did, on how "universal" they were. It is fashionable for scholars to dismiss the idea. This seems due partly to the lack of conclusive evidence in any direction and partly to (predominantly male) scholars' fear of the idea of women in power. The question may never be answered satisfactorily. Sarah Pomeroy, in her careful study, *Goddesses, Whores, Wives, and Slaves,* observes that most questions about prehistory remain unanswered. She allows herself to wonder why archaeologists have unearthed four times the number of female figurines as male statues, why Minoan wall frescoes portray many more women than men, why the lyric women poets of Sappho's time appear to have so much freedom and independence, and what meaning lies behind the strong, dominant women depicted in those Greek tragedies and myths that speak of the preclassical age. It is as foolish, she notes, to postulate male supremacy in preclassical times as it is to postulate female supremacy.[2] According to Isaac Bonewits, we may have to wait until the field of archaeology and prehistory is no longer dominated by men. Most women, however, are not waiting.

Many scholars have seemed to delight in showing certain weaknesses in the arguments of some of the more popular feminist writers on the subject of matriarchy, such as Elizabeth Gould Davis in her book *The First Sex.*[3] It's fairly easy to argue that one cannot always take myths literally, as Davis often does, nor can one assume that societies that venerated goddesses necessarily gave power to women. Such "reasonable" arguments have been used, however, to avoid dealing with the central thesis of the matriarchy argument: that there have been ages and places where women held a much greater share of power than they do now and that, perhaps, women used power in a very different way from our common understanding of it.*

---

* Editor's Note: Among the scholars who have rejected in print "*some* feminists'" acceptance of the case for matriarchy are numerous feminist anthropologists, e.g., Joan Bamberger, Sherry B. Ortner, Michelle Zimbalist Rosaldo (*Woman, Culture, and Society,* 1974); Gayle Rubin (*Toward an Anthropology of Women,* 1975); Sally R. Binford (1979; see Appendix in this volume). As Adler notes above, they categorically dismiss any discussion of matriarchy instead of considering the central questions being raised: Spirituality feminists are not particularly interested in the "archy" since that connotation of repressive rule does not seem

We face here the same problem we face in relating the modern Craft to the history of Witchcraft scholarship. In that case, scholars such as Elliot Rose and Norman Cohn argued (quite possibly correctly) that Witchcraft in European history was almost totally invented by the In-

---

applicable to the egalitarian, prepatriarchal societies that have been excavated (see Marija Gimbutas in this volume and elsewhere); rather, we are interested in the meaning of the art, artifacts, female-shaped temples, and religious and cultural practices of the prehistoric cultures, especially pre-4500 B.C. — all of which indicate that the position, power, and *concept* of woman was quite different from that during the patriarchal era. Most of our feminist sisters in anthropology will not address these issues. Why? I suggest four possible reasons. First, writing in the early and mid-Seventies, the above scholars were no doubt reacting to the unfortunate excesses and leaps in Davis' extremely popular *The First Sex*. (Although her work has generally been discredited in part or rejected entirely, I hope her memory will be honored for the catalyst her book provided for the more careful work that followed.) Second, many of these feminist anthropologists view culture and history from a Marxist perspective, in which considerations of spiritual power would be symptomatic of brain damage. (Engels' nonspiritual theory of matriarchy is also dismissed by them, but Karen Sacks' "Engels Revisited," *Woman, Culture, and Society*, is an interesting defense of his position.) Third, few topics are so certain to bring ridicule from colleagues in the anthropology department; addressing prehistoric matriarchies, or even widespread matrifocality, may be the ultimate academic taboo. Still, in order to keep their reputations clean on this issue, anthropologists must refuse to consider at least eighty years of archaeological matrifocal findings from the prehistoric era. Fourth, and most important, on a very basic level many of the perceptions of the above scholars are informed by patriarchal concepts the validity of which they have not yet examined and rejected. I have great respect for their work as descriptive analyses of patriarchy, but they repeatedly treat contemporary [patriarchal] attitudes and cultural structures as eternal "universals of the human condition," e.g., that women are *always* subservient because we bear children and because we are associated with nature more closely than are men (culture) and because "polluting" menstrual blood and "messy" lactation flow out of us. Nowhere do these scholars acknowledge the archaeological evidence that these female phenomena carried *positive* — even awesome — value for 20,000 years prior to the advent of the patriarchal era. If childbearing is *always* considered limiting and degrading, why did our Paleolithic ancestors from Spain to Siberia carve myriad statues of powerful female figures whose vulvas, large breasts and bellies cyclically yielded the very mysteries of life? One rarely sees infants hanging on these statues (a reflection of the diffusion of childcare within a clan system?); they are simply monuments to women's elemental power. If menstrual blood is *always* considered polluting, why was it, symbolized by red ocher, painted on artifacts, skeletons, and the entrance to cave sanctuaries where sacred rituals took place? If nature is *always* considered material to be conquered, as it is in the Judeo-Christian tradition, why was the Earth held sacred as the womb of the Great Mother and why did people perform sacred rituals before plucking Her plants or mining Her ore? Nature was long revered as a great power and, yes, women were associated with nature! Rather quisition. These scholars then used that argument to discount the Neo-Pagan and Craft revival and its *real* links to Paganism in the ancient world, to indigenous Paganism today, to oral traditions, folk customs, myths, and fairy tales. The situation in regard to matriarchy seems similar. Many ideas of the theorists of the matriarchy may prove incorrect, but that does not diminish the force of the central idea.

It is, therefore, important to stress that, contrary to many assumptions, feminists are viewing the idea of matriarchy as a complex one and that their creative use of the idea of matriarchy as *vision* and *ideal* would in no way be compromised if suddenly there were "definite proof" that few matriarchies ever existed. In the same way, Amazons may prove to be fictions or creations of the deep mind, or, like Troy,

---

than deny the connection between woman and nature in order to change this "sad" situation and align us with men on the side of [patriarchal] culture, as Ortner proposes, spirituality feminists say, "Yes, let us improve the status of women *and reject the patriarchal notion of the degradation of nature.*" The concept of our "dominion over nature" was, after all, an invention of patriarchal religion/culture; it is certainly not a "natural truth" of human existence. Similarly, rather than deduce that motherhood and mothering are "the most important features in accounting for the universal secondary status of women" (see Bamberger, Ortner, and Rosaldo, *Woman, Culture, and Society*), spirituality feminists suggest cultural options other than the patriarchal mode of viewing motherhood: In both prepatriarchal and contemporary matrifocal societies (see Nancy Tanner's "matrifocality," *Woman, Culture, and Society*), the same blood, pregnancy, milk, and mothering on which the above scholars blame woman's plight are regarded as powerful and honored phenomena. The element of womb envy in patriarchal oppression must be discussed *along with* the feminist call for shared parenting. The feminist anthropologists propose social change, but in surveying their theses, I am reminded of the warning issued by the post-structuralist Jacques Derrida: "We cannot utter a single destructive proposition which has not already slipped into the form, the logic, and the implicit postulations of precisely what it seeks to contest." Ortner, for example, proposes with patriarchal logic that males' physiology "frees" them to take up the projects of culture; one could just as easily observe that males' physiology "eliminates" them from a meaningful, sustained, *natural* role in human culture (but for the brief act of insemination), so they turn — with a good deal of insecurity — to *inventing* roles, meanings, elaborate puberty rites, etc. Are spirituality feminists any more immune to the Derridian paradox than the anthropologists? Probably not — *except* when we move, not from the present structure of patriarchal concepts/values/language to the uncharted waters of the future, which we also do, but to the extant forms of the *pre*patriarchal era, that is, when we consider the art, myth, and culture from a previous reality. We cannot guess what sort of government prevailed then, although Gimbutas' and Mellaart's excavations provide interesting insights, but if we can look freely (see Adrienne Rich in this volume) at the sacred, powerful forms of the female, we can say unequivocally, "This was — and is." — C.S.

they may suddenly be brought to the surface as "reality" one day. In either case, the feminist movement is giving birth to *new* Amazons, a process that is bound to continue no matter what we unearth from the past. An illustration may be helpful.

In Gillo Pontecorvo's extraordinary film *The Battle of Algiers*, Algerian women confront the French by giving out an eerie yell, a high ululation that makes the flesh crawl. These women have a great sense of power and strength, perhaps the power of the maenads. After the film appeared I occasionally heard the same cry in the demonstrations of the late 1960s, but never in the way I have heard it more recently, in meetings of women. Amazons are coming into existence today. I have heard them and joined with them. We have howled with the bears, the wolves, and the coyotes. I have felt their strength. I have felt at moments that they could unite with the animal kingdom, or ally themselves with all that is female in the universe and wage a war for Mother Nature. These women are creating their own mythologies and their own realities. And they often will repeat the words of Monique Wittig in *Les Guérillères*:

There was a time when you were not a slave, remember that. You walked alone, full of laughter, you bathed bare-bellied. You say you have lost all recollection of it, remember. You know how to avoid meeting a bear on the track. You know the winter fear when you hear the wolves gathering. But you can remain seated for hours in the tree-tops to await morning. You say there are no words to describe this time, you say it does not exist. But remember. Make an effort to remember. Or, failing that, invent.[4]

These spiritual feminists do not feel their future is contingent on a hypothesized past. They do not feel they need the words of scholars to affirm or deny their reality. "After all," I was told by Z. Budapest, "if Goddess religion is sixty thousand years old or seven thousand, it does not matter. Certainly not for the future! Recognizing the divine Goddess within is where real religion is at."

In other words, the *idea* of matriarchy is powerful for women in itself. Two feminist anthropologists have noted that whatever matriarchy *is*, "the whole question challenges women to imagine themselves with power. It is an idea about what society would be like where women are truly free."[5]

There is no consensus on what the word *matriarchy* means, for either feminists or scholars. Literally, of course, it means government by mothers, or more broadly, government and power in the hands of women. But that is not the way the word is most often used. Engels and others in the Marxist tradition use the word to describe an egalitarian preclass society where women and men share equally in production and power. A few Marxists do not call this egalitarian society a matriarchy, but most in the tradition do.

Other writers have used the word *matriarchy* to mean an age of universal Goddess worship, irrespective of questions of political power and control. A number of feminists note that few definitions of the word, despite its literal meaning, include any concept of power, and they suggest that centuries of oppression have made it impossible for women to conceive of themselves with such power. They observe that there has been very little feminist utopian literature. (The exceptions are the science fiction of Joanna Russ,[6] Monique Wittig's *Les Guérillères,* and some of the fiction published in the feminist small presses.)

Elizabeth Gould Davis and Helen Diner do see matriarchy as a society in which women have power; and they conceive of *female* power as qualitatively different from *male* power. This has led many feminists to define *matriarchal* as a different kind of power, as a realm where female things are valued and where power is exerted in nonpossessive, noncontrolling, and organic ways that are harmonious with nature.

Echoing that kind of idea, Alison Harlow, a feminist Witch from California, told me that for her the word *patriarchal* had come to mean *manipulative* and *domineering.* She used *matriarchal* to describe a worldview that values feelings of connectedness and intuition, that seeks nonauthoritarian and nondestructive power relationships and attitudes toward the Earth. This is far different from the idea of matriarchy as simply rule by women.

In addition to feminists, a number of Neo-Pagans have been exploring the question of matriarchy, and ending up with similar views about power. Morning Glory and Tim Zell, of the Church of All Worlds, told me they disliked that term "or any 'archy'" and preferred to use the word *matristic.* The Zells call themselves *matristic anarchists* and, noting the views of G. Rattray Taylor in *Sex in History,*[7] say that they consider matristic societies (generally matrifocal and matrilineal) to be characterized by spontaneity, sensuality, and antiauthoritarianism, embracing, in other words, many of the values Neo-Pagans share today.

There are a number of ways to approach the question of ancient matriarchies. Many have their roots in the historical theories of J. J. Bachofen and Friedrich Engels. Both men wrote in the nineteenth century, and although they had very different perspectives, both set forth the idea of a universal matriarchy in terms of historical laws and universal stages of evolution. The idea of a universal stage of matriarchy was, in fact, widely accepted until the twentieth century; it is now, like Margaret Murray's theory of the Witch Cult, out of favor.

Engels and the Marxists who followed him based their views on the theory of historical materialism. According to Marxist theory, a primitive egalitarianism prevailed before class society; women and men shared equally in production and power. Feminist writers such as Evelyn Reed continue to base their views on an evolutionary perspective and to define matriarchy as this kind of egalitarian society. Reed, it should be emphasized, has many original ideas in her book *Woman's Evolution*, including a novel speculation on the origin of the incest taboo as women's control of cannibalism.

J. J. Bachofen also sought universal laws of history, although he based these on religious organization, myth, and symbol rather than on materialism. In his *Myth, Religion, and Mother Right* (1861), he wrote that matriarchal societies were characterized by universal freedom, equality, hospitality, freedom from strife, and a general aversion to all restrictions. His works were attractive to poets, artists, and psychologists. Some of the feminists who come out of the Bachofen tradition, such as Davis and Diner, have dropped all reference to evolutionary theory, but accept the primacy of myth and symbolic forms. Davis has a cyclic and cataclysmic theory of history, influenced greatly by Immanuel Velikovsky. Patriarchy is seen as a degeneration, morally and even technologically.

Interestingly, it is non-Marxists such as Davis and Diner who are able to envision a dominance matriarchy with women in power, although that power is exercised in a very different fashion. Some feminist anthropologists have also noted contradictions in Davis's work; for example, she says that the rule of the matriarchies was totally benevolent, but that one reason for their downfall was the revolt of men who had been cast out. One feminist, knowledgeable in both Marxist theory and current feminist thought, told me that she was sympathetic to the argument that wars exist because of masculine aggression, but she noted, "I'm suspicious of it. I've read enough Marxist theory to feel that such a view may be a reactionary way of looking at things."

Since theories of stages of evolution in history are hard to "prove," most leading anthropologists and archaeologists outside the Marxist tradition refuse to concern themselves with them. Many feminists, likewise, tend to drop the arguments for a universal stage of matriarchy and instead simply state that Goddess worship was widespread in many ancient societies and that archaeological evidence continues to mount, with the unearthing of ancient societies such as Çatal Hüyük and Mersin, both of which may have been ruled by women. Matriarchy may not have been *universal*, and present matrilineal societies may be oppressive to women, but there *is* plenty of evidence of societies where women held greater power than they do now. For example, Jean Markale's studies of Celtic societies show that the power of women was reflected not only in myth and legend but in legal codes pertaining to marriage, divorce, property ownership, and the right to rule.[8]

Many women are also looking at the idea of matriarchy from points of view other than those of political theory, history, archaeology, and ethnography. They are reexamining those writers, poets, and psychologists who have talked for years about *feminine symbols, feminine realms,* the *anima,* and so forth. The theories of C. G. Jung, Esther Harding, and Erich Neumann are being reexamined, as well as those of poets who have claimed to get all their inspiration from the Great Goddess—Robert Graves and Robert Bly, for example. Neumann, in *The Great Mother,* asserts that matriarchy was not a historical state but a psychological reality with a great power that is alive and generally repressed in human beings today. Writers like Neumann and Graves, in the words of Adrienne Rich, have seemingly rejected "masculinism itself" and have "begun to identify the denial of 'the feminine' in civilization with the roots of inhumanity and self-destructiveness and to call for a renewal of 'the feminine principle.'"

The recurrence of strong, powerful women in myth, legends, and dreams continues, and Rich observes:

Whether such an age, even if less than golden, ever existed anywhere, or whether we all carry in our earliest imprintings the memory of, or the longing for, an individual past relationship to a female body, larger and stronger than our own, and to female warmth, nurture, and tenderness, there is a new concern for the *possibilities* inherent in beneficent female power, as a mode which is absent from the society at large, and which, even in the private sphere, women have exercised under terrible constraints in patriarchy.[9]

Philip Zabriskie, a Jungian, has also noted the power and *presence* of the ancient archetypes of goddesses and ancient women and has stated that they can be evoked in one's present psychic life.[10] It is obvious that even the Greco-Roman classical goddesses who were known in a patriarchal context are much richer images of the feminine than we have today, although it is equally true that such images can be used to repress as well as to liberate women.

As we have seen, women are looking at the matriarchy from a complex point of view. They differ as to the existence of past matriarchies, and even as to what a matriarchy means in terms of power. Some, such as Davis, see childbearing as the source of women's ancient power, the innate difference that creates a kind of moral superiority stemming from closeness to nature and life. Other feminists, starting with Simone de Beauvoir and continuing through Shulamith Firestone, see in childbearing the root of women's oppression.

Feminists also differ on the question of matriarchy as a "Golden Age," a view expressed forcefully in Davis's *The First Sex*. Some see matriarchy as, above all, an *idea* about women in freedom. They often picture the ancient matriarchies as societies governed by the kind of loose, supportive, anarchic, and truly unique principles that many of today's feminist groups are organized around, principles developed from the tradition of consciousness-raising. But others see the matriarchy rather as a place that *was* better for women, but had problems and difficulties of its own. Alison Harlow, for example, told me that she once had a vision, a small glimpse of the matriarchy:

I was standing with my mother, father, and sister as a long procession passed by. A priestess was being carried along. She pointed at me with a long wand. I was chosen. Suddenly I was taken away from everything I knew. Now, maybe I loved it, but the lack of freedom scares me. A theocracy is only good if the priestess is always right. Now perhaps they were more intuitive than us, but . . .

The matriarchy, according to Alison, was a period of thousands of years when women functioned strongly in the world.

I do not consider there was ever a matriarchy that was a utopia. I do not consider it the ultimate answer to all our problems. I do think there were values from the ancient matriarchal cultures that we would do well to readopt into our present lives. I've spent a long time trying to come to grips with what it would mean to live in a Goddess-centered theocracy, where people belonged to the Goddess, where cities belonged to the Goddess, where you are born to serve Her will. Concepts of human freedom as we understand them are not very compatible with any sort of theocracy and I am very committed to individual freedom.

If feminists have diverse views on the matriarchies of the past, they also are of several minds on the goals for the future. A woman in the coven of Ursa Maior told me, "Right now I am pushing for women's power in any way I can, but I don't know whether my ultimate aim is a society where all human beings are equal, regardless of the bodies they were born into, or whether I would rather see a society where women had institutional authority."

In any event, most women who have explored the question do see a return to some form of matriarchal values, however that may be expressed, as a prerequisite to the survival of the planet. We might note that Robert Graves wrote in 1948:

I foresee no change for the better until everything gets far worse. Only after a period of complete religious and political disorganization can the suppressed desire of the Western races, which is for some practical form of Goddess worship . . . find satisfaction at last. . . . But the longer the hour is postponed, and therefore the more exhausted by man's irreligious improvidence the natural resources of the soil and sea become, the less merciful will her five-fold mask be. . . .[11]

The idea of a matriarchy in the past, the possibility of matriarchy in the future, the matriarchal images in myths and in the psyche, perhaps in memories both collective and individual — these have led spiritual feminists to search for matriarchal lore. The road is not merely through study and research. It involves the creation of rituals, psychic experiments, elements of play, daydreams, and dreams.

NOTES

1. Friedrich Engels, *The Origin of the Family, Private Property, and the State* (New York: International Publishers, 1967); Evelyn Reed, *Woman's Evolution* (New York: Pathfinder Press, 1975); J. J. Bachofen, *Myth, Religion and Mother Right* (Princeton: Princeton University Press, Bollingen Series 84, 1973); Helen Diner, *Mothers and Amazons* (New York: Anchor Books, 1973); Erich Neumann, *The Great Mother: An Analysis of the Archetype* (Princeton: Princeton University Press, Bollingen Series 47, 1963).

2. Sarah B. Pomeroy, *Goddesses, Whores, Wives, and Slaves* (New York: Schoeken Books, 1975).

3. Elizabeth Gould Davis, *The First Sex* (New York: G. P. Putnam's Sons, 1971).

4. Monique Wittig, *Les Guérillères* (New York: Viking Press, 1969), p. 89.

5. Paula Webster and Esther Newton, "Matriarchy: Puzzle and Para-

digm," presented at the 71st Annual Meeting of the American Anthropological Association, Toronto, 1972. This paper was later published in *APHRA: A Feminist Literary Magazine* (Spring/Summer 1973) as "Matriarchy: As Women See It." A revised version, *Matriarchy: A Vision of Power* by Paula Webster appears in *Toward an Anthropology of Women*, ed. Rayna Reiter (New York: Monthly Review Press, 1975), pp. 141–56.

6. Joanna Russ, *The Female Man* (New York: Bantam, 1975); *We Who Are About To . . .* (New York: Dell, 1975); *The Two of Them* (New York: Berkley Publishing Corp., 1978), among others.

7. Gordon Rattray Taylor, *Sex in History* (New York: The Vanguard Press, 1954).

8. Jean Markale, *Women of the Celts* (London: Gordon Cremonesi, 1975). First published as *La Femme Celte*, Editions Payot, Paris, 1972.

9. Adrienne Rich, "The Kingdom of the Fathers," *Partisan Review*, vol. 43, no. 1 (1976), 29–30, 26.

10. Philip Zabriskie, "Goddesses in Our Midst," *Quadrant*, no. 17 (Fall 1974), 34–45.

11. Robert Graves, *The White Goddess*, amended and enlarged ed. (New York: Farrar, Straus and Giroux, 1966), pp. 484–86.

# Drawing from Mythology in Women's Quest for Selfhood

## Bella Debrida[1]

> Sing, O Muse . . .  Sing, Goddess . . .
> Sing me, O Muse . . .  Begin, Goddess . . .
> Sing, begin, tell me the story . . .
>
> — opening words of ancient
> Greek hymns and poetry

"In the beginning was the Word, and the Word was with God, and the Word was God"; thus the Gospel according to John would have us believe that language and rational thought originated and is identical with their conception of an exclusively male god. But John and his followers were late arrivals in the arena of speech and divinity. For eons before the Western world descended into Christianity, the peoples of ancient India had praised the power of the Goddess of Speech in their hymns. The *Rigveda*, one of the four holy books of wisdom of ancient Hinduism, dating in its written form from about 1300 B.C. and containing prepatriarchal elements, calls the creative, fecundating power of speech "matarah," "mothers."[2] Poetry belongs to the mothers. Like an untamed sister, she is virgin, unmarried.[3] Speech originates in the realm of intuition. Thought is conceived of as light; once formulated, it becomes the spoken word, the poem. The same word may mean light or song. In the beginning was Light and Song, and She was powerful.

The Muses breathed into me their divine voice, so that I might tell of things to come and things past . . .

— HESIOD, *Theogony*, 31–32

And the Sirens sang:
We know all that may happen upon the much-nourishing Earth.
— HOMER, *Odyssey*, XII.191

Outside of truth there is no poetry.

— ONITSURA, 17th c. Haiku poet

Though Greek mythology in its surviving form does not credit a goddess of speech, Greek poetry recognizes the mothers' power of song. All Greek poetry begins with an invocation to the Muse, or simply the Goddess, to inspire the poet with the song they[4] are about to sing. As the above quotations indicate, the Muse, or Muses, know all earthly and divine matters and alone have the power to inspire the poet to create song.

Did the Muse's earthly counterpart, woman, also have the power to create song? Skeptics adamantly insist, "No!" — all the while pointing to a long list of male poets in his/story and claiming that the Muse is little different from the metaphors of a later age which might take any abstract noun and personify it into a deity, often female. But the Greek "Mousa" is a woman, a goddess, not an abstract noun awaiting personification. And even patriarchal literature unwittingly discloses the intimate connection between women and their song:

Divine Kalypso . . . was now at home . . . singing high and low in her sweet voice, before her loom a-weaving.

— HOMER, *Odyssey*, V. 61–62

. . . inside her quiet house
they heard the Goddess Kirke.
Low she sang
in her beguiling voice, while on her loom . . .

— *Odyssey*, X. 221–22

Greek and Roman literature usually present respectable women weaving at their looms. Less frequently are we told what these women do while weaving: They sing and tell stories. The fourth book of Ovid's *Metamorphoses* focuses on the stories told by women while weaving.

> Women, rice-planting:
>   all muddy, save for one thing —
>     that's their chanting.
>
> — RAIZAN, seventeenth century Haiku poet

Even our own language reflects this intimate connection between woman and song. We speak of "weaving a story" or "spinning a yarn."* In many languages the equivalent verb is used in metaphorical expressions relating to the contriving of plots or deception.[5] In the *Odyssey*, literal and figurative meanings coincide: Penelope uses the pretext of weaving a shroud for her husband's father, Laërtes (which she unravels each night), as a ruse to keep her obstreperous suitors at bay.

In the *Iliad* Helen says to Hektor, the leading Trojan warrior:

> us two . . .
> we shall be made into things of song for the men [sic]
>   of the future.
>
> — HOMER, *Iliad*, VI. 358[6]

I have frequently wondered why, in a story focused on male violence and war and in which women are regarded as just another form of

---

* Editor's Note: In Part One of *The Madwoman in the Attic: The Woman Writer and the Nineteenth-Century Literary Imagination* (1979), Sandra M. Gilbert and Susan Gubar present a thorough account of the associations in patriarchal culture between pen and penis, author and authority that have inhibited women writers. If we are going to discuss the impact of literary history, however, we should not limit our considerations to the patriarchal era. It is true that script was not used as fully in the matrifocal cultures as it was later, so the records of the stories told in those societies are incomplete, but much of their sacred literature survived in oral and visual media, expressing central themes of the Goddess and the elemental power of the female that stretch back at least as far as 25,000 B.C. Jane Ellen Harrison was the first to demonstrate, in the early 1900s, that the pre-Hellenic, *women's* mythic stories were the foundation of Greek culture — "at once more primitive and more permanent" [than the later Olympian tales]. I do not believe that either sex "owns" literature or art in general; in a discussion of which sex has the greater historical claim to forming and informing the arts, men may cite the past four thousand years and women the previous twenty-three thousand years. In short, the arts today belong to women as much as anyone. We need never apologize, nor feel ourselves to be aberrations, nor fear we are venturing where we do not belong whenever we exercise our creative faculties. — C.S.

booty, Helen, who is seen by all, including herself, as the cause of this war, should be the only character in this epic poem to be conscious of and remark on the creation of poetry. This can be neither coincidental nor accidental. In light of the connection between woman and her song which the few surviving, delicate and broken threads of ancient literature allow us to piece together, this *Iliadic* passage acknowledges, however fleetingly, woman's power as the creator of song.[7]

> In the silence
> I am hearing my own voice again.
>
> — SUSAN GRIFFIN, *Voices*

What is the song she sings? The Chorus of women in Euripides' *Medea* lament that in patriarchal culture woman's song is given no voice; if it were, they say, the world would hear a tale quite different from those that men tell (11. 424–430). Alas, it is too true that most, if not all, of ancient mythology has been transmitted to us through the myopia of men's language and thought. Nevertheless, even the hostile literature of patriarchal culture could not eradicate images of women as wise and powerful.

> I have been woman
> for a long time
> beware my smile
> I am treacherous with old magic
> and the noon's new fury
>
> — AUDRE LORDE, *The Black Unicorn*

Mythology shows us woman's power. After a brief discussion of the meaning of mythology and its value for us in seeking to understand woman's aboriginal power, I will examine a mythological paradigm spanning more than a millennium for the hidden story it tells. This paradigm describes woman's journeys from the Sumerian tale of Inanna's descent to the underworld to the Greek myth of Persephone's abduction by the God of the Underworld. As I learn more of the myths of other cultures, of all periods, I become ever more convinced that all mythology reveals woman's power. However, since my own field of study has been the literature of ancient Greece, with some forays into the Near Eastern material, I will use stories from these particular mythological traditions to illustrate my general remarks.

> Space which she weaves . . . The cosmos flooded with
> The earth her vision.

> — SUSAN GRIFFIN, *Woman and Nature*

What is myth? In ancient Greek, *mythos* is simply a story; originally the word carried no implications as to a tale's truth or falsity. As early forms of rational and scientific thought assumed greater importance, *logos* acquired the meaning of a factual, historically valid account, as opposed to the more fanciful tale signified by *mythos*. Today, myth ranges in meaning from "a purely fictitious narrative" to a traditional story elucidating life experiences and reflecting both historical and metaphysical truth.[8] Using the latter as a basic, working definition, what can we as women learn from ancient mythology in our present search for self and identity? And how does this mythology pertain to women's spirituality and its political aspects?

> and from your name Eve we shall take
> the word Evil.
> and from God's the word Good.
> now you understand patriarchal morality.

> — JUDY GRAHN,
> *The Work of a Common Woman*

Most of us growing up in Western culture received images of women that are primarily negative, destructive, evil. The Bible gives us Eve, Salome, and Delilah,[9] and Greek mythology offers us another host of destructive women: Pandora, the cause of all evil; Medea, Kirke, the unnatural and unmanning Witch; Furies, Medusas, Gorgons, horrifying bogey-women, destroyers of life.

Once we begin to delve into the mythology, we find that it has been perverted. A deliberate selection process has determined who our female models may be, and even those few models have been twisted to serve patriarchal aims. By discovering our true mythological roots we can demystify, inspirit, and remythicize them; we can reclaim the power usurped by patriarchal control; we can begin to fill the overwhelming need for female models of strength and wisdom so lacking in contemporary culture.[10]

> To live our lives as travelers with roots in ourselves.

> — RUTH FALK,
> *High Adventure — Ace of Wands*

> The Goddess, from the great above, She set Her mind
>    towards the great below,
> Inanna, from the great above, She set Her mind toward
>    the great below.
> My Lady abandoned heaven, abandoned Earth, to the nether
>    world She descended,
> Inanna abandoned heaven, abandoned Earth, to the nether
>    world She descended.

— *Inanna's Descent to the Nether World (Ancient Sumer)*

The earliest surviving poetry sings of woman's journey. It is a journey to the underworld, to the land of the dead. Religious practices and other literature illuminate the meaning of this journey below as a metaphor for the cycles of the Earth, the stages in a woman's life, and the journey inward leading to discovery of the self.

Sumerian literature dating from the early second millennium B.C. speaks of Inanna's journey to the underworld where Her sister Ereshkigal rules.[11] The reason for Her going is unknown, for the literary remains are fragmentary.[12] On Her journey to the land of the dead, Inanna passes through seven gates, at each of which She is ritually stripped of Her attributes by Ereshkigal's male gatekeeper. She arrives before Her sister's throne only to be killed by "the eyes of death" and "the word which tortures the spirit" (165–66) of the seven judges of the underworld. After three days, Inanna is rescued by two life-producing creations of Her father's. Returning to the land of the living, Inanna receives back each of the attributes She had lost on Her entry and seeks a substitute to send down to the underworld in Her stead. In anger She condemns to death Dummuz, Her son-lover and the only one of Her male devotees who treats Her with arrogance rather than respect. The fragment ends here; another shorter fragment which may have been part of this poem relates Inanna's mourning over the dead Dummuz.

In the Babylonian version of the same myth, some two to three centuries after the Sumerian, two apparent modifications of the Sumerian account occur.[13] The anger and hostility implicit between the two Sumerian goddesses are openly expressed in the Babylonian tale. Of special importance is the Babylonian account that all life on Earth stops during the Goddess' absence (Ishtar is the name of the Babylonian counterpart of the Sumerian Inanna):

> Since Ishtar has gone down to the Land of no Return,
> The bull springs not upon the cow, the ass impregnates
>     not the jenny,
> In the street the man impregnates not the maiden.

Fragmentary as these stories are, important elements of later Near Eastern and Greek myth and ritual have survived with them: the relationship between two women; the journey to the underworld by a female deity; the anger of a goddess connected with this journey; the barrenness of Mother Earth during Her absence; and, especially important in Near Eastern ritual, the mourning of the dying son/consort of the Mother Goddess.

All five elements recur in quite transmuted form in the Greek Hymn to Demeter, which, dating from the seventh century B.C., was recorded at least a millennium later than its Sumerian prototype.[14] The nature of the changes occurring in the Greek version reflects, unquestionably to my mind, woman's shifting social and political position in society and the changing attitude to woman's power by the transmitters of the culture of the time.

From menses to marriage: woman's journey broken.

> Then beautiful Persephone answered her thus: "Mother, I will tell you all without error . . . how He rapt me away by the deep plan of my father [Zeus] . . . and carried me off beneath the depths of the Earth . . . All we were playing in a lovely meadow, Leucippe [there follows a list of twenty-two girls' names]; we were playing and gathering sweet flowers in our hands, soft crocuses [four more flowers], and the narcissus which the wide Earth caused to grow yellow as a crocus. That I plucked in my joy; but the Earth parted beneath, and there the strong lord, the Host of Many [Hades, God of the Underworld], sprang forth and in His golden chariot He bore me away, all unwilling, beneath the Earth: then I cried with a shrill cry. All this is true, sore though it grieves me to tell the tale."
>
> — *Hymn to Demeter,* 405–433

Unlike Inanna or Ishtar, a mature goddess and queen who travels to the underworld to visit Her sister-ruler for Her own purposes and of Her own accord, Persephone is a young girl abducted against Her will by Her uncle Hades, ruler of the dead. Even after Persephone's release, a trick by Her supposed father Zeus — secretly forcing Her to eat a pomegranate seed — constrains Her to spend part of each year in the underworld with Her rapist uncle.

Furthermore, aspects of the earlier story that belong solely to the one goddess are now split between Demeter and Her daughter. Though Persephone "journeys," the Greek hymn attributes the Earth's barrenness to Demeter's anger and grief, not to Persephone's absence. And although the reason for Inanna's or Ishtar's anger remains unknown, Demeter's has a very immediate societal cause: the rape and abduction of Her daughter. Her grief and mourning, too, are not for a dying son-god, but, on the literal level for Her abused daughter, and on a deeper level, no doubt, for Her own abused and usurped power.

Other evidence in Greek literature indicates that Persephone was not always Demeter's abused daughter but, rather, was herself, like Ereshkigal, queen of the underworld. Since She appears as such in the Homeric epics, which date from the late-eighth century B.C. and precede the *Hymn to Demeter* by less than a century, the shift from queen to vulnerable maiden is quite late and reflects the substantiated acceleration of male dominance during this period.[15]*

> & this is for colored girls who have considered
> suicide/but are movin to the ends of their own
> rainbows
>
> — NTOZAKE SHANGE, *for colored girls*
> *who have considered suicide/when*
> *the rainbow is enuf*

Yet despite the consolidation of patriarchal control, the hymn unequivocally acknowledges woman's power. Demeter, in response to a violent, anti-social act, refuses to extend Her procreative power to Earth as long as the violence of rape is permitted to go unpunished by the current race of man or gods. Her action demonstrates that the power of life may be withheld as well as bestowed; that is, woman embraces all of life: birth and death, creation and decay. Irreverence or abusive treatment of woman, of Earth, and of their life-giving qualities brings about inevitable destruction.

---

* Editor's Note: The shift to patriarchal mythology and culture in Greece occurred as the three waves of barbarian invaders migrated southeast from the Eurasian steppes, roughly from 2500–1000 B.C. Strains of the prepatriarchal mythology survived into the Homeric period, but the nature and sacred stories of the Goddess were transformed severely. See *Lost Goddesses of Early Greece* for summaries of classicists' discoveries of pre-Hellenic mythology. — C.S.

While Demeter withholds Her power, Zeus, distraught at the lack of "gifts and sacrifices" entailed in Her destruction of the "race of man," sends one after another of "all the blessed and eternal gods" (311; 325–26) to bribe Demeter into fertility. She staunchly refuses until Her daughter should be returned to Her. Zeus finally agrees, though He insures the maintenance of male control by tricking Persephone into eating the food of the dead. While woman has the power to create and nourish life, as well as the capacity to destroy it, man can impose only artificial controls upon the processes of life. He is always and forever incapable of wielding true power, a power which he does not and cannot have.[16]

> when She-Who-moves-the-earth will turn over
> when She Who moves, the earth will turn over.
>
> — JUDY GRAHN, *She Who*[17]

The mythology depicts woman's power. The religious festivals of ancient Greece honoring the Goddess, in which women only, or primarily, participated, celebrate woman's primal power as a fertile and creative being akin to Mother Earth and living in harmony with Her cycles. In their rituals the women thanked Mother Earth for Her continued beneficence and celebrated their Goddess and their cycles as women: birth, menses, sexuality, and aging. Both mythology — the journey to and return from the underworld, the barrenness of Mother Earth during the Goddess' absence, and the mourning over the dead son or absent daughter — and religious ritual respect the Goddess and woman's power, and they honor the seasonal cycles of Mother Earth and the stages of a woman's life.[18]

The *Hymn to Demeter* and the ancient rites of the Eleusinian Mysteries honor Demeter not only for Her power of earthly fertility but also for Her power to bestow blessedness in the next life to any initiate in Her rites. This aspect of Demeter's power probably originates with Her daughter Persephone, the former ruler of the underworld. In this role Persephone also recalls Ereshkigal, the powerful female ruler of the underworld in the earlier Sumerian and Babylonian traditions. The Goddess' life-giving power in the present world and Her transcendent power for blessedness in a future life were long revered.

Later literature portraying male heroes undertaking journeys similar to the Goddesses' suggests that self-understanding may be the metaphysical object of the quest below and may form the basis for bless-

edness in the next life. In Homer's *Odyssey* the hero Odysseus travels
to the underworld where he learns of events past, present, and future,
the special knowledge of the Muse, the source of all poetry. The
knowledge Odysseus acquires in the underworld aids him in continuing his journey homeward, that is, in eventually meeting his "self," and
in harmonizing him with woman, Mother Earth, and divinity. The
journey to the underworld is a journey inward, a beginning of the process of the unfolding of the self.[19] Thus mythology and no doubt the ritual associated with it honor the process of self-discovery, the natural
path of anyone's life journey.

Belief in a powerful Goddess and reverence for woman's life-centered
qualities inevitably affect the imagination and behavior of the people
living in such a culture. The archaeology indicates that, in fact, the
prepatriarchal cultures of the Near Eastern and Mediterranean lands
were peaceful, nonwarring societies.[20] A basic reverence for life in all
its aspects seems to be the hallmark of gynocentric, Goddess-worshipping culture.

As I come from the womb of my Mother, the Earth, you gave me life
. . . and you have given me a sacred pipe with which to learn from my relatives the wingeds, the two-leggeds, the four-leggeds, and those that live in
the waters, to walk the good road, which is red.
                                    — Introductory prayer to a position
                                      paper on Native American rights,
                                      July 1978

The resurgence of women's spirituality continues the tradition of
treating all aspects of life as sacred. I believe we are reaffirming for the
Western cultural heritage the hallowed nature of Mother Earth and of
all the beings She creates. In addition to specifically sacred rituals, our
entire behavior, whether overtly ritualistic or not, partakes of ritualistic
character in some sense. And since any action presupposes some attitude to life, spiritual beliefs create social and political realities.

Scholars of religion claim that all societies distinguish between the
sacred and profane.[21] I submit that their assertion depends on their
own miscomprehension, due to their assumption that Western idolatry
of a ranting Jewish God or of His dead Christian son epitomizes religious sentiment. Many Native American cultures, for instance, revere
Mother Earth and all life upon Her. Every piece of stone, every living
being, every human act participates in the spiritual and sacred process
of life. From the Ice Age through numerous ancient and modern socie-

ties, reverence for this process of life has been a cultural given. Recognition of woman's power frequently symbolizes this honoring of life.

> The bright-coiffed Hekate came near to them, and often did she embrace the daughter of holy Demeter; and from that time the lady Hekate was minister and companion to Persephone.
>
> — *Hymn to Demeter*, 438–440

Ancient mythology affirms woman's power. Yet, these stories, as we have them, all date from periods of patriarchal control, and the power these goddesses hold has already been muted, curtailed, and even perverted. In the classical Greek versions, the goddesses no longer retain any political power, and I do not doubt that the sororal hostility of the Sumerian and Babylonian accounts already reflects much patriarchal influence. Certain elements argue against a too literal role model. Others — the Goddess' power, Her freedom, the love between women — may unambiguously inspire our lives and our creativity.

> de poems gotta come outta my crotch?
>
> — NTOZAKE SHANGE, *Nappy Edges*

By reclaiming for ourselves the art of poetry, the creation of song, we can spin off from mythological insights and create our own guiding mythological visions for a new age.[22] Contemporary weavers have spun off into new visionary space drawing upon the mythology of ancient Greece, or of Nigeria, or upon their own inward journeys, sharing with us through their writings and art and music the process of their own unfolding, and creating old/new images of Goddess and woman power.[23] Defining ourselves as powerful frees us to create personally, socially, and artistically. Each insight, each action, every song sparks us onward.

NOTES

I wish to thank Judy Grahn for reading and commenting on the draft of this article.

1. Since our quests begin with our selves, our names may temper the direction of our journeys. Taking one's own name grows into a powerful self-affirmation. Mine combines the ancient Greek ending *-ida*,

meaning "child of," with my mother's name; so my name becomes Deborah's daughter.

2. The information on the Hindu power of speech is taken from L. Renou, *Etudes védiques et paninéennes,* I (Paris: E. de Boccard, 1955), pp. 1–12. A note on dates: Most early literature developed in an oral tradition; any dates given refer to the earliest known time that this material was written down, and thus became fixed. The dates provide little clue to the true antiquity of this material.

3. *Virgin* originally meant an independent, self-identified woman; patriarchal thought imposed the meaning of chaste onto the word. In the ancient Greek, too, an unmarried woman is *admete,* untamed. Thus the language unmistakably assesses what the institution of patriarchal marriage does to women.

4. Feminist linguists are discovering how social and political sexism has consciously affected even the roots of the language we speak. On the use of "they" as the singular indefinite pronoun see Ann Bodine, "Androcentrism in Prescriptive Grammar: singular 'they', sex-indefinite 'he', and 'he or she'," *Language in Society,* vol. 4, 1975, pp. 129–46.

5. *The Oxford English Dictionary, sub* "weave."

6. Ancient Greek distinguishes between "man" and "human being." Often, as in this case, the word translated as "man" or "men" actually means "human being" or "mortal."

7. Linda Lee Clader, "Helen: The Evolution from Divine to Heroic in Greek Epic Tradition," *Mnemosyne,* Suppl. no. 42, 1976, analyzes Helen's role as poet in the epic tradition, without, however, applying any feminist interpretation to her research.

8. The first definition is from *The Oxford English Dictionary.* The second is my own compilation from various theories about mythology. G. S. Kirk, *Myth: Its Meaning and Functions in Ancient and Other Cultures* (Berkeley: University of California Press, 1970) is a useful overview of the ancient mythology and some of the approaches to its study. The word *myth* usually refers to the story content and *mythology* to the study of myths. However, this distinction is not rigid, and I weave between them in this paper.

9. My mother would often remind me that the Old Testament also portrays women as good and powerful, such as Esther, Naomi, or Deborah. But as a child growing up, neither Esther nor Naomi offered me an unambiguous model for action, and never, in any of my classes, did I read of Deborah or hear her mentioned (Judges 4: 4–5).

10. Mary Daly, *Gyn/Ecology: The Metaethics of Radical Feminism* (Boston: Beacon Press, 1978), pp. 46 ff., eloquently and incisively

describes the process by which patriarchal mythology reversed the wise and powerful images of women.

11. The ancient civilization of Sumer is dated at about 4000–2000 B.C. and was located within the fork of the Tigris and Euphrates rivers, north of the Persian Gulf, in what is now Iran. Babylonia, or Akkad (its language being Akkadian), was situated up the rivers north of Sumer and is dated at about 2500 to 1500 B.C. The texts used here are from James B. Pritchard, *Ancient Near Eastern Texts Relating to the Old Testament* (Princeton University Press, 1955). See also his shorter handbook *The Ancient Near East* (Princeton University Press, 1958), and S. H. Hooke, *Middle Eastern Mythology* (Penguin Books, 1963).

12. Inanna does tell the gatekeeper that She has come to mourn for Her sister Ereshkigal's dead husband. However, given the hostility between them, this may be a ruse by which Inanna hopes to enter the underworld.

13. I say "apparent" because, due to the fragmentary condition of the texts, these elements may have been contained in the Sumerian account as well.

14. For the Greek and English of the ancient hymns see *Hesiod, The Homeric Hymns and Homerica,* trans. by Hugh G. Evelyn-White, Loeb Library (New York: G. P. Putnam's Sons, 1920).

15. Marylin B. Arthur, "Early Greece: The Origins of the Western Attitude towards Women," *Arethusa,* vol. 6, 1973, pp. 7–58.

16. The first section of Susan Griffin's *Woman and Nature: The Roaring Inside Her* (New York: Harper and Row, 1978), brilliantly evokes this essential distinction between woman's power and male control. Many Native American nations recognize the primal power of women: Woman, like Mother Earth, is power. Rather than seeking to destroy her power, Indian men traditionally learn to develop their own power, their medicine, to complement hers.

17. It is significant to me that at the time of this writing, and after I have done considerable work on Helen as a powerful early derivative of the Goddess, Mount St. Helens in Washington is asserting Her power.

18. Information on ancient Greek religious festivals is from Ludwig Deubner, *Attische Feste* (Hildesheim: Georg Olms Verlagsbuchhandlung, 1932), and Lewis R. Farnell, *Cults* [sic] *of the Greek States,* in four volumes (Oxford, 1896–1909). One must extrapolate from these compendia of dry evidence the nature of the living rituals. For recent discussion of the Demeter festivals, primarily of the Eleusinian Mysteries, from a strictly literary, anthropological, and Jungian perspective, see Carl Kerenyi, *Eleusis: Archetypal Image*

*of Mother and Daughter,* trans. by Ralph Manheim, Bollingen Series 65, 4 (Princeton University Press, 1967); George E. Mylonas, *Eleusis and the Eleusinian Mysteries* (Princeton University Press, 1961); and N. J. Richardson, *The Homeric Hymn to Demeter* (Oxford, 1974).

19. I highly recommend the *Odyssey* to any journeyer seeking a clue to her roots from ancient mythology. Despite the male hero, the power and journeys of the female figures pulsates strongly beneath the thin patriarchal veneer. Of some interest is Samuel Butler's *The Authoress of the Odyssey* (The University of Chicago Press, 1967; reprinted from 2nd ed., 1922).

20. As Merlin Stone has noted in *When God Was a Woman,* finding unbiased interpretation of the evidence in the records of traditional archaeology is like searching for the proverbial needle in a haystack. Those hearty souls wishing to embark on such an adventure may wish to look at Sir Arthur Evans, *The Palace of Minos,* vols. 1–4 (New York: Biblo & Tannen, 1964); R. W. Hutchinson, *Prehistoric Crete* (Baltimore: Penguin Books, 1962); James Mellaart, *Çatal Hüyük* (London: Thames and Hudson, 1967).

21. See Clifford Geertz, "Religion as a Cultural System," in *Anthropological Approaches to the Study of Religion,* ed. by Michael Banton (New York: Frederick A. Praeger, 1966), pp. 1–46. Mary Daly, *Gyn/Ecology,* pp. 48 ff., also notes this false distinction between sacred and profane as it is created and used by most religious scholars.

22. In my vocabulary I borrow freely from the Third Passage of Mary Daly's *Gyn/Ecology.*

23. Space does not permit credit to all the weavers; some have been mentioned in the text; many are creating around us every day; we need only to open our eyes, look within, and see.

# Our Heritage Is Our Power

## Judy Chicago

In the beginning, the feminine principle was seen as the fundamental cosmic force. All ancient peoples believed that the world was created by a female deity. This Goddess was conceived as bringing the universe into being either alone or in conjunction with a male consort, usually Her son, whom the Goddess created parthenogenetically. Procreation was not understood to be connected with coitus, and it was thought that woman — like the Goddess — brought forth life alone and unaided. Awe of the universe was transformed into reverence for Woman Herself, Whose body became the symbol of birth and rebirth. Woman's creative power was embodied in a multitude of female figurines that emphasized Her breasts, belly, hips, and vagina. These Mother Goddesses were worshipped everywhere and have been discovered beneath the remains of civilizations all over the world. They attest to a time when women not only were venerated, but actually had social and political power. All archaeological evidence indicates that these matriarchal cultures were egalitarian, democratic, and peaceful. But female-oriented agricultural societies gradually gave way to a male-dominated political state in which occupational specialization, commerce, social stratification, and militarism developed. As men gained control of the social and political forces, the power of the Goddess was diminished or destroyed. For the first time, the idea arose of life originating entirely from a male, rather than a female, source. It is possible to trace this changeover from matriarchy to patriarchy in the myths, legends, and images of the Goddess. First, Her original primacy gave way to gradual subordination to male gods; in some cases, the sex of the female deity was simply altered and all Her rituals and temples transferred to the male figure. Then the originally benevolent power of the Goddess began to be viewed as negative, destructive, or evil. Finally, the Judeo-Christian tradition absorbed all deities into a single male godhead. However, the Jews — like most early peoples — were matriarchal and worshipped a goddess. It required six centuries for Yahweh to replace Ashtoreth as the primary deity of the Jews; for a long time their temples were side by side. After the Jewish patriarchs succeeded in destroying Goddess worship, women came to be treated like chattel. The same story is repeated in culture after culture; in Crete, the powerful goddesses and queens, as a result of successive Greek invasions, were incorporated into Greek myths. Although by this time the Greeks were patriarchal, the Goddess tradition continued there, as it did in Rome. But Greco-Roman goddesses paled beside their historic antecedents. The position of Greek women had already deteriorated considerably and is clearly summed up by this famous remark by an Athenian philosopher: "That woman is best who is least spoken of among men, whether for good or evil." The destruction of the Goddess represented the destruction of women's political, social, and religious authority. However, women did not passively accept this loss of power, as is evidenced in myths, legends, and literature about the Amazons and various warrior queendoms. It is unknown whether women warred among themselves during the thousands of years of gynocracy, but history indicates that matriarchal societies probably engaged in warfare when their power was being challenged, in a vain effort to turn the tide. Roman women were in a similar position legally to that of their Greek predecessors, but in actuality they were much freer. Although they were considered "perpetual minors" and were subject to their fathers' and husbands' jurisdiction, public sentiment was at odds with the laws. These laws improved for a while as the result of a protest organized by Roman women, but their gains were later eroded. When Christianity first developed, there were a number of early religious communities where men and women enjoyed equal rights, partly as a result of their commitment to the idea that "in Christ there was neither male nor female." Throughout the Dark Ages, the Church offered women refuge from the invasions and violence that made them subject to capture, rape, and forcible marriage. Girls went to convents to be educated and either considered them their permanent homes or left to be married, frequently returning in later life. Those who wished to devote themselves to scholarship and the arts gathered there, with or without taking religious vows. During the early Middle Ages women gradually lost more of their property rights. In an effort to retain their lands, countless noblewomen established and ruled religious houses. These abbesses had the rights and privileges of feudal barons. They usually were members of the royal family and acted as representatives of the kings during their absences. They often administered vast lands; managed convents, abbeys, and double monasteries; provided their own troops in wartime; had the right of coinage; and were consulted in political and religious affairs. In the later Middle Ages, the family emerged as the most stable social force of the secular world, and women —who were central to the family—achieved greater freedom. They could own and administer property and, in their husbands' absences, managed the estates, presided over the courts, signed treaties, made laws, and, in some cases, commanded troops. The improved status of women was manifested in the growing worship of the Virgin Mary. As Christianity spread throughout Europe, it absorbed indigenous religious practices, especially the continued worship of the Goddess. In an effort to obtain converts, the Church allowed this worship to be transferred to the figure of Mary, whose image was derived from the ancient Goddess with Her son/lover on her lap. By the end of the Middle Ages, the Church was well established and was no longer willing to tolerate a female deity. Moreover, church fathers did not need women's help in spreading Christian doctrine, as they had in earlier centuries. They began to attack the last vestiges of Mother Goddess worship and to restrict women's power in the Church. In some cases, Mother Goddess worship was tied to the practice of Witchcraft, which the Church tolerated for centuries. But church fathers felt more and more threatened by the power of women in the covens. In addition, a number of heretical sects had developed where women were allowed to preach, which incensed the Church. When the Church joined hands with the State to build the social and political institutions that are the foundation of modern society, they eliminated all who resisted their authority: Witches; Christian heretics and non-Christians; lay healers, who practiced medicine despite the objections of male physicians; political dissenters and peasant leaders, many of whom were women; and those who protested the destruction of what was left of female power. Witch hunts were prevalent from the thirteenth through the seventeenth centuries. According to male scholars, no more than three hundred thousand people were exterminated, but contemporary feminist scholars are beginning to suspect that there were probably between six and nine million killed. Eighty-five percent of those executed were women. By the late Renaissance women had little independent power, for the economic and political base that had supported their medieval predecessors had disappeared. The decline of feudalism, the contraction of women's position, and the advent of the Witch hunts created a situation in which women were steadily forced into submission. By the time of the Reformation, when the convents were dissolved, women's education — formerly available through the Church — had virtually come to an end. Women were barred from the universities, guilds, and professions; women's property and inheritance rights, slowly eroded over centuries, were totally eliminated. Marriage became the only acceptable option for women. To the Reformers, the intellectual aspirations of women were not only an absurdity, but a positive peril. They never tired of repeating that women's learning should be restricted to reading and writing for the purpose of teaching the Bible to their children. Reformation leaders insisted that a woman's sole duty was silent obedience to her husband. Within the family, women did enjoy a certain respect. Their lives were busy and productive; work was centered in the home, and the activities of all the family members were crucial to its economic survival. The Industrial Revolution, however, took work out of the house, and the consequent separation between work and home had a profound effect on women's condition. Their work ceased to have importance as far as the world's values were concerned; women were expected to be the leisured helpmates of men. This, coupled with the development of the Victorian ideal of a passive and dependent wife, made women's lives so narrow, their options so few, there is little wonder that a women's revolution began. In 1792, Mary Wollstonecraft published a book which provided the foundation for feminist theory and the subsequent revolution. She argued that if women failed to become men's equals, the progress of human knowledge and virtue would be halted, and, moreover, that the tyranny of men had to be broken both politically and socially if women were to become free. In 1848, a group of American women met in Seneca Falls, New York, and addressed themselves to eighteen grievances. They demanded the right to vote, to be educated, to enter any occupation, to have control over their bodies, to sign legal papers, to manage their earnings, and to own and administer property. At first the outcry was enormous, and women were ordered back to their "place." The women persisted, however, and in less than a century they changed many laws that had restricted their lives. Moreover, they built a movement that was international. All over the world, women were agitating for their rights. It seemed that no force could stop them and that equality was in sight. But the initial thrust of the women's revolution was met by a counter force that began to push women back into the confines of the home. This time, women were restricted not by laws but by guilt and ignorance. They were told that the fight for women's rights had been won, and that their experience to the contrary was untrue. They were made to feel guilty for their aspirations and were convinced that, somehow, their desire to be free threatened men. Most of all, women were deprived of any knowledge of their foremothers' efforts. The women's revolution was obscured, as our entire heritage has been obscured. I have been personally strengthened and transformed not only by discovering the efforts women have made in the last two centuries, but also by realizing that women have fought for their dignity and their rights from the moment they first lost their Goddess and their power. *The Dinner Party* is a symbolic history of our past, pieced together — like the Heritage Floor — from small fragments which tell us something about our achievements and our condition throughout Western civilization. The women represented are either historical or mythological figures; I have brought them together — invited them to dinner, so to speak — that we might hear what they have to say and see the range and beauty of a heritage we have not yet had an opportunity to know. Sadly, most of the 1,038 women included in *The Dinner Party* are unfamiliar, their lives and achievements unknown to most of us. To make people feel worthless, society robs them of their pride; this has happened to women. All the institutions of our culture tell us — through words, deeds, and even worse, silence — that we are insignificant. But our heritage is our power; we can know ourselves and our capacities by seeing that other women have been strong. To reclaim our past and insist that it become a part of human history is the task that lies before us, for the future requires that women, as well as men, shape the world's destiny.

# PART TWO

# Manifesting
# Personal Power

# Consciousness/
# Energy/Action

. . . Many years back
a woman of strong purpose
passed through this section
and everything else tried to follow.

— JUDY GRAHN

# Consciousness/
# Energy/Action

In the early years of the second wave of feminism, we raised consciousness—from the low levels of unawareness and acceptance of patriarchal lies. This process must continue as long as the lies are perpetuated. Most people still think within the constructs of patriarchal
dualisms, e.g., mind vs. body, culture vs. nature, the conscious vs. the
unconscious, good vs. evil. In that system, women are aligned with the
"negative" half of all the pairs. Moreover, patriarchy tries hard to
equate the very nature of woman with contemptible impotence. As
Phyllis Chesler demonstrated in Women and Madness, "Most twentieth-century women who are psychiatrically labeled, privately treated,
and publicly hospitalized are not mad. . . . They may be deeply un-
happy, self-destructive, economically powerless, and sexually impotent
—but as women they're supposed to be." Again, woman as the despica-
ble "other."

In struggling to shed the consciousness of "the other," we also realized the power of creating our own consciousness. We defined ourselves. We expressed woman's relationship to our society and the world.
We began, at last, to own our souls once again.

The giant steps we have taken toward reclaiming our psyches have obviously affected our politics. Consciousness, not only of injustice but also of the possibility of a saner mode of living for everyone, is both the impetus and the sustaining force of our movement. That state of mind generates energy for our political work. In fact, a major discovery for many women has been that we can generate energy at will, using various techniques; tapping the power of the mind dispels our sense of vulnerability. Feminist consciousness emphasizes the value of process; we are not interested in using hierarchical, top-down, alienating methods to achieve reforms within patriarchal systems. Our political actions are informed by holistic ways of thinking. We see complexity and connectedness.

Consciousness can be fed from arational as well as rational sources, and women's ritual has emerged as a channel for that nourishment. Ritual empowers and sustains us in our beliefs and commitments. It is an area in which women have moved beyond myriad patriarchal conscriptions of the mind and body. We declare what is meaningful to us, and we honor it in our own ways. A deeply felt solidarity with all women results.

> I know myself linked by chains of fires
> To every woman who has kept a hearth.
> In the resinous smoke
> I smell hut, castle, cave,
> Mansion and hovel,
> See in the shifting flame my mother
> And grandmothers out over the world.

—ELSA GIDLOW

C.S.

# A Consciousness Manifesto

# Nancy F. W. Passmore

As consciousness changes, our personal and collective worlds change. An explanatory vision is a function of time and space: Things make sense according to our perceptions of them now. This is now and for now.

Today we are witnessing the merger of two explanatory approaches that Western tradition has long held to be opposites. As the frontiers of our sciences are pushed farther and farther — "*Eureka!*" — they arrive in the territory of the mystic and metaphysician. Reports of altered states of consciousness and parapsychological possibilities are not so bizarre in juxtaposition with the truly revolutionary parameters of the new physics.

## THE EVOLUTION OF THE REVOLUTION

Throughout recorded history, knowledge of the universe seems to have increased, both by the collection of facts and by the quality and precision of the way these facts are organized into a system. This progression has not, however, been a smooth linear flow. There have been certain "breakthroughs," sudden advances in human thought, in which problems were reexamined and all previous ideas modified.

Before the sixth century B.C., the universe was perceived as comfortable, reassuring, and maternal. That centennial "moment," however, produced Gautama Buddha, Confucius, Lao-Tsu, the Ionian philosophers, and Pythagoras, all of whom had a profound effect on human thought.

The Pythagoreans were empirical observers who believed that celestial bodies obeyed certain laws which could be expressed numerically. They attempted the first grand synthesis (in the West) attempting to combine religion, medicine, astronomy, and music into an explanatory whole. During the following century, Philolaus introduced the idea that the Earth moved around a "celestial fire" in the same way as other celestial bodies. Although Earth retained a "privileged" position, it was no longer the center of all things. The influence of Aristotle put the Earth back in the center of things, and his notion was followed by orthodox scientists for nearly fifteen centuries!

After the Macedonian conquest of Greece, there followed a period of orthodoxy and decline. The Aristotelian categories became the "grammar of existence," and his philosophy/spirit ruled the world of science; the fifteen-century "hold" on scientific thought resulted. Not only was progress halted, but knowledge was actually lost. In the fifth century B.C., the educated classes believed that the Earth was a spherical body, floating in space and spinning on its axis. One thousand years later, it was, in the popular view, a flat disk!

During the twelfth century A.D., there were signs of a reawakening, a remembering. Unfortunately, that was also the time of the supremely patriarchal alliance between the theology of St. Thomas Aquinas and the physics/thought of Aristotle: the worldview that furthered the Church's domination of Western Europe, and the new orthodoxy, which burned Witches and other rebels and created three centuries of sterility and stagnation for all. That logjam was ultimately broken during the Scientific Revolution and culminated in the Newtonian synthesis; a long period of assimilation followed, during which the mechanistic view of reality became accepted.

In the late-nineteenth and early-twentieth centuries, a quantum leap occurred that shattered the comfortable assurances of Newtonian "truth": It was the amazing synthesis of previously separate areas of thought/investigation. The sciences of electricity and magnetism merged, with electromagnetism accounting for light, color, and radiant heat. Chemistry was engulfed by atomic physics. Biologists uncovered electrochemical processes within living matter. The previously independent "powers of nature" were seen to be convertible into one another. They were simply different forms of "energy."

Soon matter went the same way. All the elements of chemistry were found to be composed of the same building blocks in different combinations. Finally, the building blocks themselves became nothing but parcels of compressed energy.

Meanwhile, on a macro level, the sun, previously thought to lie at the center of the Milky Way, was demoted to its place in a spiral arm. Then the whole galaxy, thought to be a sort of island-universe, was relegated to being merely a single example of thousands of millions of galaxies, each with its own suns and planets!

Einstein's theories of relativity have shown that space and time are not absolute and that matter and energy are intimately connected. The velocity of light (186,300 miles/second) dominates the whole Theory of Relativity and is the only "constant" in a universe in flux. On this constant depend all human standards of time/space. Light velocity is a constant, not because there is an absolute value in 186,300 miles/second, but because no material body (the mass of which increases with its velocity) can ever attain the speed of light.

Paralleling these ideas on a quantum level, Bohr, Heisenberg, and others showed that the presence of the observer, and the instruments of investigation, actually affect the behavior of subatomic particles. The "objective observer" hence was added to the list of post-nuclear fatalities. The formerly basic ingredients of the atomic/material universe (currently, about one hundred elementary particles have been identified) refuse bondage within the traditional either/or boundaries of dichotomous thought. They behave on some occasions as if they were particles, miniature lumps of matter, and on other occasions like waves.

According to the Theory of Relativity, time and space are not only "not absolute," but are changed by gravitational fields. An interesting phenomenon is the black hole, where mass approaches the infinitely small and gravity approaches the infinitely large (from the point of view of the observer) and has the effect of "sucking in" everything around it, including light! If we were to take two identical rulers and could move one toward a black hole, it would actually stretch, become longer than its twin, relative to the observer. Space, then, expands in a strong gravitational field. A similar phenomenon would occur with time: If we were to observe two clocks, the one close to the black hole would "run slow," relative to the observer. Time slows down in a strong gravitational field. (Once we acknowledge that time can flow at different rates, we can begin to understand how "para"normal phenomena, such as precognition, can be understood as natural and physical events.)

Gravitation, then, appears to act like Alice's "Eat Me" and "Drink Me" experiences in which she becomes larger and smaller. Einstein's ideas make more sense, and are more accessible, with an expanded awareness that allows us to experience these concepts on more than just an intellectual level.

What physicists mean by curvature of space is equivalent to gravitational fields. As space experiences a strong curvature (which may be either positive and spherical, or negative and hyperbolic), a strong distortion of space-time occurs. Matter is not, then, an independent entity dropped into a preexisting space and time. Rather, it is a barometer, an expression, of the curvature of space. The effects of curvature are important only in very large or very small scales of space/time, which is where the separate investigations of relativity and quantum theory may indeed re-merge.

## OPTIONS IN OUTLOOKS

Our personal outlooks often have not kept abreast with science, thus perhaps postponing a good deal of liberation, freedom, and "para"normal power. The recent and on-going revolution in physics has yet to be incorporated into philosophy and psychology; most of us are still existing in a kind of Newtonian head-set of causality, determinism, and materialism. The advances in science did, however, bring a different kind of revolution to human affairs, a new revolutionary potential for the life or death for the whole of humanity. The ways in which this knowledge has been dispensed (mostly by and for men) and used (e.g., as weaponry at Hiroshima and Nagasaki) seems to have focused on its most devastating possibilities. It remains (as an imperative!) to explore these themes in terms of other possible realms of consciousness, particularly those related to intuition, psychic phenomena, alpha brain waves, and the female psyche.

Every facet of Western metaphysical thought assumes a separation:

material/spiritual, male/female, nomena/phenomena, infinite/finite, *ad infinitum!* All "approved" knowledge is based on implicit metaphysics as well as empirical reality. Patriarchy is the cornerstone of feudalism, mercantilism, capitalism, and the one-way thinking of causality. To break through this thirty-five-hundred-year-old tradition requires radically new thought/experience about the patterns of reality.

Contrary to popular belief, science, like poetry, or architecture, or painting, has its genres, movements, and fashions. Historically, cycles of differentiation and specialization are followed by reintegrations on a higher level. This is analogous to the process that biologists perceive with the coded information held in the double helix of our chromosomes and the implications for conscious evolution. The decisive phase in the historic cycle appears as the confluence of previously separate branches of science or as a cross-fertilization between different disciplines or techniques. The collections of new data are selective processes guided by considerations of a metaphysical, theoretical, or aesthetic nature. Successful theories (e.g., Special Relativity) are built on data that has been available for a long time; someone simply rearranges the mosaic of "hard facts" into a different pattern. The progress of science is neither continuous nor cumulative, in the strict sense, and discoveries are often forgotten, or ignored, and rediscovered later on. Jane Roberts, in *The Nature of Personal Reality*, addresses the temporal nature of our psychological environment:

At any given time there will be various climates of belief pervading the world. Remember that ideas *are* as natural as the weather. They follow patterns, then, and obey certain laws even as more strictly physical phenomena do. Unfortunately, no one examines the nature of mental reality from such a viewpoint. You will be born in the midst of certain mass beliefs, and these may vary according to the country of your nativity. As you come into your body with all of its physical surroundings, so at birth do you emerge into a rich natural psychological environment in which beliefs and ideas are every bit as real.[1]

Literacy, and the whole Aristotelian, patriarchal worldview, tends to categorize, to label, to name, and to impose a linear quality upon our perceptions of reality. Even the act of reading/writing compartmentalizes logic, meaning, and the resultant worldview or reality-picture into segments that appear to occur sequentially, further reinforcing linear thinking.

Science and mathematics have a concept that may be helpful in traveling beyond this reality rut. Progressions that are arithmetic relate to the linear; the beta-mentality; the Western time/space perceptual dogma; the quantitative, Aristotelian physics; and assorted modes of belief that have been built upon these notions. There is another type of progression, however: the geometric. This relates to the quantum leap, the alpha-mentality, the synchronicity and relativity of space/time, the qualitative, the psychic, and the creative. The second cluster does not operate by the same laws, rules, and regulations as the first. It challenges the homeostatic inertia, the "Newtonian gravity" of the first. Although they can intersect in space and time, they are quite literally separate realities: Evoking the laws of one to explain the other is necessarily a hopeless task.

Knowledge grows by moving from the known into the unknown. Historically, perhaps, it is easier to see that science, poetry, and art open their own continuum, while simultaneously the form chosen creates its own content. This is not *logical*, in the same way that a sphere cannot be described using Euclidian geometry. Yet this sort of cross-referenced multi-potentiality seems common among scientists, artists, psychics, and other creative people.

The contemporary scientific revolution has effected the dissolution of one of the most extensive superstitious beliefs of the age: the materialistic, mechanistic, clock-work universe of nineteenth-century physics. But perhaps all of this need not even be considered on the old true/false scale; perhaps it can be used merely to temporarily suspend our disbeliefs. Remember, when Kepler postulated that the moon effected the tides on earth, Galileo dismissed the hypothesis as "occult fancy." It involved action at a distance, and, therefore, violated the "solid laws of nature" of that time. Now these laws of nature (as they were understood by classical physics only a century ago) have already been transcended; this progression should gently hint to us that many of the solid laws of our day are beliefs that obscure the otherwise obvious.

It is important to make a distinction between "progress in science" and its explanatory power. This power for explanation depends upon the kind of question being asked. History shows that the questions change with changing beliefs/values in both time and space, periods and cultures. The creative leap comes as a sudden insight or realization, often when specialized data are referred to apparently unrelated facts and the whole becomes a new synthesis.

The traditional scientific, arithmetic mode of thinking involves the creation of a theory or hypothesis and then the collecting of empirical evidence, the data. In a very literal sense, this is a common process of creating reality. The female, long accused of illogical thinking, has often shunned this process (through socialization, biology, or "accident") and can, potentially, reverse this order. I suspect that herein lies the potential for a quantum cracking of the Aristotelian-patriarchal egg. This *ability* to be receptive, intuitive, and arational can put the "data" sequentially before the "theory," the "answer" before the "question." Or as the Red Queen admonished Alice, "It is a poor sort of memory that only works one way."[2]

## WOMEN AND THE NEW CONSCIOUSNESS

Feminism is primarily a revolution of consciousness, having countless forms of political expression and action. Consciousness is where power lies, in the mass reclaiming of "the psychic powers you've always had."[3] More narrowly political movements can be infiltrated, co-opted, and generally ripped off by aliens of all kinds. The quantum leap in consciousness cannot, by its very nature, be infiltrated.

It is possible that women are especially suited to pioneer the implications and applications of the newly discovered dimensions of consciousness. We are the guardians of the human race, the medium for the incarnation of beings on this planet. Certainly the distinction between me and not-me becomes a little blurry, to say the least, when one has been inhabited as a mother. Instinctively, we honor that profound dance of matter/energy/consciousness. Long before masculist science decided it would be exciting to get involved with recombinant DNA research, women were carrying on the program of human evolution, deciding — consciously or unconsciously — which combinations of genetic material/information would become manifest. Perhaps there are *only* women and children in this world; some of us are one or the other, many of us are both.

Maybe "intuitive flashes," long denigrated as women's arational habits, are simply examples of quantum leaps beyond space/time. In any case, it is possible to allow ourselves to become more receptive to these connections. This is not a linear act of will, but an awareness of harmonies. Basic energy relationships manifest concurrently throughout an indefinite number of levels of perception, and we necessarily perceive/experience the relationship differently at different levels. What is needed is an awareness (however momentary) to help us to discard archaic systems of belief. Again, this is not an act of will, but a coming into alignment, embracing those energies/harmonics whereby the "para"normal events/experiences happen. When experience and thought are one, consciousness changes.

There are an increasing number of individuals who can perform "miracles," make things bend, levitate, disappear, or materialize with consciousness. Young children watching such performances on television also make things bend, or move, or disappear — because they believe it! It's already happening. These phenomena are merely signs, the aim being not a world full of magicians, but rather an opening toward an awareness of possibilities. By tapping inner power (via Witchcraft, meditation, certain drugs, pregnancy, fasting, or what-you-will), we allow the possibilities of consciousness, and perhaps realize in many ways the discoveries of theoretical physics:

• Time and space are not absolute.
• Matter and energy are not separate realities.
• The physical universe does not exist independently of its participators/observers.
• There is an intimate connection between the universes.
• We construct ourselves and each other; as perceived from inside space/time, these units are biogravitational, self-organizing fields. Gravity and living systems are non-linear to the extent that we self-organize.

## A CONSCIOUSNESS MANIFESTO

> Imagination is more important than knowledge.
> — ALBERT EINSTEIN[4]

There is a phenomenal amount of energy locked into this gravitational space/time. How "many" aware individuals it will take to release that energy toward a transformation in consciousness (the most essential revolution of all) is "up for grabs." The crucial issue is not quantitative, but the realization that there are no divisions, that there is consciousness in everything. There is nothing we can do to stop the expansion of awareness that there are layers of universes, but we can help it to come by allowing it to come. The interpenetration of the universes has begun, and we don't need a spaceship or other paraphernalia to participate! The *process* has already begun, and it has no end.

The classical political notion that a system moves along some definite, linear path must yield to the revolutionary concept that a system can make transitions in all directions at once.

Don't waste space/time attacking dead concepts (nor life/time reviving them!). Use anything and everything, from Witchcraft to quantum theory, to allow yourself to believe/understand how reality is created.

Realize that divisions and separations exist only in our limited perceptions. Every thought you have directly affects every event in all the universes. Awareness means participating in your own evolution. Expand to the limits $E = mc^2$! Take direct responsibility.

Failure is impossible.
—Susan B. Anthony

NOTES

1. Jane Roberts, *The Nature of Personal Reality* (Englewood Cliffs, N.J.: Prentice-Hall, 1974), p. 284.
2. Lewis Carroll, *Alice in Wonderland* (New York: Washington Square Press, 1951), p. 176.
3. Kathleen Klimek and Ann Valliant, *The Womancraft Manual* (Roxbury, MA: Womancircle, Inc., 1976).
4. Alexander Moszkowski, *Conversations With Einstein* (New York: Horizon Press, 1970).

# Consciousness, Politics, and Magic

## Starhawk

All movements seek change. The quests and struggles of our time — the spiritual and the social, the personal and the collective, the magical and the political — all come from a deep recognition of the need for major changes in our society and ourselves, for new visions and the power to make them real. But too often the struggle seems hopeless. Our energy and our creative vision are drained by the constant battle to stop the forces of destruction. The enemies are amorphous, invisible, yet omnipresent — or there are too many enemies, too many burial sites for chemical wastes, too many fingers on the trigger, too many irresponsible corporations, too many weapons already in the stockpiles, too many jobless, too many nuclear reactors, too many rapists at large, too many hopeless, and too many people in power who are unconcerned, who feel they are not part of this world. Our efforts are too easily scattered among the women's groups, the anti-nuke groups, the Third World groups, the gay rights groups, the ecology groups, the anti-corporate groups, among the whole list which we sense is somehow connected — and yet the connections too often seem unclear.

This essay is an attempt to name the links, to name what we are fighting against, to name what we are working to create. An ancient magical principle tells us that when you can name a thing you can influence it, so this is a work of magic, defined as "the art of causing change in accordance with will." The destructive forces draw their power from the consciousness that supports them. If there is hope for the continuance of life on Earth, it may well lie with magic, which has also been called "the art of changing consciousness at will."

One technique of changing consciousness is to hold two seemingly contradictory thoughts in your mind at the same time, until they are no longer contradictory. For example:

> Reality shapes consciousness.
> Consciousness shapes reality.

As you read, your consciousness is shaped by the reality of these words on the page. That reality, in turn, was shaped by my consciousness as I wrote, and my consciousness is shaped, at this moment, by all the many realities of my being and my environment.

The broad realities shaping our collective consciousness do not allow much comfort. Those of us born after World War II have never known a world in which the possibility of global annihilation was not a reality. We have never known security. We know that the pesticides on our crops cause cancer, that underground contaminants continue to spread. We have never felt confident that we would leave a hopeful future to our children. As women living in a patriarchy, our consciousness is shaped by many limitations. The threat of rape, to name only one, makes us fear the dark and the streets after nightfall, fear lonely beaches and isolated trails. That fear, in turn, shapes and limits the world we experience. Like sex, race, class, education, and health are all forces that determine the possibilities and the realities of individual lives.

We are taught to look at these realities as separate, taught that rape is a separate issue from nuclear war, that women's struggle for equal pay is not related to a Black teenager's struggle to find a job, or to the struggle to prevent the export of a nuclear reactor to a site on a web of earthquake faults near active volcanoes in the Philippines. But all of these realities are shaped by the underlying consciousness that shapes our society, our economic and social systems, our technology, our science, our religions, our views of women and men and of races and cultures that differ from our own, our sexuality, our gods and our wars, and is presently shaping the destruction of the world.

I call this consciousness *estrangement*[1] because its essence is that we do not see ourselves as part of the world — we are strangers to nature, to other human beings, to parts of ourselves. We see the world as being made up of separate, isolated, non-alive parts (not even dead — since death implies life — but inert matter), which have no inherent value.

## THE CONSCIOUSNESS OF ESTRANGEMENT

> He says that he is not part of this world,
> that he was set on this world as a stranger.
> — SUSAN GRIFFIN, *Woman and Nature*

Estrangement is the culmination of a long, historical process. Its roots lie in the Bronze Age shift from matrifocal, Earth-centered cultures, whose religions centered around the Goddess and the gods embodied in nature, to patriarchal, urban cultures of conquest, whose gods inspired and supported war.[2] Yahweh of the Old Testament is a prime example, promising his "Chosen People" dominion over plant and animal life and over other peoples whom they were encouraged to attack and conquer. Christianity deepened the split, establishing a duality between spirit and matter that identified flesh with nature and both with woman/ sexuality, and all three with the Devil as forces of evil. God was envisioned as male — uncontaminated by the processes of birth, nurturing, growth, menstruation, and the decay of the flesh — removed from this world to a transcendent realm of spirit somewhere else. Goodness and true value were removed from nature and the world as well. As Engels saw it, "Religion is essentially the emptying of man and nature of all content, the transferring of this content to the phantom of a distant God who then in his turn graciously allows something from his abundance to come to human beings and to nature."[3]

The removal of content, of value, served as the basis for the exploitation of nature. According to Lynn White, a historian of science, when the spirits *in* natural objects, which formerly had protected nature from man, evaporated under the influence of Christianity, man's effective monopoly on spirit in this world was confirmed, and the old inhibitions to the exploitation of nature crumbled.[4] No longer were the groves and forests sacred; the very notion of a sacred grove, assuming spirit in nature, was condemned as idolatrous. But when nature is empty of spirit, forest and trees become merely timber,[5] something to be measured in board feet, valued only for its usefulness or profitability.

The removal of content from human beings is, in the same way, the basis for human exploitation. The exploited are seen as less real, less human than the exploiters, a subspecies. On a biological level, it is possible that subspeciation removes inhibitions against harming one's own kind. On a psychological level, removing the human content from a class of human beings prevents identification and empathy: The oppressors see themselves as the embodiment of what value trickles back into the world; the women, the workers, the chicks-kaffirs-spics-geeks-Chinks-niggers are not seen as beings whose own lives contain inherent value, but as empty objects, valued only for their usefulness to those in power, their profitability. The removal of the Divine from nature — from *our* nature — legitimates hierarchy and domination.

Male imagery of God transfers value back to men in patriarchal society and legitimates male rule. The whiteness of God — the identification of all good with light and evil with dark, and the dualism which sees the two as opposed instead of interdependent — legitimates white rule over those with darker skin. The hierarchy is so long-standing that it does not change even when our belief in a white, male, omnipotent God falters.

As we become separate, manipulated objects, we lose our own sense of self-worth, our belief in our own content, and we acquiesce in our own exploitation. When women see men as embodying the *content* of the culture, and ourselves as not possessing inherent value, we submit to the rule of men and voluntarily devote our energies and talents to further men's desires instead of our own. Historically, Christianity has attempted to reconcile workers, slaves, women, and people of color to their position as inferiors by denying value to the conditions of this life and assigning it to some future existence in heaven, where the meek and submissive will be rewarded.

Because we doubt our own content, we doubt the evidences of our senses and the lessons of our own experience. We see our own drives and desires as inherently chaotic and destructive, in need of repression and control, just as we see nature as a wild, chaotic force, in need of order imposed by human beings.

In *The Death of Nature*, Carolyn Merchant documents the processes by which the rise of modern science and the economic needs of preindustrial capitalism in the sixteenth and seventeenth centuries shifted the "normative image" of the world from that of a living organism to that of a dead machine, which supported exploitation of nature on a scale previously unknown.[6] The "machine image" — the view of the world as isolated, non-alive parts, blindly moving on their own — grew out of a Christian context in which divinity and spirit had long been removed from matter. Modern, patriarchal science undermined belief in the last repository of spirit, killing off God after He had sucked the life out of the world and leaving nothing but the littered corpses, the hierarchical patterns of our institutions, from the Church to the army to the government to the corporation — all formed in the image of the patriarchal God with His subordinated troops of angels, engaged in perpetual war with the patriarchal Devil and his subordinate troops of demons. No longer do we see ourselves even with the dubious dignity of being flawed images of God; instead, we imagine ourselves in the image of the machine, flawed computers with faulty childhood "programming." Or, to quote my four-year-old friend Bill, we sense, when fatigued, that our "batteries are tired."

We are left in the empty world described *ad nauseum* in contemporary art, literature, and music — from Sartre to punk rock. In the empty world, we trust only what can be measured, counted, acquired. The organizing principle of society becomes what Marcuse termed "the performance principle": the stratification of society according to the economic performance of its members.[7] Content is removed from work itself, which is not organized according to its usefulness or true value, but according to its ability to create profits. Those who actually produce goods or offer services are less well rewarded than those engaged in managing, counting, or stimulating false needs. And in the business section of the newspapers, oil company V.P.s deny that their corporations are in the business of providing Americans with fuel and energy — rather, they are in the business of providing their investors with profits.

Science and technology, based on principles of isolation and domination of nature, grow crops and lumber with pesticides and herbicides that also cause birth defects, nerve damage, and cancer when they infiltrate our food and water supplies. Claiming a high order of rationality, technologists build nuclear reactors, which produce wastes that will be dangerous for a quarter of a million years, and consign the wastes to storage containers that last thirty to fifty years.

Estrangement permeates our educational systems, with its separate and isolated disciplines. It determines our understanding of the human mind and the capabilities of consciousness, our psychology. Freud viewed human drives and libido as, essentially, a dangerous, chaotic force, at odds with the "reality principle" of the ego. The behaviorists assure us that we are only what can be measured — only behavioral patterns of stimulus and response. Jung replaced a transcendent God with a set of transcendent archetypes, a slight improvement, but one which still leaves us estranged from placing value in our own images and experiences.[8]

Sexuality, under the rule of the Father God, is identified with the opposition — with the forces of nature, woman, life, death, and decay that threaten man's pristine abstraction and so are considered evil.[9] In the empty world of the machine, when religious strictures fall away, sex becomes another arena of performance, another commodity to be bought and sold. The erotic becomes the pornographic: Women are seen as objects empty of value except as they can be used. The sexual experience becomes one of domination, charged with rage, fear, and violence.

And so we live our lives feeling powerless and inauthentic, feeling that the real people are somewhere else, that the characters on the daytime soap operas or the conversations on the late-night talk shows are more real than the people and the conversations in our lives, that the movie stars, the celebrities, the rock stars, the *People* magazine people live out the real truth and drama of our times, while we exist as shadows, as if our unique lives, our losses, our passions — which cannot be counted out or measured, which were not approved or graded or sold to us at a discount and cannot be marketed — are not the true value of this world.

## THE CONSCIOUSNESS OF IMMANENCE

Estrangement permeates our society so thoroughly that to us it seems to *be* consciousness itself; even the language for other possibilities has disappeared or been deliberately twisted. Yet, another form of consciousness is possible, indeed, has existed from earliest times. It underlies other cultures and has survived even in the West in hidden streams. This is the consciousness I call *immanence* — the awareness of the world and everything in it as alive, dynamic, interdependent, and interacting, infused with moving energies: a living being, a weaving dance.

The symbol, the "normative image," of immanence is the Goddess:

the Divine embodied in nature, in human beings, in the flesh. The Goddess Herself is not one image but many, a constellation of forms and associations — earth, air, fire, water, moon and star, sun, flower and seed, willow and apple, black, red, white, Maiden, Mother, and Crone. She includes the male in Her aspects: He becomes child and consort, stag and bull, grain and reaper, light and dark. The femaleness of the Goddess is primary because it represents the bringing of life into the world. "The Goddess," as symbol, tells us that the world itself is the content of the world, its true value, its heart and its soul.

Historically, the cultures that were centered around the Goddess and gods embodied in nature underlie all the later patriarchal cultures. Images of the Goddess are the first known images of worship, found in Paleolithic sites. The beginnings of agriculture, weaving, pottery, writing, building, city-dwelling — all the arts and sciences upon which later civilizations developed — began in cultures of the Goddess.

When patriarchy became the ruling force in Western culture, remnants of the religions and culture based on immanence were preserved by "Pagans" (from the Latin word meaning "country dweller"), i.e., by country people, in folk customs, in "occult" tradition, and in covens of Witches.[10] The cultures of Native Americans and other tribal peoples in Africa, Asia, and Polynesia were also based on a worldview of immanence, which saw spirit and transformative power embodied in the natural world.

Ironically, as estranged science and technology advance, they have begun to bring us back to a consciousness of immanence. Modern physics no longer speaks of separate, discrete atoms of dead matter, but of waves of energy, probabilities, patterns that change as they are observed, and recognizes what shamans and Witches have always known: Matter and energy are not separate forces, but different forms of the same thing.

If we could change the prevailing mode of consciousness in our society from estrangement to immanence, the implications would be felt in every area of life. Immanence, expressed in the image of the Goddess, dispels the roots of estrangement. Good, true value, is not found in some heaven, some abstract otherworld, but in female bodies and their offspring, in nature and in the world. Nature is seen as having its own, inherent order, of which human beings are a part. Human nature, needs, drives, and desires are not dangerous impulses in need of repression and control, but are themselves expressions of the order inherent in being. The evidences of our senses and our experience are evidences of the Divine — the moving energy that unites all being.

Immanence is inherently anti-hierarchical. When each being carries her/his own value, there is no rationale for setting one group to serve another, for aiding one class or one race to dominate another. Joy and satisfaction cannot be postponed for an afterlife in another world; this world, this life is its own justification.

In a technological society, an economic system based on immanence would view the natural and human resources of a society as an energy network, made up of interdependent parts. Our ideas of ownership would have to change; "owning" land or oil fields or mineral rights might become as incomprehensible to us as it was to the Native Americans. If the land and wilderness were seen as having inherent value, as *beings* in their own right, we could not exploit them callously or carelessly. Nor could we exploit ourselves; we would demand that the work we do have value in and of itself and that it serve a real need if it could not offer us pleasure and satisfaction in the doing.

For women, the symbol of the Goddess is profoundly liberating, restoring a sense of authority and power to the female body and all the life processes — birth, growth, lovemaking, aging, and death. In Western culture, the association of women and nature has been used to devalue both. The immanent Goddess does not challenge the association; instead, this consciousness imparts to both women and nature the highest value. At the same time, culture is no longer seen as something removed from and opposed to nature. Culture is an outgrowth of nature — a product of human beings, who are part of the natural world. The Goddess of nature is also the muse, the inspiration of culture, and women are full participants in creating and furthering culture, art, literature, and science. The Goddess as Mother embodies creativity as much as biological motherhood. She represents women's authority over our own life processes, our right to choose consciously how and when and what we will create.

The female image of divinity does not, however, provide a justification for the oppression of men. The female, who gives birth to the male, includes the male in a way that male divinities cannot include the female. The Goddess gives birth to a pantheon that is inclusive rather than exclusive; She is not "a jealous God." She is often seen with a male aspect — Child or Consort — and, in Witchcraft, with the Horned God of animal life, feeling, and vital energy. Manifesting within human beings and nature, the Goddess and God express the content and value of human nature, drives, desires, and emotions.

When nature is seen as having its own inherent order, that order becomes the model for human organization, replacing the artificial hierarchy of order-imposed-from-without that presently governs human society and our relationship to nature. In the natural order, structures tend to be cellular and decentralized, composed of many small units rather than one large mass. Diversity, instead of uniformity, is valued, both between groups and within groups. There is no monotheistic model of an approved dogma, a "politically correct" line to take. The Goddess Herself is not a belief or a dogma; She is a symbol for a transformative understanding of what is already here, what we know, what we can become. She is a real power, the name we give the binding force that holds together the universe.

## THE ART OF CHANGING CONSCIOUSNESS AT WILL

Politically minded people often question the need for the symbol, for dragging the spiritual, the religious, into the political arena. Yet seeing the spiritual and the political as unrelated is itself a mark of estrangement. When "religion" is confined to patriarchal religions that remove the content from the world, then it is true that focus on the "spiritual" can undermine efforts for political and social change. But political movements that try to challenge patriarchal institutions without examining the consciousness that creates those structures often themselves get caught in estranged patterns. Members may give over their sense of value and content to "the Movement" and then "burn out" during those periods when it doesn't seem to be moving. Groups divide over questions of dogma, discipline, or power and dissipate their energy fighting among themselves, attacking their friends instead of enemies. Effective political action is aimed at changing consciousness and, thereby, causing change — or, to put it another way, political action is itself a form of magic, "the art of changing consciousness at will." Ignoring the spiritual aspects of political consciousness simply undermines its sources of power and benefits no one except those presently in the upper echelons of the hierarchies of patriarchal institutions.

"Magic" is a word that causes discomfort; it reeks of superstition, illusion, silliness. I use it deliberately because the words we are comfortable with, the words that sound acceptable, i.e., rational, scientific, intellectual, are comfortable precisely because they are the language of estrangement. "Magic" shocks our sensibilities. It forces us out of the old patterns.

Simply, magic is the psychology, the understanding of mind and emotion, derived from the principles of immanence rather than estrangement. As a system, its underlying assumption is that human drives and needs contain their own regulatory principles. Rather than repressing and adjusting them to a society in conflict with them, we could better spend our energies creating a society that allows us to fulfill them freely.

Magic is based on patterns of energy and their interconnections, on syntheses more than analyses. In magic we are always making connections, linking ourselves with other forms of being, identifying with what is outside of us rather than separating from it. As "the art of changing consciousness at will," magic has two important aspects: art and will.

Art implies vision, imagery, and fantasy. The practice of magic always begins with an image — not an abstraction, not an ideology, but something visual and/or tangible that speaks to a deeper part of the self than the intellect, to the unconscious as well as the conscious, to the right hemisphere as well as the left.[11] "In the realm of phantasy, the unreasonable images of freedom become rational," states Marcuse.[12] The image, the vision, can shift us out of the limitations imposed by our culture in a way words alone cannot; it can hint at possibilities of fulfillment not offered by the empty world. In Doris Lessing's fiction, the image of the four-gated city appears as an intimation of an order of being based on principles of harmony and equality not found in the cities of ordinary life.[13] The Grail appears to the court of King Arthur in a mythic tale the meaning of which has been given a Christian veneer, but its underlying Pagan structure remains clear: The Grail is the cup of the Goddess, Her breast, Her nurturing milk, spilling through the world, healing its hurts, restoring the Waste Land to fertility and life. The abstract concept of "immanence" alone can never have the emotional and healing power of the image of the Goddess to infuse the world, again, with vitality, meaning, and love, so that the *un*reasonable images of our freedom, our passion, and our creative power are envisioned and attained.

But the image, the vision alone, is not enough. Magic is nothing without *will* — determination, directed energy, and action. Determination means conscious choice, decision made in freedom. To have a will, to acknowledge our own will, means we acknowledge our right and necessity to choose actively, not to drift passively as women have so often drifted. To people who have pursued spiritual paths over the past few decades when Eastern religions have so strongly influenced the West, *will* may seem a strange, even destructive, concept. But the identification of passivity and inaction with spirituality is another form of estrangement. Transplanted and popularized versions of Eastern philosophies that teach that everything is really unfolding in perfect bliss if we could only see it, that "enlightenment" means getting off the Wheel of birth and death, and that sexuality keeps us bound to the "lower chakras" are simply more exotic forms of estrangement, and no less patriarchal and hierarchical.[14] "Going with the flow" is not necessarily going toward enlightenment; the flow of our culture right now is toward apocalypse. True spirituality, based on a spirit that is not separate from life but manifest in matter and the world, may require us to paddle upstream, and require effort and work and anguish instead of beatific bliss, if we are to have any hope of preserving the balance of life on this planet.

Energy is both intangible and tangible. Magic recognizes currents of subtle energies that flow through our bodies and through the material world, and it teaches techniques for channeling and forming them. But energy is also very prosaic: the energy to leave the house on a cold night and go to a meeting, the energy to join a march or organize a program, the energy to pound away at these typewriter keys. In order to cause change, energy must be directed.

Yet energy moves in cycles; it ebbs and flows. The practice of magic teaches us to be aware of those cycles and use them for differing sorts of work. This writing, for example, is not a steady stream; it comes in bursts, and between them, I make another cup of coffee, take the dogs out, turn the radio up or down, and let the new thoughts form themselves. Energy within groups and movements also ebbs and flows — and when it ebbs we need not feel like failures. We can use the downswing of the cycle for observation, education, and building support for the actions we take when energy is on the upswing.

Will must finally culminate in action. Consciousness shapes reality, not by mystic vibrations or subtle waves alone, but because it leads to action. Action may be direct (working for a political candidate, confronting rapists, resisting the draft, running a women's center) or it may be symbolic (organizing marches, rallies, and protests), depending on the situation. Both are necessary. When we take action, we reclaim our content, our sense of our own authority and value. We reclaim our power — not the ability to dominate another, but the power of consciousness immanent within us — the power to heal, to change, and to create.

We challenge the emptiness of estrangement whenever we make a deep connection with another, whenever we love, whenever we create community. The tools and techniques of magic, especially ritual, let us connect at a deep, nonverbal level. In ritual, we create community by sharing energy — by breathing, chanting, touching, dancing, acting playful, and sharing affection. These actions inspire creativity and restore a living value to poetry, music, and art, which are then no longer estranged commodities but "the acts of song, the acts of power"[15] that can unlock the unreasonable depths of freedom within us.

A demanding task lies ahead of us: transforming the consciousness of our culture from estrangement to immanence. Against the forces of destruction we have only our human will and imagination, our courage, our passion, our willingness to love. Yet we have reason to hope, because we are not, in truth, strangers to this world. I walk outside. I take my dogs to the park. We run through a grove of redwoods that sweat mist; a pink rhododendron, newly open, scents the air; my feet crush laurel leaves; they smell pungent; I feel the blood pound in my neck; behind the fog the sun is a cold blaze; and I am not, we are not, separate from any of it. We are of the world and of each other, and the power that is in us is a great, if not invincible, power. It can be hurt, but it can heal; it can be destroyed, but it can also renew. And it is morning. And there is still time to choose.

NOTES

1. A term I borrowed from Marx, although I use it in a broader context. See Karl Marx, "Private Property and Alienated Labor," Howard Selsam and Harry Martel, eds. *Reader in Marxist Philosophy* (New York: International Publishers, 1963), pp. 296–303.

2. This is a one-sentence summary of a vast, complex historical thesis which I do not have space to develop fully here but will explore further in the second chapter of *Dreaming the Dark: Magic, Sex and Politics,* a work in progress.

3. Friedrich Engels, "Humanism Vs. Pantheism: On Thomas Carlyle," *Reader in Marxist Philosophy,* pp. 234–235.

4. Lynn White, Jr., "The Historical Roots of Our Ecologic Crisis," David and Eileen Spring, eds., *Ecology and Religion In History*

(New York: Harper & Row, 1974), p. 25; also in *Science*, vol. 155, 1967.

5. See the essays on "Timber: What Was There For Them" (pp. 56–64) and "Forest: The Way We Stand" (pp. 220–221) in Susan Griffin's *Woman and Nature: The Roaring Inside Her* (San Francisco: Harper & Row, 1980).

6. Carolyn Merchant, *The Death of Nature: Women, Ecology and the Scientific Revolution* (San Francisco: Harper & Row, 1980).

7. Herbert Marcuse, *Eros and Civilization* (New York: Vintage Books, 1955), p. 41.

8. For a fuller view of Jung than I have space for here, see Naomi Goldenberg, "Jungian Psychology and Religion," *Changing of the Gods* (Boston: Beacon Press, 1979), pp. 46–71. Of course, many attempts are being made today to frame new psychologies based on holistic principles that approach immanence.

9. For a deeper, psychological understanding of why we blame women for death and decay and see men as clean, pure, and abstract, see Dorothy Dinnerstein, *The Mermaid and the Minotaur: Sexual Arrangements and Human Malaise* (New York: Harper & Row, 1976).

10. I use "Witch" and "Witchcraft" to denote the Pagan, pre-Christian religion of Europe, based on the immanent Goddess and Her Consort, which should not be confused with Satanism, Devil-worship, so-called "black" magic, or any other Christian heresy.

11. For a fuller discussion of right and left hemisphere perceptual differences and their relation to magic, see Starhawk, *The Spiral Dance: A Rebirth of the Ancient Religion of the Great Goddess* (San Francisco: Harper & Row, 1979), pp. 18–24 and 109–110.

12. Marcuse, *op. cit.*, p. 145.

13. Doris Lessing, *The Four-Gated City* (New York: Bantam, 1970), pp. 139–142.

14. Eastern philosophies probably function very differently in the context of their own culture, but many of their aspects that transplant most easily to the West tend to be those that fit most readily in Western, hierarchical patterns of male domination. Generally, they combine an understanding of energy principles and techniques of discipline and training with an authoritarian structure — a dangerous combination, especially when the most marketable elements are extracted, packaged, and sold to the general public.

15. Diane Di Prima, "Revolutionary Letter #32," *Revolutionary Letters* (San Francisco: City Lights, 1971), p. 44.

# The Metaphors of Power

# Barbara Starrett

We are at a crucial point. We must begin to make qualitative advances, evolutionary leaps, or we will stay in a holding pattern, moving in ever narrowing circles until we have, literally, nowhere to turn. One reason we have not been making these leaps is because we have not faced the problem of power: what it means in a masculist world; what it could mean to us.

In this essay, I am going to use *power* and *energy* interchangeably, as synonyms. But mainly I will use the word *power*, because we have backed off from the concept long enough. It is easier to consider energy without involving the ethical connotations of its uses. As a word, *energy* is more isolated from its relationships and effects, from hard choices and responsibility, and from our fears.

Power has a number of different meanings and connotations. The differences refer mainly to the uses of power. And, since language takes sides, power words often imply or trigger value judgments pertaining to those uses. We know that the obvious and overtly sexist pronouns and generic nouns operate to enforce masculist attitudes and systems. But because language is a symbol system, much more subtle methods of attitude enforcement operate covertly, through the uses and forms of words. Language can condition value structures and basic assumptions. It can control our beliefs about reality, our ways of thinking, and even how we think about thinking. That is why new realities, qualitative leaps, are difficult to articulate, why they often appear to contain contradictions: The language-symbols are seldom adequate to express ideas which are not already included within the given frame of word-connotations.

I have written before of the continuing pattern of present systems, systems which have prevailed since the dawn of patriarchy, systems which necessitate a way of thinking that can be described as objective, Aristotelian, data-centered, descriptive, measuring, hierarchical, systematic, fragmentizing, logical, sequential. It is also anti-emotional, cold, impersonal, unfeeling, sterile, and passive. It has carefully defined rules and limits; within those limits there is consistency and predictability. Outside the limits is fear and madness. We all know it well. Our socialization and education has conditioned us to absorb this mindset, and the systems, the institutions derived from it, and to block out or invalidate any other ways of thinking. I have called this mode the death pattern. For the purpose of describing the power dynamics involved in the death pattern, I would like to use another metaphor for it: the Vampire.

When the Vampire appropriates our power, he uses it within the binary structures that characterize the patriarchal death machine. In operation, this dualism is sometimes known as the adversary system. The adversary system pits one side against another, with an expected win/lose conclusion. We know that the legal structure is based on the adversary system: One attorney opposes another, not directly in order to achieve truth, or even justice, but to win. Truth and justice, indeed, are sincerely presumed to be the corollaries of victory. But the adversary system extends far beyond the courts. Scholarship, for instance, is organized around it. An idea, a proposition, a philosophy is introduced; then the analytical arguments for and against it are presented, each in turn. Political parties and candidates contend as adversaries in a warlike "campaign" for victory. The adversary nature of sports and games is obvious.

Indeed, competition, itself, is the bastard (that is, it has no mother) and direct offspring of the adversarial mind-set. Man against man, man against nature, business against business, nation against nation — all are in opposition, battling one another for jobs, money, markets, capital, labor, land, raw materials, services, status, privilege.

The adversary system makes a cynical mockery of the high ideals proclaimed by politicians, the professions, by athletes, and academicians. The *need* for the adversary, the dependence on and fear of the Opposite Other, requires a covert double-think, which is overtly manifested in the enormous split between means and end, theory and practice, policy and action.

When the adversary habit is unchecked, on a large scale, the results are war, genocide, harsh oppression. Nature, our Mother, is cruelly violated. On a small scale, the results are schoolyard, street and barroom fights, violent crime, and personal brutality. Often, however, the adversary system operates within a restraining system of laws and regulations: limits which are designed to keep the boys from going too far. Since it is difficult to reach a win/lose conclusion without overt combat, the adversary system allows a few men to act as judges and referees to decide who wins and who loses, men who may also possess the authority to punish the loser.

But in all binary concepts, as they are understood by the patriarchal culture, a judgment is involved: good/bad, black/white, mind/body. One half of the binary is always preferred to, or better than, the other half. So in the adversary system, the winner is better than the loser. The bully may be secretly admired, whether he is a wife-beater or a statesman, as long as he keeps on winning. You can be a revolutionary hero or a traitor, depending on whether your side wins or loses. Righteousness accrues to the winner, and the loser is intrinsically defective. Just as truth and justice are the result of a lawyer's victory, moral merit badges are accumulated by adversarial winners in every area.

Let us take the consideration of operative dualism one step further: What is dialectic but the same old adversarial system dressed up in the robes of history and economics? The boys of the left are covert competitors, and their adversaries are the boys who hold the spoils of the previous victories, primarily their fathers. Competitors of both the right and the left seek to enlist women on their sides, women whose energy is the fuel for the patriarchy's destructive will to win, to crush the adversary.

This male contest is, indeed, a re-volution, a re-turning, a holding pattern; but it is not e-volution, a turning from.

And e-volution is what we are about, a turning *from* the dualistic, adversarial concept of power to a new and female mode. When women, devoted to the Goddess, to Life, turn our own focused energy to economics and social issues, and look within ourselves for the way, we will not have to choose between the competitive either/or of capitalism/socialism. We will have created and evolved new, exciting, and generous ways to live, and we will keep on creating and evolving new modes, in which the means *is* the end, the policy *is* the practice, and every individual soul is the winner.

I do not mean to say that all males are masculist. A few are not. And there are plenty of women who subscribe to the patriarchal systems, including lesbians. In the masculist group I would include any woman who needs (personally, not tactically) male approval, whether that approval must come from one male, all males, or a specific group of males and whether she seeks that approval in her bed, in her home, on her job, in her head, in any group, or at large, as an audience.

The existing forms are male-owned and -operated. Women primarily tend the machinery and clean up the debris. Sometimes they *are* the machinery and the debris. The power is held, directed, and projected by males, and it is headed toward a *götterdämmerung* of destruction and annihilation. It is crucial that we know this. It is also urgent that we understand that the power held and used by the masculist society is ours: *We* are the Vampire's energy source.

But a new and radical consciousness is emerging, primarily through women, and despite our massive conditioning. Women have been "allowed," in our exclusion from important roles in the male structures, to develop other ways of knowing, thinking, and being. These ways can be described as emotional, direct, expressive, intuitive, immediate, subjective, relationship-centered. I want to make clear that this does not mean we cannot think in the masculist modes. We all can. We have been trained in them, and we have to live with and in the world as it is now structured. Some women, in order to follow their own interests or just to survive, have chosen to be better at it than their male judges and competitors. Nevertheless, the new consciousness is a qualitative leap and it is life-affirming. It cannot be contained in the masculist structures or even defined adequately in them. (I think this is one reason so many women feel more comfortable writing poetry than prose.) We have discovered, staring into that abyss, not meaninglessness but illumination, not nothingness but ourselves, not annihilation but creation.

We cherish our visions. But we must enact them. That requires power, a reclamation and use of our own power, in the world, now. We need to learn where that power is, where we want it to go, how to make it work for us, and what kinds of things deflect it from our own purposes. Quite literally, it is a matter of life and death.

Power always finds form. The generation of power, alone, is impossible because power is always used. It always goes somewhere, does something. It cannot be destroyed. But it can be transformed. When we control that transformation, when we control both *the content and the form* of power, we are reversing the process of the death patterns. We can act, rather than react.

The process of creation takes place in the mind. Yet it is not the kind of "intellectual" process we are accustomed to regard as correct. Visions are not acceptable in the laboratory or even in the classroom. Like the church, all institutions persecute their own visionaries and mystics unless the visions can be made to serve the ends of the institution. What is at stake is power. One visionary can possess the power to threaten or to support an entire institution, an entire worldview.

But consider the idea that the mind/emotions duality is false, that thinking and feeling are both aspects of the same capacity, that true mentation involves both aspects simultaneously. Patriarchal thoughtforms require the intellect alone. The emotions are feared as destroyers and contaminators of objective thought. Therefore, the patriarchy requires the systematic extinction of the emotions. The projected ideal is the computer, all intellect, all reaction.

Yet the creative process, the visionary experience that is so powerful, contains an element that makes all the difference: emotional intensity. And it cannot be separated from the intellect in that process. They operate together and are experienced as the same thing. Sometimes creation is described as the holding, at once, of extreme objectivity and extreme passion. Such descriptions are after the fact (the experience is of a unified state within which one cannot analyze what is going on) but they will do. The point is that extreme passion is necessary to creativity, and it is felt as a quality of mind.

Conviction and commitment are extra-rational. What is extra, what is added, is passion. If we believe in peace, our feelings about the victims of war have a lot to do with the strength of our belief. We can have very good reasons for our feminism, but unless we feel strongly about it, too, we are not likely to risk acting on it.

What I am leading up to is this: Passion and power, active power, are the same thing. And both reside in the mind.

We are far more powerful than we know, so powerful that only a minority of us, if we know what we are doing, could stop the death machine. That machine operates under our power, power drained from us. In our homes, in our jobs, we provide the energy. It is drained out of us by the Vampire, who gives us his approval in return. He cannot feel. And power is passion. When he appears to feel, he is bargaining, in the accepted societal forms, or we are projecting our own feeling on him. The last true emotions he has left are those appropriate to the adversarial death machine: violence, hatred, anger. When there is an excess of even these emotions, he goes to war, or hunting, or to a football game. Or he rapes. Such an excess occurs when he senses his own powerlessness. One way or another, it is life-blood he requires.

When women energize the men who spend their lives operating the death machine, we energize the entire Vampire. We transfer power to him and he uses it. For power, which is passion, always acts, always finds a form. Regardless of the rhetoric of our disenchantment, if we are drained of our energy by males, that energy/power goes to the death machine.

It has also been noted that power/passion resides in the mind. Intensity begins with thought, and to experience intensity is to experience power. But power always finds a form. *Thought* finds a form, when thought is felt. Our thoughts can create poems and ideas. Some women know that thought can also create health and healing, and that thought can make things happen, can create events and circumstances. Thought can alter reality; thought can create reality. I am not just proposing a kind of philosophical idealism. The difference lies in the view of mind as both intellect and feeling. Thought is empowered by intensity. Passion is power, and the necessary active ingredient. And we have it.

"Alpha" states need not, as we have been told, always be passive. They are similar to the creative state, in which extremes of passion and objectivity are held simultaneously. In such states, we are open but we are not passive. The difference is in the focused intensity, which is always active. For the opposite of passivity is action, not aggression, as it is for males. The mind acts its thoughts through intensity. This is creativity, and it is unlimited in its possibilities. We are unlimited in our possibilities.

It may be argued that tension is necessary for creativity, and I agree with this. But the tension exists within, and it is the eternal intensity of becoming, of expanding and breaking through boundaries, of the soul's hunger to know, to create, and to transform. This kind of tension, like molecular tension, consists, not of conflict, but of an intricate and elegant balance. It is the Kali within us all.

What I am talking about is mutation. The new consciousness is both the continuing cause and the continuing effect of a qualitative evolutionary leap; it is characterized by the astounding ability/power to will our own further evolution. The development of this power is not and will not be easy. It will require a perhaps unaccustomed self-discipline and a toughness, if it is not to be dissipated into superficial and self-indulgent dead ends. We must begin to require a great deal of ourselves.

We can create power centers both within and outside ourselves. I am grateful to Delyte Frost for this concept: Power is where power is perceived. Power resides in the mind. We can give or withhold power through our beliefs, our felt thoughts. A prelate, for example, can proclaim against abortion effectively only as long as women believe he has the right to do this. When women reclaim the power to decide for themselves about abortion, the churchman proclaims in a vacuum. His power depends on the transference of our power to him, through our belief that this is right. The Vampire must feed on our emotional collaboration. Without it, his power is gone.

Power is where power is perceived. This also means that in any given in-the-world situation, we can intentionally set up our own power centers. If we believe that power resides in those centers, it will. We will act successfully on that belief. Women's caucuses, unions, etc., will never work unless we regard them as *the* legitimate centers of power. If we really believe that power belongs in the establishment, or that we cannot or should not reclaim the power of the establishment, we will surely remain powerless. We must grant our own power to ourselves. The alternative, even by default, is to offer ourselves, our energies, to the Vampire. Our own power will increase in proportion to our belief in it.

This process works for individual women, too. When we perceive ourselves as powerful, when we believe in that power, we appropriate the power within us. The most important step to take to become an artist is to proclaim yourself an artist, and believe it. Our physical strength increases as soon as we begin to believe we are strong, to have confidence in our own muscles. When our beliefs in our selves are also supported by others, the power increases proportionately.

Another source of power is in symbols. When we invest meaning in them, we transform them into power banks upon which we can draw in an increasing circle of energy. When we support each other's beliefs, symbols, art, businesses, etc., we are recycling power among ourselves. Ideally, that power never diminishes, never dies.

Yet our experience is often that power seems to dissipate. Since it cannot be destroyed, where does it go? To the Vampire. How does it get away from us? How can we hold onto it?

The most obvious answer is that we give it away, consciously or unconsciously. The minute we depend on male approval, the very idea, the very belief, finds form, transforms the power, becomes the reality. The majority of women readily admit that their first commitment is to men or to a man. But many women who consider themselves to be quite "liberated" also transfer their energy to males, at home or at work, socially or politically. I don't mean that we can't have male friends or employers. But I am saying that it's a tricky relationship. We had better take a long, honest look at what they want from us, what we want from them.

One of the hardest, most devastating shocks of the women's movement is to learn that women, too, can damage us, can drain us. I think this happens partly because of the dreadful, massive conditioning in passivity we have all undergone. We are all contaminated with that passivity, and it is a long, hard struggle to overcome it, a struggle that must be repeated day after day, year after year. This terrible inertia is the opposite of power, of action. Within it, only negative, adversarial energy/emotions are available. The only way out is to believe our way out. But until we know this, many women, like the Vampire, seek power through other women, or else use their own power to flail with the weapons of negative emotion.

The most crucial problem for most of us is how to live within the ubiquitous realm of the Vampire and still reclaim our power and how, eventually, to defang the Vampire himself. To speak of separatism in the usual, physical way is to ignore the problem. Very few of us can support ourselves apart from the male systems. Even when that is possible, every time we go to the store, or the bank, or the post office, or to school, or to the gas station, or read a book, or turn on a radio, we are dealing in and with those systems. Most of us must also work for or within male institutions in order to live at all.

I am calling for a new kind of separatism. Not our physical presence but our emotions, energy, and power must be withdrawn from the Vampire's engulfment, and consciously used, by *us*, to create our own realities.

Our Mother, Nature, is leading the way, taking back Her energy, refusing the brutal rape of Her power. She is moving in strange, new, unexpected ways. Like Her, we must reclaim what is ours. The Vampire can only be defeated by removing his food.

The power is in our minds. The reclamation of it is an act of mind, of the feeling mind, of intensity of purpose. This means, individually and together, we must focus our thoughts, specifically, on what we really want, what we really believe. We can recognize and direct our conscious intentions toward the purposeful release of positive energy. If we behave *as if* we perceive power to reside in ourselves, we *will* perceive that power, and so will others. Power attracts power; the latent power within all women will surface and ally itself with perceived power. Most importantly, power will go where we want it to go, do what we want it to do. If it takes saying to ourselves, several times daily, "I am powerful and I can change reality," then we must say that. Sooner or later, we will believe it, and then it will work for us.

We can do this no matter where we are or whom we work for. Every woman, if she is working for the feminist vision, on whatever level, is already doing it to some degree. All of our advances have come about through her work and her belief in it. Every woman's efforts are valuable and limited only by her own vision and the intensity of her belief in that vision.

But it is necessary for some women to risk total reclamation, to risk the direct and intentional use of power, in bold, even outrageous ways. It takes only a minority of women to alter present reality, to create new reality, because our efforts are more completely focused, more total. Emily Dickinson expressed it unequivocally: "The price of all is all."

# Womanpower: Energy Re-Sourcement

# Sally Gearhart

In the past two years I have come to a firm point of conviction about what is happening to us as a woman's movement, and I want to share some of my thinking about that. I believe that politically conscious women move toward the transformation of society through one of four distinct approaches. By "politically conscious" I mean women who do not believe in the values or functions of monopoly capitalism, who want to bring that whole economic system to dust.

Strategy #1: Some women move in *revolutionary actions against the system* either through *violence* ("terrorist acts" as the press names them) or through *radical political organizing*.

Strategy #2: Far more women believe in *seizing power within*

---

© Sally Gearhart, 1976. Reprinted by permission of the author from *Woman-Spirit*, vol. 2, no. 7, Spring 1976; Dr. Gearhart presented the above essay as a keynote address at the conference titled "Through the Looking Glass: A Gynergenetic Experience," Boston, 23–25 April 1976. [Editor's Note: She has since written that her concept of re-sourcement includes a system of rotation between the "buffer areas" and the "re-sourcement areas"; see *WomanSpirit*, vol. 3, no. 10, Winter 1976. – C.S.]

*the system through consciously chosen reforms so as to make the system work for us.*

Strategy #3: A number of women put energy into *alternative organizations* or *structures*.

It is clear to me now that in terms of these first three strategies we have already lost. Daily the system anoints and assimilates more reforms into itself and regularly another multinational corporation entrenches itself into the culture of a developing nation; bombings and kidnappings frighten us step-by-paranoid-step into the police state; alternative organizations seem less and less like alternatives or cease to exist altogether. All the while the futility of our struggles becomes clearer and clearer. The dreadful has already happened. In the world of these first three strategies there is no antidote for the pell-mell rush to annihilation because all the rules there are devised and revised constantly by the dominant culture and enough of us can never become skilled enough fast enough to beat that system at its own game. Only something as powerful as that system itself can threaten it.

A fourth strategy, I believe, has the potential to be that threat. I have called the strategy "re-sourcement" because it suggests we must go to a new place for our energy. To re-source is to find another source, an entirely different and prior one, a source deeper than the patriarchy and one that allows us to stand in the path of continuous and cosmic energy. That new source is discovered only by moving inward to the self, and it is being experienced most widely these days by women who are finding our individual or *intra*personal energy flow. Once we are at home there — as more and more of us are becoming — then we can begin to develop authentic forms of *inter*personal energy or that energy which flows between people. What we have experienced with the patriarchy (the arena of the first three strategies) is *inter*personal energy which has not first been founded on, which has never been connected to, *intra*personal energy, or the internal source.

What I am calling re-sourcement is the activity of women who are reaching out for new ways of understanding and viewing reality, i.e., *they are articulating a new epistemology:* astrology, the Tarot, numerology, the I Ching, the Kabala — all these and others reinterpreted and/or redeemed from their masculist emphases and filtered anew through the channels of womanknowing, womansight; also dreams, visions, dream-and-vision-sharing, womanmusic, womanart, storytelling, rituals, dramas, celebrations, memory, games, fantasy, Witchcraft, an attention to the personal and collective unconscious, an affirmation of the intuitive, a song of praise to the non-logical, a greeting of the right-brained analogical capacity; a rediscovery and a reunderstanding of anthropological data in a reconstruction of reality that will be unequalled in history.

Second, women are re-sourcing and reformulating their attitudes toward the material world, i.e., *they are articulating a new value system, a new ethic:* the human body — discovery of its victimization by allopathic medicine, new healings, the introduction of feminist uses of the martial arts, the meaning of discipline to the female body, learnings about the laying on of hands, about loving and healing, new seeings about health, nutrition, natural cures, connections between physical health and psychological realities, questions about reproduction, midwifery, cloning, parthenogenesis, self-nurturing, and mothering; the Earth Herself and the healing of Her ten-thousand-year-long rape — the tending of the ground, farming, food production, relationship to animals, to plants, to artifacts, careful ecological reflections and commitments, connections to the biosphere, action in the face of the deeper meaning of death and life, a new assessment of the significance and destiny of a species which has ravaged its own home.

I believe that the conscious women who are exploring a new epistemology and a new value system, the women who are working in the fourth approach to social change, are all, in one form or another, attempting a *re-sourcing of energy.* They are addressing themselves to the very fundamental discovery: *that there is a source or kind of power qualitatively different from the one we have been taught to accept and to operate with; further, the understanding, the protection, the development of that source and the allowing of it to reach its full dimensions could mean the redemption of the entire globe from the devastation of the last ten thousand years.*

The more we get into re-sourcement the more we realize that patriarchal or "power-over" energy is of a victor/victim design and that the first step in the manufacture of a victim (or of a victor) is the *alienation* of the individual from her internal energy source. Further, we realize that the search for the internal source requires an absence of the dominant (external or interpersonal) energy patterns, that only in the absence of competitiveness and power-over activity can the subdued and devalued inner source find any expression. In a world where every nook and cranny has been filled with superficialized and competitivized external energy, it is no wonder that any internally sourced power has had trouble being expressed — much less valued. Hence the move on the part of thousands of women to isolate themselves (with other women of like understandings) from those power-ridden dominant energy forms; hence, that is, *the need for separatism: the separation of women from the patriarchal system in quantities great enough to make a qualitative difference in history.*

I believe that the new power (not power-over) that will emerge from re-sourcement will be *womanpower,* and that it will come from women not only because we are uniquely in tune with internal sourcing but further because there is a uniquely female capacity for collective functioning which will make possible more life-giving uses of energy in the future.

Women (probably all women but so as not to beg the question I will assume Western women) are uniquely in touch with the internal source out of at least three necessities.

1. Our historical separation from each other and from the activities of the Man's world has afforded us near constant access to the wells of *intra*personal energy. To be sure, within families and in bourgeoise social circles, women have also been relied upon to be peacemakers and relational agents, but our participation in the competitive or power-over mode has always been limited or at best "second rate"; women still have had hours-per-day and decades-per-century for visiting with ourselves within our own space.

2. Middle-class women (at least) move now in Western society toward a disavowal of sex-role socialization; many of us understand that movement to be a rejection of the most fundamental of all power-over dynamics and as well a throwing off of the self-hatred/woman-hatred engendered by sex roles. The first milestone in a developing feminist consciousness seems to mark a loving and affirmative embrace of the self as a whole entity and an internal energy flow from that holistically experienced self. We have often testified in the movement to the reality of long-dormant energy and how it can be released and expressed when it is touched by one's own self-loving hand.

3. Finally biology for sure is destiny in this sense, that as women we *are* what the patriarchy has labelled us: vessels, containers, receptacles, carriers, shelters, houses, nurturers, incubators, holders, enfolders, listeners. We are *not only* those things but neither is it accurate to say "we are also aggressors, penetrators, at-

tackers, etc.," for *if* we can be said to be those last things it is out
of context that is wholly different (and therefore manifests itself
in a totally different behavior pattern) from the one that men have
operated from in their aggression/penetration/etc. . . .

There is not much penetrating about our bodies and there is lots that
enfolds and holds and eases. We are built to receive. Let's say that loud
and clear. We are also built to give, but even our giving is in our own
mode and that mode is totally different from the mis-sourced *inter*personal energy exercised by most men (and unfortunately by many
women). Instead of probing or invading, our natural giving takes the
path of wrapping around the givee, of being available to her/him without insisting; our giving is a *presence,* an *offering,* an *opening,* a *surrounding,* a *listening,* a *vulnerability,* a *trust.* At the very most our giving takes the form of a push toward freedom for the givee, as in the act
of *giving* birth.

So in the reclaiming of our bodies, let's also affirm some propaganda:
We are what our fathers and husbands and sons and lovers have called
us, but what they have not known, or what they knew and suppressed
because of its potential paralyzing threat, is that in our listening is all
meaning, in our vesseling is the home, in our shelter is survival, in
our nurturing is all possibility. In our enfolding, in short, is ultimately
all power. But in the force and thrust of renegade and exclusive *inter-*
personal (external and externalized) energy, there can be only havoc
and destruction.

Re-sourcement calls for the energy of receptivity, the energy of the
listening ear, of the open meadow, of the expansive embrace. It calls for
an energy generated from within the individual's own territory and for
an affirmation of that energy as the genesis of both individual and
societal transformation. Women know that territory; in our centuries of
waiting we have baptized it with our blood. Now it remains only for
women to reclaim that homeland so that the redemption of the biosphere can begin.

Collectivity,* I think, and women's special capacity for it, needs to

---

* There is no word yet to carry the full meaning of women-togethering or
women-being-present-with-themselves-while-presencing-with-others. "Collective" is
inadequate for it calls up notions of a pooling, an aggregate. Further, history has
tried collective action only within settings where power-over energy has been dominant. Maybe "syzygy" (sizzagee) is the word we need, meaning "yoked" (forget
"paired") or "conjunction of organisms without loss of identity" or "a related group

be talked about elsewhere and by many of us. My own thoughts on it right now are that we are uniquely capable of it because (1) we are *in touch with* the internal energy source; (2) we are *conscious* of what we are in touch with; and (3) we have the *intentionality to share* that energy. That makes us anarchists of sorts, whose only government is self-government. Then, I'm thinking, we are uniquely capable of collectivity because we are beginning to practice — in very incomplete and frustrating ways — a new use of *inter*personal energy. We have started to look at things non-hierarchically and to take seriously the lessons we have learned on the battlefield of romantic love. As a result we occasionally find ourselves (1) respecting and/or loving one another, (2) trusting one another, and (3) beginning to dialogue with each other.

If men have ever found an internal energy flow, and even if they have been conscious of what a cosmic force they have thus tapped, they have been unable, I believe, to take the next step: intending to share that power. My continuing experience of men is that they feel they need women in order to do these things, that really respecting and loving one another, trusting one another, and dialoguing with one another are functions they cannot or will not reach out for by themselves, as men. Even the struggles of gay men toward non-power brotherhood suggest to me that collectivizing internal power may not be men's gift; they may use that power in some other way — perhaps use it creatively — but sharing it in non-power forms is perhaps at this time and place not a possibility for the male psyche.

I now realize that the power we want as women, the power that we have uniquely within us as women, the power that we are developing in order to redeem ten thousand years of extreme and misdirected relational energy, has very little to do with political parties, with money, or with revolution in the common sense of that term.

The power that is emerging from women working in the fourth strategy for change is *womanpower* itself. It is re-sourced energy that is collectively shared among women.

If our real power lies in this fourth strategy, then how do we assess the radical women's movement, at least in the United States? The fourth strategy is the politics of a rapidly growing *minority* of women, and not all those who believe in it are able to separate entirely from society in order to practice re-sourcement skills or to create a woman's cul-

---

of rational(!) integral functions." "Syzygious" would then be the adjective, and the entity resulting from women being together in this state would be a "syzygium."

ture; others of the "believers" may only be able to separate occasionally — a weekend or so out of linear time or a few moments each day in the athomeness of the self. They/we will testify that re-sourcement in the thick of the patriarchy is difficult-to-impossible — but also *crucial*.

The majority of feminists have commitments to one of the other three strategies and for a variety of good reasons. But to be working there is dangerous. We have all watched creative women go wagging off down the well-worn path toward masculist power and glory. In some part of themselves they must know that they will make no fundamental change there, that they are only riding on temporary highs (like blood sugar rushes) and only copying the very patterns that afflict us all in the first place. It hurts to see them flexing their hierarchical muscles as the system grants them power or as they join the march of every revolution in history — revolutions which have invariably failed to address the primary problem: the dominance of male over female. While women march in the service of one of the first three strategies *believing that there we can make fundamental change,* we are victims still of patriarchy and only repeat the errors of the ages.

The secret lies in that phrase, "believing . . . change." Since the majority of us do work "there," what's important, I believe, is that we understand that that work is not the essential work of the revolution, for that essential work is in re-sourcement.

The function of the first three strategies for change is to draw the enemy's fire, to operate as a kind of holding action, to stave off the knowledge and reaction of the patriarch so that time and room are bought for the essential work of genuine transformation. To be sure, each of the three strategies serves the immediate needs of some women; further, the work that is done in these areas can bring significantly closer the ideal of worldwide economic equality. Yet the *fundamental* changes, the changes that do not repeat the age-old mistakes of a competitive system, cannot come from any one or all of these three sources. If we give womanpower room and time it will work for all of us, but let's not fool ourselves that there is hope in any of these patriarchal forms.

It seems to me that women deep at work in re-sourcement, appreciating the fact that their work could not continue if that buffer state failed, need to acknowledge the protection of women working in the other three strategies. For their part, women in the buffer state — if they believe in it — need to work with the knowledge that they are protecting the re-sourcement; if they don't believe it to be the essential strategy, then they can at least affirm it as a valid part of a vast movement of women; hopefully they will lend *critical* support, openly talking about differences with and listening to women who do consider the movement's deepest task to be re-sourcement.

Criticism of this fourth strategy comes easily and is often scathing. When I allow myself to get into those criticisms, they come out like this:

1. Most obviously, since it is extra-rational in much of its expression, the re-sourcement approach seems kooky, supernatural, all a matter of faith. What these spiritualist women are asking us to believe rings too soundly of old-time religion. We can't sit around and simply contemplate our navels or wallow in self-love any more than we can lay it all on Jesus and let him take care of it. People are dying at the hand of imperialist powers and every off-the-wall fad that privileged women fall into only bolsters up the corrupt system. Not only are such crazy women not working for the revolution; they actually aid the enemy.

2. Further, it's a trap. In turning away from the direct struggles with the system itself, these energy-concerned women seem to believe about themselves as women just what the patriarchy has always wanted us to believe, i.e., that we are incapable of functioning in a male world, that we are the passive, receptive, quiet, non-violent, introverted sex, that it is our sphere to be religious and mystical. By withdrawing to the more occult or esoteric realms we yield up to men the real world, the world of power and excitement and achievement. It's an individual solution, the old "trip to the self," the attention to the personal at the sacrifice of significant social action. Women are right back inside ourselves, in the skin-encapsulated ego, isolated and alone, just as men have trained us to be.

3. Third, it's too slow. And furthermore the women involved in it tell us that things can't be pushed, that urgency contradicts the process of re-sourcement. But the world is burning and in the face of that, this fourth approach comes out as lazy, fun, mellow, the good, unstruggled-for life — as long as you can rip off the system for foodstamps or as long as you have nice white skin and aren't a single mother balancing on a piddling minimum wage between starvation and bare subsistence. But where is the real political commitment? Where is the realization that things have to change

immediately, that women have political clout if they'll only use it? There is nothing visible happening within the re-sourcement arena. We have no time to mutter little incantations or to wait for "the flow," or to hope for some supernatural occurrence. Slowly, they say, it comes slowly. By the time "it" gets here the revolution will have passed on by.

It is no wonder that feminists committed to "real" political work doubt the value of the re-sourcement approach. It is no wonder that resentment sometimes runs high. I should use my earning power or my brain or my energy struggling every day against the dehumanizing establishment while some listless unpolitical sisters chant around a solstice fire or space out on their dreams? I should spend my life and consciousness believing that dropped-out sisters will come to Something Bigger Than All of Us, that by burning their menstrual blood in the light of the full moon they will be in touch with the Great Mother and somehow make the patriarchy go "poof"? I should stifle my giggles when they speak so seriously of faith healing and procreation-without-men and obliterated matriarchies? And I should do all this, if you please, because the Tarot speaks and Taurus is at the midheaven and perseverance furthers while a little comfrey, Goddess be praised, heals it all?

The answer I am now making to all that is *yes*. That is exactly what I have to do. Even though my criticism of it is strong and vital to my consciousness, it does not shake my belief. (1) Of course it's kooky and all a matter of faith; of course it jars us. It is a whole new posture that violates every dogma of our upbringing. But not to allow it is in itself fascism. When we hear this criticism from socialist sisters, it's good to remind ourselves that Marx' fundamental view (*Early Philosophical Manuscripts*) was a religious one — beyond proof, beyond empirical demonstration; it was a view of *unalienated* humanity. (2) Of course the re-sourcement attitude affirms qualities that the system wants us to believe we have. But we affirm that we are those things *and* far more. If re-sourcement is an individual solution, then my response is, "It's about time." I suggest that no mass movement will ever be more than mimicry if it is not founded on just such an individual base. (3) Of course it's slow. But if we do not dare to slow down, to alter our own speed to be with the sisters into re-sourcement, then at least we have to remember what we've learned in these past eight years if we've learned anything at all: that, like it or not, there's no forcing any other woman into a full trot or a gallop; she *will* move at her own pace, but at her own pace we can be sure she will *move*. At this point I always remind myself that the patriarchal use of crash programs is antithetical to organic movement; in a crash program the theory goes that if you can get nine women pregnant you can have a baby in one month; it takes women, I suppose, to understand that it doesn't work that way.

On the surface re-sourcement can seem to be just another version of humanism. But I think there are two reasons why it is more than that. First, the re-sourcement is a movement of women, and that means it has *a strong and unashamed lesbian component*. At its base humanism is a socio-psychological attitude initiated by men in speaking about men, for the benefit of men; at its patriarchal roots even humanism, for all its "acceptance," cannot tolerate the love of women for each other if for a single instant that love excludes men. Secondly, re-sourcement is not "just humanism" because it hopefully retains within itself *a high radical consciousness of economic realities*. This does not mean that its proponents have to work in factories — either of necessity or in order to organize with workers — though we may do so; it does not have to mean, though it may, that women believing in the fourth strategy spend a maximum of time fighting racism. What it does mean is that through study, confrontation, and dialogue-like communication women believing in the fourth strategy (whether we ourselves are separatists or not) are aware of the privilege exercised by any who separate even temporarily from the patriarchy in order to work in isolation on a woman's culture. If I can move out of the patriarchy for my re-sourcement, then I do indeed march to a different drummer; but I have to march with the consciousness in my very bones of the cost in blood and pain and death that is somewhere being paid for my personal growth. These two characteristics not only clearly differentiate the re-sourcement strategy from humanism; as well, they distinguish the strategy from any other women's movement in history and from any other political revolution.

I've called re-sourcement a political strategy but when I ask questions usually applicable to a political movement, I find unorthodox answers. Who is the enemy? There may be no "enemy" except a system. How do we deal with "the enemy"? As seldom as possible but when necessary by opening the way for his transformation into not-the-enemy. What weapons do we use? Our healing, our self-protection, our health, our fantasies, our collective care. How do we protect our ranks? By a buffer zone of women working in the patriarchy. How do we train for the battles? By practicing our arational skills.

Most startling was the term that came to me when I asked myself, how do we gain members, i.e., what is our outreach program? The term was "religious conversion." I had to dwell on that one awhile because my memory flew immediately to all that I know of Christian conversion, the extreme of which is "if you won't believe that you're redeemed by my redeemer's blood, then I'll drown you in your own." I recalled my own "conversion" to Christianity, which really never happened. I had put it all together intellectually and then prepared myself — in vain — for the emotional undergirding that they had promised me would come. Picture me, the Bible under one arm and *The Augsburg Confession* under the other, waiting on the plains of Texas with my knees eternally flexed for the leap of faith.

Then I recalled my "conversion" to feminism which took place, I discovered, over a period of five years — actually four separate conversions and each one a revelation, each an agony, each an ecstasy. The first change was *theological*: At 5:00 in the morning someone said "God is dead" and for the first time the words had meaning. My intestines and my heart exchanged places, resettled again properly, and my life was thenceforth changed. The second movement was *personal*, two years later: Five years of celibacy had been far too long. That summer brought a *professional* transformation: One trip to California and another authoritarian teacher bites the dust. Finally, two years beyond that, the *politicization*: Still smarting from just having been royally ripped off by General Motors, I saw the National Guard maliciously beat up some of my hippie friends. Four conversion experiences. The coming of my feminism. All born right out of my self, but surrounding them all a climate that allowed the changes, a climate of intolerable conditions or supportive ones, old patterns becoming unbearable or new, special people suddenly entering my life.

I now better understand the dynamics of those changes — and my further "conversion to" or "believing in" the re-sourcement strategy. Mao has helped me with his analogy of the egg and the stone: how the egg with the internal basis for change will never hatch unless it is placed in the proper external conditions for change — heat and moisture — and how the stone, void of the internal basis, can sit in the proper external conditions forever and never hatch.

First, it is true that with each step *I* changed my life. No one changed it for me, I became no one's disciple, and I wasn't even seriously promised "sisterhood." That's what I didn't know as I waited and hoped on the plains of Texas, that *I* could change my life. (Trapped, still, in the female-as-passive role!) Second, while it is true that I changed my life, it is also true that those external conditions were a climate, not a force. They did not constitute a god or a being outside myself that required praise and worship because of the revelation he (or she!) gave to me. It has been conversion, right enough, occurring only when I am internally ready and only in an atmosphere conducive to that change.

Here's the hard part for me when I think of re-sourcement as a political strategy. We know we can't change other women, that they must convert themselves. Our job is to continue in our own growth and thus to create the atmosphere (in this case supportive and exemplary) in which their internal bases for change can break through. But if we get too far into this attitude, we will not be political at all but only "groovy," "far-out" women, each doing her own thing and assuring each other every now and again that by living our mellowed-out lives we are thus doing our bit, creating the atmosphere, *tra-la!*, in which Toots and Amy and the governor's wife and the woman hanging out diapers in Middle America are all someday going to blossom into feminists — re-sourcement feminists, at that. I suggest that unless we read and think and talk and study and practice with our vision constantly in mind and with our political sensibilities consistently sharpened, unless we somehow conceptualize that vision (knowing it will change) and ritualize the expression of it, we may forget entirely that we are a dynamic force in history.

We might also do well to build into our separatism some healthy examinations of reality and some speculations about the future. For instance, as the world situation grows worse, more people will be turning to what is called the irrational, to religion, to all the freaked and fanatic doctrines that are bound to turn up. From that perspective our job may well be to get our selves so together (both individually and collectively) with our arational skills that we'll be able to cope with the onslaught of chaos. I see, too, an ugly revival of orthodoxy within Christendom which could mean Witch hunts twentieth-century-style, complete with the use of satellite search and Kirlian photography. When I lapse into thinking how easy and mellow it is to be in the re-sourcement mode, I remind myself that when the backlash comes it will be weirdo women who will be chased down first, arrested, and separated from each other. That thought sobers me and keeps me from getting lazy. It makes me think that these days we are in a golden age of spirituality, that we will not always be so safe. I don't like to spend a lot of time in that kind of thinking, but I keep it tucked away in an accessible spot; with it available there, I cease to be worried that we won't have enough women; my concern becomes that we won't have enough women *conscious of the political nature of our re-sourced lives.*

Every now and again I get overwhelmed by the significance of the times I am living in. I have been waiting, it seems, all my life, all my lives, for the movement that is now happening among women, for the birth of the womanpower that is presently on the rise. I believe that it is on the rise *now* because the human species and its planet home are at a critical point in their interrelationship; history needs now the different energy that only conscious women can bring to it.

It was not yet time when they burned Witches one by one or even ten by ten. It was not yet time when some of our self-findings and self-lovings had to be hidden from a world that called such discoveries "perversion" and "sin." It was not yet time for countless women throughout recorded history who could not conform to the demands of their culture.

It is time now. The power is ours. And that power is not on Capitol Hill or Wall Street or in any military might. It is flowing from an authentic source, its only authentic source — from women — and that is the first time in history that it has ever happened that way; it is thus absolutely distinct from the power-over models we have been trained to respect. We will use the power that is rising within us, in the midst of us, to redeem the whole human enterprise. And if we fail in that venture, then our role may be helping our species gracefully to extinguish itself from the cosmos.

It is time.

It is ours.

We move now toward the womanwide recognition of how vast and deep an enterprise we are engaged in.

# Gyn/Ecology: Spinning New Time/Space

# Mary Daly

In the course of The Second Passage, Crone-ographers who have survived dis-covering the various manifestations of Goddess-murder on this patriarchal planet have become aware of the deep and universal intent to destroy the divine spark in women. We have seen that the perpetrators of this planetary atrocity are acting out the deadly myths of patriarchy and that this ritual enactment of the sado-myths has become more refined with the "progress of civilization." This refinement includes an escalation of violence and visibility and at the same time a decrease of visibility to those mesmerized by the Processions of fathers, sons, and holy ghosts.

The know-ing of this deadly intent has been necessary for our a-mazing process of exorcism. It is equally necessary for moving on the Labyrinthine Journey of Ecstasy, for this process is damaged/hindered by not knowing/acknowledging the dangers, traps, deceptions built into the terrain. As long as "knowledge" of the horrors of androcracy is fragmented, compartmentalized, belittled, we cannot integrate this into our know-ing process. We then mistake the male-made maze for our Self-centering way.

Since we have come through the somber Passage of recognizing the alien/alienating environment in which woman-hating rituals vary from *suttee* to gynecological iatrogenesis, we can begin to tread/thread our way in new time/space. This knowing/acting/Self-centering Process is itself the creating of a new, woman-identified environment. It is the becoming of Gyn/Ecology. This involves the dis-spelling of the mind/spirit/body pollution that is produced out of man-made myths, language, ritual atrocities, and meta-rituals such as "scholarship," which erase our Selves. It also involves dis-covering the sources of the Self's original movement, hearing the moving of this movement. It involves speaking forth the New Words which correspond to this deep listening, speaking the words of our lives.

Breaking out of the patriarchal processions into our own Gyn/Ecological process is the specific theme of this, The Third Passage. In a general sense, our movement through the preceding Passages has all been and is Gyn/Ecological Journeying. Moreover, since our movement is not linear but rather resembles spiraling, we continue to re-member/re-call/re-claim the knowledge gained in the preceding Passages, assuming this into our present/future. Hence, there is no authentic way in which the preceding Passages can be dissociated from the Third. Thus, Gyn/Ecology is not the climax or linear end point in time of the Journey, but rather it is a defining theme/thread in our Labyrinthine Journey of the inner ear, in the course of which we constantly hear deeper and deeper reverberations from all of the Passages and learn to be attuned to echoes, subtleties, and distinctions not attended to before. Yet, Gyn/Ecology is the proper name for The Third Passage, for it names the patterns/designs of the moving Female-identified environment which can only be heard/seen after the Journeyer has been initiated through The First and The Second Passages.

As the Spinster spins into and through this Passage she is encouraged by her strengthened powers of hearing and seeing. By now she has begun to develop a kind of multidimensional/multiform power of sensing/understanding her environment. This is a Self-identified *synaesthesia*: It is woman-identified *gynaesthesia*. It is a complex way of perceiving the interrelatedness of seemingly disparate phenomena. It is also a pattern-detecting power which may be named positive paranoia. Far from being a debilitating "mental disease," this is strengthening and realistic dis-ease in a polluted and destructive environment. Derived from the Greek terms *para*, meaning beyond, outside of, and *nous*, meaning mind, the term *paranoia* is appropriate to describe movement beyond, outside of, the patriarchal mind-set. It is the State of Positively Revolting Hags.

Moving through all three Passages is moving from the state of anaesthesia to empowering gynaesthesia, as dormant senses become awake and alive. Since, in The Second Passage, the Voyager became more aware not only of the blatancy and interconnectedness of phallocratic evil, but also of its reality, she is enabled to detect and name its implicit presence and therefore to overcome roadblocks in her dis-covery of being. Empowered with positive paranoia she can move with increasing confidence.

We have seen that this is the age of holy ghosts, with particular reference to gynecology. It is an age of manipulation through/by invisible and *almost* insensible presences. Some of these might be called physical, such as radiation and "white noise." Others more properly may be said to belong to the realm of the spirit, of "ghost." We are dealing here with the realm of implicit or subliminal manipulation, of quiet, almost indiscernible, intent on the part of the manipulators and quiet, unacknowledged acceptance of their ghostly presences and messages by their victims. Hence, the first chapter of this Passage will be concerned with Spooking. The Haggard* Journeyer will not be astonished to find that Spooking is multileveled. Women are spooked by patriarchal males in a variety of ways; for example, through implicit messages of their institutions, through body language, through the silences and deceptive devices of their media, their grammar, their education, their professions, their technology, their oppressive and confusing fashions, customs, etiquette, "humor," through their subliminal advertising and their "sublime" music (such as Christmas carols piped into supermarkets that seduce the listener into identifying with the tamed Goddess who abjectly adores her son).

Women are also spooked by other women who act as instrumental agents for patriarchal males, concurring, with varying degrees of conscious complicity, in all of the above tactics. To the extent that any woman acts — or nonacts when action is required — in such complicity,

---

* Editor's Note: Elsewhere in *Gyn/Ecology* Dr. Daly informs us that *Hag* is from the Old English word for Witch or harpy. — C.S.

she functions as a double agent of Spooking, for politically she *is* and *is not* functioning as a woman. Since Hags/Witches have expectations of her — righteous expectations which are almost impossible to discard without falling into total cynicism and despair — she spooks us doubly, particularly by her absences/silences/nonsupport. Finally, Spinsters are spooked by the alien presences that have been inspired (breathed into) our own spirits/minds. These involve fragments of the false self which are still acting/nonacting in complicity with the Possessors. They also take the shape of nameless fears, unbearable implanted guilt feelings for affirming our own being, fear of our newly discovered powers and of successful use of them, fear of dis-covering/releasing our own deep wells of anger, particularly fear of our anger against other women and against ourselves for failing our Selves. Spinsters are spooked by fear of the Ultimate Irony, which would be to become a martyr/scapegoat for feminism, whose purpose is to release women from the role of martyr and scapegoat.

Faced with being spooked, Spinsters are learning to Spook/Speak back. This Spinster-Spooking is also re-calling/re-membering/re-claiming our Witches' power to cast spells, to charm, to overcome prestige with prestidigitation, to cast glamours, to employ occult grammar, to enthrall, to bewitch. Spinster-Spooking is both cognitive and tactical. Cognitively, it means pattern-detecting. It means understanding the time-warps through which women are divided from each other — since each woman comes to consciousness through the unique events of her own history. It means also seeing the problems caused through space-warps — since Hags and potential Hags are divided from each other in separate institutional settings, disabled from sharing survival tactics in our condition of common isolation, spooked by our apparent aloneness. Tactically, Spooking means learning to refuse the seductive summons by the Passive Voices that call us into the State of Animated Death. It means learning to hear and respond to the call of the wild, learning ways of en-couraging and en-spiriting the Self and other Spinsters, learning con-questing, learning methods of dispossession, specifically of dis-possessing the Self of possession by the past and possession by the future. It means a-mazing the modern witchcraze, developing skills for unpainting the Painted Birds possessed through the device of tokenism, exposing the Thoroughly Therapeutic Society.

Since Spooking cannot always be done alone, and since it is a primary but not complete expression of Gyn/Ecology, the second chapter of this Passage is concerned with Sparking. In order to move on the con-questing Voyage, Spinsters need fire. It is significant that Witches and widows were burned alive, consumed by fire. For fire is source and symbol of energy, of gynergy. It is because women are known to be energy sources that patriarchal males seek to possess and consume us. This is done less dramatically in day-by-day draining of energy, in the slow and steady extinguishing of women's fire. Sparking is necessary to re-claim our fire. Sparking, like Spooking, is a form of Gyn/Ecology. Sparking is Speaking with tongues of fire. Sparking is igniting the divine Spark in women. Light and warmth, which are necessary for creating and moving, are results of Sparking. Sparking is creating a room of one's own, a moving time/spaceship of one's own, in which the Self can expand, in which the Self can join with other Self-centering Selves.

Sparking is making possible Female Friendship, which is totally Other from male comradeship. Hence, the Spinster will examine male comradeship/fraternity, in order to avoid the trap of confusing sisterhood with brotherhood, of thinking (even in some small dusty corner of the mind) of sisterhood as if it were simply a gender-correlative of brotherhood. She will come to see that the term *bonding*, as it applies to Hags/Harpies/Furies/Crones is as thoroughly Other from "male bonding" as Hags are the Other in relation to patriarchy. Male comradeship/bonding depends upon energy drained from women (its secret glue), since women are generators of energy. The bonding of Hags in friendship *for* women is not draining but rather energizing/gynergizing. It is the opposite of brotherhood, not essentially because Self-centering women oppose and fight patriarchy in a reactive way, but because we are/act for our Selves.

The term *comrade* is derived from a Middle French word meaning a group of soldiers sleeping in one room, or roommate. The concept of room here is spatial, suggesting links resulting from physical proximity, not necessarily from choice. The space is physical, not psychic, and it is definitely not A Room of One's Own. To the degree that it has been chosen, the choice has been made by another. The comrades do not choose each other for any inherent qualities of mind/spirit. Although this accidental and spatial "roommate" aspect does apply to all women insofar as all women are oppressed/possessed, it does not apply to the deep and conscious bonding of Hags in the process of be-ing. Since the core/the soul-spark of such deep bonding is friendship, it does not essentially depend upon an enemy for its existence/becoming.

At first, it is hard to generate enough sparks for building the fires of Female Friendship. This is particularly the case since patriarchal males, sensing the ultimate threat of Female Sparking, make every effort to put out women's fires whenever we start them. They try to steal the fire of Furies in order to destroy us in their perpetual witchcraze. Like Cinderellas, Hags stand among the cinders, but we know that they are cinders of our burned foresisters. We know that the cinders still Spark.

Sparking means building the fires of gynergetic communication and confidence. As a result, each Sparking Hag not only begins to live in a lighted and warm room of her own; she prepares a place for a loom of her own. In this space she can begin to weave the tapestries of her own creation. With her increasing fire and force, she can begin to Spin. As she and her sisters Spin together, we create The Network of our time/space.

Gyn/Ecological Spinning is essential for entry into our Otherworld. The Voyager who does not Spin is in mortal danger. She may become trapped in one of the blind alleys of the maze which has been uncovered in The Second Passage. That is, she may become fixated upon the atrocities of androcracy, "spinning her wheels" instead of spinning on her heel and facing in Other directions. Or the nonspinner may make the fatal mistake of trying to jump over the atrocities into pseudo-ecstasy. As a result of this escapism, this blind "leap of faith," she can only fall into a tailspin.

The force of Spinsters' Spinning is the power of spirit spiraling, whirling. As we break into The Third Passage, we whirl into our own world. Gyn/Ecology is weaving the way past the dead past and the dry places, weaving our world tapestry out of genesis and demise.

# Feminist Witchcraft: Controlling Our Own Inner Space

## Naomi Goldenberg

My own respect for feminist Witchcraft has grown over a two-year period of association with contemporary Witches. I have come to understand that modern Witches are using religion and ritual as psychological tools to build individual strengths. They practice a religion that places divinity or supernatural power within the person. In a very practical sense they have turned religion into psychology.

Witchcraft is the first modern theistic religion to conceive of its deity mainly as an internal set of images and attitudes. Although Witches do often speak of the times of the matriarchies, most are more concerned with that concept as a psychological and poetic force than as an historical verity. A popular aphorism among modern Witches is Monique Wittig's idea put forth in *Les Guérillères*: "There was a time when you were not a slave, remember. . . . Or, failing that, invent." Witches consider any thought or fantasy real to the degree that it influences actions in the present. In this sense a remembered fact and an invented fantasy have identical psychological value. The matriarchies, i.e., the times when no woman was a slave of any man, create visions of the pride and power women are working to have in their present lives. Thus matriarchies are functioning in modern covens and in modern Witches' dreams whether or not societies ruled by females ever existed in past history.

Of course, it is impossible to give definitive proof about the practices and beliefs of Witches who lived many years prior to the twentieth century. It is even impossible to decide whether or not the millions of so-called "witches" who were brutally massacred in the Middle Ages at the urging of Christian clergymen were Witches at all. Perhaps those burnings and hangings should be remembered chiefly as the most literal expression of the misogyny which smolders within the Christian tradition. Such misogyny was chiefly directed toward women who were labeled "witches" by the Medieval Church. No one can know whether the women who were executed actually practiced any Witchcraft at all, or, if they did, whether their Craft was similar to the type that feminists are engaged in today.

Scholarly arguments about the history of Witchcraft have obscured serious study of the modern phenomenon. Whatever one decides about Witches of the past, it is the Witches of the present who are building a powerful religion. It is the theories and practices of these Witches that ought to concern scholars of modern religious movements — especially scholars interested in religions with a psychological worldview.

Witches, like psychologists, understand that religions impose psychological interpretations on reality. These interpretations are conveyed through the images that religions sell to their worshipers. Witches believe that by selling women a male god, Judaism and Christianity have denied women the experience of seeing themselves as divine beings. Further, women are led to perceive it right and natural that men should rule their Earth the way God rules His heaven. For these reasons, Witches see religious and secular change as intimately linked. When enough women no longer agree that if "God's in His heaven — all's right with the world," feminist ideals of social justice can be implemented. One high priestess has even prophesied that until vast numbers of women control their own inner space by seeing themselves as divine and rejecting the notion of a male god, they will never succeed in getting the Equal Rights Amendment declared as law. This reasoning does not seem so farfetched when one reads the transcripts of ERA debates and sees how often God and His teachings are used to justify woman's subordinate place.

Witches want to change the internal picture that Jewish and Christian women have of a male god in heaven so that these women will no longer accept rule by males on Earth. Witches also want to strengthen secular feminists by providing imaginal depth for conceptual arguments. Since Witches believe that thoughts and actions form around psychological imagery, they feel that a woman will be a more effective feminist if her deep imaginal life has a feminist tone as well as her everyday political life. Like psychologists, Witches practice a Craft, the aim of which is to put people on better terms with their own mental life so that they can lead fuller, more productive lives. A major difference between Witches and psychotherapists is that Witches see the mental health of women as having important political consequences.

Although every modern coven does not call itself a feminist coven, all covens support feminist ideology to some degree. Even groups that grant men high positions and worship the Horned God on equal terms with the Goddess still permit women members more social power than has ever been available to them in Judeo-Christian hierarchies. The prominence of a female divinity in all forms of Witchcraft fosters psychological strength in all female Witches.

To understand the psychological ideals of modern Witchcraft, one must develop a feeling for the meaning of the Goddess in contemporary Witch culture. It is She who is the muse inspiring every feminist Witch and high priestess at work today. She is the focus for all the mental attitudes and abilities that the Craft helps women develop.

## THEALOGY – THE LOGIC OF GODDESS RELIGION

The teachings or doctrines of modern Witchcraft should not be referred to as theology. In Greek, *theos* is the word for a masculine god. *Thea* is the word for "goddess" and is a more appropriate root for a term referring to theories of feminist Witchcraft. The word *theology* has also come to be used almost exclusively in regard to Christian god-talk. The advent of Witchcraft, with its colorful goddess-talk, requires a new term. I hope Witches and scholars of feminist religion will adopt my suggestion and name themselves the*a*logians.

Currently, most modern Witches use the Old English word *wicca* to refer to a Witch as a "wise woman." Etymologists quibble over this usage. About the only fact on which scholars and Witches agree is that the first syllable, *wic*, has something to do with words that meant "to bend or twist." The word *wicker* and the Old English term for weave seem to be derived from *wic*. Since modern Witches are very concerned with weaving in a metaphoric sense — with weaving spells and learning how to bend the world to their will, I see nothing inappropriate in referring to a Witch as "wicca." We can consider the Old English term as having been reborn, so that it actually does mean "wise woman" in current usage.

The image of a woman weaving is a good one to keep in mind when viewing any theory or practice in Witchcraft. A woman who weaves is concentrating on changing natural materials into something useful for civilized life. She is skilled at a craft, which she has studied to the point of its becoming second nature. When she weaves, she uses this skill to bring something she alone can visualize psychically — like the shape of a basket or the design in a tapestry — into a material form which everyone else can see and use in their world. All Witchcraft begins with a psychic picture that a woman works to weave into reality.

In Witchcraft, the first thing a woman learns to visualize and bring to birth in the world is herself. She needs to have a positive image of herself at all stages of her life in order to be an effective presence at every age. Likewise, she must be able to conceive of her own growing, changing, and aging in ways that do not depress her, but instead foster acceptance and pride.

Many feminists have pointed out how difficult it is for most women in modern culture to accept themselves as they are in any point of their lives. The young girl is constantly directed to tailor her appearance and her personality to catch a man. The married woman is advised to work at staying young to keep her husband's interest, while the older woman is supposed to simply withdraw from life as beauty fades and she can no longer bear children.

Witches use their Goddess concept to give women positive self-images in all stages of life. They teach that the feminine life-force, i.e., the Goddess, appears in three forms — the maiden, the mother, and the crone.

The maiden Goddess is a woman who remains a virgin. Although she may be quite active sexually, the woman is virgin in the sense of being independent of her lovers and free to move and have adventures. All young, unattached women are virgins in this sense, as are all women who remain alone for long periods of their lives. The Goddess as virgin is known by many names. Athena, Diana, and Kore are three of the most popular.

The mother Goddess is a more nurturing presence. As the adult woman, she is the mother of all life forms. Raising children is considered only one creative possibility for the mother. She could choose to give birth to books, music, or a successful business as well. Whenever a woman nurtures either a person or an enterprise, Witches consider her a mother. She is acting like the Goddesses known as Demeter, Gaia, or Hera in pre-Hellenic mythology.

As the crone, the woman represents the Goddess of wisdom and prophecy. Older women, past menopause, fit the image of the crone — but so do all women who feel old and heavy with life experiences. The crones of the Witch community contribute invaluable insight and the perspective of age. Hecate is the most familiar name for this personality of the Goddess.

Witchcraft is the only Western religion that recognizes woman as a divinity in her own right. Mary, the only remnant of Goddess left in the Christian tradition, is recognized solely because of her son. In contrast, the maiden, mother, and crone Goddesses of Witchcraft are valued on their own terms. They are honored as independent beings with their own divine styles of experiencing life. The triple Goddess provides imagery of depth and mythic impact, which is completely unavailable to women in any other Western religious tradition.

In addition to elevating the image of woman in religious symbology, Witchcraft also improves the idea of woman in secular culture. Because each Witch is taught to see herself as the Goddess in all activities, she makes no separation between her religious ideals and her worldly behavior. The triple Goddess allows the Witch to envision herself as a regal, valuable being even when she feels unattractive or old — even when she is unattached to any man or to any child. Social pressure to remain forever young and sexy is counteracted, and a woman does not have to justify herself exclusively by the ways she complements the lives of others. Because Witchcraft honors several styles of life in its imagery, Witches can honor several styles of life in themselves. The Craft encourages a psychological range and flexibility which few other modern philosophies or techniques of self-development can provide for their female adherents.

Acceptance of psychological change is also fostered by linking the triple Goddess to the cycles of the moon. The waxing moon is the maiden, the full moon is the mother, and the waning moon represents the crone. Since the cycles of the moon are thought of as related to all human activities, they serve to remind Witches of the ebb and flow of all energy for projects and enterprise. Human effort is seen in a realistic fashion. Times of depression and withdrawal are expected, and there is no intense pressure to effect major changes in one's life or circumstances immediately. The philosophy of Witchcraft is a patient one that encourages steady, gradual transformation.

This attitude toward change guides the procedures for all rituals and spells directed toward self-transformation. At holiday gatherings, for example, Starhawk uses a cup of wine to encourage meditation about gradual change. She passes the cup around the circle and asks each covener to gaze into the wine and envision herself changed in some desirable fashion — either in outlook or in material circumstances. Each Witch then swallows just a small sip of the changed picture she has projected into the wine. No sudden alteration is expected. Nevertheless, by visualizing the change, a goal for self-development has been set. By symbolically internalizing that goal in the small swallow of wine, Witches hope to initiate a cycle of progress toward it.

With the moon as their main metaphor for growth and development, Witches have a theme of a slow and steady process in any work of psychological transformation they might undertake. A place for the waning moon encourages acceptance of inevitable setbacks and regressions as well.

# Contemporary Feminist Rituals

## Kay Turner

Comprend, we sweat out our rituals together. We change them, we're all
the time changing them! But they body our sense of good!
—MARGE PIERCY, *Woman on the Edge of Time*

The body is the image relator. In ritual, we *embody* and activate images of the archetypal, the eternal feminine, the Goddess. Images of
power, of transformation, of harmony, and of duality. One woman empowering another. The crucial exchange of gifts. I cross the circle to
give you something; you cross the circle to give her something. And so
on until we have all changed places. Power held is powerless; power
given is power for all. In feminist ritual we maintain a center of which
we are all aware. It is our collective heart which beats there. We hold
together, our center endures. Even the most painful separation, the dis-
persal which is feared but necessary, cannot disconnect us from that ritual circle. Once that circle is created and affirmed, chaos is subdued.
We survive. We thrive.

Although some theoretical attention has been given to the recent spiritual awakening within the women's movement, very little writing has been directed toward analysis of the use of ritual by women. What do these ritual acts mean to contemporary U.S. feminists? And what is their significance in terms of the women's movement?

Feminists are primarily at work revising the male-biased ideological bases of culture; some are now engaged in the creation of rituals to promote and sanction this serious turning away from the old to the new. As in traditional societies, feminist ritual provides an emotional, descriptive, intensified and sanctifying version of emergent ideological systems. Feminist ritual offers an imagistic revitalization for women and a participation in the concrete, bodily expressive creation of new images of the feminine which helps alleviate the stress of liminality.

The evaluation of culture by Michelle Zimbalist Rosaldo in her theoretical overview for *Woman, Culture and Society* serves as useful background material for answering why women have created rituals as an expression of the need for revitalization and as an impetus for political action. First, Rosaldo establishes a model for interpreting the difference in status between men and women, a model based on extensive contemporary cross-cultural analysis of male/female roles and behavior. She states that "an asymmetry in the cultural evaluations of male and female, in the importance assigned to women and men, appears to be universal."[1] This asymmetry is manifested in

the fact that male, as opposed to female, activities are always recognized as predominantly important, and cultural systems give authority and value to the roles and activities of men. . . . Everywhere, from those societies we might want to call most egalitarian to those in which sexual stratification is most marked, men are the locus of cultural value.[2]

Over the past few thousand years women have not been culturally granted a legitimate, overt way of demonstrating their power, their personhood. Only men define, possess, and confer power or authority, and power is the necessary ingredient for the creation of culture. Women are therefore consigned to live on the fringes of culture, locked in domestic zones which are rarely defined as part of the cultural territory. Rosaldo elaborates this point by using Mary Douglas's notion of "the anomalous."

Recent studies of symbolic culture have suggested that whatever violates a society's sense of order will be seen as threatening, nasty, disorderly, or wrong. Douglas has called this sort of thing "anomalous." The idea of "order" depends, logically, on "disorder" as its opposite, yet society tries to set such things aside . . . Insofar as men . . . define the public order women are their opposite. Where men are classified in terms of ranked, institutional positions, women are simply women and their activities, interests and differences receive only idiosyncratic note.[3]

Women are anomalies in many cultures and have no cultural recourse for demonstrating the reality of female power. Female power is almost without exception displayed covertly under the rubric of influence or association. But Rosaldo makes a unique claim for the possible use women may make of their anomalous or liminal positions.

Even though women's status is lowest in those societies where there is the greatest distinction between the public and domestic realms and where women are isolated from each other, "their position is raised when they can challenge those claims of male authority, either by taking on men's roles or by establishing social ties, by creating a sense of rank, order, and value in a world in which women prevail."[4] It is also clear that historically women have taken on very active roles in social systems by "manipulating, elaborating, or undermining" their domestic roles and by stressing their differences from men. In other words, by giving special attention to their anomalous status, women have been able "to take on powers uniquely their own."[5] Especially pertinent to our discussion, Rosaldo mentions the roles of nun, midwife, Witch, and religious prostitute as making particularly positive use of women's "anomalous" sexuality. "These examples suggest that the very symbolic and social conceptions [the notions of purity and pollution associated with women] that appear to set women apart and to circumscribe their activities may be used by women as a basis for female solidarity and worth."[6]

Of course it is most significant that these roles include the classic examples of women who have been allowed to utilize ritual means as a source of gaining and transferring power. Generally, men have held the rights to ritual use; in fact, the participation in ritual by men has been their most profound display of cultural authority and their most direct access to it. The performance of ritual in most societies, "primitive" and "civilized," is a simultaneous acknowledgment of men's warrant to create and define culture and, by exclusion, a sign to women to keep in their place, a place which we have already designated as outside culture and without the symbolic or real attributes of power.

Here we see a further distinction between the sacred and the profane based on the asymmetry of male-female relationships. Men have claimed sacred space as their locus for effecting control over and/or maintaining harmony with each other and the Fates. As Mircea Eliade has shown, sacred space is "manifested space"; it is created as sacred by men and in most societies women have little or no access to it.[7] Women live in the profane world, the world that is incapable of being transformed or of transforming those who live in it. Of course men live in the profane world too (in fact we all live there most of the time), but when they choose to do so (or when the "gods" command them to do so) they may enter another world, a world of the sacred, and through ritual practice they may take part in ordering that world and themselves. The sacred realm is that of being and becoming, a realm saturated with power and critically "off-limits" to the female half of the human species.

That women in the United States and elsewhere have begun to claim sacred space for themselves, to create rituals which emphasize their loyalty to each other and finally name the powers which men have found "anomalous" (i.e., nameless) is indeed an ultimate, radical (proceeding from the root) affirmation of the revolutionary potential of the feminist movement. Asserting the right to ritual means as a source of power, vision, and solidarity is the symbolic corollary of equal pay, choice of abortion, domestic freedom, the establishment of women's businesses, etc. Successful and enduring change in the status of women will come only through the parallel transformation of symbols and realities. Feminist ritual practice is currently the most important model for symbolic and, therefore, psychic and spiritual change in women.

Here I would like to describe briefly a number of feminist rituals which characterize but certainly do not exhaust the kind and variety of expression this form has taken.

In her *Spotted Bundle Enclosures,* artist Jody Pinto digs out old brick wells outside Philadelphia. At the bottom of these wells she leaves personal and found objects wrapped in animal skins. Next to these bundles Pinto makes a primitive fireplace with shards and cooking utensils. She constructs a ladder and leaves it down the side of the well as an invitation for others to come in. Reflecting on the creation of these ritual sites and her activity in them, Pinto writes, "The other day I spread wings/split a man in half/spent a year in the earth/excavated my own tomb/rolled over/cut out my heart/and ate it."[8]

Donna Henes's *Spider Woman Series* involves web-building in natural and urban environments. Henes defines web-making as the "most basic female instinct" and has made a personal ritual of web-making over the past three years.[9]

Margi Gumpert, a Witch by trade and by faith, performs a specific ritual whenever she enters a public bathroom:

I often notice that the mirror reflects an image which makes me question myself, feel critical or dissatisfied with my appearance. I don't ignore it as trivial, because I recognize that the mirror is infested with a very common political poison, *virus hollywoodius* or *televisioniensis,* subtle pressure to measure up to a pattern designed to enslave. Just to free myself of that pressure isn't a magical operation. But hundreds of other women will use that mirror. So after I have cleared my own image of that false cloud, I usually perform some sort of magical activity to neutralize the poison. I pour suggestive energy into the mirror, encouraging anyone who might look in it to see herself in her true beauty. I reinforce the suggestion with all the power of my will and call on the Goddess of Beauty Herself, blessed Aphrodite, to banish that which would deny Her, as She exists in all of us.[10]

A ritual for the Autumn Equinox is performed yearly by a group of women living in the country near Wolf Creek, Oregon:

Let friends gather, each bringing with her an article which represents a recent accomplishment — some self-chosen task she has completed. Let a circle form and each one place her article in front of her, and next to it a fruit, seed, or cone. Join hands and chant in unison the names of all present — several times till the energy is high. Then pause and chant the months of the year from the Winter Solstice to the Autumn Equinox.

Now let each one in turn hold her article while she tells her friends of her accomplishment and something she has learned from it. When all have spoken, all shall pick up the fruit, seed or cone in front of them and picture inwardly the process of its change from seed to plant to flower to seed.

Again let each woman speak in turn of what her accomplishment has meant to her growth and how she thinks it may be useful to her self and others. At this time if she feels grateful, let her give thanks. If she wants to dance, let her move. When all have expressed their feeling, with closed eyes ask yourself "What is the next stage in the process of my growth?" Ask your inner self for energy and guidance to continue.

Let all join hands, moving closer into a hugging circle and repeat:

> After the joy of harvest
> After the work of the day
> After the time of fulfillment
> Comes the time of rest.
> After the seed is planted
> Nature takes care of the rest.[11]

On the streets of downtown Boston a woman wearing a high feather headdress makes a circle of cornmeal, places three ears of corn in the center of the circle, and begins a rhythmic chant naming the goddesses of the Americas before the conquest (Tonantzin, Chicomecoaltl, Blue Corn Girl, IxChel, etc.). After the chant is finished, she calls on women passing by, invites them into the circle, and blesses them by saying in litany form an ancient Aztec poem from the *Poesia Nahautl:*

> Now o friends
> Listen to the words of a dream
> Each spring brings us new life
> The golden corn refreshes us
> And the pink corn makes us a necklace
> At least this we know:
> The hearts of our friends are true.

While the women alternate in speaking the lines of the poem to each other, they hold an ear of corn between them and tear the sheaves down exposing the fresh corn.[12]

The following ritual was recounted in *Sundance,* a journal devoted to the study and sharing of dreams.

In a past issue of *WomanSpirit* there is an article by Hallie Iglehart describing an overnight wilderness event attended by twelve women. The purpose of the venture was to share dreams, become deeper friends and explore the meaning to each of them of being women. To prepare for dreaming together, the twelve women arranged their sleeping bags into a "wheel" surrounding a central pole. In addition, each woman had two strands of ribbon attached to her sleeping bag which were then attached to the pole, making a "dream net." The arrangement is quite similar to the May Pole and Sun Dance ceremonies, except, in this case, the people are lying down, asleep and dreaming. As an approximation to a contemporary experiment in revelation, a twelve-person "dream wheel" inspires continued exploration.[13]

By way of contrast and comparison, I want to present a woman's ritual which has been practiced on the Yucatan Peninsula for centuries. A form of this ritual is still performed today but the following account was recorded in 1930 by Basauri and translated by J. Eric Thompson in his "The Moon Goddess in Central America." The ceremony is called "the song of the roses," KAIK' MIKTE.

A hollow is made in a level place and filled with water. This hollow should be of sufficient size so that a woman may take a bath in it. The woman, who hopes to benefit from the ceremony is placed in it completely naked.

Once she is in and the liquid reaches to the height of her breasts, they [other women who participate in the ceremony] cover the surface with flowers. Several women, friends of the one to be benefited, the number of which may vary, but never falls below five, take hands and dance around the bather, some singing and others saying a prayer in Maya. The dance lasts an hour, and during that time the dancers take flowers which they have already prepared, stoop down to moisten them in the water in which the principal bathes, and throw them on the breast of the woman making the ceremony (la solicitante). During the dance it is the custom to make nine turns in one direction, stop a moment to moisten the flowers, and then repeat the same number of turns in the opposite direction. When the ceremony is ended, the dancers retire, the woman remains alone in the water, and, on coming out, she takes a quantity of it, which she carries with her to employ in the preparation of her husband's or lover's food.[14]

Although the ritual is ostensibly practiced to make their lovers remain faithful, the beauty of the ceremony lies in its kinship with all ritual acts, both past and present, which describe the healing, nurturing effect of tribal sisterhood. The overt goal of the ritual is not the only reason for performing it; something significant is taking place in the act of performance, too. An individual woman is uplifted and sacralized by her sisters, her *comadres*, her C-R group, her kind.

In "The Qualitative Leap Beyond Patriarchal Religion," theologian Mary Daly makes the following statement:

The Women's revolution is not merely about equality within a patriarchal society (a contradiction in terms). It is about *power* and redefining power. Within patriarchy, power is generally understood as power over people, the environment, things. In the rising consciousness of women, power is experienced as *power of presence* to ourselves and to each other, as we affirm our own being against and beyond the alienated identity bestowed upon us within the patriarchy. This is experienced as *power of absence* by those who would objectify women as "the other," as magnifying mirrors.[15]

Daly's insistence that redefinition of power is a central goal of the women's movement is crucial for understanding the use of ritual by feminists as a symbolic model for discovering how to give and get "power of presence." One woman empowers another (or herself) through reaffirmation of the body as an instrument of communion (not alienation).

None of the rituals mentioned above would be considered effective if a transfer of power had not resulted. Yet it is of critical importance to note that power is rarely considered an object of possession which the group or individual may get hold of during ritual activity. What is stressed through ritual is the dynamic quality of power, the continual exchange of gifts which heightens the affirmative identity of all who participate. Power emanates from within as it is simultaneously received from without. For women in revolution it is imperative to create an entirely new value system, the heart of which will be a dramatic reassessment of the use of power. Ritual serves as a primary way of affirming commitment to that reassessment. The ritual setting provides a place for knowing the easy, direct exchange and sharing of power. Certainly ritual is an idealized microcosmic experience, but it may be an endurably important means of invoking a new order of things in the macrocosm. At the very least, it has been a useful mode for envisioning what a different world for women might *feel* like.

The word "feeling" deserves special mention in connection with women's rituals. In fact it is a word we must never neglect in talking about any ritual. Evon Vogt once asked a ritual participant, "Why do you go through the ceremonies? Why do you do what you do?" The participant replied, "To feel better, I want to make myself feel better."[16] In the context of ritual women are creating a space in which to feel better, to feel more, to feel the past as well as the future. Perhaps most important is the way in which ritual upholds and celebrates the validity of feeling as a mode of revelation, communication, and transvaluation. In some of the rituals described above, the flow of feelings, change in feelings, or sharing of feelings with others is a highly desirable goal in performing the ritual.

In discussing the reasons underlying the performance of ritual acts in the feminist community, we must underscore the importance of ritual as a formalized consecration of female bonding. The ritual concretization of the idea reflected in the popular feminist slogan "Sisterhood is Powerful" is extremely important in demonstrating the cohesiveness and commitment of the feminist community. A primary function of ritual is to connect the individual with the group — dramatically, indissolubly. In ritual the desire is to achieve shared meanings, shared resolutions, shared emotion, not to promote private images or dreams. The specific rites which comprise many feminist rituals reaffirm relationship, belonging, and identity. Ritual acts maintain a symbolic center of which all the participants are aware. This center is a place to which one can return for support and comfort long after the ceremony has ended. A relational or ideological bond cemented formally through ritual procedure is nothing if not enduring.

Being capable of membership in a group and finding ways of expressing that membership and acting it out are necessary for the success of
any political revolution. Let us not forget that less than ten years ago
Lionel Tiger told us "women do not bond"[17] and in so saying implied
women are incapable of creating significant political institutions. On
the contrary, we often find that the female bonds established in ritual
reinforce the female bonds that inspire social change. The use of ritual
is significant as a source for the renewal of commitment to evolving and
transforming society as a whole.

Many feminists consider the ritual setting and experience to serve as
a visionary mode. In authentic ritual experience something, an ability
to break through the present, is available which can lead to discovery
and creativity. Ritual is a potent source of invention because the participants feel the extreme intensity, sometimes the ecstasy, of openness to
possibility and revelation.

Another important consideration is the way feminist ritual purpose-
fully imparts information of a special kind, information which has been
unavailable to women and actually suppressed for hundreds of years. I
refer specifically to the ritual communication of feminine images, primarily the communication of images of goddesses. The suppression of
the Goddess in our culture has meant the loss of images which identify
personal and collective power in the female. Invocations to the
goddesses, references to their attributes, a reclamation of the wealth of
literature which remains to describe them, the putting on of their symbols — none of these ritual actions indicates a desire to return to a
golden matriarchal age as some critics have suggested. It is much more
crucial for feminists, for all women, to uncover and recover their
imagistic heritage (as represented in the powers and tales of the
goddesses) and to create new images which represent women's recent
emergence (as many women in the plastic and performing arts are now
doing) than it is to prove the absolute historical existence of a widespread matriarchy. I have no doubt that some matriarchies did exist.
The important consideration, however, is not the fact that women ruled
over men but that they "ruled" themselves and that they had culturally
approved or at least culturally active models for distinguishing their
particular powers from others. In many ancient civilizations the feminine world was not as "anomalous" as it currently is. Women had access to powerful images and used them to order and maintain their particular spheres of life.

One of the most important shrines in the pre-Conquest Mayan world was located on Cozumel Island twenty miles off the coast of the Yucatan. It was dedicated to IxChel, the pre-eminent goddess of the moon, water, childbirth, weaving, and love, who was equal in status to the great father god, Itzamna. Her shrine was visited by women from all over the Mayan world, some traveling hundreds of miles from what is now Guatemala and El Salvador. Inside the shrine a giant image of the Goddess served as an oracle for the pilgrims. The statue was hollowed out in back; a priestess would stand in that profound cavity and impersonate the Goddess, become a speaking image of the Goddess and in essence *imagine* herself the Goddess. To imagine is to make an image or become an image; impersonation of this sort was an achievement of relation with the Goddess and a means of absorbing Her powers. Images are sources of identification; they tell us who we most profoundly, most archetypally are. The Mayan women who visited the shrine at Cozumel were seeking affirmation of their own powers (primarily the power to give birth, to be fruitful) and they received it through the pilgrimage itself (the association with peers), idol worship (intense identification with an image of power), and through the ritual blessing bestowed by the personified Goddess, the priestess.

Much the same identification is sought and achieved in feminist rituals. Ritual is a special vehicle of communication for feminists; ritual speaks a visceral language of the restoration of symbols and provides an opportunity to utilize them personally. Sherry Ortner says that "Efforts directed solely at changing the social institutions cannot have far-reaching effects if cultural language and imagery continue to purvey a relatively devalued view of women."[18] The imagery conveyed woman-to-woman in ritual experience is imagery that upholds the value of women and symbolizes the varied kinds of their power. If, as Vogt maintains, "Ritual perpetuates knowledge essential to the survival of the culture,"[19] women are just now learning how important it is to their survival to store and transmit feminine knowledge through ritual means.

Much of the available data on women's rituals reveal the prominence of one individual as instigator or leader of the ritual. This is not always the case as many rituals are performed without a leader, including rituals which follow a format repeated the same way every time, rituals which rely on group spontaneity, group meditation or chanting, etc. Nevertheless, a number of women in the feminist community have emerged as ritualists, the counterpart to the shaman in traditional societies. Most women involved in introducing ritual performance, however, do not call themselves shamans or think of themselves as such; they are most widely known simply as ritualists (or practitioners or Witches if they adhere solely to the Witchcraft tradition). The comparison between shamans and feminist ritualists is instructive only in demonstrating that their goals in performance are similar and, to a certain extent, their conception of self is analogous.

If the ultimate goal of ritual experience is to effect transformation, in most cases someone must prepare the participants to undergo change. An appropriate procedure must be decided upon and followed correctly to lead the participants from one state of feeling to another. Both the shaman and feminist ritualist make preparations and later facilitate the group's progress in the actual ritual; both are capable of helping transformation to take place if the participants will trust them. I am stressing here the fact that both shaman and feminist ritualist express a powerful sense of capability, that they can serve as links, as surrogates, that they can connect different realms of reality and facilitate change by embodying change. Both roles are played by individuals who have changed and are concerned with enabling the change of others. Eliade says of the shaman: "He is, above all, a sick man who has been cured, who has succeeded in curing himself."[20] The feminist ritualist is also one who has been "sick" in the sense that oppression makes one feel sick. She who is now cured of the tyranny of oppression offers that new sense of well-being to others.

An obvious similarity between the traditional shaman and the feminist ritualist is that both do their work through performing (singing, dancing, displaying, holding, hugging) and, moreover, the performance is quite often geared to awakening and stimulating the participant's body, for both ritualist and shaman see the body, not the mind, as the locus of transformation. The body is our first and last outward reality; it defines and conditions our life experience and gives us personal identity and continuity. Both shaman and ritualist take the body to be the clearest, purest expression of self. And it is that aspect of self which must feel change before the intellectual or soul self can change. A chant I used in a ritual performance called *Seeing the Voice* expresses the bodily locus of ritual transformation:

> My hands
> Open the curtains of your being
> Clothe you in a further nudity
> Uncover the bodies of your body
> My hands
> Invent another body for your body[21]

The body is recognized as the means for making conscious interconnections and unions that were unconscious or suppressed. Ritual creates a new body, one body made of many, through which can be realized and understood the extremes of fear and love, the truly political dimensions of humanness.

Finally, the relation between the shaman and his participant community and the parallel relation between the feminist ritualist and her participant community bears notation. Richard Schechner maintains that "the deep structure of shamanistic performance is a protagonist-antagonist conflict by means of which the secret wishes of the community are exposed and redistributed. . . . The Shaman is the vessel through which all that is powerful chooses to express itself. And these powers are inherent in community itself, are the community."[22] Thus both shaman and ritualist exist primarily within a community and the powers they exemplify ultimately belong not to themselves as individuals but to the community which is the actual source of their power. The work of both the shaman and the ritualist is to make available, to clarify and intensify powers that are the essence of community. Transformation is useless in isolation.

In stressing the communal nature of the ritual experience, it may appear that the concept of the self and its nurturance are not served; as the examples given earlier indicate, some feminist rituals are performed solely for the purpose of self-revelation. From its inception the women's movement has insisted on the importance of realizing the way in which political change comes out of reinterpretation and reinvention of the personal dimension (the personal is political). All women have suffered the loss of affirmative, positive self-images as a direct result of their second-class status and consequent objectification in the male-dominant society. It is painful to consider the countless lives wasted, the talents atrophied and the sickness suffered by women who were never allowed, least of all encouraged, to know themselves and take strength and happiness in that knowledge. Surely one of the most highly regarded uses of ritual in traditional societies is the curing of "soul loss" of one form or another. Twentieth-century, postindustrial, special-privileged American women are engaged in ritual practice for much the same reason, metaphorically speaking.

For women, the ritual setting is often a place for naming individual powers and sharing the affirmation of those powers with the group or simply internalizing them through private ritual procedure. Ritual provides a mode for getting in touch with the self and staying in touch.

Also, by definition, the ritual space and activity are sacred in the sense of representing the possibility of self-transformation. Part of the power and the fear experienced in ritual is the realization that one may change, become ultimately different, as a result of the experience or that the experience may suddenly make recognizable change that has been slowly rising from the depths of the personality. Victor Turner states, "When a ritual does work . . . it can cause in some cases real transformations of character and of social relationships."[23] I would venture to say that many women have been profoundly affected and, in some cases, redirected through their experience in ritual. A lost self is recovered, nurtured and allowed to emerge fully named.

Ritual facilitates transition for the participant in specific ways. As Turner clearly states, "Practically all rituals of any length and complexity represent a passage from one position, constellation, or domain of structure to another."[24] This passage occurs in individual women most dramatically, and not without fear, separation anxiety, and trauma. Before women can enter new roles they must leave old roles behind, roles that once provided the comforts of self-definition and reality structure. Ritual participation can ease transition by rendering it in dramatic, concrete, and symbolic terms and providing a support group to encourage and enable the necessary catharsis to take place.

The transfer of values from one framework to another leaves a woman vulnerable, suspended between two life styles. It is a dangerous time for her, one which requires the support of her feminist community and the use of ritual to promote ease in the transfer. Women are realizing that this is a responsibility and a desire: to help other women cross boundaries in their lives not as aggressive individuals, proving themselves, but as new members of a community who deserve the help and protection of those who have gone before. We have all been guarded and we must all become guardians. The ritual setting allows women to know the power of guarding and the comfort of being guarded in a space that does not demand immediate resolution of the passage crisis. The crisis period may continue through many phases of recognition, adjustment, and readjustment, the assimilation of which will fall primarily on the individual. But the community has developed ritual means by which that transformation may be asserted and its painful aspects somewhat absorbed by a formal claim made on the individual — a claim that she is new, that she is one of many, that she is welcome.

For feminists, as for other practitioners of ritual, doing the ritual is more important than knowing the ritual. The efficacy of ritual is always in the acting of it, in becoming bodily involved with its elements as a source of knowing through feeling. The essence of ritual is in physical relationship, one woman to another (or one woman to herself) in the circle of affirmation they have created for each other.

This article only begins the necessary process of defining and evaluating the emergence of ritual as an important component of the greater liberation movement. To my knowledge, only Lucy Lippard's article in *Chrysalis* specifically deals with the meaning of ritual for feminists. No other theoretical material is available, although movement media sources such as *WomanSpirit, Lady-Unique-Inclination-of-the-Night,* and *Quest* have been documenting ritual practices among women since 1974. My sense of the importance of ritual for the feminist community comes out of an understanding of its historical importance for humanity. Ritual marks the ultimate ideal of relationship between self and community, the fusion, rather than separation, of these two distinct realities.

NOTES

1. Michelle Zimbalist Rosaldo, "A Theoretical Overview," in *Woman, Culture and Society,* ed. Michelle Zimbalist Rosaldo and Louise Lamphere (Stanford: University Press, 1974), p. 19.

2. *Ibid.,* pp. 19–20.

3. *Ibid.,* p. 31.

4. *Ibid.,* p. 36.

5. *Ibid.,* p. 38.

6. *Ibid.,* p. 39.

7. Mircea Eliade, *Shamanism* (Princeton: Princeton University Press, 1964).

8. Lucy Lippard, "Quite Contrary: Body, Nature, Ritual in Women's Art," *Chrysalis* (Autumn 1977), p. 38.

9. *Ibid.,* p. 43. Also personal communication.

10. Margi Gumpert, "Witchcraft," *Country Women,* April 1974, p. 27.

11. Jean Mountaingrove, "Speaking to Ourselves," *WomanSpirit,* Autumn 1974, p. 27.

12. Observed at the conference "Through the Looking Glass: A Gynergenetic Experience," Boston, 23–25 April 1976.

13. Henry Reed, ed., *Sundance,* Spring 1977, p. 262.

14. J. Eric Thompson, "The Moon Goddess in Central America" (Carnegie Institute of Washington Pub. 509, Contribution 29, 1939). Cited in *Lady-Unique-Inclination-of-the-Night,* Cycle 1, p. 49.

15. Mary Daly, "The Qualitative Leap Beyond Patriarchal Religion," *Quest*, vol. 1, no. 1, p. 21.

16. Evon Vogt, *Tortillas for the Gods* (Cambridge: Harvard University Press, 1976).

17. Lionel Tiger, *Men in Groups* (New York: Random House, 1969).

18. Sherry Ortner, "Is Female to Male as Nature Is to Culture?", in *Woman, Culture and Society*, p. 87.

19. Vogt, *op. cit.*, p. 8.

20. Eliade, *op. cit.*, p. 27.

21. Octavio Paz, "Touch," in *Configurations* (New York: New Directions, 1971), p. 63.

22. Richard Schechner, *Environmental Theater* (New York: Hawthorne Books, 1973), pp. 189–190.

23. Victor Turner, *Dramas, Fields and Metaphors* (Ithaca: Cornell University Press, 1974), p. 56.

24. *Ibid.*, p. 238.

# Honor and Ceremony in Women's Rituals

# E. M. Broner

Gender preceded modern religion. We were women before we were Jews, Christians, Moslems. It seems only natural, historical, and just, therefore, to make religion respond to our origins.

Preserved on tablet and stone are historical ceremonies. Women greeted the new moon, presided at births, held forth at funerals. We selected our mates and passed property on to our daughters. Ancient female gods were honored by their daughter priests in psalms. But after the gender of God was changed, all else changed. Woman became the ruled. Psalms were neither written to her nor by her. Her rights as a citizen were denied. She shrank as a human and was condemned as a deity. Gradually rites even excluded her. Looking casually for definitions, one finds today (in *Webster's New World Dictionary*) that *rite* is "a division of . . . churches according to the liturgy used; specifically, a patriarchate."

Many of those prepatriarchal ceremonies have survived as vestigial structures into the present, vestigial because their original meaning has been altered. The new moon ceremony is danced at the beginning of the Jewish month by male Chasidic Jews. The birthing ceremony in the Jewish religion welcomes only the birth of a boy child. The puberty ceremony welcomes only the maturation of the boy child. After death, it is the son who can mourn for his parents. Even the word *holy* in Hebrew has been reserved for males exclusively. It derived from the Akkadian name for the holy women of the temple, *kadishtu,* and has passed into Hebrew as *kadesh, holy.* The prayer for the dead, *kaddesh,* another form of *holy,* is uttered only by the male lips. That which is not holy is profane. Women priests were renamed temple prostitutes.

Ritual displays cultural authority. Kay Turner has observed that in patriarchal religions and the societies they influence ritual is used as "man's warrant to create and define culture and, by exclusion, a sign to women to keep in their place, a place . . . without the symbolic or real attributes of power."[1] The patriarchal world would remove woman from ritual.

It is my feeling that all humans mark their paths on trees, mark time with ceremony. That repetition and orderliness make for ritual. Etymologically, *rite* is from *ritual,* as is *arithmetic.* We want sums, constants. *Rhythm* is from the same root. Ritual is a collective experience, repeated and sanctified. We perform it to remind ourselves and one another that we are not alone, that we sing in chorus. We are historical, and what has happened to us is not an isolated instance. Birth has occurred before, and we women birth in a cave of women's experiences, when we are fortunate. Death has happened before, and we lament with others who have suffered losses.

The power of ritual has been explored by Barbara Myerhoff:

All rituals are paradoxical and dangerous enterprises, the traditional and improvised, the sacred and secular. Paradoxical because rituals are conspicuously artificial and theatrical, yet designed to suggest the inevitability and absolute truth of their messages. Dangerous because when we are not convinced by a ritual we may become aware of ourselves as having made them up, thence on to the paralyzing realization that we have made up all our truths; our ceremonies, our most precious conceptions and convictions—all are mere invention.[2]

*Number Our Days,* Dr. Myerhoff's anthropological study of the Jewish community center for the aging in Venice, California, shows lyrically and compassionately how central ritual is to the lives of the elderly and how expectation of a ritual even prolongs their years.

If not to prolong life, but to mark it, I began creating ritual. I made ceremony out of need before knowing an anthropological definition. Nor was I aware, in the writing and performance of a ceremony, of its aftereffects. Kay Turner would define me as a "feminist ritualist." She believes women in the United States and elsewhere have "begun to claim sacred space for themselves, to create rituals . . . as a source of power, vision, and solidarity. . . ." Turner defines ritual as political: "Feminist ritual practice is currently the most important model for symbolic and, therefore, psychic and spiritual change in women."[3]

These early forms of woman worship have faded but not disappeared. We have tenuous connections with the Mother Gods — reproductions in art books, literary allusions. I have had the warm feeling of stone in my hand when I lifted a household manifestation of female deity. I do not think of those ancient women as testing our souls or as representing a body of law that governs our lives, yet we have to know of them, to know of that origin, of that beginning, *B'Reshit,* as the first section of the Bible is called. In the Beginning. If we do not know of that earliest of beginnings, we will think of the world as having begun in the Testaments. Our allusions, speech, vision have been altered by the supplanting of one mythic context for another. We attest, testify, test ourselves. The origin of *testament* is *testes, testicle,* that most holy of objects on which men swore (the Hebrew patriarchs and their servants placed their hands there and swore the sacred oath). If we must swear by the Old and New Testes, then we worship a false idol that was "erected" while others were leveled. If we do not remember our womanly origins, then we lose our images, our language, and the meaning of the cave of self.

I, being a Jew, have written ceremonies timed to the Jewish calendar. I have written a Spring exodus, a Woman's Passover Haggadah; I have worked on High Holy Day ceremonies and a revision of Chanukah. One might ask, "Isn't that acceptable to the Jewish faith then? Isn't that being a good Jew?" No, for as Cynthia Ozick has demonstrated, a woman cannot be a Jew. In her brilliant, talmudic essay, "Notes Toward Finding the Right Question," Ozick explains that under Jewish law "women *qua* women are seen as a subdivision of humanity, not as the main class itself . . . the male is the norm and the female a class apart."[4] She describes sitting among women in her traditional synagogues:

. . . and the rabbi speaks the word "Jew." I can be sure that he is not referring to me, for to him "Jew" means "male Jew" . . . When my rabbi says, "A Jew is called to the Torah," he never means me or any other living Jewish woman.

The Jewish woman has limited access for her talents as a devotional writer, for the use of her mind. Even after the Holocaust when so much was lost, Ozick notes, the loss of the intelligence of the woman is not yet counted. Since the works of the Jewish people are not the work of all the people but of half — for woman was never allowed to contribute to that pride and monument, Torah (Law) — Ozick concludes that the law "is in this respect frayed."

## CREATING OUR EXODUS FROM DARKNESS

Perhaps in disobeying one law we create another. Perhaps in changing one ceremony, we make another. The first corrective ceremony I co-created was the women's Passover.

It is written in Exodus and in the male Haggadah: "In each generation let each man look on himself as if he came forth out of Egypt." It further directs, "And thou shalt tell thy son. . . ." How is it possible that a ceremony in which I have participated my entire remembered life makes no mention of my coming out of Egypt, and I am not commanded to remind my daughter of the exodus? In the male Haggadah four sons ask questions on which the entire seder is structured, and these questions are answered by wise men. How is it possible that with all the formalistic and informal debate and dispute, with all the revisions to the Haggadah, not a woman is mentioned?

Passover is regarded as a Freedom Holiday. Not to women. It is the time of spring cleaning, changing of dishes, shopping for special ingredients, cooking of dishes peculiar to the holiday. It is the time when we rise from the table to tend the big dinner while the men are seated and tend to the prayer.

I and my co-author of the new ceremony, Naomi Nimrod of Haifa, met to study and revise this ceremony and its attendant customs during the spring of 1975 in Israel. As the male Haggadah begins with the child singing four questions, we began with different questions: "Why is this Haggadah different from traditional Haggadoth?" "Because this Haggadah deals with the exodus of women." We altered the second question also and the next two. Instead of asking about the bitter herbs, we asked: "Why have our mothers on this night been bitter?" "Because they did the preparation but not the ritual. They did the serving but not the conducting. They read of their fathers but not of their mothers." The question that traditionally deals with leaning back on pillows to celebrate being free men, we altered: "Why on this night do we recline?" "We recline on this night for the unhurried telling of the legacy of Miriam."

In writing women into the festival of freedom—the end of slavery, the time of crossing borders—we *named* women. We chose the first prophet of all, Miriam, as our symbol. We followed her in Torah, in commentaries, and legends. We followed her prophecy of the exodus, her safe-guarding of the baby in the bullrushes until he was rescued, her dancing on the banks of the Red Sea long afterwards, celebrating exodus, her anger when she was deprived of honor, God's punishment inflicted upon her by turning her into a leper and curing her a week later to teach her the lesson of pride. We learned the lesson well— woman large yet brought low, woman supplanted by younger brother, woman disappearing, and leaving no footprint in the desert. We used the male Haggadah as the spine of our ceremony and, within it, reincorporated women. We dug up Miriam's bones from the desert. And we asked questions.

## THE SONG OF QUESTIONS

Mother, asks the clever daughter,
who are our mothers?
Who are our ancestors?
What is our history?
Give us our name. Name our genealogy.

Mother, asks the wicked daughter,
if I learn my history,
will I not be angry?
Will I not be bitter as Miriam
who was deprived of her prophecy?

Mother, asks the simple daughter,
if Miriam lies buried in sand,
why must we dig up those bones?
Why must we remove her from sun and stone
where she belongs?

> The one who knows not how to question,
> she has no past,
> she can have no present,
> she can have no future
> without knowing her mother,
> without knowing her angers,
> without knowing her questions.[5]

Passover is famous for its plagues, the ten plagues visited upon the Egyptians. Women have plenty of plagues, more than ten, more than hundreds. We rewrote the plagues to make the curses come from our experiences. We used the traditional ten as our base. We used blood; the blood which filled the river of the Egyptians and choked their water supply has also choked the history of women:

## BLOOD

> The bleeding and bearing cycle of the female
> is considered unclean by the male.
> She will be killed
> her blood spilled
> if holy places, priests and men
> are approached by bleeding women.
> And so woman is forcibly removed
> from power and rule because of blood.

We reinterpreted the noxious beasts:

## LICE

> She scratches her life
> like a lice-filled head.

We named ignorance as the worst plague of all:

## DARKNESS

> It became pitch dark
> in the history of women.
> They could not see one another.
> And no one stirred from where she sat.
> All the lights of learning were dimmed
> and the doors of the House of Study were locked.
> The woman could not read.

> The woman could not write,
> could not take part in her community,
> could not participate
> in writing her own history.[6]

All the decisions Naomi Nimrod and I made while writing the Haggadah were political, for, as Turner says, ritual is political. We made linguistic changes. We changed gender from masculine to feminine. That was political. We had to rename or name woman; we had to rename Elohim, the masculine, as Shchena, the feminine form. We shook tradition, unrhymed ancient rhymes, changed rhythms of old chants. That would be our political stand. We would not write a Haggadah of the daily news. We felt our approach would ultimately be more radical and would not yellow like yesterday's headlines.

This Haggadah, which means, "Telling," has had its own telling. It was first performed in 1976 in two places simultaneously, the first Passover seder in Haifa at the home of Marcia Freedman, a member of the Israeli Parliament, where Naomi wore her cantor father's long black robes, and in New York at the apartment of Phyllis Chesler, distinguished psychologist. The women in Israel talked all night, reclined on pillows until, as in the traditional source, the cocks crowed and it was time to say the morning prayer. We twenty Mothers of the Seder gathered in Manhattan on West End Avenue. We were varied in background, age, race, sexual preference. I trembled before the group. I trembled, as Myerhoff would later explain, in fear that this ritual would fail, that all the trappings, the seder plates, the candles, I in my priestess cap, would only be symbols and would not transcend into the private sphere of their lives. I began by calling out to them:

> I bless you, I the priestess of you
> I, your mouth, your cry, your prayer, your pain,
> your connection, your separation . . .
> I am your scribe. I inscribe your pain.
> I am your collective soul . . .
> I am born through the tunnel of your collective bodies,
> yet I am old — your ancient, your memory, your ancestor.
> My tears fill cauldrons, brews, broths, seas, eyes,
> I am the mourner for you,
> I am your wake . . .
> I blow trumpets for you, I celebrate you,
> I laugh aloud for you . . .

Trust me for I am the ghost of you.
Look, in the shadows I walk behind you . . .
Spread your legs, my daughters,
let us give birth to one another.
Let us cry out in birthing pain.
Let us uncover our shame.
Let this ceremony, let these friendships be born.

So this holiday was born and continues. On Passover 1980, we celebrated the Fifth Annual Women's Seder. Each succeeding seder has had its own special character. Each spring we become anxious to meet once again — Chesler; Letty, Robin and Abigail Pogrebin; Lily Rivlin; Bea Kreloff; I; my daughters; and other Mothers of the Seder.

When Naomi and I began work on the Women's Haggadah, we could not anticipate its reception nor the commitment of women to it. It has been read and performed by such traditionalist Jewish groups as the Pioneer women and Hadassah, as well as by Catholic nuns, and Protestant women clergy and laity seeking new ceremonies. As with all tradition, each new group that adopted it also adapted it. In 1979, one feminist seder group brought the artifacts of their lives to the table, a grandmother's fish knife, a family heirloom cooking pot, albums of foremothers. I do not believe the radicalism of the ceremony has diluted while spreading.

The holiday is anticipated as we prepare to leave the men in our families, to seclude and exclude ourselves with women in introspection, thoughtfulness, and woman's prayer.

## HONORING FORMS OF BIRTHING

As exodus is universal, so is birthing, so is pairing, so is death. Women have always been present at birth, and women were there at the final exodus as the body dressers, keeners — gods of entrance and exit. Ceremony returns to ourselves as our bodies return to ourselves.

I have gone with Harriette Hartigan, a Detroit photographer, to watch a home delivery. There were no white-masked strangers, only friendly women, a child or two, and a father-to-be, who was massaging the laboring woman. Barbara was deep into her labor, and her lover rubbed her back low and to the sides when the contractions were full upon her. Barbara called to the life within: "Come down, baby." Her three-year-old, Lenay, asked, "What's Mommy doing?" Barbara said,

"Mommy is working, Lenay." Lenay asked, "Why is Mommy making those sounds?" Barbara said, "Mommy is calling in a secret voice to the baby. Those are working and calling sounds." The child watched as the eye of the vagina opened wide in surprise, crowned with a head, with eyebrows, stuck on the nose. Barbara labored mightily and crooned and lullaby'd the life into birth. The midwife caught the baby. Barbara's body sweated like that of any road laborer; her hair was tangled and damp. She rose from the birthing bed, showered, and brushed her hair. I had brought champagne. We popped the cork, drank, and talked quietly about matters of birthing. We played the tape that we had made of Barbara calling to the baby, of Barbara calling out to her mother and to her lover. We were there to begin a new kind of ceremony.

I also participated in an old birthing ceremony. In January 1978, during a great snowstorm, I flew from Detroit to New York. It was Friday, the thirteenth, the day of the circumcision of Phyllis Chesler's son. Chesler knew the rabbi would speak of the son as if he were only of father born, grandfather connected, male ancestry descended, but would forget that the womb had held him. It was as we had anticipated. After the male ceremony, we women retrieved the baby and took him into the library. There we surrounded him with the magic circle of ourselves. I requested that we each bless him in our own voice, that we give him something useful and magical, a growing part of ourselves. I took out scissors and cut a lock of my hair. I taped it onto a sheet of red oaktag. Each woman present cut her hair—grey, black, blonde, brown hair. We lit candles and wished the baby courage to be the son of a feminist, courage to be lonely, to have laughter and friendship with his mother. We blew out the candles and presented the baby with this hairy card of great power. The storm had not abated, but I rose and flew through it back to Detroit.[7]

## WELCOMING CYCLIC RENEWAL

I have found it necessary to enrich, modify, or give warmth to weddings. I have found it necessary to make personal the funeral of a young woman friend. But the hardest ceremony for me was Rosh Hashana, the Jewish New Year.

With the help of Lily Rivlin, in autumn of 1978 (and again in 1979), we gathered, a few of us, like autumn leaves, outside of Westbeth, the artists' building in New York City on the Hudson River. We went out on the pier carrying candles, apples, honey, and a large white tablecloth that had been embroidered years ago by Lily's grandmother. The Jewish New Year is a time of atonement, a time of sending forth, of casting one's sins upon the water. If "sin" is too strong a word, it can be understood as a time of emptying our packets of what has been thrust into them, of making paper boats, writing the angry messages sent to us on their sails, and casting them into the water. *Sin* in its root form is *es, I am*. It is also a form of *yes, true, essence, presence.* By turning our pockets inside out, removing the excess, the lint from our soul, the dust that made us less ourselves and removed us from our essence, we returned ourselves to ourselves. We set sail a flotilla of ugly shapes, deformed selves, untrue and absent beings. I said:

> We cast our pain into the sea,
> salt of memory into the sea,
> regret into the sea,
> we forget — in the sea,
> hate washes its hands by the side of the sea,
> shame is cooled by the winds of the sea,
> we return, mer, mere, mother,
> to the sea.

Where the male Rosh Hashana prayer book speaks of the authority invested in the prayer, I said that I performed this "with no authority but my own and with the authority of the foremothers, of woman judge and warrior."

At this time of the year we sound the great horn, the ram's horn, in ancient staccato signals, signals of distress, warning, holiday. This time we lifted the grandmother's white tablecloth, wonderfully stained with life, used it as a talith and signaled the world that the year would begin and that women were its calendar. Ruth Sullivan of *Ms.* had xerox'd the ceremony. Bea Kreloff and Edith Teitelbaum, artists, brought holiday challah bread. Phyllis Chesler brought Sabra brandy. We, my own daughters, my holiday daughters, dipped bread into honey and ate it with apples for a sweet year. We sat on the pier in holiday.

## NOTES

1. Kay Turner, "Contemporary Feminist Rituals," *Heresies,* no. 5, 1978, p. 21.

2. Barbara Myerhoff, *Number Our Days,* New York: E. P. Dutton, 1979, p. 86.
3. Turner, *op. cit.*
4. Cynthia Ozick, "Notes toward Finding the Right Question," *Lilith,* no. 6, 1979, pp. 19–29.
5. Some portions of this ceremony appeared in "A Woman's Passover Haggadah," by E. M. Broner and Naomi Nimrod, *Ms.,* April 1977, pp. 54–56.
6. *Ibid.*
7. For a fuller account, as well as wisdom, see Phyllis Chesler's *With Child* (New York: Thomas Y. Crowell, 1979).

# Self-Images of Strength and Wholeness

Woman dancing with hair
on fire, woman writhing in the
cone of orange snakes, flowering
into crackling lithe vines:
Woman
you are not the bound witch
at the stake, whose broiled alive
agonized screams
thrust from charred flesh
darkened Europe in the nine millions.
Woman
you are not the madonna impaled
whose sacrifice of self leaves her
empty and mad as wind,
or whore crucified
studded with nails.

Woman
you are the demon of a fountain of energy
rushing up from the coal hard
memories in the ancient spine,
flickering lights from the furnace in the solar
plexus, lush scents from the reptilian brain,
river that winds up the hypothalamus
with its fibroids of pleasure and pain
twisted and braided like rope,
like the days of our living,
firing the lanterns of the forebrain
till they glow blood red.

You are the fire sprite
that charges leaping thighs,
that whips the supple back on its arc
as deer leap through the ankles:
dance of a woman strong
in beauty that crouches
inside like a cougar in the belly
not in the eyes of others measuring.

You are the icon of woman sexual
in herself like a great forest tree
in flower, liriondendron bearing sweet tulips,
cups of joy and drunkenness.
You drink strength from your dark fierce roots
and you hang at the sun's own fiery breast
and with the green cities of your boughs
you shelter and celebrate
woman, with the cauldrons of your energies
burning red, burning green.

— MARGE PIERCY

From *The Twelve-Spoked Wheel Flashing*, by Marge Piercy. Copyright © 1978 by Marge Piercy. Reprinted by permission of Alfred A. Knopf, Inc.

# Self-Images of Strength and Wholeness

*We were raised with the patriarchal messages that women are limited and incomplete beings — that we cannot comprehend the deeply spiritual or intellectual aspects of life, that we cannot exist without dependence, that we cannot defend ourselves physically, that we are partially incapacitated by our monthly "curse" — in short, that we fully deserve being considered "the other." We have discovered that these premises are false.*

> *how distant I was*
> *so distant from myself*

> — MARIANA ALCOFORADO, *The Three Marias*

*In exploring and expressing our true nature, we have experienced our bodies in ways that were denied by patriarchal sensibilities. Virginia Woolf once said that women [under patriarchy] have difficulty telling the truth about our "experience as a body," and she believed we are psychologically uncomfortable with ourselves because we are held in low esteem by society. These are spiritual problems, blockages that prevent the female body/mind from operating autonomously and evolving into wisdom. If we change social, political, and economic conditions but do not work at changing our self-images, our struggle will have been an empty gesture.*

*Paradoxically, many women began to discover their own elemental power through the terrified responses of others to feminist campaigns for justice. Angry, emotional outbursts toward us erupted at work, school, political meetings, and in relationships. Figuratively, and sometimes literally, men pointed at us and cried out accusingly, "You're scary!" At first, we looked around to see whom they could be addressing. We are scary? We who have been raised to have no sense of our selves, to function as society's invisible second sex? We have power that scares you? Hmmm, most interesting. This bears looking into. . . . So began the process of discovering, acknowledging, and honoring our powers, the fullness of our being.*

*The evolution of the female self has been a central theme of feminist spirituality and has been expressed by women in all media of art. The focus of this anthology allows only a glimpse of this rich body of art — a sampling of the poetry, some thoughts on a few of the novels, an overview article on holistic (i.e., visual/performance/ritual) art, and a piece on ritual theater. The last two are impossible to present in print, of course, but such work is being created all over the country and perhaps readers will be encouraged to seek it out. In New York, for example, performances of ritual theater are presented by Emmatroupe, directed by Eleanor Johnson; similar groups have formed in many cities. The albums and concerts by Kay Gardner have nourished thousands of women in their spiritual growth. [The healing power of Gardner's Mooncircles is rather extraordinary; many women have discovered that the combination of that music plus a comforting beverage, be it warm milk or eighty proof, can diminish the impact of nearly any painful and/or exhausting experience.] Women's empowerment and evolution is also expressed in many forms of visual art (see "Body, Nature and Ritual in Women's Art," Lucy Lippard, Chrysalis, no. 2; "Reemergence of the Archetype of the Great Goddess in Art by Contemporary Women," Gloria Feman Orenstein, Heresies, no. 5; "The Sister Chapel: A Travelling Homage to Heroines," Gloria Feman Orenstein,* Womanart, Winter 1977; and The Dinner Party, Judy Chicago).

C.S.

# Images and Models — in Process

## Juanita Weaver

Imaging creates the possible. It is a necessary first step in our efforts to bring about social change, particularly for those changes that most radically depart from our present condition. It is a powerful tool that we do not fully understand or use in our daily lives. Even those of us who want change, sense its urgency, and are working toward it have difficulty in comprehending and encompassing the enormity of what we are doing. We are attempting to radically change our material circumstances, our values, and our way of knowing. If we sometimes lose heart or become discouraged, we must realize that there may be resources we are not using. For many of us, imaging may be one such resource we have not yet discovered.

We have all heard that a picture is worth a thousand words; it may also be worth ten thousand numbers. Computer scientists have determined that a picture on a computer graphics terminal is more efficiently and quickly understood than pages of numbers or words. One of the reasons this new technology is seen as a major breakthrough is because approximately eighty percent of all information that reaches the brain originates in visual images. Humans handle visual information by intuitive processes and handle it better than words or numbers.[1] So, if one is designing a new car or a new society, working with an image makes it more understandable.

People have healed themselves using images and visualization. Some who have had cancer believe they healed themselves by picturing white blood cells attacking the cancerous cells. Isadora Duncan would hold in her mind a picture of a leaf fluttering in the wind in order to perfect a certain dance movement. Athletes have improved their game by repeated imaging of success. This same technique can be used before going to a job interview, beginning a diet, doing something you've never done before — perhaps creating a new culture. I will discuss in this brief article some of the possibilities of and roadblocks to the process of imaging/visualization; I will mention technique only in passing.

When we get in touch with our own images of new ways to live, we tap our unconscious resources, experience our own creativity, and are consequently less ready to accept external and traditional definitions and authorities that support the *status quo*. It is important for women to be able to define our own meaning because it is through that different vision, translated into our politics and spiritual quest, that we are able to create and hasten the birth of a new culture.

Anthropologists have noted that it is the function of every culture to answer three questions for its people: the individual's relationship to self, the individual's relationship to others, and the individual's relationship to the universe (which can include the concept of transcendence). We can use images to redefine these relationships in our society.

The patriarchy has defined these relationships in ways that are predicated on a mechanistic view of the universe which posits that different aspects of reality are actually separate from each other. The notion of separateness makes it possible for one aspect to be valued more than another. This results in our most common mode of relationship, that of power-over: intellect over emotion, one class or race over others, men over women, human life over the rest of creation. Consequently, we live in a world in which a person's existence is based only upon "rationality" ("I think, therefore I am."), a world in which the differences between people can form barriers we too often find impossible to cross, thus preventing real understanding, and a planet whose natural resources are wastefully plundered by humans who see themselves as the "Crown of Creation" for whom the rest of nature exists. These dynamics are harmful to everyone, not only women, and ultimately threaten the existence of our world.

Feminists believe it is crucial to change the basis of these power relationships. For example, Dorothy Riddle speaks of the consensus model of revolution, and Sally Gearhart of re-sourcement and syzygy.[2] However, it is hard to imagine a world without the power-over dynamics that presently exist between the different parts of ourselves and in all of our relationships. It is hard because in order to conjure up such images, we must create what does not now generally exist. Further, they are images that are not encouraged or validated by our present culture.

The act of envisioning a new world, a new way to be and act, is simultaneously frightening and empowering. In addition, creation may entail guilt for overturning old values and anxiety because of the newness. Still, conjuring how things can be different is what is required if we are to participate in change. Rollo May has written an entire book on the courage it takes to create something new.[3] He points out that the real courage is to continue in spite of fears and doubts. Given the patriarchal worldview, and the view of women it imposes, it is not surprising that we have doubts and confusion about images of a non-sexist and life-affirming culture. However, despite this litany of difficulties, each creation is also exhilarating. Each image hopefully brings us to a truer synthesis and is an important first step leading to action; without the idea or the dream, we have no direction.

During the past year I was part of a group of feminist activists who were searching for some way to understand what the next steps might be in our lives. We had each given years to producing feminist journals, radio shows, courses, and theory and were now, or soon to be, no longer working on them because the projects had ended or we had chosen to leave. It was apparent that after all the years of feminist labor we were still unable to find ways of supporting ourselves in work explicitly devoted to promoting a non-sexist culture, and we could not even come up with the images of what to do next. We were discouraged about the state of the women's movement and did not know where we or it was going. There was a sense that the old solutions had not worked and no new ones were in sight.

Although we were unsuccessful in creating new images, our process was on the right track. We came together to share a common experience and give each other support. We invited a therapist to our meeting to lead us in a guided fantasy. In addition, we reviewed times in our lives when we had felt powerful. The variety of experiences was enlightening; most of them did not involve power-over interactions. Although some personal insights were gained, we gave up the effort because we were discouraged by the difficulty of translating these insights into action.

We can not allow ourselves such discouragement. Our movement (and we are, of course, the movement) must create images that are particular and concrete enough for us to move toward. We are motivated by the vision, the possibility, of a more life-affirming society. But we will become discouraged if we do not also have images that give us ways of moving toward that vision in steps small enough for us to accomplish.

## RELATIONSHIP TO SELF

I would like to have a more balanced relationship between my rationality and my emotions and to nourish my spirit more. I am far from this more balanced state, but I do have some images of what I think it would be like. As I move toward this more integrated way of being, my diet will be healthier, I will exercise and meditate more, I'll have more energy and be more productive, I'll experience people more deeply (and I will do this, mind you, while loving myself at each stage of imperfection). Even though this is a partial list of my idea of a more integrated life, all the parts are feasible because I can picture them. I know my image of integration will grow and change, but the point is that I have somewhere to start.

I recently went through a series of guided fantasies in which I worked with a personal image. Several years ago I had had an image of a young and delicate yellow-green bean sprout growing in my chest. At the time, I had thought that this symbolized my creativity. I had forgotten this image until recently, and I decided that it would be interesting to do some work with a feminist therapist who was exploring personal imagery. I went through four hour-long sessions, the first half of which was devoted to relaxation and the second half to the fantasy.

I began with my original interpretation that the sprout was an image of my creativity. However, it soon acted out (for it could talk and move) images that represented much more. My sprout provided me with images that gave me information about many aspects of my life. It was a new way of experiencing myself that confirmed things I had learned in other ways and clarified others that I saw less clearly. For example, I observed again my feelings about change and how I relate to it by the ways the sprout devised to leave my body. Where it wanted to be planted and grow gave me information that had not previously been clear to me concerning some of my current and future life expectations.

At the beginning I was not completely comfortable with the process. I experienced fear of my unconscious. I think this is due, at least in part, to my inexperience with using my unconscious in creative and controllable ways. My predominant experience of my unconscious has been as a dark and uncontrollable part of my self. This is partly because growing up, I was taught not to think "bad" thoughts. I became very adept at censoring myself and distrusting myself. The self-image that most of us carry around, no matter how apparently charming or confident we are, is not lovable. The actualized and self-accepting woman is certainly the exception. To the degree that we are not self-accepting, we are insecure and suppress our spontaneous actions and thoughts. Civilization requires self-discipline but most of us have been conditioned to go beyond that and deny ourselves the right to self-expression and self-love.

## RELATIONSHIP TO OTHERS

Personal growth and happiness do not occur within a vacuum of courage, energy, and images of the possible; they are linked intrinsically to our collective growth. There are no individual solutions. My own growth and attainment of a new world will be slowed or stopped by the interference of a non-supportive environment. Only shared vision and commitment will bring about a new society.

Creating a new culture requires working politically to influence and educate organizations and masses of people, as well as requiring improvement in our personal lives. Feminist politics began by validating women's personal experiences. We need to continue and expand that process by bringing the entirety of our personal experience (intellectual, emotional, spiritual) to the evolution of new ways of being and working together. Any movement truly committed to change must deal with reality in all of its complexity. The women's movement has begun to recognize the potential of tapping our unconscious resources and translating the resulting images into form and action. For example, women have come together to form dream circles in which they try to dream a vision toward which they can work. Before sleeping they do a ritual that focuses their energies on the image they are seeking. In the morning they share the images in their dreams. Frequently, these shared dream images point the way to action.

A friend of mine, with several other women, conducts personal growth retreats and workshops. She finds it very helpful to begin the group's planning meetings with a fantasy visualizing the project they are working on. The women start with quiet time in which they can each fantasize the retreat or workshop in all of its aspects and then bring that vision to the discussion. This technique reveals to each individual desires and expectations of which she may not have been aware. Because of the clarity this exercise brings, the planning moves quickly and enjoyably.

Many feminists are experimenting with new ways of being together that replace power-over relationships and the viewing of ourselves as merely separate entities. Several years ago I received from Ruth and Jean Mountaingrove, editors of *WomanSpirit,* a plan for a political meeting that was an attempt to relate in more egalitarian and loving ways, while still making decisions efficiently. Those who attended the meeting began by asking the following questions:

1. How do our lives reflect our politics?
2. How are our lives all similar?
3. What were the laws in the gynocentric cultures? How could we live by them for a time?
4. What political structure would *we* want to live in? How could we create it in our time together?
5. What positions in that structure are desirable? How can we *all* have desirable positions?
6. What are the basic principles of our feminism? How can we live by them in our time together?

Ruth and Jean recognize that language is an imperfect tool for communicating our experience of reality; it leads us into false generalities and unnecessarily polarized positions. The five-day meeting, therefore, began with two days of nonverbal experiences, such as massage, dancing, ritual, and music to create an environment in which each person could ask for what she needed. This initial period established feelings of trust and openness in the group. The participants then were able to talk about how to share work and make decisions in a way that did not endanger those feelings. Ruth and Jean believe that such experiences can foster the evolution of a new political form.

We need to do more experimentation with ways of changing our working and decision-making processes to reflect our whole being. We must find ways to incorporate our bodies, emotions, and spirit into our political forms and actions. Once we accept the need to do this, what will our meetings look like, what will the structure and process be, how will we define power and its use? We are just beginning to find answers to these questions.

## RELATIONSHIP TO THE UNIVERSE

Our present society is based on a mechanistic and fragmented worldview which is incompatible with the deepest truths expressed in both Eastern philosophies and recent scientific findings. In the *Tao of Physics*, Fritjof Capra describes the merging of these two areas of knowledge and its potential for a "cultural revolution in the true sense of the word."[4]

The most important characteristic of the Eastern world — one could say the essence of it — is the awareness of the unity and mutual interrelation of all things and events, the experience of all phenomena in the world as manifestations of a basic oneness. All things are seen as interdependent and inseparable parts of this cosmic whole, as different manifestations of the same ultimate reality.[5]

Correspondingly, one of the most important revelations of modern physics is that the "constituents of matter and the basic phenomena involving them are all interconnected, interrelated, and interdependent; they cannot be understood as isolated entities, but only as integrated parts of the whole."[6]

The mechanistic worldview is appropriate and helpful in dealing with many of the practical aspects of our lives. However, its truths do not reflect "the big picture." It is time for us to face the complexities of the different levels of reality. While seeking on one level to open the fields of technology to women, for instance, we must also develop an image of the world quite different from the mechanistic one required by technology.

We ignore these complexities because they are confusing and new. We do not know how to integrate them into our lives. But we ignore them at our peril. Our dealing with only one image, the image of separateness and mere mechanical relationships, has led us to self-alienation and the exploitation of each other and the Earth.

## A NOTE ABOUT PROCESS

While it is necessary to have images and visions to motivate and give coherence to our actions, we must be open to revising these pictures of the future as we gain new information and perspectives. Hard-won visions have a way of becoming hard-held and hard-sold. Since, at first, they illuminate so much that was dark and provide the "rush" of any breakthrough, the vision-maker has the pride and exhilaration of being identified with the vision. Amendments to the vision can erode such pride and may be resisted for this reason. We must not fall into this trap. Our images must keep in touch with our continually deepening understanding of what it takes to bring about a more life-affirming society.

Balancing commitment to new visions and receptivity to still newer ones is not easy. Helen Lynd, a noted sociologist, has pointed out how difficult it is "to give everything one is to supporting all the truth that one can see at any given time, with full awareness that there are other possibilities and that further knowledge may enlarge and revise the hypotheses on which one has risked everything."[7] Feminists creating new visions of a better life cannot avoid the inevitable tension between the desire for certainty, stability, and a well-earned rest and the elusiveness of truth. We must honor process in the creation of our images and in the way we hold and act upon them.

## NOTES

1. Joe McLellan, "Computer Graphics," *The Washington Post Magazine,* 5 October 1980, p. 17.
2. Dorothy Riddle, "Spirituality and Politics," *WomanSpirit,* vol. 2, no. 8, 1976, p. 28. Consensus Revolution as defined by Dorothy Riddle is the process of coming together to create a qualitatively different product than what we each envisioned. It is a process of stating one's own vision, listening to those of others, and negotiating a gestalt while remembering that ultimately one can change only herself and while respecting others' process even when challenging them.
   Sally Gearhart, "Woman Power," *WomanSpirit,* vol. 2, no. 8, 1976, p. 16. To re-source is to find another source in an entirely different and prior one, a source deeper than the patriarchy and one that allows us to stand in the path of continuous and cosmic energy. Re-sourcement

is a fundamental departure because people using this strategy for change do not "fight" or "do battles"; they see those modes as part of what has to change. We use destructive weapons at a great cost to our authenticity. Syzygy refers to the process of individuals working together in interdependence, not dependence.

3. Rollo May, *The Courage to Create* (New York: Bantam Books, 1976).
4. Fritjof Capra, *The Tao of Physics: An Exploration of the Parallels Between Modern Physics and Eastern Mysticism* (New York: Bantam Books, 1977), p. 298.
5. *Ibid.*, pp. 116–117.
6. *Ibid.*, p. 118.
7. Helen Lynd, "Clues to Identity," *Varieties of Modern Social Theory*, edited by Henrik M. Ruitenbeek (New York: E. P. Dutton & Co., Inc., 1963), p. 25.

# Martial Art Meditations

# Emily E. Culpepper

Women in a patriarchal world live with the constant threat of attack and are conditioned to be ill-equipped to handle attack situations.[1] In refusing to accept that "fact of life" passively, I attended a conference in Boston in 1973 on rape and self-defense called, "Women Against Violence Against Women." The conference was a turning point for me in ways that continue to grow and multiply in my own life, the women's movement, and the world at large. There, for the first time, I saw women physically working on training themselves to fight in self-defense. It was an electrifying sight. They were determined, disciplined, and serious. Their various levels of competence clearly showed a process of development — and some of them were my size and weight! I cannot completely express with words the psychic *gynergy*[2] that this sight generated within me. I had never before seen women or girls *be*

© Emily Erwin Culpepper, 1981. This article is based on material Dr. Culpepper presented at "Through the Looking Glass: A Gynergenetic Experience," Boston, 23–25 April 1976, which was discussed, in part, in her article "Martial Art Meditations," *WomanSpirit*, vol. 2, no. 8, Summer 1976, and in "Feminism, Zen and the Way of Self-Defense," unpublished paper, Harvard Divinity School, January 1976. Printed by permission of the author.

that way. By the end of the conference, I signed up for a two-month course in self-defense.

In the first lesson, my teacher showed us how to make a fist correctly. I remember the moment vividly. Just as I was thinking, "Here I am at twenty-six learning what many grade-school boys know," my thoughts were shattered by the teacher holding up her own strong fist and saying, "This is the first weapon on your body." A weapon on *my* body?! I looked down at my own first fist. Truly, a beginning *satori*[3] ripple resonated soundlessly in my mind.

After the self-defense course, I wanted to continue this exciting form of learning. I joined an on-going Tae Kwon Do School (a Korean form of karate). In time, I began to feel my practice sessions to be energizing though strenuous, peaceful though martial, and calm though active. I realized that this body-wrenching, sweating exertion functioned in my life in the way that meditation has been described. The work is hard and slow. It was not like anything I had ever done before. Push! Exert one more ounce of energy than I thought I had. Protect that sphere of space around myself. Choose what risks are worthwhile to me. Notice! Be aware, alert, conscious. One hundred punches and the "easier girls' gym class" begins to melt and sweat right off my body. Do first form fast, ten times, and some of all that sitting around prettily like "a nice, sweet young thing" shakes and feels restless and wants to quit sitting in my soul. Spar! Resist that kick, make my own moves, and the laughter received for wanting to play baseball bounces off the louder snap and swish of my uniform. Sometimes I am tired and resist going to class — "I went three times this week already!" — but I go and discover that the gaping lack of expectation from my past becomes an emptiness in which a thought of patient determination can arise.

> My hand WILL go through this brick.
> And with it will go weakness, and hand lotion,
>     pink dresses, and the fear of catcalls.
> I kneel here, grimly reverent,
> As though at an altar of revolution —
> Or doom.[4]

No, *satori* is not too exaggerated a word to evoke turning the tables on the oppressor in my mind and feeling the push of it in my body.

When a woman realizes fully that she could fight back if ever she were attacked, she is experiencing the power of her be-ing.[5] That revelation, that sense of increasing power, has led many women to study various styles of martial arts and self-defense, in both women's schools and mixed schools. Invariably, the language we use to describe the place such study has in our lives includes words such as "path," "way," "transformation," "revelation," "self-discovery," "self-affirmation." Our perception of this process is not a static, one-time-only concept; it is an organic, vital wisdom of living.

We are establishing a new way for women to handle themselves in the world.

— NANCY LEHMAN[6]

Studying a martial art develops the body but at the same time self-discipline is formed. . . . It is hard work . . . but over a long period of time a rhythm is built up and a self-expectation that extends into one's life. The excitement . . . of watching oneself transform, is perhaps the most exciting thing one can participate in.

— NANCY HALDEMAN[7]

Those of us who have studied Tae Kwon Do for some time have come to realize that we use our training constantly. . . . The female body is supposed to be a beautiful object. Women often internalize this attitude and view their own bodies as things. . . . The body is separated from the self in a schizoid way rather than being felt as an integral part of the self. . . . Self-confidence depends on an integrated self-body.

— PAT GILLIGAN[8]

As we proceed, each of us at our own pace, finding our own path, we discover that this "way" nourishes itself. The realization that radical change is possible and the enlightenment coming from its myriad unfolding ramifications are not all that sustain us as we struggle onward. The doing of the work itself, the performing of the techniques, the experience of working out — all offer us further insights and produce in us further sensations of pleasure, peace, harmonious sense of self, felt wisdom, and oneness. Of course, this occurs as we struggle through ups and downs, pain, extremity of effort, confusion, depression, fragmentation, and doubt.

An immediately trying aspect of my study was to develop the determination and discipline to go to class and to continue to go. Only by going to class — often, at first, when the *thought* of the exertion seemed tiring and enervating, when the awkwardness and pitifully incorrect efforts of the last class seemed depressing and perhaps insurmountable — only by going did I gradually begin to learn real discipline, determination, and perseverance. This involves forgiving myself for the times that I did not go rather than using that as an excuse to discontinue, not letting it remain in my mind as "proof" of my unworthiness. I learned to succeed by living moment-by-moment. I learned to go to class by putting on my coat, picking up the bag with my uniform in it, starting to move toward the studio, starting to be on the way there — rather than letting my mind race ahead and agonize over anticipating "too much work for how low my energy is today." I began to practice the discipline of telling my friends that a certain time in the evening is the time for myself, for my karate class. Slowly I learned how to be realistic about when I was too sick to go, or when some other activity should take priority. Developing the ability to make these judgments included learning to resist being overcome by the self-doubt that I secretly might be avoiding, shirking, letting up on my discipline. Gradually I found a kind of shelter or restfulness in this discipline. The rest of my day might have been happy or depressing, hectic or slow, hot or cold — but here, now, the familiar uniform is pulled on, the known exercises are done, pushing a little bit past the last time I stretched. The work is the same yet new. It begins, resumes, continues. My rhythms harmonize. My body balances and turns and spins. My brain floats in my skull. My body exerts herself freely.

I have learned to concentrate, to focus my attention on the task at hand, rather than letting my awareness be scattered. I have developed ways of breathing that flow better with the motions and allow for the moments inbetween the moving to be more truly restful. Five even breaths between this sequence of kicks and that sequence. Other concerns are outside, in the dressing room somewhere. I might put them back on again with my clothes, but I can consider them with a revitalized focus: "What am I doing?" I can contemplate more clearly now rather than being bogged down in "I have to's."

I start to see how I can thwart myself in many ways. My resolves that are so easy to put into words come out more ambivalently in physical execution. I work on fixed sparring with a partner, planning several counterattacks to work on: Out goes my ridge-hand and uppercut. "I didn't do that right; I take it back; I'm terrible; what a wavy line and weak move I made!" screams my face as it contorts almost involuntarily into a sour expression of dissatisfaction. That is an important mixed message and split flow of energy I struggle to learn to control. It takes strength and confidence away from my move. I am holding back something when I have the kind of divided energy that can pop out into such an expression. I work toward executing techniques with equanimity. I notice that at times when I am partly holding back, I am also likely to break my gaze, to look away from the opponent, to give the opponent an advantage. Over and over I drill on maintaining a steady, even, alert gaze.

In studying a martial art, each woman will learn different things about herself. This active meditating brings each of us face-to-face with the lessons we need to learn about ourselves, the consciousness-raising insights without which we can continue in conditioned patterns of fooling ourselves. A test gets announced, and I am dismayed at the tailspin of emotions this touches off in me. I realize that I have a very hard time evaluating myself. Why should I think everyone's techniques are better than mine? Why feel after all this time that I'm still a total klutz? Bluntly stated, I know this is an askew impression, but what is the correct self-evaluation? "Passing or failing a test is not the real goal of why I'm here," I mutter to myself. Yet, I do want to progress; I want to achieve; I want. If I do not plumb this turmoil, it will control me and divide me against myself. I continue to work, trying to utilize my discipline to look deeper into myself, to discover what my fears and obstacles, attachments and strengths are. My taciturn teacher praises my performance — and I realize I find her direct praise difficult to hear. I stretch my mind both to let go of this and also to understand why it is sometimes so.

And where is the teacher in all this? She demonstrates the techniques, "Watch: See this line, that shape, this move," — but verbal explanations are kept at a minimum. "Try it yourself." I push myself, find my second, third, fourth wind to repeat over and over. She calls us through move after move. I spent months sometimes secretly feeling that she could give "it" to me, some trick, some "thing" she knew about how to perform the particular moves. And if she wasn't giving it to me, didn't I resent that? How could she just say, "*Do it! Practice it!*" when I was clearly doing it and still not feeling I was getting it. Eventually, the thought formed in my brain that I'd have to get it myself, do it myself — just what she had been patiently saying and encouraging the class to do all along. A teacher does not give one the art. She is a medium of transmission, but paradoxically, the "object" is an essence that must be found in one's self.

Often after class, I have more energy than before. The overall nature of this physical work and mental focus is increasingly satisfying and frequently exhilarating. Theoretically, this phenomenon has been explained as a function of the way athletics stimulates our right brain, which is often underutilized.[9] In *Powers of Mind*, Adam Smith noted the similarity between the way athletes describe a special sense of acute awareness or "right" feeling and descriptions of enlightenment in meditative traditions, especially zen.[10] To me this is not a result of just the physical workout or the mental and emotional workout. Rather, it flows from the dynamic experiencing of the oneness of my body/mind/soul.

The practice of a martial art has helped me unravel the strands of patriarchy and weave a new fabric of my existence. The lessons of the patriarchy were learned within my very muscles, my bones, my sinews. For too long I moved and thought in patterns that were not what I imagined them to be. I thought I was learning to be gentle; instead I was learning an excess that was weakness. I have begun to unpattern myself, to *uncondition* my very flesh and spirit as I condition myself in this new art.

Women are coming to realize that we often have been separated from the most ordinary knowledge about our female selves — our center, our power, our be-ing in the world. Self-defense is one of the ways we can come to know and touch our true selves. The crucial process of centering has taken on flesh for me in the learning of a martial art. I move and jump and kick and spin, becoming at times a swirling around an "unmovable center." I am hit by an opponent's roundhouse kick, yet there is more and more a center that does not crumple. This sensation transfers itself into my relationships with friends and strangers. I realize that I am often aware more quickly now of emotions and responses within myself and more fully aware of the be-ing of others. I know and respect myself more than before. There is a center from which I find the strength to speak up, to act, to make change. I feel my aliveness all through my body and am not limited to a clicking-away reason/logic in a corner of my skull. My awareness and my universe are expanding.

I am alone in my work, yet I am not alone. Coming alive out from under patriarchy, it is a healing and inspiring sight to behold my sisters striving, training, changing, growing strong. The trials of living in this dangerous patriarchal world do not vanish with the euphoria sometimes flashing through one as a move snaps out with a sudden harmony of strength and form and accuracy. No, patriarchy doesn't vanish forever — and yet, its ultimate voidness is known all through in such moments as each woman experiences the wholeness of her be-ing. These women are truly beautiful — uniforms wet with sweat, eyes fierce with determination, muscles stretching and straining, their strength pushing against mine and mine against theirs. Workingout together, we know that we are not trying to succeed at the expense of making another look bad. The honor in our efforts is clear, like water in our dry throats, a steadiness calling forth steadiness. In my pre-feminist living, such women did not exist. Now, we are creating our selves.

NOTES

1. I speak from the perspective of having made the ethical decision that I have the right to defend myself. I have come to this moral stance through the realization that we live in a society that is willingly and actively killing women, who have been socialized to be victims. In an earlier paper, I have examined the process of this ethical reflection by myself and by other women studying self-defense. See: "Reflections on Ethics and Self-Defense: Establishing a Firm Stance," unpublished paper, Harvard Divinity School, 1974.
2. *Gynergy* is a word I have created to express the female energy that both comprehends and creates who we are. See my article, "Female History/Myth Making," *The Second Wave,* vol. 4, no. 1, Spring 1975.
3. *Satori* is a Japanese word that refers to the moment of enlightenment, the freedom from enslaving illusions and the realization of the true nature of our being.
4. From an untitled poem by Gail Murray, in *The Female State: A Journal of Female Liberation,* no. 4.
5. *Be-ing* is a way Mary Daly began writing this word, first in *Beyond God the Father: Toward A Philosophy of Female Liberation* (Boston: Beacon Press, 1973) to express the active, verb nature of existence.
6. *Black Belt Woman,* vol. 1, no. 1, Sept. 1975.
7. *Black Belt Woman,* vol. 1, no. 2, Nov. 1975.
8. Lafferty and Clark, "Self Defense and the Preservation of Females," *The Female State,* no. 4.
9. Hal Aigner, "Why Sports Get You High," *WomenSports,* Dec. 1974.
10. Adam Smith, *Powers of Mind* (New York: Random House, 1975), see especially Chapter 4.

# From Sacred Blood to the Curse and Beyond

## Judy Grahn

Because a group of people once gave me two apple trees for my yard, I arrived at my own definition of the difference between *power* and *control*. This happened to me as a result of understanding the nature of apples, how they come about. An apple is something real which is created; this is *power*. Only an apple tree can make an apple, no one else can. The wealthiest magnate on Earth cannot make an apple no matter how he might stand in the sun, or squat or contort his flesh. He does not have the power of an apple tree to make apples and neither does anyone else. He can own them. He can fence them, transport them, plant and prune them; he can bulldoze them, line them up in military formation, poison them, grind them up, bore them to death, set fire to them, graft them and use them; and this is *control*. He can never, from the substance of his body, make an apple as an apple tree can; this is *power*.

## POWER AND CONTROL UNITED

In the time of the societies that flourished before the rise of the doctrines of patriarchy, male supremacy, white supremacy, ownership supremacy — the world outside of *that* noisy world — power and control
were one entity and vested in the same being. Power was greatly respected for what it is, the production of interlocking life, and it was
given *worth-ship*. This word has come down to us as *worship*.

The Goddess-centered religions, which immediately preceded and
were imitated by the Zeus-Yahweh-Jehovah-Allah-Christ pantheon of
our times, especially venerated plants, the fruits of plants, and trees.
For example, Asherah, the great goddess forcefully displaced by the
early Hebrew patriarchy, was portrayed at her shrines as a tree, the
tree of life, the apple maker.

Since the apples that human bodies make are baby human beings,
human power was worth-shipped for its origins, the physical stuff of its
existence. Menstrual blood, the yoni, the uterus, milk, the placenta,
and umbilical cord were all treasured and gave us the concepts of
sacredness, worth-ship, and the analogies by which words are attached
to ideas and imparted to people as language and wisdom.

The erect penis and semen also came in for a share of attention,
though not nearly to the extent of the female physical paraphernalia of
creativity, birthing, and menstrual powers.

"The transformation mysteries of the woman," as Erich Neumann
admitted, "are primarily blood-transformation mysteries that lead her to
the experience of her own creativity and produce a numinous impression on the man. This phenomenon has its roots in psychobiological development. The transformation from girl to woman is far more accentu-
ated than the corresponding development from boy to man. Menstruation, the first blood-transformation mystery in woman, is in
every respect a more important incident than the first emission of sperm
in the male. The latter is seldom remembered, while the beginning of
menstruation is everywhere rightly regarded as a fateful moment in the
life of woman. Pregnancy is the second blood mystery. According to the
primitive view, the embryo is built up from the blood, which, as the
cessation of menstruation indicates, does not flow outward in the period
of pregnancy."[1]

Among cultures more ancient than our recently patriarchal one, menstruation is equated with flowers and with fruit, for instance, apples

and pomegranates, and also grains. As the flower opens its (red) petals and forms fruit, so does the ever-creative yoni. The matriarchal analogy encompasses all: As we humans are so are the trees and so is the Earth, and as they are so are we. This is the original equation. Flowers were seen as wombs, or as the menstruation of a tree or plant. As the tree flowers and makes fruit, so does the human womb flower and make fruit. So the moon was said to menstruate when she disappears from view. So the rain was sometimes said to be the menstruation of the sky. As the rest of nature is, so are we.

Menstruation being analogous botanically to the flowering of plants and trees, people used particular flowers to display this connection between women flowering and other things flowering. In many contemporary cultures, the flowers that were held sacred as symbols of the womb are still honored, even though their original meaning has been submerged. In Egypt and India, it was the lotus; in Japan and China the many-petaled chrysanthemum; in Greece the female mysteries of Demeter and her daughter Kore were seen in the pomegranate or the poppy; and for the European-based cultures which spread to the Americas, it was the red, red rose.

## The Basic Powers of Menstruation

The menstrual analogy was recognized and developed long before the agricultural era. Hunter-gatherer peoples smeared red ocher around the mouths of sacred caves in a clear, precise statement: The Earth is our Mother.

The paintings within the caves were most usually portrayals of bison, deer, and other herbivorous animals with fat, pregnant bellies and in positions of giving birth. Sometimes an internal diagram within the painting pointed out the animal's womb. Sometimes branches are laid across the belly. These have been described by male-oriented observers as spears, and perhaps in a few cases where hunters are also present in the painting, they are spears. Many more are plants or branches, probably having birth-aiding properties.

The paintings, incredibly delicate and realistic, were sometimes accomplished by using hollow reeds through which the paint was blown to get a fine, even spray of color. It is impossible to believe that these portraits of birthing were not done by women, just as the antler bones carved thousands of years ago with tiny moons, waxing and waning, are surely a woman's record of her own flow as she perceived it joining the moon's flow.

Menstruation is the most regular thing to happen to human beings, and herein lies the genuine power of menstruation, and what it has meant to human history. Women, given a setting in which modern stress and disruption of our natural time is absent, menstruate with amazing regularity. Our periods become coordinated with each other's and with the moon's twenty-eight-day cycle.

Engineers have said of the power of the lever that if a person only had somewhere to stand, he or she could move the Earth. For women — and for the origins of human science — the moon was such a place and menstruation such a lever. By paying attention to the motions of an observable natural body (the moon) and noting the like motions and changes of their own bodies fixed in the same cycle, women saw and learned to capture the concept of time.

This concept was expressed in lunar calendars, which Rosemary Dudley explains in "She Who Bleeds, Yet Does Not Die":

In India, the lunar calendar, possibly one of the first of its type, is still in use today. The month is divided into two fourteen-day periods: the dark half and the bright half. The total of twenty-eight days is both a menstrual and lunar cycle, with the full moon as a cosmic representation of pregnancy, and the new moon standing for the promise of rebirth. These beliefs are apparently universal, for the lunar markings found on prehistoric bone fragments are thought by many to represent women's cycles.[2]

The lunar calendar was followed by the stellar, or star-based, calendar and only recently, at the beginning of the patriarchal era, has time been reckoned by the sun, and Sun-days given more attention than Moon-days.

By carving the moon cycles onto bone, by putting counting sticks into a basket, by tying knots in string, and by stringing beads in a particular manner to account for their own periods and the moon's, women created counting — and accounting. The shell bead, a symbol of woman's genital, along with the cowrie shell, were valued so highly they were used for trade, aesthetics, status, and counting. Beads are still used for counting and remembering in the abacus and in that "garland of roses," the rosary.

All rites are menstrual; that is, they are periodical. It is the periodicity of menstruation that has made it so important to human affairs. This gave us *time*, a way to measure exact time as more than the simple dark and light of days. Menstruation and its connection to the regular movements of the moon gave us time in large exact measurement and, thus, a way to remember a specific past and to divine a specific future. Without menstruation and the sciences of measurement women developed from watching first the moon and then the stars, there would be no clocks or watches, no astronomers, no mathematicians or physicists, no astronauts, none of the architecture and engineering which have been born from exact measurement and proportion. We could build a nest, like a bird, but not a pyramid, not a square or rectangular or round or any other regular, geometric shape. Geometry was a gift of menstruation.

## The Belt of the Shamaness

As women learned to control the products of our bodies, another result was the art of magic, which developed from such physical properties as blood power. The smell of blood has a tremendous effect on animals, attracting some and repelling others. In hunting cultures, knowledge of how to use menstrual blood as a powerful positive/negative force gave women a special magic for hunting and tracking and trapping, and for playing tricks on the animal family.[3] Shamanism, and its sister sorcery, grew from such arts. We can hear echoes of its ripe old voice in Western culture; in English Witchcraft, for instance, Witches were accused of making familiars out of snakes by feeding them on milk and drops of blood.

Like animals, plants react strongly to blood. In general, they love it. This gave women a special influence with them, as this description from *The Wise Wound* of an ancient Greek agricultural rite reveals:

> . . . the great women's autumn festival [was] the Thesmophoria, from which men were excluded, though there are indications that they might be admitted in women's attire. The Thesmophoria . . . was when the women went down into caves in which pigs had been thrown early in the summer, and recovered the remains which they mixed with the seed grain, on the third day scattered on the fields. It is probable that the origin of this festival was a specifically menstrual mystery. The women, who according to some authorities, invented agriculture, did so because only they had the secret of the strong fertility of the seed corn. The reason for this was that originally the women mixed the seed corn with menstrual blood, which was the best kind of fertiliser, before planting it. Since the men had no magic blood of this kind, they could not

grow corn as well as the women could, any more than they could grow babies.[4]

It may be that the first clothing was a menstrual belt and fiber pad, used not for modesty, certainly, and not even for neatness, but worn to catch the valuable substance of the monthly blood in order to use it in applied sciences. The products of our own bodies birthed the sciences.

## The Woman's Friend

The oldest word for menstruation means "the Woman's Friend." In some cultures, the Woman's Friend was originally called *tupua*, a Polynesian word meaning valuable, sacred, wonderful, magical; the word/concept *taboo* later derived from that. At base, *taboo* means *menstrual*.

The days of menstruation were set apart from other days. In Babylonia they were called *sabbatu*, from which the word/concept *Sabbath* evolved, a sacred, periodic day valued because She (collectively) menstruated, producing the power of the blood. At base, Sabbath means *period*. Repeated practices that women developed in order to teach, confirm, and make social the powers of menstruation were called by words derived from *ritu*, menstruation.[5] At base, *rituals* and *rites* mean *public menstrual practices*.

The female genital, source of blood for the magic of hunting and for the magic of agriculture, source of keeping track of time, source of counting and remembering and measuring, source of geometry and babies and umbilical cords and the knowledge of tying, of connections, and placing, of flowering and fruiting and desiring — the female genital was worth-shipped, the female body was held valuable as a source and as a force, held valuable because of the sciences its mind produced and the wealth of culture that followed after.

Goddesses have abounded to represent these powers. In the past, goddesses have been portrayed naked with prominent genital triangles, with red dots over the third eye, with knots, beads, shells, red paint, red flowers, and with beautiful, decorated belts, belts, belts.

The name for the Goddess in most cultures stems from "womb" or "vulva." For instance, Hera means "womb," and Pallas Athena means "vulva-vulva"[6]; Venus, "venerate," and "venial" are all related. The words for the female genital, woman, Goddess, and queen all stem from the same roots: cwen, quim, gens, yomi, gyne, combe, cwm, gune, gana, jani, yoni. At base the name for female is Womb One. In modern

American English the magical, still-used name for the old Goddess-powers is *Cunt*. Her power and Her control of it have been driven underground, and She is held in contempt, but Her name still retains magical and emotional strength as a curse; otherwise it would not have survived as a forbidden word.

## Communion with the Goddess

The menstrual rituals that have been passed down as patriarchal church rites through the centuries were created when agricultural women taught a menstrual-birth analogy: As the mother makes the child with her own flesh so does the Mother-Earth make us with Her flesh — in the form of grain. To teach this principle to the people of their communities, the women, or sometimes the girls at menarche, made bread in the shape of a female, or specifically of the yoni, or the round moon. This special bread, whether made of rice, millet, corn, wheat, or rye, was and is eaten in a public *cere*mony, from Ceres, the Latin name for Demeter, the goddess who gave us grain and the word *cere*al.

The special products of women's bodies were taken in various Goddess ceremonies of worth-ship. In *Communion with the Goddess,* Lawrence Durdin-Robertson describes one of these ceremonies: "The Eucharist of Isis consisted of the bread which she had given mankind and the milk which had flowed from her bosom: the chalice from which the initiate drank this potion was a cup formed in the shape of a woman's breast."[7] The chalice also represented the uterus since blood was taken in some ceremonies, original blood from the original, menstrual source. As Durdin-Robertson explains, "The altar, in the [religion] of the Goddess, is the place where she or her priestess gives 'the power of the altar' (or the 'power of the blood'). Here this potency is given in a natural and living way in her monthly courses. And so the great symbol of the power of the altar in Matriarchal religion is the natural and beautiful symbol of the Moon."[8] The altar itself is the lap of the mother, a high flat place covered with a cloth, or skirt, whereon are placed the sacred products of women's bodies. The word "eucharist," for communion, comes from another name for the Goddess, Charis.[9] At base all communion began as communion with the Goddess; the Christian eucharist is the imitation of a cereal-sharing menstrual event.

## The Universal Red Flag

To declare publicly the altered, charged, menstrual state or *tupua,* women all around the world for ages have marked themselves with red pigment. In India and other places, the forehead is believed to be the site of the soul and is painted with a red dot during religious ceremonies. An Apache woman on the grand occasion of her first menstruation has her face painted red by a shaman, after she dances all night long, ritually. For some other Native American women, red leg stripes have signified the onset of menstruation. Among some Australian people a menstruating woman wears red paint from the waist up, or in some tribes wears it only around her mouth. This is the same tradition for many European and American peoples; although there are no formal rites, at puberty girls often begin wearing lipstick and red nail polish to signify the major change they are undergoing, in station, from childhood to womanhood: the acquisition of the power of the blood.

Menstruation is the flower of a woman, the bloom of her potential, the signal for her to take on the offices of womanhood. When these offices have been restricted, made powerless and despised by others, she herself will despise her first menstruation as representing the beginning of a lowering in status and a bitter lot in life. She may be emotionally divided from her mother at this time, too. When the offices of womanhood are unlimited, powerful, and respected by others, she will celebrate her menarche more than a first communion, more, even, than her first marriage.

## POWER AND CONTROL DIVIDED

From the flower of menstruation came truly wondrous human apples, as women learned to control and understand the natural forces of time, space, animals, and plants through the power of what our own bodies regularly produced. The men wanted this too, and the second great saga of the blood power story should open with the honestly jealous sentiments of a native Australian man: "But really we have been stealing what belongs to them, for it is mostly all woman's business; and since it concerns them it belongs to them. Men have nothing to do really, except copulate, it all belongs to the women . . . the baby, the blood, the yelling, the dancing, all that concerns the women; but every time we have to trick them."[10]

### *"Don't Laugh at the Menstruating Men"*

Mythologically, after Hera, "the Womb," arose Hero, the "male Womb." One of Herakles' (Hercules') tasks in acquiring control of the

Mothers' powers was to steal the female belt — that is, the menstrual offices — of the Amazon queen Hippolyta.

The envy that men felt or feel for the powers produced from women's bodies underlies much of their (collective) behavior. Men began imitating menstruation with their own bodies and pretending to give birth. They set about gaining control of blood, and of the life forces, by imitating women's physical nature. One of the most astonishing and important stories on Earth concerns the jealousy men feel toward menstruation and the solutions they have found to this.

In the Changa tribe of Australia, the men have developed a rite imitative of menstruation. They plug up the male anus in a ritual, and afterward claim that men have a wondrous power: Men have no need to defecate. Then they hide in the brush so no woman will see them shitting and discover the trick. The women, however, are completely aware of what is happening, and in *their* initiations they tell the daughters what the men are doing, instructing the girls not to laugh at them. The women realize that the secret is actually theirs; they say that when a woman becomes pregnant her source of blood is stopped up and that this is the original plug.[11]

Men have developed blood mimic rites in which they slit the underside of the penis to make an imitation of the female genital. The idea is that when the split penis is held upright against the man's abdomen it resembles a menstruating vagina. This extreme operation, or subcision, is done in New Guinea, Australia, the Philippines, and Africa. In some places in New Guinea, the word for the cut penis is the same as a word meaning "the one with the vulva"; in others the blood that is periodically caused to flow from the wound is called "man's menstruation." Another people say that the blood flowing from the wound is no longer the man's blood: Since it has been sung over and made strong, it is the same as the menstrual blood of "the old Wawilak women."[12]

The circumcision prevalent in our society is physically less extreme than subcision but the principle remains the same. From the beginning, the acquisition of blood power by imitation has been the basis of the practice. In *The Sacred Fire* B. Z. Goldberg explains, "Jews, when a male child is born to them, on the eighth day of the boy's life, will perform the *bris*. Even when the boy is born already circumcised, some incision must be made so that blood will come forth, for in the blood of this organ the covenant between Israel and Jehovah has been consecrated."[13] All circumcision, even in a hospital setting, is a male surgical "rite" which helps consolidate masculine solidarity.

## The Red Rose and the Briar

When the child-woman Snow White pricks blood from her finger, the analogy is obviously to her menarche, or first menstruation. But blood pricked from the finger is more than a fairytale euphemism for menstrual blood. It is also a way to acquire blood for magical purposes, without using authentic menstrual blood. The pricked blood becomes a substitute for the natural power of the monthly blood flow and all that it gave rise to in human culture. Used in an imitative way, the pricked blood gives the user control over the ancient menstrual powers.

Pricking flesh to acquire blood artificially is the only way that men can "produce" it. In the European romantic legend of two heterosexual lovers, the female red rose is paired with the male briar, or "prick." *Prick,* when used as a slang, taboo name for the penis, is a descriptive-magical term for access-to-power, just as *Cunt* is a name for female-power. The briar is the male rose.

As the male imitation of menstruation in a society is acted out more blatantly and as men come into more control of the powers women created and formerly controlled, authentic menstruation itself is driven underground. The blood that women produce monthly is hidden, forbidden, declared "unclean" and shameful. *Women are excluded from the very offices we developed, especially during menstruation and pregnancy.* All over the world patriarchs have taken extreme care to prevent pregnant and menstruating women from handling any of the religious paraphernalia used at the altar, or even at times from entering the church at all.

Plugging up of the anus, subcision, circumcision, cutting off the fingers in sacrifice, the slash in Christ's side and his blood-dripping crown of briars, the bloody bandage on the traditional hero — all are versions of male imitative "menstrual" magic, and all have a similar underlying formula: The ability to shed blood equals the control of life powers.

## Mr. Clean and Mrs. Unclean

Circumcision is rationalized as being hygienic; so was the practice of leeching in former centuries and countless other surgical procedures. Male blood-letting is considered "cleansing," while at the same time natural female blood is considered "dirty."

The concept of ritual uncleanliness was used by men to suppress woman's sphere of influence. The patriarchal label "unclean" has nothing to do with either good housekeeping or medical health. It was used to demean matriarchal customs. For instance, the pig was held sacred to Demeter and other versions of the Goddess, so early Jewish and Muslim patriarchs declared pigs *unclean*, that is, forbidden, to their followers. Christian patriarchy absorbed the essence of the edict; in the historical slang of a number of European languages the word "pig" means woman, especially a sexually active woman; it also means the vulva itself.

Most physical body properties and "earthiness" are included in the general patriarchal concept of *unclean*. Anything suggestive of menstruation and birthing, any dripping, oozing, squirming, colorful, animal-smelling, earth-smelling, mucousy body exudates have become part of the masculine anti-physical and anti-matriarchal philosophy. At base, *unclean* means *unpatriarchal*, and *unclean* means *menstrual* in the patriarchal mind.

## The Fall of Women

From its splendid history as a great public socializing force, characterized by dazzling astrological/astronomical temples (time/places), festivals, special clothing, jewelry, body paint, choreography, flowers, incense, baths, and feasts — from a position central to human culture and the door through which females entered into the full status of adulthood with political and scientific clout — menstruation has been violently reversed over the centuries into a private, shameful act, equated with being slightly ill or weak. The hysterectomy has been used at times to eliminate it altogether. The status and social control women have had has fallen with the fall of menstruation.

A new controlling force temporarily arose in history, centered on "male menstruation," that is, mock menstruation or Heroism, womb imitation. Because the male sex can acquire the blood for blood power only by the use of pricking instruments such as briars, thorns, knives, swords, whips, razors, and the like, all of which involve large or small amounts of pain and trauma, a reverse analogy has happened whereby there is a cult of pain and disability associated with menstruation and childbirth. Menstruation, the original, natural source of blood flow, became falsely called "the wound."

The story of menstruation is a story of the great contortions societies have suffered and are suffering as men consolidate their newborn authority by imitating, replacing, and violently overthrowing the former authority of women, which derived from the powers of women's own bodies. Power and control are split, and no longer are the provinces of woman, hers just because she produces them. "Producer" and "owner" are not the same; the latter controls the fruits and flowers of the former.

## POWER AND CONTROL—REUNITED?

Despite any goddess or any ancient menstrual rites, despite Demeter, Mawulisa, Kundalini, Frigga, Ukemochi, Kwan Yin, and all Their temples, sciences, and history, I, knowing nothing of them, reacted to my first menstruation in a vastly different way than the spirits of these goddesses could possibly sanction. Like billions of other young women in the violently antiwoman cultures of recent centuries, my menarche was a subject of horror to me, signifying weakness, failure, disability, shame, and a terrible fall in status. From being relatively equal with boys, I became overnight inferior to men. Worse, I was subject to intense, thirty-six-hour-long cramping, compounding my feeling of physical loss and helplessness.

### Reclaiming the Queen's Belt

My rubbery, pinkish menstrual belt I considered the ugliest thing I had ever seen, and I loathed having to own it. Menstrual pads were to be treated in a most unshamanistic manner, wrapped in toilet paper before being sneaked into the trash, so no strange eyes would be directed to the dread stuff my disloyal genital had produced. As with other women, my self-respect and feelings of female pride would reflect what society saw—a great bleeding wound to be hidden.

Then, suddenly, in the middle of my life, history shifted slightly, allowing a few cracks in what-is to show us what-was and what-can-be. As a consequence of the women's liberation movement and the movement of women into the salaried work force, women-established and -owned health centers and home-birth centers have sprung up. Women are working with each other on the issues of menstruation, health, birth control, birth procedures, and millions of elements of our buried history.

Some women are meeting or living together in rural settings, trying to find what-can-be from remembering women's rituals. They have reported that their periods become coordinated with each other's and with the moon when nothing else interferes. Women also report that diet affects not only pregnancy but also menstruation. The feminist health centers have advocated for years using internal sponges rather than manufactured tampons, which have recently been implicated in "toxic shock syndrome."

Eventually, even while living a high-pressure city life, I tried out what other women advised. My life changed.

The physical change came first. I learned that modern industrialized (that is, male-developed) methods of processing foods have deprived us nutritionally of the live elements present in fresh, whole foods, which prevent cramping and depression during menstruation and which prevent hot flashes and depression during menopause.

Vitamin and mineral deficiencies have been well-documented by a popular health magazine, *Prevention*,[14] as causes of menstrual pain and depression, among other things. Many women have reported the elimination of menstrual discomfort through the use of calcium and dolomite supplements and through cutting down on salt intake. For others, including myself, the solution to former agonies of severe cramping is vitamin E taken daily along with eating plenty of whole grain breads, brewer's yeast, and cereals that still have their living cells intact and full of B vitamins.

### First the Bread in "Bread and Roses"

The priestesses of ancient times would be enraged if they could see what has happened to their sacred breads and meals, if they could see how stripping the life elements out of flour to give it a "shelf life" has led so many women to believe that their menstruation is truly a "curse" put on them by a vindictive universe or God. Otherwise, why would something natural hurt so badly?

It doesn't. My own menstrual pain — twenty-five years of it — was once barely bearable after the consumption of a dozen Midol or similar stultifiers in one day, losing work, being foggy-brained for three days, and trying to sleep through the worst of what was a periodic misery. If no one else had "cursed" my period, I certainly did. I believed menstruation was an endurance contest designed for me to lose. Now, after discovering from other women three years ago that my problem was not me, but was the inferior quality of most contemporary bread, I eat quite differently — and I love my period. Sometimes I need one aspirin for it. Mostly I take nothing except long soaking baths. I try to spend time by myself because I feel pleasantly introverted and a little spaced-out (or in). Other women are attempting to find this personal seclusion as well.[15] Often this state includes strong feelings of renewed purposefulness to life, self-respect, and good will and gentleness toward other beings.

## And Then to the Real Roses

I see the moon with new eyes; I hear the word "temple" with a growing understanding. I hear stories that women are again drinking their own blood, or feeding it to their plants as the women of old did. I know women who are trying to rediscover or reconstruct the old rituals, or construct new ones, or challenge the patriarchal imitations which exclude women.

A friend who lives on a tiny income (as so many women do) tells me that, as her eleven-year-old daughter nears menarche, she has planned to give her a special party. All the women, of all ages, who know her daughter will be invited, and everyone is to bring a present. "What sort of present?" I wonder. "Just bring whatever you would have wanted to receive on this occasion in your own life."

I am seized with a desire to weep and a determination to make my present something of major proportions, substantial, to call the other women and urge them: Let's make this occasion count. What shall our presents be, I wonder? What could we give her that would help reinstitute her offices, and ours, and prevent any further erosion of our powers? How to keep her from being sacrificed; how keep her from ever wanting to deny her body, or to deodorize, demenstrualize, deuterize herself for what the patriarchal voices will call "progress," "advanced technology," "efficiency," or "industrial necessity"?

The salaried job world has long been built around a solar calendar, with attendant patriarchal attitudes toward menstruation, childbirth, pregnancy, childcare, and male-oriented menstrual products, advice, and operations. Patriarchal technology and womb-imitation will continually attempt to usurp, eliminate, or replace the female body functions of breast-feeding, birthing, menstruation. These are temporary imitations of female magic, and we will fight them, absorb them, and outlive them. Ultimately, we will reverse patriarchy and redistribute power and control. But while the machinations continue, they agonize our lives.

I want my friend's daughter to be wise to the many traps, and to want to regain control over not only her own body, but also her share of the cultural wealth its history has provided to humanity. To have control of the powers of bread *and* roses means for women to re-acquire scientific control, especially in the areas of power women developed and have been subsequently excluded from — in mathematics, architecture, engineering, physics, chemistry, healing, philosophy, justice, distribution of goods, and the interpretation of religious-ethical-aesthetic-ecological *rites*. Let us set our sights on the moon. Again.

NOTES

1. Erich Neumann, *The Great Mother* (New York: Princeton University Press, 1955), p. 31.

2. Rosemary J. Dudley, "She Who Bleeds, Yet Does Not Die," in *Heresies*, no. 5, p. 114.

3. Penelope Shuttle and Peter Redgrove, *The Wise Wound: Eve's Curse and Everywoman* (New York: Richard Marek Publishers, 1978), pp. 182–183.

4. *Ibid.*, p. 182.

5. Dudley, *op. cit.*, p. 112.

6. Shuttle and Redgrove, *op. cit.*, p. 178.

7. Lawrence Durdin-Robertson, *Communion with the Goddess* (Clonegal, Enniscorthy, Eire: Cesara Publications, 1978), p. 41.

8. Lawrence Durdin-Robertson, *The Cult of the Goddess* (Clonegal, Enniscorthy, Eire: Cesara Publications, 1974), pp. 22–23.

9. Lawrence Durdin-Robertson, *The Goddesses of Chaldea, Syria and Egypt* (Clonegal, Enniscorthy, Eire: Cesara Publications, 1975), p. 215.

10. Paula Weideger, *Menstruation and Menopause* (New York: Dell Publishing, 1977), p. 115.

11. *Ibid.*, p. 116.

12. *Ibid.*, p. 117.

13. B. Z. Goldberg, *The Sacred Fire* (Secaucus, New Jersey: The Citadel Press, 1974), p. 167.

14. *Prevention* Magazine (Emmaus, Pennsylvania: Rodale Publishing Company).

15. Ruth Mountaingrove, "Menstruation: Body and Spirit" in *WomanSpirit*, vol. 2, no. 8, Summer 1976, p. 64. See also Mary Beth Edelson, *Blood Power Stories*, 1973.

# The Healing Powers of Women

# Chellis Glendinning

When I was a freshman in college, my menstrual period stopped. After six months with no blood, I went to the infirmary, where the doctor suggested I have a pelvic examination. I couldn't imagine what such an exam might be like, but I knew I didn't want one. I told him I'd think about the possibility and, by the time I had walked across campus to my dorm, miraculously, blood was running down my leg.

A story of mind over matter? Perhaps. I did produce the flow on call. But even more, that episode in my life is the story of matter over mind, the matter of modern medicine and its fear-inducing control over women's minds . . . and bodies. In *Vaginal Politics*, Ellen Frankfort astutely describes the politics of the gynecologist's office: "I was the child, he was the adult; I was naked, he was dressed; I was lying down, he was standing up; I was quiet, he was giving the orders."[1]

I look back at that moment of resistance and wonder at the uninformed instinct that kept me from giving myself over to modern gynecology. When I finally did so one year later, I encountered a belief system that viewed me as a being in need of forceable alteration, a being

---

not of strength and wholeness but of weakness and subordination. When I participated in its practices, I was given the pill and subjected to dangerous hormonal upset, continual vaginal infection, and an unnecessary Dilatation and Curettage (D&C) operation, and later the Dalkon Shield intrauterine device (IUD), which brought me Pelvic Inflammatory Disease (PID), four years spent in or near bed, and a narrow escape from a hysterectomy.

Because I am a woman, the power I have over my life in this society significantly diminished when I came of age as a sexual being and potential mother. In the doctor's office my sense of myself as a strong and whole person was assaulted again and again when practitioners of modern medicine gave me misinformation about procedures and treatments and challenged my instincts about my own body until, in fear and ignorance, I gave in to their dictates.

## PREPATRIARCHAL HEALTH CARE

Healing has not always operated on the model of the externally produced "cure" that informs contemporary medicine. The symbols, artifacts, artwork, and myths that have survived from prepatriarchal eras indicate that our ancestors believed all forms of life and all experiences to be connected by one life energy, and their ways emphasized an energetic alliance between the spiritual and material aspects of life. Prepatriarchal cultures were, in their totality, healing experiences, and women were essential contributors to this state. They were the original healers, the midwives, herbalists, myth-makers, spiritual guides, psychic and death guides.[2]

In pre-Hellenic Greece, for instance, they made offerings of honey and barley cake for the Earth Mother, Gaia, whenever they plucked medicinal herbs from Her surface.[3] They said that their herbs came from the Goddess Hecate's garden,[4] and women in childbirth drank *artemisia* tea from the herb named for the Goddess of the Waxing Moon, Artemis.[5] At various oracular shrines, priestesses maintained a tradition of healing associated with Athena; Athena's "all-heal" was the mistletoe, and She was often called by the name *Hygieia*.[6]

Hygieia evolved into a separate deity and survived into the patriarchal, Olympian period of mythology. However, the patriarchal social order that had been brought into Greece by three waves of barbarian invaders eventually extended into the realm of medicine, and the new deity Apollo established his adopted son, Asclepius, as the chief healer.[7]

In Olympian mythology, Hygieia was co-opted as a "daughter" of Asclepius, as were the healing goddesses Panacea and Aegle. Epione was transformed into his wife.

During the early years of the Asclepian tradition, around 600 B.C., many of the prepatriarchal practices were maintained, especially the notion that the healee plays an active role in the healing process. Healing took place through a ritual called incubation, sleeping in a dream temple to learn to heal one's self. Quiet time, cleansing baths, herbs, and consultations with healing guides called *therapeutes* were used to ready the healee before entrance into the temple.[8] Healing was, in effect, a spiritual experience in which energy was released from the unconscious to become accessible in external reality. The power of the rite lay in its ascription of healing to the life energy and in its ability to awaken one's unique connection to that energy.

In time, though, the shift from holistic to dualistic values taking place in Greek society transformed the Asclepian tradition. Practitioners at the sanctuary began to shift focus from the healee's potential for self-healing to the *therapeutes'* knowledge of and involvement in this process. This new medicine was named after the practitioner Hippocrates, a clinical observer who made detailed compilations of symptoms from descriptions of healings written on the walls of the sanctuary.[9] He recognized the value of the life energy and wisdom of the unconscious, and also that of empirical evidence and conscious knowledge.

## THE PATRIARCHAL ASSAULT

As patriarchal consciousness proliferated, Hippocratic medicine lost touch with the life-force as healer. It came to overemphasize "objective" reality and became detached from the healee's wisdom for self-healing. Like the society surrounding it, medicine became professionalized, hierarchical, competitive, and male-dominated. It drew lines that compartmentalized the human body into organs and systems supposedly separate from each other. It disconnected political, economic, social, emotional, and psychic factors from physical well-being. Through the years patriarchal medicine evolved into a tradition obsessed with disease, not healing, with the doctor's training and accomplishments, not the healee's experience and wisdom.

The change was particularly disastrous for women. Called allopathic medicine (meaning treatment opposing, *allo*, the suffering, *pathos*), its "heroic" treatments of drugs or surgery assaulted the delicate balance of the female body, rather than catalyzed its natural tendency to heal itself. In keeping with patriarchal politics, the new medicine viewed the female body and its processes as sick, dirty, and in need of alteration. Moreover, it excluded women, the original and perhaps most natural healers of all, from contributing to the healing arts. The results of these changes in health care have been deadly for millions of women in modern times.

The techniques of allopathic medicine are based on the aggressive notion of countering the obviously diseased part(s) by cutting them out or irradicating the symptoms with drugs. The many examples of allopathic assaults on the female body testify to a basic lack of understanding of and respect for women's biology. They include the birth control pill, the IUD, unnecessary hysterectomies, unnecessary radical mastectomies, drugs like DES, unnatural childbirth, and an epidemic of Caesarean section deliveries. Assaulted by such practices, the original healer has been transformed into the most likely patient.

In *Complaints and Disorders: The Sexual Politics of Sickness*, Barbara Ehrenreich and Deirdre English expose medical science as one of the most potent sources of sexist ideology in modern culture. Beginning back at the Asclepian temple, they tell us, Hippocrates bewailed women's "perpetual infirmities," and ever since, medicine has echoed the prevailing patriarchal notion that man represents wholeness, strength, and health, while woman is weak, incomplete, and a "misbegotten male."[10] Phyllis Chesler noted in *Women and Madness* that the accepted female role in patriarchal society is the same as the psychiatric establishment's definition of mental illness: dependence, passivity, sexual inactivity, "help-seeking," and fear.[11]

Damned if we act passive and weak and damned if we don't, women have never been allowed to participate in a meaningful way in the patriarchal business of health care. Since the Hellenic period in Greece, women have been excluded from medical education and practice. In medieval times men excluded women from admission to universities and, "catch-22," established laws prohibiting all but university-trained doctors from practicing. Today's "liberated" females are allowed to become doctors, but in 1970 only 9.4 percent of physicians (including both medical doctors and doctors of osteopathy) were women,[12] with most of those channeled into "appropriate" expressions of the female role: childrearing (pediatrics), providing help and compassion (psychiatry), and putting people to sleep (anaesthesiology).[13]

## RECLAIMING THE POWER TO HEAL AND BE HEALED

Throughout the patriarchal era, some women have always fought to participate in their own health care, to protect the ancient healing ways, and to affirm their strength and wholeness. While most women succumbed to political, cultural, and economic pressures to fulfill the narrowly defined roles of mother, wife, and nurse in patriarchal culture, other women — the wise women — harked back to the strong female models of prepatriarchal days. They were the healers, herbalists, midwives, and psychics, maintaining connection to the magic and mystery of life and to the forces of natural, healing ways.

Documentation of their work, "witchcraft," by patriarchal historians has been pejorative and malicious since the sight of strong women is perceived, and rightly so, as a threat to patriarchal oppression. Wanton murder of millions of women as "witches" took place in Europe and America from the fourteenth through the seventeenth centuries. Although the Church and State portrayed "witching women" as satanic demons, the majority of medieval wise women actually served the peasant communities as healers, herbalists, and midwives; they were the physicians of the people. The herbal remedies they concocted had been tried and tested for centuries, maybe longer, and derivations of them — ergot, belladonna, digitalis — are important today in pharmacology. So effective were their practices that in 1527 the renowned European physician Paracelsus burned his official pharmaceutical texts, declaring he had learned everything he knew from the wise women.[14] The wise women frightened not only the medical establishment but also the entire feudal system through their network of underground communication and their function as political matrices in the peasant communities.[15] In *Malleus Maleficarum* (c. 1486), the witch-hunters' manual, we read, "No one does more harm to the Catholic Faith [i.e., the patriarchal Church/State] than midwives."[16]

Despite all odds, women have continued to this day to practice the old healing ways. Throughout Europe and America, contemporary wise women have maintained many of the ancient symbols, myths, health practices, and rituals, and they have often engaged in political activity to protect their ways. Other practitioners have focused on single healing approaches, like midwifery, herbalism, healing circles, or laying on of hands, modes which were aspects of prepatriarchal life. In recent years within the feminist movement, reclaiming the power of healing has taken two distinct forms: (1) redefining patriarchal assumptions about the female body and taking back control of its care, as exemplified in the women's health movement; and (2) bringing back ancient healing practices and inventing new ones that respect the power of the life energy.

## SPIRITUAL DIMENSIONS OF FEMINIST HEALING

Since the beginning of the contemporary wave of feminism, an unofficial guild of feminist healers has been emerging. They are women who use health practices that have roots in prepatriarchal culture. Refusing to see allopathic medicine as the only alternative for health care, many women are reclaiming the old ways and becoming psychics, herbalists, body therapists, energy healers, ritualists, midwives, dream-interpreters, and death guides. Some of the techniques they practice have survived from prepatriarchal times in other parts of the world, such as Chinese acupuncture and herbalism, Japanese *shiatsu* massage, and Lomi Lomi Body Work from Hawaii. Other women are practicing non-allopathic approaches invented during the patriarchal era, such as homeopathy, the Bach Flower Remedies, and Reichian therapy.

Although holistic healing has been thought of as esoteric and unreal by a society and medical tradition that claims to be all-knowing and all-controlling ("If we don't have the cure now, we'll get it in the next fifteen years; just send your dollars . . ."), feminist healers view the process of healing as involving the finer functions of the mind. To them psychic healing, energy transmissions, improvement by botanicals, "faith," or visualizations are natural functions of life, not unfathomable and, therefore, fearful mysteries. Even patriarchal science ironically supports the natural ability of women to heal (and perhaps to be healed) in recent research done by Diane McGuinness and Karl Pribram, neuropsychologists at Stanford University. According to their studies, women are more accurate than men at perceiving "subliminal" messages, more empathetic, and more attentive to sounds and their emotional meanings.[17] All of these qualities contribute to receiving and understanding the often subtle changes of the healing process, and even to having psychic abilities.

To many feminists, what the patriarchy refers to as "altered states of consciousness" are ours by nature. Traditionally, changes in consciousness have been experienced through spiritual initiation — through fasting, exercise, sickness, hardship, aging, intoxication, meditation, nature, passion, song, dance, ritual, and sleep. They have also been experienced in the *natural course of living* — being alive; relating to one another, to plants, animals, the stars, and the Earth; in menstruation, childbirth, menopause, and dying. Evidence from prepatriarchal art and ritual suggests that we are capable of being in tune with our selves to a degree at which we can only guess today[18]; what we consider "far out" is potentially a matter of course. The addictions of contemporary patriarchal society, such as coffee, sugar, nicotine, cocaine, alcohol, Valium, and television, and its narrow concept of "normal" being (completely rational, controlled, organized, intellectual) are dulling us from our true power as living creatures. Many women agree that psychic experiences, feeling and seeing the energy of the universe, and opening to the depth of experience possible in birthing, menstruation, menopause, and death are natural aspects of being alive. The healing modalities feminists are exploring today are reflective of this understanding. I shall describe five of them: midwifery and natural childbirth, guidance in death, laying on of hands, dream work, and healing retreats.

## MIDWIFERY AND NATURAL CHILDBIRTH

Today's hospitals generally offer women a sterile, unsupportive, and highly technological experience of birthing. Drugs are administered to anaesthetize the woman from her own body's messages, and in recent years an epidemic of Caesarean section deliveries has emerged in response to the doctors' desire to control every aspect of birthing.[19]

In response to this unnatural approach to childbirth, women all over the country have been reclaiming the role of midwife in an effort to return the transformative power of birthing to women. Before patriarchal medicine developed obstetrics, women had always been each other's best friends in times of childbirth.

Making home births and midwives available has not been easy in the patriarchal context. In 1972, the Santa Cruz Birth Center in California disbanded when some of its members were arrested for practicing medicine without a license. Since then, despite continual arrests, the movement for natural childbirth has grown. Midwifery schools have sprouted across the country, and more and more women are having their babies at home with midwives attending. So many women have become midwives outside the medical system that the American Medical Association has sanctioned a certified nurse-midwifery program.

"Home birth is the wave of the future," says Tonya Brooks, founder of the Association for Childbirth at Home International. "Every time a woman has her baby at home and realizes that she can be causal over her birthing, you can never again convince her that she cannot do it."

## DEATH GUIDES

Just as women in prepatriarchal times helped each other to birth, so they helped each other and their male companions to die. Today, guiding one through the ultimate transition has become a more acceptable practice because of the work of one woman, Dr. Elisabeth Kübler-Ross. In the Sixties in a class at the University of Chicago, Dr. Kübler-Ross began to explore the extreme taboo found in America surrounding the dying process, death itself, and grieving. In her work with dying patients, she discovered that if people are encouraged to express, rather than repress, the denial, anger, disappointment, and sorrow they feel, they will arrive at a state of peaceful acceptance of their own death.

Today, Dr. Kübler-Ross heads Shanti Nilaya, a healing center in California, where people from all over the world learn to express negative feelings so that their lives and deaths become positive, transformative experiences. Her work has spawned offshoots, such as the Jamie Schuman Center headed by Mary Ball in New Jersey. Many women are active in the emerging hospice movement to provide comfort and honesty in the dying process, and feminists around the country are spontaneously forming support groups for each other when terminal illness strikes a member of their community.

## LAYING ON OF HANDS

The purest, least complicated, and perhaps oldest technique for invoking the life energy's powers to heal is laying on of hands. The feminist approach to such healing is that channeling energy is not an esoteric skill; rather, it is a remembrance, and we are all capable of learning how to use it. Undoubtedly, most people think of laying on of hands in connection with the Christian church, but its true roots extend back to pre-Christian practitioners: the wise women of prepatriarchal times.

Today the approach is used widely within the feminist and holistic health communities. The well-known spiritual healer Olga Worrall uses laying on of hands at the New Life Clinic in Baltimore, Maryland. At the New York University School of Nursing, Dr. Dolores

Krieger teaches a method of laying on of hands she calls Therapeutic Touch. Under her guidance, nursing students (called "Krieger's Krazies" on campus) learn to detect imbalances in the body and channel energy to correct them. Until her death in 1980, Doris Breyer in San Francisco used her own method of channeling energy to break through chronic physical and emotional blockages in the body and reach greater potentials for living.

## LISTENING TO DREAMS

Most people think that Sigmund Freud and Carl Jung invented dream therapy. Actually, women in prepatriarchal times respected the dream world as an essential plane of existence and valued the visions, symbols, and messages they received from it. Patriarchal culture, with its fear of the unconscious and things dark and mysterious, characteristically relegated dreams to a level of trivia. In one sense, the psychoanalysts are to be congratulated for re-popularizing a fascination with the wisdom of the unconscious, and it is important to note that some of the most prolific and experimental of those practitioners have been women, such as M. Esther Harding, a Jungian who pioneered modern women's spirituality in her books *The Way of All Women* and *Women's Mysteries,* and Marie-Louise von Franz, who grappled with the Jungian concept of "the feminine" (receptive, nurturing, reflective, cyclical consciousness) in many lectures and books.

Today's feminist dream workers look beyond the polarized and sexually defined view of women as conscious expression of "the feminine" and see themselves as the potential embodiment of all human characteristics, role definitions aside.

Techniques used to make contact with the dream world are varied. Many women keep elaborate dream journals so they can remember their nightly visitations, observe the evolution of symbols and motifs, and even keep track of precognitive dreams. The Senoi technique has become popular, too: It emphasizes morning dream-sharing, conscious participation in the dream world to face and work through difficulties, and following through unfinished activities in the dream, whether in the world of the dream or in daytime life. In the Gestalt approach, each character in the dream signifies an aspect of the dreamer's psyche, and its practitioners encourage learning about the self by acting out the statements and interrelationships of the characters. Many women have also incorporated dreams into their rituals, forming dream circles for dream-sharing or for collectively working on specific problems in their dreams, such as how to achieve certain political goals, where to look for strength and, as at the Asclepian temples, what to do for personal healing.

## HEALING RETREATS

Sometimes the stressful conditions of our lives in the patriarchy are too overwhelming, and we need to get away. Recognizing this fact, many women have started healing retreats where women can escape to a nurturing environment to regain strength and perspective. Nourishing Space in Arizona and Willow in northern California are examples of country land where women are invited to retreat in the presence of other women and nature.

Other healing retreats are short-term gatherings offering specific workshops, often on holistic health, communal meals, and time to be alone in a beautiful setting. Womanshare is a women-operated farm in Oregon that opens its gates several times a year for weekend retreats on spiritual healing, women's sexuality, country living, and other areas of concern. Rosemary Gladstar's retreats in northern California are another example. An herbalist, Gladstar began her bi-annual "Healing Ways for Women" gatherings in 1976, dedicated to "the magic that happens when we gather, questing for inner harmony and 'new age' answers to age old questions."[20] Happening each spring and fall, usually around the time of the equinoxes or Halloween, the retreats bring together well-known women healers to teach classes on cancer prevention, sexuality and spirituality, laying on of hands, ritual, locating one's spirit guide, herbs for gynecology, and much, much more. Organic food, some of which is from her own garden, moon rituals, and a talent show entertain and nourish the three hundred participants.

## HEALER AS GUIDE, HEALER AS POLITICAL ACTIVIST

Treelight Green is a feminist body therapist in Oakland, California, who combines many approaches of healing, ancient and new. Her work is an integrative physical therapy incorporating deep tissue massage (Lomi Body Work), breathing techniques, meditation, Gestalt verbal therapy, and exercise. Since 1973, Treelight's practice has included seeing clients for private one-and-a-half-hour sessions, teaching, working collectively with other therapists, and participating in health conferences.

"When I work with a woman," Treelight says, "I assume she knows most about herself. I'm not an authority figure who has all the knowledge. I'm a guide who helps each woman unfold in the best way for her."

Sometimes Treelight asks her clients to do breathing exercises to bring energy into their bodies. Sometimes she does massage to help them release chronic muscle tensions. Sometimes she guides them in meditation to quiet their minds or discover symbols for guidance. Sometimes she facilitates their acting out the aspects of themselves they least understand or appreciate. Sometimes she helps them change their diets. Her goal is to help women move beyond the patriarchy's limited view of the female, open up blockages in their bodies and deal with held-in emotions, discover their own sources of wisdom, and bring a powerful sense of themselves into all areas of their lives — to become whole.

As a feminist and a healer, Treelight emphasizes the political nature of her work. She recognizes the roots of much of her own practice in nonwhite cultures, and she assures accessibility of her practice by offering a sliding scale and by working for barter. As a middle-class woman, Treelight expresses thanks for the lessons she has learned from women different from herself. Often, she has found, women of color and working-class backgrounds show a deep understanding of the step-by-step process of healing and are more in tune with their needs than are middle-class women.

One way Treelight has worked is through a collective called In Process, three women who offer retreat-workshops using body therapy and guided meditation to focus on personal, political, and spiritual issues in women's lives. A unique offering of the group is the Class Background Meditation, in which participants are led into a guided fantasy of what life in all classes might be like. After they discuss what they have found in the meditation, they play out the differing stances in "class" groupings within the larger group. According to Treelight, whenever she finds herself in the working-class grouping, she notices her body and emotional experience transforms, and she becomes angrier and more tense. She also witnesses that many women, as a result of this exercise, realize a profound understanding of the divisive nature of patriarchal society and go on to seek new solutions in personal and political ways.

# HEALING OURSELVES

For women to heal ourselves is a political act. To reclaim ourselves as whole and strong beings is to say "No" to the patriarchal view of women as weak and "misbegotten." To call upon the natural healing ways is to say "No" to the patriarchal obsession with controlling, directing, and enacting "cure." To heal ourselves is a reclamation of the power we all have as living beings to live in harmony with the life energy and to fulfill our potentials as creatures among many on this planet.

Women all over the country have been breaking away from the hold of the patriarchal medical establishment to use natural approaches to heal themselves of menstrual irregularities, PID, cystic breast syndrome, alcoholism, arthritis, overeating, anxiety, and even cancer. The first resource that every woman who breaks away must call upon is courage. Often her imbalances are the direct result of the stresses of patriarchal society or the manipulations of allopathic medicine. Other times their source lies elsewhere, yet the harshness of patriarchal society worsens them. In her most vulnerable moment and time of greatest need, a woman who is sick and wants to heal herself must muster all her courage to divorce herself, as much as she chooses, partially or completely, from the promised cures of modern medicine. She faces leaving behind the sense allopathic medicine offers of solidity and absolutism. The urban hospital stands before her with its high technology, leatherbound volumes of facts and figures, pills for all occasions, and male priesthood in white and green. In letting go, she places herself outside the patriarchal context, and suddenly *anything can happen.*

From this point of departure, she can see beyond the compartmentalized patriarchal view of health and disease. She can begin to recognize how family life, work situation, diet, emotional state, her view of herself, and her spiritual awareness contribute to or detract from her health. With this recognition, she can choose a healing modality (or several) that best suits her. She may choose acupuncture, a new diet, herbs, a move to the country, meditation, feminist therapy, bioenergetics, ritual, Bates eye exercises, or some combination of available treatments — with or without a simultaneous allopathic treatment. What all holistic approaches share is that each, in its own way, encourages or catalyzes the life energy to correct imbalances in the body, mind, and spirit. What they all require is participation in the healing process.

What they offer is the opportunity to recover our sources of wisdom and establish new expanses of being and living. The political implication of self-healing includes not only the empowerment of the self, but also the creation of new definitions of our potentials as members of human society.

## HEALING OUR WORLD

The question of healing in today's world goes beyond the issues of health care and holistic medicine. It includes not just violations against women by allopathic medicine, but also the comprehensive imbalances and excesses of patriarchal society. It includes all aspects of living on this planet because the hierarchical, destructive nature of the patriarchy makes every part of our lives sick. To heal is to become whole. To move beyond the narrow view of women as weak, dirty, and ineffectual; to realize how well being is determined by sexism (and racism and classism, as well) in a male-dominated culture; to take control of our bodies and lives — these are fundamental political acts.

When women are faced each day with enforced Caesarean deliveries, birth control that maims and kills them, and doctors who think them dirty, when we encounter rape, violence in the streets, job discrimination, sexual slavery around the world, pollution, and nuclear madness, we realize that reclaiming the integrative ways of our ancestors must involve our healing powers on all fronts — from the medical to the social to the environmental to the political to the psychological to the spiritual. Healing the divisions that were imposed during the patriarchal era is *the survival issue of our time and our planet*. A world that systematically sickens its women cannot survive.

NOTES

1. Ellen Frankfort, *Vaginal Politics* (New York: Bantam Books, 1973), p. xxiii.
2. Erich Neumann, *The Great Mother* (Princeton, New Jersey: Bollingen Series/Princeton University Press, 1972), pp. 286, 296.
3. Lewis R. Farnell, *The Cults of the Greek States,* vol. iii (Oxford: Oxford University Press, 1907), p. 15.
4. Jane Ellen Harrison, *Myths of Greece and Rome* (London: Ernest Benn Ltd., 1927), p. 38.

THE HEALING POWERS OF WOMEN

93

5. *Ibid.*, p. 37.
6. Robert Graves, *The Greek Myths*, vol. i (London: Penguin Books, 1960 [1955]), p. 176.
7. *Ibid.*, p. 177.
8. C. A. Meier, *Ancient Incubation and Modern Psychotherapy* (Evanston, Illinois: Northwestern University Press, 1967), p. 54.
9. C. Kerenyi, *Asklepios* (New York: Bollingen Series/Pantheon Books, 1959), p. 48.
10. Barbara Ehrenreich and Deirdre English, *Complaints and Disorders: The Sexual Politics of Sickness* (Old Westbury, New York: The Feminist Press, 1973), p. 6.
11. Phyllis Chesler, *Women and Madness* (New York: Avon Books, 1972), p. 39.
12. U. S. Dept. of Health, Education and Welfare, "Decennial Census Data for Selected Health Occupations: U.S. 1970" (Washington, D.C.: Government Printing Office, 1975), pp. 22–23.
13. Jerry Weaver and Sharon Garrett, "Sexism and Racism in the American Health Care Industry: A Comparative Analysis," *International Journal of Health Services*, vol. 8, no. 4, 1978, p. 689.
14. Thomas Szasz, *The Manufacture of Madness* (New York: Delta Books, 1971), p. 85.
15. Barbara Ehrenreich and Deirdre English, *Witches, Midwives and Nurses* (Old Westbury, New York: The Feminist Press, 1973), pp. 7–8.
16. Heinrich Kramer and James Sprenger, *Malleus Maleficarum* (New York: Dover Publications, Inc., 1971 [1486]), p. 66.
17. Daniel Goleman, "Male-Female Contrasts: The McGuinness-Pribram View," *Psychology Today*, Nov. 1978, p. 59.
18. Sandra Roos, "Roots of Feminine Consciousness in Prehistoric Art," unpublished ms., pp. 19–21.
19. Gena Corea, "The Caesarean Epidemic," *Mother Jones*, July 1980, pp. 28–42.
20. Rosemary Gladstar, "Healing Ways for Women" brochure, Fall 1978.

# Expanding Personal Power Through Meditation

## Hallie Iglehart

O! Now this I cannot bear. My soul replies not. Indeed, worse than
anger is this indifference!

> —from an Egyptian papyrus
> on the role of the mind in
> spiritual and social survival,
> c. 2000 B.C.[1]

When a dominant culture insists that power lies only outside the individual, in hierarchical organizations, people eventually cease to believe
in their own inner power. They can no longer hear their inner voice.
This inner wisdom, or soul, has many names — the merging of the conscious and unconscious mind, the whole brain, holistic thought, the life
energy of the universe, the larger Self, the One Mind. All of these labels are expressions of union, simultaneous union between one's physical and mental selves and between one's self and the life forces around
us. This sense of union with the larger powers of life is tremendously empowering. Hence, the connection between inner wisdom/

strength/power and outer power is one that the patriarchy does not want women to make.

This dimension of our reality is currently being explored by countless feminists who see the ultimate political goal of feminism as a new way of being, *in addition to* creating new laws and customs. Employing such methods as meditation, ritual, holistic healing, and historical and psychic research, we are learning to trust the depth of our inner wisdom and to integrate this guidance in our personal and political actions. We act from deep conviction, from a source of power that can never be co-opted.

## WOMEN AND INNER POWER

Throughout the ages, women have been associated with inner wisdom. Sandra Roos, an art historian, has noted that much of Paleolithic art reflects holistic and female-centered thinking:

One of my favorite expressions of holistic art from the Upper Paleolithic period is the large number of what are called "vulva images" . . . circular images slashed by a line. These were incised in rock as reliefs, either by themselves or as part of the anatomy of a female figure, the pubic triangle. These pieces are holistic on many levels at once. The slashed circle is not only a continuous motif that implies infinity and encompasses everything; it also refers to woman, her vulva, and her womb. The visceral association is with the source of life. This image doesn't isolate any one body of experience, but encompasses a whole series of experiences, from the most finitely sexual to vast infinity.[2]

In the Upper Paleolithic and Neolithic eras, women's magical ability to create life and food, plus their menstrual coordination with the cycles of the moon, were regarded as evidence of their intimate relationship with the mysteries of the universe. Thus women were revered as shamans, healers, priestesses, and oracles — as they are in many contemporary cultures, including Native American, Balinese, Black American, Haitian, East Indian, African, and others. In Western industrial societies, women's attunement to inner wisdom is recognized in the skills of nurses and psychics, the wisdom of old wives' tales, and the devotional commitment of female worshippers in religions. Needless to say, these characteristics are not as highly respected in a patriarchal world as are the assumed powers of doctors and clergymen.

Women seem to have a special capacity for meditation. While men are raised to be rationalist, unempathetic, and aggressive, women are encouraged to be quiet, introspective, receptive, and intuitive (which often means our ability to process suprarational bits of information in a gestalt sense). In addition, brain researchers have found that women are better at perceiving "subliminal" messages than are men.[3]

Most meditations, however, that evolved within a patriarchal framework are unsuited and/or destructive for women.[4] Many of these practices were developed by men to increase their sensitivity and receptivity, qualities already encouraged in women. Such meditations are usually rigidly proscribed, hierarchically transmitted, mystified, otherworldly, and ascetic. They tend to fragment the mental, physical, and emotional being. Often focusing on withdrawing from the world, they emphasize quiet and control.

We are too used to being quiet and controlled, and we have been withdrawn from the world outside our homes for too long. We need meditations that help us discover, trust, and express our inner wisdom, love our bodies, and use the full power of our inner strength and emotions to guide and inspire us in our personal/social/political lives. We do not need to learn how to overcome these parts of ourselves. The personal and political implications of using meditation to help take back control of our own psyches, bodies, and lives are enormous.

Meditation as practiced within a patriarchal framework is often a validation of and training for the hierarchical, life-denying (read also female- and nature-denying), sexist, racist, and classist power structure that feminists are trying to change. There is a fine line between "quieting" ourselves and suppressing ourselves. With feminist meditation, we develop our power — not "power-over" someone or something else — but "power-within," a force emanating from deep within each of us, radiating out into the world, and connecting and interacting with others.

## WHAT IS FEMINIST MEDITATION?

Meditation is really more ordinary than most people think. Meditating is anything we do that encourages the free flow of our energy — a state in which all aspects of our consciousness are focused and integrated. Many people "meditate" while they are driving a car, sitting on the toilet or in the bath, or engrossed in a project or problem. By identifying and validating such spontaneous meditations, and by using the focus of specific meditative tools, we can tap our inner wisdom.

Feminist meditation emphasizes practical uses of self-discovery and the development of each person as a whole being with integrated mind, body, and emotions. People who use meditation with these guidelines in mind take more control over their lives, are far less likely to give over their spiritual or political power, and are able to apply their own extensive inner wisdom to everyday life.

Feminist meditation encompasses a wide range of techniques and can be learned from teachers, friends, or one's self, for no one is an "expert," and each of us has different needs and sensitivities. Some of these methods are mindful breathing, centering, and visualization practices from Asia; others are from Western psychology (particularly the Gestalt practice of acting-out different parts of oneself, Jungian active imagination, and hypnosis). Dreamwork (especially the Malaysian Senoi methods and dream programing), advice from one's spirit guide (an anthropomorphized representation of one's inner wisdom), and affirmation techniques are used interchangeably with bodywork such as massage and laying on of hands, swimming, running, and various other healing and physical activities.

I have spent much of the last ten years exploring and experimenting with various forms of Eastern and Western meditation, finally evolving womanspirit meditations for myself and my classes. The struggles, changes, and discoveries that I have gone through reflect my own gradual rejection of patriarchal attitudes toward women and the body/mind/emotions. Learning to trust my own judgment and intuition about what forms of meditation (if any) to use has been as important as meditating itself. I focused successively (sometimes for many years at a time) on various meditations and syntheses of these meditations. I now use different forms according to the situation and my own or the group's orientation. Some are practical, problem-solving techniques; others help me consciously open up to the life-force of the universe. With these meditations I have moved toward a more refined awareness in everyday life, with which everything becomes a meditation.

I see my own meditative development as a process of taking back control over my inner self — the root of my being which I had previously given over to "experts." This discovery and growing trust of the inner self is one of the most joyful and sustained experiences I have known, for as I go deeper into myself, I come more in contact with the larger Self within me, the point of union with the life energy shared by all forms of life.

## INDIVIDUAL AND COLLECTIVE EMPOWERMENT THROUGH MEDITATION

One of the most important uses of meditation for women is the developing personal power through self-discovery and knowledge. Margo Adair, a teacher of Applied Meditation, believes women cannot be successfully assertive without first exploring our inner realms of consciousness:

Some of our past experiences cause us to hold constricting beliefs and perpetuate realities we no longer want. For instance, we can know intellectually that as women we are strong. However, we can still hold messages on an unconscious level that we were given as we were growing up that say we are weak. We act in the world in terms of our previous experience, which is stored at inner levels of consciousness. So, from the inner level we get the message that we are weak, and from the outer level — the intellectual level — we say to ourselves that we are strong. We find ourselves divided and acting in ways that are not assertive. We can become more assertive by going into the inner levels of consciousness with meditation and changing the old pictures that we have.[5]

For some women, self-discovery and empowerment come through meditations that explore personal mythology. One's personal mythology is made up of stories, dreams, songs, experiences, pictures, poems, feelings, symbols, and objects that describe or represent her self-development. A personal mythology represents, in a condensed form, the true heroic form of a lifetime of values and experiences. From numerous personal mythologies has arisen women's new collective mythology of stories, role models, and fables for this new era of women's power.

Evolving a personal mythology can be tremendously validating and inspiring. Carolyn Shaffer has described how meditating on her personal mythology triggered unexpected creativity and a whole new phase of her life:

Looking back, I can credit my becoming a writer to that first exploration of my personal mythology in Hallie's womanspirit class. I shared, as part of my mythology, my experience as May Queen when I was an eighth-grader at a Catholic elementary school. In writing about the experience several months later, I found myself going into a meditative state and tapping rich sources of inner imagery. I experienced such incredible joy and satisfaction that I began seeking other things to write. Within a month or two, I was confident enough in my abilities as a writer to apply for a position with a small community newspaper. Within a year, I was associate editor of the newspaper, and six months after that was named editor-in-chief of a regional magazine. When circumstances freed me of these demanding responsibilities, I began fulfilling my own personal and professional dream—writing a book about contemporary women and spirituality. Before that initial acknowledgment and exploration of my personal mythology, I had been afraid of creative expression and had avoided it whenever possible. By allowing myself to explore my own inner store of myths and images, I overcame my fear and discovered that that which I had most feared was, ironically, to become my most satisfying work.

Under patriarchy, spiritual experiences are isolated from practical and political concerns and often arise during a period of self-denial and isolation. Feminist meditation grounds the ecstatic experience of kinship with all life by asking meditators to apply this experience to practical considerations of everyday life and the well-being of the planet as a whole.

In recent years, this essential connection has been strategically expressed at numerous feminist conferences, demonstrations, and other political gatherings. To close the 1978 San Francisco Take Back the Night March against pornography and violence against women, Starhawk, Lee Schwing, Nina Wise, and I created a ritual. Using chanting, movement, and meditation, we encouraged the 5,000 participants to feel their individual and collective power, to transform anger and frustration and channel that power into sustained action. I ended the ritual with a meditation, asking people to imagine themselves leaving the March feeling powerful and focused, visualizing what they would do the next day, the next week, and throughout the year to develop their own power and creative action in counteracting violence against women.

## MEDITATION FOR CREATIVITY AND PROBLEM-SOLVING

Meditations have provided me with some of my most creative and effective rituals, teaching, and writing. For ideas on a particular project or day's work, I may talk with my spirit guide, program my dreams, or do a ritual to release my creative energy. The answers may come immediately, or within a few days, but they always arrive, often surprising me with their insight and creativity.

Ruth Eckland, a photographer, documents environmental activism and refugee programs. She describes how photography itself becomes a meditation:

> On a white table, I observe reflections of light through rose glass filled with water. My gaze floats down and hovers detached above the patterns—mauve fly wing shadows, edges on the verge of dance keeping the filament washes stretched to subtle tensions, visually tuned to create an effect of stereoscopic movement. The shutter closes. I have captured, crystallized a point of awareness. The meditation of photography has taught me to focus. My perception and the object fuse.

Many women find that ongoing meditation within a feminist framework helps them develop a sense of their own power and uniqueness and their connection with other women; it also inspires them to encourage this experience in others. Carolyn Shaffer, the originator and a coordinator of the conference titled "The Great Goddess Re-Emerging" at the University of California at Santa Cruz in 1978, attributes her inspiration for that successful event to a meditative state:

> I received the idea for a conference on "The Great Goddess Re-Emerging" while composing a letter at my typewriter. I slipped into a receptive state and found my mind flooded with images of women sharing their wisdom about women's spirituality. I thought, "Why not bring these women together at a conference?" The rightness of the idea and the strong, positive charge I felt overrode my fears and hesitations—those other voices that asked me who I thought *I* was to propose such a conference. Even though I did not have the credentials or the contacts to pull off such an event by myself, I knew I could at least set the idea in motion. The details would take care of themselves. I immediately proposed the idea in the letter I happened to be typing to the program coordinator of the U.C. Santa Cruz Extension. If I had not learned to move easily into these receptive states and, just as important, to trust the intuitions that emerged from them, I would not have been able to initiate the Goddess Conference, one that undoubtedly opened other women to their own inner strength and wisdom. I was, in a sense, passing on the torch, since my own opening to meditation and women's spirituality had come through a number of people and events.

## SELF-AWARENESS THROUGH MEDITATION

Directly focusing through meditation on universal experiences, such as life, growth, and death, can precipitate psychic breakthroughs, leading to a fuller involvement with the world. In a restaurant one morning soon after I had spent five days with Dr. Elisabeth Kübler-Ross focusing on living, dying, and death, I had an intense conversation with a friend about violence in the patriarchal world. Suddenly my physical, mental, emotional, and spiritual perceptions of the world changed radically. (Interestingly enough, I had previously been saying that I wanted to experience spirituality in mundane life.)

For several hours, everything and everyone I saw seemed composed of a density and an internal light far greater than any I had ever experienced. I was aware that I saw everything without judgment and that my rational mind, though still chattering with its usual busy thoughts and plans, seemed a far, faint, distant voice. I could see directly into other people's beings through their eyes, and plant forms emanated a powerful life-force, vibrating with an intensity and intelligence I had never noticed before. I found myself not only able to function perfectly in the world, but with a far greater joy, love, and absorption than usual.

This experience was the first step in an ongoing exploration of my connectedness with all life and with my own power. I now feel closer to all living beings and have a clearer sense of what I need to do to help change the world and myself. I am certain that the five days of various meditative and other practices dealing with life, pain, death, anger, fear, hatred, love, and spiritual communion, as well as the conversation I was having, helped open me to this experience. As in the Take Back the Night March, confronting painful issues released a tremendous amount of energy that had previously been tied up by fear, guilt, and unexpressed anger. It is easy to see why the patriarchy would prefer to repress our emotions, for they are keys to our power.

## HEALING AND MEDITATION

One of the most common results of suppressed emotions and fear is physical and mental illness. The holistic health movement has shown that our health is a reflection of the state of our life energy and is directly affected by our thoughts and emotions, as well as by the environment, how we handle stress, and how we care for our bodies.[6]

Meditation is an important tool both as preventive medicine and for healing disease. Regular meditation, even just for a few minutes a day, helps reduce stress, regenerate energy, and focus one's thoughts and emotions. It is an essential tool for feminists as preventive medicine against physical and emotional "burn-out." Through meditation, we can learn to pace ourselves, get a perspective on our lives and our work, and solve problems concerning our health.

Although preventive medicine is the best medicine, meditation can be used for healing even after one is ill. The individual can use her meditation techniques to probe the cause of and cure for her or another's sickness, usually through inner dialogue, psychic reading, or dreams.

In ancient Roman times, three to four hundred temples were built around the Mediterranean as sites for receiving healing dreams, a practice modern women are rediscovering. A friend of mine, Judith Todd, had a hip problem of some twenty years. It grew worse until she was unable to walk more than a half-mile. After a year of acupuncture and other physical treatment, she went to see Anne Barnett, a psychic teacher, healer, and hypnotist. Anne taught her how to go into trance and visualize the hip as completely well. After practicing this visualization once a day for three weeks, Judith dreamed that Anne was standing behind her talking about emotions. When Judith awoke, her hip was much better and continued to heal rapidly.

Healing can be brought about either by visualizing or affirming that the sickness is changing into health or by focusing on and applying the healing energy of one's hands. I have found laying on of hands, by myself or with others, to be one of the most powerful meditations I know. As I tune into the life-force of the universe, I physically feel it coursing through my body and direct it to unite with others. Mental, emotional, and physical distractions recede, and the group truly becomes one whole being.

## GROUP MEDITATION

Whether for healing, problem-solving, or focusing, the energy of group meditation is one of the most powerful and profound forms of feminist work. Sharing meditation insights validates and reinforces individual experiences, and we learn to trust our inner wisdom and recognize the cohesiveness of our visions. We experience, in a visceral way, the union of the individual and the collective, and find that the whole is far greater than the sum of all its parts. As in the Take Back the Night Ritual, we can collectively focus our group psychic energy for political goals. Meditation techniques, such as visualization, holding hands in a circle, or bodywork, help minimize friction and unproductive communication. Each person feeds on the collective energy and, at the same time, is a channel for it.

At a rainy weekend-long meeting of the Oregon Women's Land Trust several years ago, sixty women met in one house to work out the values, organization, financing, and long-term goals of obtaining land for women. Differences and tensions often erupted as questions about money, class, race, city-versus-country, visions, collectivity, accountability, and priorities were discussed. Throughout the weekend, we would stop and hold hands, stretch, or massage one another's shoulders for several minutes. There were several instances when the group could have fragmented beyond repair if we had not done this. We managed to stay together and establish the structure, process, publicity, and paid jobs of an organization which, in three years, acquired hundreds of acres of collective land for women.

## A WORLD OF FEMINIST MEDITATION

Meditating individually and collectively, we build a vision that helps us create the kind of world we want to live in, rather than waiting until after we have dismantled this one. Simultaneously, we become the kind of people we want to see living in our world.

I see this world as one in which each individual feels her own power emanating from within, a power that gladly and cooperatively interacts with that of others. Thus, each person has a sure knowledge and understanding of her own inner wisdom and how to express that wisdom in action. It is a world in which creativity, love, play, and intuition join forces with intellectual, emotional, and physical strength to create new forms of harmony and peace, both within the individual and the group.

In this world, we are all spiritual and political leaders, gurus, teachers, and students. We use meditation, along with other spiritual and political tools, to tap our power and inner strength. We learn that we are our own sources of wisdom and that we cannot be oppressed from within or from without. The powers that we respect are not separate from ourselves:

> And you who think to seek for me —
> Know that your seeking and yearning will avail you not
> Unless you know the Mystery:
> That if that which you seek you find not within you,
> You shall never find it without.
> For behold: I have been with you from the beginning,
> And I am that which is attained at the end of desire.[7]

# 304 *Self-Images of Strength and Wholeness*

NOTES

1. Bika Reed, *Rebel in the Soul, A Sacred Text of Ancient Egypt* (New York: Inner Traditions International, 1978), p. 15.
2. From an interview to be included in *The Catalog of Womanspirit* by Hallie Iglehart.
3. See Daniel Goleman, "Special Abilities of the Sexes: Do They Begin in the Brain?" *Psychology Today*, Nov. 1978, p. 59.
4. However, many of the meditations were originally developed in matrifocal and egalitarian societies. Feminist scholars, teachers, healers and priestesses are currently researching the roots of ritual from the Upper Paleolithic period to present times, the *I Ching*, Tarot, Tantric meditation, psychic communication, healing and group focus through meditation, and other original forms.
5. From interview for *The Catalog of Womanspirit* (see above).
6. See *The Holistic Health Handbook* (Berkeley: And/Or Press, 1979), for a wide selection of theoretical and practical articles.
7. Charge of the Star Goddess (from the Western Pagan tradition).

# Feeding the Feminist Psyche Through Ritual Theater

# Batya Podos

Six women lie sleeping in a circle of candlelight. They are women of no particular time, wearing remnants of their past lives — torn jeans, animal skins, a mini-skirt, a necklace of glass beads, feathers. Some of them are barebreasted. One by one they begin to awake. They greet each other with curiosity and affection. They groom each other, pat each other fondly, sing random notes to each other until their voices weave together into a single chord. For the next hour and a half they will live inside their circle, never leaving it, never breaking the bond of energy that exists among them. They oil their bodies, pound out rhythms on the ground, chant each other's names aloud. They paint their faces and bodies with magical symbols of power, reenact their battles, dip their hands in blood. The ritual they are performing is no darkly mysterious rite in a hidden grove under the full moon, but is an adaptation of Monique Wittig's *Les Guérillères* performed as part of a Master of Arts thesis project at San Francisco State University in 1977. The candlelight, scented oils, the litanies of names chanted continuously, the repetition of sounds and symbols, and circular move-

---

ments — all add to the sense of timelessness, help weave the spell of the play around the audience, and tap each person's subconscious memories.

The roots of theater lie in spiritual and magical ritual and date back far beyond the classical Greek drama we have come to associate with its beginnings. Pageants, festivals, ceremonies, and seasonal celebrations were all parts of early theater and were linked to the daily spiritual life of the people who participated in them. There was no separation between spiritual consciousness and the consciousness of everyday life.

The Greeks gave us the first written dramas. These were performed in the context of religious festivals dedicated to the god Dionysus. The classic tragedies were designed to teach moral lessons and provide "catharsis" — a purge or purification of the emotions that would bring on spiritual renewal. These ideals were used later by the Christian church in the Passion Play — the portrayal of various aspects of the life of Christ — to instruct the illiterate populace in the doctrines of the Christian religion and to bring them into spiritual communion with God.

Contemporary ritual theater reaches back into its own earliest beginnings. Its context is the spirit but not perceived in terms of some celestial energy apart from the world; its context is spirit *in* the world, the integration of the spiritual with every aspect of daily life. In terms of the feminist psyche, not only must ritual theater seek to provide a transformative spiritual experience, it must educate an audience whose spiritual experiences, self-definitions and world perceptions have been taught and nurtured by a misogynistic society — an audience that has been denied knowledge of its own history and power. For that reason it works within a framework of symbolic vocabulary that will speak to the subconscious understanding that lies within each one of us. It is through the reintegration of female imagery and symbology into consciousness that catharsis is accomplished.

The possibilities of ritual theater to transform consciousness and the meaning of that experience in terms of a feminist vision cannot be explored without first distinguishing between ritual theater and other, more traditional theatrical experiences, as well as other works of feminist or political theater. To delineate feminist ritual theater, I will use my own work as a playwright and director in recent years: my adaptation of *Les Guérillères* by Monique Wittig in 1977, my adaptation of *The Myth of the Triad of the Moon* by Charlene Spretnak in 1978, my original production of *Ariadne* in 1979, and my original production of *The Story of Athena and Other Tales Our Mothers Never Told Us* in 1980. All of these plays were produced in or near San Francisco.

First of all, and prime in importance, ritual theater involves the cathartic experience — the emotional purge that leads to self-revelation and transformation. This comes from new knowledge revealed about the self and, in terms of feminism, this knowledge takes the form of the revelation of powers hitherto unknown — particularly concerning our historical and prehistorical past. When confronted with this new knowledge about ourselves, we are transformed. We have a new sense of who we have been in the past and who we might be again. For my purposes as a playwright, this is accomplished most effectively by bringing to life ancient matrifocal and Goddess-worshipping cultures, by reexamining ancient mythologies, and by creating a female context that provides images and symbols of the power of women that are not readily available in our present-day culture. Ancient myths can be seen as symbolic interpretations of actual historical events, explanations of historical transitions over a period of time. They are a key to the consciousness of the people and cultures from which they originated. By researching the changing mythic patterns and finding that they are linked to corresponding patterns in history, our perceptions of history as it has been taught us are changed, and assumed historical "truths" are challenged.

Many elements add to the creation of ritual theater. The first of these is the use of non-linear language. Time is not measured by our daily standards. The past, present, and future are experienced simultaneously and are used interchangeably. The energy is cyclical. Getting from point A to point B is not as important as spinning a web of events. The energy can be compared to the energy within a magic circle, but instead of spiraling up into a "cone of power," it spirals out over the audience. In fact, the entire play can be seen in terms of a magical spell, and the various devices — the mythic setting, the timelessness, the repetition of words and movements — can be seen as trance-inducing elements to aid the audience in reaching the subconscious.

Repetition is itself an important part of the ritual drama — the repetition of words, phrases, whole passages and the repetition of musical segments, of certain movements, patterns of movements, groupings of performers. In the adaptation of *Les Guérillères*, a litany of women's names was repeated endlessly throughout the entire piece. One woman after another would pick up the names so that someone was always chanting. This way the litany drifted in and out of consciousness. It became omnipresent, like the sea. (Occasionally the ear follows the roar and the swell of the waves, occasionally the sound is forgotten in other conversation or activity, but always it is there.) In *Ariadne,* Ariadne's thread was the repeated image, and throughout the play references were made to the thread as the thread of life and to Ariadne as a spinner and a spider so that the thread actually became the connecting link from one scene to another.

Symbols themselves are redefined in terms of positive female imagery. The earth, caves, darkness, the sea, the hidden, enclosed, and circular — all have been used as symbols of the feminine but not always as sources of female power. We have been told that we are "of the darkness" while men are "of the light," that our nature is earthbound while theirs is celestial. In *Ariadne* the darkness becomes a character in itself, played by the chorus. They are the labyrinth that Ariadne must enter to be initiated into the mysteries of the Great Goddess — and the mystery of her own self; they are the labyrinth where the minotaur lives who is the guardian between the doors of life and death. The darkness here becomes the transformative space that leads to rebirth and renewal. It is only feared and despised when we do not understand its nurturing qualities. Historical images associated with matrifocal cultures, such as the bull, the labyris, the spiral, are also part of the context of ritual theater. They provide our historical links, give us a base in our historical past.

The symbols, the circular sense of time, the non-linear language, and the repetition are all devices designed to reach the audience at its subconscious level. Certain symbols, words, and actions will trigger certain emotional responses, appeal to our mythic senses and unify us in our perceptions and understandings. The goal is to bring the audience into the fullest emotional experience possible, to exhume the ancient memories from the subconscious where they have lain dormant and unrealized. The goal is to remind the audience of what they used to know about their relationship to the world but have forgotten — to remind them of who they used to be. This is the self-knowledge that opens the door of transformation. And transformation is the single most important purpose of ritual theater — transformation through self-revelation and personal experience.

In the feminist context these are shared experiences. The personal realization extends itself to the larger shared community of womanhood. An audience lends itself readily to such experiences. It is not a passive entity — a watcher from the outside — but a full participant in every aspect of the action. In order for the ritual to succeed, to have any purpose at all, the audience must be transformed in some way.

Ritual theater provides a historical and spiritual link to the timeless shared community of womanhood. The link is made strong by evoking sustaining images of female power. The ultimate symbol of this power is the Goddess. Historically, we know that goddess figures have been found dating as far back as 25,000 years before the birth of Christ. We know that throughout the ancient world cultures were built and sustained on a belief in the Great Goddess in Her many and various aspects. We know that remnants of Her worship exist throughout the world today despite the many recurrent efforts made to destroy Her power and often, as in the case of the Witch burnings of the Middle Ages, Her worshippers. We know that the memory of Her and the memory of women as free and powerful beings lives on, even though it is often buried so deeply that it no longer reaches out to us.

As in ancient cultures, where there was no separation of spiritual consciousness from daily living, the Goddess is not spirit separated from the flesh but is manifest tangibly in the world — *is*, in fact, the world and every living thing. She is also the transcendent force of eternal female energy. It is this spirit that ritual theater attempts to invoke. In *Ariadne,* Ariadne is both Goddess and woman. As the High Priestess of Minoan Crete, she is considered the living representative, the fleshly personification, of that eternal female energy. She is also a young girl growing into a woman, a loving sister to her half-brother the minotaur, and a devoted daughter to her mother Pasiphae, High Priestess before her. There is no contradiction, no separation between her spirit and her earthly body.

The ancient Minoans understood women as divine, each one of us being the living representative of the Goddess. That powerful connection is not something dropped on us by heaven but is generated from within. The invocation of that power through performance illuminates both players and audience with a new understanding of themselves — a new strength and wholeness. In order for the ritual to succeed, both the players and the audience must experience it. In the four years I have worked with ritual theater, I have never worked with a cast who was not in some way profoundly affected by the rehearsal process and the experience of the play. Techniques like improvisation, sense memory, inner dialogues, and visualization make each rehearsal another link in the process that will connect the ritual experience with the players' daily lives. If the play does not become true to the players, it will never be true to the audience.

Ritual theater draws upon the power of our experiences made larger than ourselves. It creates a common language through symbolic action, a set of shared, mythic experiences that touch our deepest memories. No definition of terms is necessary. We see, we experience, we understand, we remember.

The images of power we draw on exist in our own consciousness. Ritual theater helps part the curtain behind which they have been hiding, calls them back into existence, and makes them tangible and real. By telling the truth about our ancient past, by discovering our own lost history, we are neutralizing over 2,000 years of lies about the nature of women. We not only empower ourselves with this knowledge, but we defuse those assumptions by making them impotent. When the lies about women no longer hold us in their thrall, when we no longer believe them ourselves because we are filled with the power of our own history, we have affected a change of primary importance: We become, once again, whole and powerful persons.

When Ariadne says to Theseus, "I never loved you. I never went with you willingly," she is not only changing our accepted historic and mythic context, but she is making a lie of the image of women giving up everything for the love of a man. In *The Story of Athena and Other Tales Our Mothers Never Told Us*, the Goddess Athena says to the women in the audience:

Listen. I know you think that I have betrayed you, that I haven't a thing to say for you, that I side with men against you, but you must understand that history has made me what I am. If I had been some small household goddess, if I had been married to a new and greedy god, I would have disappeared. There would be nothing for you to remember or your children to read about. Yes, I put on the armor. Yes, I learned an enemy's language. Yes, I gave up my lovers. But I survived! Cities have been built for me, a whole people still call themselves after me, and over 2,000 years after the fall of my civilization you know who I am because there is nowhere in Greece my name isn't written. I have been transformed, yes. But so have you. Do not judge me until you look at your own lives. I have never lost my power. I have never forgotten who I am.

With this declaration, she is not only reclaiming history but is affirming the power of every woman in the audience. She is also acknowledging the pain of the compromises that we make to survive. When these feelings are given validity, when we have a chance to see in front of us our own possibilities, to confront our personal and collective power, we experience a tremendous affirmation of our inner selves. We begin changing our perception of ourselves in the world. We begin to see the "being" of what is possible.

Our transformations through the dramatic experience of ritual theater bring us new insight and awareness on intellectual, emotional, and psychic/spiritual levels. We are now more able to recognize the distortions that are given us as truth. We are able to see ourselves more clearly in terms of our present lives and the way we relate to our modern culture. By unlocking the past, we open ourselves to a deeper understanding of who we are in the present and, therefore, who we might become in the future. Ritual theater is a vehicle for this understanding, a medium through which we share these experiences.

When Ariadne sings

> I am the spinner, the weaver of mysteries.
> I stitch together the patterns of time;
> I weave the seasons one into another;
> I spin out the web of the world's design.

she speaks of the primal creative power present in every woman, the eternal flow of female energy that is our source of power and strength. It exists for us to tap, to use to create new forms of consciousness and to effect change. The Goddess is the mirror of ourselves. By invoking Her, we invoke our own inner creative energy. By invoking the true past, we have a guide to the future, a path to follow toward transformation—not only of ourselves but of our culture and the world.

# See For Yourself: Women's Spirituality in Holistic Art

# Mary Beth Edelson

I began to paint and draw images that spoke of women's power, the power of our bodies, in 1961, when I was pregnant with my first child. In a very specific way, images of numinous women as the triad, the One who is in charge, emerged in my work. I experienced what was happening in my body as holy, as sacred. The work that I conceived during this period reflects this attitude, symbolized by the use of concentric circles with energized perimeters that became spirals and were placed either on the heads of women or their breasts, or vagina, or womb.

As time went on, I defined these images as Goddess and my passion for Her grew by leaps and bounds. Initially the information came as academic study and intellectual exercise, but the intensity behind gathering the information came from experiencing "The All Powerful One," "The Spiritual One," as female. I wished to communicate these experiences, as well as the images and symbols that they were generating for me, to others.

I was also exorcising the hold that patriarchal forces had placed over me. With the releasing of this hold on my psyche, I was receiving energy and an expanded self-image. As Carol Christ succinctly puts it, "The real importance of the symbol of Goddess is that it breaks the power of the patriarchal symbol of God as male over the psyche."

The summer, especially while lying in the sun in front of the ocean, had always been a fertile and creative period for me. Concepts for the following year's work often fermented at that time, but one particular summer had been a blank, nothing had grown for me to shape in the coming year. However, the night that I returned from the ocean I imagined a circle of towering goddesses in my mind's eye silhouetted against a night sky in my back yard. The next morning I set out to make them.

The circle became a series of stylized figures cut from plywood called *The Goddess Tribe*. When the tribe totally surrounded the viewer, their bonding suggested communications: sound, whispers, and chants. As individuals their physical presence suggested an exploration of various aspects of feminine realms including bringing up the sun, wholeness, passages to other states, celebration, soaring, dominion, and dancing. Their stance, in spite of the stylized rigid form they inhabited, was that of an activist. When mounted on the wall, the physicality of their eight-foot-high forms towered over and controlled the space. Thirteen in all, they were heavily painted and then scratched back through to reveal the underlayers.

## PRIVATE RITUALS

While continuing to make art objects, I was also integrating private rituals, and later public rituals, into my various art processes.

I document my private rituals with a camera that I set on time release so that I do not need to have anyone else there. Another person would change the psychic space — and would, quite naturally, make me aware of another presence. At these times, I want to concentrate all my energies on kinds of communications other than interpersonal, communications that have to do with getting in touch with myself and then beyond myself and into wider spaces. I carefully prepare what I am going to do beforehand so that I do not have to concentrate on what I am doing; then I try to flow with the ritual, and that flow changes whatever I plan.

The private ritual came to me as a personal rite, first performed either alone in nature or with my children in nature and later photographed in the early Seventies as a part of my art process. Setting aside a special time, I said to my children, "This activity is out of the ordinary; we are going to act out our gestures and ritualize our behavior. The art will stand as a record of the unity and wonder that we experienced." I was trying to tie them to the Earth, to help them feel in a direct way that nature is not outside, but a part of them. We merged — mother, child, and nature — becoming one again for a moment.[1]

In the same spirit as *The Goddess Tribe,* I created a series of photographic images of my body as a stand-in for Goddess. They were private rituals done in nature in the Outer Banks, North Carolina. The photographic images were defining images — not who *I was* but *who we are* — the spirit in bodily form, sexuality, body, and mind all in one, presented assertively, in the aggressive form that they came to me. The body is where we live, the home of our spirit. I was summoning Goddess to make house calls, talking to Goddess with the body, and ending the dialogue with being. These photographic body rituals were an outward visual image to present to my community of the manifestation and recognition of the Goddess within.

In this same series, the naked photographs of *Moon Mouth* declared and insisted on woman as primary. Although she exposed her female body, she was not a nude tantalizer, but powerful, wild, and in control. A risk was taken by exposing the body, not only its naked form, but also exposing the body's energy to energy forces in nature.

These early works wanted to take a clear political stance — they needed to be assertive to get their points across, but as time went on I could build on the clarity of my earlier works and become more lighthanded.

While I say that this series, or any other series, of my rituals takes us from a chrysalis through stages of fulfillment and development, these words are only meant as indicators or stimulators. It is my intention that the works not be seen as having fixed interpretations or single meanings, but that they be layered and subject to the interpretations of the viewer/reader and that they will change in time.

The following are brief descriptions of some of the ideas behind eight of my private photographic rituals:

*The Sacred Manic Goddess Makes Tracks: Or How to Walk Away* (four photographs). It has always been difficult for me to walk away from a conflict. Somehow I always felt that the "other" held me there, that I had an obligation to stick it out. I was trying to teach myself how self-destructive such an attitude can be and to give myself permission to avoid the conflict, to protect myself by simply walking away. *The Sacred Manic Goddess* runs through the woods and into an arched opening in a castle ruin and disappears.

*Great Mother Sea Us* (three photographs). She has walked out of the sea — paces back and forth along the shore impatiently waiting for us to come. We hope Her acknowledgement will enable us to nourish/be nourished: to "see/sea."

*Crossing Over* (three photographs). The risk was taken and this time we went too far. A death mask howls out at us.

*Frozen Moment* (three photographs). Literally taken in the freezing cold at night in Iceland. Her dark side is given full reign as She hunkers and threatens all who might come into Her territory.

*Rising Firebird Energy* (four photographs). The first images are low with cave-like openings, but they rise up through fire and form wings. The last image is a flaming bird in flight.

*Stone Speaks* (series of three photographs). Nestled in among large rocks on the coast of Maine, She opens Her mouth as wide as possible as She moves, allowing the rocks to speak through Her. This piece is dedicated to having the courage to say the hard thing — to speak out.

*The Balancing Edge* (a series of three photographs). A woman standing on the edge (of the world) and flying by balancing on one foot. She is full of shamanic powers and hopes to balance life.

*Spirit of Rock* (in two photographs). The first photograph is a massive boulder in the woods and the second is a spirit, in the same monolithic form, supposedly passing in and out of the rock behind it. Representing the spirit of our oneness with nature and the great round as a rock: *prima sculptura*.

## HOLISTIC ART

My work also evolved more holistically, integrating sculpture, drawings, photographs, collaborations, artists' books, and public ritual performance into a living environment — a comfortable space that invited participation.

My interest in a holistic approach, or multiplicity, led me to develop structures for my work. The structures help contain in order to avoid dispersion. I don't like to leave anything out. If I do, it's like drawing a human body without arms or legs, as if the entire anatomy were too much to consider. The art market has found singular, non-holistic work easier to package, but that is the opposite of my encompassing approach.

Lucy Lippard, a distinguished art critic, has called the release of this multiplicity by women artists "a political act":

In the early seventies we all struggled against the notion that an artist who couldn't narrow herself down simply couldn't "make up her mind,". . . . Gradually we began to theorize concretely about our inclination toward "collage" impact and to understand how natural it was for us to do so in simultaneously diverse styles and mediums. . . . Feminism's central contribution to recent art, then, has been not a single line, but a web of patterns and structures that underlie more superficial intentions.[2]

An expression of this multiplicity and its drive toward holism is an exhibition I created entitled *Dark Shelters/Light Natures.* To enter the exhibition space, you walked through a passage, "cave curtain," that separated the exhibition space from the outside world. By emphasizing and demarking the separating of this space from other spaces, I can suggest a more complete and holistic environment. In the interior space, one was confronted by *Toothless,* a cave/shelter-shaped sculpture with an electric blue chair inside; human scale, it appeared empty, but full. *Toothless* was named after the Celtic Goddess of destruction and creation, Sheela-Na-Gig, who is portrayed with a spreading vagina interpreted as the *vagina dentata.* The toothed vagina is a symbol of the irrational fears and fantasies that some men have of castration or of women as devourers. I was challenging men to face this fear, to come inside and see there were no teeth — and to contemplate that fact. It also expressed a challenge for women to confront their feelings about themselves, their mothers, and other women.

Some men, particularly middle-aged men, came out of the space with tears in their eyes. I was amazed at the gut-level response from people who are usually so guarded with their emotions. When you sat inside of *Toothless,* your view was *Northern Dawn,* a thirteen-foot impenetrable, monolithic black canvas structure with a thin slit in the bottom of the flat mound shape, emitting light which defined the perimeters of the dark sculpture, suggesting an *aurora borealis.* It was a reassuring sight and a calming, peaceful site. Small individual lights with handmade clay shades (echoing the shape of *Toothless*), which reduced and directed the light, were the only sources of illumination in the gallery. They were placed over each of the photographs of private rituals lining the walls.

While the exhibition is obviously my personal view of a holistic environment, I hope that the works together create an atmosphere that includes the viewers'/participants' notions of a fulfilling space. I think of this space as sacred and as a temporary *communitas*. I have tried to incorporate both spiritual and political statements in the works while presenting a cohesive visual space that encourages people to visualize how things could be. I also included handmade books as you entered the "cave curtain."

A holistic approach allows almost infinite diversity. You can present contradictory information without being confusing. I like the notion of contradiction because I don't want my symbols and images to become solidified or dogmatic. For example, in the exhibition *Proposals for: Memorials to 9,000,000 Women Burned as Witches in the Christian Era,* I used a fire ladder as both a symbol of spirituality (or being able to rise above) and as a reference to the fact that during the Middle Ages to get rid of a woman accused of witchery quickly, she was tied to a ladder and thrown into a bonfire. The ladder symbol was charged with very positive and very negative connotations.

I often use books in order to give a complete view, to present many sides and contradictions. On the other hand, some of my books are purely visual without a verbal message, emphasizing sensual, seductive surfaces, and drawings. For a while, I rejected using seductive materials, thinking seductiveness was dishonest. I was being too puritanical, cutting myself off from a vital element and risking energy being lost from that separation. Being seductive is one of the vital elements of life. Another effect books can have is to put people at ease. Visitors can nestle comfortably with the books in the gallery. Galleries are often cold spaces where the message is that you can come in, stand for five minutes looking, and then you must leave. Books help break that time limit. Also my books are not under plastic. Obviously they have been worked on for months, but the public is trusted to handle them and treat them with respect.

Another area of public participation is my *Story Gathering Boxes.* The boxes contain paper tablets with topics stamped on them that relate to the particular exhibition in which they are placed. I have collected Stone Stories, Mother Stories, Story of Your Life, Goddess Stories, Blood Power Stories, Old Myths/New Myths, etc. People coming to the exhibition are asked to write on these topics and leave the cards for others to read. I have collected over one thousand stories to date and hope to publish them one day.

In order to create ritual space in a gallery, I make certain assumptions from the women's culture, my culture. Without shared symbols, the rituals would become empty exercises. My information is not limited to feminism, but *feminist culture* does provide a center and a validation for the ritual performances.

The early movement provided us with some common symbols for protesting and the very important structure of consciousness raising, but many women saw the latter as a one-time experience. After the initial wave, pulling in and devising my own personal mythology/symbology and my own private rituals seemed to be the only avenue open at the time for exploring Goddess, female energy, nature, and spirit through my art. This meant, however, that my art explorations were coming from intuitions and not from a culture. It was only after the emergence of dialogues, conferences, and publication on women's spirituality that the possibility of building a holistic culture arose, along with the possibility of incorporating this culture in my art processes. It is this evolving culture that allowed me to present my first public ritual performance within the context of a shared culture.

But this privileged position has been a long time coming.

## PUBLIC RITUALS

Lucy Lippard has observed that ritual performance is part of the development of contemporary art and speaks toward a more direct human involvement and communication in our various art processes. Of a particular ritual I performed, she has written:

In the public rituals, her task is much more difficult. Although the world ritual is used very loosely these days as a form rather than as a container, it still implies a value system. There is a distinction between a ritual and a spectacle or a festival. When a ritual doesn't work it is a self-conscious act that isolates the performer as an exclusive object of attention. When it does work, the form's importance diminishes to become only one element in a communal impulse connecting all the participants and all the times this action has been performed in the past or will be performed in the future. A true ritual not only fulfills a need but generates the need to fulfill it again and again. (I seem to be describing addiction; perhaps a better term is stability. Much contemporary art seems to be looking for a way back through the passages to a time and place when art had meaning to many people.) Edelson's most recent ritual is called *The Nature of Balancing* and is about balancing our lives, especially in relation to nature. Like her other work it is concerned with "timelessness," incorporating past, present and future rather than looking nostalgically (and dangerously) backwards. And it balances again between two "sides" (cultural and political) of feminism.[3]

I reluctantly began doing public performances because it appeared that acting-out was a more complete way to communicate certain aspects that could not be presented in any other format. In my own performances, I try to consider the audience's response. At the beginning as people become caught up in the experience, particularly when the subject matter is rage and other unacceptable public emotions, a great deal of tension can be produced, but at some point I allow for a release of that tension through humor or some lightening device so the audience can relax with what is happening; finally, I try to create a comforting, nourishing experience, hoping people will leave the performance feeling better about themselves and others.

The validity of exhibiting in public what has been sacred in private and experienced without any notion of theatrics has been my most constant questioning in regard to making my rituals public. For some years I kept these rituals to myself, or my family or small groups of like-minded friends, sharing the experience with others only by telling them about the processes afterwards. My public rituals are still few and far between. They spring from the need to directly experience the content — when the information would be misrepresented if it were presented any other way, and when all other available media fall short of telling the whole story. I use public rituals only when I feel I must.

In my early performances, I tried to re-create the liturgy of the feminist movement as I perceived its evolution through the Seventies. Briefly, the liturgy presents our move from isolation to our earliest attempts at communication through our anger, rage, and protests, and then to our community, celebration, and the grounding of our activism, basically the story of how we came together. When the liturgy is chanted, we seldom break into words — the communication is made through sounds. From releasing our anger, we gain control and find ourselves. As we define ourselves, we discover our commonality. Through these processes, we are able to reassure and enjoy each other; we unleash our sensuality and begin celebrating. The liturgy or ritual performance, mirroring this process, ends with celebration of our emergence and the beginning of a new culture. I believe some transformation on a small or large scale should be experienced during the performance. Unless that change happens, the performance is not successful.

The performances have dealt with a range of topics that are both spiritual and political. *Proposals for: Memorials to 9,000,000 Women Burned as Witches in the Christian Era* retold some of their stories: The ritual consisted of chanting the names of women and men who were burned as Witches. Again, this ritual performance took place within a complete environment designed to intensify the experience: A gate served as the passage entrance to an eleven-foot-high fire ladder circled with stone-like handmade books and enlarged photographs of rituals in a Neolithic cave—all memorials to these martyrs.

*Burning Spiral,* an earthwork and performance, began in a cornfield where we cut down rows of cornstalks and placed them in three 200-foot-long rows that were two feet wide. We then braided the rows together by hoisting the entwined cornstalks on our shoulders and weaving our bodies in and out of each other. This finished, we rested, and at sunset placed the braided cornstalks on a sloping hill in the shape of a large spiral and burnt it. The fire and smoke spiraled on the ground and in the air. Some sat in the spiral while it was burning.[4]

## WORKSHOPS

The participants in my performances usually become involved through workshops that I give with small groups or at universities. This means, of course, that the performers are not professional. That is an essential aspect of ritual: We are actually experiencing and not just acting. The audience can also identify with the performers because they can visualize themselves in their place. The more I perform the rituals, however, the more professional they become, even when I am starting out with a new group each time.

To stimulate the creative juices at the beginning of my ritual workshops, I take the participants through highly visual guided images in which we all attempt to pull inside our innereye. Sitting in a circle, we then share what we imaged. These images are then used to build our own creative rituals at that time or are tucked away for future use. The workshops are structured to search out the territories that feminist rituals have covered in recent years, as well as to present a historical overview. They delve into what our rituals mean to us today and what they convey to others. Using discussions, chants, readings, research, recalling (remembering our past), and dreams, as well as our intuition, we share information to gain insights into this young field, as we actually experience these processes. Other information that I share includes *Anatomy of a Ritual,* an analytical look at the structure of rituals, and elaboration on various contemporary rituals through slides and video tapes. All the aforementioned is filtered through a creative, ever-changing approach.

During the workshops we prepare our own rituals as a result of these processes and then begin rehearsing them for a public presentation. The emphasis is on building a non-hierarchical situation, a situation in which skills are shared. The participants have access to information so that they can conduct their own workshops and hopefully pass on a non-hierarchical status. A danger that has been discussed is that an institutionalized dogma will evolve out of women's spirituality, out of our rituals, and that we will become hierarchical. Human nature being what it is, this is always a possibility, but if we keep our processes alive and well and continue to support their evolutionary growth, we can avoid this pitfall. The workshops are not obsessed with an end product. The processes we select for relating to one another, and how these processes affect *what* we have to say and *how* we say it, are a main focus.

The following are excerpts from writings by participants in ritual performances and workshops:

Mary Beth Edelson's exhibitions consist of photographic images and sculptural forms evoking ancient symbols, Goddess, female iconography, and the four "universal" elements of earth, air, fire, and water, all of which overlap and interrelate, creating an environment that is at once simple and highly complex. I participated in a group ritual in which these images and forms literally come "alive" in both humorous and highly impassioned ways.

The sacred ritual, *The Nature of Balancing,* with symbolic images of birds and flying, moved contemporary women toward unity and empowerment. In it, the "movers" (performers) pass through frustration and rage to awareness; they attempt individual flight which is thwarted by a solid wall; finally, through unity, they achieve a balance and fly. We gathered over each other embracing and building a mountain. As we unfolded, each of us stood and took the hand of the next, helping her to rise. In a circle with arms circling each other's shoulders, we extended one leg up and straight behind as we leaned forward balancing on the other leg. Then, balancing as a whole we swayed deeply and strongly from side to side, making a movement we could never have made alone. We flew. The "flying," at last accomplished, is dependent on each woman giving and taking support to sustain balance.

I was deeply moved. I had gone to Mary Beth Edelson's first meeting curiously, as an artist interested in meeting another artist. I had liked her photographs and her exhibitions. But, frankly, the rituals of my experience had been hokey at best or boring. Edelson's discussion of her work with ritual, however, captured my imagination, and I resolved to join the ritual and find out more.

The ritual was developed in a collaborative manner. Based on Edelson's inspiration, experience, and research, the ritual "filled out" with our responses and ideas and with a physical awareness of the movements we could accomplish. The full shape and form of the ritual, and its content, developed as we worked.

In retrospect, I realize that the four weeks of rehearsal were, for me, a form of initiation. I experienced a growing recognition that performing a ritual and the content of a ritual could be significant to me. The night we performed I was aware that I was being watched, was performing, and yet I experienced the ritual intensely. As we moved through each phase, I felt a deep bond with women's history and experience, with the search and consciousness expressed in the ritual. The ritual affirmed my experience as a woman, an artist and an individual and inspired a new consciousness. I was changed.[5]

— REBECCA BALLENGER

Another participant wrote:

Darkness: We lie where floor and wall meet, clinging to the wall, motionless. Gradually, wet primordial sounds, vocally recreated, fade in.

All is fusing: Mind becomes body; thought becomes movement. I am woman/artmaker/art simultaneously, any alienation from my body or my artwork fading as idea and instinct unwittingly express themselves in movement. Gyrating, our bodies gravitate toward the center of the room. I discover I am not alone. Slowly we merge into one undulating sea of energy. Connecting, we calm our movements, ebbing in the shape of a half-circle, a harbor, a crescent moon. Our overlapping bodies breathe together, woman-spirit asleep and ready for dreaming.

To the greatest extent possible in the rehearsal time, the method emulated the collective/developmental creative process we were depicting. Though she [Edelson] began with a vision of the (approximate) end result, she allowed process to mold and shape the event over time, and welcomed suggestion and improvisation. The performance, based on a creation myth, presented the natural evolution of primordial life force as female and as developmental.[6]

— CAREY CACCAVO

## CHANGING RITUALS BY ARTISTS

The unique and sometimes zany way in which some women think is given full reign in our art/rituals, where we have the opportunity to re-create the world in our image. Artists bring the creative process to ritual. This process adds to its contents, stimulates ritual's evolution, and helps to avoid repetitious stagnation. The following works are ever-changing and evolving ritual performances by visual artists.

*Book of Gulls* (twelve drawings and related text: silverpoint, ink, and type-writers; 1978, as yet unpublished). I went to the beach daily for twelve suc-cessive days to feed the seagulls, keeping a journal for the duration, noting my observations of the gulls' habits, their variations, and other related infor-mation. Each day I did at least one drawing of a gull. As the days progressed, I realized that while on the one hand the piece was about seagulls and their habitation of the Connecticut shore where I lived, it was still more about the archetypal act of nurturing. I became acutely aware of the mythic quality of birds in general, and as I performed the daily task of feeding, observing, and writing, I allowed my fantasies to play with the con-cept of bird as woman, bird as Goddess, bird as avenger, bird as spirit, and bird as symbol of transformation and transcendence. A very simple feeding activity, then, became a structure upon which to hang not only an elemen-tary empirical investigation, but also a mythic identification, personified by my intuitive self as a vehicle of flight and passage . . .

— MARY FISH

*Androgyny and Memory: The Queen of the World Passing into Alchemy* (A melodrama intended to satirize patriarchal notions of "high art"; Temple of Olympian Zeus, Athens, Greece, 1978). Three women, wrapped in clas-sical robes and wearing plastic cat masks, drape themselves around the base of one of the remaining columns. With heads abruptly turned away from the ruin and toward the crowd of curious tourists, the feline goddesses remain frozen to the stone. Suddenly, to the rhythm of their clicking tongues, the goddesses perform a quick tap dance and then return to the original tableau.

I use satire in an attempt to restructure experiences to become more suita-ble for the acceptance of goddess myths.

— JANE ELLEN GILMORE

*Personal Maintenance/Preserved Flowers;* April 1978. A performance in which I sat in a chair for several hours without moving. The chair was at the end of a corridor facing a film image. The film was of me sitting on a toilet, legs spread apart with close-up shots from above of my hands as I pried long red fake fingernails off of each finger with a pair of scissors. The fingernails fell between my legs into the toilet. The film was projected above a bank of live flowers which I had picked and dipped in wax. The performance took place at the opening of a large group show. Because of my stillness, silence, and lack of activity, most viewers chose to see and refer to me as an object. Many indulged in comments and insults which were directed at me as a passive receiver. This would never have happened had I assumed an obviously aggressive demeanor. As I sat watching the film, being aware of the crowd, I focused on the audience as individuals, hoping my silence would contribute to their own self-awareness in the situation. I thought about the helpless discomfort of an unwillingly passive role and how that produces frustration, acts of self-destruction, and violence in women's lives. I concentrated on understanding vulnerability as a place from which knowledge and strength can grow. I concentrated on transforming the victim's position.

— ALYSON POU

*Winter Solstice;* 1977. yes. reverence to her. the chant on the winter solstice on the full moon on the beach in the snow in the full spirit of the great round. on the darkest night of the year in the dark of the snow which obscured the moon and in the company of nine cars of city state and federal police who forbade the fire on the order of a superior who had the authority to forbid. but the moon asserted herself in the huge white waves which contained us in their rhythm and glow and rocked the chanting into a trance of chanting really chanting. or maybe i myself was in a trance from the very beginning anyway carrying totems and images of people i loved in the pockets of my spacesuit chanting my own rites of passage for myself. and the fire asserted itself too in the form of a delayed due to extreme cold chemical reaction causing a spontaneous combustion in the sacrificial bowl. it was perfect. a surprise chance to see ourselves only eyes showing between ponchos and parkas. chanting in circles around the tiny fire in the wooden bowl under the white canopy which also appeared spontaneously. and more chanting. and altered chanting. and invocations and glorifications and in general much reverence to her. to her to us to each other. and then at a certain point which we all realized together the chanting was over. for this time and the chanters lined up and passed the unlit fire log by log hand over hand over beach over fence back into the truck. and hugged and kissed each other and me and separated in the dark in the snow back in cars and bus back into the other world.[7]

— DONNA HENES

*Invitation to a Burning;* 1980. For the Spring Equinox 1980, I presented a participatory ritual *Invitation to a Burning* at the Los Angeles Woman's Building. I made a "body" out of clay, muslin, pigment, and wax and stuffed it with dead vegetation. It represented our winter of oppression, our old bound selves. In a candlelight ceremony we burned the body, and women leaped over the flames together. Afterward we filled the clay husk with earth and planted seeds sacred to women: barley, flax, and poppies. These seeds sprouted and flourished while the piece was on display — they created a new "body" representing women's new-growing spirit. Seeds from the performance were sent to the international women's gathering in Copenhagen in 1980. Women planted "Liberty Gardens" to celebrate womanspirit rising everywhere.

— FAITH WILDING

*Performance: Diction Dictionary* (South American creation myths featuring women as the creative force, the genetrix; 1980). The performance begins with sweeping the space and evocation of the celestial housewife who brought the world into being and women's everyday maintenance activities. Using a globe as a kick ball, curves for rivers, stones, and seeds I built a symbolic landscape. At the end I wrapped myself in strips of paper evoking the productivity of the writer (the way some of Sappho's poems were found as the wrappings of a mummy).

— ANN-SARGENT WOOSTER

*Feminist Rosary;* 1980. Although I am not a Catholic, I have always been fascinated by the rosary and decided that we needed a feminist version of it. I got an ordinary Catholic rosary and had the crucifix replaced with a Mary medallion. Then, from a standard instruction booklet, I learned the rosary's underlying structure so that I could isolate out the patriarchal content and construct a new cycle of prayers of "songs" honoring the Great Goddess (which I adapted from Wicca rituals in books by Z. Budapest, Starhawk, and Margot Adler). On the "stem" I say various blessings and invocations to prepare for entering the magic circle. The circle itself is conveniently segmented by four single beads on which I invoke the powers of the cardinal directions and the solstices and equinoxes. Between these, while silently chanting a repetitive incantation to cast and maintain the magic circle, I meditate on the meaning of the great Pagan festivals at the cross-quarter points: Samhain, Candlemas, Beltane, and Lammas. Thus, the Feminist Rosary has become a powerful personal code of the traditions, time/space cycles, and sources of strength that lie hidden in our deepest spiritual heritage.

— MIMI LOBELL

*Interior Scroll;* Performance, 1975. Interior scroll is an event for the body as a source of wisdom — vulvic space as "interior knowledge." Poised naked I slowly draw out from my vagina a narrow, five-foot-long scroll and read the text printed there.

The image is about the power and possession of naming. The physical movement has to do with the passage of interior thought to external signification. The scroll makes reference to an uncoiling serpent; I associate Her with ticker tape, rainbow, torah in the ark, chalice, choir loft, plumb line, bell tower, umbilicus, and tongue.

— CAROLEE SCHNEEMAN

NOTES

[Part of this article appeared in different form in an interview with Mary Beth Edelson by Alyson Pou, *Atlanta Art Papers,* vol. 4, no. 4, July/Aug. 1980.]

1. *Your 5,000 Years Are Up!* by Mary Beth Edelson. Notes from the unpublished manuscript, 1973.
2. Lucy R. Lippard, *Seven Cycles: Public Rituals* by Mary Beth Edelson, Introduction, p. 6., 1980.
3. *Ibid.,* p. 8.
4. Mary Beth Edelson, *Intermedia,* edited by Hans Breder and Stephen C. Foster, University of Iowa, 1979.
5. Rebecca Ballenger, *Artery,* William Paterson College. "Participants Speak" by Rebecca Ballenger and Carey Caccavo, Fall 1980.
6. Carey Caccavo, *Artery,* William Paterson College. "Participants Speak" by Rebecca Ballenger and Carey Caccavo, Fall 1980.
7. Donna Henes, "Winter Solstice," *The Great Goddess,* no. 5, *Heresies: A Feminist Publication on Art and Politics,* Sept. 1978.

# Images of Spiritual Power in Women's Fiction

# Carol P. Christ and Charlene Spretnak

## PART ONE BY CAROL P. CHRIST

Women's stories have not been told. And without stories there is no articulation of experience. Without stories a woman is lost when she comes to make the important decisions of her life. She does not learn to value her struggles, to celebrate her strengths, to comprehend her pain. Without stories she cannot understand herself. Without stories she is alienated from those deeper experiences of self and world that have been called spiritual or religious. She is closed in silence. The expression of women's spiritual quest is integrally related to the telling of women's stories. If women's stories are not told, the depth of women's souls will not be known.

Through recognizing the crucial importance of stories to selves, the dilemma of women is revealed. Women live in a world where women's stories rarely have been told from their own perspectives. The stories celebrated in culture are told by men. Thus, men have actively shaped their experiences of self and world, and their most profound stories orient them to what they perceive as the great powers of the universe. But since women have not told their own stories, they have not actively shaped their experiences of self and world nor named the great powers from their own perspectives.

As women become more aware of how much of their own experience they must suppress in order to fit themselves into the stories of men, their yearning grows for a literature of their own, in which women's stories are told from women's perspectives.

The simple act of telling a woman's story from a woman's point of view is a revolutionary act: It never has been done before. A new language must be created to express women's experience and insight, new metaphors discovered, new themes considered. Women writers who name the gap between men's stories about women and women's own perceptions of self and world are engaged in creating a new literary tradition. And just as consciousness-raising is a story-telling ritual, so too are feminist literary readings ritual events. As women writers share their naming of experience, they forge connections to other women, who hear their own unnamed longings voiced, their perceptions of the world and its powers given form.

This new literature created by women has both a spiritual and a social dimension. It reflects both women's struggles to create new ways of living in the world *and* a new naming of the great powers that provide orientation in the world. In order to call attention to the spiritual dimension of women's quest, which is sometimes overlooked in the urgency of the struggle for new social roles, I have made a distinction between the spiritual and social quests. In making this distinction, I do not intend to separate reality into the spiritual and the mundane, as has been typical in Western philosophy. I believe that women's spiritual and social quests are two dimensions of a single struggle and it is important for women to become aware of the ways in which spirituality can support and undergird women's quest for social equality.

Women's *social quest* concerns women's struggle to gain respect, equality, and freedom in society — in work, in politics, and in relationships with women, men, and children. In the social quest a woman begins in alienation from the human community and seeks new modes of relationship and action in society. She searches to find nonoppressive sexual relationships, new visions of mothering, creative work, equal rights as a citizen.

Women's *spiritual quest* concerns a woman's awakening to the depths of her soul and her position in the universe. A woman's spiritual quest includes moments of solitary contemplation, but it is strengthened by being shared. It involves asking basic questions: Who am I? Why am I here? What is my place in the universe? In answering these questions, a woman must listen to her own voice and come to terms with her own experience. Because she can no longer accept conventional answers to her questions, she opens herself to the radically new — possibly to the revelation of powers or forces of being larger than herself that can ground her in a new understanding of herself and her position in the world.

As I see it, the powers of being that orient and ground women's quest are best understood as "forces or currents of energy," to use Doris Lessing's term, which operate in all natural and social processes. These forces are the energies of life, death, and regeneration and being, non-being, and transformation, which are most obvious in nature, but which also operate in the social world. These forces are not only life-forces, but forces of death and destruction. In nature the life- and death-forces are intertwined. Every individual is finite and eventually must die, but life also re-creates itself from death. The dead heron, which in Margaret Atwood's *Surfacing* provides food for swarms of insects that devour its flesh, is a graphic symbol of death transforming into life. It is not individuals, but the process of life transforming into death into life that is eternal — or seems so from a human perspective. The individual can gain a sense of transcendence from recognizing participation in these larger life- and death-forces.

It is important for women to name the great powers or powers of being from their own perspective and to recognize their participation in them. Women need to recognize that their participation in the life- and death-forces in all natural processes means that they have as much right to exist and to affirm their value as every other being. Women also need to name their movement for greater equality as a movement rooted in the powers of being and life. Women's spiritual quest provides orientation for women's social quest and grounds it in something larger than individual or even collective achievements. If a woman has experienced the grounding of her quest in powers of being that are larger than her own personal will, this knowledge can support her when her own personal determination falters.

Women's Spiritual Quest takes a distinctive form in the fiction and poetry of women writers. It often begins in an *experience of nothingness*. Women experience emptiness in their own lives — in self-hatred, in self-negation, and in being a victim; in relationships with men; and in the values that have shaped their lives. Experiencing nothingness, women reject conventional solutions and question the meaning of their lives, thus opening themselves to the revelation of deeper sources of power and value. The experience of nothingness often precedes an *awakening*, similar to a conversion experience, in which the powers of being are revealed. A woman's awakening to great powers grounds her in a new sense of self and a new orientation in the world. Through awakening to new powers, women overcome self-negation and self-hatred and refuse to be victims.

Awakening often occurs through *mystical identification*, which women's traditional attunement to the body and mothering processes have prepared them for. Women's mystical experiences often occur in nature or in community with other women. Awakening is followed by a *new naming* of self and reality that articulates the new orientation to self and world achieved through experiencing the powers of being. Women's new naming of self and world often reflect wholeness, a movement toward overcoming the dualisms of self and world, body and soul, nature and spirit, rational and emotional, which have plagued Western consciousness. Women's new naming of self and world suggests directions for social change and looks forward to the realization of spiritual insight in social reality — the integration of spiritual and social quests.

Though a woman's spiritual quest may proceed linearly from the experience of nothingness, through awakening, to mystical insight, and new naming, this order is not necessary. The moments of women's quest are part of a process in which experiences of nothingness, awakenings, insights, and namings form a spiral of ever-deepening but never final understanding.

## *Kate Chopin's* The Awakening (1899)

The awakening of Kate Chopin's character, Edna Pontellier, a married woman in her late twenties, is sparked by a mystical experience in the sea. Set within the highly conventional French Creole society of her husband's friends and associates, Edna's quest ends tragically with her return to the sea where she swims out to her death. Recently reclaimed as a feminist classic, *The Awakening*[1] poses a challenge to critics because of its ending: Is Edna's death the triumph of a strong woman who chooses to die rather than face spiritual annihilation or the defeat of a woman too weak to fulfill her quest? My view is that the ending of the novel reflects spiritual triumph but social defeat. It provides eloquent testimony that women's quest must be for full social and spiritual liberation.

Chopin describes Edna's awakening in a passage that occurs near the beginning of the story and is repeated again at its end. The passage begins, "a certain light was beginning to dawn dimly within her, — the light which, showing the way, forbids it" (33). The dawning yet forbidding light suggests revelation, but also portends the tragedy that follows Edna's enlightenment. The passage continues:

At that early period it served but to bewilder her. It moved her to dreams, to thoughtfulness, to the shadowy anguish which had overcome her the midnight when she had abandoned herself to tears.

In short, Mrs. Pontellier was beginning to realize her position in the universe as a human being, and to recognize her relations as an individual to the world within and about her (33).

Here the spiritual dimension of the novel is clearly articulated: It concerns Edna's recognition of the nature and potential of her own soul and its relation to the cosmos, "the world about her." This realization seems so simple some might not call it "spiritual." But Chopin clearly intends the reader to compare Edna's awakening to those religious awakenings commonly called conversions, as is evident from her ironic comment, "this may seem like a ponderous weight of wisdom to descend upon the soul of a young woman of twenty-eight — perhaps more wisdom than the Holy Ghost is usually pleased to vouchsafe to any woman" (33–34).

The sea is the medium of Edna's awakening. Walking by the sea, Edna senses the limitless potential of her soul and begins to question her life.

But the beginning of things, of a world especially, is necessarily vague, tangled, chaotic, and exceedingly disturbing. How few of us ever emerge from such a beginning! How many souls perish in its tumult!

The voice of the sea is seductive; never ceasing, whispering, clamoring, murmuring, inviting the soul to wander for a spell in abysses of solitude; to lose itself in mazes of inward contemplation.

The voice of the sea speaks to the soul. The touch of the sea is sensuous, enfolding the body in its soft, close embrace (34).

A symbol of infinite and fearful power, the sea is also empowering. When she first learns to swim, "She did shout for joy, as with a sweeping stroke or two she lifted her body to the surface of the water. A feeling of exultation overtook her, as if some power of significant import had been given her to control the working of her body and her soul" (70). Swimming in the ocean is both a physical and spiritual experience; Edna feels control over her body *and* over her soul.

She turned her face seaward to gather in an impression of space and solitude, which the vast expanse of water, meeting and melting with the moonlit sky, conveyed to her excited fancy. As she swam she seemed to be reaching out for the unlimited in which to lose herself (71).

Edna's experience is a classic mystical experience of temporary union with a great power, and the experience provides her with a sense of illumination.

The element of danger in Edna's experience — a portent of her suicide — is a common feature of mystic experience. Mystical experience shatters an old self, and the mystic who faces nothingness risks becoming lost there — the conventional supports of the self shattered but were lacking the revelation that could lead to the creation of a new self on the other side of nothingness. For a woman the risk is that when the patriarchal definitions of her being are stripped away, she will be faced with radical freedom; she will have no guidelines to tell her how to act. She must have courage, clear-sightedness, and awareness of the consequences of her choices or she may lose herself.

Edna's mystical experience reflects wholeness. She is not transported out of the body into a transcendent world. Instead, the experience is extremely physical, even sensual, and in it she finds revealed the power of her body as well as her soul. For her physical, sexual, social, and spiritual awakening occur together.

Edna's awakening starts her on the path of women's social quest, a search for new ways of living in human community. Unfortunately, her quest is not fully supported by any of her friends, and at the end of the story, Edna, confused and despairing, returns to the sea and swims out to her, achieving spiritual freedom at the expense of her life. The tragedy of the novel is that spiritual and social quests could not be united in her life.

## Doris Lessing's The Four-Gated City (1969)

Doris Lessing's immense and unwieldy five-volume series, *The Chil-*

*dren of Violence,* charts a spiritual journey from a woman's perspective. Though Lessing's intention was to write about a generation, in choosing Martha Quest as the heroine of her story she made women's experience central in it. Martha's quest begins in an experience of nothingness. It is uniquely shaped by her experience of motherhood, and her guide on her journey is another woman, Lynda, through whom Martha incorporates the dark side of women's experience. *The Four-Gated City,*[2] the last volume in the Martha Quest series, might be compared to a Sufi "teaching story," which, as Lessing has written, is designed to assist "the interior movement of the human mind."[3]

Martha's development follows definite stages. Martha begins to remember the times alone with herself when she has gained insight. She learns to protect her right to those times. She experiences motherhood and, through children, broadens and deepens her understanding of herself and the times in which she lives. She pays debts and relives past experiences that she had not integrated or understood. She confronts her mother and understands how she had struggled to create an identity different from her mother's. She experiences depression and confronts a mythology of liberation offered by the culture — psychology — and finds it lacking. She decides to pursue her own inner growth of a relationship and thus frees herself from the mythology of sexual love. Finally, she explores the region of "madness" with her friend and guide, Lynda, and gains visionary powers.

Martha's month in the basement with Lynda, exploring regions of nonordinary reality, is a rite of passage. Her earlier apprehensions of another dimension of reality are confirmed. The center of her life shifts decisively as the region of nonordinary reality and the insight it offers become the goal of her quest; it is the city she had dreamed about. It is important to note the sisterhood and sharing between Martha and Lynda. Each is a guide and teacher for the other. Lynda shares with Martha her knowledge of the nonordinary regions, based on her long experience with them. Martha shares with Lynda the strength to cope with ordinary life. It is as if two separated parts of women's experience, mother and witch or madwoman, are joined. From the integration of the separated comes a new power.

At the conclusion of the novel, the house in which she has lived for twenty years has been sold and Martha prepares to leave. Once again she has no definite plans. Martha's thoughts about her future sum up the insights she has gained on her journey. "She had learned that one thing, that most important thing, which was that one simply had to go on, take one step after another: this process itself held the keys" (588). Martha has learned to trust her capacity to grow and learn from any situation. There is no other person, no place outside herself, necessary for the process of insight that she has learned to value above all else.

Looking at Martha's quest in its entirety, we see that her spiritual consciousness is defined by the "watcher," the part of herself that observes, understands, becomes conscious of the deeper dimensions of her experience. The watcher has a less aggressive relation to reality than ordinary male consciousness, but it is not passive. When she describes the watcher as a soft, dark, receptive intelligence, Martha does not mean it is merely a passive receptacle. The watcher is an active consciousness. Far from being undifferentiated passivity, it is a form of consciousness that must be developed through discipline. Waiting is the major discipline of this consciousness. Waiting is not a passive activity; Martha waits with purposefulness. She does not know what she is waiting for, but when it is given to her, she takes active steps to explore it. Thus she discovers Lynda's territory in one of her waiting periods and explores it further on her own.

Martha's knowledge of self and world is always concrete. She uses books only to verify her insights, to confirm something she knows or half knows. Her knowledge is not abstract, nor unconnected to ordinary life. Nothing she knows is arbitrary, surprising, or unrelated to something she had known before. Her self-knowledge and knowledge of the world are intimately related.

Martha feels part of a process that transcends her conscious control. Since she is not concerned to change the process or herself, but only to understand, she desires nothing in particular. She trusts that whatever happens, wherever she goes, the process of living will provide her with opportunities to deepen her insight.

An observing, connected, deepened consciousness is the source of Martha's prophetic power. As she understands what is happening in her self, in the children, and in the world in which she lives, she comes to understand what will happen as a development of what already is happening. This form of prophecy is organic, not exoteric, an insight into processes everyone is involved in, not revelation from an external source.

Though Martha's journey strikes a responsive chord in many women, Lessing's view of the relation between the spiritual and social quest is disturbing. Like Martha, Lessing seems to believe that nuclear catastrophe is inevitable. And this apocalyptic vision leaves her pessimistic about social change and somewhat detached from women's social quest for equality in relationships, work, and politics. There are many days when I find Lessing's pessimism compelling and can easily envision the nuclear accident she describes. However, I want women to be more than witnesses and prophets of disaster or hope, more than mothers or nurturers of "new children." I believe it is possible that women's new naming of self and world can stem the tide of violence and disintegration Lessing so convincingly depicts.

## Margaret Atwood's Surfacing (1972)

The spiritual quest of the unnamed protagonist of Surfacing[4] begins with her return to the Canadian wilderness, where she had lived as a child. Ostensibly, the protagonist is in search of her missing father, who is presumed dead. But the search is really for her missing parents, her mother having died a few years earlier, and for the power she feels it was their duty to have communicated to her. The external detective story of the protagonist's search for her father is paralleled by an internal search — half obscured by her obsession with her father — to discover how she lost the ability to feel. The two mysteries intersect when she recognizes that "it was no longer his death but my own that concerned me" (123).

Confronting her past and the powers of nature, she discovers a power within herself and stays alone in the wilderness to complete her quest. When the time to leave the island comes, she hides, escaping from her friends. "I am by myself; this is what I wanted, to stay here alone" (196). "The truth is here" (197). The choice of solitude is not so much a rejection of community as a recognition that certain experiences and truths are so alien to ordinary consciousness that the individual must withdraw in order to experience them.

After the others have left, the protagonist has time and space to plumb more deeply the knowledge and experience that has been given her. Lying alone at the bottom of her canoe she has a vision of the great powers of the universe, the divinities who have guided her journey: "Through the trees the sun glances; the swamp around me smolders, energy of decay turning to growth, green fire. I remember the heron; by now it will be insects, frogs, fish, other herons" (194). The great powers of the universe transform the swamp; they transform the heron from death to life. The life power rises from death. This is the meaning of the incredible words she had spoken earlier, "nothing has died, everything is alive, everything is waiting to become alive" (182).

The protagonist recognizes her body as both *revelation* and *incarnation* of the great powers of life and death. "My body also changes, the creature in me, plant-animal, sends out filaments in me; I ferry it secure between death and life, I multiply" (194). The female experience of the transformation of parts of her body into plant, animal, and infant is perhaps the most complete human incarnation of the great powers. The protagonist's vision of the universal transformative energy of life into death and death into life is reflected in her characteristic perception of the fluidity of the boundaries between objects, plants, animals, humans. Joe has "fur" like a bear, canoers are "amphibian," the fetus is "plant-animal" sending out "filaments."

After her vision, the protagonist enters the final phase of her visionary journey: transformation itself. She realizes that she can see her dead parents, and perhaps the gods themselves, if she follows the path she is beginning to sense. "The gods, their likenesses: to see them in their true shape is fatal. While you are human; but after the transformation they could be reached" (181). Her transformation is frightening. Though she knows it is beyond "any rational point of view" (196), it is neither mad nor illogical. Whereas before she had abandoned false memories, now she will give up all identity as a human. Before she had experienced the fetus transforming her body, now she will change herself into a different state.

She ritually breaks her connections to the human world — burning or purifying clothing, books, one of everything in the cabin. She is purified and transformed by immersion in the lake. Like the fetus in her womb, she changes in water. "The earth rotates, holding my body down as it holds the moon; the sun pounds in the sky, red flames pulsing from it, searing away the wrong form that encases me" (206). The powers guide her away from the garden, the house, into the woods. She becomes wild. She is animal: "I hollow a lair near the woodpile, dry leaves underneath and dead branches leaned over" (207). Having undergone transformation, she experiences mystical identification with all forms of life: "Leopard frog with green spots and gold-rimmed eyes, ancestor. It includes me, it shines, nothing moves but its throat breathing" (208). She experiences direct union with the great powers of life and death in nature. All boundaries between herself and other forms of life are abolished. She *becomes the transformative energy*: "I lean against a tree, I am a tree leaning . . . I am not an animal or a tree, I am the thing in which the trees and animals move and grow" (210).

Later she sees a vision of her mother feeding the birds; then her mother disappears, the birds remain. She is translated. This vision confirms her sense that her mother's gift is connection to nature. As Barbara Hill Rigney says, "Almost witchlike, with her long hair and wearing her magically powerful leather jacket, the mother feeds wild birds from her hand, charms a bear, and is in tune with the seasons."[5] In a similar vein, Adrienne Rich calls the mother as she appears "Mistress of the Animals."[6]

The next day she sees what her father saw. What he has seen "gazes at me with its yellow eyes, wolf's eyes, depthless but lambent as the eyes of animals seen at night in the car headlights" (216). The eyes of the wolf remind her that her father's gift is the power of seeing, or insight. The protagonist is terrified as she realizes that in the state of transformation individual human identity has no meaning. Her father's vision is impersonal, but it is also strangely comforting because it means that the life power survives a particular identity. With the vision of the parents, the protagonist's circle is complete. Her parents' power has been communicated to her.

The vision granted, the gods then retreat into "the earth, the air, the water, wherever they were when I summoned them" (218). Translated back to human form, the protagonist returns to the cabin and opens a can of beans, symbolizing her return to modern human life. Though she is no longer in direct contact with the powers, she has gained wisdom and consciousness of her own power through her encounter with them. She marks her new power with a declaration: "This above all, to refuse to be a victim . . . give up the old belief that I am powerless" (222). The source of her newly discovered power is twofold. First, she renounces the fictitious memories that held together her delusions of innocence and powerlessness. Letting go and allowing her true past to surface is itself a source of tremendous energy. Second, her grounding in her own past and in the powers of the universe provides her with a sense of authentic selfhood.

Though Atwood has effectively portrayed a woman's spiritual quest, she has left the question of its integration with the social quest open. Still, it seems fair to assume that Atwood's protagonist has experienced a spiritual and psychological transformation that will give her the inner strength to change her social and political relationships. She no longer sees herself as inevitably powerless and victimized. By naming anew the great powers and women's grounding in them, *Surfacing* provides women with alternatives to patriarchal notions of power that can aid their struggle to change the social world.

## PART TWO BY CHARLENE SPRETNAK

*Maxine Hong Kingston's* The Woman Warrior (*1976*)

Maxine Ting Ting Hong Kingston's first book, *The Woman War-rior*,[7] is subtitled *Memoirs of a Girlhood Among Ghosts*. Although the National Book Critics Circle named it the best non-fiction book of 1976, the author has said, "I did a lot of conjecturing — this could have happened, that could have happened. I feel I could just as well call it fiction. Other people have."[8] Other people have also celebrated the strong and passionate style, and the graceful interweaving of family history and myth, of concrete and abstract turns of speech. To my mind, there is no doubt that *The Woman Warrior* is an autobiographical *novel*.

Hong Kingston opens her story with an account of her own menarche ritual. Her experience is familiar to many women who have come of age under patriarchy: Menses is presented to her as potential disaster. The narrator's mother shares with her, for the first and only time, the story of a martyred aunt who defied patriarchal mores. In response to her act of sexual freedom, the aunt and her family were attacked by outraged neighbors; the aunt gave birth that night in a pigsty and, some hours later, committed infanticide and suicide in the family well. Thereafter, her name is never mentioned, her very existence denied. The narrator's mother ends the story with a warning: "Now that you have started to menstruate, what happened to her could happen to you. Don't humiliate us. You wouldn't like to be forgotten as if you had never been born" (5). Such was the celebration of womanhood and the female body.

Later in the novel, the narrator imagines that she spends her seventh through twenty-second year with a magical, elderly couple on a mountaintop, training to be an invincible swordswoman. "She [the narrator's mother] said I would grow up a wife and a slave, but she taught me the song of the warrior woman, Fa Mu Lan. I would have to grow up a warrior woman" (20). In that fantasy, the narrator experiences her menarche entirely differently than she had in real life: The kindly old woman explains to her, "You're an adult now. You can have children" (30). The young warrior notes, "Menstrual days did not interrupt my training; I was as strong as on any other day" (30).

During her training, the narrator grows in spiritual purity, i.e., skillful mindstates, and in physical prowess. She explains, "I learned to make my mind large, as the universe is large, so that there is room for paradoxes" (29). She learns to "control the sword's slashing with my mind" (33). Finally she is ready to return to her people and avenge their cruel exploitation by a corrupt baron, who "sat square and fat like a god" (43). The warrior demands that he repent, but he merely tries to be charming: "Oh, come now. Everyone takes the girls when he can. The families are glad to be rid of them. 'Girls are maggots in the rice.' 'It is more profitable to raise geese than daughters'" (43). She cuts off his head.

In the baron's house, the warrior finds a room filled with "cowering, whimpering women" (44). They had been the baron's concubines and could not escape on their tiny, bound feet. The warrior calls the villagers to come and identify their daughters, but no one claims any. She gives each woman a bag of rice and never sees them again, but tells us of their evolution:

They rolled the bags to the road. They wandered away like ghosts. Later, it would be said, they turned into the band of swordswomen who were a mercenary army. They did not wear men's clothes like me, but rode as women in black and red dresses. They brought up girl babies so that many poor families welcomed their visitations. When slave girls and daughters-in-law ran away, people would say they joined these witch amazons (45).

A theme that winds throughout the book is the conflict between the narrator's inner power and that of her mother. The latter's message to her daughters is that they must, above all, behave in a way that will attract husbands. Yet she herself is anything but docile: "She could make herself not weak. During danger she fanned out her dragon claws and riffled her red sequin scales and unfolded her coiling green stripes. Danger was a good time for showing off" (67). The feminist literary critic John Leonard has called this character "the mother to end all mothers"![19] Looking back on her childhood, the narrator considers the power of the chants about women warriors and wonders if her mother, who taught the chants to her daughters, may not have known their "power to remind" (20).

In spite of all the woman-hating proverbs and the denials of her true female self, the narrator decides, "From afar I can believe my family loves me fundamentally" (55). She has made her mind large enough for paradoxes.

*E. M. Broner's* A Weave of Women (*1978*)

All of E. M. Broner's books to date are concerned with formalizing the connections among women. With powerful, poetic prose Broner insists that women *honor* one another, that we treat each other with courtesy and respect. This deeply felt love, for ourselves and other women, is the basis of spirituality in her stories; it is the secure foundation from which power grows.

*A Weave of Women*[10] takes place in the Old City of Jerusalem. The weavers are fifteen women who come from Israel, Europe, and America. This diverse, yet closely knit, group reflects Broner's philosophy: "I think women transcend all people. We have a past and we have a present that transcends all nationalities. Men are nationalists."[11] Broner has said that she wrote *A Weave of Women* in "a priestly voice" to encourage women in ceremony, hymn, or psalm to realize that life is a real or symbolic battle, that we must become warriors, and that we must abide by our own calendar and rhythms.[12] In this novel, the battles of women's lives are depicted in a society even more stubbornly patriarchal than our own; hence we are inspired by the defiance and triumphs of the characters. They nurture their power and take control of their circumstances in spite of formidable odds.

The warp and woof that form the intriguing texture of *A Weave of Women* are the diversity of character and personal history of the women interwoven with the healing, empowering rituals that they create for themselves. When a woman is wounded by patriarchal oppression, her sisters do not sigh passively; when a woman experiences a triumph in her life, her sisters do not let it slip by unmarked. The women create rituals for birthing, for cooling off, for forgetting false self-images, for ridding themselves of demons, for burying their dead, for accepting change, for girding for battle, for seeking revenge, for honoring their bodies, for beginning a journey, for excommunicating a woman who betrayed them in many ways, and for sending forth sisters to a new time and place in their lives.

Broner also addresses the question of whether feminists need deny their entire ethnic heritage because it has been shaped and owned by patriarchy. No, we need not. Just as the women learn to decipher the patriarchal bias in the daily newspaper (e.g., when they read that a young scholar has stoned a foreign "whore," they rush to the hospital, knowing that a traveler has been brutalized for an act of sexual freedom), so they learn to decipher the biblical accounts of Hebrew women. Broner's interpretation of the story of Esther is both wise and often hilarious. Esther is shown to be a courageous woman who trusted her inner power and made difficult choices:

She could either ignore her origins [in Ishtar] or she could act upon them. She could ignore the fact that once her powers were vast and her influence wide, or think only that her statues are broken and her name whispered. She could ignore the fact that once she was queen of heaven, mistress of the fields, and the great destroyer, or act upon that knowledge (125).

Again and again, Broner lyrically tells us that *women have choices*. The central choice is how we shall regard our selves, the phenomenon of the female body/mind. In order to shed patriarchal images and evolve into their own truth, the women create a "counterholiday," Holy Body Day. Having spent much time together, their menses occurs almost simultaneously and they proclaim "the twenty-first day after the onset of menses" as their holy day. They begin with a prayer to the Goddess: "Blessed are thou, O Mother of the Universe, from whose body we descend, who has kept us alive, preserved us and brought us to this time, this season" (257). The women go together to the bathhouse, and later they "speak of the legends of their bodies" (258). They compose and sing *The Women's Song of Songs*.

At the end of the story, the women found a pioneer settlement in a deserted Arab village on the outskirts of Jerusalem. They have staged demonstrations, infiltrated the Knesset (parliament) by electing a woman warrior, struck back at attackers, divorced tyrants, founded a Girls' Town, mourned their dead, loved their friends, healed their wounds, and strengthened their will. They have done all of this with the spiritual power they acknowledged and encouraged and *honored*. Broner's ceremonious women never theorize about collective power; they feel it and they live it.

## Women's Work

The novels we have discussed are stories of women *directly* exploring and experiencing the spiritual content of their lives. The characters have rejected the patriarchal mode of spiritual quest that would have them implore a priestly caste to intervene and shape their spirituality. The women's insistence on owning their own souls is truly a revolutionary act. Having gradually come to trust her own inner power, each of the protagonists could be imagined to echo the words of a contemporary woman warrior who is guided by her spiritual convictions, Sonia

Johnson: "Somehow I evolved into a person who ceased to ask permission."[13]

Many nineteenth-century women novelists shared such convictions, and it is one of the tragedies of our movement that most of their writing was devalued and dropped from the history of American literature so that we, at the beginning of the second wave of feminism, knew of no tradition of nonpatriarchal spirituality among American women. In leaving patriarchal religion, many women have felt they were stepping into a fearsome abyss; we had to start from "square one," just as our earlier sisters had. This should not have been. Recently, however, feminist literary scholarship has uncovered numerous nineteenth-century novels that express themes extremely familiar to contemporary proponents of postpatriarchal spirituality: that women, even those believing in a supreme male deity, must find their spirituality within themselves, not by listening to ministers; that women can improve their position by discovering and using their inner power; that women can and should teach each other about possibilities; that women's friendships with women are extremely important, and one does not find her true identity through marriage and children; that women must accept themselves as women, not permanent children; and that women and men are essentially different in some very basic aspects of the psyche.[14] The novels bearing such themes have sometimes been dismissed as "sentimental" by many contemporary feminist scholars, but they are ignoring the strong connection, often voiced by Elizabeth Cady Stanton and other activists of the period, between women's spiritual convictions and their political networking and actions.

Woman's spiritual power — *as defined by woman* — has been a focus of several novels in recent years, and many more are in progress. These are stories of struggle. The enormous task of surmounting patriarchal barriers to female spirituality is only the beginning of a challenging process. Once a character begins to nurture her inner power, how shall she use it? What are her ethics? What is her vision? Will her triumphs and inner peace buoy her through periods of despair — or will she walk into the sea? And at some point in such novels the reader may join the author and the protagonist in wondering — perhaps furtively — *Is this struggle really worth all this effort?* It cannot be otherwise, for we will never go back to asking permission.

NOTES

1. Page references to *The Awakening* are from the Capricorn Books edition, 1964.
2. Page references to *The Four-Gated City* are from the Bantam Books edition, 1970.
3. Doris Lessing, "What Looks Like an Egg and Is an Egg?" *The New York Times Book Review*, 7 May 1972, p. 42.
4. Page references to *Surfacing* are from the Simon and Schuster edition, 1972.
5. Barbara Hill Rigney, *Madness and Sexual Politics in the Feminist Novel: Studies in Brontë, Woolf, Lessing, and Atwood* (Madison: University of Wisconsin Press, 1978), p. 111.
6. Adrienne Rich, *Of Woman Born* (New York: Bantam Books, 1977), p. 245.
7. Page references to *A Woman Warrior: Memoirs of a Girlhood Among Ghosts* are from the Alfred A. Knopf edition, 1976.
8. "Writing Out the Storm: An Interview with Maxine Hong Kingston," Timothy Pfaff, *California Monthly*, Oct. 1979.
9. John Leonard, "In Defiance of Two Worlds," a review of *The Woman Warrior*, *The New York Times*, 17 Sept. 1976.
10. Page references to *A Weave of Women* are from the Holt, Rinehart and Winston edition, 1978.
11. "Women and Ritual: An Interview with Dr. Esther Broner," V. Lynn McGee, *New Women's Times*, 7–20 Dec. 1979.
12. Personal correspondence from Dr. Broner.
13. "Sonia Johnson: Life After Excommunication," Christine Rigby Arrington, *San Francisco Chronicle*, 3 Dec. 1980.
14. See Nina Baym, *Woman's Fiction: A Guide to Novels by and about Women in America, 1820–1870* (Ithaca: Cornell University Press, 1978). Baym goes farther than most scholars in acknowledging the themes of women's spiritual power, as distinct from their cultural interactions with clergy, but she generally labels this power "psychological."

# PART THREE

# Transforming
the Political

# The Unity of Politics
# and Spirituality

Truthfulness anywhere means a heightened complexity. But it is a movement into evolution. Women are only beginning to uncover our own truths; many of us would be grateful for some rest in that struggle, would be glad just to lie down with the sherds we have painfully unearthed, and be satisfied with those. Often I feel this like an exhaustion in my own body.

The politics worth having, the relationships worth having, demand that we delve still deeper.

— ADRIENNE RICH

Selection is reprinted from ON LIES, SECRETS, AND SILENCE: Selected Prose, by Adrienne Rich, with the permission of W. W. Norton & Company, Inc. Copyright © by Adrienne Rich, 1978.

# The Unity of Politics
# and Spirituality

*Both politics and spirituality are concerned with power — power created, maintained, and utilized in alignment with a particular view of life. A person with an unexamined mind is powerless in the face of emotional vicissitudes that run an entire cycle, no matter how painful, because s/he has not developed the quiet detachment necessary to make choices about one's mindstate. That mindstate, e.g., anxious, fearful, greedy, hostile, determines one's worldview and the kind of political system that s/he deems necessary. For instance, many people who function continually with unskillful, negative mindstates insist that human beings are naturally base and so require totalitarian policing. Hence, power over others can be built on ignorance, but eventually that ignorance and that kind of power can be dispelled by truth.*

*Politics built on the lie of natural male supremacy is death-oriented and corrupt with exploitation of "the other." The damage wrought by patriarchy cannot be halted by patchwork reforms of that system, nor will technological "fixes"* save the Earth and us. Only the acceptance of a postpatriarchal, holistic attitude toward life on Earth *will bring about truly comprehensive change. Feminist spirituality is a means of both evolving that attitude and activating the processes which will lead to that change.*

*The pieces in this section are arranged in chronological order to document some of the historical growth of the idea that our politics and our spirituality, our outer and inner power, are intrinsically linked. The essays from journals have been ordered according to the time they actually appeared in the feminist network of bookstores and mailboxes, and hence began generating discussion, since that was often much later than the official date of publication.*

*Many of the theorists in this section address the means by which to bring about political change. We are not interested in masculist, linear approaches that would first attack the defects in the status quo and only later would consider the creation of a new society. Our models of change, our meetings, and our public actions all express on our own terms an encompassing political struggle. We address the issues and the connections among the issues. We are building a revolution of the psyche as well as of the society. The postpatriarchal options that we are evolving have roots in the peaceful, egalitarian, body-honoring, Earth-revering, gynocentric cultures. To remember our potentials and to begin to live these possibilities with our sisters and brothers as we initiate change is our political process. Always, we work to expand our circles.*

*We see clearly where we are now, and we know that it is winter. And suddenly, through this shocking cold, we remember the beauty of the forest lying under this whiteness. And that we will survive this snow if we are aware, if we continue. And now we are shouting with all our strength to the other sleepers, now we are laboring in earnest, to waken them.*

— Susan Griffin, Woman and Nature

C.S.

# Sisterhood as Cosmic Covenant

## Mary Daly

The church often has been envisaged as *a space set apart* from the rest of the world, having a special meaning for people and functioning as haven and sanctuary. It is still not uncommon for people to experience the physical interior of a church building in the way described by Eliade as an experience of sacred space.[1] Even the frankly nonreligious person in our culture tends to value certain "holy places" of her or his private universe, places associated with happy memories, usually. Often it is a ritualized and superstitious sense of specialness that attaches to "holy shrines" that has nothing to do with individual or communal insight and growth. A church construed as space set apart, then — whether the term is intended to mean a building, an institution, or an ideological "sacred canopy" — has certain propensities for serving as an escape from facing the abyss. It then becomes a place for spinning webs of counterfeit transcendence.

Yet the image of a space set apart is not worthless. I have already suggested that this revolution provides a space — mainly a province of the mind — where it is possible to be oneself, without the contortions of mind, will, feeling, and imagination demanded of women by sexist society. But it is important to note that this space is found not in the effort to hide from the abyss but in the effort to face it, as patriarchy's prefabricated set of meanings, or *nomos,* crumbles in one's mind. Thus, it is not "set apart" from reality, but from the contrived nonreality of alienation. Discovered in the deep confrontation between being and nonbeing, the space of liberation is sacred.

When sacred space is discovered, the possibility of deterioration into escapism or of absolutizing the space into a particular form is there. However, the real danger is that women will succumb to *accusations* of escapism or single-mindedness by those who do not see the transcendent dimensions of feminism. Reduction of women's liberation to escapism because of "personal hang-ups" is still a potent weapon, especially when couched in psychological jargon. Women are vulnerable to accusations of absolutizing the movement, and we are accustomed to listen only too well to the voices of alienation. Yet there is something to be attended to here, since the accusation is a typical *reversal* of the real problem, which is the constant temptation *not* to face the universality of sexual caste and the awesome demands of living in the new space.

Since the new space is set apart precisely from the nonreality of sexist alienation and since we are *in* it only insofar as we confront nonreality, it is not static space but constantly moving space. I have said that its center is on the boundaries of patriarchy's spaces, that is, it is not *contained.* R. D. Laing wrote something that is of help in understanding this:

The truth I am trying to grasp is the grasp that is trying to grasp it. . . . The Life I am trying to grasp is the me that is trying to grasp it.[2]

Our space is the life source, not the "container" of contrived covers of life. But whereas Laing was writing of an individual leap or journey through inner space that society would call madness, we are engaged in a journey that is not only utterly individual but also ultimately communal. The kind of communality that it has springs from the fact that there is discovery of "the me that is trying to grasp it." Laing, however, while he does perceive the destructiveness of the social setting, remains to some extent caught in an intrapsychic point of view. The problem remains that even if many persons are "cured," this of itself isn't enough. As Phyllis Chesler remarks, throughout his book *Sanity, Madness, and the Family* "he remains unaware of the universal and objective oppression of women and of its particular relation to madness in women."[3]

Our space set apart does mean individual freedom, but this becomes possible in recognizing and refuting the structures of objective oppression. I have said that our struggle is not on the enemy's terms. It is self-actualization that is communal, that has as a necessary condition deep rejection of the structures of destruction.

The ever moving center of our space — the opposite of "dead" center — moves because it is ourselves and we are moving, becoming, in a "noospheric net" never dreamed of by Teilhard de Chardin or other prophets of male futurism. This center is the Archimedean point of support, the fulcrum from which, if enough women discover it and do not lose courage, it may be possible to move the world.

## EXODUS COMMUNITY

Because of this constantly moving center, the space of the women's revolution can be called an *exodus community*. The church has been characterized by this name, but both the formulations and the social and psychic realizations of the meaning of this image have been limited and limiting to human aspiration. The church as exodus community allegedly has gone forth from bondage toward liberation on the basis of a promise made by Yahweh to the fathers of the people of God. The voyage has not been spectacular, and this is in no small measure due to the fact that there is something contrived about promises handed down from on high. Yet, as in the case of *space set apart*, the image has value when taken out of its paralyzing context and allowed to spark forth our own insight. The moving center which is the energy source of the new sisterhood as exodus community is the promise in ourselves. It is the promise in our foremothers whose history we are beginning to discover, and in our sisters whose voices have been stolen from them. Our journey is the fruit of this promise — a journey into individualization and participation, leaving behind the false self and sexist society. Since one cannot physically leave the planet, however (and extraterrestrial space trips as programmed by the prevailing society will be super-sexist, with the accommodation of space stewardesses, perhaps), our mode of departure has to be appropriate to the situation. We can depart mentally to some extent by refusing to be blinded by society's myths. We can depart physically and socially to a degree also, but simple withdrawal will not change the wider situation. The adequate exodus requires com-

munication, community, and creation. The truly moving space will not
be merely unorthodox or reformist, but will be on its way beyond
unorthodoxy as well as orthodoxy, discovering and bringing forth the
really new.

To those within patriarchal space, and perhaps especially within its
religions, it may look as though radical feminists have broken a "promise" by not "living up" to the expectations that have been outgrown. In
fact, by living out our own promise, we are breaking the brokenness in
human existence that has been effected by means of the constructs of
alienation. To put it another way, we are breaking the dam of sex
stereotyping that stops the flow of being, that stops women and men
from being integrated, androgynous personalities. The admission of the
fact of this brokenness into our consciousness brings to light the promise burning within, the potential toward the "fearful symmetry" that
the poet glimpsed, and that our culture keeps hidden in the forests of
the night. It also puts us in touch with "the flow of the inexhaustible
Encompassing" about which the philosopher Jaspers has written, without which there is only "the random swirling of dead husks of words,
producing a semblance of external order and meaning in endless, arbitrary variation."[4]

The dawning of this promise within, this rushing of the waters of
life that have been dammed and damned by our culture, since it puts
us in touch with ourselves and with the "Encompassing," brings us into
the deepest possible community. It is the community that is discovered,
rather than "formed," when we meet others who are on the same voyage. There is, then, a "covenant" among us, *not* in the sense of an
agreement that is *formed* and precisely formulated, but in the sense of
profound *agreement that is found*. The word "covenant," then, cannot
fully say the reality—it is part of the language that splits, cuts off, divides and tries to paste back together again. If, however, we can get beyond the limits imposed by our inherited nonspeech, we can use the
sound to signal something more. The covenant is the deep *agreement*
that is present within the self and among selves who are increasingly in
harmony with an environment that is beyond, beneath, and all around
the nonenvironment of patriarchal splits and barriers. For lack of a better word, this may be called the "cosmos," and the sense of harmony
has its source in participation in being, which means being in touch
with the deepest forces in the cosmos. Out of this contact comes new
speech. "Covenant" has always been bound up with language. Sisterhood as cosmic covenant means beginning to re-name the cosmos.

"Covenant" also has the meaning of a common-law form of action to recover damages for breach of contract. Women's form of action to recover damages begins with a declaration. Those women were not joking when they claimed that all you have to do to become a Witch is to say three times to yourself: "I am a Witch; I am a Witch; I am a Witch."[5] This is something like speaking an unspeakable word. It is an exorcism of the internalized demon that divides the self against the self. It is a way of saying, "I am, I am, I am." With this declaration one joins the new coven and discovers the covenant.

## COMMUNICATING COMMUNITY

Part of the self-understanding of the Christian church has been that it is a community with a "mission." As Moltmann suggested, the promise (*promissio*) implied a mission (*missio*).[6] There is a consistency of ideas here, though not in the sense that Moltmann intended. A promise handed down from an anthropomorphic deity to the forefathers does imply a mission — an extension of the command. In the history of Christianity the mission has often meant bloody conquest "for Christ." One need think only of the "conversion" of the "barbarians" of Europe or of the Crusades to be reminded of the thrusting and conquering propensities of the Christian conception of mission. Even the peaceful missionaries who have gone to "heathen" lands have felt justified in using questionable tactics to impose "true" beliefs upon others and in so doing have "righteously" allied themselves with economic imperialism. The imagery and the behavior implied in mission, then, is phallic. It is only necessary to think of the word in a very common contemporary military context — "bombing mission" — to perceive the direction implied by the word (outward, thrusting, exploding in many directions from one source). Moreover, the example conveys the burden of violence with which the history of the word is weighted down. Mission, then, is not communication but compulsion, whether this be understood as physical or psychological compulsion and coercion.

Since the promise which is the source of sisterhood is within women's being and since the cosmic covenant based on that promise is an agreement that is discovered, the mode of communication of this community cannot be expressed adequately by the term "mission." The truth embodied in the term is the "sending" aspect of communication, but this is a relatively superficial aspect of communication, and the word "mission" is essentially wrong because it one-sidedly stresses this aspect. The communication involved is not a thrusting of an objectified "message" to another nor a thrusting of oneself or any model upon the psyche of another. Insofar as there is "sending" at all it is mutual — an interpenetration of insights coming from discovery of participation together in being, in the cosmos. It is, as two women observed, a process of "cosmosis."[7]

The expansion of the new space of women's awareness, then, is not an imperialist expansion that pushes back the territory of others. Rather, insofar as it *is* where being is discovered in confrontation with nothingness, it is an invitation to others to leave the patriarchal space of alienative identity — the sacred circle of eternal return — and enter new space. The Roman church has often "excommunicated" those who disagreed with its dogmas. One woman remarked that the community of sisterhood, which has no hierarchy and no dogmas, involves a process which is the opposite of this. That is, it expands by "incommunication."[8] Those who discover the covenant *find themselves* in the new space. The old territory, then, is not encroached upon: One does not bother to invade nonbeing. Rather, it is left behind by those who follow the promise within, which is the promise of integrated, transformed, androgynous* being.

## EARTH, AIR, FIRE, WATER: ECOLOGY AND THE COSMIC COVENANT

George Wald has pointed out that we have something to learn from the history of the dinosaurs, who had very small brains for their size. Since the proportion of brains to brawn was very low, they disappeared. Whereas within the individual human being, the proportion of brains to brawn is high, technology has inversed the proportion and we are coming again into the situation of the dinosaurs. Cars, not the people in them (for we realize that the people are not altogether in control), kill more than 50,000 Americans a year. On a more disastrous level,

---

* Editor's Note: Since this passage was published in 1973, Dr. Daly has written, "I no longer use the term *androgyny* in any positive sense, since I consider it to be a false and misleading term for the integrity of female-identified be-ing" (*Chrysalis*, Issue 6, Nov. 1978). Many other feminists agree with her, having found that *androgyny* is *really* used to mean "Why can't a woman be more like a man?!" We do not believe that the active aspects of our behavior are in any way "masculine" nor that our quiet, observing, *connecting* states are "passive" (see the Introduction to this volume). — C.S.

Wald points out that the discovery of a nuclear reaction — the process of turning hydrogen into helium — which could mean that we could shortly make our own sunlight, is turned mainly into a weapon that threatens our lives and the life of the planet. Again, the trips to the moon have been negligible for high-level scientific content, but are expected to be useful for future weaponry. Our self-destructive use of brawn need not have been:

It is our western culture at work, our western culture with its beautiful Judeo-Christian ethic. It is our culture alone among the cultures of the earth that sees it that way, that has brought the technology of killing and destruction much further than any culture on the earth ever dreamed of doing before.[9]

There are some points to be added to George Wald's insightful statement: This "beautiful Judeo-Christian ethic" of missions — missions to convert "pagans" over their dead bodies, missions to the moon, missions to drop hydrogen bombs and ultimately to end life on the planet — is the culmination of the masculine-feminine schizophrenia which is causing the race to rape itself to death. The brain which the brawn is overshadowing is essentially not technical reason but ontological reason, that realm where power, justice, and love meet in harmony. The cosmic covenant is the discovery of this harmony.

Farsighted thinkers have pointed out that the moral imperative of respect for life, formerly understood in quantitative terms, must now be understood in terms of the *quality* of life.[10] This has obvious implications, such as the need for population control and for bringing a halt to the waste of resources and pollution of the environment. Such needs are not understood by the *machismo* mind. Marcuse uses the category of obscenity to describe the behavior of the "affluent monster." He points out that "this society is obscene in producing and indecently exposing a stifling abundance of wares while depriving its victims abroad of the necessities of life . . . in its prayers, in its ignorance, and in the wisdom of its kept intellectuals."[11] Meanwhile, of course, the affluent society *pretends* to be *improving* the quality of life, disguising what is actually happening by its usual techniques, which I have called "reversal."

Marcuse observes that the Establishment abuses the term "obscenity" by applying it, not to expressions of its own immorality but to the behavior of another:

Obscene is not the picture of a naked woman who exposes her pubic hair but that of a fully clad general who exposes his medals rewarded in a war of aggression; obscene is not the ritual of the Hippies but the declaration of a high dignitary of the Church that war is necessary for peace.[12]

Marcuse's perception is acute, and he rightly calls for "linguistic therapy" which would free words from almost total distortion of their meanings by "the Establishment." Yet I must point out that the therapy will never be radical enough if the basic obscenity is perceived as capitalism rather than sexism. The very word "obscene" itself, as used by "the Establishment," suggests the locus of the essential perversion and victimization. Marcuse's own insightful juxtaposition of the naked woman and the fully clad general reveals the basic reversal in phallic morality which is still observable in socialist as well as capitalist societies. Such social criticism does not go far enough. It employs revealing instances of the powerful elite's *sexist* behavioral, imaginative, and linguistic distortions while still perceiving these distortions' radical source in capitalism and their cure in socialism.

Another sentence from the same essay of Marcuse is symptomatic of this phenomenon of shortsightedness. He writes:

Thus we are faced with the contradiction that the liberalization of sexuality provided an instinctual basis for the repressive and aggressive power *of the affluent society* [emphasis mine].[13]

It should be stressed — and this is what feminism is doing — that the so-called liberalization of sexuality "provides an instinctual basis for the repressive and aggressive power" *of the sexist society*. For, of course, it is not a genuine liberation of sexuality that displaces the obscenity of generals and projects it upon naked women, and the essential disease is *not* affluence in itself. The lifting of taboos on genital sexuality does nothing to liberate from sex roles. Marcuse himself says that this relaxation binds "the 'free' individuals libidinally to the institutionalized fathers."[14]

Such expressions of insight into the sexist nature of the oppressive society, strangely coupled with failure to direct the critique *directly* and *essentially* at sexual oppression, is characteristic not only of intellectuals such as Marcuse but also of more "popular" expressions of social criticism. Such films as *The Godfather, The Ruling Class,* and *Deliverance* can be seen as brilliant exposés of the social disease which is patriarchalism. One could almost believe that the writers and directors must be committed feminists. Yet the functioning of these productions, with their amazingly revelatory juxtapositions of sex and violence and their exploitation of phallic symbolism, has not been directed intentionally to the service of feminism. Perhaps one could call such "understanding" of sexual alienation "subintentional." Recognition of the real enemy's identity is so close to the surface of consciousness of the writers and directors of such productions that some feminists tend to find the experience of reading such books and watching such films almost unbearable. "They know not what they say," it would seem. Then it is clear that women will have to speak forth the identity of that which is destroying us all. The subintentional revelations of male critics indicate that some receptivity to this knowledge may be possible — that the capacity to hear is closer to consciousness than we would have expected. The time for us to speak is precisely now.

In writing of the "new sensibility," Marcuse dreams of new people who will have broken identity with the "false fathers" who built Auschwitz and Vietnam, the ghettos and temples of the corporations. He says that "they will have broken the chain which linked the fathers and the sons from generation to generation."[15] But this is precisely the point: What *is* the substance of the chain that has "linked the fathers and the sons," culminating in the Auschwitzes, the Vietnams, the corporations, the ecclesiastical and secular inquisitions, the unspeakable emptiness of the consuming and consumed creatures whose souls are lost in pursuit of built-in obsolescence? This is precisely the chain that derives its total reality from the reduction of women to nonbeing. The strength of the chain is the energy sapped out of the bodies and minds of women — the mothers and daughters whose lifeblood has been sucked away by the patriarchal system. The chain that has drained us will be broken when women draw back our own life-force.

The power to regain our own life comes from the discovery of the cosmic covenant, the deep harmony in the community of being in which we participate. The false harmony coerced by the chain of fathers and sons which dominates our constantly deteriorating environment has many manifestations. In economic terms it can be seen as a false concord based upon a false dichotomy of supply and demand. In America, the dominant elite creates the false consciousness of the public, whose alienation is so total that their very being is lost in the commodities they are trained to live for and devour. This is a translation into the realm of economics of the myth of eternal return. It means living out the endless circle of meaningless desires, never fulfilled, pouring human being into the insatiable chasm of nonbeing.

In contrast to this hell-bent "harmony," the concord which is the cosmic covenant is found in the process of rupture with the continuum of rapism, our imposed artificial environment. The power of imagination is unchained and we see, hear, feel, breathe in a new way. Our perception reaches beyond the ugly and the beautiful of the great chain of nonbeing.

In the refusal of our own objectification, those who find the covenant find something like what Buber called I-Thou. This happens first among women, as sisters, and as we have seen, the discovery contains a dynamic that makes us aware of the Verb who is infinitely personal, who is nonreifable, present and future in the depths of our present-future I-Thou. This Verb is the Eternal Thou. The contagion of this refusal of objectification extends outward toward male liberation, opening up the possibility for I-Thou between women and men, and among men. This Great Refusal of rapism clearly means refusal to rape earth, air, fire, water, that is, refusal to objectify and abuse their power.

More than this, it means that the covenant embraces our sister the Earth and all of her nonhuman inhabitants and elements. It embraces, too, our sisters the moon, the sun and her planets, and all the farthest stars of the farthest galaxies. For since they *are*, they are our sisters in the community of being. The question arises of how to speak of our relation to these nonhuman sisters who speak their word, but in a nonhuman way. Paul Santmire has suggested that in order to speak of the relationship to nature we might modify Buber's articulation of the I-Thou, I-It distinction and speak of a "third type" of relation, which can be called an I-Ens (I-Being) relation.[16] The I-Ens, writes Santmire, is intimate, fluid, and present. The Ens is characterized by givenness. It is not perceived as an object to be used, but is beheld in its own splendor, which gives rise to wonder. It therefore does not fit into a utilitarian description of the world. Along with givenness, the Ens exhibits mysterious activity and beauty. The "I" of the relation is characterized by wonder, and can experience both dread and delight. In this relation there is a sense for the presence of the Deity; there is an awareness of the dimension of depth.[17]

But the I-Ens, which Santmire has described with great sensitivity and lucidity, is not the "normal" relation to nature in sexist culture. It is a momentary delusion of poets, madmen, and lovers who must be lured back to "normality," which is utilitarianism. But the cosmic covenant of sisterhood *has* the potential to transform the extraordinary relation of the poet to nature into the ordinary and "normal" relation, changing our environment from a culture of rapism to a culture of reci-procity with the beauty of the Earth, the other planets, the stars. Out of women's becoming in the process of confronting nonbeing can come an ever more conscious participation in the community of being. This means that we will look upon the Earth and her sister planets as being *with* us, not *for* us. One does not rape a sister.

## NOTES

1. See Mircea Eliade, *The Sacred and the Profane* (New York: Harper & Row, 1961), pp. 20–65.
2. R. D. Laing, *The Politics of Experience* (New York: Ballantine Books, 1968), p. 190.
3. Phyllis Chesler, *Women and Madness* (Garden City, N.Y.: Doubleday, 1972), pp. 92–93.
4. Jaspers and Bultmann, *Myth and Christianity* (New York: Noonday Press, 1958), p. 13.
5. From a statement of the New York Covens, quoted in *Sisterhood Is Powerful*, edited by Robin Morgan (New York: Random House, 1970), p. 540.
6. Moltmann, *Theology of Hope* (New York: Harper & Row, 1967), p. 203.
7. Linda Barufaldi and Emily Culpepper, "Pandora's Box," in *Women and Religion*, 1972, p. 51.
8. Conversation with Janice Raymond, Nov. 1972.
9. George Wald, "The Human Enterprise," in *Population, Environment, and People*, edited by Noël Hinrichs (New York: McGraw-Hill, 1971), p. 222.
10. See Elizabeth Farians, "Population, Environment, and Women," in *Population, Environment, and People*, pp. 97–103.
11. Herbert Marcuse, *An Essay on Liberation* (Boston: Beacon Press, 1969), pp. 7–8.
12. *Ibid.*, p. 8.
13. *Ibid.*, p. 9.
14. *Ibid.*
15. *Ibid.*, p. 25.
16. H. Paul Santmire, "I-Thou, I-It, I-Ens," *The Journal of Religion*, vol. 48 (July 1968), p. 266.
17. *Ibid.*, p. 272.

# The Personal Is Political

## Sheila D. Collins

Women have come to an understanding that the personal is political
through the consciousness-raising process. In the course of this process
we came to learn that the problems we thought were purely personal —
that we thought were due to our own peculiar upbringing or to our
own inabilities or neuroses — were, in fact, shared by every other
woman. We began to see that our relationships with our mothers, our
fathers, our male and female peers, our bosses, our husbands, and our
children followed similar patterns and met with similar resistances. We
realized that while each woman's life follows a distinctive course, there
is a general pattern that unites us all. We realized that women inhabit
a different culture from that inhabited by men. We realized that our
relationships with men, no matter how intimate, were governed by certain unequal distributions of power — educational, economic, social, political, and physical.

As we moved out from the family unit to analyze our role as women
in the larger society and in the world, we began to see the same kinds

of general patterns emerging, the same kinds of resistances to our growth displayed, the same kinds of power games operating. Through the consciousness-raising process women have come to see that our position in the home or in the larger society is not so different (paradigmatically speaking) from the position of the Latin American peasant vis-à-vis the ruling elite or the Black welfare mother in relation to the affluent white. We have come to see that the football games so enjoyed by the men in power in this country are but a mirror image of the wargames played in the Pentagon, and that the white European or American male theologian's claim to "scholarly objectivity" and "academic excellence" is but a weapon in the arsenal by which they protect their privileged position of power against the threatening incursions of Third World liberation theology or feminist theology. We understand now that those in positions of ecclesiastical, political, or economic power who still insist that the worst sin is egoism, pride, or self-interest are not applying those categories to themselves but to those whom they would keep subordinate.

Racism, sexism, class exploitation, and ecological destruction are four interlocking pillars upon which the structure of the patriarchy rests. The structures of oppression are everywhere the same, although the particular forms in which oppression is manifested may at first glance look different. The democracy of the Athenian *polis*, to which the Western world has always looked as its ideal, was made possible only through the restricted domestic labors of the slaves and wives of the Athenian property owners. Western "freedom" and affluence depend on the domestication of women and the exploitation of a low-paid labor base made up of minorities and women as well as unlimited access to foreign sources of natural resources which are taken from the ground without regard for the rights of the Earth or the people who live on the land.

The feminist experience has thus enabled us to penetrate the superficial differences to see the systemic and psychic links between the various forms of injustice. Feminists hold that the alienation of woman from man — because it was the first and still is the longest lasting form of human alienation — can be seen as a primordial paradigm from which all other unjust relationships derive.

Because we are aware of our own subjugation and objectification by men, feminists are particularly sensitive to the way in which others are objectified and oppressed. It is no accident that the feminist movement in this country from its very inception was linked with the abolitionist movement, that the modern feminist movement grew out of the civil rights movement of the 1960s, and that groups like the YWCA and the National Women's Political Caucus, which have been strongly influenced by the feminist perspective, have taken strong stands against racism as well as sex inequality and have been working for the rights of welfare and working-class women as well as equal rights for the middle class.

The feminist experience and its understanding of history, then, provide us with a handle on the human condition, with a way of understanding and explaining the fact of human evil. Because it is able to see the connections between the various forms of human evil, it is able to offer a vision of the health and wholeness to which the entire biblical experience points but which has never been adequately delineated before, either by Christian idealism or by Christian realism. By locating the source of human sinfulness in the patriarchal worldview, we are able to find metaphors which help to explain and to connect the various manifestations of sin, both personal and corporate, in a way that was not possible before.

Such metaphors are summed up in a series of dualisms, the two halves of which are related to each other as superior to inferior, superordinate to subordinate. Male/female, mind/body, subject/object, man/nature, inner/outer, white/black, rational/irrational, civilized/primitive — all serve to explain the way in which the patriarchy has ordered reality. As we have seen, the left-hand side of each equation has assumed a kind of right of ownership over the right. The relationship is one of owner to owned, oppressor to oppressed rather than one of mutuality.

The links between the various forms of alienation and oppression are clear when we begin to analyze and then compare the psychic relationship that exists between each of the pairs listed above. For example, in Western culture and in the Judeo-Christian tradition, male and female have been related to each other as mind to body. The male owns or subordinates the female just as the mind controls and manipulates the body. In the Western theological mind, woman was body, while man was mind or the spiritual, rational will. The divine *Logos* which was carried over from Greek philosophy into Christianity was distinctly male. It was thought by the Church Fathers to represent the essence, or the original archetype of life, while bodiliness, femaleness, and sexuality occurred as a result of the Fall.[1] In the early Church tradition it was man who represented the subject of creation, while woman was a distinctly subhuman object. She was irrational nature, rampant sexuality, the primitive dark, bestial side of life, while man represented the light, civilizing, rational superego. Salvation was located in an otherworldly return to the spiritual essence and in a repudiation of nature and the body.

In the same way that man subordinated and stereotyped woman, so each dominant group has subordinated and stereotyped those whom they have conquered or whom they wish to conquer. To the Israelites and their modern equivalents the Baal- and Astarte-worshipers represented all that was irrational, sexual, bodily, primitive, and dangerous. In the eyes of the Yahwistic writers they were not real people with a mixture of traits, but idolaters, objects of scorn and derision. Jezebel became a symbol of female infamy through this objectification process. It was not until the nineteenth century when women, realizing the way in which they had been stereotyped and objectified by male culture, could begin to make anything like a realistic assessment of Jezebel's character. Here is what one commentator in *The Woman's Bible* wrote about Jezebel:

All we know about Jezebel is told us by a rival religionist, who hated her as the Pope of Rome hated Martin Luther, or as an American A.P.A. now hates a Roman Catholic. Nevertheless, even the Jewish historian, evidently biassed [sic] against Jezebel by his theological prejudices as he is, does not give any facts whatever which warrant the assertion that Jezebel was any more satanic than the ancient Israelitish gentleman, to whom her theological views were opposed. . . .
I submit, that if Jezebel is a disgrace to womankind, our dear brethren at any rate have not much cause to be proud of Elijah, so, possibly, we might strike a truce over the character of these two long-buried worthies.[2]

The social and psychic models of dominance and submission which operated for men against women and for the Israelites against the Pagans continue to operate today wherever one group oppresses another. For the white racist, the Black takes on all the characteristics which we have seen attributed to women. He is bestial, irrational, sexually dangerous, dumb, yet also passive, slow, emotional, and shiftless. In essence, the Black is objectified, made into a subhuman species. The peasant, the Oriental, and the African have been similarly labeled. Countless Vietnam veterans have spoken of the fact that they were able to kill the Vietnamese because they thought of them as "gooks," as a mindless subhuman species, rather than as people like themselves. Indeed, they have testified that the army taught them to think of the "enemy" in this way. As the song from *South Pacific* goes, "You have to be taught to hate." Much of man's aggression, his impulse to murder and exploit, has been taught him by his culture and by the worldview which dictates the values he assigns to objects and persons. Contrary to popularizers of the notion that man is inherently aggressive and bellicose (such as Robert Ardrey and Desmond Morris), most reputable biologists, psychologists, and anthropologists conclude that war is a learned or conditioned behavior — a product of human culture. Psychologists at the Canadian Peace Research Institute find the person involved in war doesn't even have to be especially aggressive. Their research indicates a high correlation between militarism and conformity or obedience to orders. In order to teach our children to be peacemakers, they contend, we should teach them to be nonconformist as well as nonaggressive.

It is a well-known observation that fascist regimes combine an authoritarian worldview with a hierarchical social system, an appeal to puritanical "personal morals" and strict sex-role differentiation. War, ecological disaster, the subordination of women, slavery, racism, and colonialism can all be seen as extensions of the deep-seated psychic dualism which arose with patriarchal culture. To say that such sinfulness stems from humanity's inherent selfishness, pride, or egoism is to mistake a symptom for the disease itself.

The wholeness that feminists are proposing is a wholeness based on a multidimensional vision of the world, rather than on the single vision which has dominated Western culture and most theological thought. Such a multidimensional vision means the ability to grasp complexity, to live with ambiguity, and to enjoy the great variety that exists in the world. Wholeness does not imply the eradication of differences as the old assimilationist model did or as the fear of a monotonous unisexual creature implies. On the contrary, wholeness of vision may lead to a multiplication of differences, as people are able to choose freely the person they want to be rather than following a pattern of one they are *expected* to be. Only through an affirmation and celebration of our differences can we come to an understanding of the ties that bind the total creation together.

There can be no essentially just (holistic) ethical decisions made if the voices, the feelings, and the life conditions of the formerly mute and inarticulate ones go unheeded. For example, solutions to the abortion dilemma, family planning, day care, and the like, must be made with regard to the total condition of woman's position in society and with full regard for her own feelings and the way in which she experiences her body. No just solution to the abortion dilemma can be made until woman's role has been equalized with man's. Just decisions in this realm, therefore, will never be made by men who do not share the same kinds of conditions and liabilities as women do who, up to now, have been among the mute and inarticulate. Similarly, Western powers cannot make just decisions as to how development money is to be spent for the so-called underdeveloped nations, unless the voices of the peasants, the oppressed, and the poor are considered of equal value to those of the ruling elite.

Not until the white Westerner comes to an appreciation and affirmation of the physical characteristics, spiritual qualities, lifestyle, and culture of those whom he has formerly looked down upon as "primitive" or "underdeveloped" or "savage," can he discover the common humanity which binds them together. Only after males can appreciate and affirm women and women's culture, only after males realize that they might yet learn something about life from females, can true reconciliation be achieved between them. A holistic ethic affirms singleness within community, diversity within unity, the validity of *both/and*, rather than *either/or*. It is the only kind of ethic worthy of a pluralistic world.

## NOTES

1. Rosemary Ruether, "The Scope of Women's Liberation," unpublished paper presented at a conference on "Manhood and Womanhood in the Church," Yale Divinity School, 4 March 1970.
2. Ellen Battelle Dietrick, "Comments on Kings," *The Woman's Bible*, ed. Elizabeth Cady Stanton (New York: European Pub. Co., 1895); reprinted by Arno Press, Inc., 1972, pp. 74–76.

# Dimensions of Spirituality

# Judy Davis and
# Juanita Weaver

We dare to raise the issue of spirituality for women, to begin to redefine it, and to say it is of vital importance to the women's movement.

## SPIRITUALITY

Feminist spirituality has taken form in sisterhood — in our solidarity based on a vision of personal freedom, self-definition, and in our struggle together for social and political change. The contemporary women's movement has created space for women to begin to perceive reality with a clarity that seeks to encompass many complexities. This perception has been trivialized by male-dominated cultures that present the world in primarily rational terms. Reality is not only rational, linear, and categorized into either/or — it is also irrational and superrational. Because we do not have a new word for this struggle to comprehend this totality and incorporate that understanding into our action, we are calling it spirituality. We choose the word spirituality because this vision presupposes a reverence for life, a willingness to deal with more than just rational forces, and a commitment to positive life-generating forces that historically have been associated with a more limited definition of spirituality.

Women's new experience with spirituality has erupted after several thousand years during which Western history was defined basically by men in the Jewish and Christian traditions. Today, we have hints of a time when men did not hold the power and control over women that they do now, a time when women were held in highest esteem because they possessed the power to create life. Today there is a new reality arising from the self meeting self and a freedom of imagination and strength building through life-sharing. This vision is present in feminist art, in the re-examination of matriarchal cultures, and the development of new political insights and forms working toward a synthesis of the "old theologies." All of these expressions point to a new possibility of something special and extraordinary that all women can share collectively. They promise renewed hope in life and growth. Our vision strives for fundamental change in cultural beliefs, society's institutions, and human relationships — beginning with the rejoining of women to women. Women conscious of this spirituality are on the move.

This awareness in the women's movement is not happening in a vacuum. A mechanistic worldview and faith in pure rationality is breaking down throughout the society. The fact that our rational conclusions are heavily influenced by our class, race, sex, and our particular unconscious, has become common knowledge over the past fifty years. Even scientists — supposedly the most rational of human beings — are listening to plants communicate their pain and anxiety over the possibility of outside forces causing them harm. Scientists have been studying psychic phenomena and astral projection for years and recently have begun to study Kirlian photography — the photographing of a person's aura or force field. There can be no doubt that a multi-dimensional reality exists for people today.

In its broadest context, spirituality is being open to reality in all of its dimensions — in its rational, irrational, and super-rational complexity, and acting on that understanding. This requires a radical departure from the present compartmentalized ways of perceiving and determining action. The body/mind dichotomy, the separation of spiritual from secular, technical and instrumental knowledge from the emotional and artistic, one class, race, and sex from another, has resulted in a world filled with starving, alienated, and warring people. We cannot, for very real practical reasons, continue in this way. What we mean by spirituality is this radical change in the way we think, perceive, experience, and act. It is an inclusive way of looking at and moving in the world. Spirituality is central to the women's movement because it is a struggle to deal with reality as it is, without imposed limitations.

## POLITICS

What is the relationship between spirituality, as we have defined it, and politics? Politics, by its very nature, is partisan; spirituality affirms the inter-relatedness of all things. An awareness of this inter-relatedness must inform our sense of revolutionary urgency, as expressed in political ideologies, strategies, and lifestyles. Our spirituality — the awareness of oneness and openness to new sources of power — should help us deal with the inevitable tensions between goals and process, compromise and ideology, survival and revolutionary integrity.

It is the recognition of this intimate relationship between spirituality and politics that makes the women's movement different from other movements. We recognize that the function of rational categories is to divide and separate so analysis and thought can take place. However, while conceptualization, as we now know it, still requires the use of discrete categories, we are determined not to lose sight of a deeper reality while searching for new forms.

Our movement is not only about gaining more political and economic power from our opponents. Women have suffered from power-over politics and can use that knowledge in the struggle to develop new power relationships. Ours is a fight in which the means are as important as the ends. This understanding of the processing nature of our revolution can make us freer to create new possibilities in the relationships between ourselves and our sisters in the movement who have different beliefs, and our old school chums who are still dim as to what all the fuss is about. We are in the process of re-evaluating power, recognizing the many kinds of power that exist.

Concern for spirituality does not mean false innocence, fear of power, or the avoidance of compromise often necessary for life. The attainment of power is necessary to change the position of women. What we are calling for is a new perspective on power, an effort to use power differently, and an openness to new sources of power and energy.

One of the places within which women are organizing and fighting for power and change is within the institutional Jewish and Christian patriarchal traditions. Special task forces, caucuses, women's centers, consciousness-raising groups, and commissions on women and religion exist in all major Protestant denominations. Roman Catholic women are similarly active. Jewish women in the counter-cultural chavurot movement are connected nationally by the Jewish Feminist Organization. There are similar groups in "secular" organizations, such as the National Organization for Women, and the American Academy of Religion. These women seek to feminize male-dominated systems and to gain equality of work, pay, and representation. The struggle to legitimate the ordination of eleven Episcopal women is the most publicized of these efforts.

Some "political feminists" have seen spirituality as identified only with what patriarchy has said it to be — that is, a lot of male words, doctrines, laws, decrees and female suffering, poverty, chastity, and obedience. They have feared that women's traditional preoccupation with spiritual matters — if repeated in the women's movement — will divert us from political and economic struggles. Their political analysis has shown how religion has kept people from dealing with the social structures that oppress them. Many have decided that religion is but a reflection and expression of a particular culture, and that therefore religion, as we know it, oppresses only because it reflects a patriarchal culture. Questions of spirituality usually are considered unresolvable until better social conditions are realized.

Other "cultural feminists" have been rediscovering a spirit perhaps inherent in women and present in prepatriarchal cultures. Some have said that our ability to give birth points to feminine creativity *prior to* the biblical male creation story symbolized in Adam's giving birth to Eve. They have said women were the first inventors of agriculture and healing, that there is a buried, subconscious, inherently female spirit capable of great power and understanding which women artists are expressing in art, music, and in new understanding of our psyches. Still others have said women are intimately tied to the Earth and the universal moon and menstrual cycles, and have practiced herbal medicines, read astrology charts, and created Witch covens.

## SPIRITUALITY AND POLITICS

The so-called division between cultural feminism and political feminism is a debilitating result of our oppression. It comes from the patriarchal view that the spiritual and the intellectual operate in separate realms. To deny the spiritual while doing political work, or to cultivate the spiritual at the expense of another's political and economic well-being, is continuing the patriarchal game.

Both trends in feminism are creating new communities and traditions from which to gain insight, strength, and friends to help in changing society. Our spirituality must be inclusive of both the political and cultural, rational and superrational — unionists, theorists, musicians, herbal healers, and Earth Mothers. It is a Being together that is larger than the sum total of our individual parts, because together we can transcend our partial, divided selves. It is a holistic understanding of the world, a way of binding us together again, a way of being in love with ourselves and the world while we work to change it. It is not a denial of the intellect but a heightened use of the mind to analyze economic and psychological power in order to strategize how to change it. It includes also the irrationality of the unconscious and psychic powers, of fate, of luck, of sudden insight, of unexplainable coincidences, and of why love is healing. It is not a validation of things as they are, but a constant questioning and restlessness that is always open to new visions.

Many questions are raised by this vision of spirituality. Even though many women, inside and outside institutional religious structures, have given up the humble, silent, guilt-ridden stance before a male god, there is wide exploration as to what constitutes a valid replacement for our formerly inadequate religious lives. What forms will our struggle take as women work simultaneously inside and outside the crumbling patriarchal structures? How will we come to hold power and use it differently in a new social order? How will we avoid the danger that new knowledge and experience gained won't be co-opted and misused by existing institutions?

These and other questions are explored in women's spirituality. It's part of a new beginning, bringing us closer to transforming the world from what we know it to be to what we want it to become. It is the renaming of ourselves and the world — the rediscovery of our essential unity.

# Politics, Spirituality, and Models of Change

# Dorothy I. Riddle

Change is the one constant in our lives. We ourselves, our relationships, our work, our society are continually being transformed and transmuted by our daily experiences. We may try to impose change on others or may experience others trying to change us. Our awareness of change may be very general, as in the "things were sure different when I was growing up" reminiscences. Or, alternately, we may be aware of the immediacy of choices made or not made and their consequences.

Depending upon whether we feel in control of our changes or at the mercy of them, change may excite or frighten us. Usually, we learn to feel in control of our lives when we have a sense of predictability about the future – a predictability that is in contradiction to our reality of constant flux. In order to deal with the contradiction, we often try to establish set rules for behavior or to group people or concepts into neat categories. This kind of organizing behavior gives us an illusion of constancy and control.

Unfortunately, the organizing behavior that helps us feel secure is

© Dorothy I. Riddle, 1981. This essay is based on material Dr. Riddle presented at the conference titled "Through the Looking Glass: A Gynergenetic Experience," Boston, 23–25 April 1976. Printed by permission of the author.

exactly what prohibits either personal growth or the evolution of systems. Trying to maintain the *status quo* is what leads to rigid, stagnating individuals or unresponsive, oppressive institutions. Most of what we find oppressive in institutions, for example, began as creative ideas that were unable to change as needed.

Politics is our attempt to either bring about or resist change on a collective, societal level. Politics involves how we channel and direct the collective power or energy that we have. Political change is the collective equivalent of personal growth. Collective focus brings about change in institutions, just as individual focus brings about change on a personal level.

When we become frightened of domination or economic upheaval, our collective process becomes conservative — i.e., we struggle to maintain the *status quo* and resist change at any cost. Any deviation from the known or familiar is viewed as a threat which might force change; therefore, it is attacked. On the other hand, when we feel at ease (e.g., physically superior, economically secure), our collective political process may become more liberal and open — i.e., we are open to considering new alternatives.

Politics has to do with the "what" of the process of change. Spirituality, on the other hand, is the process component, the "how" of the process of change. Our spirituality has to do with our sense of who we are and the ethics of how we use our power for change. Thus, every process of change has both a political and a spiritual dimension.

Traditionally, we have tended to focus either on spirituality or on politics, either on process or on product; but they are interrelated. Spirituality focuses from society to the individual, emphasizing uniqueness and individuality. Politics focuses from the individual to society, emphasizing our membership in a group. At the same time, spirituality focuses on our interconnectedness and sense of oneness, while politics focuses on our differences which result in our experience of separateness.

## WHAT IS THE "RIGHT" CHANGE?

The ingredients of any process of change include an awareness of the need for change, a belief or vision that change is possible, and a commitment to action. The first ingredient is primarily a political process — one of analysis. The second is primarily a spiritual process — one of imaging a potential new synthesis. Within the third ingredient, both spirituality and politics are combined since action contains both process (means) and product (end) components.

Since both ourselves and our context are constantly changing, there can be no one static code of behavior or "right" action. Whatever is now the "right" action must include some component of what we have just learned. New knowledge brings with it new responsibility.

As we grow and change, we become aware of new inequities and new abuses of power. As our awareness grows, we then have an obligation to change those inequities. However, before that awareness, we could not be responsible for creating the change since we could not imagine it. As our awareness changes, we need to create new standards of what is appropriate and acceptable.

Our political analysis provides us with the awareness that sparks change, the goal toward which we strive, which of necessity changes as we move toward it. Our spiritual philosophy provides us with guidelines of *how* to achieve our goal. For example, a commitment to unity (or nonduality) reminds us that there must always be a third alternative, rather than just two (viewed as right and wrong). A commitment to equality (or nonhierarchy) reminds us that each of us knows what is best *only* for ourselves. Our responsibility to others is not to do for them or even to tell them what to do, but rather to facilitate their own knowing what is best for them and their trusting of that inner knowledge.

Ultimately, it is not a matter of what we specifically do, but the intentionality behind what we do. For example, if we act with the intention to foster fear or self-doubt in another person, then we are abusing our power. Similarly, if we engender the belief in another that they cannot make their own decisions, or that they do not have control of their lives, or that they should be afraid of differences between themselves and others, then we are abusing our power. However, if we act with the intention to foster empowerment or self-respect, then we are not abusing our power. We are acting ethically whenever we act with a belief in the ability of each person to decide best for themselves and with a delight in, rather than fear of, uniqueness or difference.

## MODELS OF REVOLUTION

When we talk about creating a revolution, we are implying that we want to bring about a complete and radical change in the way in which we live and relate to each other. Violence, or intense and extreme force, is usually seen as necessary for any successful revolution. However, if we wish to create a nonviolent society (in the most general, nonoppressive sense), then we must find a model for using our power to bring about change that is itself nonviolent. In order to develop such a model, three possibilities can be considered: conquest revolution, cultural feminism, and consensus revolution.

## Conquest Revolution

Conquest revolution is a model of change based on an awareness of the need for change in others, individually or collectively. Any ultimate vision is static, since the need for control supersedes any willingness to allow for the ambiguity of continued change and growth. The goal is postulated as the one "right action"—i.e., whatever action is considered as "politically correct." Force is viewed as both appropriate and essential in order to assure ultimate success.

In conquest revolution, the spiritual dimensions of flexible vision and concern about process are virtually neglected. This is a model which assumes that the ends justify the means, or that "might makes right." An everyday example of the conquest revolution approach might be driving one's car as hard and fast as possible with no maintenance, grinding gears, and stripping the rubber from the tires. The car is then abandoned when it is no longer functional, and it is blamed for falling apart. The conquest model is exclusively goal-oriented and pays no attention to the intentionality behind action.

This model is particularly compelling because it is the most familiar to us and seems the most efficient. The feeling of control and superiority from conquest, or having power over another, results in an instant "high" from intense confrontation which is very exhilarating. Unfortunately, having power over another is a self-perpetuating way of relating. Violence breeds violence. Violence is not self-limiting nor is the abuse of power in any form. The more power we have the more we typically want. It is important that we understand that power-over behavior is addictive and, as with any other addiction, we must choose to change it if we are to relate in non-power-over modes.

Power-over relating, or the conquest model, is maintained by several myths. The first of these is the myth of the half-person. This myth states that we are each half-persons and that we need another person in order to make us whole. We can see this being acted out in the ritual of heterosexual marriage and the words that go along with the marriage vows. What happens when we believe that we need someone else to make us whole is that we then give over the power of self-definition to that person. We become dependent upon that other in order to function as a whole.

The second myth is that of scarcity, i.e., that there is not enough to go around. If we believe that we must compete for scarce resources, then we will also believe that we must hoard whatever we have rather than sharing it. Our own focus is what determines our feeling of scarcity or abundance. If we believe that we must have more than we already have, then no matter how much we have we will feel that scarcity exists. It is only when we become aware that we can have whatever it is that we need, and that by sharing we in fact increase what we have, that we can move beyond the feeling of scarcity to a feeling of abundance.

The third myth is that of linear time, i.e., that time follows itself in a past-present-future sequence which is static and set. If we accept this myth, then we will believe that our past shapes and limits our future. When we become aware of the fact that time is not linear and that the past, present, and future all exist at the same time, then we can understand that we are continually changing not only our future but our past.

In actuality, the means that we use shape who we are. We cannot separate the means from the end. The end toward which we are moving is constantly changing and the only thing that we have in the present is the means. If we ignore another's pain, we perpetuate the objectification of others which leads to violence. If we set aside our own needs, then we once again invalidate our own sense of what is important and do violence to ourselves.

## Cultural Feminism

Cultural feminism is the process-oriented model that feminists have developed to provide balance to the product/goal focus of conquest revolution. This model of change is based on an awareness of the need for change in ourselves. The ultimate vision is more flexible than in conquest revolution but may not be clearly linked to the present in a way that results in constructive action. There is often a resistance to setting any particular goal or set of standards for fear that such a goal would assume priority over concerns about process.

Here the focus is almost exclusively on the spiritual dimension, assuming that since "the personal is political," personal changes will somehow lead to societal changes. Thus, the focus is on how we are with ourselves and with each other, rather than on where we are going.

Using the car illustration, we might maintain the car well but not drive it much.

The lack of attention to the political dimension can result in an individualistic emphasis without any built-in accountability. There is a sense of "anything goes" since it is all "a learning process." The lack of political analysis can result in a sense of passivity that ignores political reality and is noncritical of the violent nature of our present society. This kind of attitude can be just as harmful as "might makes right" since it keeps us from learning how to set and maintain limits and prevents our developing the integrity that comes from holding ideals and standards.

Cultural feminism has served an important historical role in adding the spiritual dimension to conquest revolution. It reminds us that we are important as individuals and that our personal lives do make a difference. However, it has not developed effective techniques for being able to limit and change the consequences of conquest revolution tactics.

We need both the richness and strength that come from valuing diversity and the focus that comes from setting and achieving goals. We need both freedom for process and responsibility for the product.

*Consensus Revolution*

Consensus revolution is an integration of the product focus of conquest revolution and the process focus of cultural feminism. As a model of change, it assumes that the need for change lies both within ourselves and in the society. The vision is both a given and is continually in the process of change, being composed of a series of visions to help us move into a qualitatively new space which we cannot now envision. The theme of consensus revolution is to value both product and process equally, to live out the fact that we become whatever we do.

Consensus revolution is a process of identifying and stating one's own needs and then releasing them to be met in ways never before imagined. It is a process of sharing one's vision with others and negotiating a gestalt which incorporates that vision without becoming attached to any one vision as better. It is the process of coming together to create a qualitatively different product than what each could create separately. It is working toward specific societal changes while remembering that ultimately one can change only oneself. It is, figuratively, both maintaining one's car well and using it to arrive at a specified destination.

In developing a model of consensus revolution, we need to keep in mind several aspects of creating change. When we oppose someone in direct conflict, we force that person backwards and by doing so we add energy and revitalize that negative position. We come to harm only if we stand still, and fear freezes us in a position from which we cannot move. Anger makes us blindly charge ahead while we are still attached to the past and not free to come up with new visions and alternatives. Sometimes we have to choose to move backwards or sideways in order to gain the necessary perspective or momentum to carry us past a particular difficult point.

The process of consensus revolution follows the cycle of change that involves creating, developing, and ending. Any cycle of change is both an end in itself and a means to an end not yet conceived. It is analogous to the constant process of creating and sloughing off cells in our own bodies.

Creating a vision is crucial to deciding where we are going to focus our energy. We cannot begin without a vision, yet we also need a vision that can be changed as we live it out. Our different political beliefs may come from slightly different perspectives on a shared vision. While the conquest model postulates the group leader as the one who *has* the vision, the consensus model views the leader as someone who helps the group achieve or *keep focused on* their vision.

In developing our vision, we need to be continually learning about our process of working together. We tend to work best in small groups where we can develop mutual trust and have accountable leadership. We need time and space in which to experience alternatives together and re-energize. We need to remember that the creative process is nonrational and to experiment with various tools that will help us be in touch with intuitive knowledge. We need to remember that time is ultimately nonlinear, that on some level we already know all we need to know. We need practice in knowing when to wait and when to move ahead, when we are centered and in focus and when we are defensive and on guard.

Probably the most crucial part of the cycle of change is that of being able to end or release a vision. Unless we are able to release or eliminate, we become constipated with old forms. The trick is that we need to be able to release or end without necessarily knowing what will come next. We are only really free if we can risk everything on the next step. Releasing is difficult because we are taught to want control of the process, to want to know what will happen next. However, if we must know what will happen next, then we limit our own experience to only that which we can imagine now. Another habit that makes releasing hard is belief in "the more the better." If we look at our own eating patterns, for example, we know that this is not so. If we continue eating more of what we like, we can eventually kill ourselves with overeating.

Our societal fear of endings comes from a basic misogyny. Esoterically, the female principle is the giver of form and, therefore, the giver of death or the end of that form. Rather than fearing the end, we need to take responsibility for integrating into our creations a sense of the need for an end. The basis of all esoteric teachings is that death holds no fear. We need to remember that death is a transmutation, a changing of form, rather than a termination. We also need to develop ending rituals to give ourselves the gift of summation, i.e., the gift of knowing what it is we have learned during that cycle.

Learning to consciously and deliberately end means taking our power seriously — our power to create, our power to develop, and our power to end. We have the power to harm or to heal, to abuse or to love.

## THE NEED TO END VIOLENCE

Violence is the abuse of power either actively by harming another, or passively by allowing oneself to be harmed or by ignoring one's own needs. It is crucial for us to understand the complexity of trying to define violence. There is no one action that is violent or nonviolent. It is the intentionality behind that action which makes it either violent or nonviolent. If someone is about to harm me, my acting to stop them from harming me is not violent. If I harm them more than is necessary in order to stop them, that excess is violent. Similarly, if I were to do nothing and allow myself to be harmed, that would be violent.

Our spirituality is what helps us understand that violence is counterproductive. Violence is possible only when we objectify others, i.e., distance ourselves from them. As long as we are aware of our unity with others, we are aware of the fact that in harming another we also harm ourselves. Unless we wish to remain violent, violence is never justified because we become what we do. Claiming that we can create peace through violent means is a *non sequitur*.

Violence is the cornerstone of the conquest model of revolution. It is such an ingrained habit that we are often not aware of the violent images (e.g., "I could just kill him") or the emotional patterns (e.g., revenge) with which we perpetuate the cycle of violence. We need to take responsibility for having in a certain sense created violence by giving up power or not taking ourselves seriously. Similarly, we need to take responsibility for ending the present cycle of violence.

From the three models of change, we can see that the key to a nonviolent process of change is a balance and integration of the spiritual and political dimensions of our lives. Violence is a method of creating change that denies the spiritual dimension of connectedness with others, thereby perpetuating the abuse of power. In order to create a qualitatively different society, we need to use a consensus model of revolution that allows us to end violent habit patterns and evolve toward a way of being which we cannot now comprehend.

# The Politics
# of Feminist Spirituality

# Anne Kent Rush

Integration of self-change with institutional change is a revolutionary practice in our society. Segmentation is the basis of patriarchal socialism or capitalism — separation of women and men, of theory and practice, of learning and working, of experience and belief, of production and product, of means and ends, of mind and body, of race, of age, of "class," and, interestingly enough, of religion and government.

The integration and recognition of the relationship between all these processes is the basis for the sanity and power of feminism. Any activities, theories, or organizations which connect parts of our lives are usually considered dangerous to the establishment, e.g., pointing out the relationship between sexism, racism, and capitalist production is a crime against existing institutions because the state perpetuates belief in their unrelatedness. Making these connections gives us power because the institutions cease to be abstractions, becoming understandable and then changeable factors in our lives.

Feminism is vitally concerned with the development of political-personal theory, but it never remains a politic of idealism because it is si-

From *MOON, MOON*, by Anne Kent Rush. Copyright © 1976 by Anne Kent Rush. Reprinted by permission of Random House, Inc.

multaneously concerned with the application and testing of our theories. It is (hopefully) reality in constant evolution, theory as the articulation of our own experience. Feminism is concerned with the reintegration of all these segmented parts and, therefore, the creation of a way of life ecological to the whole person. Thus, feminism is committed to the eventual replacement of patriarchy and capitalism with more coherent forms as a necessity for social and personal survival. It is a collective, nonhierarchical, nonsegmented, experience-based, ecological, evolutionary process — and as such it is *revolutionary* because these aspirations contradict the processes of patriarchal capitalism.

This is why the idea of women's religion is so anathematic to our current system. Not to worship the male principle would mean to turn away from everything this system deifies, and on which it has succeeded. These are the reasons Witchcraft was (and is) a crime punishable by oppression and death, a crime against the state.

Witchcraft, a religion of the people, was a spiritual movement which revered women and the lunar creative power; it was based on the interconnectedness of all things, the understanding of the necessity of and nonhierarchical respect for all elements of the life process. The dark of the moon, the period and principle of meditation, "death," and visions, was equally revered with the brightness and outward focus of the full moon principle.

Witchcraft became the focus of all the might and destruction the incoming patriarchal religions could muster:

Bring no more vain oblations; incense is an abomination unto me; the new moons and sabbaths, the calling of assemblies, I cannot away with; it is iniquity, even the solemn meeting. Your new moons and your appointed feasts my soul hateth; they are trouble unto me; I am weary to bear them . . . Come now, and let us reason together, saith the Lord.

— ISAIAH, I, 13:18

Rebellion is as the sin of witchcraft.

— SAMUEL, I, 15:23

Witchcraft as a way of life was forced to become a secret cult. As early as pre-Greek cultures we have records of Thessalonian sorcerers who debased Witchcraft. Later Greek classical literature is full of references to the matriarchal-patriarchal struggle. In a pronouncement of the General Council of the Church in the ninth century, there is a section on evidence against women who held allegiance to Diana-Hecate and who professed to ride to their meetings on certain beasts. The

Church Council of Treves in 1310 condemned any woman who claimed to ride with Herodiana.

The struggle raged on for centuries, and matriarchal knowledge became more and more suppressed. There are voluminous records, even up to the Salem trials in the early United States, which tell of the fate of women who dare to worship their own power. In a 300-year period, over 300,000 Witch practitioners were put to death for adhering to their religion and for defying the patriarchal establishment. Witchcraft, the religion of integration, had to be discredited and eliminated before the "success" of patriarchy could be insured.

It stands to reason, with so many centuries of brutal religious persecution, that women today should have a deep fear of conceptualizing our own spirituality. Women who try are severely penalized. Reverend Carter Heyward in New England was persecuted and harassed for her ordainment as a female Episcopal priest in 1974. Z. Budapest was put on trial in Los Angeles for her activities as a Witch in 1975.

Because of all this, it is essential that we *do* create our own spiritual practices. Our spiritual beliefs define what we respect, what we love — and what we ultimately perceive as our highest values. For a feminist, or for any woman, to perpetuate a patriarchal religion and to worship a male god is for her to deify her oppression.

The rituals being created today by various women are part of the renaissance of female spirituality, that is, of the ultimate holiness or life-sacredness of women and the female creative process. Within a world which for centuries has tried to brand women as "unclean," as "devils" or as the "immoral corruptor of man," this healing process is a vital one.

It is my belief that *reforming* patriarchal religions, such as Hinduism, Judaism, or Christianity, is not possible, just as reforming capitalism is not possible. The very institutions are contradictory to feminism. Women need to once again create new theory and practices for ourselves in order to reunite the spiritual element with the social-political.

At the same time, just as with feminist change within a capitalist society, I recognize that complete change is not always instantly possible. It does seem to me, though, that it may be possible to create women's religions within this culture even before the rest of the institutions have caught up with them, and to use these spiritual groups as vital centers for creating radically different ways of living. Women's spiritual groups can become birth centers for social change.

The task of our age is to draw on our spiritual heritage and, through reestablishing our collective female consciousness, to develop a way of life which doesn't need hierarchy at its base and which returns us to our efforts to live out the knowledge that we are all one. This evolution is dependent on our willingness to be unconventional, to free our imaginations and our bodies from our cultural restrictions and to unite at a deep level with other women.

The rituals we are creating today are beginnings of this process. They are attempts to bring spirituality, that is, our connection with the creation of our own destiny, back into the practice of the people.

You say there are no words to describe this time, you say it does not exist. But remember. Make an effort to remember. Or, failing that, invent.

— MONIQUE WITTIG, *Les Guérillères*

# Metaphysical Feminism

## Robin Morgan

A reflective interest in experience. A psychological curiosity about love
and religion. Surely the former is a fitting description of the changing
consciousness of any woman as she begins to examine her own life,
with her own tools of expertise. Surely the latter could be an apt expression for the two-fold obsession of women through the ages: human
and divine love. (The metaphysical poet John Donne was, in fact, positively "womanly" in his preoccupation with this two-fold love, seeing in
human love the best approach to cosmic love, as women have done for
centuries.)

To go on: psychological curiosity, the desire to startle and to approximate poetic to direct, even colloquial speech, and above all, *the blend
of passion and thought,* feeling and ratiocination. Psychological curiosity — and courage — is more required by the politics of feminist consciousness than by most political movements. The desire to startle is,
naturally, experienced by all ignored peoples, but the desire to approximate poetic to colloquial speech seems especially and poignantly rele-

From *GOING TOO FAR: The Personal Chronicle of a Feminist,* by Robin
Morgan. Copyright © 1968, 1970, 1973, 1975, 1977 by Robin Morgan. Reprinted
by permission of Random House, Inc.

vant to feminism. What else has our embryonic culture been attempting but to articulate in accessible terms that which previously has been unknowable or at least unspeakable? And that wonderful phrase "passionate thinking" — certainly this describes the electric leap of shared and connecting consciousness at its most intense. "Passionate thinking is always apt to become metaphysical, probing and investigating the experience from which it takes its rise." "The *dialectical* expression of personal drama."

When I think, then, of metaphysical feminism, I think not only of an all-encompassing feminist vision which goes literally beyond the physical (yet never leaves it behind) but which is in its very form related to those seventeenth-century English poets. An obsession with love has been at the heart of women's concerns — and in fact of feminists' concerns — for millennia, no matter how steadfast certain antithetical feminists remain, fixed in an anti-emotional polar response to what they see only as "feminine sentiment." How often have feminists called, too, for the "peculiar blend of feeling and ratiocination" in our battles against the patriarchal dichotomizing of intellect and emotion! It is the insistence on the *connections*, the demand for synthesis, the refusal to be narrowed into desiring less than everything — that is so much the form of metaphysical poetry and of metaphysical feminism. The unified sensibility.

Not the least devastating gesture of patriarchal power has been to cast the cosmos itself — the life-force, energy, matter, and miracle — into the form of a male god. Feminists have already observed that this has had a less than salutary effect on women. We could spend fifty volumes delineating the destruction done in the names of such gods, and we can also look around us. At this writing, Christian armies and Moslem forces in Lebanon are slaughtering each other *and* civilians (for which read: women and children and the aged) in the streets of Beirut, even as Catholic and Protestant antagonists draft grammar-school children to snipe at one another across the blood-scummed cobblestones of Londonderry in Northern Ireland. Both of these "religious wars" are misnomers in the political sense, but in a deeper sense they are perfectly named, since both are about the contest between the two great modern patriarchal religions: capitalism and communism. For it is not only the Judeo-Christian tradition which has shored up the patriarchy for five thousand years; it is every male-conceived and -dominated faith.

I confess to a particular antipathy for the Catholic Church, despite my loyalty to good theater wherever it can be found, and my long-standing passion for Gregorian chant.[1] I don't mean to let the rest of Christianity (or my own religion of origin from which I am so apostate, Judaism) off the hook easily. But it *is* hard to overlook or forget nine million women burned as Witches over a period of three hundred years by Christianity, and largely by the Catholic Church.[2] Even today, in Catholic South and Latin America, illegal abortion and childbirth compete for the highest cause of death among women. In the United States, the church is financing Birch Society-led campaigns to undo the moderate progress women have made in gaining self-determination over our own bodies. So much blood spilled on the cathedral steps, because that perfect microcosm of patriarchy—that hierarchy of octogenarian celibate males running around in drag—still thinks it can rule on the lives and bodies of millions of women, whatever our ages.

Which should not, I grant, keep us from justly condemning the gray, co-optative mask of modern Protestantism (clamped over the self-righteous expressions of Luther and Knox); the virulent woman-hatred in fundamentalist Christianity; the woman-fear and woman-loathing rampant in Judaism to this day (as if the scars of that religion's matriarchal origin and its overthrow were still not eradicated from the Jewish collective unconscious); the female-as-temptress or the female-as-nonentity in, respectively, the exoteric and esoteric sophistries of Buddhist, Zen, or Western existential thought; the vitriol spewed on women for centuries in Moslem cultures.[3]

Very well. We do not exist or, since this is the choice, we are the devil's gateway, we are evil. What else, we may ask, is new? And for every female mystic who has somehow managed through her own genius, like Teresa, to reach her transcendence even through the labyrinth of patriarchal means—millions of us have stared with horror at the disbelievable reality of our own ankles stockinged in flame, have peeled open the parchment of our lips that the world might read the scream stuck in that throat. What else can we hear but that unspent scream—even if they did have anything to say to us now?

So we left their churches, and are still leaving. And the birth of what has been called female spirituality is a new phenomenon in the women's movement.[4] This has given me much personal joy—and at present it is worrying me sick. Because once again spirituality is becoming confused with religion—thus going nowhere near far enough.

## ANOTHER PARABLE

How can we love?
How can we *not* love?

— *The Three Marias,*
*New Portuguese Letters*

The sea organisms crawled up onto the land to commit ecstatic suicide, to escape triumphantly from existing, to return to infinite pure energy, motionless.

But life forced itself to flow through even the gasps they drank in of what they assumed was death: air. Despite themselves, they became air-breathing organisms. Every step taken toward nonexisting brings us closer toward existing.

It is the fault of something female.

Nature, we have heard, abhors a vacuum. Speaking then through male anguish at his own womb envy, nature discovered existential despair. But male anguish expressed this despair as misogyny. What else to feel when faced with this female endless birthing, this repeated insistence on life and life-giving and life-re-creation? What *is* this maddening tendency to bear and bear and bear, as if each woman were somehow somewhere in herself singing "I never met a universe I didn't like"?

He only wants her to understand his wretchedness. He persecutes her to make her understand why death is the answer, he tortures her to raise her consciousness to the suicidal, to make her as truly aware as he is. She won't despair. She won't die. She creates agriculture, domesticates animals. Culture is born.

He appropriates her gods, her whole cosmic space, to the merciless, negative, bleak, terror-filled void in which he is trapped. She curses his gods — but does not die. She calls to him. She sees his beauty writhing, contorted in pain. He sobs with longing to share what she is, sees, owns, the whole Earth as female, the solar system female, the universe female, all that he smells and touches and which holds him and bore him and will outlive him — female, eternally rutting and conceiving and laughing and producing.

For what? What is there to celebrate here, in this dimension? Is there no way to kill her out of this gross procreation? Can none of his entropy conquer her energy? If he cannot stop her, can he at least successfully pretend that he *insists* she do precisely what she is doing? Can he tell himself he *demands* she conceive? Rape is born, his own parthenogenetic child. Laws are written controlling her body's freedom. She creates pottery, baskets, songs. She investigates the power of herbs. Art and science are born.

Is there no way to stop her? Is there no way to evade this inexhaustible deathless pursuing consciousness? He devises nirvanas of escape. Oriental philosophies which pretend she is illusion, Occidental philosophies which pretend she is existentially meaningless. And all the while she smiles and conceives. Children. Grapefruits. The thimble. Barnacles. The printing press. City squirrels.

He is more and more trapped into his systems. He invents new and efficient ways of murdering what she produces — wars, chemicals, political systems which destroy her creations or treat them as products. He is consumed with self-loathing for having become the weapon of himself and never the victim in his global attempt to commit suicide. She weeps for him and gives birth to a new star, hoping its nova will divert him from his misery.

He invents names for her creatures, deliberately mixed around. He calls the human ones insects, vermin, pigs, cows. Then he kills them, and their animal namesakes, too. He forgets what and who and why he is killing. He knows only where he came from — that womb of Earth, and where he is going — that same insatiable womb with its infinite capacity for orgasm and for creation as it sucks him in and spews him out and laughs lovingly *lovingly* at him as if he were her plaything.

Only when he has totally forgotten who he is and why he hates her so; only when she herself has almost forgotten herself; only when his pain has at last infected her so that she almost has begun to listen, almost understand his message of nonexistence, his longing for peace and death and the silence of a collapsed nonwomb whose energy and matter are once and for all time separated — only then does she slowly rouse herself to remind him.

That time is now.

NOTES

1. This fondness extends itself to secular music of the Middle Ages, as well; nevertheless, I was gratified to learn that the structure of Gre-

gorian chant is based on very old musical forms dating back to "pagan" matriarchal religious ritual. (See *Music in History*, McKinney and Anderson, American Book Company, New York, 1940). This comforts my conscience almost as much as the music delights my spirit.

2. The *New York Post* of 18 August 1976, carried the Associated Press story of a twenty-three-year-old woman, Anneliese Michel of Klingenberg, Germany, who died after having undergone exorcism rites by two Catholic priests. *Time* magazine (6 September 1976) also reported and expanded the story. It appears that civil authorities are now investigating the exorcism procedures, which were originally recommended by an eighty-one-year-old local priest who believed Ms. Michel was possessed of demons which sent her into violent seizures. With the permission of Bishop Josef Stangl, two exorcists—Fr. Arnold Renz and Fr. Ernst Alt—were called in. Fr. Renz, not one averse to publicity, claimed during a television appearance that Ms. Michel was possessed by six spirits, including Lucifer, Nero, Judas, Cain, and Adolf Hitler—a case of overkill, one would think. The exorcism rituals continued for ten months; Ms. Michel's seizures grew more frequent and intense and her weight dropped to seventy pounds. The priests called in no medical assistance. Finally she died, "of malnutrition and dehydration," according to the medical report. Bishop Stangl told the press that he was considering a church investigation into the "possible negligence" of the priests; he said his decision on this would be forthcoming upon his return from a health-resort holiday. Bishop Stangl's diocese is Würzburg, where in one year alone during the seventeenth century, more than three hundred witches were burned alive for "trafficking with the devil." Further medical background was uncovered about the dead woman, whose seizures had been diagnosed unmysteriously when she was in high school: Anneliese Michel suffered from epilepsy.

3. The Associated Press recently reported from Istanbul that two orthodox Moslem villagers, Tahir Akcay and Mehmet Veysi, shot and killed their wives for their failure to uphold fasting traditions during the holy month of Ramadan. This was in September of 1976.

4. Not as new as it might seem, perhaps. In a provocative paper entitled "Jane Lead: The Feminist Mind and Art of a Seventeenth-Century Protestant Mystic," Catherine F. Smith of Bucknell University suggests that the connections between feminism and a mystical tradition extend quite a way back, even though this linkage has been ridiculed, when recognized at all, by male-biased scholarship. She writes: "The patriarchal limitations of mystical thought are not the main point when women writers are concerned. Rather, mysticism has given

women a voice, a literary form capable of describing both their reduced condition and their native powers. It has also provided them
with an indirect language for protesting sexual politics." Quoted by
permission.

# The Politics
# of Women's Spirituality

## Charlene Spretnak

The language you speak is made up of words that are killing you.
— MONIQUE WITTIG

It should be pointed out that we are dealing here with a number of linguistic ironies: There is no author*ess* behind this article, yet it speaks of the eras of the God*dess*, the priest*ess*, the mythic hero*ine* — all of whom pre-dated their male counterparts. It should be pointed out that these derivative words were created and assigned by usurpers: They are designed to trivialize and negate the validity of our past. It should be pointed out that we understand the power of *naming ourselves*: This understanding is laced with rage that we should *have to* create new words to replace our ancient names, which were annihilated. It should be shouted out that we will not be confused, subdued, or crushed by mutilated words, patriarchal constructs, and the boundaries of the rational *hemi*sphere of the brain. Read between these lines, under them, around them, over them, and through them — with the thread of your

© Charlene Spretnak, 1978. Reprinted by permission of the author from *Chrysalis: A Magazine of Women's Culture*, no. 6, Nov. 1978.

own experience and power, weave your connections and your interconnections with one another. In this way is women's spirituality created.

The underlying rationale for patriarchal societies is patriarchal religion. Christianity, Judaism, Islam, and Hinduism all combine male godheads with proscriptions against woman as temptress, as unclean, as evil. We were all made to understand that Eve's act of heeding the word of the serpent caused the expulsion of the human race from the Garden of Eden. We were made to understand that, as a result of her act, it was decreed by God that woman must submit to the dominance of man. We were all raised in cultures that reflect this decree: Men enjoy the secular and spiritual positions of power; women cook and clean for them and supply them with heirs.

Most of the four billion people currently living in accordance with the patriarchal order do not question it: Things have been this way for a long time; it must be the natural order. But what if the patriarchy is only a few thousand years old? What if, for tens of thousands of years before that, societies were built around the concept of the Great Goddess? If this is the case, our entire overview of history is altered: We once passed through a very long phase of matrifocal culture; we are now passing through a phase of patriarchal culture (which appears to be self-destructing after a relatively brief run); and the future phase is ours to design.

## MANIFESTATIONS OF OUR RECLAIMED SPIRITUALITY

*Anat, Aphrodite, Artemis, Asherah, Astarte, Athena, Attor, Au Set, Blodeuwedd, Britannia, Britomaris, Changing Woman, Demeter, Dictynna, Gaia, Hathor, Hecate, Hera, Ananna, Ishtar, Isis, Ix Chel, Kali, Kuan Yin, Magna Mater, Nut, Pandora, Persephone, Rhea, Rhiannon, Saraswati, Selene, Tara, Themis, White Goddess*

Ours is the oldest spiritual tradition on Earth. Now we understand the symbolism in patriarchal myths wherein Apollo slays the python at Delphi, wherein evil comes to weak-willed Eve in the form of a snake, wherein Saint George fiercely slays the giant snake-like dragon, wherein Saint Patrick rids Ireland of the snakes — for in matrifocal spirituality snakes were a widespread symbol of cyclical renewal and regeneration, continually growing and shedding their skins. We understand why the animal declared unclean by the Judaic fathers was the pig, which had long been held sacred to Demeter and other Mediterranean forms of the Goddess for its prolificacy.

The great silence has been broken at last. Women are coming together to cultivate the powers that can result from exploring matrifocal heritage, personal and collective mythology, natural healing, meditation, dreamwork, celebrating the cycles of nature (i.e., our surroundings and our own bodies), and ritual. As we all bear scars from having been raised under patriarchy, the ability to heal ourselves and each other psychically and physically is essential to the growth of women's culture. Ritual can generate and transform tremendous fields of force. That energy is always there for us to tap and manifest. Rituals created within a framework of women's spirituality differ in form and content from the empty, hierarchically imposed, patriarchal observances with which most of us grew up. They involve healing, strengthening, creative energy that expands with spontaneity from a meaningful core of values.

## CURRENT PERCEPTIONS WITHIN THE MOVEMENT

For some feminists the merging of spiritual and political power seems impossible. Furthermore, it seems distasteful. After all, one is "serious," the other "inconsequential." A representative example of this view appeared in the widely reprinted "Will the Women's Movement Survive?" by Naomi Weisstein and Heather Booth (*Sister*, vol. 4, no. 12). The authors present a thoughtful, concerned analysis of problems now faced by the movement: cultural recidivism, erosion of past victories, the withering of our alternative institutions and organizations, and our consciousness in the context of social change and revolutionary stalemates. While admitting that there are many weak areas in the movement today, they declare: "We must take active, positive, imaginative steps to give our movement new momentum. We must act. All of us, together, can surmount our current difficulties and come back with a stronger, saner, sounder movement." *Brava!* Sounds like a passage from *WomanSpirit* magazine. . . . Up with positive, imaginative solutions; down with the old weaknesses and insanity. Weisstein and Booth conclude the article with the conviction that we *can* do it: "Let us, all of us, carry our movement forward, past defeat, past ignorance, past conflict, past exhaustion, to change the lot of humanity, to drive on through to that better world, that just and generous society." Right. Let's go.

It is in their discussion of consciousness, however, that the shadow of dualistic thinking falls. The authors see women's spirituality only as a passive, suicidal "collapse into mysticism." Our spirituality is newly reclaimed, unfamiliar, and, therefore, "other." There are no role models, no points of reference in *recorded* history for women who are politically active *and* in touch with the full range of their powers. But we are not who the patriarchy says we are. We are giving birth to ourselves as wise warriors. The old boundaries are meaningless to us. We are all. It is this impulse toward a unified, expanded sensibility that Robin Morgan advocates in "Metaphysical Feminism" (in *Going Too Far*) as "the insistence on the *connections*, the demand for synthesis, the refusal to be narrowed into desiring less than everything."

In proposing strategy to bring more women into the feminist movement, Weisstein and Booth suggest that all we need is a coordinated plan of recruitment. They overlook the largest mobilized force trying to defeat us: patriarchal religions. The churches have contributed an enormous amount of money, time, and organizing toward the goal of crushing us, especially on the issues of abortion and the ERA. How is it that masses of women follow their lead? *Because patriarchal religion and social structure are believed to have always been the natural order.* Feminism is seen as unnatural, as a threatening aberration. Women whose lives revolve around Judeo-Christian teachings will never embrace feminism unless we reach them with the historical truth that the system they are holding up is itself the recent aberration. (Mary Daly's *The Church and the Second Sex*, an overwhelming documentation of the pervasive anti-woman bias, and *Beyond God the Father*, the groundwork for a creative alternative, would be strategic accompaniments to historical evidence of when and how patriarchal religions really began, which is perhaps best presented in Merlin Stone's *When God Was a Woman*.)

Finally, regarding the author's concluding exhortation (cited above), I would like to point out that we will never get "past exhaustion" unless we know how to heal ourselves; that we will never get "past ignorance, past conflict" unless we go beyond patriarchal, dualistic modes of thought, and that the new world to which they hope to "drive on through" will soon look remarkably like the old world unless a new consciousness is built that reflects our oneness with each other and our environment. These are not "other."

Another example of perceiving the alliance between politics and spirituality as impossible appeared in an exchange of letters and articles that spanned three issues of *Off Our Backs* (Fall 1977). At the end of this exchange, some members of the *Off Our Backs* collective published this statement: "We don't agree that a women's religion is any kind of answer to the patriarchy. Religions, even women-identified ones, have misled the oppressed rather than encouraging them to struggle against their situation." Reducing our new totality, our swelling awareness and strengths, to the construct of conventional "religion" is a self-defeating denial. Once again, the concept of a woman with both spiritual and political power is almost inconceivable. Yet she is being born.

## FUTURE DIRECTIONS

Our directions are circular, an ever-expanding spiral. Where are the lines dividing present from future, humans from nature, body from mind, being from being? Within our circle the great silence has been broken. But what about out there?

The Paleolithic woman/Goddess statues, the original mythology, the matrifocal cultures should appear in textbooks in every school. We must write the books. Our sisters in patriarchal religions should be encouraged to make an *informed* choice about whether those systems have validity and historical legitimacy. Whether or not their conclusion is ours, we should know that those women are aspects of ourselves and we of them.

What divides women from women within the movement? We all want a better world. We are all political. We all understand long-range struggle. As we break down the systems that oppress us, we must begin to form the future. Right now. Already the connection has been made between transformative ritual and political mobilization: At anti-nuclear demonstrations and at conferences on violence against women, women have led rituals that involve the transformation of rage and depression into constructive, activist energy. Participants enter the closing ceremony exhausted and discouraged; they leave feeling exhilarated, bonded with each other, and optimistic about organizing. What will political meetings, organizations, strategies be like once we acknowledge spiritual power? Spirituality enables us to feel a deep connection between one another. It heals and avoids the fragmented sense that often plagues political movements, in both personal and collective terms. Our bonding is profound. Do we know that yet?

Like feminist goals in education, law, health care, etc., feminist goals in spirituality are ultimately humanist. Some of our brothers want to work with us; can we recognize them? What divides us from a humanist future? We must expand our vision and propose options for restructuring. Floods of them. Futurism is already another patriarchal game: proposals, recommendations, decisions that have nothing to do with us. Nothing to do with new ways of knowing and being. We must develop a cohesive cosmology; we must design models of affirmation and integration.

Women's spirituality exposes revisionist history and reveals the truth about our past; it replenishes and sustains us in our struggle; and, more than being just a tool to aid us while we fight for a better life, it *is* a key to the better life. We are forming a new sensibility of that which cannot be quantified — of that which gives birth to possibilities, which is difficult to control, which does not serve hierarchical ordering — and, therefore, has been fiercely denied. We refuse to acquiesce any longer to being the "other," the "non-being." Ours is a working, activist philosophy of existence — *on our own terms.*

At the center of our expanding spiral is a creative self-love and self-knowledge. We have barely tapped the power that is ours. We are more than we know.

Blessed Be
It Is You Who Is a Hera
It Is You Who Is Wise and Strong
It Is You Who Are The Power
and Flow of Change
Blessed Be

# Feminist Spirituality: The Politics of the Psyche

# Judith Antonelli

There is a great deal of doubt expressed in various segments of the women's movement as to the relevance of feminist spirituality to politics. The strongest critics of spirituality see it as escapist, as focusing on inner subjective reality as opposed to external objective conditions — thus taking away from the "real" political work that needs to be done. Those who have written in defense of spirituality have mostly emphasized the necessity to work on *both* the inner and outer aspects of reality, refusing to reduce feminism to a choice of either/or. However, this in itself does not challenge the notion that spirituality and politics are two separate categories.

One of the reasons why spirituality is viewed as apolitical by some women is that up until the feminist movement, radical politics have been materialist — i.e., dealing only with visible, physical reality. Whether communist, socialist, leftist, or anarchist, radical politics have focused on *control of the means of production* as the central issue in freeing ourselves from oppression. The women's movement, while ex-

panding on this to include other issues such as reproduction, has generally aligned itself with the materialist view of reality. For an issue to be
considered "political" by materialists, it must be analyzed from this perspective; unseen forces are not acknowledged as having any influence.
Spirituality is seen simply as "an opiate of the people" — i.e., as a way
of diverting people's attention from their oppression in the here and
now. While this can be said of patriarchal religion, it is not necessarily
the essence of spirituality itself.

Spirituality is a worldview based on energy, a perception which includes the nonvisible and nonmaterial. It deals with the collective
psyche (soul) of humanity. Ritual, astrology, the Tarot, dreams, and
mythology are symbolic languages emerging from the unconscious. Psychic energy (life-force, creative principle) is inherently female, and
this realization is the essence of *feminist* spirituality.

Materialist revolutions do not work to dig out oppression by its roots.
They change social structures from the top down; "benevolent dic-
tators" have decreed that equality in wealth and sexual roles shall be
the norm. The difference between socialist and capitalist fascism (that
is, authoritarianism or state power based on repression) is that at least
the socialist fascists want everyone to be fed. That's worth something —
but not enough. In fact, it may be more insidious, since when you're
starving amidst wealth, oppression is an obvious fact.

Nonrational, spiritual reality is not acknowledged in socialist societies. Religion is condemned, although the reverence for Mao and Fidel
certainly resembles the worship of God the Father in capitalist countries. Mental illness is also still present, which indicates some kind of
suppression of the nonrational, unconscious mind. Competition, na-
tionalism and patriotism, imperialism, an emphasis on industrialized
production, and technological control of nature continue after
"revolution": China is working on the bomb; Cuba has political pris-
oners. Moreover, heterosexual, monogamous marriage and, thus, the
patrilineal nuclear family are the only sanctioned form of sexuality.
The repression of the varied forms of sexual expression indicates the
suppression of sexual, or life, energy — i.e., the female principle. Materialist (or socialist) revolutions are, therefore, still patriarchal.

Materialist politics are much like behaviorist psychology in that underlying causes, usually unseen, are dismissed as impossible, for all that
exists is the visible. Human behavior is viewed as completely conditioned by the external environment, and people are thus treated as abstractions, machines, or white rats. Karl Marx and B. F. Skinner are

truly brothers under the skin. Therefore, materialist politics take the symptom — that most people in the world are denied the right to a comfortable material existence — and treat it as the problem. Clearly, destruction of the world by a small group of white men in order to achieve more wealth than they can ever possibly use does not make sense. We are talking here about a drive for power, a need for domination, that must be examined in psychological, motivational terms if we are to truly understand it and dismantle it. Although motivational psychology has generally been used by the patriarchy to discredit political struggle, feminists can now use it as a tool to explain oppression.

The female principle is primary in nature. Woman possesses a power that no man can ever have: the capacity to give birth to new life, as well as the ability to experience an unlimited amount of pleasure in the sexual act. She is the creator of life, while his role in conception is, at best, a secondary one. Patriarchy is based on the "phallacy" that the male is creator. Man's original awe and envy of woman becomes, under patriarchy, resentment and hostility. The only way man can possess female power is through woman, and so he colonizes her, suppressing her sexuality so that it serves him rather than being the source of her power.

Patriarchy creates a split in consciousness. When body and mind are split, one must confront the fact that woman can create with her body *and* her mind, while man can create only with his mind. In compensation, to cover his own lack of completeness, to make himself feel superior, man claims all rational-intellectual processes as his own, devaluing all bodily, emotional, and intuitive functions, while simultaneously saying that these functions are *all* that women are capable of. Patriarchy is based on fear of the female and the suppression of all "female" qualities: woman, nature, the body, feelings and emotion, instinct, intuition, and, finally, life itself.

Patriarchy is indeed a male neurosis. Every social institution under male dominance is an expression of man's womb envy, designed to take woman's power away from her and place it in the hands of men. In squelching female energy, patriarchy creates a culture that is destructive and death-oriented. If man denies his dependence on the female and tries to usurp her, making himself primary, he can only be the destroyer of life; he is not able to create life. While woman sheds the Blood of Life each moon at menstruation, man can only shed the blood of death through warfare and killing. Imperialism can be seen as the logical extension of rape; invasion of a people's homeland, as well as ecological destruction, is psychically analogous to the rape and invasion of a woman's body. Now that man has all but conquered woman, nature, and Earth, he is already beginning colonization of the moon, another symbol of the female principle!

The essence of a spiritual view of politics lies in the perception that matter is a manifestation of energy, that material reality reflects and symbolizes psychic reality. An obvious example is that emotional conflicts often emerge in the form of physical illness. This is not to deny that material reality also gives rise to energy patterns — for life is a cyclical process, not a linear one, and therefore *both* can be true. However, I am here focusing on just *one* aspect of the cycle — the fact that the spiritual gives rise to the material — in order to make my point that spirituality is indeed political (i.e., that it deals with the distribution of power).

There are many political examples of how material reality is symbolic of psychic reality. The torture of animals (instinctual beings) and the predominance of right-handedness (dominance by the brain's left hemisphere) are indicative of the hyper-rationalism of our society. One of the most glaring examples, however, is in racism: the oppression of people of color by the white race. Black and white have a very strong psychological significance in terms of the intuitive/rational split. Blackness, darkness, the New Moon, and the night have all been symbols of the unconscious, instinct, inner-directed energy, the void from which all creation begins. Whiteness, brightness, the Full Moon, and the daytime symbolize conscious awareness, ego, rational intellect, outward energy. It is no accident that as our world grows more rational and more ego-dominated, white supremacy over dark-skinned peoples increases also. Fear of blackness and what it represents psychically is one of the roots of racism, as well as of the notion (especially prevalent in allopathic medicine) that white is clean, sterile, and pure — while black is seen as a symbol of sadness and death.

Symbolic language, then, is very important for us to decipher. There is a wealth of information in mythology, for example, which tells us about the transition from matriarchy to patriarchy. Myth *is* hystory,* but in allegorical, not literal, form. The predominance of a Mother Goddess represents matriarchy: the predominance of the female principle, a society in which women control the means of production and re-

---

* I prefer this spelling to the term "herstory" because it indicates the linguistic connection to "womb" (from the Greek word). Both are "where we come from."

production, and where female clans are the basic social unit. Patriarchy, the institution of laws which break the mother-child bond and assure men of knowledge of their paternity, begins when the son kills his mother and paves the way for the ascendance of a father god, who represents the predominance of male power. Women today who are trying to bring back Goddess worship are not worshipping idols, escaping through mysticism, or revering an external god-substitute. The Goddess represents nothing less than female power and woman's deification of her own essence. It is external only to the extent that this power is contained within the cycles of nature as well as within ourselves.

Every oppressed people needs a sense of its hystory; therefore, researching our matriarchal past is not escapist, but a very important political act. We must develop an analysis of history from the perspective of the balance between the female and male principles. Knowledge of our past shapes and clarifies our vision of the future. We can gain much of this knowledge intuitively, for the collective unconscious contains our memories of matriarchy.

Developing our psychic power is also political. To think that we can rely only on physical techniques of self-defense is naïve in light of the fact that men have the military weapons and the technology to wipe us out instantly as soon as they recognize the threat we pose. We *must* develop psychic power as a means of self-defense. Living in the country must also not be seen as privileged and escapist. It is imperative that women learn survival skills such as living off the land, growing food, and healing with herbs. We must begin to put good nurturing energy into the Earth in order to counteract man's manipulation of her. Who knows how many "natural catastrophes" have been the retaliation of Mother Nature for all the damage that has been done to her?

If we are to survive the massive destruction that is the inevitable outcome of male supremacy, we *must* attune ourselves to psychic reality. Dismissing spirituality as apolitical, relegating it to a different sphere than the material, is shortsighted and feeds right into the rationalist fears that work to maintain the patriarchy.

# The Unnatural Divorce
# of Spirituality and Politics

# Hallie Iglehart

An unnecessary and destructive chasm exists between "spiritual" and "political" feminists.* It is unnecessary because we are saying the same things about the abuse of power-over relationships, the right to physical and mental health, the destruction of the environment, the importance of the personal and the political, the individual and the collective, and the necessity of the overthrow of the patriarchy on all levels. We have

---

© Hallie Iglehart, 1978. Excerpted from *Quest: A Feminist Quarterly*, vol. 4, no. 3, Summer 1978; reprinted by permission of the author.

* The patriarchal use of the terms "political" and "spiritual," and of "inner" and "outer," "material" and "psychic," as separate and opposing phenomena is inaccurate. However, we are just emerging from patriarchal dualism and do not yet have words adequately describing a synthesis of these areas of human existence. Also, since the areas womanspirit focuses on are predominantly extra-rational (but not excluding the rational, as the patriarchy would have us believe), any description of them in analytic terms is limited. It is something like trying to describe color with sound — some communication is possible, but many essential elements of the experience are missing. Many of the misunderstandings between "political" feminists and "spiritual" feminists come from this language problem. When we use rational, dualistic terms to communicate womanspirit, we must remember their inadequacy and allow our intuition and imagination to fill in the gaps. Ultimately, we need a new definition of feminism which includes all forms of change.

the same goals and values, but sometimes use different words to describe them or tools to actualize them. The split between us is created and maintained by patriarchal dualistic concepts of "spirituality" and "politics." It is destructive because it prevents the synthesis of the "spiritual" and "political" approaches necessary to establish the kind of world we want to see. When we do make this synthesis within ourselves and within the feminist movement, we will have more power than we ever imagined possible.

With this article, I hope to begin to bridge the gap between "spiritual" and "political" feminists by addressing some of the criticisms of womanspirit (also known as feminist spirituality, women's spirituality, etc.) by describing how it is politically expedient for the patriarchy to have us believe that our "political" and "spiritual" interests are opposed, and by showing how a synthesis of the two is developing through womanspirit.

Objections to womanspirit seem to fall into three main categories: all spiritualities and religions are oppressive; spirituality is escapist; and it is a wasteful use of womantime and womanenergy. These attitudes reflect a shallow view of history,[1] and of spirituality and its relationship to political power. The oppression associated with religion and spirituality is real — in a patriarchy. The oppression of political power is real — in a patriarchy. To dismiss all spirituality as oppressive, however, is akin to dismissing all politics as oppressive. Refusal to recognize and deal with both oppressions is self-destructive. Moreover, we cannot build a strong movement without recognizing the value of all of our work, and without communicating and working together.

## WOMANSPIRIT GOALS

The womanspirit movement seeks to reclaim the spiritual-political powers neglected or suppressed throughout the patriarchal era, to develop a feminist force that attacks the patriarchy from all directions, and to create new ways of being and relating. For its first few years, womanspirit has focused on rediscovering and strengthening our "spiritual" powers and knowledge through consciousness-raising and skills-sharing. We have been studying prepatriarchal history and art, collective mythology as a history of the process of patriarchal takeover, personal mythology as a tool for self-empowerment and self-knowledge, natural healing as effective and people-oriented medicine, and ritual as a community-creating device and a focusing of psychic power. In all these areas, we use the skills of meditation and psychic powers both for "inner" clarity and for effectiveness in the "outer" world. We also integrate a third layer of awareness and practice — a sense of who we are in the universe and our place in the community of Earth, animal, and sea.

By combining our intuitive powers with our intellectual skills, and by practicing psychic and psychological preventive medicine, we can conserve and resource our energy. And by devising tools for developing creativity and vision and concretizing these visions, womanspirit creates the new world now, rather than waiting until it is too late.

## THE DUALISTIC SPLIT: "SPIRITUAL" VS. "POLITICAL"

Feminists who rely heavily on theory, analysis, and material values (important approaches, but not all-important), often dismiss feminist spirituality as having little "political" relevance. In so doing, they fall into one of patriarchy's main traps, that of dualism: "If it's spiritual, it can't be political."

Emphasizing dualisms makes it easier for the patriarchy to isolate people from our own power and to keep us struggling against one another. Feminists early on recognized that the patriarchy used dichotomies such as "feminine" and "masculine," "black" and "white," "personal" and "political" to weaken us. Womanspirit goes a step further and asserts that "spiritual" and "political" powers are inseparable, that the abuses of both kinds of power are the result of the patriarchal mentality which views them as antithetical. Within these dualities is the supposition that one person cannot win without the other losing, and that we must constantly be on our guard to protect what little we have.

Dualities do exist, but they are no more a true description of existence than multiplicities or holism. A holistic view recognizes that we are all one and that to harm any part is harming ourselves. A multiplistic view (i.e., recognizing many experiences) encompasses many factors at once and approaches any situation from all sides, so that there is no *one* politics, no single solution. In this society, however, the polarities of dualism have become so exaggerated that the multiplicities lying between them (and the wholeness itself) have been forgotten — indeed, declared nonexistent.

In some societies, the interconnection of the "material" and "spiritual" worlds is recognized and valued.[2] In them, "politics" and "religion" work together to create a harmonious, egalitarian society. "Spiritual" power in more integrated societies grows from the study of the self as a microcosm of society and the cosmos, and of "psychic" forces and the rhythms of nature. This "spiritual" power interacts with and affects material reality. Its predominant expression is effective, non-oppressive, non-manipulative power; it attunes itself to the existing situation, sees how best to work with what is at hand, and uses the available energy. In our dualistic, overly material technological culture, this interconnection is denied, to the benefit of those with material power. Sexist, racist, and ethnocentric attitudes dismiss this spiritual-political wisdom as superstition, ignoring the concrete evidence of the power of the spirit to affect material reality.

These dualistic elements are manifested in the feminist movement by a competitive "more political than thou" attitude and by the demand to justify an inherently extra-rational mode (womanspirit) in rational terms. This demand reflects an ethnocentric attitude that politically valuable tools cannot be developed outside the established political feminist arena, i.e., in spirituality. In proscribing certain approaches, these attitudes make it difficult for the movement to grow and to encompass more women and more areas of life.

## SPIRITUAL OPPRESSION

One of the primary ways the patriarchy uses dualism to keep us oppressed is by telling us that we are not psychically oppressed and that psychic oppression and power are unrelated to material oppression and power. Debating whether psychic or material oppression is greater keeps us fighting each other rather than fighting together against our common enemy.

Psychic oppression is so great in the West that we hardly know what the spirit is. Ironically, spiritual growth is smothered by the very institutions which purport to foster it. Religion in the common understanding of the Judeo-Christian-Muslim monopoly emphasizes sin, guilt, authoritarianism, fear, and promises of future well-being rather than self-knowledge, love of self and other, and integration of inner power with outer power. In addition, these religions as institutionalized exclude women, the Earth, and the body, and separate the emotions from the spirit, thus denying any chance of wholeness. Religion in these terms becomes an escape from dealing with our own authority and responsibility and with the complicated interweavings of the daily issues of mind, spirit, body, emotions, religion, politics, and society. The patriarchy knows that people in touch with their spirit are powerful

people, and does all it can to convince us that the spirit, like power, is
something to fear rather than something to love and from which to
grow.

Long after people have rejected traditional religion, the combined social, political, and economic forces of patriarchal education, advertising,
and entertainment continue their spiritual oppression by constantly demanding that we function merely analytically and competitively. The
resulting suppression of compassion, emotional and psychical communication, self-love, and the union of self-power with collective power
(all components of healthy spirituality) is an essential tool in maintaining power-over relationships and sexual, racial, class, and other oppression.

Every time we discredit ourselves and one another, give over our
power to another, or cut ourselves off from our inner strength, we feed,
consciously or unconsciously, patriarchy's power. We lose contact with
our spirituality and its connection to our "outer" power.

Many instances of connection between material and psychic oppression are subtle and complicated. Others are overt and clear. It is common knowledge that established religion is often big business, as
witnessed by the riches of many of the churches, and the willingness of
believers to turn over large sums of money to churches and gurus.
Some doctors receive $45 each time they pull the switch to administer
electric shock — a strong incentive to abuse the treatment.[3] Cultural,
economic, social, and spiritual phenomena all affect one another. We
are not the victims only of psychic or only of economic oppression.
Wherever there is material oppression, there is psychic oppression and
vice versa.

Thus far, the feminist movement has primarily worked on the "material" level, and we have accomplished much in a few years. Yet many
women are put off by the exclusively "political" emphasis of the movement, sensing the necessity of developing other parts of our lives within
a feminist framework. The feminist movement, without a healthy spirituality, can never be effective because it addresses only one part of
our oppression.

## SPIRITUAL POWER

Just as material and spiritual oppression go hand in hand, so do political and spiritual power. The womanspirit movement emphasizes a consciousness that inner must always be combined with outer, that the psy-

chic is inseparable from the material, that political power cannot exist without spiritual power, and offers tools for developing our inner power. We are actively creating new forms of cooperative, creative, and effective power; we need ritual, psychic integration, and healing methods that relate to us as integral parts of the natural forces.

It is inaccurate to analyze separately any of the areas on which womanspirit focuses, since one of the strengths of womanspirit is that its many methods interweave and strengthen one another. For instance, beginning a meeting with a circle of hands is at once a meditation, a ritual, and a healing. Some methods, however, do focus more on one area than another, and I discuss here, as examples, two of these areas, meditation and healing.

## Meditation

Meditation is a key force in developing clarity and self-authority, conserving energy, gathering and directing power, and as preventive physical and psychological medicine. Meditation is not mysterious or foreign. It is anything that centers us, allows the exclusively rational mind to rest and the more holistic and intuitive mind to come to the fore. Many of us meditate but do not realize it, believing meditation to be a secret, "spiritual" discipline learned only from a teacher. All of us meditated as children. Artists, scientists, inventors, musicians, and others develop meditative techniques to help them tap their creative and holistic minds.[4] Some of us have developed daily experiences such as taking a bath, running, or daydreaming, into meditation.

Meditating daily, whether through a focusing device such as breathing, visualization, or sound, helps clear away extraneous thoughts, fears, or tensions. The more practical, problem-solving meditations offer specific information and ideas for projects, work, and relationships that might otherwise remain unresolved. Most of these centering and problem-solving meditations take only a few minutes but save much of the energy we waste in over-analysis, unwise decisions, infighting, and splits over ideology and personalities.

The resistance to experiments so effective and presumably unthreatening is astounding. One of the primary fears about meditation, as with spirituality in general, is that people will become so involved in their inner selves that they won't want to, or be able to, act in the world. Like some aspects of both spirituality and politics, meditation has been, on occasion, perverted. But the popularity of meditation, New Age spiritualities and the revival of fundamentalist religions is a reflection of our great hunger for contact with our inner selves. This need will not go away. These spiritualities, however, have about as much relationship to womanspirit as dictatorships, capitalism, and New Left politics have to political feminism. We grew out of them, we have been oppressed by them; they are models for what we do not want. But sometimes we use some of the techniques (e.g., theory and analysis, meditation and yoga) in a new context, with new values and a new purpose.

A technique as simple as spending a few minutes in the beginning of a meeting breathing and holding hands in a circle — an essential part of womanspirit meetings — makes the work go faster and more effectively. The participants leave the circle energized, focus on the work at hand, and communicate with one another on several levels. Disagreements are more easily dealt with, and the united forces of the individuals produce far more creative and powerful ideas and strategies. A concrete electromagnetic energy begins to travel around the circle. This energy is not mysterious: It is the force that is tapped in healing techniques around the world, from acupuncture in China to laying on of hands in Black communities in this country. In a circle of hands, people literally are affected by the collective energy.

The meditative mind, whether using breath awareness, problem-solving, dreams, psychic techniques, the *I Ching*, or the Tarot, is focused. It gives us space to reflect, to let go of counterproductive ego or reactive impulses. It does not avoid questions or criticism but considers them and makes clear and creative choices. Meditation also allows room for the intuitive mind. Rationalizations, doubts, and fears recede so that the more holistic mind can offer its perspective.

Employing meditation along with logic and verbalization is a deeper and more energy-conserving approach to problems than exclusive reliance on the rational mind. Some of the most creative ideas for organizing, teaching, and writing, for example, can come from meditation. Sometimes meditation makes outer communication unnecessary or paves the way for outer communication that would have been ineffective previously. Perhaps someday meditation will be unnecessary. In the meantime, womanspirit uses meditation as a tool — and for its inherent value — for it will help us win the revolution.

A vivid example of the power of this technique is the experience of the Psychic Action Committee of the Conference on Violence Against Women in San Francisco. The conference covered about thirty different areas, ranging from lesbian self-hatred to pornography to child abuse. It attracted a remarkably wide range of ages, classes, races, and backgrounds. The Psychic Action Committee of four women was asked to create two workshops and a ritual for closing the conference. None of us had ever worked together before; some of us had never met; and we all came from different backgrounds and approaches. We had in common only a commitment to integrate our "spiritual" values and tools with our "political" ones.

We began each of our planning meetings by spending a few minutes holding hands in a circle, focusing on our breathing, and doing a relaxation exercise. This helped after a long and hassled day, set aside any thoughts distracting us from the work at hand, and, on a psychic level, helped us break down the barriers between us.

In four meetings, we designed two two-hour workshops for two hundred women and planned a ritual that could direct the energy of a thousand women who had spent a weekend dealing with violence. Both the workshops and the ritual not only accomplished all our purposes but were also achieved through meetings shorter by half and more enjoyable than most of the other planning meetings. Two of the conference coordinators told us how different our meetings were compared with some of the others, which were sometimes hindered by conflict and communication problems.

## Healing

An equally essential tool is healing. It includes not only "curing" someone after she is sick (the main focus of patriarchal medicine), but also preventing illness through attention to cycles, diet, warning signals, self-knowledge, and energy.

Too many of us are helpless in the face of patriarchal medicine. How can we say we are effecting political change when we consistently give up our bodies, our health, and our authority to a male-dominated power structure incapable of healing us no matter how much power we gain within it?

Patriarchal medicine is based on a distrust of the body's own healing powers, and on denial both of our individual healing potential as well as that of nature. It is dominated by an excessive use of surgery and chemicals, and a methodology that separates the body from the mind and emotions and treats each organ separately. Socializing this medicine, having more women doctors, or obtaining more control in hospitals and clinics are not the only solutions to our health problems. We do not need *more* of a medicine that often makes us sicker, disempowers us, relies excessively on chemicals and surgery, and is ignorant of natural healing. While Western medicine has some useful approaches and techniques, most (such as drugs and surgery) are extremely traumatic and should be used only as last resorts, as in Chinese medicine. Preventive medicine, medicinal herbs, laying on of hands, psychic healing and an understanding of the interconnection of emotions, mind, and body provide a far more effective and self-empowering basis for our medicine.

Natural healing relies primarily on the healing powers of the Earth and the entire human being. It is the predominant form of medicine in the world, although it is quickly being threatened in newly industrialized countries by drugs and surgery. Until the Crusades, natural healing was the only form of medicine in the West for tens of thousands of years and has been practiced primarily by women.[5] It still prevails in this country among people with less access to established medicine — such as older and poorer people, and in some rural communities, ethnic groups, and first-world cultures.

Self-empowerment is one of the most dramatic aspects of natural healing. There is incredible power in discovering that expensive and alienating cancer surgery, mechanical abortion, or antibiotic treatment is often unnecessary, and that cure through natural methods both works and regenerates. The discoveries are accompanied by an overwhelming sense of personal and collective victory — knowledge and power not often experienced in the day-to-day struggle against the patriarchy. As each woman goes through the natural healing process, she adds to the growing collective knowledge. And most importantly, we get well rather than sicker.

Bodywork (some versions of which are known as laying on of hands, acupressure, energy work, massage, polarity therapy, *shiatsu*) is an important aspect of natural healing because of its accessibility, universality, effectiveness, and relationship to power. In this country, laying on of hands, familiar to first-world cultures and old-fashioned healers, is now being used by white, middle-class bodyworkers. Bodywork demands a direct knowledge of one's own body energy, sensitivity to another's, and an understanding of the energy that moves through all living things and through the furthest reaches of the universe. It is powerful, but easily tapped.

Vital, equal, and intimate relationships are rare; we can develop more of them. Having shared bodywork, it is much more difficult for us to become alienated, paranoid, or overly competitive with one another, for we have touched souls and power. Because we are much closer on many nonverbal levels, verbal communication is easier, we understand each other much more quickly, and move to yet another level of creativity. For example, a workshop on self-hatred and suicide and cooperation at the 1977 Feminist Forum in San Francisco was so full of pain that women began massaging one another. At that crucial moment, the experience of being touched, soothed, caressed, and cared for did more to heal permanently the self-hatred than any discussion would have. It was an essential first step in breaking down the patriarchal fiction that we are worthless and unlovable.

## CONCLUSION

The womanspirit movement is a necessity, not a luxury. Without it, we are operating with only half our potential tools and power. What we think we want is based on what we think is possible; one of womanspirit's most important functions is to create and implement a feminist vision. We need tools such as meditation, personal mythology, natural healing, dreamwork, study of matriarchal history and mythology, and ritual to reach beyond the possibility laid out for us by the patriarchy. We cannot wait until after the revolution for the new order to rise up, phoenix-like, out of the ashes of the old. We need to lay the groundwork now through lifetimes of hard work in researching, experimenting with, and practicing a new integration of "politics" and "spirituality." We need new ways of healing, self-knowledge, self-power, new ways of being and relating to ourselves, one another, the Earth, and the cosmos. If we neglect them, we will create only a new version of the overly competitive, dualistic, rational, technological patriarchy.

Ultimately, the goals of spirituality and of revolutionary politics are the same: to create a world in which love, equality, freedom, and fulfillment of individual and collective potential is possible. If we unite the two approaches to these common goals, we will experience this fulfillment.

NOTES

1. Space considerations prevent me from describing here our heritage of spiritual and political unity during Paleolithic and Neolithic times and its loss through the patriarchal takeover. For information on this sub-

ject, see Merlin Stone, *When God Was a Woman* (New York: Dial Press, 1976); Anne Kent Rush, *Moon, Moon* (New York: Random House/Moon Books, 1976); and Adrienne Rich, *Of Woman Born* (New York: W. W. Norton and Co., 1976), pp. 84–110.

2. See, for example, Sandra Roos, "Roots of Feminine Consciousness in Prehistoric Art" (unpublished manuscript, 1976); Patricia Garfield, "Learned from Senoi Dreamers," *Creative Dreaming* (New York: Ballantine, 1974); John Nance, *Gentle Tasaday: A Stone Age People in the Philippines Rain Forest* (New York: Harcourt Brace Jovanovich, 1977).

3. See, for example, *Madness Network News*, vol. 3, no. 1, April 1975.

4. Patricia Garfield, "Learned from Creative Dreamers," *Creative Dreaming* (New York: Ballantine, 1974).

5. Barbara Ehrenreich and Deirdre English, *Witches, Midwives and Nurses: A History of Women Healers* (Old Westbury, N.Y.: The Feminist Press, 1973).

# Ethics and Justice in Goddess Religion

## Starhawk

The religions of the Great Goddess, which are presently undergoing a rebirth and a re-creation, especially among women, are sometimes accused by those unfamiliar with their philosophy and practices of lacking a conception of justice or a system of ethics. This paper is written to explore and clarify the ethics and morality inherent in a worldview centered on immanent divinity found within nature, human beings, and the world.

Most writers on contemporary Goddess religions, womanspirit, or Witchcraft cite the past to offer a historical basis for the present traditions. I am not going to do that here. Historical points are always arguable, and while the past may serve us with models and myths, we need not look to it to justify the re-emergence of the feminine principle. Whether or not there was a religion of the Great Goddess in prehistoric times, there is one today. Whether or not women ever ruled in matriarchies, women are taking power today. Whether or not contem-

© Starhawk (Miriam Simos), 1979. Starhawk presented the above essay at the annual meeting of the American Academy of Religion, New York, 15–18 Nov. 1979; reprinted by permission of the author.

porary Witchcraft has its roots in the Stone Age, its branches reach into the future.

And it is with the future that any system of ethics and justice must be concerned, because the ethics of the unarguable, historical, well-documented, and patriarchal religions and cultures have brought us to a point at which our chances of destroying ourselves and poisoning the biosphere seem much greater than our chances of preserving life into the future. Never before have we as a species had the potential for causing such widespread social, biological, and irreversible destruction, yet never before have we had such potential for the alleviation of poverty, hunger, disease, and social injustice, and for the fostering of individual freedom, growth, and creativity. The choices we must make, although they are rarely posed in these terms, are essentially ethical choices.

The conceptions of justice in the Western, patriarchal religions are based on a worldview which locates deity outside the world. Of course, within each tradition there are exceptions, but in the broad view of Christianity, Judaism, and Islam, God is transcendent, and His laws are absolutes, which can be considered in a context removed both from the reality of human needs and desires and the reality of their actual effects. They are the laws of heaven — and must be followed whatever their consequences on Earth. So, as I write this paper, the newspaper greets me with headlines stating that the Pope has reiterated the ban on birth control. I doubt if any Catholic, in good conscience, would hold that God wants to doom the poor to inescapable hunger and poverty. Yet such is the effect of this absolute morality. Because when we believe that what is sacred — and, therefore, most highly valued — is *not* what we see and sense and experience, we maintain an inherent split in consciousness that allows us to quite comfortably cause pain and suffering in pursuit of an unmanifest good.

The major difference between patriarchal religions and the evolving Goddess religions — perhaps even more central than the image of the divine as female — is the worldview that includes regarding divinity as immanent: in the world, not outside the world, as manifest in nature and in human beings, human needs and desires.

In such a system, justice is not based on an external Absolute who imposes a set of laws upon chaotic nature, but on recognition of the ordering principles inherent in nature. The law is the natural law. We break it at our peril, not because we fear hellfire or damnation or a Day of Judgment after the end of the world, but because its consequences are also inherent in the structure of the world. So, if I "break" the law of gravity by jumping out of a third-story window, I may break my neck in consequence, not because the Goddess is punishing me for my effrontery, but because that is the way the law of gravity works. So, if we continue to spray our forests with mutagenic chemicals that leach into local water supplies, we will continue to see increases in miscarriages and birth defects. If we continue unsafe storage of nuclear wastes, rates of cancer will continue to rise. That is the way it works.

The Goddess is manifest not just in human life, but in the interwoven chain of relationships that link all forms of life. We are not given dominion over the birds of the air and the fish of the sea; rather, human life is recognized as part of the animal world. We are conscious, but consciousness itself is *of* nature, not separate from nature. And we do not have the right to damage or destroy other species in order to further purely human aims. Witches, of course, are not Jains, nor are most of us vegetarians. The Goddess in Her aspect as the Crone or Reaper and the God in His aspect of the Hunter embody the principle that all of life feeds on other life. Death sustains life. But the hunt, the harvest, the reaping of herbs — or of profits — must be practiced with respect for the balance of life and its continuation in the greatest possible richness and diversity of forms. The herds are culled, not obliterated. When herbs are cut, only a few are taken from each separate clump, so that they may grow back in future years. Human communities limit their numbers to what the land can support without straining its resources or displacing other species. We do not, for example, have the ethical right to destroy a species — even the lowly snail darter — in order to build a dam, regardless of how much money has already been invested in the project. When we consider ourselves as a true part of the fabric of life, then each time we irrevocably destroy an aspect of life we have destroyed an aspect of ourselves.

Diversity is highly valued — as it is in nature — in a polytheistic worldview which allows for many powers, many images of divinity. In ecological systems, the greater the diversity of a community, the greater is its power of resilience, of adaptation in the face of change, and the greater the chances for survival of its elements.

Diversity is also valued in human endeavors and creations. Ethics are concerned with fostering diversity rather than sameness, and they are not concerned with enforcing a dogma or a party line. Individual conscience — itself a manifestation of the Goddess — is the final court of appeals, above codified laws or hierarchical proclamations.

Such a statement makes many people uneasy. If ethics are based on the individual's sense of right and wrong, then don't we open ourselves to the horrors of a Hitler, to crime, anarchy, and blind selfishness? Yes, if the individual self is seen out of context. But in Goddess religion, the individual self is never seen as a separate, isolated *object*: It is a nexus of interwoven relationships, an integral and inseparable part of the human and biological community. The Goddess is manifest in the self — but also in every other human self, and the biological world. We cannot honor and serve the Goddess in ourselves unless we honor and serve Her in others.

In Witchcraft, the coven structure fosters the dynamic balance between the individual self and the interrelated community that is necessary for true personal responsibility to develop. A coven, the congregation of the Craft, is a small group, not more than thirteen in membership. Coveners participate in rituals together and develop an intimate bond of trust and support. Because the group is small, each individual personality stands out and affects its direction. Yet within the group there is community; it becomes a laboratory in which we experience the divine in others, in diverse and usually strong-willed individuals rather than as an abstract glow of appreciation for humanity in the mass.

Each individual self, then, is linked by ties of blood and affection to a family, and by the bonds of love and trust to the coven, which in turn is a part of the larger human community, the culture and society in which it is found, and that culture is part of the biological/geological community of Planet Earth and the cosmos beyond, the dance of being which we call Goddess.

Inherent in Goddess religion, then, is an ethical imperative to work toward relationships and communities that serve the Goddess manifest: the interplay of diversity and richness of life in its fullest expression. No one can live out the fullness of self when she is hungry or condemned to a life of poverty and discrimination, when as woman her roles are circumscribed and she is not free to be strong, creative, to control her own body and her own sexuality, to be a leader, and to be in touch with her internal power; when the color of her skin limits her freedom and opportunities; when her life is overshadowed by the fear of war or the threat of ecological disaster. Whenever the Goddess is diminished, self is diminished; and given the conditions of our society, a commitment to the Goddess carries with it an inherent demand to work for social change. Regardless of how fortunate and privileged we as individuals are, regardless of how many growth seminars we attend, how often we meditate, how many miles we jog each day, or how often we meet with our coven and perform the rituals of the changing seasons, we cannot fulfill ourselves in a world of starvation, pollution, and hopelessness. As Witches, the rituals we perform reinforce that identification of self with Larger-Myriad-Self, so that it becomes not an intellectual affirmation but a deep, constant psychological state. They do not offer an escape from the world of suffering, but a source of healing and energy we can use to heal the wounds of the world. And their mood — in spite of the suffering we recognize — remains one of joy and wonder, of celebration of life.

Because divinity is manifest in human beings, our needs and desires are not seen as evil or negative, but as sacred evidences of the life-force. Witchcraft is not a religion of self-abnegation. We celebrate our hunger, our creativity, our successes in the world, and our sexuality.

Sexuality is sacred not just because it is the means of procreation, but because it is a power which infuses life with vitality and pleasure, because it is the numinous means of deep connection with another human being, and with the Goddess. Witches value diversity in sexual expressions and orientations, recognizing that different people have very different needs and capacities. Sexual ethics are based on honest recognition of one's own impulses and desires and honoring one's true feelings rather than either repressing them or feigning a level of desire which does not exist.

Force or coercion of any sort, however, is extremely unethical. Sexuality is sacred because through it we make a connection with another self — but it is misused and perverted when it becomes a means of treating another as an object, or treating oneself as an object, or attaining power *over* another. Sex is not an obsession, it is the moving energy of the Goddess wherever it is honored and recognized with honesty — in simple erotic passion, in the unfathomable mystery of falling in love, in the committed relationship of marriage, in periods of abstinence and chastity, or in its infinite other appearances which we will leave to the reader's imagination.

Coercion, however, is often more subtle than physical rape or overt economic pressure. It includes psychological pressures which influence people to ignore their needs or repress their impulses, political pressures to focus one's sexual drives in "acceptable" orientations, and social pressures. By these standards, the attitudes promulgated by most of the "major" religions are extremely coercive and immoral. When the indi-

vidual self and will are considered sacred, no one has the right to interfere with another's exercise of free choice or control of energy, mind, or
body.

The issue that comes to mind here is abortion. While the so-called
"right-to-life" movement tries to pose this question as one involving the
rights of fetuses, Goddess religion recognizes that to value life as an un-
tempered absolute is ridiculous — it is to maintain the right of every
cancer cell to reproduce blindly, of every sperm and every egg to unite
a new embryo, of every flea and cockroach to populate the world endlessly. Life is interwoven in a dance of death, the limiting factor that
sustains the possibility of new life. The predator is as necessary to an
ecological balance as the prey — because it is the richness and diversity
of the interplay between species that manifests the Goddess.

Human life is valuable and sacred when it is the freely given gift of
the Mother — through the human mother. To bear new life is a grave
responsibility, requiring a deep commitment — one which no one can
force on another. To coerce a woman by force or fear or guilt or law or
economic pressure to bear an unwanted child is the height of immorality. It denies her right to exercise her own sacred will and conscience,
robs her of her humanity, and dishonors the Goddess manifest in her
being. The concern of the anti-abortion forces is not truly with the preservation of life, it is with punishment for sexuality. If they were genuinely concerned with life, they would be protesting the spraying of our
forests and fields with pesticides known to cause birth defects. They
would be working to shut down nuclear power plants and dismantle
nuclear weapons, to avert the threat of widespread genetic damage
which may plague *wanted* children for generations to come — if there
are generations to come.

"All acts of love and pleasure are my rituals" is a saying from the
Goddess, and in Her religions sharing love and pleasure with each
other are considered among the best things human beings can do with
our time here. An ethical society would encourage all that allows that
expression to be most honest, all that makes us free to listen to our own
deep desires.

Justice, then, in Goddess religion operates in the world as it is inherent in the world and the ecological balance of the biosphere. Consequences may not be distributed fairly on an individual level: It is not
the owner of the chemical company who will give birth to a defective
child, nor are we comforted by the belief that he will burn eternally in
an afterlife. Consequences are suffered collectively, because it is our

collective responsibility as a society to change those practices that destroy the lives of individuals and the interplay of life-forms around us. No external God, Goddess, angel, or convoy of visitors from another planet will do this for us: *We* must create justice and ecological and social balance; this is the prime concern, the bottom line, the nitty gritty of ethics in a worldview that sees deity as immanent in human life and the world we live in.

Life, being sacred, demands our full participation. The ethical person engages in life and does not withdraw from it. Our ideal is not monastic seclusion or asceticism, but the fully human life lived in the world, involved in community. To be human is, by definition, to be imperfect, and Goddess religion holds out no superhuman standard of perfection which we are expected to emulate and at which attempt we inevitably fail. One acts ethically not out of a sense of guilt or self-hate brought on by constant failure, but out of pride: honor of the divine within.

Life demands honesty, the ability to face, admit, and express oneself. It demands integrity — being integrated, having brought together and recognized our conflicting internal forces, and being integrated into a larger community of selves and life-forms. Life demands courage and vulnerability, because without them there can be no openness and no connection; and it requires responsibility and discipline, to make choices and face the consequences, to carry out what we undertake. And, finally, life demands love, because it is through love, of self and of others, erotic love, transforming love, affectionate love, delighted love for the myriad forms of life evolving and changing, for the redwood and the mayfly, for the blue whale and the snail darter, for wind and sun and the waxing and waning moon, caring love for the Cambodian child and the restless ghetto teenager, love of all the eternally self-creating world, love of the light and the mysterious darkness, and raging love against all that would diminish the unspeakable beauty of the world, that we connect with the Goddess within and without.

Yet Witches, like everyone today, face life in a society that makes ethical actions difficult and a purely ethical life impossible. We all, by participation in the life of our culture, participate in exploitation, destruction, and pollution. It is a conflict with no easy resolution. Some Witches have removed themselves from the city, not to withdraw from the world but to explore the possibilities of creating new communities. Most of us, however, continue to drive our cars, run our electric type-writers, buy coffee, and eat bananas, while recycling our garbage sporadically, if at all.

If I have a personal guiding principle, it derives from my friend Mary, who used to go with her small son out to open land north of Los Angeles where they could walk under live oaks and play in the stream that ran down from the coastal foothills. A rough, beer-drinking crowd frequented the area and left the stream littered with cans and trash. Mary always brought some large bags with her, and when they were leaving she and her little boy would fill them with beer cans. It was a discouraging task, as the supply was so vast that their efforts barely seemed to make a difference. I asked her once why she bothered to try. "I know I can't clean it all up," she said, "but I believe in picking up the garbage that you find in your path."

Each of us must determine for ourselves what path is ours and where it takes us; the garbage is not hard to recognize. And that is what I would like to offer as an ethical guide for a modern age.

# Applications of Spirituality as a Political Force

I will no longer lightly walk behind
a one of you who fear me:
                            Be afraid.
I plan to give you reasons for your jumpy fits
and facial tics
I will not walk politely on the pavements anymore
and this is dedicated in particular
to those who hear my footsteps
or the insubstantial rattling of my grocery
cart
then turn around
see me
and hurry on
away from this impressive terror I must be:
I plan to blossom bloody on an afternoon
surrounded by my comrades singing
terrible revenge in merciless
accelerating
rhythms . . .

I must become the action of my fate.

— JUNE JORDAN

# Applications of Spirituality as a Political Force

*Putting into practice the theory expressed in the previous section, we conceive and structure our political actions in ways that reflect and nourish our elemental power. The more we explore and acknowledge our true nature, the more effectively we can dispel the patriarchal lies about women and the injustices that those lies support. We are also exposing the patriarchal rationale behind ravaging the Earth and poisoning the biosphere.*

*The strategies and actions in these articles cover a wide range of options for political activism. There is no one "correct" way to approach all the issues, but all of the actions—from the Sixties' tactics of confrontation employed by WITCH to the Eighties' tactics of convincingly presenting sane, humane alternatives to patriarchal barbarism—have in common the informing principle of acknowledging the power of mind, i.e., the spiritual impulses that underlie concern for life on Earth. "Purely political" movements that have denied the existence or importance of such impulses have discovered that no amount of rhetoric alone can sustain long-term political struggle. (Of course, some of the more successful political movements that are outspokenly "anti-religious" have built a great deal of their philosophy around an idealism and a code of unselfishness and oneness that is clearly spiritual.)*

Spirituality is a sustaining force in our politics not only because it affirms our true nature but also because it helps us channel energy — the power within us that we were conditioned not to acknowledge — toward political goals. Most of those goals are not easily attainable. The opposition grows increasingly intense, and the struggle sometimes seems almost overwhelming. While admitting the uphill, fatiguing nature of our political work, Gloria Steinem observed to Ms. readers in 1980, "Fantasies seem to bolster our psychic strength." Indeed. This is why women participating in demonstrations against pornography, harassment of homosexuals, nuclear madness, etc., are urged to envision our world without those atrocities. Will it. We consider it absolutely essential to birth the new way of being in our hearts and minds, as we actively oppose the present system.

> Seize structure.
> Correspond with the real.
> Fuse spirit and matter.
> Know your own secrets.

> — MURIEL RUKEYSER

Feminist activism is responding to a basic conflict between truth and ignorance. The existence of patriarchy depends on their keeping people, including feminists, ignorant of other options for being, e.g., pretending that patriarchal religion represents the only and the natural way to relate to self, others, and nature. We defiantly unravel their falsehoods, and we weave new possibilities with the female wisdom that we have always carried within us.

C.S.

# WITCH: Spooking the Patriarchy during the Late Sixties

WITCH was born on Halloween 1968, in New York, but within a few weeks covens had sprung up in such diverse spots as Boston, Chicago, San Francisco, North Carolina, Portland (Oregon), Austin (Texas), and Tokyo (Japan). A certain common style — insouciance, theatricality, humor, and activism, unite the covens — which are otherwise totally autonomous, and unhierarchical to the point of anarchy.

Nor will any of their leaflets or statements elaborate on what that means.

Washington, D.C., WITCH — after an action hexing the United Fruit Company's oppressive policy on the Third World *and* on secretaries in its offices at home ("Bananas and rifles, sugar and death/War for profit, tarantulas' breath/United Fruit makes lots of loot/The CIA is in its boot") — claimed that WITCH was "a total concept of revolu-

---

tionary female identity" and was the striking arm of the Women's Liberation Movement, aiming mainly at financial and corporate America, at those institutions that have the power to control and define human life.

Chicago WITCH covens showered the Sociology Department at the University of Chicago with hair cuttings and nail clippings after the firing of a radical feminist woman professor, and the Chicago Witches also demonstrated against a transit fare hike. They, as well as Witches in New York, San Francisco, North Dakota, and New England, disrupted local Bridal Fairs. The fluidity and wit of the Witches is evident in the ever-changing acronym: the basic, original title was Women's International Terrorist Conspiracy from Hell, but on Mother's Day one coven became Women Infuriated at Taking Care of Hoodlums; another group, working at a major Eastern insurance corporation, became Women Indentured to Traveler's Corporate Hell; still another set of infiltrators, working at Bell Telephone, manifested themselves disruptively as Women Incensed at Telephone Company Harassment. When hexing inflationary prices at supermarkets, a Midwest coven appeared as Women's Independent Taxpayers, Consumers, and Homemakers; Women Interested in Toppling Consumption Holidays was another transfigutory appellation — and the latest heard at this writing is Women Inspired to Commit Herstory.

> Rebellion is as the sin of witchcraft
> — SAMUEL, I, 15:23

## NEW YORK COVENS

WITCH is an all-women Everything. It's theater, revolution, magic, terror, joy, garlic flowers, spells. It's an awareness that Witches and gypsies were the original guerrillas and resistance fighters against oppression — particularly the oppression of women — down through the ages. Witches have always been women who dared to be: groovy, courageous, aggressive, intelligent, nonconformist, explorative, curious, independent, sexually liberated, revolutionary. (This possibly explains why nine million of them have been burned.) Witches were the first Friendly Heads and Dealers, the first birth-control practitioners and abortionists, the first alchemists (turn dross into gold and you devalue the whole idea of money!). They bowed to no man, being the living remnants of the oldest culture of all — one in which men and women were equal sharers in a truly cooperative society, before the death-dealing sexual, economic, and spiritual repression of the Imperialist Phallic Society took over and began to destroy nature and human society.

WITCH lives and laughs in every woman. She is the free part of each of us, beneath the shy smiles, the acquiescence to absurd male domination, the make-up or flesh-suffocating clothing our sick society demands. There is no "joining" WITCH. If you are a woman and dare to look within yourself, you are a Witch. You make your own rules. You are free and beautiful. You can be invisible or evident in how you choose to make your Witch-self known. You can form your own coven of sister Witches (thirteen is a cozy number for a group) and do your own actions.

Whatever is repressive, solely male-oriented, greedy, puritanical, authoritarian — those are your targets. Your weapons are theater, satire, explosions, magic, herbs, music, costumes, cameras, masks, chants, stickers, stencils and paint, films, tambourines, bricks, brooms, guns, voodoo dolls, cats, candles, bells, chalk, nail clippings, hand grenades, poison rings, fuses, tape recorders, incense — your own boundless, beautiful imagination. Your power comes from your own self as a woman, and it is activated by working in concert with your sisters. The power of the coven is more than the sum of its individual members, because it is *together*.

You are pledged to free our brothers from oppression and stereotyped sexual roles (whether they like it or not) as well as ourselves. You are a Witch by saying aloud, "I am a Witch" three times, and *thinking about that*. You are a Witch by being female, untamed, angry, joyous, and immortal.

# On Common Ground: Native American and Feminist Spirituality Approaches in the Struggle to Save Mother Earth

## Judith Todd

Until the seventeenth century, Europeans commonly regarded the Earth as a living, female being. This concept tended to restrain activities that would abuse the Earth, such as mining. But one variant of this view saw the Earth, like women, as benevolent, passive, and subject to man's dominion. When patriarchal society came to depend on metals, this perversion of the ancient reverence for Mother Earth allowed Her rape in the form of mining and squandering of natural resources to support burgeoning industrialization, first in Europe and then in North America. By contrast, Native Americans knew that nature is primarily benevolent, but not passive. She is sacred and powerful and must be treated with respect and love. Both Native Americans and proponents of feminist spirituality understand that if Mother Earth is not regarded with reverence, the balance and harmony of nature is destroyed, and human life eventually will be destroyed also.

## KNOWLEDGE OF THE LIVING MOTHER EARTH

The dualistic and hierarchical elements in today's mechanistic worldview are derived from Greek and Judeo-Christian roots. A certain proclamation in the Old Testament may have had more far-reaching effects than any other statement in Western patriarchal history: "Man shall have dominion over the Earth and all the creatures of the Earth." Other writings of the Old and New Testaments imply separation and duality between spirit and matter, man and woman, heaven and Earth. These dualities are not equally valued polarities in dynamic tension; rather, one half of the duality is clearly valued above the other according to this hierarchy: God-Jesus-men-women-children-animals-plants-Earth.[1] The spectrum of good (orderliness) and evil (chaos) fits easily onto this hierarchy, with God, of course, at the good end, leaving women more closely associated with the Earth, nature, and disorder, the evil end. The normative implications of this scheme for human actions are clear. Man, being closer to God and orderliness, shall have dominion over women, children, and the Earth so as to impose order on their inherently chaotic (evil) natures. This view of the Earth later facilitated the European patriarchal assault on the untamed New World.

The harsh Judeo-Christian attitude toward the Earth was ameliorated through the centuries by contact with the surviving Pagan view of nature as beautiful, bountiful, and whole. The resulting blend took various forms. Carolyn Merchant, a historian of science, has demonstrated that some versions of the view of the Earth as a living female being served to prevent mining and misuse of natural resources.[2] However, a dominant version in the sixteenth century, the pastoral view, regarded nature as *passively* female, which implied that man could manage Mother Earth, use Her as a commodity, and manipulate Her as a resource. Merchant explains the implications of this view for urbanized, sixteenth-century Europe:

Nature, tamed and subdued, could be transformed into a garden to provide both material and spiritual food to enhance the comfort and sooth the anxieties of men distraught by the demands of the urban world and the stresses of the marketplace. It depended on a masculine perception of nature as a mother and bride whose primary function was to comfort, nurture, and provide for the well-being of the male. In pastoral imagery, both nature and women are subordinate and essentially passive. They nurture but do not control or exhibit disruptive passion.[3]

The pastoral view of the living Mother Earth also actively contributed to the way in which the New World was settled and "civilized." New World explorers sent back descriptions of this lush, new territory, enticing settlers to partake of the bounties of the vast, "virgin" land. Traders came to kill game and sell pelts in Europe. Metals such as copper, silver, and gold also lured newcomers to America. The analogy between mining Mother Earth's body and sexual intercourse with a woman was made commonly during the sixteenth and seventeenth centuries. Merchant cites John Donne's Elegie XIX, "Going to Bed," which describes man's attitude toward the new American sources of minable wealth:

> License my roaving hands, and let them go,
> Before, behind, between, above, below.
> O my America! my new-found-land,
> My Kingdome, safelist when with one man man'd
> My Myne of precious stones, My Emperie,
> How blest am I in this discovering thee![4]

One can imagine the same exuberance being expressed today by discoverers of coal or uranium in the American Southwest.

The pastoral tradition, along with the original Judeo-Christian attitude toward the Earth, provided fertile ground for the new ideas of Francis Bacon in the seventeenth century. Bacon advocated that nature be dissected and probed by man's instruments until She reveal Her secrets so that they could be used to serve mankind's purposes. Bacon was well aware of the interrogation and torture of Witches, and he used language calling up images of the Witch hunts to expound the ideology of the new science. Merchant, quoting from a number of Bacon's works, describes the methods Bacon advocated:

The new man of science must not think that the "inquisition of nature is in any part interdicted or forbidden." Nature must be "bound into service" and made a "slave," put "in constraint" and "molded" by the mechanical arts. The "searchers and spies of nature" are to discover her plots and secrets.[5]

Here the view of nature as a living female being does not tend to restrain Her mistreatment but, because of the prevailing fear and hatred of women as Witches, the female connection with the Earth actually sanctions Her abuse in the form of scientific manipulation and economic exploitation.

René Descartes and other Frenchmen writing in the 1620s and 1630s ushered in the next critical phase of the Scientific Revolution, which marked what Merchant terms the death of nature. Déscartes dropped the organic imagery and depicted nature and human bodies in mechanical terms. All of nature, in the mechanistic worldview, is composed of interchangeable, inert atoms. The view of the Earth as a clump of inanimate matter, a mere cog in the machine of the universe, provides no sanctions against digging in the "dead" Earth crust or exploiting natural resources, so the mechanistic worldview made manipulation the order of day and culminated in today's ravaged Earth.

As we have seen, knowing that Mother Earth is a living being rather than a large clump of inanimate matter is not sufficient to prevent abusing Her resources. Nor will the abdication of man's position of "dominion over the Earth" insure the proper regard for nature. I believe we should beware of contemporaries who proclaim themselves "stewards" of the Earth. Granted, a farmer or rancher who considers himself to be the steward of the land he "owns" and who refrains from using chemicals or overtaxing it is much preferable to one who strains the land for all the produce possible and dumps insecticides into it, but the line between stewardship and dominion can be exceedingly fine, depending on the rest of the person's worldview. Many Christian theologians have explained recently that the concept of unbridled dominion over nature was an error in interpretation and that everything will be fine now that "responsible stewardship" is being stressed instead. Feminists are skeptical of this shift because the very notion of stewardship requires separation and dominion of the stewards over the stewarded.[6] If the land is seen as inanimate or as inherently passive, then what is to stop a "practical minded" steward from convincing himself that chemical insecticides or "low-level" radioactive contamination are not the best course?

What is best for the land may be just leaving it alone. But inherent in the concept of stewardship is the idea that the land somehow *needs* to be stewarded; simply leaving it alone, unmanaged, unmeasured, is not considered. In speaking of foresters, for instance, Peter Matthiessen has observed that they share with big lumbermen a kind of ". . . 'management' mentality that tends to abhor the concept of unmanaged wilderness."[7] In contrast, Matthiessen reports that Calvin Rube, a Yurok leader, objects to designating Yurok sacred land as "wilderness." That land, in Rube's view, is not "wild" but ". . . 'natural,' complete, a perfect place . . . full of strength and beauty. . . ."[8] In the traditional Yurok view, then, the land can be left alone. To call something "wild" implies that it needs taming. Similarly, to call oneself a steward — rather than just a creature — of Mother Earth implies that the Earth lacks sufficient wisdom to function independently of human management.[9]

## PHILOSOPHY AND FORMS

There is another worldview. It contrasts substantially with the mechanistic worldview, the pastoral view of nature, and even with the attitude of neo-stewardship toward the Earth. This worldview is *in essence* common to prehistoric Native Americans, contemporary traditional Native Americans, European adherents of the (prepatriarchal) "Old Religion," and contemporary weavers of feminist spirituality — or womanspirit. I emphasize that what is common to all four views is their essence, i.e., their basic metaphysical assumptions, not the various expressions, which differ even within each group (e.g., among the many Native American tribes). According to this worldview, Mother Earth is active, alive, sacred, and to be treated with respect, not to be used up or manipulated to satisfy human greed. In the pantheons of both prepatriarchal Europeans and Native American groups, goddesses are at least as numerous, powerful, and important as gods. Father Sun represents a male deity in balance with Mother Earth, but there is no omniscient, invisible, heavenly Father God, separate from and superior to the Earth and Her creatures. There is the Great Spirit, or All That Is, no more male than female, Who participates in the existence of all things in nature. Time (to the extent there is a concept of time at all)[10] is cyclic, not linear; events unfold, develop, intermingle, and repeat in different forms, rather than occurring in a linear sequence. All things are interrelated, and change in one entity ultimately affects all others, however spatially distant.

The interrelatedness of all things in a living, organic universe implies the need for humans to be sensitive to the rest of the natural world in order to maintain its harmony. Our mechanistic legacy insists that objects in the world can be affected only by movement of other external objects. By contrast, the traditional Native American/womanspirit worldview sees that human thoughts, will, and emotions also affect things and events. Hence there is plenty of room in this view for what patriarchal science calls "para"-psychology or the "super"-natural. There is, of course, no supernature. There is only nature — and our minds, thoughts, and wills are part of it. The Hopi and other tribes emphasize the importance of being happy and having positive thoughts; by doing so, one keeps one's mind in harmony with nature.

For tens of thousands of years before Europeans arrived, many Native American tribes lived on this continent in tune with the cycles of nature without wasting precious resources. In some 450 years, the pastoral and mechanistic worldviews brought by the newcomers have licensed squandering Mother Earth's resources so that we now think we have a shortage of electrical power and gasoline to power our machines. There is no shortage of power in that sense; conservation and use of appropriate technology can sustain us. The shortage is of spiritual power, which was lost to European cultures during the patriarchal onslaught that later all but destroyed Native American cultures.

Indeed, the main difference between Native American spirituality and Europe's Old Religion is the amount of time it took for the patriarchy to nearly destroy it. The Old Religion was crushed throughout Europe by burning Witches; burning libraries; forbidding people to congregate at streams, hills, or other sacred sites; building churches on top of ancient sacred stone circles, hills, or other Pagan shrines; and generally intimidating people into conforming to the patriarchal view of the world. Women bore the brunt of this attack. Some nine million women were burned to death or otherwise killed.[11] The records reveal that in several villages only one woman was left alive.[12] But men, too, were killed for practicing the Old Religion, or just for being effeminate.

In the New World the process was similar. Native American religious practices were forbidden on pain of imprisonment, torture, or death. People were whipped to death or doused with kerosene and burned for practicing their native religion. Even after the various Native American groups were safely contained on separate reservations, religious persecution continued. Children were forcibly kidnapped, sent to white boarding schools, and forbidden to practice their traditional spiritual ways.

The white patriarchy was intent on squelching Native American spirituality for two reasons. They realized that the Native peoples' strength, their social integrity, depended on their spiritual worldview. The Native Americans would not become part of the great American "melting pot" as long as they were tribally cohesive. Perhaps more importantly, it was difficult to deal with them about rights to land use as long as they felt themselves to be part of a tribe with ancient historical roots, rather than merely independent individuals.

The second reason the patriarchy wanted to destroy Native American spirituality is the same as their reason for destroying the Old Religion: They feared it. That fear was the legacy of patriarchal Europe. First, Native American spirituality recognized phenomena — such as the ability to communicate with natural forces psychically — that the materialist, mechanistic worldview denied existed. To be faced with such beliefs again was unnerving; they had to be eradicated. Second, Native American spirituality, like prehistoric Paganism, embodied a reverence for Mother Earth that was not at all consistent with the march of industrialization and capitalistic progress.

This latter factor is particularly relevant to today's patriarchal blitz of nature. The march of capitalism and colonialism once depended heavily on metals and mining. John C. Mohawk has outlined Western civilization's progression from the ancient agrarian period through more modern times and the role of metals in this process.[13] Once kilns that could melt metal were developed, metal was useful in making weapons. When the local supplies of tin, copper, and iron were used up, these metals had to be obtained from sources outside the area. Trade routes were developed to supply the metalworkers and, in turn, the trade routes needed military protection to ensure the transport of metals. It then became profitable to colonize other lands to get the raw materials, since owning one's own mine is both easier and more dependable than trading.

Eventually, European colonization spread to the Americas and followed the lure of metals buried within the "virgin" lands.[14] By that time, the Old Religion with its spiritual awareness of the sanctity of the living Mother Earth had been rather thoroughly destroyed; natural human feelings of connectedness with the Earth had been suppressed so that no European remnant of a spiritual worldview stood in the way of industrialization and capitalistic exploitation. But here, in the hearts and minds of the Native American peoples, was that same loathsome Earth-reverence again. It had to be contained and, hopefully, destroyed lest it resonate with the white population, remind them of their own ancient, prepatriarchal spiritual heritage, and prompt their consciences to check the progress of patriarchal "civilization." As I shall discuss later, the patriarchy's fear of Native American spirituality's power to do these things was not unfounded.

## SOME CURRENT ENVIRONMENTAL ISSUES

It is ironic, and surely no coincidence, that even though Native Americans now own just 2.3 percent of this land, that 2.3 percent contains a staggering proportion of the known energy resources within U.S. boundaries: thirty percent of the oil; thirty percent of the strippable coal; a significant proportion of natural gas, timber, and geothermal energy; and about sixty-five percent of the available uranium.[15] Multinational corporations, such as Gulf Oil and Exxon, want control over those resources for the sake of their profits, while the federal government wants dominion over those resources to service its war machine. Clearly, then, the pressure is intense on the remaining traditional Native Americans to give up their land.

In these days of "energy shortages" and governmental policies to produce synthetic fuels, coal mining is increasingly important. While thirty percent of the strippable coal in this country is on Native American land, most of it lies within the San Juan Basin in the Southwest.[16] This ancient homeland of the Hopi people includes Black Mesa, which contains twenty-three billion tons of coal. According to ancient Hopi prophecies, strangers will come to take what is under their land. The Hopi are warned that the intruders must not be allowed to take it.

The precious subterranean substance referred to in the prophecies could be the vast amounts of coal. There are also underground water tables which are being depleted by one power plant alone at the rate of twenty-four hundred gallons/minute.[17] Uranium — one-sixth of the world's supply — also lies underground in the San Juan Basin. Uranium mining in that area has already resulted in the accumulation of fifty-six million tons of uranium "tailings" (milling waste products) on Navajo lands.[18] Many huge piles of tailings, which retain about eighty percent of their original radioactivity, are not even fenced off, and children play on them. Not surprisingly, more than one hundred babies born recently in the Laguna Pueblo, site of the world's largest uranium strip mine, have suffered birth defects.[19]

Because of its vast reserves of coal and uranium, the San Juan Basin has been designated a "national sacrifice area" by the National Academy of Sciences. It has also been suggested that the Black Hills of South Dakota be so designated because of their large stores of uranium. Uranium exploration, which drains and contaminates the underground water tables, is already under way there. The rate of birth defects on the Pine Ridge Reservation is at least three times the national aver-age.[20] In one month in 1979, thirty-eight percent of the pregnant women on that reservation suffered spontaneous abortion; sixty to sev-enty percent of the currently newborn babies at Pine Ridge suffer breathing difficulties due to jaundice or undeveloped lungs.[21] These tragedies have occurred even before the mining is expanded to a large-scale operation, and the traditional Lakota people intend to prevent it. In the words of a Lakota spokesperson, Russell Means, his people's prophecies indicate, ". . . once the Black Hills are lost to us — even on paper — we are lost as a people."[22]

## FIGHTING NUCLEAR MADNESS

If there is such a thing as "the most urgent" of all urgent ecological issues, it would be uranium mining and nuclear power and weapons. This issue is a common focus for Native American and womanspirit po-litical efforts.

At anti-nuclear demonstrations, Native American speakers and drums inspire feelings of determination and solidarity in the demon-strators. The Native American presence reminds us of the spiritual her-itage of this land and of the whole history of the white patriarchy's decimation of the land and native peoples. The courageous stance of traditional Native Americans, in spite of 450 years of brutal oppression, inspires hope that we *can* survive the awesome powers of the multina-tionals and the U.S. government. Winona La Duke, a founder of Women of All Red Nations (WARN), has expressed the feelings of many Native American women about the battle over uranium mining and related issues: ". . . we view ourselves as an integral part, almost a representation, of the Earth. The Earth is our mother — a woman. As women are exploited, so is our mother. And we must fight both battles simultaneously."[23]

Feelings of solidarity with the Native American struggle to protect Mother Earth from mining interests are felt very strongly by a Santa Fe feminist group called Women for Survival. According to Mishwa, a spokesperson, working as women in the Southwest for the Earth's sur-vival means working with Native Americans, those who live closest to the Earth.[24] Hence, a primary function of Women for Survival is to support political action by Native American people. Women for Sur-vival is a member organization of the Mount Taylor Alliance, a multi-ethnic, multi-cultural group in Albuquerque whose purpose is to preserve traditional culture, land, and water. Their work with the Alliance has included conducting a drive to supply food, blankets, and clothing for Navajo in the Red Rock uranium mining area and providing childcare and other support services at the Dalton Pass spiritual protest against uranium mining in April 1980.

Mishwa notes that Native American spirituality is not separated from political struggle; there is an element of spirituality in everything Native Americans do. For example, in courtroom situations they speak as if in prayer. The presence of Women for Survival in such courtroom situations is purely supportive; they serve as a kind of buffer between this Native spiritual attitude and the white, male court authority.

All the members of Women for Survival agree that womanspirit is important for their political activities. They are evolving their own spirituality and ritual form, learning from all kinds of peoples; elements of their rituals are taken from Wicca, Jewish tradition, and Medicine Circles. "Our spiritual beliefs and practices," says Mishwa, "give us strength to do the physical and emotional parts of political struggle."

On the West Coast in March 1980, members of the San Francisco coven Raving, including Starhawk, author of *The Spiral Dance*, plus many members of the Bay Area Pagan community joined with local groups, including a Marxist spirituality collective, to produce a Three-Mile Island Memorial Parade. The march was a moving ritual/street theater pageant, divided into two sections: images of devastation, past and future victims of the nuclear industry, and the grim future in store if we continue on the nuclear path — then, joyful, positive images of a nuclear-free future, including contingents dressed as the four elements (earth, air, fire, and water) with floats representing sources of renewable power. Information was presented on banners, placards, and in a pamphlet that was handed out *en route*, rather than in boring speeches. Over five thousand people turned out, including survivors of Hiroshima, Native Americans, and veterans of the atomic tests during the Fifties and Sixties. The march culminated in Golden Gate Park in a simple ritual in which an effigy of a nuclear tower was destroyed in a tug-of-war, releasing a flight of balloons and paper doves. The day ended with community picnicking and networking in the park.

During the same month, a three-day conference was held at the University of Massachusetts at Amherst on "Women and Life on Earth: EcoFeminism in the '80s" at which some four hundred women gathered to share information and strategy on issues such as toxic wastes, nuclear power, and appropriate technology. The conference reaffirmed the importance of women's energy in healing the Earth (although, as Elizabeth Dworan insightfully noted in *New Women's Times*, this notion ". . . is considered no less than heresy . . ." by the EPA).[25] Dworan cited Nancy Jack Todd's discussion during the conference of the interconnections between all things in nature: ". . . until we know in a spiritual, poetic, and ethical — as well as a scientific — way, what these connections are, we had better take a giant step backward in the development of all but the most nurturing, renewable, earth-bound technologies."[26] The EcoFeminism conference also affirmed the importance of women's vision in re-establishing a harmonious, healthy environment for future generations.

One expression of that vision is the tremendously powerful Environmental Ritual, which has been led on the West Coast by Chellis Glendinning, a long-time political activist and womanspirit healer. The form of the ritual came to Glendinning in a dream, and the content was influenced by the work of Elisabeth Kübler-Ross and Joanna Rogers Macy. In her work with terminally ill patients, Kübler-Ross identified stages of attitudes which people experience toward their own death: denial, bargaining, anger, depression, and finally acceptance. In order to move from denial through to acceptance, one must express all repressed emotions. Glendinning noted that contemporary American culture as a whole might be said to be in the denial stage regarding our deteriorating ecology. Joanna Rogers Macy facilitates groups that deal with people's feelings about the environment. Macy concluded that the difference between mourning a person's death and confronting one's environmental despair is the outcome: Rather than letting go and saying good-bye, one can find hope and strength for the necessary political activism.[27] Glendinning's Environmental Ritual creates a setting for people to acknowledge the horrifying environmental conditions, express their rage and despair about those conditions, and then transform the released negative energy into a sense of collective and individual power to bring about change. Joanna Rogers Macy is now using the Environmental Ritual in her workshops throughout the country. This ritual is also part of the survival training programs offered by Interhelp, a peace organization, based in northern California, whose purpose is to bring people with divergent political views together around the issue of nuclear disaster. The Interhelp organizers believe that our survival in the future will depend on the unity we have now, and they see the Environmental Ritual as a powerful tool in discovering and strengthening that unity.

## POSITIVE RE-VISIONING

History has exposed the lie that the only way out of our present "energy crisis" is to colonize and gain control over ever more resources. We now see that such an approach is precisely what got us into our present crisis and state of ecological destruction, while nearly annihilating Native American cultures. The energy corporations and the government would have us believe that we have no choice but to continue raping the Earth, that we must hand our fate, and that of Mother Earth, to the interests of the multinationals. That is not our only choice. We can stop the stripmining and uranium mining; employ conservation measures; develop appropriate, non-exploitative technologies; and take responsibility for restoring balance and harmony on the Earth.

Native American and feminist spirituality are among the strongest sources of hope in today's ecological nightmare. They provide inspiration and strength and protect us from political "burn-out." The patriarchy has long feared and attacked Native American spirituality because they recognized it as the backbone of traditional cultures that would not make deals with the government. Centuries earlier in Europe, the patriarchy had feared and attacked the Old Religion because it illuminated the interrelatedness between human life and Mother Earth, thereby getting in the way of industrialization, capitalism, and technological "progress." The worldview held by these two traditions was never completely destroyed on either continent, and its spark is being rekindled today as a powerful force in the current struggle and in providing positive images for future generations.

The importance of positive re-visioning is a theme of feminist spirituality at anti-nuclear events. The patriarchy is doing so many destructive things that we could spend all our energies scurrying around saying "Stop uranium mining," "Stop stripmining," "Stop polluting," "Stop. . . ." These things must be done, but focusing only on the negative invites "burn-out" and simply is not enough. We need to give at least as much energy to envisioning positive alternatives. Obviously we must support conservation, solar power, and appropriate technologies and must speak out continually against nuclear madness. On a more subtle but equally important level, it is imperative that we imagine and think positively about the future, however negative the current information. Optimistic, creative mental attitudes, expressed in individual and collective actions, will actually help bring about the results we envision.

Such positive visioning corresponds with the Hopi attitude toward life in general and their own prophecies in particular. Hopi mythology tells of three previous World Ages, each destroyed by cataclysm after humans replaced their attitude of respect and love of the sacred Earth with selfishness and greed.[28] We now live in the Fourth World and are nearing its end. The Hopi prophecies foretell a time of purification, which will include weather changes, earthquakes, and other natural upheavals, famine, pestilence, civil wars, and possibly international nuclear war.[29] These times have already begun; however, the severity of these purifying events depends on what human beings do, think, and will in the meantime. We still have choices. The choices we make, the mental attitudes we have, and our intentions will determine the extent of the upheavals Mother Earth must bring about in order for purification to occur and the Fifth World Age to begin.

At the end of our current World Age, say the Hopi prophecies, a vast spiderweb will be woven all across this land.[30] Perhaps that spiderweb is the network of powerlines carrying electricity across our continent. Here the Hopi prophecies and Christian mythology ironically intersect, for that huge spiderweb is resting on the arms of millions of crosses. The cross is the Christian symbol of the torture, death, and rebirth of the One who is said to have sacrificed His life for our sins. The cross is also a universal prepatriarchal symbol for the Earth. Only now it is Mother Earth who is tortured, sacrificed, and it is She who will be reborn into the Fifth World, as the Hopi prophecies foretell.

NOTES

1. Sheila D. Collins, *A Different Heaven and Earth* (Valley Forge: Judson Press, 1974), p. 66.
2. Carolyn Merchant, *The Death of Nature: Women, Ecology and the Scientific Revolution* (San Francisco: Harper & Row, 1980), p. 3 *et passim*. My paper necessarily glosses over centuries of history in order to trace general trends in European-derived worldviews. Please see Merchant's book for an excellent detailed discussion of the shift in worldviews from the organic to the mechanistic, and the impact of this shift in perspective on our environment.
3. *Ibid.*, pp. 8–9.
4. *Ibid.*, pp. 40–41.

5. *Ibid.*, p. 169.

6. Charlene Spretnak, radio interview conducted by Linda Parry, WBAI-FM, New York, Dec. 1979.

7. Peter Matthiessen, "Stop the GO Road," *Audubon*, vol. 81, Jan. 1979, p. 59.

8. *Ibid.*, pp. 58–59.

9. To a certain extent, the Earth possesses self-regulating capabilities to adapt to the needs of life systems; scientists who have observed this phenomenon call it "the Gaia hypothesis," their conclusion that the Earth is, indeed, a living entity. See J. E. Lovelock, *Gaia: A New Look at Life on Earth* (Oxford: Oxford University Press, 1979). Lovelock's attitude toward the Earth represents yet another example of the fact that a person can see the Earth as a living being and still not conclude that technological destruction of the environment should be stopped. Indeed, Lovelock, a subscriber to the view of man as Earth's steward, seems more concerned that we not "over-react" (p. 115) by enacting legislation that would hamper technological pursuits. Ironically, he seems to suggest that *because* Gaia is alive, She can handle the pollution, chemical dumping, and even nuclear wars created by Her occasionally misguided human offspring and will go on living no matter what we do. Lovelock's conclusion: not to worry.

10. The Hopi, for example, have no word for time and their verbs are without tense. For a discussion of this aspect of the Hopi language, see Benjamin Lee Whorf, "The Punctual and Segmentative Aspects of Verbs in Hopi" and "An American Indian Model of the Universe" in his *Language, Thought and Reality: Selected Writings of Benjamin Lee Whorf*, edited by John B. Carroll (Cambridge: M.I.T. Press, 1956), pp. 51–64.

11. Andrea Dworkin, *Woman Hating* (New York: E. P. Dutton & Co., Inc., 1974), p. 130. The genocide of people who practiced the Old Religion was a political act. Hence *any* action to reclaim that ancient spirituality is itself a political act.

12. Rosemary Radford Ruether, *New Woman/New Earth: Sexist Ideologies and Human Liberation* (New York: The Seabury Press, 1975), p. 102.

13. John C. Mohawk, untitled position paper, presented at a conference titled "Technology: Over the Line?," the One-Year Project of the Foundation for National Progress, San Francisco, 1980, p. 6 *et passim*.

14. The white patriarchy's use of metal weapons was one of the two reasons it was so successful in destroying Native American spirituality in less than 500 years, while the process took some 4,000 years

in Europe; by the time they got here, metal weapon technology was well developed. The second reason it took longer in the Old World was that they could not simply decimate whole populations of women because they still needed at least a few women for propagation; Native Americans, on the other hand, served no such purpose, so whole villages — even whole tribes — could be wiped out with impunity.

15. Estimates for these figures vary depending on the source: for example, estimates of the percentage of uranium that is owned by Native Americans range from 55% to 90%. I suspect this variation depends, in part, on what the writer includes as "Indian land." The 65% figure I have used here seems a safe compromise and is the one cited by Michael Gardner in "The Archaeological Wonders of Chaco Canyon," *The Sierra Club* Bulletin, Nov./Dec. 1979, p. 10. The source for the statement that Native American land makes up 2.3% of the territory within the U.S. is the U.S. Federal Trade Commission, Bureau of Competition, *Staff Report on Mineral Leasing on Indian Lands* (Washington, D.C.: U.S.G.P.O., 1975), p. 5.

16. Gardner, *op. cit.*, p. 10.

17. Sherman Goldman and Alex Jack, "An Interview with Richard Kastl," *East West*, Dec. 1977, p. 32.

18. San Francisco Bay Area Coalition Against Uranium Mining and the American Indian Movement, *What You Should Know about Resource Development and Native American Nations* (San Francisco, May 1980).

19. *Ibid.*

20. Greenpeace, untitled information pamphlet, 1980.

21. San Francisco Bay Area Coalition Against Uranium Mining and AIM, *op. cit.*

22. American Broadcasting Company, *The Uranium Factor: ABC News Close-Up*, May 1980. Means' statement echoes the attitude of traditional aboriginal people in Australia who are currently faced with the same struggle to save their land from mining interests. (Approximately 15% of the world's uranium is buried on their land.) Wesley Lanhupuy, manager of a legal group representing the Aborigines in their efforts to regain legal title to their traditional lands, says: "The land — without it we are nothing. . . . We would be deceiving the land if we gave it away for money and deceiving our ancestors who passed the land on to us." See Henry Kamm, "Australian Mining Stirs Aborigines' Rancor," *The New York Times*, 19 Oct. 1980. (Also see the text of Means' speech at the Black Hills International Survival Gathering in July 1980, published in *Mother Jones*, Dec. 1980, pp. 22–38. I agree with his eloquent indictment of the ma-

terialist "European mind" if the phrase is amended to "European *patriarchal* mind." The prepatriarchal European worldview was not materialist and was essentially like his own.)

23. Article in *Rain* Magazine, cited in *Ain't Nowhere We Can Run: A Handbook for Women on the Nuclear Mentality*, Susan Koen and Nina Swaim (Norwich, VT: WAND, 1980).

24. I gratefully acknowledge that the information about Women for Survival was obtained primarily from a telephone interview of Mishwa by Chellis Glendinning in San Francisco, 8 Nov. 1980; I am also grateful for correspondence from Carolyn Shaffer, who attended "Native People vs. the Energy Companies: The Rape of the Southwest," a slide show that Mishwa presented at The Women's Building in San Francisco on that date.

25. Elizabeth Dworan, "EcoFeminism: The Next Step," *New Women's Times*, 23 May–5 June 1980, p. 6.

26. *Ibid.*, p. 6.

27. Chellis Glendinning, "A Ritual for Despair," *WomanSpirit*, vol. 6, no. 24, May 1980, pp. 13–14; also in *New Age*, Nov. 1980, pp. 52–53.

28. Frank Waters, *Book of the Hopi, as told by Oswald White Bear Fredericks* (New York: Ballantine, 1963), pp. 3–27.

29. Dan Katchongva, *From the Beginning of Life to the Day of Purification: Teachings, History and Prophesies of the Hopi People, as told by the late Dan Katchongva, Sun Clan* (Los Angeles: Committee for Traditional Indian Land and Life, 1972). If this publication is unavailable, see Waters, *op. cit.*, pp. 402–412 or Goldman and Jack, *op. cit.*

30. Thomas Banyacya, Hopi Traditionalist spokesperson, quoted in Mohawk, *op. cit.*, p. 1.

# Spiritual Dimensions of Feminist Anti-Nuclear Activism

## Gina Foglia and Dorit Wolffberg

There is a crisis evolving on our planet that has been labeled "ecological" because it has finally reached a level at which the very process of nature is being violated. Species of animals are being extinguished. Poisons are being introduced into the eco-system. These interruptions are breaking a cycle that has sustained life and ensured survival for billions of years; the result is deadly. As women, we are as intimately connected to the rhythms of life and death, as we are to the rhythms of our own bodies. As women who are conscious of our heritage, we use this intimate knowledge in reversing the breakdown.

While the goals of feminism are often expressed in terms of women reclaiming power in society, it is also imperative that this process of re-feminization of culture include a change in the actual perception of life on the Earth. Consciousness must be expanded so that the larger ecological patterns can be understood. There can be no dividing up into

© Gina Foglia and Dorit Wolffberg, 1981. Printed by permission of the authors. The authors wish to acknowledge assistance from Lorie Dechar and from "the wonderful women in the Office of [Inner] Space Management at CUNY-Queens: Dinah Foglia, Jean Trush, Miriam Youngerman."

"us and them" because we, life on Earth, are all interrelated and, at this point, are vitally dependent on one another.

The values that govern our culture are the values of separation. These are patriarchal in nature and lead toward the continued exploitation of people and of the Earth. Susan Koen and Nina Swaim, authors of *Ain't Nowhere We Can Run: A Handbook for Women on the Nuclear Mentality,* propose:

The solution involved in restoring balance to the world is not as simple as swinging the pendulum in the other direction or tipping the balance point towards the female half which is currently ignored in the world. . . . We have to begin to envision a world in which balance comes from the existence of a dynamic system. . . . In such a world, the either/or dichotomies which predominate today's world would be replaced by a celebration of both/and perspectives. Thus, what is needed is a change of both form and content, a generation of new constructs which support holism rather than separation and compartmentalization, which will foster harmony between people and nature rather than domination of nature by man. Right now these constructs exist in the imagery, visions and fantasies of feminists, and are finding their way into the actual behaviors of some people.[1]

This tendency toward imbalance and separation affects every aspect of our personal and social lives. The wholeness of the individual is a necessary prerequisite to the healing of society. The teachings of patriarchal culture, however, encourage a lack of trust in one's own power and judgment; people are subsequently made dependent on the so-called expertise of others. They are kept alienated from themselves and, hence, weak and easily controlled. It is very difficult for people who consistently rely on external validation of themselves to change their attitudes about anything. Just as they are alienated from themselves, they are alienated from their bodies, and women suffer more than men from those values that make our bodies someone else's domain, whether it be a rapist or a doctor. Humankind in general is sadly alienated from the Earth, the very source of our shelter and food. Men have taken this alienation to heart, however, as they exploit the Earth's surface and her depths, as they rape her to fill their pockets. The Earth is treated as they treat all women, but they call her domination "progress" and slap themselves on the back.

Obviously, this is not progress. Progress will only begin when society realizes that it is imbalanced and chooses to heal itself. The healing must involve the balancing of female and male energy and awareness.

## ECO-FEMINISM

Nature has evolved over eons into a complex, self-perpetuating, and self-preserving whole. When substances are introduced into this natural system that change its basic components, the system is forced to alter. To survive, it must change or else it must rid itself of the interfering element. An example of this process is genetic mutation.

The feminist anti-nuclear movement deals with problems so basic to survival that our philosophies of the most basic meanings of life, i.e., our spiritual convictions, are called into the search for a solution. The movement is political in a much more profound sense than we usually associate with "politics." Our struggle is not just between one group of people and another, but is the struggle between those forces which seek to compete with and overcome nature and those forces which understand that living in harmony is the only means of survival. While each individual in the movement may subscribe to a different relationship with the unifying principle of the universe, the movement as a whole has looked back to the matrifocal spiritual symbols for strength. We were all taught that religions that worshiped nature were "primitive," but we know now the importance of those earthbound values. We also know that it was women who were the priests in the very ancient holistic religions, and we believe that our time has come again.

From the very beginning, women involved in the larger environmental movement have used holistic constructs, whether or not they were couched in religious terms. Rachel Carson, author of *Silent Spring*, the first major work available on the destruction of the environment, makes constant reference to the "web of life." She draws connections between the various levels of life, their interdependence and the devastating effect of disruption on the cycle. The very fact of the interconnectedness is spiritual, an expression of the common bond of every element in the universe.

On 21 March 1980 in Amherst, Massachusetts, a conference was held that attempted to apply these holistic principles to its content and structure. The conference was called "Women and Life on Earth: Eco-Feminism in the 80's."* Its goals included learning how ecological is-

---

* Editor's Note: With the encouragement of women who worked on the first eco-feminist conference, in Amherst (Women and Life on Earth, 160 Main St., Northampton, MA 01060), two similar gatherings were held in the months that

sues affect women and how we have responded, exploring the relationship between feminist and ecological concerns, creating a sense of unity and an on-going functioning network, and encouraging strategies through which all women can act to affect the future and quality of life on Earth. The tone of the conference was beautifully expressed in the opening statement written by Grace Paley and Ynestra King:

We here are part of a growing movement of women for life on Earth. We come from the feminist movement, the anti-nuclear movement, the disarmament movement, the holistic health movement. We have come because life on Earth and the Earth itself is in terrible danger. We feel a great urgency. We don't have much time, but we have to move against those (mostly men) who've formed patriarchal government and power which poison and pillage our farms, forests and rivers, have destroyed our cities and armed our children against children of our sisters. They do this every day as part of their ordinary work.

We all know there has to be another way of being — of living and working on this Earth. There is and because of the physical and historical facts of our experience we women know it.

We're here to say the word ECOLOGY and announce that for us as feminists it's a political word — that it stands against the economics of the destroyers and the pathology of racist hatred. It's a way of being, which understands that there are connections between all living things and that indeed we women are the fact and flesh of connectedness.

We own the real power of our numbers and political consciousness and the symbolic power of our history and our life in the mythologies of creation. We intend to use these powers as health makers to forcefully resist the destroyers, the poisoners.

The world has to have a future. We intend — furiously and with some joy — to connect this assaulted planet to that future.[2]

---

followed. A conference titled "Women and the Environment" took place at Sonoma State University in northern California on 25 April 1981; the motto was "Think globally; act locally." In October 1981, Women and Life on Earth, London (82 Lady Margaret Rd., London N19) held a conference with the same title as the one in Amherst. A *Proceedings* volume from each conference has been published by each of the three groups.

I was unable to attend the conferences in Massachusetts and England, but I can say that the California gathering was a memorable community event with workers and participants of all ages and races and both sexes — a multiplicity of eco-feminist activists! Speakers were Angela Davis, China Galland, Anna Gyorgy, Winona La Duke, and Peggy Taylor; fifty workshops were offered. The conference was initiated by Susan Adler and produced by a women's collective called CREATE (637 Dexter St., Santa Rosa, CA 95404). At the end of the day, male volunteers cooked a huge dinner for the collective and all the other workers. — C.S.

The spirituality that is inherent in the ecological structure was the force underlying the entire conference. It came through in the issues which ranged from health and surviving in the wilderness, to urban organizing and militarism. It came through in the connections made among the women, who interacted with love and generosity and an openness to each other's sometimes conflicted viewpoints. Even though we were not homogeneous, ranging from scientists to grassroots activists, we were able to put our different perspectives into the larger pattern so that a common working ground could be established. As strategies were being planned, this holistic process was experienced as a sense of power, both personal and collective. It informed each definition and value judgment. It was embodied in actions in the theater, the art, the poetry, the music, the mythology, and the rituals. We are whole people made up of many aspects, and a solution to our alienation can only be reached if we are treated as such.

The conference had a profound effect on many of the women who attended, and it did not dissipate quickly. Some of us felt affected in a way that reached beyond reason, even beyond emotion. We were made well aware of the role that all women have to play in the survival of the Earth and returned home with a clarified sense of responsibility.

## WE ORGANIZE AND WE ACT

As feminists in the anti-nuclear movement, the two of us have chosen to work primarily with women. Many of us in the movement are lesbians, and we extend this aspect of our lives into our wider definitions of politics. Others of us have worked with mixed groups and have found that both the groups and the decision-making processes were frustrating and unproductive. While the anti-nuclear movement as a whole is realizing the importance of feminism, there is sexism in the men involved, and their personal values dominate the political action. Many woman-identified women are looking for a different way in which to express concern and have impact on others. We are developing the means by which we work from a different perspective than men. Both within the groups and within the society at large, we attempt to view people as multidimensional. The effect we choose to have on others involves concentration on developing personal strength, as opposed to creating fear. We also recognize that it is more effective to approach a task with fewer numbers and more commitment than it is to insist that everyone be the same. The language used is of a cooperative, instead of competitive, nature and we are able to accept diversity of opinion and approach. The environment is always a supportive one, and it is a pleasure to meet.

There are feminist anti-nuclear groups all over the United States. In the Northeast alone there are approximately twenty-five. These groups have formed the Northeast Womyn's Alliance Against Nuclear Power and Destruction. Its meetings are held monthly to work together on and to evaluate actions. In October 1980, the Alliance formed twelve principles by which we express our beliefs. The following is the first:

As feminists, we are committed to the elimination of patriarchy in all its forms. By patriarchy, we mean a social, cultural, political, and economic order that has at its base woman-hating, homophobia, hierarchical structures, and a negation of values considered "feminine." We seek a society where values of cooperation, strength, collectivity, and a deep respect for all life are upheld. We seek to live in harmony with all nature.

The meetings are filled with sharing of ideas, sharing of food, sharing of feelings, and sharing of symbols. Anger can be expressed so that the feeling need not build into pain. At the end of each meeting we form a circle and sing songs like this one:

> Wearing our long wing feathers as we fly,
> Wearing our long wing feathers as we fly,
> We circle around, we circle around
> The boundaries of the Earth.

## The Groups

The Alliance is not a homogeneous organization. Each local group is different and works autonomously; we will describe two of them. We, the authors, are members of Women Opposed to Nuclear Technology (WONT), a group based in New York. WONT is presently involved in performing an original theater piece entitled "Spin the Earth Web, Sisters." It involves music, poetry, dance, and ritual providing information about ecological destruction as well as an emotional relationship with that information. The members of the group work together in local and centralized actions, while individual members become involved in forms of civil disobedience and different aspects of organizing.

The members of LUNA, a group based in Boston, have distributed the following statement:

LUNA is Lesbians United in Non-Nuclear Action. What brings the women of LUNA together is a deep commitment to anti-nuclear action and, ultimately, to our survival and to the survival of the Earth. Our action grows from a healing and generative energy. This energy is manifested in our work. Our process reflects an effort to consciously unlearn patriarchal ways of relating. We begin weekly meetings with "rounds," during which each woman tells the state of her life at that particular time. We work to respect the diversity represented in the group by careful listening. Energy circles are a time to connect our energy and express our love for each other. Annually we meet at a lesbian feminist collective farm to renew ourselves. We try to bring our presence, our spirit, to everything we do.

*The Actions*

On 3 May 1980, three hundred women gathered in Hartford, Connecticut to speak out against United Technologies, a multinational corporation involved in arms production. We chose to approach the action in a nontraditional way, planning to avoid the usual rally and speakers. We called it a gathering, and it began with the formation of various groups at different points in the city. Each group then walked toward the center of Hartford, performing street theater, handing out leaflets, interviewing, singing. On the leaflet handed out by WONT was the following poem, superimposed on the delicate image of a sunflower:

SUNFLOWERS

skyward they climb
resolute as tigers
their unblinking golden eyes
like trumpets in the sun

crying yes! abundance
is pouring from the sky
and rushing in the wind
and muttering through the soil

the only shortage is "man's"
inability to dance
like sunflowers in a reel
with all nature

—Lorie Eve Dechar

On the back was a bibliography and a listing of local resources. The purpose in creating a flyer of this type was to present the public with a positive image and viable options, instead of something that would make them react with defensiveness to fear.

Our groups converged in a park in the center of Hartford; we then walked through the downtown area, past United Technologies, and completed our circle at the park. There we heard each other speak, shared our creativity, and held a ritual. The ritual was learned from a Native American woman and consisted of each woman pouring a handful of cornmeal and tobacco into a fire while making a silent wish. After the last woman was finished, we intoned this chant:

> We all come from the Goddess
> and to Her we shall return
> like a drop of rain
> flowing to the ocean.

Immediately, a short rain began. No clouds had been seen earlier that day, and not one was to be seen after. This rain was taken as a sign and made our energies soar.

Two weeks after the Hartford action, the Northeast Alliance met to evaluate its work. We asked questions: For whom was the gathering? Did the process flow as smoothly as we had hoped? Was responsibility taken and shared as easily as we hoped it could be? We decided that the action was a success (we even got good press coverage), but that there was a lot we could learn from it. At that same meeting, we began planning our next action. That was the 24 May occupation/blockage of the nuclear power plant at Seabrook, New Hampshire. Not all of the member groups of the Alliance took part in this action, but those that did formed their own cluster of affinity groups and called themselves Lesbian Tide.

While we were a part of a much larger coalition at Seabrook, we did maintain autonomy in our living space and for a large part of our decision-making. The difference between the process of Lesbian Tide and that of the mixed camp was marked. While the women understood that talk about feelings and community was an integral part of dealing with the stresses of political activism, it took the mixed groups four days of growing pressure to finally "call a meeting" for that purpose. Modes of communication were entirely different; the women's meetings were full of support and serious listening even when there was disagreement, while the men tended to compete even when they were agreeing with

Spirituality as a Political Force

each other.* The women's space was a warm and cooperative home, complete with a healing tent where one could receive massage and herbs along with the traditional forms of medicine. The evenings were spent re-energizing with songs and spirit. Hebrew chants telling about the Sabbath Queen, the symbol of re-creation and transcendence, were shared along with American Indian chants. Before leaving camp for the first confrontation with the military, the entire cluster joined together in an energy circle. We were silent while we received the good feelings of those who couldn't be with us.

The action as a whole was somewhat disappointing and frustrating, due to low numbers and a breakdown in the decision-making process. This caused the women of Lesbian Tide to re-evaluate our choice to be part of a mixed action and reaffirmed our belief in the process that we had chosen to use. We decided that even in the face of adversity it was important to stick to our convictions, whether it be about the matter of consensus in decision-making (in which decision would be made more slowly) or our definition of what the term violence might really entail.

On 16 and 17 November 1980, the Women's Pentagon Action took place in Washington, D.C. For several months before that weekend, the regional offices of the Action in New York, Washington, and Amherst distributed a unity statement explaining the reasons for the Action and expressing the connections among the issues and among the

---

* Editor's Note: See Diane McGuinness, "The Nature of Aggression and Dominance Systems," *Absolute Values and the Search for the Peace of Mankind: Proc. of the Ninth Internatl. Conference on the Unity of Sciences*, Miami Beach, FL, 27–30 Nov. 1980 (New York: Internatl. Cultural Foundation, 1982). Numerous psychologists' studies reveal that (1) males in all-male groups organize themselves into a linear dominance system, and females in all-female groups organize themselves into clusters that have no internal dominance order, although hierarchical dominance often occurs among the clusters (Knudson, 1973, observations of pre-schoolers); and (2) crowded situations intensify hostility and competitiveness among males, but increase cooperativeness among females (Freedman *et al.*, 1972, observations of college students; supported by Ross *et al.*, 1973; Stokols *et al.*, 1973; Epstein and Karlin, 1975); Baum and Koman (1976) found that even creating an *image* of social density was sufficient to elevate hostile feelings in males. Perhaps males' psychobiological disposition toward establishing a pecking order plus feeling hostile and competitive in large groups explains some of the exasperations that many women encounter at large, multi-day demonstrations involving men. Men, however, would seem to be better off in mixed groups, as psychologists have found that male hostility and punitiveness diminish in such circumstances. ["Woman is the civilizer." — an age-old saying] — C.S.

groups of women who would be converging. It cited the horrors of the nuclear arms race and then emphasized our collective power and the positive, holistic nature of our approach:

We are gathering at the Pentagon on November 17 because we fear for our lives. We fear for the life of this planet, our Earth, and the life of the children who are our human future.

We are women who come in most part from the northeastern region of our United States. We are city women who know the wreckage and fear of city streets; we are country women who grieve the loss of the small farm and have lived on the poisoned earth. We are young and older; we are married, single, lesbian. We live in families, as students in dormitories, and some are single parents. We work at a variety of jobs. We are students, teachers, factory workers, office workers, lawyers, farmers, doctors, builders, waitresses, weavers, poets, engineers, homeworkers, electricians, artists, horseloggers. We are all daughters and sisters.

We have come here to mourn and rage and defy the Pentagon because it is the workplace of the imperial power which threatens us all. Every day while we work, study, love, the colonels and generals who are planning our annihilation walk calmly in and out the doors of its five sides. To carry out their plans they have been making three to six nuclear bombs every day. They have accumulated over thirty thousand. They have invented the neutron bomb which kills people but leaves property and buildings like this one intact. They will produce the MX Missile and its billion dollar subway system which will scar thousands of miles of our western lands and consume its most delicate resource — water. They are creating a technology called Stealth — the invisible unperceivable arsenal. They have just appropriated twenty million dollars to revive the cruel old killer nerve gas. They have proclaimed Directive 59 which asks for "small nuclear wars, prolonged but limited." They are talking about a first strike. The Soviet Union works hard to keep up with United States initiatives. We can destroy each other's cities, towns, schools, children many times over. Five other countries now own at least one nuclear bomb. France will produce the neutron bomb. We are in the hands of men whose power and wealth have separated them from the reality of daily life and from the imagination. We are right to be afraid.

At the same time our cities are in ruins, bankrupt; they suffer the devastation of war. Hospitals are closed, our schools are deprived of books and teachers. Our young Black and Latino youth are without decent work. They will be forced, drafted to become the cannon fodder for the very power that oppresses them. Whatever help the poor have received is cut or withdrawn to feed the Pentagon, which needs about $500,000,000 a day for its murderous health. It will extract $157 billion dollars this year from our own tax money, $1800 from a family of four.

With this wealth our scientists have been corrupted; over forty percent work in government and corporate laboratories that refine the methods for destroying or deforming life.

The lands of the Native American people have been turned to radioactive rubble in order to enlarge the nuclear warehouse. The uranium of South Africa, necessary to the nuclear enterprise enriches the white minority and encourages the vicious system of racist oppression and war.

As we write this, a warhead with the power of 750 Hiroshimas is blown out of its silo in a wood near a small town in Arkansas.

There is fear among the people, and that fear, created by the industrial militarists, is used as an excuse to accelerate the arms race. "We will protect you . . ." they say, but we have never been so endangered, so close to the end of human time.

We women are gathering because life on the precipice is intolerable.

We want to know what anger in these men, what fear which can only be satisfied by destruction, what coldness of heart and ambition drives their days.

We want to know because we do not want that dominance which is exploitative and murderous in international relations, and so dangerous to women and children at home — we do not want that sickness transferred by the violent society through the fathers to the sons.

What is it that we women need for our ordinary lives, that we want for ourselves and also for our sisters in new nations and old colonies who suffer the white man's exploitation and too often the oppression of their own countrymen?

We want enough good food, useful work, decent housing, communities with clean air and water, good care for our children while we work. We expect equal pay for work of equal value. In our old age we expect our experience and skills to be honored and used.

We want health care which respects and understands our bodies. We want an education for children that tells the true history of our women's lives, that describes the Earth as our home to be cherished, to be fed as well as harvested.

We want to be free from violence in our streets and in our houses. The pervasive social power of the masculine ideal and the greed of the pornographer have come together to steal our freedom, so that whole neighborhoods and the life of the evening and night have been taken from us. For too many women the dark country road and the city alley have concealed the rapist. We want the night returned, the light of the moon, special in the cycle of our female lives, the stars and the gaiety of the city streets.

We want the right to have or not to have children, we do not want gangs of politicians and medical men to say we must be sterilized for the country's good. We know that this technique is the racist's method for controlling populations. Nor do we want to be prevented from having an abortion when we need one. We think this freedom should be available to poor women as it always has been to the rich. We want to be free to love whomever we choose. We will live with women or with men or we will live alone. We will not allow the oppression of lesbians. One sex or one sexual preference must not dominate another.

We do not want to be drafted into the army. We do not want our young brothers drafted. We want *them* equal with *us*.

We want to see the pathology of racism ended in our time. There can be no peace while one race dominates another, one nation dominates the others.

We want the uranium left in the Earth and the Earth given back to the people who tilled it. We want a system of energy that is renewable, which does not take resources out of the earth without returning them. We want those systems to belong to the people and their communities, not to the giant corporations that invariably turn knowledge into weaponry. We want the sham of Atoms for Peace ended, all nuclear plants decommissioned and the construction of new plants stopped. That is another war against the people and the child to be born in fifty years.

We want an end to the arms race. No more bombs. No more amazing inventions for death.

We understand all is connectedness. The Earth nourishes us as we with our bodies will eventually feed it. Through us, our mothers connected the human past to the human future.

With that sense, that ecological right, we oppose the financial connections between the Pentagon and the multinational corporations and banks that the Pentagon serves.

Those connections are made of gold and oil.

We are made of blood and bone; we are made of the sweet resource, water.

We will not allow these violent games to continue. If we are here in our stubborn hundreds today, we will certainly return in the thousands and hundreds of thousands in the months and years to come.

We know there is a healthy sensible loving way to live, and we intend to live that way in our neighborhoods and on our farms in these United States and among our sisters and brothers in all the countries of the world.

Twenty-two hundred women attended the first day of the Action, Sunday, which consisted of two series of workshops. In the morning there were informational discussions; in the afternoon strategy and action were discussed. The topics were women and militarism, feminism and ecology, women and work, women and violence, women and racism, women and sexual orientation, women and poverty, women and health, and women and the arts. That evening a memorial ritual was held for Yolanda Ward, a civil rights activist in Washington who had recently been slain.

The second day of the Action was attended by thirteen to fifteen hundred women and consisted of four stages: mourning, rage, empowerment, defiance. We began with a silent vigil walk through Arlington National Cemetery; many women wore black veils. It was a time of personal contemplation about the massive numbers of people who have been killed by militarism. The procession was led by four sixteen-foot-high puppets from the Bread and Puppets Theater, one all black and in black clothing, one red, one gold, one white. Beautiful twelve-foot-high puppets of Demeter and Persephone were also with us, as they had been at the eco-feminism conference.

The black puppet led us from the cemetery to the Pentagon. Just behind her were tall banners with symbols of life and well-being and women wearing corresponding symbols of death and destruction. Many women played instruments and noisemakers — drums and lots of pots and pans! At the Pentagon we lined the four sides of the parade ground, a grassy area, and listened to a statement by Grace Paley. As the last stage of our mourning, we planted cardboard gravestones with the names of women and the ways they have died. We made loud wailing and mourning noises, and the black puppet performed a ritual in front of every gravestone. Then beautiful white bird puppets, each so large that it took three puppeteers to operate, flew around the parade ground.

The red puppet moved forward, signaling rage, and women ripped off their mourning veils and became angry, shouting and making noise. Then the gold puppet, with the white puppet, led the way to encircle the Pentagon. We sang as we circled and formed in groups at each corner of the building. There we chanted "om" or other words and meditated on cracking the Pentagon walls and what they stand for. Witches from New York State created a large women's symbol with cornmeal; inside of it was a pentagram of cornmeal; inside of that was a pentagon of ashes, which they swept away into the pentagram.

The music and drumming and singing began again, and many women then performed civil disobedience, for which training sessions had been offered in communities and in Washington on the day before the Action. They blocked the doorways and read from the unity statement. They shouted "Shame!" every time a militarist came out. Women from Vermont wove a web of multi-color yarn across one of the main entrances, blocked mainly by Black guards. As the guards ripped down the web, the women simply rewove it, saying, "We won't do white males' dirty work anymore; why should you?" Eventually, the Black men stopped destroying the web. Several white guards were called in, and together they arrested approximately one hundred fifty women at various sites. There was no ritual closing because the temperature dropped suddenly and snow and sleet began to fall. Was nature herself closing our theater work with her own ritual of cold fury?

A web of women and women's organizations continues to grow around the issues raised by the Women's Pentagon Action.* During those two days, women in New Mexico, California, Iowa, Massachusetts, and Damascus, Arkansas (site of the Titan missile "mishap"), held vigils at which they read the unity statement and their poetry, sang songs, and performed rituals. Internationally, women held vigils, presented the unity statement to the U.S. embassy in their country, printed news releases, and sent statements of solidarity to the organizers in Washingon, D.C. Telegrams were received from Australia, Canada, England, Germany, Japan, Scotland, and Sweden, reaffirming that our concerns are above and beyond national boundaries.

## OUR FEARS, OUR DREAMS

Even as we carry out political activism and plan our new society, we continually ask ourselves, "Do we have a chance?" We ask when we evaluate the impact of an action. We ask each time we share our confrontations with those who do not even see the danger. There are many moments of despair, and even panic, as we go about our daily lives and see the overwhelming lack of respect that people have for one another. We are bombarded by the filth created by technology and people's increasing dependence on it. We are frightened that life on Earth will not survive. We are also frustrated by those parts of the larger anti-nuclear movement that we feel are confounding progress, going about their protest in ways that will not change society but will maintain the

---

* Editor's Note: Readers concerned about stopping the nuclear arms race — and its window-dressing, the nuclear power industry — may wish to support the Women's Action for Nuclear Disarmament (formerly the Women's Party for Survival), founded by Dr. Helen Caldicott (56 N. Beacon St., Watertown, MA 02172). The Women's Pentagon Action, which takes place every November, maintains a year-around office at 29 W. 21st St., New York, NY 10010. — C.S.

same values that we see as destructive. They perpetuate the values of separation by not addressing sexism, racism, classism, and homophobia. We feel that unless the society we are attempting to create is qualitatively different from the one we now have, there is no point to our revolution. We will destroy ourselves sooner or later.

Obviously, if all we felt were despair, we would be paralyzed and could not act. We cope by having faith in the rightness of our purpose and of our process. We have chosen an unpopular cause and have become deviant. Those of us who are lesbians have given up the privileged status of heterosexuality and have taken on a personal struggle with oppression. A great strength can come along with these choices. It is the strength of freedom and self-control. We will define who we are and what we consider necessary and significant. We will choose how we pray, whom we will love, what we will buy, and what we will produce ourselves. As women, we are actually reclaiming the right to control our own lives. In doing so, we are beginning the process of rebalancing and healing ourselves. If we can gain control over our own lives, we can help others to learn to do the same. It is said that we only evolved from animal to human when we became self-conscious. Perhaps it can also be said that we can only begin to reach our human potential when we become self-responsible.

In trying to determine what sort of world we would actually like to see, it makes sense to look around at what is already going on. It seems that what is being sought through revolutionary actions is the best balance between personal freedom and social responsibility. After working in a movement that has been able to work without leaders and hierarchical methods of designating responsibility, it appears that what is necessary for a truly free society is a capacity for internal discipline and social generosity. This can only be accomplished by healthy and balanced individuals.

The women who are devoting themselves to the feminist anti-nuclear movement recognize that we cannot separate the personal from the political. We cannot expect to wait until society is healed in order for us to begin living in a healthier way. We cannot expect others to live by the new values if we ourselves do not become an example. Therefore, we attempt to practice in our own lives an elimination of unnecessary waste and destruction of resources, a way of relating to all people that encourages cooperation and tolerance, a sensitivity to the needs and fears of others, and the understanding that our methods are as important as our goals, if not more so. We are attempting to change our own consciousness so that each action is based on these new values that have been internalized. When this happens, there is no need to remember all of the details of how to behave. There is a deliberate recognition that the universe is in multidimensional flow, in constant motion, and we all flow within it.


NOTES

1. Susan Koen and Nina Swaim, *Ain't Nowhere We Can Run: A Handbook for Women on the Nuclear Mentality* (Norwich, VT: WAND, 1980), p. 60.
2. Ynestra King and Grace Paley, Opening Statement, "Women and Life on Earth: A Conference on Eco-Feminism in the 80's," Post-Conference Mailing No. 1, 18 April 1980.

# Spiritual Techniques for Re-Powering Survivors of Sexual Assault

## Carolyn R. Shaffer

The roots of rape run deep, imbedded in and nourished by a culture of male violence, protected by the silence of social taboo. For years women did not speak publicly of rape, incest, and other forms of sexual assault. Rapes become ugly secrets festering unseen in our bodies and our minds. They shamed us in our own eyes and made us ever more vulnerable to attack. We blamed ourselves, or kept quiet for fear others would blame us.

We are changing. For over a decade women have been speaking out on the atrocity of rape. We have challenged and, in some cases, changed the law and police and medical practices. We have learned to defend ourselves, individually and collectively. We have organized anti-rape squads, telephone hotlines, and rape counseling centers. By breaking the silence and taking action, we have cracked the narrow patriarchal mold that has shaped our lives. We have declared ourselves no longer victims.

And yet forcible rape continues to rank as the most frequently committed violent crime in America. According to the F.B.I., the number of reported rapes nationwide has increased steadily for more than a decade and jumped twelve percent during the first six months of 1980, as compared to the previous year. To avoid assault, we continue to curb our sexuality, stay home after dark, walk warily even in daylight, and dress and speak with care for fear our T-shirts or our tones of voice might be misinterpreted as invitations to sex. When attacked, we still find it difficult not to blame ourselves. The difference today is that we are no longer isolated. We have the physical, social, and spiritual resources to empower and re-power ourselves.

Any form of sexual assault upon a woman is a political act in that it expresses and reinforces women's degraded position in our male-dominated culture. By the same token, the actions women take to prevent sexual assault, to initiate criminal — and sometimes civil — charges against the rapist, and to re-power ourselves after an attack are equally political. By asserting our power, we challenge deep-seated cultural assumptions about the submissive nature of the female and, in a very real sense, change the power dynamics between women and men.

In a culture that touts violent, aggressive acts as manly and views weak, submissive behavior as womanly, sexual assault is a logical extension of normal male-female relationships. The stereotype of the rapist as a crazed monster driven by inordinate or perverse sexual desires bears little resemblance to reality. According to studies of convicted rapists, most sexual assaults are premeditated and committed by men who are sane, sexually well-adjusted, and as likely to be friends, acquaintances, lovers, or relatives of their victims as strangers attacking women on dark streets. To challenge rape, which Susan Griffin aptly labeled the "All-American Crime" (*Ramparts,* Sept. 1971; also in *Rape/The Power of Consciousness*), is to challenge patriarchal culture itself.

## RECOVERY FROM RAPE: A SPIRITUAL JOURNEY

To *will* does not mean that the world will conform to our desires — it means that *we* will: We will make our own choices and act so as to bring them about, even knowing we may fail. Feminist spirituality values the courage to take risks, to make mistakes, to be our own authorities.

— STARHAWK, *The Spiral Dance*

Rape is more than a physical and emotional shock; it is a brush with death and, in this sense, a profound spiritual experience for the victim. The raped woman's very existence has been threatened. She feels she can count on nothing, not the safety of her home, not even the solidity

of the earth beneath her feet. Even when a rapist is successfully prose-
cuted, the victim often remains shaken at the deepest level of her
being. To recover fully she must re-power herself spiritually as well as
physically and emotionally. She must reaffirm — or perhaps discover for
the first time — that essential part of herself which can never be victimized, her place of power within. In reclaiming her power, in refusing to be objectified and victimized, she will have engaged in a profoundly political act.

The means by which a woman can re-power herself are many. She
can curse her rapist or forgive him, shout and scream or quietly center
herself through deep breathing; she can cast spells, repeat affirmations,
visualize the rapist being caught and herself becoming whole; she can
take control of her dreams and/or take her attacker to court; she can invent and perform a full-scale magical ritual or simply hold hands and
talk and cry with a friend. Her choice may be to do nothing more than
give herself permission to feel depressed, scared, and angry. The
methods she chooses are not as important as the fact that *she* chooses
them.

The last thing a rape victim needs is someone telling her what to do.
A therapist, friend, or doctor who, with even the best intentions, makes
decisions for the victim is, in a sense, repeating an act of violation by
once again taking away the assaulted woman's power. Feminist spirituality departs radically from traditional religion and standard forms of
therapy in that it assumes each woman knows what is best for her and
has the right to make her own decisions. The feminist counselor or
priestess views herself strictly as resource and catalyst. She listens to the
assaulted woman, offers information and options, asks her preferences,
and, once the woman has decided, supports her totally in her choices.

"In feminist spirituality there is no formula for the victim of sexual
assault; no spell, though there are lots of spells; no one thing to do,
though there are lots of things to do," explains a priestess, whom I will
call Maya, experienced in ritual magic and theater. "Whomever you
work with — the woman who wants to hex or the woman who wants to
heal — if it takes a year to do it, you have got to support her through
that period in the way that works for her."

Maya found her ability to set aside her own biases and personal preferences tested when two of her friends were raped in separate incidents. Each asked Maya to help her, but in diametrically opposed ways.
One woman, a member of a circle of women Maya was coaching, was
brutally beaten during her rape, responded to her rapist with anger, and

asked Maya, as an experienced ritualist and Witch, to hex him. The second woman, one of Maya's closest friends, chose a path of total forgiveness. Feeling that hatred toward her attacker would be self-destructive, she chose to restrain her angry emotions and focus on healing herself. Maya respected both women's wishes completely even though she felt certain that, in the first case, the energy of the hex would, in some form, return to her, and, in the latter case, the process of recovery would be slow and frustrating.

The two radically different approaches to re-powerment chosen by Maya's friends indicate the range of spiritual techniques available to women who have been sexually assaulted. The hexing involved a full-scale magical ritual, requiring several days of preparation and involving about twenty women, all friends of the rape victim. The operation was focused, intense, cathartic, and complete in itself. "The hex served as a catalyst for the woman to cleanse herself," explains Maya. "She got what she wanted and was able to move out of the energy created by the rape and become renewed." For the friend who chose to restrain her emotions, the recovery process took a year and was interrupted by a series of illnesses. "I made myself available to her in every way I could," said Maya. "I performed psychic healings on her, helping her cleanse her energy and ground out her illness. I gave her space to cry, to talk, to feel the emotion of what was happening. Sometimes we just sat together holding hands and felt healing energy flow through us." Eventually, the friend shed her illnesses and became whole and strong again.

As powerful and cathartic as group ritual can be, it is not appropriate for all women. Some, like Maya's close friend, prefer to release their fear, grief, and anger in small spurts, rather than a single emotional outburst. A rape victim, especially, may feel too vulnerable to engage in intense group activity.

One very private way a woman can re-power herself is by working with her dreams. Karen Hagerman, a licensed clinical psychologist on the staff of Bay Area Women Against Rape in Berkeley, finds dream-work remarkably effective for rape victims plagued with nightmares. Many learn to reverse roles in their dreams, switching from victim to attacker. "Dreams are the language of the unconscious," explains Hagerman. "Like rituals, they tap the symbolic content of the mind." Hagerman sometimes recommends a dream incubation ritual to women who seek guidance in resolving specific issues around their rape experience. Ideally, the ritual involves several days of preparation. First, the woman visualizes a guide and draws a picture of this being; then she reflects on the problem and writes out her thoughts; finally, she pictures a special dreaming place and sketches that. For the dreaming itself, she goes to her special place — either physically, if it exists on that level, or in her imagination. Often, insights and solutions blocked by the woman's conscious mind will surface in her dreams.

The trauma of sexual assault can emotionally blind a woman to large areas of her life and cripple her with rigidly patterned behavior. Dreamwork and other forms of therapy may help, but her block can be so severe that the trauma itself will remain undetected even after years of such work. A psychic counselor, a clairvoyant who can read the symbolic content of a person's subtle energy field, will often uncover, in the course of a single reading, suppressed memories that have plagued a person for years by creating unexplained physical symptoms and obsessive patterns. In one case, a woman seeking psychic healing for a goiter remembered, with an intense outburst of emotion, an incest experience from childhood. The trauma of the incest had evidently triggered not only the growth of the goiter but a psychic split between the woman's spiritual being and her body. When the psychic counselor proceeded to heal the split by realigning the woman's spiritual, emotional, and physical selves, her blocked memories flooded back. Although this caused her extreme distress at the time, it led to the cure of her goiter and, coupled with months of therapy, enabled her to regain emotional health and wholeness.

"Readings see everything and therapy can miss the boat," remarks Wendy Everard, a clairvoyant and a trained therapist who has worked with many victims of incest and rape. This fact, she explains, almost led her to give up therapy in favor of psychic readings. She learned, however, that handing people information about themselves or making their decisions for them does not work well, yet she is convinced that psychic readings can speed up the therapy process immensely. Everard claims that, with women who have been sexually assaulted, often simply acknowledging a previously blocked memory of the event can release much of the pent-up emotional charge around it.

Another psychic reader, Levanah Shell Bdolak, who is a priestess as well, frequently gives her clients ways of working on their own to release the energy from emotional blocks. When rape is involved, she often suggests a visualization in which the woman puts the rapist in a suitcase, locks it, and blows it up, sending all his energy back to him and reclaiming her own energy for herself. She recommends that the woman repeat this as many times as necessary to free herself of obsessive playbacks of her memory of the assault.

Bdolak does not believe in hexing. According to her, in traditional hexing the person sends her own energy out to the rapist or other target with the risk that it will rebound, in some form, to her. Maya, the priestess mentioned earlier, attributes a concussion she received in a traffic accident two months after her hexing ritual to this bounce-back phenomenon. For her it was an unmistakable signal that the hex had been effective and the cycle was complete. While Maya does not regret her decision to hex, she admits she would do so again only in the direst of circumstances and would perform the operation differently. Bdolak suggests that, instead of hexing, the woman turn the rapist's own energy against him. She need simply imagine herself a mirror reflecting back his hostile thoughts and feelings. But, Bdolak adds, this works best after the sender has neutralized her own feelings of anger. If the woman finds this difficult, she can ask a neutral person to gather and return the rapist's energy for her.

Other Witches and priestesses, including Z. Budapest, founder of the Susan B. Anthony Coven No. One in Los Angeles, recommend hexing, although they may not quibble with Bdolak's approach if the effect on the rapist is the same. Budapest, who helped initiate the Anti-Rape Squad in Los Angeles in the early Seventies and has worked with countless victims of sexual assault, includes a hex for a rapist in her *Holy Book of Women's Mysteries, Part I* and claims that, to her knowledge, such hexes have resulted in the capture of at least three rapists and the death of one of these.

In her book, Budapest also includes instructions for two simple yet dramatic post-rape rituals. In one the friends of the assaulted woman give her a scented bath, rubbing her back, speaking to her soothingly, and strewing the water with flowers they have freshly gathered. In the other, intended for a woman who has been raped in her own bed, the participants ceremonially burn the bedsheets and take the mattress outside to be bleached pure again by the sun.

Most of us have little experience with authentic ritual. Those we have encountered at church or at public functions are often mere formulas, either devoid of content or feeling or laden with guilt and judgment. Authentic ritual follows no formula, although it contains a simple, yet essential structure. This structure is natural to the act of celebration and is found, wholly or partially, in everything from birthday parties to protest rallies. It embodies five basic elements: setting apart and purifying a special place; invoking the greater powers, whether these be the elemental forces, the Goddess and/or God, or simply universal energy; raising the level of energy, through chanting, dancing, music, or such, until a point of emotional catharsis is reached; celebrating, usually with food, drink, and merriment; and, finally, completing the process by consciously opening the circle and sending the energy generated by it out to serve a purpose in the world. Working within this basic structure, any group of women willing to speak, move, chant, and dance from their hearts can create rituals of re-powerment for themselves, their sisters, and the world.

## THE END OF RAPE: NO VICTIMS TO BE FOUND

We will not live as victims. We must dig deeply into the roots of our experience, extract all such feelings and throw them into the face of the patriarchy, replacing them with our strength and power, thereby entering a new dimension of life — leaving all rapists behind with no victims to be found.

— MARGO ADAIR, teacher of Applied Meditation

A woman is hospitalized. For years she has suffered sexual abuse at the hands of her therapist. Her spirit finally rebels. She perceives herself as a victim and goes mad with rage. Night after night, her sisters, the members of her coven, visit her. In a private room they chant with her, help her breathe, bring her back to center; they guide her on journeys into her unknown depths, help her release anger and fear, then celebrate her victories with cakes and wine and good talk. "Without my sisters and the Craft I would be in a back ward today, alone and in pieces," she tells me softly. "They gave me what no hospital, no therapist could give: They made it possible for me to retain my integrity." The woman is no longer hospitalized, no longer victim. Today she is a warrior exposing with a lawsuit the abuse she received in the name of medicine; she is an artist incorporating visual art with sacred, healing dance; she is Goddess and woman, transforming the world as she transforms herself.

Women today are not fighting back alone, nor are we healing only ourselves. As Susan Griffin observes in *Rape/The Power of Consciousness,* "Our very selfish motion, to heal ourselves, to tend to our own wounds, may turn out to be the most radical motion of all, one that heals not only ourselves but eventually all, and thus transforms the social order absolutely." Increasingly, we are making the connection between our private pain and our collective oppression, and we are responding publicly.

On a sunny June day in 1980, scores of women gather in a meadow near the top of Mount Tampalpais. This peak, located several miles north of San Francisco and considered sacred by the Native Americans, had been the scene of the brutal murder of a young woman the previous spring and of other murders and numerous rapes over the years. The women hold hands in a circle. They breathe together in silence. A priestess steps forward and speaks:

> We are here to remember our sisters who have died on this
> mountain.
> We are here to remember that although we have been
> compared to this Earth,
> We are not allowed to walk it in safety,
> And we are not allowed to walk it alone.

The circle of women send their pain and anger into the Earth, asking that it be changed into energy for action; they invoke the women of the past, the ancient queens, the priestesses of the Goddess, the healers, the women burned as Witches, the women who tended the land, all women past and present who have been oppressed and have fought back. They chant again and again, "I am a woman, my will is unbending," sending the words and their energy out in webs to surround and reclaim the mountain.

We are learning we need never be victims. Rape will not disappear tomorrow, even as we continue our long-range struggle to spread post-patriarchal mores throughout the legal system and society in general. Assaults are perpetrated in order to paralyze and cripple our psyche — *but they cannot.* Our spirituality has taught us the reality of transformation: By not ignoring pain and anger but, rather, acknowledging it, naming it, and feeling it so totally that the energy bound within us is released, we are free to live fully once again. Nothing can stop our movement toward a new culture in which, ultimately, rape — whether of women or of the Earth — will be unthinkable.

# The Christian Right's "Holy War" Against Feminism

## Charlene Spretnak

On behalf of America, a Declaration of National Moral Emergency
was signed in April 1980 by six fundamentalist ministers, two federal
legislators, two military leaders, a professional football player, and his
coach. What prompted those men to warn that "America is facing the
greatest crisis in her history . . . the struggle for her very survival as a
free nation" is the political activism surrounding such issues as the
ERA, abortion rights, and gay rights.[1] Christian Voice, a right-wing national lobbying organization, concurs with their analysis: "America's
rapid decline as a world power is the direct result of those [three]
things."[2] Feminists have often been accused by both liberals and con-
servatives of *going too far*, but now the Christian Right has upped the
ante: Feminists are "moral perverts,"[3] "godless humanists,"[4] and "enemies of every decent society."[5]

Most of the men who signed the Declaration are leaders of a national
political movement that has happily married ultraconservative political
goals to fundamentalist interpretations of the Bible. The Christian
Right is also known as the Fundamentalist Right, the New Right, and

the "Good News" movement. Their growth during the past four years has been phenomenal, and pollsters now estimate their numbers at sixty million.[6] They were a formidable force at the 1980 Republican Convention, squashing feminist issues and blocking Howard Baker — and almost George Bush, as well — from the Vice-Presidential nomination, although they did not have enough clout to secure it for their favorite son candidates, U.S. Senator Jesse Helms (R-North Carolina) or Rep. Philip Crane (R-Illinois). [Since all signs indicate that Helms will run for President eventually, voters should be interested to learn that he publicly, at least twice, referred to the feminists demonstrating outside the GOP's convention hall as "garbage."[7]]

Although not widely admitted, there have been avowals of building a third party by some leaders of the Christian Right who feel that the Republican Party is no longer "marketable" and "just won't do."[8] However, the current mood of the Republicans is quite compatible with the political goals of the Christian Right — that is, to take nearly all the public funding out of social services (which are supported by "socialistic Christian liberals" and "demonic secular humanists") and put that money into a greatly increased defense budget, plus large tax cuts. This plan reflects a seamless merger of the ultraconservative view of life ("I do not care about anyone beyond the perimeter of my own yard") and the sustaining religion of *laissez-faire* capitalism, Calvinism ("If you are truly righteous in the eyes of God, you are rich — or at least middle class"). Christian Right delegates to the 1980 Republican Convention were numerous, and their movement intends to control the 1984 convention completely, as well as to sweep the 1982 elections.

The philosophy of the Christian Right has little in common with the traditional political dynamics of Democratic and Republican interactions. Opponents are not considered to be "misled" or even "plain wrong," but rather are "evil" and "immoral." Anyone who does not live and vote within their tightly proscribed boundaries is labeled an enemy of God. Combining the apocalyptic fervor of fundamentalism with the doomsday language of the Far Right, they articulate their position on "moral issues," which is their code word for feminist issues, in the fanatical language of a holy war: "Pray that God will not unleash His wrath on this nation before we, as His soldiers, have the opportunity to turn this immoral and unthinkable evil [Planned Parenthood] away from His eyes." "Secular humanists are leading us to the gates of Sodom and Gomorrah." "Unless there is drastic change, our days are numbered." "God is saying to us, 'I'm going to give you one more chance to save this country.'" "God help us if we fail!"

Their blanket term for all feminist legislation that would protect and advance the status of women in the areas of education, economics, health care, government, and — yes — religion is "assaults on the family." Howard Phillips, national director of the Conservative Caucus, which successfully targeted many liberals for defeat in 1978 and 1980 and replaced them with Christian Right legislators, traces the roots of current "assaults" to the nineteenth century when "liberation of the wife away from the leadership of the husband began." He cites as detrimental women's attaining inheritance and property rights, sexual freedom, and the vote! He evokes the halcyon days before the Nineteenth Amendment when our country operated on the principle of "One *family*, one vote."[9]

Citizens who do not agree with such "pro-family" sentiments are held to be anti-family and sinister. Obviously, the Christian Right intends to "bring back the family" by making life hellish for anyone who lives outside the state of matrimony. In addition, their entire "pro-family" campaign is informed by a crucial distinction: They are not simply advocating the traditional family of two-heterosexual-parents-plus-offspring(s), a situation which millions of feminists find workable and fulfilling; rather, the Christian Right is specifically campaigning for the *patriarchal* family. Rev. Jerry Falwell, a Baptist minister who is the national president of Moral Majority, Inc., a "moral/political organization," explains why the Equal Rights Amendment is "immoral": "A definite violation of holy Scripture, ERA defies the mandate that 'the husband is the head of the wife, even as Christ is the head of the church' (Ep. 5:23). In 1 Peter 3:7 we read that husbands are to give their wives honor *as unto the weaker vessel,* . . ." [my italics].[10]

All areas of the Christian Right's platform reflect the patriarchal model for relationships: dominance and submission. Since women and children are to be under the control of husbands/fathers, the man in a family is *completely responsible* (male liberation activists, take note) for any family member's deviation from the proscriptions. Falwell appeals to macho sensibilities by blaming "weak men" for many of today's family problems.[11] Similarly, the Christian Right declares that they do not want America to have mere military parity with the Soviet Union; they want superiority and *dominance*. In the realm of environmental problems, they will entertain no logical presentation of current perils because the Bible says God gave humans the right to "subdue" the earth and to "have dominion" over it. Economically, their insistence on unregulated capitalism certainly ensures the perpetual domination of the haves over the have-nots. Finally, their openly declared goal by the year 2000 is to impose their will on every aspect of American life. Toward this end, Rev. Bill Bright, president of Campus Crusade for Christ International, exhorts, "America will not be politically sound until all positions of political power are held by born-again conservative Christians."[12]

## "BORN AGAIN" OR BORN YESTERDAY?

The relentless absolutism of the Christian Right rests on patriarchal religion. Hence, a historical perspective reveals that they have built their house of straw. Since the Christian Right vilifies feminism for undermining "God's line of authority in the home"[13] and "attacking God's plan for the family,"[14] it is crucial for their purposes that people believe the Bible represents "God's natural law" which has existed since Day One. But, in fact, the notion of the supreme deity, i.e., ultimate power, being male is a relatively recent invention. Abraham, the earliest patriarch of the Judeo-Christian tradition, is dated by biblical scholars at only 1800 B.C.; Goddess artifacts have been dated at 25,000 B.C. (Patriarchal gods were brought into Goddess-oriented Greece around 1900 B.C. by barbarian invaders.) "The will of God" is a concept that has been used for countless political ends, not the least of which have been in the realm of sexual politics. While it is probably perfectly accurate to proclaim, as does the Christian Right, that the patriarchal God the Father abhors women's liberation, it would be just as accurate to assert: The Goddess Supports the ERA! In short, it is fine to believe in God, but that tradition was born yesterday and has very shallow historical legitimacy for claiming to possess the eternal law for all humankind.

It also has the blood of a lot of women on its hands; misogyny has always been inherent in the Judeo-Christian core symbols and doctrines. The new, patriarchal religion co-opted the older mythic symbols and inverted their meaning: The female, Eve, was now weak-willed and treacherous; the sacred bough was now forbidden; and the serpent, symbol of regeneration and renewal with its shedding skins, was now the embodiment of evil. The Goddess religion and its "Pagan" worshippers were brutally destroyed in the biblical lands. The Old Testament is the military and cultural record (albeit considerably laundered) of a massive political coup. It is important to note that we did not emerge into patriarchal religion from a dark, immature period of primitivism; Goddess-centered cultures, including Minoan Crete, were highly evolved and had sophisticated moral codes that acknowledged our oneness with Mother Earth.

Later the Church found that it could not attract converts in the heavily Goddess-oriented Mediterranean and Celtic cultures without a Goddess on its banners: Mary, Mother of God, formerly God herself. From the fourteenth through seventeenth centuries, the Church burned millions of women as "witches." They were the women who defied patriarchal oppression by observing the Old Religion, celebrating nature's holidays (solstices and equinoxes) instead of the Church's, and practicing contraception, abortion, midwifery, and healing among the peasants, thereby constituting a communication network that the patriarchal Church/State found threatening. [Do these issues sound familiar?] If the Christian Right attempts a Witch hunt of harassment against feminists, as many analysts have predicted for the Eighties, it will not be the first time. *But this time we are organized.*

Even if the guardians of patriarchal religion and culture were murderously "overzealous" in the Old World, the Christian Right is fond of reminding voters that their way is the American way because the Declaration of Independence and the Constitution contain references to God the Father. This is true. We all voted a straight patriarchal ticket for thirty-five hundred years because no one else was on the ballot; however, we now see the possibility of freedom and dignity for *both* sexes.

## WHOSE MORALITY?

> you are what is female
> you shall be called Eve
> and what is masculine shall be called God.
>
> and from your name Eve we shall take
> the word Evil
> and from God's the word Good.
> now you understand patriarchal morality.
> — JUDY GRAHN[15]

The Christian Right calls itself "pro-moral" and calls everyone else immoral, or at best amoral. They believe that America has been taken over by a "satanic" conspiracy of "secular humanists," which includes all feminists. In spite of facts such as the national poll in May 1980, which found that Americans favor the ERA by a margin of two-to-one, the Christian Right maintains that no one except secular humanists supports the ERA and they comprise only three to four percent of our population.[16]

Their main refrain against humanists is that they are "anti-morals." Jerry Falwell, who has a weekly television audience of fifteen million for his "Old-Time Gospel Hour,"* likes to explain to his listeners, "Feminists tell us that nothing is absolutely right or absolutely wrong."[17] As with all their other pronouncements on feminism, this is an absurd lie. For years feminists have been saying loud and clear that the patriarchal practices which demean and oppress women are outrageous, immoral, and *wrong*. It is *wrong* to tell a girl from birth that her only hope in life is to please and cajole a man and to block her from becoming active, assertive, and confident in her own right. It is *wrong* for parents to favor their sons over their daughters in funding and encouraging education. It is *wrong* to discriminate against women and minorities in hiring, wages, and promotion. It is *wrong* to portray women, girls, and boys as pornographic toys for men. It is *wrong* to sentence women to back-alley abortionists who often maim their "patients" and leave them to die in a pool of blood. It is *wrong* to condone by silence the enormous amount of wife-beating, incest, rape, and forced prostitution that is committed against women. Is the Christian Right concerned about these atrocities? Very selectively. They are indignant primarily because some women have been sleeping with women, some women have received safe, affordable abortions, and some women have been trying to legislate equal rights: three patriarchal sins of the first degree.

To see the smug expression on Jerry Falwell's beefy face when he expounds on the "moral depravity" of feminists is to witness male privilege incarnate. When he adjusts the sleeve of his expensive three-piece suit and intones, "I believe God will hold us accountable if we do not stop abortion," the unctuous piety calls to mind attorney Florynce Kennedy's ten-year-old observation that still says it all: *If men could get pregnant, abortion would be a sacrament.*

---

* Arbitron, a television research organization employing the statistical methods of the social sciences, determined that Falwell's weekly audience, as of November 1980, was actually 1.6 million viewers (*The New York Times* News Service, 23 May 1981).

The one issue on which the Christian Right overlaps with the feminists is pornography. However, with their characteristic double-think, the former pretends that the opposite is true. Leaders of the Christian Right continually cite in one breath "the Hugh Hefners, the Larry Flynts, the Gloria Steinems, and the Betty Friedans" as the agents of decadence in our country. (*Ms.* is considered by them to be a "filthy" magazine.) At a press conference during America's Pro-Family Conference held in Long Beach in July 1980, I pointed out this contradiction to Rev. Tim LaHaye, founder of Californians for Biblical Morality and a co-founder of the national Moral Majority, and asked him why the Christian Right does not join the anti-porn marches that feminists have conducted in every major city in recent years. LaHaye's face froze with horror.

## MANIPULATING WOMEN'S FEARS

In a classic feminist essay, "Safety, Shelter, Rules, Form, Love: The Promises of the Ultra-Right,"[18] Andrea Dworkin analyzed the psychology that successfully motivates Christian Right women to campaign against equal rights. Promising to place enforceable restraints on male aggression and abandonment, they offer *form* (a simple fixed, predetermined social, biological, and sexual order that banishes the confusion and mystification with which women experience the world since they are kept ignorant of most practical knowledge and skills necessary to function autonomously), *shelter* (exploiting the belief that women without men are homeless, they claim to offer protection from that fearsome state), *safety* (they acknowledge the reality of danger — assault, shame, disgrace — and promise that if a woman is obedient, harm will not befall her), *rules* (living in a world she has not made and does not understand, a woman needs to know what she is supposed to do next), and *love* (a concept of love based on formal areas of accountability: If a woman is pleasing and obedient to God and her husband, she will be provided for).

At America's Pro-Family Conference, these themes abounded in both the printed material and the speeches by the national leaders of the Christian Right. Women were encouraged to buy cassettes and/or books with titles such as *How to Live with a Difficult Man* [no parallel title is sold to husbands], *The Role of the Godly Woman, Profile of a Godly Mother, Women's Lib vs. God's Plan, Understanding the Male Temperament* [no parallel title is sold to husbands], *Lord, Change Me!,* and *The Spirit-Controlled Woman* [my emphasis]. The philosophy is the same as that presented in the "Totaled" Woman seminars that have been taught in many church meeting halls in recent years: A woman survives by ministering to her husband's every need and suppressing her own needs and impulses toward wholeness. (Conversely, feminists believe that empathy, caring, and support should be manifested by *both* persons in a marriage.) Beverly LaHaye, whose *The Spirit-Controlled Woman* is described as "the study of why women act the way they do and what the Holy Spirit can do to strengthen a woman's weaknesses," operates Family Life Seminars out of San Diego with her husband. Their business includes a cassette-of-the-month club with a cassette album that delivers the whole message on the cover: The dominant figure in a collage is a well-dressed, macho-type husband staring forcefully straight ahead and oozing "family leadership" out of every pore; behind his left shoulder, in somewhat smaller proportion, stands his wife gazing at him hopefully.

Phyllis Schlafly, head of the "Stop ERA" movement and the right-wing Eagle Forum, which got its start with funding from the John Birch Society, predictably told the "pro-family" conference that the ERA is "an attack on God's plan for the family." However, when she speaks to "positive women" specifically, she is openly Machiavellian about the sexual politics of a patriarchal marriage: A successful wife can "motivate" her husband and "teach him, restrain him, reward him, and have power over him that he can never achieve over her with all his muscle."[19] In other words, careful manipulation is advised to compensate for total economic dependency. (The Christian Right opposes laws for community property in marriage and divorce as an invasion into family matters.) Ironically, Schlafly calls feminists "man-haters" because of our critiques of male power plays, but expresses unmistakable contempt for men themselves that runs through all her analyses. In her opinion, it was the women's demonstrations that "gave the men the backbone they needed" to overthrow the leftist government of Goulart in Brazil in 1964 and, again, that gave men "the courage they needed" to overthrow Allende in Chile's coup of 1973.[20] [Both sets of demonstrations were covertly directed by the Right.] Some observers have suggested a correlation between the fact that a major solution by the liberals for family protection, i.e., Social Security, failed Schlafly and her mother (their father/husband had never been employed long enough to accrue any benefits for them after his death) and Schlafly's lifetime commitment to tightening the screws on patriarchal roles for men.[21]

As millions of women have come to realize, neither the fundamentalists' model of obedient servitude nor Schlafly's shrewder version is a path toward fulfillment — or even mental health. Because many women struggle against their "natural destiny" under patriarchy, they outnumber men by far in tranquilizer addiction and in seeking psychotherapy. Depression among women is often widespread in sub-cultures that are ultrapatriarchal, such as the Mormon Church. Therapists in Salt Lake City have reported that Mormon women constitute three-quarters of their patient load and commonly suffer from low self-esteem and lack of fulfillment outside the home.[22] In Utah, suicide among teenage females, teenage marriages, divorce, and rape occur at much higher rates than the national averages.[23] Schlafly tells those women and others in similar straits, "We get our esteem from Jesus, not society"[24] — a curious claim from someone who spends most of her time flying around the country making speeches and media appearances and who glories in being known as the most powerful woman in the Republican Party.

The Christian Right also enlists numerous followers by raising the specter of *the bad mother*. They imply that a woman is failing her children unless she holds ultraconservative, fundamentalist views. Their largest anti-gay campaign is called "Save Our Children"; the Pro-Family Forum's pamphlet on the public schools is titled "Is Humanism Molesting Your Child?"; and Schlafly warns that a daughter's life can be "shattered by a chance encounter with a 'consciousness-raising session.'"[25] She exhorts women to align with the Christian Right in order to safely distance themselves as far as possible from feminists, whom she describes as "marital misfits"[26] who dislike children and despise mothering them.[27] Once again, such slandering clashes with reality. Millions of feminist mothers, while doubting perhaps that we can completely eradicate sexism in our lifetimes, are fighting with great determination for our children's future in a better world.

With the publication of *Wealth and Poverty* in early 1981, George Gilder added another dimension to the Far Right's manipulation of women: If women attempt to alter their dependence on men, civilization will collapse! Gilder explains that feminists are overestimating the male nature by believing men can live and love in egalitarian situations; actually, he claims, men are incapable of participating in familial and sexual love unless they can maintain a sense of masculine dominance.[28] He insists that a wife's earning more than her husband necessarily destroys his role, his reason for being, and causes the breakdown of the family.[29] Independent women upset this scheme, of course, and he is distressed that "the equal-rights campaign discriminates in favor of female credentials over male aggressiveness and drive."[30] How influential is Gilder? The Reagan administration has bought cartons of his book to distribute to Congress and throughout the Christian Right; David Stockman, Budget Director, considers *Wealth and Poverty* "a coherent, comprehensive philosophical base for what we're trying to do."[31] Within a few weeks of its publication, Schlafly began telling Congressional committees, "It's time to reassert the dignity and social good of the male provider role."[32] Also during that period, California State Senator John Schmitz, a national director of the John Birch Society, explained to the press, upon attaining an appointment to the California Commission on the Status of Women in order to abolish it, that a society which tinkers with the necessarily dependent role of women suffers problems such as rape and other crime: "Women civilize men. To the extent they reject that function, they have to be held responsible for the decline in civilization."[33] How can women, who have no authority in patriarchal society, possibly be blamed for the direction society takes? If women *are* the civilizers — and many radical feminists would agree — then logically the civilizers should direct society, or at least hold half the power since a society controlled by a predominantly aggressive group can only become violent and self-destructive. When Schlafly asserts that women have the responsibility to "spin the fabric of civilization,"[34] we wonder whether she has been reading Mary Daly. However ironic, though, the point of convergence is slight: The members of the New Right/Christian Right agree that woman possesses considerable elemental power, but they insist that she must use it to serve man rather than to shape society. The only "logic" behind this is, as usual, the desire to control women.

## WHO THEY ARE

The Christian Right consists of several national organizations with interlocking directorates. All of them exploit single-issue causes through a centralized fund-raising operation of direct mail campaigns that dwarf any similar efforts by the liberals of either party. Using computerized mailing lists that have been repeatedly cleaned and expanded over recent years, they raise millions of dollars and can send out emotional calls for millions of citizens' letters to flood Congress on specific issues.

The largest expansion of those lists has occurred through the efforts of right-wing fundamentalist ministers on evangelical television programs, "the electronic church." There are now about fifty Christian television stations and four Christian networks; programs are also televised via 3,000 cable stations. The three Christian Right ministers with the largest audiences are M. G. Pat Robertson of "The 700 Club," Jerry Falwell of "Old-Time Gospel Hour," and Jim Bakker, a former employee of Robertson's, of "Praise the Lord Club." Robertson has an audience of five million, an annual budget of $100 million, and owns the Christian Broadcasting Network in Virginia Beach; Falwell has an audience of 15 million, an annual budget of $60 million, and a television station in Lynchburg[35]; Bakker is also said to take in at least $1 million per week but his PTL network, headquartered in Charlotte, North Carolina, has suffered financial problems.[36] All three push the same political causes; all three run a fundamentalist college; and all three depend on holding their audiences and the flow of contributions. There are competitive tensions among them, which Falwell has acknowledged by predicting that the "top eight" television evangelists will be whittled to "three or four" within the next few years.[37]

Falwell himself has ensured that he is a long-range contender by joining forces with the leaders of the Far Right to form Moral Majority, Inc. in 1979. Moral Majority now lobbies in every state except Utah on single-issue politics and elective offices; many of their members were delegates to the 1980 Republican Convention. Their rolls include 72,000 ministers, who reach countless others. They publish a biweekly newspaper, *Moral Majority Report,* with such articles as "Women at West Point Called a Waste," "Falwell Says NOW Not Representative of Women," and "All in the Family" (urging opposition to Senator Cranston's Domestic Violence Prevention and Services Bill). They also sponsor "I Love America" rallies at state capitols; in the unratified states rally-goers are issued buttons saying "Stop ERA" and signs saying "Protect the Family; Stop ERA." A fourteen-year-old participant at Falwell's "I Love America" rally in Springfield, Illinois, in May 1980 told the *Chicago Sun-Times,* "God made woman to submit herself to man. Men are superior," she explained, "and that's how it's supposed to be."[38]

Moral Majority was founded with the help of Paul Weyrich (director of the Committee for Survival of a Free Congress, and President of the Free Congress Foundation, Inc., which publishes the *Family Pro-*

*tection Report* and holds training sessions for right-wing candidates) and Howard Phillips (director of the Conservative Caucus, which has an extensive lobby and campaign network nationwide). The executive director of Moral Majority, Inc., is Robert Billings, who also serves as an officer of Weyrich's two Free Congress organizations, was President Reagan's religious liaison representative during the 1980 campaign, and became an assistant to the Secretary of Education in early 1981. Falwell serves as president and is their most vocal spokesperson.

Billings' son, William, heads the National Christian Action Coalition, which publishes *The Christian's Political Action Manual*, a guide to organizing congregations by precinct, mastering campaigning techniques, lobbying ("front door" and "back door") and handling the press (e.g., "Rather than deny charges, attack the man who made the charges."). William Billings cites Weyrich, Phyllis Schlafly, and John Terry Dolan (chairman of the National Conservative Political Action Committee) for inspiration and assistance in his writing the *Manual*. He also organized the Christian Voters' Victory Fund, which publishes the *Family Issues Voting Index*, a report card of the voting on "pro-family" issues by the House and the Senate that identifies "immoral" legislators. The *Index* has been reprinted in newsletters of other Christian Right organizations, such as *Concerned Women for America*. Billings shares an office building with the Christian Voice Moral Government Fund, whose legislative director is a former-hippie-turned-Moonie-turned-right-wing-fundamentalist, Gary Jarmin.

Dolan's NCPAC is infamous on Capitol Hill for running exaggerated "attack ads" against liberal lawmakers of both parties; his Ronald Reagan Victory Fund spent $4 million in 1980.[39] With the help of Jesse Helms, NCPAC was founded in 1975 by Richard Viguerie, the wizard of direct mail fund-raising who is known as the godfather of the New Right. His clients include Phillips' Conservative Caucus, Weyrich's CSFC, the National Tax Limitation Committee, Gun Owners of America, and scores of others. Viguerie, who publishes *The Conservative Digest* and was a central figure in the formation of several ultraconservative organizations during the Seventies, states flatly, "Without direct mail, the conservative cause would not exist today."[40] His company, RAVCO, and its subsidiaries keep twenty-five million names on three thousand reels of magnetic tape and send out one hundred million pieces of mail per year.

Weyrich appears on Robertson's and Bakker's television programs, and many of the Christian Right ministers of the electronic church feed their lists of contributors into Viguerie's computers, and it's all so handy. . . . An intriguing aspect of this most perfect of political marriages is who approached whom: The Far Right politicos approached the fundamentalists. Phillips, Weyrich, Viguerie, and Dolan are all veterans of Young Americans for Freedom, an "old" Right campus organization. They were impatient with the Republican Party by the mid-Seventies and were all working on ultraconservative causes in Washington. Weyrich founded the Heritage Foundation, with money from Joseph Coors, and became acquainted with Robert Billings during the latter's unsuccessful bid for a Congressional seat in 1976. Billings, who had started many "untainted" Christian schools throughout the Midwest, had been urged to run by Ed McAteer, then national field director of the Christian Freedom Foundation and recently retired Southeast sales manager for a soap company. When Weyrich realized the outreach that Billings and McAteer had among the conservative Christians in their regions, he urged Billings to return to Washington after the election and represent "the Christian viewpoint" as a lobbyist to counteract the effect of the liberal National Council of Churches. Weyrich's fellow-YAFfer, Howard Phillips, who had been appointed by Nixon to dismantle the U.S. Office of Economic Opportunity and had authored the veto statement that defeated then-Senator Mondale's Child Development [childcare] bill in 1972, broke away from the American Conservative Union and founded the Conservative Caucus in 1974. He later hired McAteer as field director, and the latter became "the connection" who brought the fundamentalist ministers of the Southeast to the Weyrich-Phillips-Viguerie network.

Until that point, the rhetoric of the New Right did not contain catch phrases like "pro-moral," "pro-God," "pro-family," and "God's line of authority in the home." In exchange for several million voters, however, the New Right adopted strategic terms from the fundamentalist lexicon and built the Christian Right movement. McAteer has since founded the Religious Roundtable, a point of convergence for the communication lines of fifty-six Christian Right organizations, but it is Weyrich and his cronies who still call the shots. On alternate Thursdays, leaders of the Christian Right come to Weyrich's office where they meet with "the operations people." These meetings have become known as the Library Court Group, in which, as Weyrich explains, "It has been our job to tell them, 'Okay, here is what to do.' "[41]

Such an arrangement makes for strange bedfellows. For instance, Jerry Falwell was reported by the *Washington Post* to have "made unkind remarks about persons of the Jewish faith and said Catholics were incomplete Christians" at a rally in Richmond.[42] It must be trying for the right-wing fundamentalist ministers to drive into Washington for strategy briefings from an Eastern Rite Catholic (Weyrich), a Russian Jew (Phillips), and a Roman Catholic (Viguerie). [Some years ago, Viguerie took his daughters out of his Catholic parish's catechism classes after he learned they were being shown films on ecology; later he quit the parish entirely after his pastor delivered sermons on the plight of the migrant farmworkers led by Cesar Chavez.[43]] Distasteful to them or not, the right-wing fundamentalists have a successful alliance with the Catholics on outlawing abortion and with the Mormons on blocking the ERA and other pro-feminist legislation. The Mormon Church, one of America's wealthiest corporations with a daily income from investments of $3.5 million, has anti-ERA lobbies in every unratified state. In Florida, they were investigated for violation of election laws because they sent $60,000 in small checks from California Mormons to four anti-ERA candidates just before the 1978 election and had not registered as a lobby with Florida's state government.[44]

## POLITICAL STRATEGIES

Realizing that most Americans do not read a great deal (less, for instance, than Western Europeans), the Christian Right delivers its messages primarily through electronic media: right-wing ministers on evangelical television programs, cassettes of speeches from their conferences and "teaching tapes," and sophisticated computer-generated mailings of personalized letters to voters/donors. Phyllis Schlafly, for instance, distributes videotapes of her anti-ERA speeches, which encourage women to attend her training sessions for anti-ERA organizers.

They also produce a multi-media presentation, *America, You're Too Young to Die*, which they advertise through church, civic, and political gatherings in thousands of communities. It is a seventy-five-minute show that begins with color slides of Americana projected on three large screens, accompanied with excerpts of ballads and Protestant hymns sung by ten performers; the second segment features ominous music and images of decadence; the third features films of dozens of missiles and interviews with Pentagon hawks who feel that the U.S. has become vulnerable to Russia and must vastly increase the defense budget immediately. Interspersed with the slides on decadence (e.g., pornography theaters, sexually exploitive ads, satanic "masters" such as

Charles Manson, and glassy-eyed cult members) are a statue of the Buddha, numerous bloody fetuses that fill the screens with red — plus these feminist images: Gloria Steinem's face, the cover of *Our Bodies, Our Selves,* and women marching behind a "Lesbian Feminist Liberation" banner. At the end of the presentation, the audience is asked to pray to God for help in ridding our country of the "elements of depravity" they have seen on the screen. A female singer kneels and plaintively tells God that she understands such current horrors as the ERA are punishment for our sins and for our moving away from Him.

Once sufficiently incensed, citizens are asked to "correspond regularly with your legislators." Often the letters that emanate from Viguerie's company include petitions that the recipient is asked to circulate and then mail to her/his Senator and Representative — or else a simple statement on an issue, which the recipient is asked to paraphrase in brief letters to Washington. Membership in many Christian Right organizations includes a pledge to write often to lawmakers, while *never* revealing any group affiliation. An extremely shrewd pyramid scheme for generating letters is "prayer chapters," used by Beverly LaHaye's Concerned Women for America and similar grass-roots lobbies. Seven members form a prayer chapter, and the chairpersons of seven chapters constitute a prayer unit. Members are asked to pray daily for the "Key 16" ("the sixteen elected officials who make decisions that affect each one of us and our families: five at the national level, five at the state level, and six at the local level") *and* to be ready to receive "special news alerts" via the unit leaders which call for letters to be sent to all or some of the Key 16. (Concerned Women for America often recruits members by inviting them, via church bulletins, to large "prayer breakfasts.") The collective *consciousness* that the Christian Right is building concerning their political activities and goals should not be overlooked.

Another tactic is registering voters *in the churches* after services. Moral Majority claims to have brought three million new voters into the electoral process in that way. Surveys have revealed that a majority of the unregistered voters are evangelicals, since they believe earthly life is merely a Devil-ridden, transitory experience that one must bear before being united with Jesus in the afterlife. Although apolitical, these people naturally respond to their newly politicized ministers telling them that America is facing a "death struggle" with "satanic elements," such as feminists and humanists.

Whipping up such fears on a massive level of demonstration was the motivation behind the Washington for Jesus March in April 1980, which brought 200,000 "true believers" to the Capitol Mall. It was sponsored by Reverends Robertson, Bakker, Falwell, and John Giminez, who conceived the idea; by Senator Paul Laxalt (R-Nevada) and Representative Larry McDonald (D-Georgia), who is an official of the John Birch Society; by Anita Bryant; and by several political lobbies such as Christian Voice, One Nation Under God, Religious Roundtable, and Moral Majority. All of the official publicity denied that the march was political, but several aspects belied that: Marchers were recruited and organized by voting precincts and were to present petitions to their federal legislators. Each participant was asked to sign a "prayer commitment" citing their address (more fodder for Viguerie's computers) plus the name of their Senators and Representative. Occasionally the apolitical veneer cracked and the truth poked through. For instance, in an unguarded moment on Robertson's "The 700 Club" television program, a supporter of the march, Iverna Tompkins, explained, "Is it political? Yes, it's political. We are against those who would turn the country over to women. God is against it."[45]

In Congress, the Christian Right has proposed several "pro-moral" bills, the best known of which are Jesse Helms's attempt to reinstate prayer in schools and Paul Laxalt's Family Protection Act. In 1963 the U.S. Supreme Court ruled that group prayer in schools violates the First Amendment since no school district nor other governing body has the right to impose religious practices, even if they are "voluntary." The Helms bill sought to remove school prayer from the jurisdiction of the federal courts. The Senate passed it in 1979, but the following summer the House was sharply divided during hearings on the issue. Even many fellow Republicans were outraged at Helms's attempt to erode the Supreme Court's jurisdiction and, in the patriarchal language of Rep. Harold Sawyer (R-Michigan), "virtually emasculate the Bill of Rights."[46] [Interesting that our leaders consider the Constitution a masculine, virile entity. . . .] The Christian Right is determined to impose patriarchal religion on the public schools; beyond the Helms measure, they also talk about a Constitutional amendment.

Laxalt's Family Protection Act was originally introduced in September 1979. Its thirty-eight proposals would legislate the values of the Christian Right in education (prayer sessions in public buildings; textbook censorship; union-busting against teachers; tax-exempt status for Christian, i.e., white, schools, and tax credits for parents who send their children there), welfare (no food stamps for students), "First Amendment guarantees" (remove Christian schools and operations from any federal accrediting or regulating), taxation (additional exemption credit for childbirth or adoption — for married couples only), and domestic relations (no federal funds for child-abuse or spouse-abuse services; no federal funds for the Legal Services Corporation's assistance in cases concerning abortion, desegregation, divorce, or gay rights). Uncharacteristically, the Christian Right actually acknowledges in this bill the need of millions of Americans for daycare services, but wants it to be handled privately by employers; they would also extend the tax credits for childcare to cover volunteer work of a religious/political nature. In truth, a few provisions among the thirty-eight make sense, such as the "multigenerational household incentive" which would offer tax credits or exemptions for persons over sixty-five, but the overall package is a right-wing fundamentalist nightmare, one that will recur in Congress throughout the Eighties.

One of the major subterfuges of the Christian Right's political strategy is to pretend they are merely saving us all from "the federal power grab": Schools, public services, labor-protective laws, and civil rights for women and minorities should all be left up to each state. It is extremely important to realize that the Christian Right is organized at *all* levels of government and fully intends to take over state and local systems — even down to district school boards. (It was a group of Baptists led by a Mormon who forced the school board in Concord, California, to place a partial ban on *Ms.* magazine in June 1980, hoping to set an inspiring precedent; ACLU sued.[47]) While rarely revealing their affiliations, members of the Christian Right have lobbied against ERAs at state levels, as well as against state laws concerning domestic violence (a newsletter from Concerned Women for America explained that battered women do not really want refuge centers because such a program would be inflationary![48]), the prosecution of rape, and community property during marriage and divorce. The well-funded opposition to these progressive laws is an instance of what Sonia Johnson, the excommunicated head of Mormons for ERA, has aptly labeled *patriarchal panic.*

Another sleight of hand is the Christian Right's manipulation of their single-issue campaigns. People donating money for a specific, emotionally presented cause, e.g., anti-abortion, anti-gun-control, are not told that each single-issue drive operates under the umbrella of comprehensive right-wing goals. For instance, the very few right-wing legislators who always vote pro-abortion, presumably from libertarian leanings, are never targeted for defeat because their ultraconservative votes on every other issue are valuable to the Far Right. Similarly, Gun Owners of America, founded by Viguerie in 1975, ignores opponents of gun control who are liberal or progressive and supports only those who are ultraconservative. In short, what you see is not necessarily what you get from the Christian Right.

## COMPREHENSIVE GOALS

Although feminism is one of the major targets of the Christian Right, there are many others. They oppose unions; busing, desegregation, and affirmative action; national health insurance; federal subsidies for social services or public education; "dangerous" humanist institutions, such as ACLU and NEA (and, of course, NOW); the Departments of Education and Health and Human Services; and nearly all federal regulatory agencies such as OSHA, EEOC, EPA, FTC, FDA, and Ralph Nader's proposed Consumer Protection Agency. Shortly after President Reagan was elected, the Heritage Foundation sent him a lengthy "blueprint for a conservative American government" that recommended cutting the food stamp program, abolishing the Department of Energy, and withdrawing the Justice Department from suits involving busing.[49] During the same period, Senator Orrin Hatch (R-Utah), a Congressional favorite of the Christian Right, announced that his top priority as the new chair of the Senate's Labor Committee would be to press for a Constitutional amendment banning all affirmative action programs.[50] Imposing their *laissez-faire* utopia would amount to turning back the clock at least a hundred years — with one exception: They are outspoken proponents of nuclear energy and weaponry.

Their selective religiosity allows them to piously defend ultraconservative priorities over Jesus' gospel of love: "Love thy neighbor as thyself" becomes "Kill a Commie for Christ." A Christian Right candidate for Congress, Rev. Bob Thoburn of Virginia, once explained that even graduated income tax is among their "unbiblical" targets, as are "fourth-rate powers" of the Third World:

The welfare state is contrary to the Bible. The purpose of civil government is to punish criminals, protect our property rights, and maintain a strong defense. The government's function is not to redistribute wealth; the income tax is unscriptural. . . . The free market is the biblical approach to economics. . . . We should have let the military win in Vietnam in a couple of weeks. The most powerful nation in the world could have easily licked a fourth-rate power like them.[51]

John Terry Dolan would reduce the function of government even further and appropriate the federal budget as follows: "Ninety-nine percent for defense — keep America strong — and one percent for delivering the mail. That's it. Leave us alone."[52]

They have no intention of leaving *other* people alone, of course, and actually intend to reinstate the House Committee on Unamerican Activities (also known as the House Internal Security Committee)! They encourage discrimination against homosexuals; they hope to block every option for women other than being "the weaker vessel" in a patriarchal marriage; and they insist that all children in public schools be taught creationism alongside evolutionism. (Bills requiring the teaching of creationism are pending in more than fifteen states.) It is extremely unlikely that they would allow in textbooks any of the creation myths other than Genesis, even though the oldest creation myth in Europe, that of Gaia, the pre-Olympian Earth Mother Goddess Who brought forth the world parthenogenetically, long pre-dates the Bible. Censorship, in fact, is a favored tactic of the Christian Right. The American Library Association reported more attempts to ban or restrict materials from school libraries in 1979 than in the last twenty-five years; immediately after the November 1980 election, the rate of such incidents jumped 500 percent, from about four a week to four a day.[53] Since they consider public schools and universities to be hotbeds of humanists, the Christian Right wants to monitor and control public education but not fund it with tax money; their commitment, rather, is to building a vast network of Christian academies and colleges.

Paul Weyrich has proudly labeled the members of the new right-wing coalitions "radicals working to overturn the present power structure in this country."[54] They believe the way is clear for fundamentalist groups to influence elections and policy-making because they interpret the First Amendment in a one-way direction that protects churches from government but not vice versa. Many Constitutional experts, however, believe that the Founding Fathers had in mind a complete separation of church and state. In the matter of tax-exemption, the IRS' rules prohibit politicking by any tax-exempt group whether religious, environmental, cultural, etc. Numerous fundamentalist, Catholic, and Mormon congregations seem to be in violation, and lawsuits are pending.

In addition to the Christian Right's fondness for censorship, conformity, and control, their leaders, e.g., Viguerie and Phillips, speak gleefully of "punishing" and taking "revenge on people who go against us."[55] Just after the November 1980 election, Paul Weyrich publicly warned Vice-President Bush that he had better "hew the line" of the ultraconservatives, and John Terry Dolan publicly warned President Reagan that he had "not only a moral obligation . . . but a political obligation" to heed the "massive conservative mandate."[56] [Actually, the voter turn-out in that election was the lowest in thirty-two years, and only one out of four eligible voters voted for Reagan.]

They have begun, as do all fascist movements, by attacking the most traditionally powerless groups: women, Blacks, homosexuals, welfare recipients, laborers. [See "The Nazi Connection" by Gloria Steinem, *Ms.*, Oct. and Nov. 1980.] Their ends justify any means because of the Christian Right's disconcerting belief that they have the obligation to follow "God's law" rather than civil law whenever they decide the two conflict. They even possess the obligatory conspiracy theory: The government, schools, and media have been taken over by a handful of secular humanists/feminists — who believe in a "godless, socialist one-world government." To intimidate citizens who are not "true believers," the Christian Right employs a password: "Are you born-again?" is being asked in all parts of the country in challenging tones that call one's national loyalty into question.

Although alarmed by the feminists' international networking, the Christian Right itself has an eye on overseas expansion. Several of the leading right-wing fundamentalist ministers were flown to Taiwan by that government and treated as statesmen in July 1980. Bill Bright's Campus Crusade for Christ International has launched a $1 billion campaign to carry his "I Found It" crusade worldwide. To export the Christian Right's entire package, though, would require certain modifications. Their ace tactic, direct mail, would not be efficacious in most Third World countries where right-wing dictators have kept the majority of the populace illiterate and poverty-ridden, but adapted productions of their multi-media presentation would probably draw sizeable crowds. . . .

## WHAT WE CAN DO

To protect ourselves and our children from the onslaught of the Christian Right, we need activist coalitions that match the size and strength of theirs. They are neither "moral" nor a "majority"; they are

490     *Spirituality as a Political Force*

simply well organized. But wherever they appear — at their "I Love America" or "God Bless America" or "America, You're Too Young to Die" rallies — there also we will be, picketing, leafleting, and exposing the hidden agenda of right-wing oppression behind their talk of "freedom" and "liberty." Whenever their candidates appear on radio or television, in newspapers or magazines with their "Christian" gospel of sexism, racism, classism, and homophobia, our letters-to-the-editor and telephone calls to call-in programs will follow. The necessity of alliances in forming such a resistance movement is increasingly apparent to those who are being targeted; a week after the November 1980 election, leaders of the AFL-CIO announced that labor would have to "work hard now at establishing political coalitions with minority, women's, religious and other groups with political muscle."[57]

Women and men both within and without patriarchal religions must speak out individually and collectively. The mainline denominations must declare again and again that the right-wing fundamentalists do not own the Judeo-Christian tradition nor "the Christian vote" — and feminists must make clear that *the patriarchy does not own spirituality and morality*. Just prior to the Washington for Jesus March in April 1980, a coalition of mainline Christian and Jewish leaders, known as the April Alliance, released statements to the press on the "arrogance" and the danger of the Christian Right's attempt to steamroll over the diversity that constitutes America and to impose their repressive desires on Congress. Similar stands must be taken publicly by national, regional, and local leaders of the Judeo-Christian community. Since the hate campaign of the Christian Right against opponents is often quite vicious, clergy women and men are not likely to speak out *unless* they receive letters of support and encouragement from their congregations. Some of the mainline churches are also considering buying television time and even stations in order to fight the right-wing minorities on the electronic turf. In October 1980, many clerical leaders joined with Norman Lear to form People for the American Way (P.O. Box 2000, Marion, OH 43302), a coalition dedicated to waging "media war" against Christian Right oppression; their first project was a series of television "commercials" produced by Lear.

In Dallas, a local coalition of feminists, gays, and clergy called "The Thinking Majority" protested the National Affairs Briefing, a Christian Right convention sponsored by McAteer's Religious Roundtable and the Rev. James Robison Foundation in August 1980. Ronald Reagan, John Connally, Phyllis Schlafly, and Jerry Falwell were among the speakers. As usual, the crowds were attracted through covert publicity in church bulletins rather than public media, so the protesters learned of the event only a month beforehand. Still, they held a press conference and radio interviews, staged a counter-rally nearby, and leafleted the convention.

Letter-writing alone will not carry the day, but right now our legislators at all levels are being deluged with voters' letters orchestrated by the Christian Right. Their rank-and-file write *regularly* to their "Key 16." We must do the same; brief letters or postcards will suffice. Starhawk, a feminist activist and author, has suggested that we use the network we already have as a letter-writing network: The first ten minutes of any kind of feminist, labor, Black community, etc., meeting should be spent on writing letters to a specific legislator on a specific topic. Begin by phoning the reference desk of your local library to get the addresses of your legislators. To find out how your federal Representative and Senators voted recently on controversial subjects, send $1 to the National Women's Political Caucus (1411 K Street, NW, Washington, DC 20005) and/or write to Americans for Democratic Action (same address). The latter also publishes *A Citizen's Guide to the Right Wing* and the monthly *Legislative Newsletter*.

Alert citizens can force the covert lobbying groups of the Christian Right to register with state governments as political lobbies. Many states have laws requiring such registration by any group spending more than $100 to influence legislators. The Mormons were lobbying intensely in Virginia "as independent citizens" until Sonia Johnson forced them to go public by her presenting the state with some of their 85,000 anti-ERA pamphlets, plus evidence of their renting offices and buses to bring demonstrators to Richmond. Similarly, Chris Miller, while running for re-election to the Texas legislature in 1976, exposed the illegal [unregistered] lobbying of a right-wing group called Women Who Want To Be Women.

Political action on a large scale takes money, as the Christian Right — especially Richard Viguerie — knows so well. The Federal Election Campaign Act of 1973 was passed in the wake of revelations that a mere 153 individuals contributed $20 million to Richard Nixon's 1972 campaign. The Act limits an individual's contribution to a federal candidate's campaign to $1,000, and that of a candidate's political action committee to $10,000. However, "independent" PACs can raise money and contribute it freely. For example, Dolan's NCPAC was one of five committees that together raised more than $35 million for Reagan's campaign in 1980.[58] Viguerie and Dolan tell potential contributors that modest but regular donations are needed to counteract "big labor" money; actually, NCPAC took in three times as much money as did the AFL-CIO's COPE in 1977.[59] The Christian Right's coffers have swelled because they reach people who are usually apolitical and they practically extort contributions with fear-raising, emotional tactics. As best we can, we must financially support the liberal and progressive PACs and bring new people to their mailing lists. Small contributions by many is the key.

To counter the offensives of the Christian Right, we must keep informed of their tactics and campaigns. An excellent starting point is *The Fear Brokers* (Beacon Press) by former U.S. Senator Thomas J. McIntyre (D-New Hampshire) and John C. Obert; McIntyre was targeted for defeat in 1978 by Howard Phillips' Conservative Caucus and was replaced by a CC field coordinator, Gordon Humphrey. The smear tactics of NCPAC are being challenged in a counteroffensive media campaign by Democrats for the Eighties, chaired by Pamela Harriman (P.O. Box 3797, Washington, DC 20007). George McGovern has founded Americans for Common Sense (P.O. Box 472, Washington, DC 20044) to develop sound alternatives to right-wing extremism. In addition, Group Research, Inc. (419 New Jersey Ave., SE, Washington, DC 20003) publishes a monthly newsletter on the Far Right.

The most active organization closely monitoring the Christian Right and other versions of the New Right is Interchange Resource Center (2027 Massachusetts Ave., NW, Washington, DC 20036). Allyne Kell, director, and Georgia Fuller, assistant director, publish the bimonthly *Interchange Report* and occasional bulletins; they also facilitate the building of anti-Far-Right networks of moderates, liberals, and progressives at state and national levels. Senator Robert Dole (R-Kansas) has labeled the Interchange alliance "one of the greatest single threats to the conservative movement that we have ever faced during the past decade."[60] Sound good? Contributions from individuals, groups, and foundations are a sound investment in our future. Interchange is a resource clearinghouse and welcomes information from all parts of the country about New Right/Christian Right activities.

In early 1981, Women USA (76 Beaver St., New York, NY 10005; P.O. Box 8214, Washington, DC 20024) was founded by Bella Abzug, Yvonne Brathwaite Burke, Maggie Kuhn, Brownie Ledbetter, Patsy Takemoto Mink, and Gloria Steinem. Those six activists have volunteered their lobbying and organizing skills to establish an effective network of women to fight the Right. The main project of Women USA is a toll-free "hot line" (800-221-4945; in New York State, dial 212-344-2531), which advises callers of current issues, often suggesting specific actions, such as sending letters or telegrams. The hot line is supported by contributions, and Steinem has urged feminists to donate ten percent of our income to feminist organizations, noting that some of the most powerful Christian Right groups got that way through the ten-percent tithe.

The Christian Right calls the Eighties "the Decade of Destiny." They are well along the way to achieving their avowed take-over. Many of us previously dismissed them as being merely fanatical and not a serious threat. They are both. The time is due, if not overdue, to speak out against and resist the march of the Christian Right. It is not "God's army" we are fighting — it is misogyny, bigotry, greed, and fear. Those are the enemies.

## NOTES

1. *Declaration of National Moral Emergency*, 29 April 1980, signed by Bill Bright, Philip Crane, W. A. Criswell, Jerry Falwell, Jesse Helms, D. James Kennedy, Albion W. Knight, Tim LaHaye, Tom Landry, J. Wm. Middendorf II, James Robison, and Roger Staubach.
2. Quoted in *Interchange Report*, vol. 1, no. 2, June 1979.
3. George Romney, speaking of ERA supporters during an interview by Harry Cook, Knight-Ridder Wire Release, 19 Dec. 1979.
4. This phrase and variations of it appear in nearly all material from the Christian Right; see especially Tim LaHaye's pamphlet and book *The Battle for the Minds*.
5. Meldrim Thomson, Jr., national chairman of the Conservative Caucus, quoted by M. Eileen McEachern, "Don't Call Me Ms.," *The Boston Globe Sunday Magazine*, 12 March 1978.
6. A Gallup poll of December 1979 determined that 60 million Americans are "born again" Christians; not all those evangelicals are right-wing, but subtracting the liberals is thought to be equalized by adding the number of other ultraconservatives in the Christian Right movement who are right-wing but not "born again" (e.g., many Catholics).
7. Jesse Helms expressed this opinion during both his speech and his press conference at America's Pro-Family Conference, sponsored by a coalition of Christian Right organizations, Long Beach, CA, 12 July

1980. I taped it, as did reporters from major newspapers; it should also be part of the cassette the conference sold of Helms's speech, unless it was edited out.

8. Richard Viguerie, quoted in *A Citizen's Guide to the Right Wing*, Americans for Democratic Action, Spring 1978; Howard Phillips, quoted in an article by Alan L. Otten, *The Wall Street Journal*, 29 May 1975; John Terry Dolan, quoted in "The New Right Brigade," Myra MacPherson, *The Washington Post*, 10 August 1980.

9. Howard Phillips, speech at America's Pro-Family Conference, Long Beach, CA, 12 July 1980.

10. Jerry Falwell, *Listen, America!* (Garden City, N.Y.: Doubleday/Galilee, 1980), p. 151.

11. *Ibid.*, p. 129.

12. Bill Bright, quoted in unabridged article on the Washington for Jesus March, Interchange files; shortened version appeared in *Interchange Report*, vol. 2, no. 1, Spring 1980.

13. Wm. Billings, executive director of the National Christian Action Coalition, "What It Means to Be Pro-Family," flyer for America's Pro-Family Conference, Long Beach, CA, 12 July 1980.

14. Phyllis Schlafly, speech at America's Pro-Family Conference, Long Beach, CA, 12 July 1980.

15. Judy Grahn, *The Work of A Common Woman*, collected poems (New York: St. Martin's Press, 1978), p. 137.

16. The nationwide poll was conducted by William R. Hamilton and Staff for NOW; at America's Pro-Family Conference, 12 July 1980, Tim LaHaye announced that there are only 275,000 humanists in our country, and Jerry Falwell cited 3–4% as their proportion.

17. Falwell, *ibid.*

18. *Ms.*, June 1979, pp. 62–64 and 69–72.

19. Phyllis Schlafly, *The Power of the Positive Woman* (New York: Jove/HBJ, 1977), p. 17.

20. *Ibid.*, pp. 222–223.

21. "Phyllis Schlafly's Formula for a Better Life," Gail Sheehy, *San Francisco Chronicle*, 12 March 1980.

22. Utah Governor's Commission on the Status of Women, *Utah Women: A Profile*, June 1978, p. 42.

23. Sonia Johnson, *Patriarchal Panic: Sexual Politics in the Mormon Church*, paper presented at the American Psychological Association Meetings, New York City, 1 Sept. 1979.

24. Schlafly, speech at America's Pro-Family Conference, Long Beach, CA, 12 July 1980.

25. Schlafly, *The Power of the Positive Woman*, p. 7.

26. *Ibid.*, p. 212.

27. Schlafly, speech at America's Pro-Family Conference, Long Beach, CA, 12 July 1980.

28. George Gilder, *Wealth and Poverty* (New York: Basic Books, 1981), p. 136.

29. *Ibid.*, p. 88.

30. *Ibid.*, p. 137; also see p. 147.

31. "The 'Prophet' Reagan's Men Are Reading," David Treadwell, *San Francisco Chronicle* (from *The L.A. Times*), 22 March 1981.

32. "A Clash Over Worker Sex Harassment," *San Francisco Chronicle*, 22 April 1981.

33. "Outraged Women Rap Appointment of 'Anti-Libber,'" Nancy Day, *San Francisco Examiner and Chronicle*, 21 March 1981.

34. Schlafly, *The Power of the Positive Woman*, p. 177.

35. *Group Research Report*, vol. 18, no. 7, July–Aug. 1979, p. 26.

36. See Dick Dabney, "God's Own Network," *Harper's*, Aug. 1980; also see Ed Briggs, "The Electronic Church," *Richmond Times-Dispatch*, five-article series beginning on 29 March 1979.

37. Briggs, *ibid.*

38. "'I Love America' Rally Turns to Hating ERA," *Chicago Sun-Times*, 7 May 1980.

39. "The New Right Brigade: John Terry Dolan's NCPAC Targets Liberals and the Federal Election Commission," Myra MacPherson, *The Washington Post*, 10 Aug. 1980.

40. "Viguerie: Into Politics by the 'Back Door,'" *Washington Star*, 23 June 1975.

41. "T.V. Evangelists and Small Group Lead 'Christian New Right's' Rush to Power," Dudley Clendinen, *The New York Times*, 18 Aug. 1980.

42. "Churches Press Virginia Senate," Karlyn Barker, *The Washington Post*, 16 Feb. 1980.

43. "The Godfather of the New Right Feels the Torch Is Passing," *Washington Star*, 23 June 1975.

44. "State to Probe Mormon Contributions" and "Mormon Money Worked Against Florida's ERA," Linda Cicero, *The Miami Herald*, 20 and 22 April 1980.

45. The quote was broadcast on 16 Feb. 1980, reported by James S. Tinney, *The Washington Afro-American*, 19 April 1980.

46. "Cold Shoulder to a Prayer Proposal," *San Francisco Chronicle* (reprinted from *The Washington Post*), 30 July 1980.

47. "Magazine Ruled Off-Color But Not Off Limits," *San Francisco Examiner*, 27 June 1980.

48. *Concerned Women for America Newsletter*, March 1980.

49. "Conservative Researchers Expect New Prominence," B. Drummond Ayres, Jr., *The New York Times,* 17 Nov. 1980.

50. Interview with Senator Orrin Hatch, broadcast on NPR, 7 Nov. 1980.

51. *Sojourners,* April 1976.

52. MacPherson, *op. cit.*

53. "Caution: These Pages May Be Banned in Your School," Lisa Cronin Wohl, *Ms.,* Sept. 1980, p. 82. Also, "Behind the Crusade to Ban Books," James Mann, *San Francisco Chronicle,* 16 June 1981.

54. Quoted in *The Fear Brokers,* U.S. Senator Thomas J. McIntyre and John C. Obert (New York: The Pilgrim Press, 1979; Beacon Press, 1981), p. 47.

55. *Ibid.,* p. 156.

56. "New Right Warns Reagan to Heed Mandate," Gaylord Shaw, *San Francisco Chronicle,* 6 Nov. 1980; the first post-election press conference held by Reagan and Bush, at which they were asked about Weyrich's warning, broadcast on NPR, 6 Nov.; "Bush Says Religious Groups Won't Control Reagan," *San Francisco Chronicle,* 11 Nov. 1980.

57. "What Labor Fears Now," Phillip Shabecoff, *San Francisco Chronicle* (from *The New York Times*), 12 Nov. 1980.

58. MacPherson, *op. cit.*

59. Federal Election Commission files, cited in *The Fear Brokers,* p. 62.

60. Quoted in *Interchange Report,* vol. 1, no. 2, June 1979.

# The Voice of Women's Spirituality in Futurism

# Baba Copper

Speculation about possible futures has been a necessary part of human survival for a long time. The act of formulating and communicating an image of the future — a projected possibility — itself becomes a part of that future. Modern future studies have a profound impact on the fabric of our society, greater by far than the simple studies of supply and demand that past agricultural or commercial planners performed. Futurists in all fields — from commodity sales to government planning to science fiction — shape our lives through their predictions. Whether the methodology used is a projection of statistical trends or simply the expansion of a hunch into a theory, futurists have great power over the directions a complex technological society takes. Our highly interdependent world culture must relate with a futurist orientation to the finite environment we inhabit.

Future studies only recently have become a recognized academic field. The discipline largely explores an elite vision of a technologically sophisticated future and is dominated by white males. The academic futurist, as well as his corporate and governmental colleague, projects the political, economic, and social institutions more or less as they exist today. Social change is treated as a problem to be controlled, usually by the creation of institutions to manage change in the interests of the men who subsidize the planning.

Few of these futurists are in touch with the dynamic shifts in consciousness that are exploding within the masses for whom they plan. Comfortably unchallenged by a feminist perspective, they exchange their ideas at conferences or commissions on the future. (For example, the thirty-eight members of the Commission on the Year 2000 were all men; and in its first eight years, the journal of the World Future Society, *The Futurist*, has published nearly 500 articles but included only twenty-one authored or co-authored by women.) Futurist writers such as Daniel Bell, in *The Coming of Post-Industrial Society*, and Alvin Toffler, in *Future Shock* and *The Third Wave*, keep a firm hold on the public imagination. The popular image of the future remains captive to the proliferation of complicated machines which dehumanize our environment, to the increased regimentation of our lives as consumers and workers, and to the acceleration in loss of personal and political power.

Recognition of these patriarchal limitations has encouraged feminists to develop new analytical tools in relation to the past and the future. A new sense of prideful competence and creativity among women has exploded in a vigorous acknowledgment of responsibility for naming the future. In "Feminist Visions of the Future," Jane Dolkart and Nancy Hartsock proposed, "Visions can structure our priorities, provide a measure of our successes, hold a source of energy for change."[1] Feminist journals such as *Quest* and *Country Women* have devoted whole issues to future visions; female science fiction writers such as Ursula LeGuin, Marge Piercy, and Joanna Russ have explored totally new directions in speculative fiction; futurists such as Hazel Henderson, author of *Creating Alternative Futures* and *The Politics of the Solar Age: Alternatives to Economics,* and sociologists such as Elise Boulding have brought new perspectives on ecologically sane limitations of technology to the ivory towers of the male planners.

## THE DYNAMICS OF FUTURISM

Every era has had futurists, although they may not have been labeled as such. Fred Polak, a sociologist of history, argues in *The Image of the Future* that history can be seen as nothing more than the "read-out" of the input of futurists.[2] In ancient times, prophets and philosophers lobbed ideas into the future that have exploded centuries later among peoples quite unfamiliar with their originators (e.g., Marx, Jefferson, Thomas More). In the nineteenth century, artists discovered the power of futurist projections: Religion lost its hold over the imagination of people as the consensus image of the future shifted from the postponed rewards of the Kingdom of Heaven to the more immediate magic of machines. The love affair between artists and the ideology of science, which promises the liberation of humanity through the defeat of nature, has spawned the irrationally seductive images of the future that we have now — space wars and computer people.

All futurists, past and present, do battle with the assumptions that sustain consensus reality. Although most people are convinced that what they see as "natural" is also eternal, their attitudes shift regularly as a result of the efforts of those who project the future and those who redefine the past. The present is the point of action between experience from the past and expectations for the future. If we have accepted false interpretations of past experience, such as minimizing the importance of the contribution of women, then we prejudice the actions we take in the present. If we expect a negative future in which we have no control over our lives or the world into which we bring our children, then our present will reflect this. Our motivation and direction of action are dependent on our attitudes, especially the ethical criteria we apply to the information we accept from the past.

## THE ETHICS OF GENDER POLARITY

Most people are unaware of the beliefs with which they guard the boundaries of their experience. For instance, few recognize that their acceptance of the polarization of human traits into "masculine" and "feminine" is a fallacy that has a direct negative impact upon their lives, whether they are male or female. Society rewards certain character traits and penalizes others. If, for instance, empathy and nurture are appropriate to females, but not to males, then we cannot expect male-dominated societies to be cooperative — either with each other or with the rest of nature — since cooperation flows directly from the exercise of these two human traits.

In the ancient struggles waged by men to shift matrifocal social structures to a new focus on patriarchal property rights, male gods were invented to legitimate a system whereby a female's labor and reproductive capacity belonged exclusively to one man. Ethical strictures that buttressed that political system became religious law. Thus, culturally prescribed character traits that protected male ownership of women were codified into a double standard of ethics for men and women.

Ethics is defined as the science of ideal human character. It is the skeleton upon which we project the living flesh of culture. The division of human characteristics into polar opposites of masculine and feminine, with the differentiation reflecting a gender-based value hierarchy, has had disastrous significance throughout patriarchal history. The character traits associated with the exercise of dominance, violence, and control have become the idealized model for males, even as the social results of that limited personality are deplored. The absence of "feminine virtues" — devalued as corollaries of submission — from the decisions and choices surrounding power insures the repeated triumph of tyranny.

Most modern future planning is being done by men who have not questioned the rationality of a belief system that insures character trait specialization by sex. The futures they project are still captive to the masculist values of excessive control, linearity, order through hierarchy, and competition.

## CONSENSUS REALITY

Having identified the fallacy of gender polarity, feminists have turned to deeper probings of the values and priorities that inform cultural choices. Feminism is a strategy of noncompliance with male control over the naming of culture. Adrienne Rich has expressed it this way: "Feminism means finally that we renounce our obedience to the fathers and recognize that the world they have described is not the whole world. Masculine ideologies are the creation of masculine subjectivity; they are neither objective, nor value-free, nor inclusively 'human.' "[3]

The radical changes of consciousness that feminists are discovering have sprung from the exchange of experiential truths between women. This process has been cathartic in detaching women from allegiance to traditional definitions of their past as well as their future. Susan Griffin has written of the revolutionary nature of *thinking* and *feeling* a new world: "I see that what I saw before as real was delusion. Every motion I make to heal myself widens my visions. This comes upon me as joy, as an experience of gladness that the world can be what I imagine.

Rape is an invention. Rape can be unimaginable. I feel safety. I know what this state is. I feel blessedness. I say we can pronounce this world differently. Our world can become, flesh."[4]

These are words of discovery. The inventors of this vision are feminists who are functioning as futurists. Consensus reality — the dominant cultural expectations within a given time and place — is sustained by a shared state of consciousness. The *change* of consciousness that feminists articulate is a frame of reference which differs radically in its ethical roots and in its definitions of experience from that which sustains current consensus reality.

The general acceptance of the social inevitability of rape reflects a fundamental assumption about human nature that has not been questioned by men or women within patriarchal cultures for centuries. With the possible exception of tiny groups of aboriginal peoples living out Stone Age ethics, rape is a part of the social reality of all societies. No religious prophet, no social utopian, no visionary artist before 1915 articulated a clear image of any other possibility. By not questioning the mass belief that man, alone of all the creatures, must sexually violate others, humans have denied themselves any other possibility. Although the fear of rape has limited the freedom of all women in all patriarchal societies, there have been no reform movements that projected the eradication of rape as a primary priority of social change. This is not to say that male social reformers or religious leaders have condoned rape. However, when the connection between intercourse and violence is seen as fundamental or "natural," then that violence becomes part of the state of consciousness that informs expectations. The absence of an image of human sexual interaction devoid of rape has continually reinforced the power of the mythology that supports rape.

I have used the example of a world without rape as a way to illustrate the potential of projected futures. The future is shaped by our image of it. Those who successfully manipulate the habits of consciousness that limit human possibilities are futurists. By normalizing a *change* of consciousness, the futurist expands the do-able, the thinkable.

Any collective assessment of reality is sustained by an interlocking set of beliefs about what is "natural" or real. These beliefs are exchanged and reinforced among people at all levels of awareness. Belief systems organize our attention, enabling us to choose among myriad stimuli. We cannot always question the origins of our responses to what is desirable, what is beautiful, what is right, what is unchangeable. These are all part of what we think of as "natural." We have strong beliefs about what is fundamental, what is important, what is appropriate, what is taboo or unthinkable. These beliefs are based on the prevailing cultural interpretations of the past, as well as our personal experience. We dignify them to ourselves with privileged labels such as *custom, instinct, tastes, traditions, laws of nature, human nature, fundamental truths, morals,* or *ethics.* They are our springboards for action.

## VALUES OF FEMINIST SPIRITUALITY

More than a critique of patriarchal reality, feminism is spiritual transition, a politics of *being* in which a change of consciousness is integrated with modes of living. New values and priorities emerge from this process. Along with the most visible aspects of feminism — solid political goals such as the Equal Rights Amendment, equal pay for equal work, adequate childcare — women have focused attention on the internalized bonds that keep us alienated from each other and ourselves. Cathartic self-valuing and the unlearning of rivalry and competition between women are the first steps toward new definitions of "natural" ways for women. Detachment from the objectification and standardized goals of beauty or fashion has allowed women to respect our bodies in ancient ways, acknowledging the sacredness of female mysteries: rhythmic bleeding in a lunar cycle, nurturing another life in our bodies, transforming blood into milk. By affirming the natural rhythms of womanhood, women are reawakening to the sacredness of all nature and our responsible relationship to Her infinite complexity.

The re-emergence of Goddess imagery has provided a focus for a nonlinear metaphor of female humanness, as defined by women. The female experience of time is grounded in the periodicity of woman's body and the natural phenomena of lunar and solar cycles. The conceptual model of time as a spiral releases the human experience of synchronicity (sometimes misnamed "coincidence") from the invisibility of rationalistic denial. As a result, change becomes less inaccessible; its latent repetitious patterns can be addressed. The Tarot, *I Ching,* and astrology are attempts to systematize patterns of change within a nonlinear model of time.

The futurist who predicts by "throwing the bones" and the academic futurist who is armed with computers, statistics, and analyses, differ largely in their understanding of time. The future creates its own anticipation via the futurist. Predictions shape the future to the degree that they are acted upon in the present. There is considerable under-standing of the political use of futurist thinking among women who are exploring the psychopolitical potential of feminist spirituality. Naomi Goldenberg insightfully points out, "[Modern] Witches consider any thought or fantasy real to the degree that it influences actions in the present. In this sense a remembered fact and an invented fantasy have identical psychological value."[5]

By visualizing how we want to be in relation to each other, feminists are changing the way we interact. New definitions of honor between women emphasize the importance of non-competitive bonding, reci-procity, and nurturance of other women from the surplus of internal re-sources that are woman's nature. Sharing, mutual validation, and emo-tional support of women by women begins a needed healing. New definitions of commitment and fidelity are part of the search for an ethic unpolluted by echoes of ownership.

Feminist values emphasize the importance of self-acceptance of the body. By scorning the rewards of power and acceptance that flow from men to the women who adjust their looks to fit a male-defined ideal, feminists reduce the power of male cultural control. Women are reach-ing for honorable interpersonal interactions that do not include "saving face," self-sacrifice, vengeance, manipulation, lies of expedience, or the need to "die for Honor" — as in duelling or wars.

The emerging ethic of feminist spirituality is colored by the experi-ence of motherhood, which directly or indirectly affects the character of all women. The process of child-rearing has many lessons that inform the female value structure. Children are teachers of alternative frames of reference, playfulness, and nonverbal means of communication. Flexibility and fairness are among the lessons of motherhood. Authority without controlling dominance — the sometimes elusive ideal of good mothering — is learned through the process of letting go, by which the mother meets the developing capabilities of her child's growth. The ideals that are evolving from women's newly self-conscious search for our own value priorities are rooted in authentic female experience.

## EXAMINING SEXUAL "MORALITY"

The patriarchal moralist often has been the strongest cultural voice of loathing for female sexuality. Women are developing a new con-sciousness of the importance of gaining control over our own bodies, as well as valuing them. As a corollary to this, feminist analysis has rejected the religious strictures on female sexuality misnamed "morality." Feminist spirituality celebrates the sexual/sensual nature of woman. New ethics specifically exclude the suppression of female sexuality imposed by adherence to the patriarchal system of ownership of women and children. The "moral issues" of chastity, virginity, romantic love, chivalry, nonreciprocal sexual fidelity and monogamy, suppression of childhood sexuality, masturbation, female "carnality" and, above all else, lesbianism — all these are being recognized as dominance strategies.

Pauline Long, a feminist futurist, predicts, "Sexuality will not yield just a pleasant pastime, but become a matter of sacred reverence and put us in touch with our wholeness."[6] Sexuality and love have new connections as the result of the validation of the "feminine" qualities of empathy, affection, and intuition. The mode of knowing through awareness of inner voices and the voices of nature have interwoven women. The future, as well as the naming of culture, is emerging from the clouds of powerlessness and sexual suppression as women apply, in Rich's terms, "the synthesis of reflection and feeling, the personal struggle and critical thinking, which is the core of the feminist process"[7] to the definition of love.

## CONCEPTUAL PROBLEMS IN COMMUNICATION

The difficulties of communicating the female experience within androcentric conceptual categories are great. The separations that we have been trained to expect between the "political" and the personal (i.e., the subjective, the interior or the psychological) confuse any description of authentic female experience. Women, children, and the place of their confinement — the home — have been philologically contained by men as "personal life." This relegation of the politics of sexuality and the home has successfully obscured cracks in the foundations of patriarchal civilization for centuries.

Helen Holmes, a feminist futurist, has noted:

When women are really free to open out and to let their thoughts range without restraint, without fear of interruption, without a view to gaining male esteem and its accompanying power, then I believe that there can be an outwelling of some of the ancient wisdom of the species. Even when women have not permitted themselves to speak out, or when they have not been permitted to speak out, their actions often speak. All their species-nurturing behavior, all their calling-forth of the good in others, through the centuries have expressed these ancient truths. But, alas, for women to achieve any influence in policy-making in today's world, such behaviors and words must be thoroughly suppressed.[8]

Polar absolutes are rejected by feminists as obscuring the more complex truths. Feminism acknowledges the validity of each unique identity or experience; it affirms concern for wholeness and integration. Diversity is seen as an enriching opportunity for synthesis rather than a problem demanding differentiation, categorization, or ranking. Women are claiming the myriad manifestations of female deity, and these are assimilated into the psychology of the seekers as fast as they are conceptualized. Pluralistic invention provides a safe place for each woman's personal growth and self-discovery. Further, beliefs cannot be isolated from temporal action, but the masculist polarization of the spiritual and the political leaves female experience in a kind of conceptual limbo.

The patriarchal sacred texts, in which ethical codes are frozen in time, place authority and responsibility outside of the individual — in law, custom, and traditional roles. The feminist, on the other hand, has moved from being the object to being the active verb in her relationship to her self as well as to others. The miracles of her body, her capacity for nurture and endurance, the magnitude of her powers, talents, and aptitudes — all are sacred. She devotes tremendous energy to negotiating new ethical expectations between women. Because codified behavior often involves covert dominance demands, feminists have developed a willingness to submit one's actions to feminist analysis and interpersonal questioning. Groups of women usually function on the basis of consensus, rather than majority rule. Much attention is given to the balancing of the distribution of power between women, with recognition given to the subtle inequities generated by residual patriarchal socialization. When women gather to explore their dreams, to experience the sense of political-spiritual continuity latent in Witch identification, to exchange affirmation and support, to encircle with talk and experience an abstraction such as loyalty, to sing and dance in celebration of the season — the process itself *is* the spiritual content.

## FEMINIST SPIRITUALITY IN FUTURIST FICTION

The ethical assumptions that sustain patriarchal consensus reality, i.e., the "givens" by which mankind has circumscribed human nature, are shifting under the influence of feminist vision. Speculative fiction has been a strong force in the process of freeing women from the limiting patriarchal expectations of the future. Beyond the redefinitions of appropriate female tasks and traits, futurist fiction provides a stage on which the feminist imagination can project female solutions to human problems and needs.

An example of visionary fiction in which ethical concepts are stretched by both poetic and linguistic means is *The Kin of Ata Are Waiting for You*. In this fantasy about a simple society in which dreams and rituals focus the life of the people, Dorothy Bryant introduces the concepts of "nagdeo" and "donagdeo". "Nagdeo" is that which is good, whole, positive, or constructive but the opposite is left undefined, as if it could not be conceived fully. These two words are woven into the reader's expanding understanding of the spiritually integrated culture of Ata. "But each person finds for himself what is donagdeo. To force anyone to do or not to do something is also donagdeo. Nothing is forbidden. Nothing is taboo."[9]

Two utopian visions of female-named futures that embody much of the feminist ethic are *Herland*, written in 1915 by Charlotte Perkins Gilman, and *The Wanderground*, written in 1978 by Sally Miller Gearhart. Both books recognize woman's need to acknowledge that we are nature's creatures and are dependent upon Her complex well-being. In modern terms, Herland is a labor-intensive, low-density agrarian village society of "people highly skilled, efficient, caring for their country as a florist cares for his costliest orchids."[10] Wanderground is more "primitive"; there the women rely on highly developed psychic powers for communication, transportation, and other needed technologies. Life in both worlds is communal and nonauthoritarian, with the mechanics of decision-making shared or rotated. In both, age is respected and acknowledged for the accumulation of experience it represents.

The underlying assumptions of these futurist characters about their rights and responsibilities to the world around them are exemplified by their attitudes toward the coming generation of young. " 'The children in this country [Herland] are the one center and focus of all our thoughts. Every step of our advance is always considered in its effect on them — on the race. You see, we are *Mothers*,' she repeated, as if in that she had said it all."[11] In Wanderground the girl-children are educated in the Remember Rooms through trance assimilation of personal memories of the past. "Once upon a time," began Bessie, "there was one rape too many. Once upon a time . . . the earth finally said 'no!' There was no storm, no earthquake, no tidal wave or volcanic eruption, no specific moment to mark its happening. It only became apparent that it had happened, and that it had happened everywhere."[12] It was called the Revolt of the Mother.

Both *Herland* and *The Wanderground* are books that evoke strong positive emotions among women readers, similar to the responses described by Griffin in the quotation cited earlier when the possibility of the non-inevitability of rape occurred to her. Although written sixty years apart, both rely on the same feminist analysis and renaming of the past to release women from dominant cultural expectations of the future. The ethics, i.e., the characteristics and choices which the women of these imaginary lands exercise to shape their cultures, are remarkably similar.

## TOWARD A POSTPATRIARCHAL FUTURE

If our attitude toward the future is colored by either indifference or revulsion, our present is afflicted. Mothers, as a category, have a direct investment in the future. On the other hand, women as a class suffer from some of the same limitations on our sense of time as do all oppressed people. Positive future orientation — with clear goals and priorities tailored toward an achievable, self-defined control over our circumstances — is a luxury. Feminist spirituality speaks directly to this dilemma. It is providing a process, a theater of ethical and emotional growth, where women can begin to unravel the socialized restraints on our instinctual drive for survival and cultural wholeness. Women's inner knowledge is beginning to inform the future. The forms of this process are political, the source is ethical independence, which some women find in Goddess-identification or a Witch coven or a solstice circle.

The application of feminist ethics must extend to the task of curbing the ecological and social destabilization resulting from technological overkill. Men have reached the point where evolutionary choices are emerging in their conscious decision-making. The ability of modern science to intentionally or unintentionally modify our life-sustaining matrix is no longer acceptable. Policy that reaches directly into the shelter of women's wombs is being made without the input of mothers, by men whose gender-limited character traits restrict their ability to empathize with the well-being of either nature or future generations.

Further, the ethical criteria that feminists are evolving have not yet been fully applied to the issues of child-rearing and education. Since we know that the past has been falsely reported and interpreted in order to justify male-dominant institutions and roles, mothers can no longer train daughters to be submissive, nor encourage the physical and mental underdevelopment it demands. Feminist mothers who raise children to be "well adjusted" or "successful" within patriarchy are failing to live their ethic. Mothers teach their daughters how to mother by teaching them the values and identity that in turn shapes the mothering that the daughters may do. A shift in mothering to the living and teaching of feminist spiritual values probably cannot be done without personal sacrifice and new support systems among women. However, collective, female-controlled child-rearing goals of gender-balanced character traits and feminist values are essential in the movement away from species extinction.

Finally, the re-definition of death must be part of the transition we make away from the patriarchal hold upon our imagination. Death is part of the future of all who live. Present cultural responses to this fact diminish living. Our vision of the future becomes entangled in the three central mythologies of the linear model of time: novelty, "progress," and personal extinction. The worship of novelty and "progress" creates contempt for past wisdom and protects the new from ethical evaluation. The pulsations of all life, the repetitions, the vibratory cycles are part of the human experience for us to recognize. Our expectation of personal obliteration denies this knowledge and keeps us dancing to anti-life compromises and meaningless life choices.

Writing of the future, Peggy Kornegger has observed, "Women understand that changes in consciousness (and in perceptions *of* consciousness) are at the core of revolutionary change and that those deep, soulshaking, transformations are also the most profound energy sustainers. It is the spirit of hope within us that will keep us going when all else fails. To see being as indestructible energy, death as continuation not obliteration, and revolution as psychic as well as political movement is the vision of feminist spirituality."[13]

NOTES

1. Jane Dolkart and Nancy Hartsock, "Feminist Visions of the Future," *Quest*, vol. 2, no. 1, Summer 1975, p. 2.
2. Frederik Polak, *The Image of the Future*, translated and abridged by

Elise Boulding (New York and Amsterdam: Elsevier Scientific Pub. Co., 1973).

3. Adrienne Rich, *On Lies, Secrets, and Silence* (New York: W. W. Norton & Co., 1979), p. 207.

4. Susan Griffin, *Rape/The Power of Consciousness* (San Francisco: Harper & Row, 1979), p. 25.

5. Naomi Goldenberg, *Changing of the Gods: Feminism and the End of Traditional Religions* (Boston: Beacon Press, 1979), p. 89.

6. Pauline Long, "Politics of Sexuality," *Politics of Matriarchy*, Matriarchal Study Group, London, p. 37.

7. Adrienne Rich, *ibid.*, p. 304.

8. Helen Holmes, "Reproductive Technologies — A Women's Analysis," *Technology — Over the Invisible Line?*, Foundation for National Progress, 1980, p. 1.

9. Dorothy Bryant, *The Comforter* (Berkeley: Evan Press, 1971), p. 53; reissued as *The Kin of Ata Are Waiting for You* (Berkeley and New York: Moon Books/Random House, 1976).

10. Charlotte Perkins Gilman, *Herland* (New York: Pantheon Books, 1979), p. 18.

11. Charlotte Perkins Gilman, *ibid.*, p. 66.

12. Sally Miller Gearhart, *The Wanderground: Stories of the Hill Women* (Watertown, MA: Persephone Press, 1978), p. 158.

13. Peggy Kornegger, "Cosmic Anarchism: Lesbians in the Sky with Diamonds," *Sinister Wisdom*, no. 12, Winter 1980, p. 9.

# Women's Collective Spirit: Exemplified and Envisioned

## Grace Shinell

Ten years ago political women began a movement from a circle. We sat in circles to encompass our group identity; yet, we spoke only from a personal viewpoint; we questioned each other only to clarify, not to criticize. We did consciousness-raising as a political/spiritual process. Ever since, the direction of our movement has puzzled observers, for it is the truly revolutionary direction of the expanding circle. A few examples of that circular pattern will show how all-encompassing has been our movement to date. An extended consideration of social development from earliest times also reveals a pattern of collectivity, effected by women as a political strategy and intensified as a spiritual process.

In the modern movement we began with self-centeredness. An early awareness, developed in our consciousness-raising circles, was the need of every woman to create a positive self-image in sharp relief to the cultural denial that she had experienced. The attainment of a proud, personal independence is still the goal of the moment for many feminists. These women frequently make the conclusive and defensive statement that they cannot work in collectives, and yet they are often drawn for personal reasons into our circles. Their self-interest may be evident and at times resented, but the pattern is set: The discovery of self leads increasingly to the discovery of others.

From self-centeredness, feminists are pushing forward. Some are overturning the established structure, denouncing in one breath materialism and spirituality; others of us are envisioning our future with hindsight, exercising the dynamic energy of spirituality, underplaying the static energy of material considerations — including the material revolution so passionately urged by our politically committed sisters. We are not countering each other's efforts. Assuredly, the revolution will continue as we continue traversing different planes of a cycle, which in balancing energies has twisted, not into two factions — one political, one spiritual — but into a two-sided approach. Our path is a magical double spiral, which allows travelers in opposite directions to surpass each other without confrontation. That is the present direction of our movement, evolved out of the generative interaction of the circle: our sisterhood.

The functioning reality is that political feminists must be spiritually bonded; spiritual feminists must be politically bonded. Because spirit registers through and is expressed as union, the most common expression of spirituality is oneness — in political terms: collectivity. Modern experiments of collectivity conducted in unsupportive, even hostile, environments under the added duress of righting inequities that are fostered by the surrounding culture have proved as enduring and no more difficult than most relationships. The nature of the collective relationship, however, is far more political and spiritual than our individual ways of relating. For this reason alone collectivity has a specific appropriateness in political and spiritual life. It has, additionally, an even greater general appropriateness and usefulness to women, for the entire history of human development reveals that collective strength is a strength that women have in far greater measure than do men.

## WOMEN ARE NATURAL SOCIALISTS

Because the factors that distinguish the sexes have been so often misrepresented to the detriment of women, feminists have often settled for claims of equality. Yet we all know that sex differences do exist. What needs to be affirmed is that women, who are named for two organs of creativity — the womb and the hand[1] — have no reason to feel inferior to those who have been so aptly and simply named man. In addition to the many ramifications of her biological primacy, woman distinguishes herself from the day she is born in socially meaningful ways: While infant girls smile more often, boys startle more often; when only three days old, girls are more responsive to another infant's cry than are boys of the same age.[2] The greater physical coordination of girls, which may be linked to greater left-right brain coordination,[3] is demonstrated in infancy. Although mothers have not needed scientists to tell them that girls sit up, crawl, walk, and, most significant, talk earlier than do boys, these sex differences in "response tendencies and behaviors" have been delineated in repeated testing, providing "evidence for the existence of sexually dimorphic patterns which would be difficult to attribute to the influence of social or cultural learning."[4]

However these sex differences may be accounted for, they are of enormous social and cultural significance. While widely recognized, their potential value, particularly in regard to survival, has been minimized in favor of aggressivity and other sociobiological theories supporting male supremacy. Although neither popularized nor officially heeded, the work compiled by feminist biologists in connection with the Genes & Gender Conferences in 1978 and 1979 has dispelled many of these misogynistic constructs, among them the popular "killer ape theory" of human progress. Dr. Ruth Bleier, a professor of neurophysiology, is one of the contributors to *Genes & Gender II* who disputes the evolutionary potential of killer apes, hominids, or *homo sapiens* by pointing out that "unbridled aggressivity and territoriality" logically lead into an "evolutionary dead end of intraspecies conflict, competition, and annihilation." She suggests instead, ". . . the qualities of sharing and cooperation that characterize present-day gatherer-hunter societies were always basic and necessary features of evolving human societies."[5]

What should be no less obvious from a study of human social development and related biological factors is that women will create cooperative societies when free to do so; the historic fact is that men have created competitive societies being entirely free to do so. Given history, even men who most ardently advocate socialism and other forms of cooperative economies would do well to trust only women to bring them about.

Sexual differences may be considered socially acquired; the awesome probability is that some of them are innate. The results are guaranteed in either case. Within the foreseeable future, which has become very short now, women will not have the know-how or wherewithal to breed or rear men differently, and we cannot desire equality with them or in their institutions, given the present character of each. We had better take advantage of the way we are constituted. We can start by recollecting.

## THE HIDDEN SOCIAL UNIT THROUGHOUT HISTORY

In her major work, *Woman's Evolution from Matriarchal Clan to Patriarchal Family*, the Marxist anthropologist Evelyn Reed affirmed the matriarchal clan as the first form of social organization, stating, "The mothers alone were equipped with the maternal and affective responses that were extended into the human world in the form of social collaboration."[6] As this pivotal statement indicates, Reed maintains that it was female collectivity within the clan, not matriarchy within the family, that inspired and continued to develop human social organization until the relatively recent imposition of the patriarchal family. Moreover, Reed clearly establishes the high level of women's social contribution in primitive times. She draws on standard anthropology sources to illustrate the remarkable ingenuity and cooperative productivity of early women, concluding, "The households they managed were not merely kitchens and nurseries; they were the first factories, laboratories, clinics, schools, and social centers."[7]

The needed reassessment of the traditional story of social genesis, which credits the noble hunter with selectively (i.e., competitively) evolving the larger brain of *homo erectus*, leading to the development of human social organization and all subsequent inventions, has been undertaken by many other feminist anthropologists. Sally Slocum succinctly counters:

. . . I suggest that longer periods of infant dependency, more difficult births, and longer gestation periods also demand more skills in social organization and communication — creating selective pressure for increased brain size without looking to hunting as an explanation. . . . Hunting cannot explain its own origin. *It is much more logical to assume that as the period of infant dependency began to lengthen, the mothers would begin to increase the scope of their gathering to provide food for their still-dependent infants.* . . . It is an example of male bias to picture these females with young as totally or even mainly dependent on males for food. Among modern hunter-gatherers, even in the marginal environments where most live, the females can usually gather enough to support themselves and their families.

Slocum pointedly adds, "We need not bring in any notion of paternity, or the development of male-female pairs, or any sort of marriage in order to account for either families or food sharing."[8]

Reed extends this assessment of female independence by verifying among modern gathering-hunting tribes a socially beneficial separatism. She further maintains that women originally imposed taboos upon hunters resulting not only in separate eating arrangements and a work-role division still much in evidence, with women the more significant producers of all necessities, but also in a total segregation of the sexes. In her view, this arrangement is enforced protectively by women and intensified by the necessity to nurse children to a state of growth and health where they no longer need milk. The lengthy period, during which nursing mothers mark themselves with red ocher and in other ways disengage from heterosexual relations, extended at least four years and sometimes as long as ten or twelve years.[9] Under these conditions, primitive women are not forced to attend helpless infants to the exclusion of all other productivity; rather, they continue to contribute their work to the community, to fully nurture their children whose development is unimpeded, and to preserve their own health by preventing successive pregnancies.[10] Through incest taboos, resulting in male exogamy, whereby men are required to leave their kinship group, localized and periodic separatism became widespread and permanently instituted.[11] These arrangements resulted in a prevailing female social unit, obscurely termed matriarchal, which still exists in some areas of the world, and for which a better term might be "sororal commune."

The following description of a modern gatherer-hunter tribe is revealing for it contains a reference to the hidden social unit throughout history — the sororal commune — and an implication of a related economic structure:

. . . among the Mundurucu, both men and women agree that the truly enduring bond is between mother and daughter. . . . Mothers and daughters work together, they relax in each other's company, they are seemingly inseparable. This unit carries over to the relations between sisters, who are expected to form enduring residential groups. Sisters must be loyal to one another, they must share, they are a unit. . . .

The solidarity of the mother-daughter and sister-sister dyads extends itself in diminished degree to a union of all women of a household and, ultimately, of the village. One of the chief sources of this cohesiveness is, very simply, the work process.[12]

The productive pattern of the sororal commune is evident not only in primitive society. These sisterhoods of workers can also be seen to advance from the first agriculturalists and artisans in the seventh millennium B.C. to highly civilized scientists and artists in the third millennium B.C. Whereas modern history demonstrates the limited applicability and frequent social and economic failures of brotherhood within an antithetical patriarchal structure, ancient history illustrates the encompassing application and overall success of sisterhood within a supportive communal structure.

Curiously, the sororal commune as an ancient and potentially viable form of social structure is overlooked. The evidence for its existence is not lacking (least of all today), but perhaps we have been distracted from envisioning and exemplifying this ideal feminist society by a too intense consideration of a problematical, inapplicable matriarchy. Free of the matriarchal misalliance, we are free to esteem what feminists are actually doing. Informally, or in process, with varying levels of effort and success, we are relating, not as mothers and children, but as sisters. Current, functioning sororal communes exemplify a realistic, alternative social unit. We also have in this form of women's government an exercise of innate or acquired proclivities and abilities, which are specifically possessed in a greater degree by women than by men and which can be shown to constitute a collective spirit among us. Moreover, this spirit has always distinguished us favorably from men.

## THE TRIBE AND TRIBADISM

Before examining the historic development of the sororal commune, an important dimension of sisterhood must be recognized fully. Without the politically motivated prohibitions against homosexuality enforced by patriarchal brotherhood, sisterhood must be firmly understood to include a sexual relationship, providing the emotional-spiritual ties and life-supporting strength of the sex bond. From the root for tribe (Greek *tribe*: "the act of rubbing"; cf. *tri-báo*: "tri-based") comes a cognate term, tribadism, exclusively defined as lesbianism. The hidden sexual preference throughout history, which can be logically ascribed to the sororal commune — the hidden social unit throughout history — is tribadism. That tribadism has gone unremarked is obviously no proof of its absence; rather, the suppression of women's sexual preference for one another is to be presumed and was evidently enforced by patriarchy in every way possible, including the religious and medical advocacy of clitoridectomies.[13] Although there is a lack of information regarding lesbianism in primitive society, which can be tragically accounted for, within the closeness of women sharing every phase and aspect of life together, the lesbian bond may be supposed as the normal sexual union in prepatriarchal eras.

Without apparently intending to signify homosexuality, Helen Diner nevertheless provides a good description of the social arrangements that would most obviously support homosexual bonding and particularly reinforce a homosexual preference among women:

> Growing males were made to leave the community as soon as possible, and marriage outside the clan was arranged. They were then barely tolerated outsiders in their new clan, subject to the mother-in-law taboo.
>
> The women, however, remained inseparable. No daughter was given up. Husbands were admitted only as guests, occasionally forming male associations on the periphery of the clan. . . . The blood bond between the women was much stronger than any sexual ties connecting them with their men, not only in the great mother clans of Sumatra, northern India, and among the Indians of North America, but also in the matriarchal parts of Africa.[14]

The antiquity and prevalence of this arrangement has been noted in many other sources,[15] yet the possibility of homosexuality is seldom assessed by anthropologists or historians. Women's separatism and, within that separatism, a socially beneficial collectivism has not been adequately recognized either, although the development is historically and presently verifiable. The Neolithic and Bronze Ages (7000–1500 B.C.), however, offer the most inspiring examples of social progress that can be attributed to the governance and spiritual guidance of sororal orders. In this period, the first cultures developed into civilizations, the first towns grew into temple cities.

## THE HISTORIC ROLE OF WOMEN'S COLLECTIVITY

One of the world's oldest towns was unearthed in southern Turkey (ancient Anatolia) at a site called Çatal Hüyük. Described by its excavator, James Mellaart, as a birthplace of architecture, the buildings of this Neolithic town had to be constructed in block units, for the walls abut each other without intervening passages. Such construction infers communal agreement and, in this instance, communal agreement was arrived at within the context of spiritual life. The only section excavated is designated the religious quarter because of its apparent character: Out of 139 rooms excavated in building Levels II through X, at least forty rooms were used for religious purposes; in one period, rows of shrine rooms alternate with rows of living apartments.[16] Burials in the religious quarter routinely include tools indicating that sacred duties did not exempt anyone from work in the afterworld or in life in Çatal Hüyük and further revealing the type of work contributed by women as compared to that done by men: Spatulae, ladles, awls for sewing, bodkins for basketry, knives, and hoes contrast with fire stones, arrow and spear heads, sickle blades, and knives.[17] Collectivity is also indicated in what must have been specialized workshop organization, rather than cottage industry. Archaeologists express admiration for the evident advanced technology in crafts and for the quality and refinement of everything produced. The excellent monochrome pottery of later Near Eastern locales has origins at Çatal Hüyük, where wooden vessels were also varied and sophisticated in design, woolen textiles were skillfully manufactured, and copper and lead were smelted into tools and beads. Significantly, a huge oven suggests that bread was made for a community and not baked only over family hearths.[18] Mellaart concludes, "The basis for the spectacular development of the Neolithic at Çatal Hüyük was evidently laid by efficiently organized food production and conservation,"[19] which he unstintingly credits to the "triumph of agriculture" over the age-old occupation of hunting. He denotes as well a corresponding increase in the influence of women, substantiated by "the almost total disappearance of male statues in the cult."[20]

Mellaart also excavated Hacilar, 230 miles northwest of Çatal Hüyük. In his report on this site, he again notes the absence of hunting equipment, a contrasting emphasis on spinning, leatherworking, and agriculture, and he characterizes the kitchens as elaborate. "All this," he remarks, "is reflected in the statuary: the male is virtually absent, and so is any sexual emphasis."[21]

Although it is impossible from this evidence to conjecture the existence of patriarchal families, the pattern of a definite relationship among women emerges. The enduring bonds of motherhood and sisterhood are to be discerned at Çatal Hüyük in the ceremonious interments of women, who were placed together along with their children, whereas the bones of a very few men were buried separately.[22] Burial rites are generally held to be indicative of religious beliefs. Of the religion of sixth millennium Anatolia, James Mellaart surmises, "The principal deity was a goddess who is shown in her three aspects — as a young woman, a mother giving birth or as an old woman."[23] But there is also another type of figure found enshrined in 5800 B.C. at Çatal Hüyük, which Mellaart describes and associates as follows:

The double goddess with two heads, two pairs of breasts, but a single pair of arms (and a body united below the waist) is the earliest representation yet of a concept familiar to Anatolian religion, recurring later at Hacilar I and Kultepe.[24]

As with Anatolia, southeastern Europe also had agricultural stability, according to Marija Gimbutas, through which the region developed a cultural momentum before it was "cut short by the aggressive infiltration and settlement of semi-nomadic pastoralists" from the Eurasian steppes during the fourth millennium B.C.[25] Gimbutas describes the Old Europeans as "sedentary horticulturalists prone to live in large well-planned townships." She adds, "The absence of fortifications and weapons attests to the peaceful coexistence of this egalitarian civilization that was probably matrilinear and matrilocal. . . ."[26] Gimbutas extensively documents the predominating finds of female figurines among which are double-headed "goddess" figures united in one body.[27]

Moving thousands of years forward to the Cycladic Islands off the shore of Turkey, we find female relationships still idolized and, increasingly, infiltrated. Spyridon Marinatos, a distinguished archaeologist, describes the symbolic remains of this allied culture in terms still revealing the ancient matrilinear triad and even suggestive — although not to Marinatos — of tribadism:

Another representation, also attested in the early period, shows two goddesses side by side. They are closely juxtaposed and often embrace each other. As well as the two figures from Teke there is a second Cycladic group, hitherto unnoticed, in which women embrace each other. . . . [Marinatos makes specific reference to a triad of enclasped mother and daughter with infant son.] This type of group is also found among the Archaic Greek terracottas from Crete. They are best identified with the Cretan Mniepes, whose cult was still alive in Sicily in the days of Diodorus. . . . The holy trinity is also found in the Creto-Mycenaean religion. The triads are not like the Egyptian, with father, mother, and child, but in Crete the goddess is often attended by two young women and later we find either a god between two goddesses or a goddess between two men. . . .[28]

Mellaart, too, recognizes the immemorial transmission of the double goddess concept from Anatolia to Crete and comments:

It probably represents the two aspects, mother and maiden, of the great goddess, predecessors of the "Two Ladies" of the Knossos texts, the famous ivory from Mycenae and the Demeter and Kore of Classical Greece.[29]

The island of Crete, with her millennia-long history of ever greater cultural improvements under a peaceful,[30] spiritually directed government, indeed reflects the double goddess concept. Visual and written documentation makes manifest a pattern of communal living and of spiritual governance through sororal orders.

The fresco evidence clearly shows that the governing occupants of Knossos, the principal city of Crete with approximately 30,000 inhabitants, were women. Males appear as cupbearers, bull leapers, boys under instruction, and in one highly significant depiction, the "Temple" fresco, they mob the courtyard through which a single file of women passes, while only women can be seen within the great House of the Labrys. That the women depicted were held under the rule of any male authority is very doubtful. M. A. S. Cameron, who has begun a scholarly examination of these frescoes, challenges the assumption that the women of Knossos are shown in "court dress," citing Helga Reusch's comparative study of Cretan frescoes in relation to Greek mainland paintings of women subjects. According to Reusch's analysis, the dress depicted is, above all, that of the principal Cretan deity, a goddess, and of her priestesses.[31] J. D. S. Pendlebury, an excavator and curator of Knossos, has contributed the most telling assessment, however: In viewing these frescoes, he admits to "a curious, unpleasant feeling of the inversion of the sexes . . ."[32] In fact, women and men continue to be recorded as separate classes in even the late (1500 B.C.) Linear B Knossos tablets and, although women or goddesses are clearly revered, men are never depicted in exalted positions[33]; rather, they are most often shown in groups and, in at least two instances,[34] these groups appear to be under the direction of women.

The women, too, most often appear in groups. On the Linear B tablets, they are also listed in occupational units. There are a few titles that may have distinguished them from one another: potnia ("Lady"?), Ariadne ("very holy") and klawiphorous ("key bearer").[35] From the assignation of these titles, they seem to be applicable to more than one individual at a time. In general, there are no signs of glory or garish greatness. Even the name of the mythological dynasty of Crete, Titan, does not have the meaning of great or gigantic. It means white, the color of milk (hence the derivative Greek words *titthe*, "female nipple," "grandmother"; *titene,* "queen"; *titax,* "king"). Appropriately, in all of the frescoes, women are painted the color of milk, which emphatically distinguishes them, as do their titles, from men.

Even though the temporal authority and sacerdotal duties of Cretan women are evident, they are seldom noted. Even their residences are repeatedly mischaracterized as palaces,[36] although no sovereign is ever depicted or recorded. Among these holy women, there may have been an officiating priestess whose existence is indicated by the small subterranean "throne room." This "throne" is a simple high-backed chair carved from stone; connected to it, along the same wall and on either side of the adjacent walls, are stone benches for the other members of the convening group, who, to judge from the artifacts found in place, functioned as an ecclesium. On the numerous milk stones[37] used to make seal impressions, these priestesses appear in ecstatic communion with their sisters.

The idea of sisterhood is overwhelmingly exemplified in image and myth throughout the Bronze Age Mediterranean world. Apart from a few heroes with sidekicks (Gilgamesh and Enki; Theseus and Pirithous, Achilles and Patroclus), there is no tradition of brotherhoods in this same mythic legacy to match the numerous examples of sisterhoods: Eumenides, Erinyes, Muses Graeae, Gorgons, Harpies, Lamiae, Sirens, Fates, Pleiades and, in the realm of history, Naditu, Danaides, Maenads, Bacchae, and Amazons. That most of these sisterhoods have been cast as threatening to men is not at all surprising considering the evidence of invasions establishing that northern patriarchal barbarians disrupted the old, peaceful way of life in the Mediterranean and ushered in four centuries of Dark Ages.[38] From this period probably emerged the many private mysteries performed exclusively by women in classical times through which their communion and spirit were renewed in spite of the oppressive patriarchal rule under which they lived: the autumnal Thesmophoria; the Lanaea held in January to arouse the sleeping vegetation; the giving of sacred objects by whiterobed virgins in a ceremony known as the Skirophoria; the Festival of Things Insolent or Things Unwanted, Things Beyond and Outside, called the Hybristika; the celebration by only women and girls of Dionysus' rebirth every third year; the Tegean Festival of Ares, "Entertainer of Women"; the mother and daughter rites known as the Brauronia; and the Eleusis Vigil kept through the night by women.

That women could maintain their sisterhood through spirituality under the harshest of conditions shows that their strength was their spiritual sisterhood—not property, not physical power, not class privilege, not even political rights. As long as women were able to work together, whether in families, convents, or harems,[39] they continued to be socially productive and they could not be utterly reduced and dispirited as modern women have been. In the aptly titled *The Underside of History*, Elise Boulding details the ". . . hardiness of women, particularly of how they created an entire system of formation and education for children and adults of differing cultures . . .". "The real infrastructures of the first millennium A.D.," she specifically remarks, "were created by women in the face of continuous and destructive use of force by men." Boulding describes at length the means through which women established "learning-teaching dialogues" under a variety of circumstances to generate cultural rebirth.[40]

## MODELS OF COMMUNION

That women will continue to create from what has been destroyed is demonstration of an immutable pattern formally taught in much earlier "learning-teaching dialogues" and personified by the ever-regenerative Goddess. The mystery lessons begun among women in earliest times led successive generations to an enlightened understanding of natural processes and induced a heartening of regard for the female principality—the creation and continuity of life. These teachings also led spiritual seekers to the general relativity of pantheism and undifferentiated love, to a shedding of individual identity and a fusion with others. This sort of spiritual concordance is to be distinguished from what has been taught and personally exemplified by politically motivated, patriarchal religious leaders. A major difference is that among ancient women, any assumed divinity does not appear to have been a status of individual power; rather, the ability *to divine* is indicated by tradition and attributes. Interestingly, the talents assigned to ancient holy women—divining, hypnosis, and therapeutic touch—are currently gaining scientific validation.[41] The more relevant point, however, is that the actual functioning roles of sibyls, salmas, pythonesses, water bringers, and lightbearers required communion, not dominion.

This distinction is also to be noted in the practices of patriarchal monotheism, which uphold the authority of a father god as compared to the old "idol-worship" of pantheism, which sanctified all forms of life. A distinct preference for abstract symbols, such as the double spiral, and for animal and vegetable images, rather than individualized human idols, signifies a devotional relativity, not an investiture of omnipotence in a single form. Furthermore, the wanton human sacrifice and destruction of the Earth frequently called for by father gods in historic times and perpetrated by their male adherents cannot be justified by parallel allegations. Funeral practices of an unknown nature do not provide evidence for Goddess-inspired human sacrifice. This specious charge is not even supported by mythic accounts or other representations until the barbarian patriarchal takeover and then, in addition to what may be allegories of vegetation godhood,[42] there are innumerable instances of condoned female sacrifice, murder, and rape. The so-called demonic aspect of ancient goddesses is also a misreading, often deliberate, of their powers of transformation. One of the best known of these, the Hindu goddess Kali, shares her name with the Greek Blessed Isle Kalliste ("Fairest") and in the Hindu pantheon has an equivocal position with Shakti, "Fairest of the Three Worlds," i.e., the transcendent plan.[43] Withal, the ancient hags were life-givers who honored life, although form was an illusion that could be playfully treated, and in their hagiocracies, no one was deputized with concrete power. Power flexed. It was, after all, understood to be just energy, which is obtained from interaction. The modern world would be a far more peaceful place if men could understand what it is to be truly pregnant with power.

The female-principled theology of the Copper and Bronze Ages was not only profoundly egalitarian and of necessity taught by groups in groups, the various religious traditions were also solidly based on an accessible, beneficial form of practice — yoga. Far from a mind-boggling power trip, yoga is an example of the kind of relaxing physical and spiritual practice that life-bearing women would devise, and there is every reason to believe that it was originated among women. To correctly perform body yoga exercises, the center of gravity must be in the hips, as it is in women, not in the shoulders, as it is in men. Moreover, yoga can be traced back to gynocentric religions in India and Egypt.[44] In this connection, the long and awesome association of women and snakes originates in the iconolatry of kundalini yoga. Kundalini ("coiled line") is a pre-invasion Indian goddess, who raises *ki* ("earth") energy, zoomorphized as a serpent. The famous snake goddesses of ancient Crete are, therefore, likely to have been governing kundalini priestesses, which suggests the basis of that society's extraordinary providence and peacefulness over millennia.

An important element in yoga is the transmission of spirituality through sexuality. Unlike male-dominated religions, the ancient female-principled religions were not life-denying; goddesses, their priestesses, and devotees were sexual beings, who neither denied heterosexuality nor homosexuality and who even engaged in sex collectively. The charge of promiscuity, however, is a patriarchal value judgment, which, as we know, was originally laid down by Church fathers in an attempt to enforce female virginity, life-long coupling, and two-sex bonding in support of a propertied family and class structure. Unfortunately, the patriarchal advocacy of monogamy heightens possessiveness. Like monotheism, it stresses attachment in an individual and a personal relationship, rather than nondiscriminating oneness in universal relativity and love.

Doing so many things differently is clearly an effect of thinking differently. As the first educators, women even taught their thinking differently, and their method can be seen to incite a collective spirit. Consider, for instance, that in the gynocentric Aegean world of the second millennium B.C. writing was used only for inventories and for occasional dedicatory inscriptions. In spite of the availability of clay tablets, knowledge was not recorded.[45] It was taught orally and it was learned by heart. The outcome was a very different perception and display of intelligence.

In the oral tradition of teaching, comprehension did not usually occur in concrete or finite terms — in facts, details, conclusions — which often produces troubled and contentious intellects. Instead, oral teaching fostered mental clarity and concentration, which could be developed into contemplative and transcendent mental states. It encouraged listening to others and a recognition of and reliance on intuition, rather than empirical deduction, judgmental evaluation, individual analysis and expertise. Oral teaching drew on a common past. A sense of heritage induces more than self-respect; it induces collective identity and a regard for the transmission of wisdom through life processes. The kind of knowledge that becomes valued is the kind that has scored high in life's testing, i.e., in living relationships, and the highest grade in such a system of education is oneness.

Thus, allegory and symbolic images, not investigations, analysis, or graphs and charts, were ingeniously used to teach omniscience, not science, and relativity, not objectivity. A communion of understanding based on common knowledge was voiced in a lyrical, uncritical choice of words, which must have had its echo in personal conversation. Through poetry, heartfelt values and spiritual concepts and sensibilities were unfolded. The apportioning of these benefits cannot be reckoned; such beneficences can only be counted as shared. Under these circumstances, group concourse takes place through harmony and rhythmic flow, not through personal challenge and hustle. Even this was emphatically taught through inspired movement: dance. From a wise perception of Jane Ellen Harrison's, Elise Boulding surmises, "Through dancing, concepts of order, leadership and religious projections are developed. The Cretans danced their way into culture and civilization. . . ."[46]

Speaking only from personal experience, during lunch hours in the gym, we girls danced with each other in the middle of the basketball court, while the boys careened and vied around us. Girls were taught to dance by other girls, boys learned to dance from us.

Is it possible to dance our way back into community, culture, and civilization, while the boys career and vie around us? Only time will tell, but dance we must — circling — doing a figure 8 through a maze of contradictions, dodging confrontation, tugging the hands of faltering sisters, the group rhythm transporting us round. Just that is our most practical, political strategy — for our greatest, tested strength is our collective spirit.

NOTES

1. The word woman appears to have suffered a hysterectomy and to have become confused with a word that it logically preceded and promptly superseded: Anglo-Saxon *wifman,* meaning "of man." A line of development can be traced from Sanskrit *vama,* meaning "woman," through Goth and Old High German *wamba,* meaning "uterus," to Middle English *wambe* or *wombe,* "womb." Combined with Latin *manus,* "hand," from Sanskrit *manu,* the source of the all-inclusive term "mankind," woman emerges as an apt, distinctive term.

2. Laurel Holliday, *The Violent Sex* (Guerneville, CA: Bluestocking Books, 1978), pp. 18–19, 21, citing studies by Lewis, Korner, Freedman, Maccoby, Bell and Darling.

3. See Daniel Goleman, "Special Abilities of the Sexes," *Psychology Today,* Nov. 1978, pp. 48–120, for reports of recent electroencephalograph testing demonstrating greater left-right brain coordination in females.

4. Holliday, *op. cit.,* p. 18, quoting June Reinisch, "Fetal Hormones,

the Brain and Human Sex Differences," *Archives of Sexual Behavior,* 1974, 3:51.

5. Ruth Bleier, "Behavior and Evolution," *Genes & Gender II,* p. 64. Although in this essay, Bleier addresses mainly the use of distorted science to prove "assumptions about innate differences," she agrees that an early "division of labor, based on a straightforward sexual reproductive difference" was a distinct possibility (p. 65). By all accounts, women and men have developed differently with some enduring effects.

6. Evelyn Reed, *Woman's Evolution from Matriarchal Clan to Patriarchal Family* (New York: Pathfinder Press, 1975), p. 48.

7. *Ibid.,* p. 128.

8. Sally Slocum, "Woman the Gatherer," *Toward an Anthropology of Women,* ed. Rayna R. Reiter (New York: Monthly Review Press, 1975), pp. 43, 45–46.

9. Reed, *op. cit.,* pp. 81–83, 135.

10. See Lila Leibowitz, "Perspectives on the Evolution of Sex Differences," *Toward an Anthropology of Women,* p. 28, for refutation of theories of male dominance and pair bonding among primates, which raises questions concerning what may be considered natural. See also Leibowitz, "'Universals' and Male Dominance among Primates" in *Genes & Gender II,* eds. Ruth Hubbard and Marian Lowe (New York: Gordian Press, 1979), pp. 35–46. Leibowitz cites Jane Lancaster's observation of vervet monkeys attesting to coalitions of females, which form against the predatory or frightening behavior of males.

11. Reed, *op. cit.,* pp. 68–69, 355–360.

12. Yolanda Murphy and Robert F. Murphy, *Women of the Forest* (New York: Columbia University Press, 1974), pp. 122–123.

13. See G. J. Barker-Benfield, "A Historical Perspective on Women's Health Care — Female Circumcision," *Women & Health,* vol. 1, no. 1, Jan./Feb. 1976, p. 14, for information that clitoridectomies were medically advocated in the United States and Europe as late as the 1930s with the intent of denying the "juvenile pleasure" of clitoral orgasm.

14. Helen Diner, *Mothers and Amazons* (Garden City, N.Y.: Doubleday, 1973), p. 83.

15. See the already cited Reiter anthology, Reed, and Murphy; additionally, J. J. Bachofen, Robert Briffault, James Frazer, O. T. Mason, and Lewis Morgan.

16. James Mellaart, *The Neolithic of the Near East* (New York: Scribners, 1975), pp. 100–101; *Çatal Hüyük* (New York: McGraw-Hill, 1967), pl. 6, pp. 69–70, 77, 80.

17. *Çatal Hüyük,* p. 209.

18. *Ibid.*, pp. 22, 63, 211–212, pl. 6. See *Excavations at Hacilar* (Edinburgh: University Press, 1970), vol. I, pp. 30–31.

19. *Çatal Hüyük*, p. 221.

20. *Ibid.*, p. 176. The few statues judged to be masculine cannot be identified as genitalia are never shown. Although shrine walls are impressively ornamented with goddess images, including life-size reliefs of female figures side-by-side, pp. 109–117, 125, human males are never represented. If they are replaced by bull effigies, these bulls are frequently birthed by human female figures, a piety to be later rendered scandalous in the Greek version of the Pasiphae and minotaur myth. According to this myth, the bull child appears to be a projection of Mother Earth's powers in regions threatened, as Anatolia and Crete were, with volcanic activity, and not a deity in his own right.

21. *Excavations at Hacilar*, p. 170.

22. *Çatal Hüyük*, p. 60.

23. James Mellaart, *Earliest Civilizations of the Near East* (New York: McGraw-Hill, 1965), p. 92.

24. *Çatal Hüyük*, pl. 70–72.

25. Marija Gimbutas, *The Gods and Goddesses of Old Europe, 7000–3500 B.C.* (Berkeley: University of California Press, 1974), p. 18.

26. Marija Gimbutas, "The First Wave of Eurasian Steppe Pastoralists into Copper Age Europe," *Journal of Indo-European Studies*, vol. 5, no. 4, Winter 1977, p. 281.

27. *The Gods and Goddesses of Old Europe*, pl. 86, Fifth Millennium B.C. Vinča Culture.

28. Spyridon Marinatos, *Crete and Mycenae* (New York: Harry N. Abrams, 1960), p. 38. The female trinity was widespread and enduring. See Anne Ross, *Pagan Celtic Britain* (New York: Columbia University Press, 1967), p. 207. She notes in particular: "Trios of goddesses are well-known in insular mythology, and although the representational form of this concept is apparently the well-known mother goddess type, any one of the single goddesses invoked or portrayed in Roman Britain could appear in threefold form."

29. *Çatal Hüyük*, pl. 70–72.

30. See James Walter Graham, *The Palaces of Crete* (Princeton: Princeton University Press, 1962), pp. 8, 13, 19. There is no evidence of martial activity or a defense system on Crete, according to Graham.

31. M.A.S. Cameron, "The Lady in Red," *Archaeology*, vol. 24, no. 1, Jan. 1971, p. 43. Any interpretation of deification must also be clarified, particularly in regard to the assumption that there was a principal Cretan goddess.

32. J.D.S. Pendlebury, *The Archaeology of Crete* (New York: W. W. Norton & Co., 1965), p. 200.

33. The so-called "Priest-King" fresco shows a smiling, flower-wreathed youth, pledging his heart with one hand and with the other apparently leading an animal. Also the tradition of "Wanax" (consort?) Minos belongs to the Homeric Achaean occupation period on Crete, not to the earlier gynocentric culture.

34. The "Parisienne" and "Temple" frescoes at Knossos.

35. R. W. Hutchinson, *Prehistoric Crete* (Baltimore: Penguin Books, 1968), pp. 211, 231; John Chadwick, *The Mycenaean World* (London: Cambridge University Press, 1976), pp. 74, 92–93.

36. See Graham, *op. cit.*, p. 28. In a singular instance, he applies the ancient Cretan word *labyrinth* of which there is specific mention on a Knossos tablet in a dedication to the "Lady of the Labyrinth"; also Vincent Scully, *The Earth, The Temple and The Gods* (New Haven: Yale University Press, 1962), *passim,* for theory that the great temple edifices were built as entrances into the Goddess' body, the Earth itself; Hans George Wunderlich, *The Secret of Crete* (New York: Macmillan, 1974), for interpretation of Knossos as a necropolis!

37. Hutchinson, p. 23, "Engraved seals and beads continued to be handed down as ornaments, amulets, or milk-charms for nursing mothers (even up to the present day, when they are called 'milk stones'), but their original history and significance has been lost."

38. Lord William Taylour, *The Mycenaeans* (New York: Frederick A. Praeger, 1964), p. 177.

39. Elise Boulding, *The Underside of History* (Boulder: Westview Press, 1976), pp. 230–231, clarifies: "When the word harem is used in connection with a royal court, the historian means to signify the women's court." She further suggests that the patriarchal "pathological form of what may have originated as a separate and parallel government of women by women in the temples of the major priestesses should not be mistaken for the whole institution." She cites Anna H. Leonowen's information in *Siamese Harem Life* (New York: E. P. Dutton, 1953) detailing a harem that educated women physicians, judges, artists, scholars, and warriors and that numbered some 9,000 women.

40. Boulding, *op. cit.*, p. 341 and Chapter 8.

41. See Gay Gaer Luce, *Biological Rhythms in Human and Animal Physiology* (New York: Dover Publications, 1971), p. 13, for Dr. Y. Rocard's experiments at the University of Paris. Rocard has conditioned many individuals to detect minute (milligaus) changes in the Earth's magnetic field through the use of divining rods. Dolores

Krieger, of New York University's Division of Nursing, has been
teaching therapeutic touch for more than five years.

42. See Theodor Gaster, *Thespis* (New York: W. W. Norton & Co.,
1977), pp. 30–33; also John M. Allegro, *The Sacred Mushroom and
The Cross* (New York: Doubleday, 1970), pp. 157–158. There is
much evidence to show that patriarchal gods were originally figurative elements of harvest rituals not unlike the Greek Alous Festival
and Halloween. Jehovah's name was extracted from the harvest lament *halaleulia;* Allah's from *alalu;* whereas according to Diodorus,
the more ancient Egyptians shed tears and cried to Isis at the first
cutting of the corn. See also Gordon Wasson, Albert Hoffman, and
Carl A. P. Ruck, *The Road to Eleusis* (New York: Harcourt Brace
Jovanovich, 1978), for a theory of hallucinogenically induced, death-
like experiences and other mushroom-beheading allegories.

43. Ajit Mookerjee and Madhu Khanna, *The Tantric Way* (Boston:
New York Graphic Society, 1977), p. 75.

44. See Kenneth Grant, "Cults of the Shadow," *Kundalini, Evolution
and Enlightenment,* ed. John White (Garden City, N.Y.: Doubleday, 1974), p. 395. See also Mookerjee and Khanna, p. 12; they state
that yoga influence is evident in the ancient oriental and Mediterranean cultures.

45. Literacy was also widespread in these cultures. See Boulding, pp.
193–194, for legends in Sumer, India, Egypt, Crete, Libya, Greece,
Latinum, and Britain crediting women with the invention of writing.

46. Boulding, *op. cit.,* p. 246. See Hutchinson, p. 263, for description of
a dance, which, according to myth, Theseus observed Cretan women
doing, the *Geranos,* or crane dance; he adds that flocks of cranes actually perform a circling dance, the outer ring moving to the right,
the core group to the left.

# Appendix: Two Debates

As the evolution of post-patriarchal spirituality thrived throughout the second half of the seventies, various aspects of the movement were examined and debated. This process of questioning and considering our options as we continue to create them is vital to our politics if they are to touch our lives deeply.

In this section are two debates on much-discussed topics in feminist spirituality. The first, "Does Hierarchy Have a Place in Women's Spirituality?," begins with an essay that Gloria Z. Greenfield, a former priestess of the Pomegranate Grove, wrote in 1978 for Chrysalis: A Magazine of Women's Culture in which she proposes that the notion of high priestesses is counterproductive to feminist goals of independence and self-determination. Although high priestesses are not a widespread phenomenon in feminist spirituality, the examining of power is always worthwhile. For a response, I have invited Z. Budapest, a high priestess for the past ten years, to explain her work.

The second debate, "Are Goddesses and Matriarchies Merely Figments of Feminist Imagination?," begins with Sally R. Binford's critique of spirituality feminists' understanding of prehistory, which appeared in Human Behavior in 1979. The responses by Merlin Stone and myself seek to clarify the nature of the new interest in Goddess-oriented cultures. Binford also contributed a counterresponse in which she stresses economic power among the goals of feminism; the post-counterresponse suggests that we choose "both/and" rather than "either/or" when we consider spiritual and economic power.

C.S.

# I. Does Hierarchy Have a Place in Women's Spirituality?

## Spiritual Hierarchies: The Empress' New Clothes?

## Gloria Z. Greenfield

During the spring of 1976, the first national women's spirituality conference, entitled *Through the Looking Glass: A Gynergenetic Experience*, took place in Boston; approximately 1500 women from North America participated. The intention of the conference was to provide a space where the issues and concepts of women's spirit could be explored and developed. Resource women, ranging from theologians and high priestesses to radical psychologists, were brought in from across the country to share their knowledge and act as workshop facilitators. The conference had a strong effect on the women's movement in general and on many individual women in particular. As co-organizer, I was extremely affected; nineteen months later, I have strong criticisms of the outcome of the conference, and I question the general direction of the women's spirituality movement.

Transforming the concept of *spirit* into an institution, such as the "women's spirituality movement," can be as dangerous as it is confusing. Primarily, the danger and confusion stem from a vague grasp of the nature of spirit. This leads to a focus on learned ritual rather than on self-determined movement.

Spirit is defined as the *principle of conscious life; the vital principle in man* [sic], *animating the body or mediating between body and soul; an attitude or principle that inspires, animates, or pervades thought, feeling, or action.** It is no surprise, then, that the Latin derivation of spirit (*spiritum* from *spiritus*) is *breath.*** Without breath, there is no life.

An apparent danger with spirituality lies in accepting the patriarchal premise that the life-force comes from an Other, a *higher being.* Such dogma ensures the perpetuation of a basic hierarchical system, demanding gratitude (taxation) to a sovereign for one's existence. The medium of exchange is energy. This energy is often manifested by adhering to a fixed lifestyle and set of values; the more intensely one adheres to the lifestyle and set of values, the more protection and direction one anticipates from the higher being. A key to liberation is the individual's realization that she must control her destiny. The revolutionary act begins with the taking of self-control; once an individual assumes this act of responsibility, she participates in the formation and development of her environment. The environment encompasses both domestic and community space. In other words, when the individual perceives herself as the commander of her own life, she becomes an active participant in her community.

Unfortunately, not all sectors of the women's spirituality movement emphasize this. Rather, some emphasize the perpetuation of a hierarchical structure: the following of *high priestesses.* A distinction is made between *seeker* and high priestess. The seeker is seen as an individual who is ignorant of the mysteries of life, while the high priestess is received as the holder of all truths. She is the personification of the Great Goddess, and she guards her knowledge with oaths of secrecy.

The dynamic involved in this relationship negates any revolutionary intention. The high priestess holds the supposed key to life, while the seeker strives to prove her integrity and worthiness of receiving such knowledge through devotion to the high priestess. As the high priestess

---

* *The Random House Dictionary of the English Language, Unabridged Edition,* New York: Random House, 1971.

** *The Englishman's Latin Dictionary,* E. P. Dutton & Company, New York: date unknown.

encourages this mystical and esoteric image, she is received with awe. This was illustrated during an outdoor women's music festival, when an outburst of rain threatened the event's continuation. A well known high priestess was requested by a representative of the audience to stop the rain: She responded with a smile. Her choosing to smile, rather than articulate the fact that she was incapable of such an act, secured her position as a higher being. Will this woman be expected someday to part the Red Sea for womankind? Responsibility for such occurrences must be claimed by both high priestess and seeker. The high priestess chooses to be perceived with awe; the seeker chooses to perceive the high priestess as almighty.

One may wonder how this dynamic can occur within the women's movement. It is quite common, though quite destructive, for movements to "star-trip" those of their members who are associated with media communications. However, spokespersons and musicians, for example, depend on an effective presentation of their training/knowledge to their respective movements. Spokeswomen often place themselves in accountable situations via questions and answers. Many feminist musicians are encouraging their audiences to sing along, demystifying the music. This does not occur with the high priestess because the very nature of her role depends on the maintenance of hierarchy. Although she may give lectures on the background of Goddess-worship, does she give workshops on the acquired skills which differentiate her from the seeker? Some contend that the seeker is unprepared to acquire such powerful skills for fear that she will misuse them. This implies an emphasis on *power-over*, rather than power within. It is analogous to the horizontal fear of women gaining economic strength, because we might use that great power of money with ill intent. Both contentions presume that women will act with neither integrity nor responsibility, which justifies the patriarchy's exclusion of women as valuable members of society. The psychic skill belonging to a high priestess can be compared to the medical skills of a doctor. Both acquired their respective skills through training, and both protect their position by mystifying the nature of their skills.

As individuals with integrity, we must be responsible for our actions. Every action is an execution of a personal choice. Either we choose to define ourselves, or we choose to be defined by patriarchal values. We choose to be free by fighting the source of oppression and reclaiming self-control, or we choose to accept degradation and oppression by inaction and compliance. By assuming that a higher being directs our lives, we disclaim responsibility. Often I hear women comment: "Whatever the Goddess wants will happen." The implication feeds into nonproductivity and noncommitment. Self-motivation dwindles as we perceive ourselves as puppets of pre-destiny.

Not all women involved in women's spirituality choose to accept hierarchy. Having reclaimed self-control, some are exploring new ways of communicating. In this exploration, various tools (i.e., the Tarot, dreams, psychic travel) may be employed *as a means* rather than an end. These women have found their spirit, *the attitude or principle that inspires, animates, or pervades thought, feeling, or action.* Their spirit was right there, waiting to be recognized.

# Response by Z. Budapest

## THE VOWS, WOWS, AND JOYS
## OF THE HIGH PRIESTESS
## OR
## WHAT DO YOU PEOPLE DO
## ANYWAY?

I have been a Dianic High Priestess for ten years now. My coven, The Susan B. Anthony Coven Number One, is one of the oldest spiritual groups of revolutionary women in this country, or maybe the world. It's wonderful to lay back, to sigh a sigh of relief — ten years! Not many women's groups have lasted that long in the patriarchy. How did we do it? What have we accomplished in a decade of the Goddess movement?

Such continuity certainly did not come about from assigning power to "higher" beings. In ten years we have had thousands of politically conscious women participate in our rituals. The results speak highly: I have three large flour-sacks of letters from women who changed their lives because of this Goddess exposure. This long tenure didn't come about by "hugging" information either; if there is continuity, there is teaching going on. "Oaths of secrecy," as in the old tradition of Wicca, have been discarded by me and many other feminist Witches. How can you spread information if you have to keep it secret? The "new" women's religion doesn't need extra baggage. As for hierarchy, Oh Goddess! We carried over our normal revolutionary customs, namely, all are equal, somebody facilitated, and somebody was the High Priestess. Taking responsibility has been hard, but the ten years have testified that many were trained through practicing while "on the job."

I asked Starhawk, a very active High Priestess herself, about hierarchy and she responded:

I don't know anyone in the Craft setting herself up as a guru-type, and I know even fewer Witches who would be impressed in the least with any-one who did. Leadership and hierarchy are strictly coven matters — and covens vary. Some are more authoritarian, some are quite collective. That's as it should be — because people need different situations in order to develop and grow. Diversity is a Craft value.

For myself, I prefer a coven of equals in which all are leaders. Praise Goddess, I've got one — but it didn't come about instantly or easily. Leadership skills are something women, in this culture, need to learn. We don't get them automatically or by accident; everything in the main-stream culture is set up to keep us from ever getting them, from ever coming into our own power. To discuss that question fully would take a volume. Let me just say that sometimes we need to be trained in order to eventually lead, and that training can take place within a coven. Sometimes we need role models, other women who are leaders. I feel we should encourage women to be strong, to take power-that-comes-from-within (not power-over).

## HISTORY OF THE SUSAN B. ANTHONY COVEN NUMBER ONE

In 1971 we were a political group who wanted to accomplish the goals of women's liberation. We decided to combine our spiritual skills with our revolutionary activism in order to speed up the process of ar-riving at those goals. The traditional Pagan community had never seen such a blend of independent/politico women Witches before. They argued that we were "just using the Goddess for politics" and accused us of being "political, not real Pagans." To this we replied, "Witches have always been political." The legend of Aradia, the first avatar who taught the oppressed to use magical skills to defeat their oppressors, is evidence of such politics. If you define politics as a statement of power relationships among people, it can easily be seen that all religions are "political." In the Goddess religion, the natural, nurturing relationship between mothers and their children is promoted as a model of human relationships. It is not a religion which advocates hierarchical, power-over relationships. The Judeo-Christians, on the other hand, relate to a god who is angry, punitive, vindictive, and who constantly chastises "his" children. Worship of this god is the prototype for competitive, blaming, guilt-ridden relationships among people.

In the early Seventies, it was heretical to say, "The Goddess is using us to bring about social and spiritual change," or to say, as we also did, "We are the Goddess." In those days, High Priestesses were housewives during the six weeks between sabbaths. Only briefly, in circles, were they permitted to acknowledge themselves as Goddess. Priests talked about "their High Priestesses" the way they were accustomed to talking about "their wives." The emerging Dianic tradition shook up the crowns on many heads.

In the mid-Seventies, we faced different opposition: "How can you have balanced energy with no men?" In 1976, we invited priestesses in Ukiah to attend our Midsummer women's circle. As we headed for the woods, many women from traditions other than Dianic followed. As I looked back from halfway up the mountain, I suddenly understood what the men feared. There they were, a small group of men left to themselves with nobody to reflect their glory that evening. In the circle of sixty-eight women, it became clear to all why we didn't need men to raise energy or "balance" ourselves. As they danced naked on the mountaintop in complete freedom and leapt over Midsummer fires, they understood that nothing was wanting there. We all felt blessed. Since then, in many parts of the world, Dianic covens have been founded, bonds have formed, and we have learned about each other and rejoiced.

## RELIGION = POLITICS = RELIGION

The police also discovered the Dianics, however. When we opened the Feminist Wicca, our occult supply store, we were constantly watched by the Los Angeles Police Department. One day they arrested me for reading the Tarot for an undercover policewoman. There was a silver lining to this crisis, however: Women's religion was suddenly seen as politically threatening to the patriarchy. Although it was a dubi-

ous way to become well known, Goddess religion was being responded
to very seriously. There were mass demonstrations in my behalf. Losing
the case made us more aware of how political religion really is. We
fought the rap for three years before giving up. The Boston conference,
later in 1976, seemed almost like a victory celebration. Thousands of
women celebrated their personal connections with the Goddess. Morgan McFarland led a beautiful ritual, and some danced naked in the
church where the conference was held. We birthed renewed energy for
the longer-lasting struggles to follow.

There was opposition within the feminist movement toward the spiritual movement. Those who didn't share the experiences wondered why
intelligent women would want to "worship the Goddess." They missed
the crucial meaning: It is self-worship. If the Goddess is seen as being
"out there" (or "up there"), it is because all living things are a part of
Her: trees, stars, moon, honeybees, rocks, and us. Just as She has thousands of different names, She can be worshipped in thousands of
different ways. It will take time for women to get rid of patriarchal
ways of worshipping. If some see Her as sitting up on a cloud with Her
magic wand blessing them, maybe this is a step toward seeing Her inside themselves. In the Susan B. Coven, we teach that women are the
Goddess every time we make a choice.

Soon composers started making Goddess songs, and sculptors made
Goddess images. The Woman's Building in Los Angeles had an exhibit
of altars that women had built for themselves. Our Goddess teaching
had inspired women artists, and they are now teaching through their
own culture. Such things, however, cannot be learned in one intro-
ductory workshop; they may take years and must be taught in a very
personal way.

As High Priestess, I wrote, gave lectures, and promoted Goddess-
consciousness by ordaining priestesses, hiving new covens, and initiat-
ing new members yearly. (I also worked at holding the coven together
and at making it possible for us to work and have fun at the same
time.) I regularly mail 3,000 copies of our newsletter, *Themis,* sometimes with only the help of my roommate. One of my more frightening
duties was finding a place of worship. The coven has been arrested
twice for trespassing in Malibu. At our old covenstead, we worshipped
undisturbed for three years until one night some rich neighbors noticed
the light of about one hundred of our candles burning. My students
got a taste of what it's like to belong to an unpopular religion when six

police cars came after us with shotguns, looking for "female sacrifices." Two years later, the police knew our names and did not arrest us; they just made us leave. They had received a complaint from a house lower down on the mountain. I angrily stomped my foot, pointed to the house which had twice called the police on us and said, "The third time YOU GO!" (This place today is known as the Great Malibu Landslide.)

## SHOULDN'T WE WOMEN HONOR EACH OTHER?

High priestess means Female Elder. It is an honor that can be earned by starting a group and serving them. One aspect of conducting successful rituals is knowing how emotion and drama can be effectively combined to facilitate each woman's discovery of the Goddess within herself. Some people call this our inner creative child. The task of the High Priestess is to improvise, to tune into the energy that is present, and channel it when needed so that everyone feels good afterward. It is also hard work, in some ways more difficult than performing as a singer or actress. Singers or actresses have scripts, rehearsals, and an agreed-upon program. The High Priestess uses her own inspiration most of the time. Imagine what it is like to lead a circle of 250 women without a microphone. High Priestesses do not get paid for this work; what they get is honor. My ministry is my gift and my divine act; it is where I am Goddess. I have conducted seventy-nine sabbaths now, with anywhere from 17 to 250 women in each circle. My money to live comes from sales of my books, campus speeches, and Tarot readings.

The notion of High Priestesses being higher beings and not seekers as well is utter nonsense. People may respect or even feel a sense of awe for a High Priestess in much the same way they do a good teacher. We are so indoctrinated with the patriarchal way of seeing everyone as either one-up or one-down that sometimes a healthy respect for elders is misinterpreted as a bad thing. How are women going to learn from our mothers and crones if we don't honor and respect each other?

My focus is in battling the forces of patriarchal history. Most other High Priestesses are doing the same. Starhawk marches against nukes; Batya Podos writes and acts in her plays in order to teach about the re-emergence of the Goddess. Most covens, like the Susan B. are teaching- and service-oriented. We facilitate religious experience.

## CONCLUSION

Questioning the operation of the Goddess movement is healthy; constructive criticism is always welcome. The real challenges facing us are apathy among women, which is an outgrowth of self-loathing unhealed in our womansouls, lack of trust among us, which prevents the exchange of information, and lack of smarts about money, which keeps us poor. Most deadly of all is a lack of a sense of history, for the patriarchy would love to divide, conquer, and burn us again. We need courageous leaders at this point in our history, but let us never forget that we are all the Goddess.

# II. Are Goddesses and Matriarchies Merely Figments of Feminist Imagination?

## Myths and Matriarchies

### Sally R. Binford

*Once upon a time, about 4,000 or 6,000 years ago, women were powerful, free, and in control of their lives. Society was organized along matriarchal lines, and political decisions were made according to female principles that, as we all know, are sensitive, just, and loving. In the context of this culture, women invented ceramics, agriculture, and weaving. Women also knew how to control their fertility; there were means of contraception available that were nontoxic and completely reliable. Since we wanted the babies we had, our relationships with our children were relaxed and loving. We worshiped the Goddess in temples of great beauty, and priestesses conducted rites celebrating our sexuality. The world was at peace.*

*Soon, however, this blissful life was disrupted by patriarchal males who were bent on negative uses of power and who harbored a predilection for warfare. They destroyed our temples and suppressed our rites.*

*The Goddess was replaced by a vengeful male god, and in order to assure his dominance and assuage his jealousy, all records of matriarchal rule and goddess worship were destroyed. Since this takeover, women have been oppressed. The patriarchs took away our knowledge of contraception and forced us into motherhood; they taught us to be ashamed of our sexuality. They denied our inventions and claimed them as their own.*

*For centuries, males controlled access to historical records and wrote of the past in ways that denied our former greatness. This conspiracy has been carried on by anthropologists who have consistently denied the existence of a state of prepatriarchal matriarchy. Their very denial of a matriarchal stage in the human past is suspect; indeed, it is one more striking example of suppression of the truth. If only we can reclaim our past, we can once again be strong and free. We can rediscover herbal methods of birth control and healing and reassert control over our lives. There is an abundance of mythic material that confirms the existence of formerly powerful matriarchies; and art objects — from the Venus figurines of the Paleolithic through Indian temple engravings — reveal the long-suppressed existence of goddess worship. The strength we gain from the knowledge of our past will help us to reclaim our former greatness.*

Feminist anthropologists are faced with a formidable task. Not only have we had to deal with the macho interpretations of prehistory offered by Robert Ardrey, Desmond Morris, and Lionel Tiger, who attempt to rationalize male supremacy, but we also have to cope with the flip side of the myth-as-history coin currently in vogue in some feminist circles. The myths of Eve's apple, Pandora's box, and Freud's penis envy have been replaced by the myth of Former Matriarchal Greatness and the Overthrow of the Mother Goddess. The tenacity with which many women cling to this belief is enormous. As an anthropologist, I am fascinated and can explain it only as a religious phenomenon.

Indeed, in some places, belief in former matriarchies has taken an explicitly religious form. In Los Angeles, for example, a group of Mother Goddess worshipers have formally organized themselves into a church, complete with temple, priestesses, and rituals.

In the many discussions I have had with partisans of this myth over the past several years, I am persuaded that logic, reason, and arguments based on knowledge of the data cut no ice at all. The only experience I have had as an anthropologist that is analogous in its lack of susceptibility to reason is trying to argue the evidence for biological evolution with hardcore fundamentalists, whose faith also renders them impervious to information.

These beliefs are not limited to a lunatic fringe of the women's movement. Academic institutions have recently become involved in the Mother Goddess/Matriarchy madness. A recent conclave at the Santa Cruz campus of the University of California was organized for the very purpose of resisting the interpretations of professional archaeologists. Amid charges of a conspiracy by the anthropological establishment, author Merlin Stone — a leading proponent of the faith — urged untrained women to march through Europe and the Middle East on their own excavation expeditions in order to discover long-suppressed truths.

A less inflammatory conference was held last summer at the University of Washington to discuss whether or not ancient matriarchies and powerful female religions really existed.

Since faith is dictated by a need to believe that is stronger than reason, I entertain no hope of persuading the true believers. What follows is an attempt to restate the major articles of faith of the New Feminist Fundamentalism and to weigh these against current anthropological understandings of the evolution of culture so that those still uncommitted may have a basis for evaluating the claims of the new faith.

1. Matriarchy (rule by women) preceded patriarchy (rule by men) in the evolution of cultures.

This is one of the fundamental cornerstones of the faith and is supported largely by mythic material collected by Johann J. Bachofen and other early armchair anthropologists. The resurrection of the misguided thinking of the opening decades of the nineteenth century by the propagators of the faith has done little to enhance the reputation of feminist thought. According to early armchair anthropologists, human society went through the stages of savagery, barbarism, and then (at last) civilization, by which they meant Western European society.

Living non-Western cultures were seen as cultural fossils surviving from an earlier stage. Each stage was characterized by a mating pattern: Promiscuity was rampant among the savages, while the slightly more advanced barbarians were polygamous. The civilized pattern was, of course, monogamy. According to this formulation, inheritance and tracing ancestry varied with cultural level also: Savages scrambled for what they could get; barbarians inherited rights and goods from their mothers; while Western civilization was sublimely patrilineal. Political power, it was assumed, was distributed randomly, if at all, among savages; often to women, among matrilineal barbarians; and with the appearance of civilization, patriarchy took its rightful place in the world.

This neat tripartite scheme was demolished when anthropologists began doing serious field research. Field-workers learned that rules of residence, ways of reckoning kin, methods of manufacturing and distributing goods and services (technology and economy), and patterns of assigning political power varied in much more complex ways than early theorists could have imagined. As prehistoric archaeologists and cultural anthropologists gathered more and more data, the simplistic notion of a matriarchal stage in the human past had to be discarded.

In recent years, several women authors such as Elizabeth Gould Davis in *The First Sex* and Merlin Stone in *When God Was a Woman* have revived the notion that humanity experienced a golden age of matriarchy in the past. This belief has been combined with the assertion that there is a conspiracy against its acceptance, making those who question the faith subject to suspicion of being co-conspirators. I am the last to deny that anthropology — perhaps even more than other academic enterprises — is dominated by sexist males. I am, however, equally persuaded that if a male anthropologist discovered evidence of past matriarchies, he would publish his findings rather than suppress them. The existence of a past stage of matriarchy would lend support to the thesis that patriarchy is the more advanced cultural form in evolution; it would also support the notion that matriarchies had inherent weaknesses that allowed them to be replaced by patriarchies. Further, the unique discovery of matriarchal cultural systems would also guarantee research grants, and I cannot believe that any academic male social scientist would suppress his findings on principle, thereby denying himself funding.

One of the basic objections to the mythic matriarchal past — apart from the lack of evidence to support it and the consistent body of data that argues against it — is the use of myth as history by the propagators of the faith. We do not attempt to reconstruct biological evolution or the history of the universe by recourse to myth, and the data of cultural evolution are no more amenable to this kind of methodology than are these other attempts to understand evolutionary processes. Myths are not appropriate primary data for reconstructing the past. The Persephone myth, for example, elucidates little about either Greek history or the causes of seasonal variations in temperate zones. The story of Noah's Ark tells us nothing of past geological processes.

2. Matrilineal inheritance and kinship systems are evidence of former matriarchal societies.

The confusion of matrilineality (reckoning inheritance and descent through the female line) with matriarchy (the rule of women) is an almost essential component of the New Fundamentalist faith. In fact, matrilineal institutions tend to be associated with certain patterns of male warfare rather than with female political authority. The Iroquois, for example, were warlike and strongly matrilineal. Their principal investigator, Lewis H. Morgan, wrote that Iroquois men "regarded woman as the inferior, the dependent, the servant of man, and from nurture and habit, she actually considered herself to be so."

In most matrilineal societies, the authority figure is the mother's brother rather than her husband. This may make for decisions that favor the woman's family rather than her husband's, but decision-making still rests with males. The presence of matrilineal institutions may have modifying effects on male dominance for individual women, but matrilineal kinship and inheritance in no way confer political authority on women. In *Sexual Politics,* Kate Millett points out: "Matrilineality does not constitute an exception to patriarchal rule, it simply channels the power held by males through female descent."

3. There existed in the past safe and "natural" methods of birth control; rediscovering our matriarchal heritage can help us to control our fertility.

The principal method of controlling fertility in our own culture and in non-Western cultures for the great stretch of history and prehistory has been to limit the number of female children permitted to reach puberty. Since it is females who bear the children, it is the number of *females* in a population that determines the rate of population growth.

Other factors contributing to lowered fertility rates among women have included long periods of nursing, often several years; diets high in protein and low in carbohydrates; and strenuous physical labor (normally, hauling wood and water is women's work). There are also widely practiced means of abortion in non-Western cultures, almost all of which are thoroughly unpleasant and as dangerous to the woman as to the fetus. These include jumping on the woman's belly, the woman ingesting poisons, striking the woman across the belly with a large object, and insertion of various sharp objects in the woman's vagina. All of these methods of fertility control are consistently backed by infanticide, with heavy emphasis on female infanticide. Marvin Harris documents the extent to which female infanticide has been the species' dominant method of population control and the ways in which this practice is linked to male dominance. Once female infants are defined as nonpersons, their removal becomes less psychologically difficult.

The widespread practice of female infanticide as the major reliable means of population control also helps to explain why almost every culture manifests deep-seated fears of uncontrolled female sexuality. The anthropological literature teems with images of *vagina dentata,* insatiable female gods, and malevolent nymphomaniacal spirits. Women's sexuality is linked to childbearing, and it doesn't take a degree in demography to see that uncontrolled female sexuality without reliable contraception and abortion leads to uncontrolled population growth.

In fact, the rise of feminism can be linked historically with recent attempts to control fertility. The invention of the rubber condom in the 1840s directly correlates with the first major burst of feminist activity in Great Britain and the United States. The rise of the suffragette movement in this country during and after World War I coincides with the invention and spread of the diaphragm. The women's movement of the 1960s concurred with the widespread use of birth control pills.

The danger of discounting recent technological advances in birth control by romanticizing the past is very real. I hold no brief for the reckless testing of the Pill on Third World women, and no one is more critical of gynecologists as a group than I, but let us not discount the significance to women of *relatively* safe means of contraception along with the use of antibiotics in fighting infection from abortion.

4. Prehistoric art reveals the existence of the worship of the Mother Goddess and documents the former power of women.

To assume that the representation of the female figure in art signifies matriarchal power is so fraught with fallacy that I find it difficult to take it seriously as an argument. Does *Playboy*'s artwork imply that it represents a matriarchal cultural system? The Venus figures of the Upper Paleolithic appear to be the earliest example of a common human fascination with the female form. There exists, by the way, a great deal of cave art from the same period that is not discussed either by male art historians or by women seeking to document the existence of the Mother Goddess — representations of female genitalia that would be right at home in any contemporary men's room.*

Art always exists as an integral part of a cultural system, and it bears systemic relations to that culture's mode of production, to its political system, to its ideology. The method of assigning one's own meaning to certain symbols and then tracing them over broad geographic areas and through tens of thousands of years of cultural change is, to put it mildly, not a reliable means of reconstructing the past. It would be possible to take any artistic representation — cattle, for example — and construct a theory about a religion based on the worship of livestock. Enough cattle exist in prehistoric art and in all later periods for a plausible argument to be made that humanity once worshiped cattle but that the history of such worship has been suppressed. What sounds plausible, using such methods, is not necessarily true.

In summary, the New Feminist Fundamentalism is based on assumptions that cannot be supported; these include the notion of matriarchy as a stage in cultural evolution, the equating of matrilineality with matriarchy, the romanticizing of "natural" birth control, and the assigning of unitary significance to art forms that appear in widely differing contexts.

I can find no valid reason for the need to believe in a golden age of matriarchy. Certainly, if we did once live in matriarchal societies, we blew it by letting the patriarchs take over. How did this happen? One of the most intriguing "explanations" is offered by Elizabeth Gould Davis: Because of their carnivorous diet, men grew enormous penises, and women were so turned on that they voluntarily surrendered their power. I cannot accept this as a serious piece of history — only as a thoroughgoing putdown of women.

The overwhelming body of evidence from anthropology and from history argues against a universal stage of matriarchy. There are those

---

* Editor's Note: This "Playboy theory" of the female statues from the Upper Paleolithic period has also been proposed by John Onians, "The Origins of Art," *Art History, Journal of the Assoc. of Art Historians*, vol. 1, no. 1, 1978 (London). For a learned response, see Marija Gimbutas, "Vulvas, Breasts, and Buttocks of the Goddess of Life, Death, and Regeneration: Commentary on 'The Origins of Art,'" *The Shape of the Past: Studies in Honor of Franklin D. Murphy*, published by the Institute of Archaeology and Office of the Chancellor, University of California at Los Angeles, 1981. — C.S.

who will contend that this statement simply indicates how brainwashed I have been by my male colleagues. This must mean that my female colleagues have also been intellectually victimized. Another putdown of women!

It is often argued that the reality or truth of a former matriarchal stage is irrelevant, that the idea is a useful one around which women can rally. I take strong exception to this. In order to cope intelligently with the present and the future, we must understand the past. We must come to terms with the cultural processes that have caused male dominance to be so widespread and long-lived. Anthropologist Joan Bamberger argues this point cogently in a contribution to *Women, Culture and Society:*

Myth and rituals have been misinterpreted as persistent reminders that women once had, and then lost, the seat of power. This loss accrued to them through inappropriate conduct. . . . The myths constantly reiterate that women did not know how to handle power when they had it. The loss is thereby justified so long as women choose to accept the myth.

The final version of woman that emerges from these myths is that [woman] represents chaos and misrule through trickery and unbridled sexuality. . . . The myth of matriarchy is but the tool used to keep woman bound to her place. To free her, we need to destroy the myth.

The evolution of women's culture is a field that needs serious study; the nature of male dominance and its causes are significant areas of inquiry. Some anthropologists have given these problems serious consideration. A giant step was taken by the authors of *Toward an Anthropology of Women,* edited by Rayna R. Reiter. *The Female of the Species* by M. Kay Martin and Barbara Voorhies and *Cannibals and Kings* by Marvin Harris are other examples that come to mind.

The true believers in the fundamentalist faith of the Fall from Matriarchy and the Overthrow of the Mother Goddess contribute nothing but confusion and misinformation, and their insistence that those who question their assertions are part of a sexist conspiracy does little to enlighten us. In this period of backlash and antifeminism, an investigation of the relationship between women's control over their own reproduction and the forces that seek to keep women "in their place" might be of much greater utility. It is no accident that women's oppression is most often expressed as a "right to life." The historical and cultural antecedents of such thinking need to be explored and understood.

It is hoped that efforts to understand the evolution of women's culture will continue and that these efforts will be based on current information and sound methodology. The assertion of a mythic past as history and questioning the goodwill of those who doubt its validity constitutes an attitude that has much in common with the orthodoxy of Freudian psychology, fundamentalist Christianity, and other religions based on blind faith.

# Response by Merlin Stone

Entering into a discussion about whether or not ancient Goddess worship existed, as the author of "Myths and Matriarchies" (I refer to it as M & M) suggests, is much like inviting us into a discussion of whether or not World War II actually occurred. As long as the author of M & M chooses to blind herself to the evidence of *seven thousand* years of artifacts and the *three thousand* years of historical (i.e., written) material, as discovered, deciphered, and described by archaeologists and historians (those listed in the *ten pages* of bibliography of *When God Was a Woman*) — how can her statements even be considered seriously?

Being extremely busy with the publication of my new book, Volume I of *Ancient Mirrors of Womanhood: Our Goddess and Heroine Heritage*, I really do not have time to rewrite or repeat all that is included in this new work (some 430 pages of additional evidence, approximately 215 in each volume), as well as the 240 pages of *When God Was a Woman*.

The author of M & M's own reference to belief in Goddess reverence as "madness" not only reveals an intolerable religious bigotry but perhaps explains her problem in absorbing and comprehending this massive body of information.

# Response by Charlene Spretnak

In the Fall Equinox 1979 issue of *WomanSpirit*, an article by Sally Binford was reprinted from the May 1979 issue of *Human Behavior*. The theme of the article was advertised on the cover of *Human Behavior* as "Matriarchy Unmasked." Since the article was one of the most misleading that I have come across in several years of researching Goddess mythology, I immediately sent a letter to the magazine. The letter, which is printed below, was never published in *Human Behavior* because the magazine went out of business and that May issue was their last.

3 May 1979

## MATRIARCHIES VS. GODDESSES

Dear *Human Behavior*,

Sally Binford raised some important points and exaggerated many others in her article "Myths and Matriarchies" (May 1979).

Her most serious error was to blur the crucial distinction between two separate areas of research: (1) Archaeologists, classicists, and historians of religion have amassed abundant evidence that Goddess religions pre-dated patriarchal religions in many parts of the world; (2) Whether or not those societies who revered a form of the Goddess were matriarchies is unknown.

In Greece, for instance, the earliest artifacts, altars, and linguistic references to the pre-Hellenic deities (Hera, Demeter, Artemis, Athena, etc.) long pre-date the appearance of the Hellenic, i.e., Olympian, gods. (See the works of Farnell, Harrison, James, Nilsson, Kerenyi, Willetts, and Zuntz.) However, most feminist Goddess-researchers share Binford's exasperation with "loose talk" of a "Golden Age of Matriarchy" in Greece or elsewhere; nor is this belief common in the feminist population at large.

Binford often did what she warns against: taking assumption as fact. She cited as fact Marvin Harris' much-questioned deduction that, because some primitive patriarchal societies practice female infanticide, it must have been *the* primary means of population control in all prehistoric societies, as well. She also accepted Joan Bamberger's assumption that, if there were matriarchies, they collapsed internally through women's "inappropriate conduct." Several scholars have suggested that the wave of "Aryan" invasions that moved down from the Eurasian steppes into the Mediterranean and all the way east to India conquered many Goddess-worshipping cultures, which *may* have been matriarchal to some degrees and were clearly matrifocal.

Finally, Binford altered Merlin Stone's quote to suit the theme of her article. At the U.C. Santa Cruz conference, Stone did not "urge untrained women to march through Europe and the Middle East on their own excavation expeditions." Rather, she suggested that feminist researchers *do* get training and "learn ancient languages such as Akkadian and Hittite" in order to study the ancient texts directly (*The L.A. Times*, 10 April 1978). This recognition that many of the standard translations concerning Goddess religions reflect the patriarchal bias of our society (e.g., "holy women" translated as "temple prostitutes") is quite different from Binford's sarcastic claim that feminist researchers believe there is a willful "conspiracy" among male researchers.

Binford closed with a call for further research; I feel the entire feminist community would agree. One very basic area of investigation would be whether societies who worshipped a goddess differed in any ways from societies who worshipped a god.

CHARLENE SPRETNAK
author of *Lost Goddesses of Early Greece:
A Collection of Pre-Hellenic Myths*

Sally Binford's article contains a number of lesser and greater errors. Her central premise — that feminist researchers and their hapless followers subscribe to "the golden age of matriarchy" theory — is simply

554 Appendix: Two Debates

false. Merlin Stone, for instance, is rightfully intolerant of women stretching the facts — *because we don't have to*. In dismissing improbable fabrications of unqualified, universal matriarchy, Stone has often asked rhetorically, "Why build our house of straw when we have bricks?" Likewise, I emphasized in the introduction to *Lost Goddesses of Early Greece* that too many clues to our prehistoric past have been lost for us to reconstruct the totality of those cultures with any certainty. This recognition of the *limits* of our knowledge is a theme that has prevaded all the major books published on Goddess religion during the past few years, e.g., the works of Stone, Rich, Gimbutas, Fisher, Christ, Goldenberg. The two major feminist magazine spreads on this topic, i.e., *Heresies,* no. 5 and *Chrysalis,* no. 6, also explored what we *do* know about the Goddess-oriented past, but they did not publish fantasies of wishful thinking.

## PART ONE

Other errors appear throughout the four sections of Binford's essay, each covering a supposedly groundless "article of faith of the New Feminist Fundamentalism". In the first section, "Matriarchy preceded patriarchy in the evolution of cultures," Binford correctly observes that cultural patterns in prehistoric societies are now acknowledged to have been much more complex than early researchers had thought. She then makes the unsupported statement that the hypothesis of a matriarchal stage in history had to be dropped because of modern research. Surely this assertion would bring a barrage of objections from many contemporary archaeologists and cultural anthropologists. The case definitely has not been closed. Moreover, she ignores the massive accumulation of evidence that the pre-invasion societies were largely *matrifocal.* (See the Editor's Note in "Meanings of Matriarchy" in this volume.)

Binford also suggests that we would/should be embarrassed if unequivocal proof of widespread matriarchy were discovered because (1) "it would lend support to the thesis that patriarchy is the more advanced form in evolution," and (2) "it would also support the notion that matriarchies had inherent weaknesses that allowed them to be replaced by patriarchies." Binford's first worry here is a surprisingly pure example of patriarchal thought; how could anyone possibly propose that our present, i.e., patriarchal, culture with its ever increasing alienation, materialism, suicidal destruction of nature, and sexist corruption is inherently superior to earlier cultures that were harmonious (e.g., citizens of Goddess-oriented Crete and Old Europe enjoyed millennia of peace in unfortified towns) and egalitarian (see *Woman's Creation: Sexual Evolution and the Shaping of Society* by Elizabeth Fisher)? Binford's second worry here ignores the proof of barbarian invasions, which I mentioned in my letter to *Human Behavior*. (See Marija Gimbutas' article and Footnote 1 in the Introduction, both in this volume.)

The final problem in the first section of her article is Binford's refusal to accept any historical references in mythology. Numerous classics scholars since 1903 would disagree. They have noted that certain patriarchal elements, e.g., the rape of Persephone and the forced marriage of Hera, were not part of these goddesses' mythology prior to the barbarian invasions; they have concluded that their inclusion in the myths is a historical reference to the rape of the Goddess-oriented culture and to the trauma of occupation. These classics scholars were/are not idiots; they were/are women and men who held/hold professorships at Oxford, Cambridge, and universities on the Continent. They were/are certainly not propagators of any blind faith.

## PART TWO

In the second section, "Matrilineal inheritance and kinship systems are evidence of former matriarchal societies," Binford briefly cites an example of matrilineality within a patriarchal culture (the Iroquois). True, many other examples of this situation have been recorded by observers. This could mean either (1) matrilineality is a remnant of gynecratic societies that has survived in some cases into the patriarchal era, with the adaptation that the mother's brother is held superior, or (2) matrilineality has never existed without the domination of the mother's brother and patriarchal conditions for women. Binford allows only the second possibility; I say we just don't know.

## PART THREE

In the third section, "There existed in the past safe and 'natural' methods of birth control; rediscovering our matriarchal heritage can help us control our fertility," Binford presents Marvin Harris' sexist, ill-founded theory of population control as if it were fact. Harris, an anthropologist at Columbia University, wrote *Cannibals and Kings*, which was excerpted in *The New York Times Sunday Magazine* in an article he titled "Why Men Dominate Women" (13 Nov. 1977). He, and Binford, assert that "the principal method of controlling fertility in our own culture and in non-Western cultures for the great stretch of history and prehistory" has always been female infanticide. Harris builds his case on numerous citations of female infanticide in patriarchal societies, from nineteenth-century foundling homes back to the warring, nomadic bands. Why is this billed as "startling new evidence"? Why should there be surprise at the low value placed on female lives under patriarchy? (Even today a new cycle of female infanticide is beginning as couples can opt to abort their baby if an amniocentesis test shows that the fetus is the "wrong" sex; guess which sex is aborted more often with this procedure. This type of abortion is far different than an abortion performed for valid reasons held by the mother. That such abortions are being made available by the medical establishment and that so many young couples believe they must produce a son to justify their lives are two extremely disturbing examples of patriarchal corruption in our society.)

None of Harris' "proof" supports his conclusion: that it has always and everywhere been this way. Using extremely shoddy methodology, he takes the incidences of female infanticide in primitive, historic, patriarchal societies and extends this fact backward into prehistory with no justification whatsoever. He is purposely vague. Are his warring bands the barbarian invaders who swept into Old Europe from 4500 to 2500 B.C., and later into the Aegean area, imposing their thunderbolt god and their patriarchal social order? One doesn't know. Certainly Harris doesn't know. He can only fantasize that the many instances of woman-hating which he cites from patriarchal societies were always and everywhere in existence.

Many of Harris' backward extensions directly contradict the findings of archaeologists. If people have *always* believed "menstrual blood pollutes," then why was red ocher painted on artifacts and corpses in Neolithic graves and on vulva-like entrances to caves wherein archaeologists tell us that group worship took place and statues of the Goddess were the only representations of deity found in those societies? The mysterious menstrual blood was sacred. Throughout the Upper Paleolithic period the surviving statues show that our ancestors were in awe of women's mysteries, i.e., bleeding painlessly in rhythm with the moon, drawing both females and males from their bodies, providing food for the young from their breasts.

In the many Goddess-oriented societies, where the supreme deity was female, the priests were female (see the artifacts from the Minoan and other Neolithic cultures), and the participants in the central rituals were female (see Gimbutas' article in the volume and Harrison's *Prolegomena to the Study of Greek Religion*), just how plausible is a theory which posits that "women were defined as nonpersons" (Binford's words) and hence were easy objects of infanticide?

Binford brushes over any real possibility of herbal contraception or abortion. A more serious error, however, is her interpretation of "why almost every [patriarchal] culture manifested deep-seated fears of uncontrolled female sexuality" and why "the anthropological literature teems with images of *vagina dentata*, insatiable female gods, and malevolent nymphomaniacal spirits." Binford, rather amazingly, maintains that these are expressions of fear of overpopulation! I and many feminist researchers maintain that these are patriarchal expressions of intense fear of woman's elemental power, of envy and resentment of her mysteries.

## PART FOUR

In the fourth section, "Prehistoric art reveals the existence of the worship of the Mother Goddess and documents the former power of women," Binford again exhibits patriarchal attitudes. She allows that the powerfully exaggerated, procreative female statues of the Upper Paleolithic period show a certain "fascination with the female form" but she points out that so does *Playboy*. It is truly pathetic when a woman cannot perceive the difference between the powerful Paleolithic figures and current pornographic portrayals of women as coy, vulnerable toys.

The rest of this section revolves around the serious error that I cited at the beginning of the letter to *Human Behavior*: Ignoring the decades of research by classicists and archaeologists, Binford holds that if there is no hard evidence of matriarchies then, likewise, there was no Goddess. She simply cannot sweep so much cross-cultural evidence of Goddess-worship under the rug.

# Counter-Response by Sally R. Binford

Regarding the above exchange, I wish to discuss two major points within the context of feminist politics: (1) an assumption underlying much of the writing on mother goddesses and matriarchies; and (2) the relevance of religious/spiritual concerns to the struggle for women's rights.

Feminist authors concerned with demonstrating religions based on the Great Goddess often share the assumption, which is sometimes made explicit, that there are enormous psychological and biological differences between the sexes; women are by nature sensitive, loving, and nurturing, while men are aggressive, brutal, and violent. As anthropologist Gayle Rubin points out, this is precisely the assumption of conventional sexists, and it cannot be supported by either biological or social science. One of the major thrusts of feminism has been the refutation of these culturally defined sex differences and the adamant refusal of women to accept such definitions of themselves.

The task of women today is to break free of the strictures of the "feminine" as set forth by our culture and not to embrace them in the name of spirituality. The most exciting aspect of modern feminism is that we are free to explore what women are really capable of, rather than to accept the mothering role set out for us by men for centuries. Clichés about the nurturing, gentle nature of women, whether offered by Sigmund Freud, Carl Jung, Norman Mailer, or feminists themselves, are the same in content and oppress all women.

It is with more than twenty years of experience as a professional anthropologist that I warn my feminist sisters of a syndrome common to the disenfranchised and oppressed: the evocation of a Lost Age. The Ghost Dance of the Plains Indians and the Cargo Cults of the South Pacific are examples of this, as is the current concern with mother goddesses and matriarchies.

The function of myth is the same in all societies: to rationalize the *status quo*. Those with power in our society buy into the myths of manifest destiny, the free enterprise system, and women as keepers of hearth and home. The powerless dream of and long for a mythic past and waste precious time attempting to document its reality. The bottom line of power and authority has to do with who owns and allocates goods and services, not with the gender of the deities we choose to worship.

If women allow themselves to be consoled . . . by the invocation of hypothetical great goddesses, they are simply flattering themselves into submission (a technique often used on them by men). . . . Mother goddesses are just as silly a notion as father gods. If a revival of these cults gives women emotional satisfaction, it does so at the price of obscuring the real conditions of life. This is why they were invented in the first place.

— ANGELA CARTER, *The Sadeian Woman*

What the study of the past can teach us is that as long as women do not have a fair share of the economic pie, as long as we do not control our own reproductive capacity, our access to power is severely limited. It is time to struggle with real issues of power and not to fritter away our energies rebuilding myths and doing our own versions of the Ghost Dance.

# Post-Counter-Response
## by Charlene Spretnak

I do not agree with the above Marxist feminists' (Binford and Carter) interpretation of the myriad statues, frescoes, bas reliefs, seal rings, and other archaeological evidence of the Goddess and prepatriarchal images of women. First of all, the evidence is not merely wishful thinking or empty dreaming; Merlin Stone's bibliography in Volume Two of *Ancient Mirrors of Womanhood: Our Goddess and Heroine Heritage,* for instance, includes over 500 books and articles on the history and implications of Goddess spirituality. Second, the artifacts and myths have sparked the interest of feminists because they are images of *power;* they encourage empowerment and wholeness, not weakness or submission. Both pre- and postpatriarchal expressions of the female dispel the dying patriarchal views of woman as "the eternal fluffy feminine" à la Freud and Jung. But why does Binford insist that we must stop considering ourselves sensitive and loving? Surely a strong, independent woman can possess such traits. Moreover, if myths are created solely to justify the *status quo,* as the above authors assert, it would seem that the powerful female symbols and myths dated in the prepatriarchal era carry a message for us.

Contrary to Binford's and Rubin's beliefs, women do indeed differ psychologically and biologically from men. Current non-sexist research by leading neurophysiologists supports this unequivocally. However, the variances being discovered are far different from the patriarchal projections of sexist stereotyping. (See Footnote 3 in the Introduction to this volume.)

As for the "real conditions" of life, feminist spirituality contributes to a truly comprehensive analysis because it acknowledges the politics of the psyche in patriarchal oppression. We see an intrinsic interconnection among sexism, racism, class exploitation, and ecological destruction: As long as a notion of ultimate authority, i.e., God, is perceived as male and white (a notion that permeates even atheistic societies today), persons fitting that description will continue to relate to everyone else as "other," less than fully human, and, therefore, deserving of injustice and abuse. The Goddess, conversely, is not an authority figure; She is, among other things, a symbol of harmony and oneness among humans, animals, and nature. Having accepted the patriarchy's symbol for their politics of separation, i.e., God the Father, for nearly 4,000 years and having witnessed the oppression and destruction their system has wrought, we can now appreciate the insight of Virgil's observation: "We make our destinies by our choice of gods."

If, after studying the worldwide extant evidence of the Goddess as Creator, Transformer, Mother, Daughter, etc., a woman can conclude only that the artifacts in the museums do not really exist or that they are merely "silly," that's fine. But other women find silly the belief that any economic analysis alone could address all the complex dimensions of life. Nonetheless, "let a hundred flowers bloom, let a thousand schools of thought contend."

---

Editor's Note: It should be stated that not all Marxist feminists share Binford's and Carter's anti-spirituality view, although most probably do; for example, there is a group of feminist women and men in San Francisco called the Marxist Spirituality Collective (Box 11503, SF 94101). Also, *Quest: A Feminist Quarterly* has published a good deal of Marxist feminist theory in juxtaposition with essays on feminist spirituality. — C.S.

# Afterword

# Feminist Politics and the Nature of Mind

We are not mind. We know this because we can observe the mind. We can watch thoughts arising and falling away. We can hone our attention so finely that we can observe the very birth of a thought: vibration in the mind, vibration by energy of matter (cells) which is energy. We can see patterns among the thoughts. Many of the patterns have been culturally imposed. Viewing them within a framework of feminist theory suggests certain possibilities: First, as the oppressed class worldwide, women have been raised with greater psychological insecurities than we may have recognized; second, the values of patriarchal culture have been internalized so thoroughly that the resultant thought patterns are viewed as human nature; and, third, with the recent scientific findings that female and male brains are physiologically and functionally quite different, it becomes clear that cultivating the female mind, with its impulses toward empathetic comprehension, communion, and harmony, is essential to humankind's surviving the myriad forms of patriarchal destruction, such as the "necessity" of a nuclear arms race.

## SHEDDING INSECURITY

When I went away to college in 1964, I noticed a curious phenomenon: Altercations in the men's dormitories, no matter how vociferous, seemed to be fought and dispensed with; altercations in the women's dormitories seemed to hang in the air for weeks, months, or even years. Later, when I had acquired a feminist perspective, I understood what I had seen. Men, in general, are raised in the warmth of cultural affirmation; their roles, their behavior, their very being are validated by family, school, church, and state. So sacrosanct is the notion of manhood that no challenge to a man's opinions or actions could possibly threaten his sense of who or what he *is*. Women, conversely, are not permitted by patriarchal culture to develop a healthy, autonomous sense of self; we are to be only someone's daughter, someone's wife, someone's mother — the good girl dancing nicely around the edges of men's lives. With no firm grounding in the power of our own being, challenges to our opinions or actions may be perceived as attacks on our very structure of identity, calling forth protective "overkill" of retaliation and resentment.

Unfortunately, this same pattern is still being played out in many feminist political groups. During the past few years, I have been invited to speak about prepatriarchal mythology to feminist audiences in several parts of the country. When I inquire of my hosts on those lecture trips about the state of the movement in their city, I am usually told that some of the local feminist organizations are thriving and are continuing to sponsor political actions, but that many others are in splinters. Groups have divided and divided again. Women are not speaking to one another. The distinction between being opponents on an issue and being enemies is rarely acknowledged. Emotional exhaustion, labeled "burn-out," is common and *Protect Yourself* has become the motto of the veterans.

Guardians of white, male supremacy depend upon such splintering of revolutionary movements to maintain the *status quo*. There is an old saw that oppressed groups always fight more among themselves than against their oppressors. We can see that women's insecurities are largely implanted by patriarchal design: We are *supposed* to interact with one another only with a frail ego, self-hatred, and no truly positive (rather than defensive) sense of self. Allowing ourselves to love ourselves, however, is the antidote. Once we acknowledge the power of our own nature, alternative ways of being develop. Women's spirituality is a way to that power.

Throughout our formative years, almost all women experienced some degree of rejection or discrimination by family and/or teachers for the patriarchal sin of having been born female. In the more brutal cases, which are legion, the rejection was an intense and daily ordeal. Obviously, the self-hatred, seething rage, and crippling insecurity that result from such cruelty are not going to be erased with five minutes of meditation. Yet feminist meditation and ritual do create new psychological patterns of self-love and affirmation of the larger realities — i.e., humans are not meaningless clumps of alienation stomping around waiting to die, as much of patriarchal philosophy and literature contends; we are one with all life forms in the living, breathing universe, and our potentials far exceed patriarchal confines. Reclaiming our psyches is a political victory over patriarchal conditioning. We choose not to function as pathetically wounded victims who can merely attempt ineffectual forays into liberation. We choose to make ourselves healthy, strong, and whole, to acknowledge our own elemental power.

An essential element of skillful living is the cultivation of full awareness of the present moment. Usually our minds jump back and forth to the past or the future; much time and psychic energy are lost to "playing back tapes" of negative events from the past. A certain spiritual tradition includes an exhortation that emphasizes living fully in the present moment: "When you walk, walk. When you run, run. Whatever you do, don't wobble!" For feminist politics, or any politics, we could adapt that to: "When you argue, argue. When it's time to move forward, *move forward*." It is possible to carry around on one's shoulders an enormous load of past negativity; the weight of it sets one's face in hard lines and presses in on thoughts that might otherwise be active and creative. Clinging to the past limits possibilities in the present. Traveling unencumbered brings freedom and inner power, which fuel the political actions of the movement.

## REPLACING PATRIARCHAL RESPONSES

We have recognized the importance of our refusing to be victims of patriarchal injustices in society — but we must also refuse to be victims of patriarchal modes of thought.

Every feminist victory in law, education, business, medicine, publishing, etc., is good for all of us. That is a simple platitude, often spoken, sometimes believed. Beneath the surface, however, patriarchal responses may linger: envy, resentment, antagonism. Rigidity and a culturally acquired desire to destroy "the other" often masquerade as "principles" during attacks on a woman; psychological and verbal violence, "trashing," is a patriarchal mode of "broadening" someone's political views. The pervasive masculist impulse "Be like me — or else!" remains a source of destructive tension. Rather than pretend that such divisive reactions do not exist, we should recognize them as behavior patterns learned from patriarchal culture. Since we can observe and direct our minds, we can choose to change the patterns. Every thought plants a seed for future thoughts.

We know that winning justice for women is an ongoing struggle and that the fight will intensify as we face reactionary forces during the Eighties. There is, at the same time, a struggle in our minds between unskillful (i.e., patriarchal) and skillful (i.e., holistic, postpatriarchal) mindstates. Several Eastern spiritual traditions, and a couple of Western ones, include the concept of the impeccable warrior, or hera/hero: one who moves through life battling uncompromisingly with the demons of fear, envy, hatred, aggression, etc., that would imprison the mind on low levels. The impeccable hera can expand her awareness to sharp perceptions of the diverse energies in a situation or focus it on a single thought with great one-pointedness. She is not bound to reactive thought modes, such as feeling that if someone is petty and dishonorable toward her, she has no choice but to return the base behavior threefold. She is a powerful opponent because she will not get drawn into an antagonist's cycles of negativity. She knows when formidable force is called for, when a gentle tap, and when nothing but time and space are needed. She does not accept the masculist view of life that we must kill or be killed. The impeccable hera is firm in her commitments and determination, but she will have no part of a rigid, self-righteous posture of more-ethical-than-thou. She knows lightness and humor and understands that the cosmic dance involves sad and funny missteps, as well as grace. She knows compassion and love and the unity of all sentient beings.

The spiritual concept of "right living" has nothing to do with trying to be "good" in order to reap rewards in some ephemeral afterlife. It has concrete effects here and now, which many women have experienced. The more impeccably a person lives — and thinks — the more invincible she becomes to other people's negativity. This is simply an experiential realization that thought creates an actual field around us.

Positive thought attracts positive solutions, resolutions, actions, creativity, and growth; negative thought attracts more negativity. Spiritual teachers, including Witches, have known about thought fields for centuries. Today scientists, too, are discovering them in laboratory experiments.

The options are very narrow for a life lived through reactive thought patterns. Many girls are psychologically tyrannized by a patriarchally conditioned mother or father who is ashamed at not having produced a son. Psychiatrists have noted that such victims often grow up to "become" the brutalizing parent: intolerant, spiteful, punitive. This is not because they cannot see any other models for adulthood, but because the reactive patterns of revenge are so thoroughly ingrained that they dominate behavior. A child's mind, in such situations, naturally dreams of revenge, of tyrannizing the tyrant and doing everything back to him or her. As an adult, this is usually not possible (the parent is deceased, lives far away, is protected, etc.), so the unexamined mind acts out the reactive patterns on co-workers, political colleagues, friends, and, most unfortunately, on daughters.

The hatred and self-hatred perpetuated among women under patriarchy by reactive, vengeful thought patterns constitutes an atrocity of chain reactions that has stretched for centuries. In many patriarchal societies today, a bride must still move into the home of her husband's family and become the servant-like daughter-in-law in a house of strangers. During the early Seventies, I lived in a country with such a system and observed the devastating cycle of vengeance — never against the oppressors, always against other women. The daughter-in-law endures several decades of servitude, degradation, and cruelty from a tyrannical mother-in-law, who in turn was brutalized in her youth by *her* mother-in-law. If the victim has had the "luck" to marry the eldest son, one day she will rule the household and take revenge for several decades on her sons' wives. The culture encourages such behavior as a fact of life with common proverbs: "The hated daughter-in-law goes on producing the beloved grandsons." If just *one* woman in each family would rise above the closed circle of reactive thought patterns and would treat her own class, i.e., women, with love and compassion and support, the women in that country could begin to reclaim their own psyches and then take action. Love is the catalyst, the revolutionary offensive. It is happening, slowly, at first in the cities. The situation there is more extreme than in our own country but is not without broad parallels in the realms of family, education, employment, activism, and friendship.

The goal of maintaining skillful mindstates is not to suppress rage and somehow transform it into ladylike niceness. Rage is an entirely appropriate response to being violated, psychically or physically, individually or collectively. But unchanneled rage does not lead to sustained political action. With a political perspective, rage can move into anger, which can move into an unswerving commitment that *this outrage against women WILL NOT GO ON*. That commitment is fed by a sense of inner and collective power, which meditation and ritual can help to fortify. During the Vietnam War, many would-be activists dropped out of political work because they found their rage or depression about the war so intense that it overwhelmed their lives. The women and men who did stop the war did not indulge in emotional states of a consuming intensity; they kept their eyes on the goal, worked steadily for years to broaden their base of public support and to pressure the government — and they won.

I do not know anyone now who lives as an impeccable hera during every moment of her life. We are all fighting our own demons. (If only we could see how similar the struggles are!) I have seen many women, however, who are evolving quite consciously in that direction with age. Their spiritual practice is the *awareness* of body/mind. Laughingly, they shed patriarchal bindings; lovingly, they discover their own true natures.

## CULTIVATING THE FEMALE MIND

After I had assembled this book with its chorus of women's voices singing of our elemental power, our own body knowledge, I came across a prophetic passage that many of us probably read in 1976:

In arguing that we have by no means explored or understood our biological grounding, the miracle and paradox of the female body and its spiritual and political meanings, I am really asking whether or not women cannot begin, at last, to *think through the body*, to connect what has been so cruelly disorganized—our great mental capacities, hardly used; our highly developed tactile sense; our genius for close observation; our complicated, pain-enduring, multi-pleasured physicality. . . . There is for the first time today a possibility of converting our physicality into both knowledge and power.
— ADRIENNE RICH, *Of Woman Born*

Since I had recently read many articles on new brain research, the intellectual half of my mind commented as I read: "Yes, that's correct. We do process more information more quickly; we do have a much finer tactile sense; we do excel at perceiving facts in context." At the same time, my whole body/mind experienced a rush of affirmation: *Yes! Yes! Yes! That possibility is happening! That is women's spirituality!*

I hope this book will explain the "why" and "what" of women's spirituality. The "how" resides within every woman. Particular rituals, meditations, and practices can be found in books and periodicals cited in the bibliography. And "there's plenty more where that came from": the female mind, thinking through the body.

> I think woman is organically opposed to war.
> — TATYANA MAMONOVA,
> exiled Russian feminist activist

Most of us have always suspected, and some of us have seen very clearly, what the neuropsychologists have determined recently about the female mind (see Introduction). What may be news and is surely dismaying are their discoveries about the male mind: The psychophysiological tendencies of men's minds [speaking of statistical *averages*] correlate with patriarchal values. Although men excel at many visual-spatial tasks, daylight vision, and gross motor movements, when it comes to grasping oneness and at-large bonding (i.e., active empathy with people beyond one's circle), most men are simply not playing with a full deck. That is, the competitive, violent society we live in is not merely a product of conditioning. That is, having comparatively little capacity for empathy, many of the men at the Pentagon, the White House, etc., if left to their own devices, will probably *never* understand that they are one with the children on whom they drop napalm. ("The Oriental does not put the same high price on life as does the Westerner." — General Wm. Westmoreland) They will probably *never* understand that they are of the same life energy as the low-income, pregnant woman who desperately needs an abortion. ("There are many things in life that are not fair." — President Jimmy Carter, signing a bill to cut back federal money for abortions) They will probably *never* understand that it is their sisters and brothers — *us* — who will be poisoned by their leaking plutonium,* their deadly chemical wastes, their

---

* The dangers of nuclear power far exceed any need for it; nuclear energy and weaponry are a product of the "manipulative animal's" penchant for playing with

proliferating warheads. Unless women's voices are heard, we will all be pulled into their death wish. Very soon.

> We women are the fact and flesh of connectedness.
> — GRACE PALEY and YNESTRA KING

Cultivating the female mind, acknowledging the female source of wisdom and harmony — these practices must extend beyond our own bodies and our own circles. Of all the patriarchal outrages — e.g., racism; harassment of homosexuals; increasing violence against women; forced prostitution; pornography; non-personhood for women in legal, educational, and medical areas; economic oppression — it is nuclear power and weaponry that promise irreversible effects. Our activism is not a matter of "either this issue or that"; all of the above stem directly from our society's acceptance of patriarchal values. As we work in each area, we will voice the *connections* among the issues.

> To reach union with the Tao, man needs to abide by the female.
> — ELLEN MARIE CHEN, commenting
> on the *Tao Te Ching*, Book 28

How to save us all from annihilation, how to birth a just world of inner and outer peace and harmony. . . . One essential element of our strategy should be achieving broad public awareness that the human race *does* have a heritage of long eras of peace among societies that lived by holistic values. There are so many books on the history of wars, why none on the history of peace in the prepatriarchal cultures? Well-meaning anti-nuclear and peace activists often say, "We are trying for something new in the history of man [sic]: peace." This is not so. Peaceful and progressive societies thrived for millennia where gynocentric values prevailed, e.g., Minoan Crete and Old Europe. In short, we have lived sanely before, we can do it again.

A second element must be our self-regeneration. To avoid being

---

and controlling the ultimate toy. According to Arthur Rosenfeld of the American Council for an Energy-Efficient Economy, the U.S. could practically *export* oil if we would simply retrofit our buildings and homes and manufacture only energy-efficient cars and large appliances, none of which would involve spartan living conditions. In turning an anthropologist's ear to the conversations of male physicists and other energy-technologists, Laura Nader has reported that conservation is demeaned as "feminine" and solar power as "not intellectually challenging," while fission and fusion, a flirtation with danger and death, are considered glamorous and thrillingly risky, "the biggest crap game of all" (see *Physics Today*, Feb. 1981).

overwhelmed by the dimensions of our struggle, we should carefully maintain our most essential political resource: us. Addressing what we would call "burn-out," Elizabeth Cady Stanton, an indefatigable hera of the first wave of feminism, warned her colleagues, "To develop our real selves, we need time alone for thought and meditation. To be always giving out and never pumping in, the well runs dry too soon." Feminist process, then, involves living the new possibilities *now*, as we struggle.

Can we adopt yet another political slogan? Here is one that will contribute to our long-range success in whatever personal or public areas we may address: *Watch Your Mind.* Trust your body knowledge. Feed your natural tendencies toward multi-layered perceptions, empathy, compassion, unity, and harmony. Feel your wholeness. Feel our oneness. Feel the elemental source of our power. Discard the patriarchal patterns of alienation, fear, enmity, aggression, and destruction. It is not necessary to force them away; by merely focusing awareness on the negative, masculist thoughts as they begin to arise and then opting not to feed them any more psychic energy, their power becomes diminished and they fade. The wisdom of our body/mind can wash over those artificial habits of thought as waves rising from our center.

We have choices. We have will. We have insight and awareness that can be acknowledged and developed — or denied. We can move far beyond the patriarchal boundaries. The authentic female mind is our salvation.

C.S.

# Notes on the Contributors

MARGOT ADLER is a writer; a reporter for National Public Radio in New York City; host of *Unstuck in Time*, a talk show on WBAI-FM; author of *Drawing Down the Moon: Witches, Druids, Goddess-Worshippers, and Other Pagans in America Today*; a practicing Pagan and a priestess in a British-based tradition of Witchcraft.

JUDITH ANTONELLI is interested in various dimensions of spirituality and the psyche, especially the connections between religion and ethnicity. She practices polarity therapy and astrology and is currently doing research for a book on fascism and the occult.

SIEW HWA BEH is a graduate of the Film Studies Program at the University of California at Los Angeles and founded *Women and Film* in 1970, which she edited for five years. She was a performing artist in her homeland, Malaysia; she is now an investor, a traveler, and a writer.

SALLY R. BINFORD is an anthropologist and prehistoric archaeologist whose publications include a book on archaeological theory and over thirty articles and monographs. She has taught at Northwestern University, the University of California at Los Angeles and at Santa Barbara, and the University of New Mexico.

E. M. BRONER is a novelist, playwright, scholar, and author of five books, including the novels *Her Mothers* and *A Weave of Women*. In 1980, she became a fellow in literature of the National Endowment for the Arts

and attended the U.N. Mid-Decade Conference of the International Decade of the Woman, held in Oslo and Copenhagen.

ZSUZSANNA BUDAPEST is a psychic, playwright, lecturer, High Priestess, and
founder of the Susan B. Anthony Coven No. One of Dianic Witchcraft.
She is author of *Selene: The World's Most Famous Bull-Leaper* and *The
Holy Book of Women's Mysteries*, which incorporates her earlier *The
Feminist Book of Lights and Shadows*.

PHYLLIS CHESLER is a professor of psychology, has lectured widely in the
U.S. and abroad, and practices therapy in New York. She is author of
*Women and Madness, About Men, With Child: A Diary of Mother-
hood*, and co-author of *Women, Money and Power*.

JUDY CHICAGO is one of America's leading women artists; she has pioneered
feminist breakthroughs in art and was a co-founder of the Woman's
Building in Los Angeles. For the past three years, she has exhibited *The
Dinner Party*, a symbolic history of the feminine in Western civilization.
She is the author of *Through the Flower, The Dinner Party*, and with
Susan Hill, *Embroidering Our Heritage*.

CAROL P. CHRIST is an associate professor of women's studies and religious
studies at San Jose State University. She is author of *Diving Deep and
Surfacing*, co-editor of *Womanspirit Rising* and is currently working on
*Symbols of Goddess and God in Feminist Theology*, for which she received a grant from the National Endowment for the Humanities.

SHEILA D. COLLINS is a teacher, theologian, poet, and administrator of programs that further community organizing and development; her activism
has centered around the interrelations among sexism, racism, and class exploitation. She is author of *A Different Heaven and Earth: A Feminist
Perspective on Religion*.

BABA COPPER is an artist, a co-founder of the Union of Feminist Utopian
Futurists, a Crone futurist, and a member of the rural community of
Heraseed, where she and other women are learning to reconnect with
food production, to restore the soil, to be more self-sufficient, and to create
survival skills for the future.

EMILY E. CULPEPPER is a rebellious white woman from Georgia and proud
to be a lesbian. Her doctoral dissertation at the Harvard Divinity School
considers feminist myth-making as a force for social change. Her film, *Period Piece*, explores images and folklore about menstruation.

MARY DALY is a philosopher, theorist, professor, and author of *The Church
and the Second Sex, Beyond God the Father: Toward a Philosophy of
Women's Liberation*, and *Gyn/Ecology: The Metaethics of Radical Feminism*.

JUDY DAVIS is a graduate of Union Theological Seminary in New York.
She has worked in the feminist movement for more than a decade as an
organizer, ritualist, teacher, and writer; she also worked in the church for

seventeen years. She lives in Washington, D.C., and Penland, North Carolina.

BELLA DEBRIDA has been spiraling into cronehood, completing a Ph.D. in classical Greek literature, acting, writing, and teaching classes on gynocentric culture. Her vision: One morning all women will wake up, in unison cry "No!" to patriarchal ways, and reassert their power.

SOPHIE DRINKER was a musician and a historian of music. Her research on the origins of music led her to considerable knowledge of the history of Goddess-worship, which she presented in *Music and Women: The Story of Women in Their Relation to Music.*

MARY BETH EDELSON is first and last an artist, one who weaves the fabric of her art into her life. This framework has led her to a holistic approach to art in which the contents and concerns lead to the form, whether that be sculpture, painting, drawing, video, artists' books, environments, or photography, whether that be public or private.

GINA FOGLIA is involved in eco-feminist activities on and around Long Island, New York. She is a fibre artist; a horticulturist; a co-founder of Arethusa, a woman-owned business; and was a member of the collective that produced the Goddess issue of *Heresies* in 1978.

SALLY GEARHART is a lesbian-feminist activist and an associate professor of speech at San Francisco State University. She appeared in the gay documentary *Word Is Out* and is author of *The Wanderground* and co-author of *A Feminist Tarot.*

MARIJA GIMBUTAS is a professor of European archaeology at the University of California at Los Angeles. She is author of *The Gods and Goddesses of Old Europe, 7000 to 3500 B.C.: Myths, Legends and Cult Images,* plus numerous articles and two forthcoming books on the Goddess.

CHELLIS GLENDINNING is a holistic health practitioner and writer. She has taught at the Esalen Institute, the University of California at Berkeley, and elsewhere. Her articles appear in national newspapers and magazines and in feminist and holistic health publications.

NAOMI GOLDENBERG is an associate professor of religious studies at the University of Ottawa. She studied at the C. G. Jung Institute in Zurich and has written several feminist critiques of Jungian psychology. She is author of *Changing of the Gods: Feminism and the End of Traditional Religions.*

JUDY GRAHN is a founding mother and strong supporter of women's independent publishing. She is best known for her poetry, especially *The Common Woman, She Who,* and *A Woman Is Talking to Death,* and is currently researching sources of women's power and Gay history.

GLORIA Z. GREENFIELD is a founder and financial administrator of Persephone Press, a lesbian-feminist publishing house producing innovative material to foster lesbian sensibility and new ways of thinking. She is an expatriate of the women's spirituality movement.

HALLIE IGLEHART has been leading feminist spirituality groups since 1973 and group rituals at conferences, including the U.N. Mid-Decade Conference of the International Decade of the Woman in 1980. Her articles have appeared in many feminist publications, and she has recently finished a guidebook for women's spirituality groups.

JUNE JORDAN is a poet, novelist, and essayist. She is the author of several award-winning books; her most recent collection of poetry is *Things That I Do in the Dark*.

ROBIN MORGAN is a poet, theorist, and feminist activist whose books include *Monster, Lady of the Beasts, Sisterhood Is Powerful,* and *Going Too Far: The Personal Chronicle of a Feminist*. She has written and lectured widely on the subject of feminist culture and spirituality and is working on a cycle of verse plays, a novel, and a book of feminist theory.

NANCY F. W. PASSMORE is editor and publisher of *The Lunar Calendar: Dedicated to the Goddess in Her Many Guises,* an annual from Boston. A freelance metaphysician, she views internationality, liberty, love, truth, and beauty as the transformative vision currently evoking the Goddess within.

MARGE PIERCY is author of six novels and seven volumes of poetry. Themes of women's spirituality are prominent in *Woman on the Edge of Time* and in much of her poetry, especially *The Moon Is Always Female,* which contains The Lunar Cycle poems.

BATYA PODOS is a playwright, director, and producer who has been developing a style of ritual theater over the past four years that invokes the historical, mythical, and spiritual aspects of the Goddess. Her original, full-length play *Ariadne* was published in 1980.

ADRIENNE RICH is author of ten books of poems, of which the most recent is *The Dream of a Common Language,* and two of prose, *Of Woman Born: Motherhood as Experience and Institution* and *On Lies, Secrets and Silence: Selected Prose, 1966–1978.*

DOROTHY I. RIDDLE is currently teaching community mental health consultation and training psychologists to work in rural areas. She has given a number of lectures and workshops over the past eight years on the importance of integrating spirituality and politics.

ANNE KENT RUSH is author of *Moon, Moon, Getting Clear: Body Work for Women, The Basic Back Book,* co-author of *Feminism as Therapy,* and editor and illustrator of *The Massage Book*. She runs Moon Books, a feminist publishing company in Berkeley.

CAROLYN R. SHAFFER is a freelance writer and editor in the San Francisco Bay Area; her work has appeared in *New Age, Plexus,* and elsewhere. She was the originator of the conference titled "The Great Goddess Re-

Emerging" at the University of California at Santa Cruz in 1978 and is currently writing a book on women, power, and spiritual leadership.

NTOZAKE SHANGE is a poet and playwright. She is best known for the choreopoem *for colored girls who have considered suicide/when the rainbow is enuf, Nappy Edges,* and "Sassafras."

GRACE SHINELL is a member of the Women's Ancient Studies Group in New York City and is a zen student. Her varied collective experience includes participation in the collective that produced the Goddess issue of *Heresies* in 1978.

SABRINA SOJOURNER is a student of the Yoruban tradition of the Goddess and is a Witch. She holds an M.A. in theater arts and has taught women's studies at San Francisco State University.

CHARLENE SPRETNAK is author of *Lost Goddesses of Early Greece: A Collection of Pre-Hellenic Myths* and "Problems with Jungian Uses of Greek Goddess Mythology," *Anima,* Fall 1979.

STARHAWK is author of *The Spiral Dance: A Rebirth of the Ancient Religion of the Great Goddess.* She has been teaching and practicing Witchcraft for twelve years and is a licensed minister of the Covenant of the Goddess. She has completed a forthcoming novel, *To the Wild Places* and is currently working on *Dreaming the Dark: Magic, Sex and Politics.*

BARBARA STARRETT is a poet, essayist, teacher, and psychotherapist. Divorced, the mother of five, she holds a B.A. in philosophy, an M.A. in English literature, and a Ph.D. in symbolics. She is author of *I Dream in Female: The Metaphors of Evolution and the Metaphors of Power.*

GLORIA STEINEM is a founder of the National Women's Political Caucus and a founder and editor of *Ms.,* to which she contributes articles on a wide range of feminist issues.

MERLIN STONE is an art historian, sculptor, and author of *When God Was a Woman* and *Ancient Mirrors of Womanhood: Our Goddess and Heroine Heritage.* Her articles on reclaiming knowledge of the ancient reverence for the Goddess have appeared in *Spare Rib, Heresies, WomanSpirit, Ms., Chatelaine,* the London *Times,* and *F* in Paris.

JUDITH TODD is a doctoral student in the History of Consciousness Program at the University of California at Santa Cruz. She has published several articles on feminist spirituality and our relationship with the Earth, a subject that has interested her since her childhood on an Indiana farm.

KAY TURNER is a doctoral candidate in the Folklore Program at the University of Texas at Austin. Her dissertation research is on the cross-culturally encountered yet little studied tradition of women's home altars. She edits *Lady-Unique-Inclination-of-the-Night,* a feminist journal of the Goddess founded in 1975.

JUANITA WEAVER is a founder of *Quest: A Feminist Quarterly* and the Feminist Radio Network. She has given several workshops and seminars on women's politics and spirituality. She works for the Women's Business Enterprise within the Small Business Administration in Washington, D.C.

DORIT WOLFFBERG is a feminist anti-nuclear activist currently living in New York. She is a social worker in a state institution for the retarded, working with profoundly retarded, multiply handicapped adult women.

# A Bibliography of Feminist Spirituality

Editor's Note: The focus of this list is pre- and postpatriarchal spirituality; it does not include the many well argued feminist books that urge reforms within patriarchal religion. Some of the titles are recommended with certain reservations, but all make valuable contributions. The literature on prepatriarchal spirituality is so vast that I have limited its representation here to books giving a comprehensive view of a certain area or period; readers specifically interested in that topic and in Goddess spirituality through the ages are referred to the bibliography in Volume Two of *Ancient Mirrors of Womanhood: Our Goddess and Heroine Heritage* by Merlin Stone. — C.S.

Adair, Margo. *Meditations to Facilitate Our Organizing for Social Change.* San Francisco 94101 (P.O. Box 11503): Marxist Spirituality Collective, 1979.

Adair, Margo. *Applied Meditation for Intuitive Problem Solving.* Forthcoming.

Adler, Margot. *Drawing Down the Moon: Witches, Druids, Goddess-Worshippers, and Other Pagans in America Today.* New York: The Viking Press, 1979; Boston: Beacon Press, 1981.

*Anima: An Experiential Journal,* periodical, 1053 Wilson Avenue, Chambersburg, PA 17201.

Ashe, Geoffrey. *The Virgin.* London: Routledge & Kegan Paul, 1976.

Atwood, Margaret. *Surfacing* (novel). New York: Simon and Schuster, 1972.

Bachofen, J. J. *Myth, Religion, and Mother Right.* Princeton: Princeton University Press, Bollingen Series 84, 1967 (1854).

Bambara, Toni Cade. *The Salt Eaters* (novel). New York: Random House, 1980.

Bolen, Jean Shinoda. *The Goddesses in Everywoman.* Los Angeles: J. P. Tarcher, Inc., 1982.

Boulding, Elise. *The Underside of History: A View of Women Through Time.* Boulder, CO 80301 (1898 Flatiron Court): Westview Press, 1976.

*Bread and Roses: A Women's Journal of Issues and the Arts,* vol. 2, no. 3, Autumn 1980; P.O. Box 1230, Madison, WI 53701.

Briffault, Robert. *The Mothers.* London: George Allen & Unwin Ltd., abridged edition, 1959 (1927).

Brindel, June Rachuy. *Ariadne: A Novel of Ancient Crete.* New York: St. Martin's Press, 1980.

Broner, E. M. *A Weave of Women* (novel). New York: Holt, Rinehart & Winston, 1978; Bantam Books, 1980.

Broner, E. M. *The Ceremonial Woman.* Forthcoming.

Bruteau, Beatrice. *Neo-Feminism and Communion Consciousness.* Chambersburg, PA 17201 (1053 Wilson Ave.): Anima Publications, 1979.

Bryant, Dorothy. *The Kin of Ata Are Waiting for You.* Berkeley and New York: Moon Books and Random House, 1976 (1972).

Budapest, Z. *Selene: The Most Famous Bull-Leaper on Earth* (fiction). Oakland, CA 94608 (4400 Market St.): Diana Press, 1976.

Budapest, Z. *The Holy Book of Women's Mysteries,* 2 vols. Oakland, CA 94611 (2927 Harrison St.): Susan B. Anthony Coven No. 1, 1979.

Caldicott, Helen. *Nuclear Madness: What You Can Do.* Brookline, MA: Autumn Press, 1978.

Campbell, Joseph. *The Masks of God,* 4 vols. New York: The Viking Press, 1968, 1970, 1971.

Capra, Fritjof. *The Tao of Physics.* Boulder, CO: Shambhala Publications, 1975; New York: Bantam Books, 1977.

Capra, Fritjof. *The Turning Point.* New York: Simon and Schuster, 1981.

Carol, Chris. *Silver Wheel: Thrice Thirteen Songs.* Portland, OR 97212 (3934 N.E. 18th): Olive Press, 1979.

Carson, Rachel. *Silent Spring.* New York: Fawcett Books, 1962.

Chesler, Phyllis. *Women and Madness.* Garden City, NY: Doubleday & Co., 1972.

Chew, Willa. *The Goddess Faith.* Hicksville, NY: Exposition Press, 1977.

Chicago, Judy. *The Dinner Party: A Symbol of Our Heritage.* Garden City, NY: Doubleday & Co., 1979.

Chopin, Kate. *The Awakening* (novel). New York: Avon Books, 1972 (1899).

Christ, Carol P. and Judith Plaskow, editors. *Womanspirit Rising: A Feminist Reader in Religion.* San Francisco: Harper & Row, 1979.

Christ, Carol P. *Diving Deep and Surfacing: Women Writers on Spiritual Quest.* Boston: Beacon Press, 1980.

Christ, Carol P. *Symbols of Goddess and God in Feminist Theology.* Forthcoming.

*Chrysalis: A Magazine of Women's Culture,* no. 6, Fall 1978. (This periodical is no longer being published; hence no address.)

Colegrave, Sukie. *The Spirit of the Valley: Taoism and Androgyny in Chinese Thought.* London: Virago Press, 1979.

Collins, Sheila D. *A Different Heaven and Earth: A Feminist Perspective on Religion.* Valley Forge, PA: Judson Press, 1974.

Daly, Mary. *Beyond God the Father: Toward A Philosophy of Women's Liberation.* Boston: Beacon Press, 1973.

Daly, Mary. *Gyn/Ecology: The Metaethics of Radical Feminism.* Boston: Beacon Press, 1978.

Dames, Michael. *The Silbury Treasure: The Great Goddess Rediscovered.* London: Thames & Hudson, 1976.

Dames, Michael. *The Avebury Cycle.* London: Thames & Hudson, 1977.

Davis, Elizabeth Gould. *The First Sex.* New York: G. P. Putnam & Sons, 1971.

de Beauvoir, Simone. *The Second Sex.* New York: Alfred A. Knopf, 1952 (1949).

Diner, Helen. *Mothers and Amazons: The First Feminine History of Culture.* Garden City, NY: Anchor Press/Doubleday & Co., 1973 (1929).

DiPrima, Diane. *Loba* (poem). Berkeley: Wingbow Press, 1978.

Downing, Christine. *The Goddess: Mythological Representations of the Feminine.* New York: Crossroad (Seabury Press), 1981.

Drinker, Sophie. *Music and Women: The Story of Women in Their Relation to Music.* New York: Coward-McCann, Inc., 1948; Washington, DC 20031 (Box 31061): Zenger Publishing Co., 1977.

Durdin-Robertson, Lawrence. *The Goddesses of Chaldea, Syria and Egypt.* Clonegal, Enniscorthy, Eire (Huntington Castle): Cesara Publications, 1975.

Durdin-Robertson, Lawrence. *The Religion of the Goddess* (formerly titled *The Cult of the Goddess*). Clonegal, Enniscorthy, Eire: Cesara Publications, 1975.

Durdin-Robertson, Lawrence. *The Goddesses of India, Tibet, China and Japan.* Clonegal, Enniscorthy, Eire: Cesara Publications, 1976.

Durdin-Robertson, Lawrence. *Communion with the Goddess* (five volumes on temples, images, symbols, and priestesses). Clonegal, Enniscorthy, Eire: Cesara Publications, 1976–78.

Edelson, Mary Beth. *Seven Cycles: Public Rituals,* 1980; 110 Mercer Street, NY, NY 10012.

Edelson, Mary Beth. *The Sacred Manic Goddess Makes Tracks* (working title). Forthcoming.

Ehrenreich, Barbara and Deirdre English. *Witches, Midwives and Nurses.* New York: The Feminist Press, 1973.

Erdoes, Richard. *The Woman Who Dared* (novel). New York: Fawcett Books, 1978.

Evans, Arthur. *Witchcraft and the Gay Counterculture.* Boston: Fag Rag Books, 1978.

Falk, Nancy A. and Rita M. Gross, editors. *Unspoken Worlds: Women's Religious Lives in Non-Western Cultures.* San Francisco: Harper & Row, 1980.

Falk, Ruth. *High Adventure: Ace of Wands* (novel). Forthcoming.

Ferguson, Marilyn. *The Aquarian Conspiracy: Personal and Social Transformation in the 1980s.* Los Angeles: J. P. Tarcher, Inc., 1980.

Fisher, Elizabeth. *Woman's Creation: Sexual Evolution and the Shaping of Society.* Garden City, NY: Anchor Press/Doubleday & Co., 1979.

Forfreedom, Ann, editor. *Women Out of History: A Herstory Anthology.* 1972 and 1974; out-of-print; query at the address in the following entry.

Forfreedom, Ann and Julie Ann, editors. *Book of the Goddess.* Sacramento, CA 95819 (P.O. Box 19241): The Temple of the Goddess Within, 1980.

Freedman, Marcia. *Four Essays in Feminist Ethics.* Jerusalem: Bat Kol Press Collective, 1981 (in Hebrew and English).

Galland, China. *Women in the Wilderness.* New York: Harper & Row, 1980.

Gage, Matilda Joslyn. *Woman, Church and State: The Original Exposé of Male Collaboration against the Female Sex.* Watertown, MA 02172 (P.O. Box 7222): Persephone Press, 1980 (1893).

Gearhart, Sally and Susan Rennie. *A Feminist Tarot.* Watertown, MA 02172 (P.O. Box 7222): Peresphone Press, 1977.

Gearhart, Sally. *The Wanderground* (fiction). Watertown, MA 02172 (P.O. Box 7222): Persephone Press, 1978.

Gidlow, Elsa. *Moods of Eros* (poetry). Mill Valley, CA 94941 (685 Camino del Canyon, Muir Woods): Druid Heights Books, 1970.

Gilman, Charlotte Perkins. *Herland* (novel). New York: Pantheon Books, 1979 (1915).

Gimbutas, Marija. *The Gods and Goddesses of Old Europe, 7000 to 3500*

B.C.: *Myths, Legends and Cult Images*. London: Thames and Hudson, 1974; Berkeley: University of California Press, 1974.

Gimbutas, Marija and Barbara Bradshaw. *The Great Goddess, Giver of All*. Forthcoming.

Gioseffi, Daniela. *The Great American Belly Dance* (novel). Garden City, NY: Doubleday & Co., 1977.

Goldenberg, Naomi. *Changing of the Gods: Feminism and the End of Traditional Religions*. Boston: Beacon Press, 1979.

Grahn, Judy. *The Work of A Common Woman* (poetry). New York: St. Martin's Press, 1980.

Grahn, Judy. *Another Mother Tongue: Stories from the Ancient Gay Tradition*. Watertown, MA 02172 (P.O. Box 7222): Persephone Press, 1981.

Grahn, Judy. *Blood and Bread and Roses*. Forthcoming.

Grahn, Judy. *The Motherlords*. Forthcoming.

Graves, Robert. *King Jesus* (novel). New York: Creative Age Press, 1946.

Graves, Robert. *The White Goddess*. New York: Farrar, Straus & Giroux, 1966 (1948).

Graves, Robert. *The Greek Myths*, 2 vols. Harmondsworth, England: Penguin Books, 1955.

Griffin, Susan. *Woman and Nature: The Roaring Inside Her*. New York: Harper & Row, 1978.

Griffin, Susan. *Rape/The Power of Consciousness*. San Francisco: Harper & Row, 1979.

*Hagborn*, periodical, P.O. Box 894, Albany, NY 12201.

Harding, M. Esther. *Women's Mysteries, Ancient and Modern*. London: Rider & Company, 1971 (1955).

Harrison, Jane Ellen. *Prolegomena to the Study of Greek Religion*. London: Cambridge University Press, 1922 (1903).

Hawkes, Jacquetta. *Dawn of the Gods: Minoan and Mycenaean Origins of Greece*. New York: Random House, 1968.

Hawkes, Jacquetta. *The First Great Civilizations: Life in Mesopotamia, the Indus Valley, and Egypt*. New York: Alfred A. Knopf, 1973.

Henderson, Hazel. *Creating Alternative Futures*. New York: G. P. Putnam & Sons, 1978.

Henderson, Hazel. *The Politics of the Solar Age: Alternatives to Economics*. Garden City, NY: Anchor Press/Doubleday & Co., 1981.

*Heresies: A Feminist Publication on Art and Politics*, no. 5, Sept. 1978; P.O. Box 766, Canal Street Station, NY, NY 10013.

Heyob, Sharon Kelly. *The Cult of Isis among Women in the Graeco-Roman World*. Leiden: E. J. Brill, 1975.

Hitching, Francis. *Earth Magic*. New York: Wm. Morrow & Co., 1976.

Hobson, Gary, editor. *The Remembered Earth: An Anthology of Contemporary Native American Literature. Albuquerque, NM: Red Earth, 1978.

Hollander, Annette. How to Help Your Child Have A Spiritual Life: A Parents' Guide to Inner Development. New York: A & W Publishers, 1980.

Holliday, Laurel. The Violent Sex: Male Psychobiology and the Evolution of Consciousness. Berkeley, CA 94708 (1101 Keeler Ave.): Bluestocking Books, 1978.

Homebrew: A Journal of Women's Witchcraft, periodical, P.O. Box 6, Berkeley, CA 94704.

Hungry Wolf, Beverly. The Ways of My Grandmothers. New York: Wm. Morrow, 1980.

Iglehart, Hallie. The Catalog of Womanspirit. Forthcoming.

James, E. O. The Cult of the Mother-Goddess: An Archaeological and Documentary Study. New York: Frederick A. Praeger, Inc., 1959.

Jong, Erica. Fanny (novel). New York: New American Library, 1980.

Kerenyi, Carl. Eleusis: Archetypal Image of Mother and Daughter. New York: Schoken Books, 1977 (1967).

Kingston, Maxine Hong. The Woman Warrior (novel). New York: Alfred A. Knopf, 1976.

Koen, Susan and Nina Swaim. Ain't Nowhere We Can Run: A Handbook for Women on the Nuclear Mentality. Norwich, VT 05055 (P.O. Box 421): Women Against Nuclear Destruction, 1980.

Kolodny, Annette. The Lay of the Land. Chapel Hill, NC: University of North Carolina Press, 1975.

LaChapelle, Dolores and Janet Borque. Earth Festivals: Seasonal Celebrations for Everyone Young and Old. Silverton, CO 81433 (P.O. Box 542): Fine Hill Arts, 1974.

LaChapelle, Dolores. Earth Wisdom. Los Angeles: Guild of Tutors, 1978.

Lady-Unique-Inclination-of-the-Night, periodical, P.O. Box 803, New Brunswick, NJ 08903.

Leading Edge Bulletin: Frontiers of Social Transformation, periodical, P.O. Box 42247, Los Angeles, CA 90042.

Lederer, Wolfgang. The Fear of Women. New York: Harcourt Brace Jovanovich, 1968.

LeGuin, Ursula. A Wizard of Earthsea (novel). New York: Bantam Books, 1975.

Lerman, Rhoda. Call Me Ishtar (novel). New York: Holt, Rinehart & Winston, 1977 (1973).

Lessing, Doris. The Children of Violence (novels), 5 vols. New York: Alfred A. Knopf, 1952–1969.

Levine, Faye. Solomon and Sheba (novel). New York: Richard Marek Publishers, 1980.

Levy, G. Rachel. *The Gate of Horn: Religious Conceptions of the Stone Age and Their Influence upon European Thought*. Atlantic Highlands, NJ: Humanities Press, 1968 (1948).

London Matriarchal Study Group. *Menstrual Taboos*. London W.C.1 (Flat 6, 15 Guilford St.): Matriarchal Study Group.

London Matriarchal Study Group. *Politics of Matriarchy*. London W.C.1 (Flat 6, 15 Guilford St.): Matriarchal Study Group.

Lone Dog, Louise. *Strange Journey: The Vision Life of a Psychic Indian Woman*. Healdsburg, CA: Naturegraph Publishers, 1964.

Lorde, Audre. *The Black Unicorn* (poetry). New York: W. W. Norton & Co., 1978.

*The Lunar Calendar: Dedicated to the Goddess in Her Many Guises*. Boston, MA 02215 (P.O. Box 511, Kenmore Station): The Luna Press, annual.

Mariechild, Diane. *Mother Wit: A Feminist Guide to Psychic Development*. Trumansburg, NY 14886: The Crossing Press, 1981.

Meeker, Joseph, editor. *The New Natural Philosophy Reader*. Forthcoming.

Merchant, Carolyn. *The Death of Nature: Women, Ecology and the Scientific Revolution*. San Francisco: Harper & Row, 1980.

Monaghan, Patricia. *The Book of Goddesses and Heroines*. New York: E. P. Dutton, 1981.

Monaghan, Patricia. *The Sun Goddess: A Survey of Myths and Legends of the Solar Female*. Forthcoming.

Morgan, Robin. *Lady of the Beasts* (poetry). New York: Random House, 1976.

Morgan, Robin. *Going Too Far: The Personal Chronicle of a Feminist*. New York: Random House, 1977.

*The Mother Church Bulletin*, periodical, P.O. Box 2188, Satellite Beach, FL 32937.

Neumann, Erich. *The Great Mother: An Analysis of the Archetype*, translated by Ralph Manheim. Princeton: Princeton University Press, Bollingen Series 47, 1963 (1955).

Niethammer, Carolyn. *Daughters of the Earth: The Lives and Legends of American Indian Women*. New York: Macmillan Publishing Co., 1977.

Pagels, Elaine. *The Gnostic Gospels*. New York: Random House, 1979.

Patai, Raphael. *The Hebrew Goddess*. Philadelphia: Ktav, 1967; New York: Avon Books, 1978.

Pepper, Elizabeth and John Wilcox. *A Guide to Magical and Mystical Sites: Europe and the British Isles*. New York: Harper Colophon Books, 1977.

Piercy, Marge. *Woman on the Edge of Time* (novel). New York: Alfred A. Knopf, 1980.

Piercy, Marge. *The Moon Is Always Female* (poetry). New York: Alfred A. Knopf, 1980.

Podos, Batya. *Ariadne* (drama). East Palo Alto, CA 94303 (430 Oakdale Rd.): Frog-in-the-Well Press, 1980.

*Quest: A Feminist Quarterly,* vol. 1, no. 4 and vol. 4, no. 3; 2000 P Street NW, Washington, DC 20036.

Reed, Evelyn. *Woman's Evolution: From Matriarchal Clan to Patriarchal Family.* New York: Pathfinder Press, 1975.

Renault, Mary. *The Bull from the Sea* (novel). New York: Pantheon Books, 1962.

Rich, Adrienne. *Of Woman Born: Motherhood as Experience and Institution.* New York: W. W. Norton & Co., 1976.

Rich, Adrienne. *The Dream of A Common Language* (poetry). New York: W. W. Norton & Co., 1978.

Rich, Adrienne. *On Lies, Secrets and Silence: Selected Prose, 1966–1978.* New York: W. W. Norton & Co., 1979.

Roberts, Jane. *The Nature of Personal Reality.* Englewood Cliffs, NJ: Prentice-Hall, 1974.

Ross, Anne. *Pagan Celtic Britain.* New York: Columbia University Press, 1967.

Roszak, Theodore. *Person/Planet: The Creative Disintegration of Industrial Society.* Garden City, NY: Anchor Press/Doubleday & Co., 1979.

Rothenberg, Jerome, editor. *Technicians of the Sacred: A Range of Poetries from Africa, America, Asia and Oceania.* Garden City, NY: Anchor Press/Doubleday & Co., 1968.

Rothery, Guy Cadogan. *The Amazons in Antiquity and Modern Times.* London: Francis Griffiths, 1910.

Ruether, Rosemary. *New Woman/New Earth: Sexist Ideologies and Human Liberation.* New York: Seabury Press, 1975.

Rush, Anne Kent. *Moon, Moon.* Berkeley and New York: Moon Books and Random House, 1976.

Russell, Jeffrey B. *A History of Witchcraft: Sorcerers, Heretics and Pagans.* London: Thames and Hudson, 1980.

Shaffer, Carolyn. *Spirited Women.* Forthcoming.

Shange, Ntozake. *For Colored Girls Who Have Considered Suicide/When the Rainbow Is Enuf* (choreopoem). New York: Macmillan Publishing Co., 1977 (1975).

Shinell, Grace. *Memory Serves: Radical Applications of Heritage.* Forthcoming.

Shuttle, Penelope, and Peter Redgrove. *The Wise Wound: Eve's Curse and Everywoman.* New York: Richard Marek Publishers, 1978.

Silko, Leslie Marmon. *Ceremony* (novel). New York: The Viking Press, 1977; Signet Books, 1978.

Sobol, Donald J. *The Amazons of Greek Mythology*. New York: A. S. Barnes & Co., 1972.

*Sojourner*, vol. 6, no. 5, January 1981; 143 Albany St., Cambridge, MA 02139.

Spretnak, Charlene. *Lost Goddesses of Early Greece: A Collection of Pre-Hellenic Myths*. Berkeley: Moon Books, 1978; Boston: Beacon Press, 1981.

Spretnak, Charlene, editor. *The Politics of Women's Spirituality: Essays on the Rise of Spiritual Power within the Feminist Movement*. Garden City, NY: Anchor Press/Doubleday & Co., 1982.

Starhawk. *The Spiral Dance: A Rebirth of the Ancient Religion of the Great Goddess*. San Francisco: Harper & Row, 1979.

Starhawk. *Dreaming the Dark: Magic, Sex and Politics*. Boston: Beacon Press, 1982.

Starhawk. *To the Wild Places* (novel). Forthcoming.

Starrett, Barbara. *I Dream in Female: The Metaphors of Evolution and the Metaphors of Power*. Vineyard Haven, MA 02568 (P.O. Box 1516): Cassandra Press, 1977.

Stone, Merlin. *When God Was a Woman*. New York: Dial Press, 1976; HBJ Harvest Books, 1978.

Stone, Merlin. *Ancient Mirrors of Womanhood: Our Goddess and Heroine Heritage*, 2 vols. New York, NY 10014 (P.O. Box 266, Village Station): New Sybilline Press, 1979 and 1980.

Suhr, Elmer G. *The Spinning Aphrodite: The Evolution of the Goddess from Earliest Pre-Hellenic Symbolism through Late Classical Times*. New York: Helios Books, 1969.

*Thesmophoria* (formerly *Themis*), periodical, 2927 Harrison St., Oakland, CA 94611.

Turner, Kay. *Contemporary Feminist Ritual, 1965–1979*. Forthcoming.

Van Vuuren, Nancy. *The Subversion of Women as Practiced by Churches, Witch-Hunters, and Other Sexists*. Philadelphia: Westminster Press, 1973.

Washbourn, Penelope, editor. *The Seasons of Woman: Song, Poetry, Ritual, Prayer, Myth, Story*. San Francisco: Harper & Row, 1979.

Weinstein, Marion. *Earth Magic: A Dianic Book of Shadows*. NY, NY 10022 (P.O. Box 1202, F.D.R. Station): Earth Magic Productions, 1980.

*The Wise Woman*, periodical, P.O. Box 19241, Sacramento, CA 95819.

Wittig, Monique. *Les Guérillères* (novel), translated by David LeVay. New York: The Viking Press, 1971 (1969).

*WomanSpirit*, periodical, P.O. Box 262, Wolf Creek, OR 97497.

*Women and Life on Earth*, periodical mailings, 160 Main St., Northampton, MA 01060; also *Proceedings* of their eco-feminist conference held in Amherst, March 1980.

*Women in the Wilderness*, periodical mailings, Star Route, Box 274, Muir Beach, CA 94965.

*Wonder Woman*, introductions by Phyllis Chesler and Gloria Steinem. New York: *Ms.*/Holt, Rinehart & Winston, 1972.

Charlene Spretnak holds degrees from St. Louis University and the University of California at Berkeley. She is a founder of the national Feminist Writers' Guild.*

She writes on various aspects of pre- and postpatriarchal spirituality and is the author of *Lost Goddesses of Early Greece: A Collection of Pre-Hellenic Myths.*

---

* The Feminist Writers' Guild is a political and service organization with active chapters and/or contact persons in more than twenty states to date. For information, send a self-addressed, stamped envelope to:

Laura Tow, National Administrator
Feminist Writers' Guild
P.O. Box 9396
Berkeley, CA 94709